Third Edition

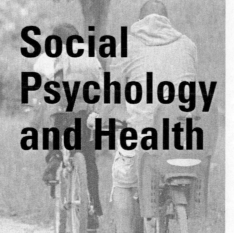

Social
Psychology
and Health

MAPPING SOCIAL PSYCHOLOGY

Series Editor: Tony Manstead

Current titles:

Open University Press
McGraw-Hill Education
McGraw-Hill House
Shoppenhangers Road
Maidenhead
Berkshire
England
SL6 2QL

email: enquiries@openup.co.uk
world wide web: www.openup.co.uk

and Two Penn Plaza, New York, NY 10121-2289, USA

First published 1995
Reprinted 1996, 1997
Second Edition 2000
Reprinted 2007, 2008 (twice), 2009
First published in this third edition 2011

A catalogue record of this book is available from the British Library

ISBN-13: 978-0-33-523809-5
ISBN-10: 0-33-523809-2
eISBN: 978-0-33-524052-4

Library of Congress Cataloging-in-Publication Data
CIP data applied for

Typeset by RefineCatch Limited, Bungay, Suffolk
Printed in the UK by Ashford Colour Press Ltd., Gosport, Hampshire.

Fictitious names of companies, products, people, characters and/or data that may be used
herein (in case studies or in examples) are not intended to represent any real individual,
company, product or event.

The *McGraw-Hill* Companies

Third Edition

Social Psychology and Health

Wolfgang Stroebe

Open University Press

Dedication

To my friends of the interdisciplinary social science working group (ISAG: Hans Albert, Bruno Frey, Klaus Foppa, Wilhelm Meyer, Karl-Dieter Opp, Kurt Stapf, Viktor Vanberg) for more than 30 years of discussion, always lively, often stimulating.

Praise for this book

"The third edition of Social Psychology and Health is a welcome update of a venerable book that has done much to define and inform the field of health psychology. Eminently accessible to professionals, students, and laypersons alike, Wolfgang Stroebe's review and discussion of contemporary theory, research, and practice couldn't come at a more opportune time. An aging population, stress occasioned by rapid social change, a sedentary lifestyle, and increased costs of dealing with the consequences have brought matters of health to the forefront as never before. With its focus on understanding and modifying health-related behavior, this book is essential reading for anybody interested in the manifold health issues created by overeating, smoking, alcohol and drug abuse, insufficient physical activity, and a host of other harmful life-style practices."
Icek Ajzen, Department of Psychology, University of Massachusetts, Amherst, USA

"Wolfgang Stroebe's third edition of Social Psychology and Health is skilfully integrated across multiple health problems and theories of causation, prevention, and amelioration. The book offers absolutely first-rate reviews of new and classic research. It is a must-read volume for researchers and a superb choice as a textbook for university courses in health psychology and public health."
Alice Eagly, Professor of Psychology, Northwestern University, USA

"When the first edition of Social Psychology and Health emerged, I was very impressed. This excellent book became my standard response to students asking for an accessible and thorough introduction to this topic. The third edition continues Professor Stroebe's definitive treatment of the topic. This edition features important new evidence and provocative discussions of relevant policy and practice. The book is easy to read, insightful, and compelling. It's a 'must-read' for anyone who wants an introduction to scientific investigations of social psychology and health."
Professor Greg Maio, Cardiff University, UK

"This outstanding volume brings to bear cutting edge social psychological knowledge on the vastly important domain of health behavior. It illustrates the richness, profundity and diversity of insights that social psychological work of recent decades affords when it comes to understanding individuals' habits and challenges in maintaining and preserving a healthy, and productive life style. A must read for health professionals and policy makers as well as educators, parents and others for whom improving health of individuals and communities is of interest and concern."
Arie Kruglanski, Distinguished University Professor, University of Maryland, USA

Contents

Preface

This third edition of *Social Psychology and Health* has been so extensively revised that it essentially represents a new book. The parts which remain from the old text have been updated, a great deal of new text has been added, and more than a third of the original references have been replaced. The book has also grown in size, and the coverage of many of the areas has become more comprehensive. All this has been achieved within the old structure. Thus, hardly any of the chapter and section headings have been changed, and the number of chapters has remained the same.

There are at least three reasons for this extensive revision. First, there have been revolutionary changes in the social psychological understanding of behaviour. Whereas traditionally, social psychologists have explained behaviour as 'reasoned', the result of conscious deliberation, informed by beliefs, attitudes and social norms, there is increasing evidence that behaviour is often influenced by automatic response tendencies, which operate outside of the control of the individual. Because such automatic response tendencies can play a powerful role in undermining attempts at health behaviour change, it is extremely important to discuss this work in a book on health behaviour. It is surprising that with few exceptions health psychologists have so far neglected this work in their research. Second, health psychology is a very active research area. In the decade since the writing of the second edition, a substantial body of research has been published, much of which has had bearings on the topics covered in this book. Third, the book uses a great deal of epidemiological literature and this type of descriptive evidence does not age well. What has not changed, however, is the basic scientific perspective which shaped this book from the beginning. Although health psychology is an interdisciplinary endeavour, involving various areas ranging from medicine to sociology and economics, and although these perspectives are well represented, the main focus of this book is on social psychology and health. Therefore much of the health research presented here has been guided by social psychological theories and conducted by social psychologists.

In writing a book one draws on the support of others. I would like to express my gratitude to Henk Aarts, Guido van Koningbruggen and Esther Papies, all members of URGE (Utrecht Research Group on Eating), with whom I collaborated on all of my eating research and who have influenced my theoretical thinking in this area. I also owe thanks to John de Wit for his helpful suggestions on my section on HIV/AIDS. Finally, I would like to thank the members of the Interdisciplinary Workgroup on Social Sciences (ISAG). The biannual meetings of this workgroup during the last three decades have made me appreciate the value of economic analyses of social behaviour.

Wolfgang Stroebe

Changing conceptions of health and illness

Good health and a long life are important aims of most persons, but surely no more than a moment's reflection is necessary to convince anyone that they are not the only aims. The economic approach implies that there is an 'optimal' expected length of life, where the value in utility of an additional year is less than the utility foregone by using time and other resources to obtain that year. Therefore, a person may be a heavy smoker or so committed to work as to omit all exercise, not necessarily because he is ignorant of the consequences or 'incapable' of using the information he possesses, but because the lifespan forfeited is not worth the cost to him of quitting smoking or working less intensively . . . According to the economic approach therefore, most (if not all!) deaths are to some extent 'suicides' in the sense that they could have been postponed if more resources had been invested in prolonging life.

(Becker 1976: 10, 11)

The modern increase in life expectancy

Progress in medical science has been impressive. Knowledge of the body and understanding of disease processes have advanced continuously from the seventeenth century onwards, slowly at first but very rapidly since the turn of the twentieth century. This increase in medical knowledge appears to have resulted in a substantial increase in life expectancy. In 2007 the life expectancy at birth in the USA was 77.9 years as compared to 48 years in 1900 (Matarazzo 1984; CDC 2010). This increase in longevity has been due mainly to the virtual elimination of most infectious diseases as causes of death that were common at the turn of the twentieth century (e.g. pneumonia and influenza, tuberculosis, diphtheria, scarlet fever, measles, typhoid, poliomyelitis). Thus, whereas approximately 40 per cent of all deaths were accounted for by 11 major infections in 1900, only 6 per cent of all deaths were due to these infectious diseases in 1973 (McKinlay and McKinlay 1981). Between 1981 and 1995 the death rate due to infections

TABLE 1.1 The 10 leading causes of death in the USA: 1900, 1940, 1980 and 2007

Cause of death	1900	1940	1980	2007
Pneumonia and influenza	1	5	6	8
Tuberculosis (all forms)	2	7		
Diarrhoea, enteritis and ulceration of the intestines	3			
Diseases of the heart	4	1	1	1
Intracranial lesions of vascular origin	5	3		
Nephritis (all forms)	6	4		9
All accidents[a]	7	6	4	5
Cancer[b]	8	2	2	2
Senility/Alzheimer's disease	9			6
Diphtheria	10			
Diabetes mellitus		8	7	7
Motor vehicle accidents		9		
Premature birth		10		
Cerebrovascular diseases			3	3
Chronic, obstructive pulmonary diseases			5	4
Cirrhosis of the liver			8	
Atherosclerosis			9	
Suicide			10	9
Septicaemia				10

[a] This category excludes motor vehicle accidents in the years 1900 and 1940, but includes them in 1980 and 1992.
[b] This category encompasses cancer and other malignant tumours in the years 1900 and 1940 and changes to malignant neoplasms of all types in 1980 and 2007.
Source: Matarazzo (1984); Gardner *et al*. (1996), CDC (2010)

somewhat increased, mainly due to the appearance of a new infectious disease (AIDS). However, in 1996 the trend changed and infectious disease deaths began to decrease again (Armstrong *et al.* 1999). Table 1.1 illustrates the significant shift in causes of death during this century.

Because this decline in mortality from infectious diseases happened during a time when medical understanding of the causes of these diseases had vastly improved and when vaccines and other chemotherapeutic medical interventions became widely available, it was only plausible to attribute these changes to the efficacy of the new medical measures. However, this may be yet another example of a premature causal inference from purely correlational evidence. After all, during the same period conditions of life also improved considerably in most industrialized societies. For large populations in western societies the problem of malnutrition has been solved and some of the most serious threats to health associated with water and food have been removed by improvements in water supply and sewage disposal.

As can be seen from Figure 1.1, which depicts the fall in standardized death rates for the nine common infectious diseases in relation to specific medical measures for the USA, the decline in mortality from these major infectious diseases took place *before* effective medical interventions became available. McKinlay and McKinlay (1981: 26) concluded from their analysis that 'medical measures (both chemotherapeutic and prophylactic) appear to have contributed little to the overall decline in mortality in the United States since about 1900 . . . ' Similar conclusions were reached by McKeown (1979) on the basis of an even more extensive analysis of data from England and Wales.

Today, the major killers are cardiovascular diseases (i.e. heart disease and stroke) and cancers, with cardiovascular diseases accounting for approximately 30 per cent of deaths in the USA and other industrialized countries. Although deaths from cardiovascular diseases increased during the first half of the twentieth century, this pattern has changed. During the last four decades there has been a small but steady decline in deaths due to heart disease and stroke in the USA and several other industrialized countries.

Improvements in medical treatment undoubtedly contributed to this decline, but the significant changes in lifestyle that occurred in the USA during that period were also responsible. Goldman and Cook (1984) even estimated that more than half of the decline in heart disease mortality observed in the USA between 1968 and 1976 was related to changes in lifestyle, specifically the reduction in serum cholesterol levels and cigarette smoking.

Unfortunately, despite advances in medical treatment and significant lifestyle changes, deaths due to cancer have increased since 1950 in most industrialized countries. This increase has been almost entirely due to an increase in lung cancer which is responsible for more than one fourth of all cancer deaths (Breslow 1990). However, from 1990 to 1995, there occurred for the first time a continuous and sustainable decline in cancer mortality in the USA of 0.6 per cent per year (Cole and Rodu 1996). Nearly 40 per cent of this decline resulted from a reduction in lung carcinoma mortality and is thus likely to be due to the reduction of smoking in the USA.

To summarize, the significant increases in life expectancy at birth that occurred during the twentieth century in most industrialized countries seem to have been only partially attributable to improvements in medical treatment. There is substantial evidence that a purely medical explanation of these changes would be too narrow. Changes in sanitation, nutrition and lifestyles contributed importantly to the increase in life expectancy.

From disease control to health promotion

The marked decline in mortality due to infectious disease during the twentieth century, the vast improvement in average living conditions in western industrialized

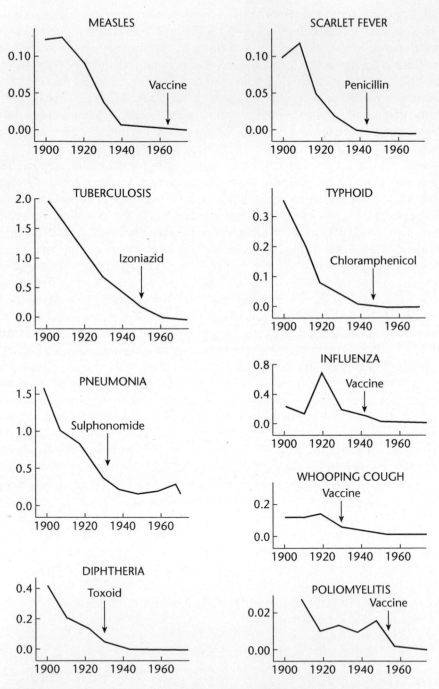

FIGURE 1.1 The fall in the standardized death rate (per 1000 population) for nine common infectious diseases in relation to specific medical measures in the USA, 1900–1973
Source: McKinlay and McKinlay (1981)

nations and the substantial increase in life expectancy have stimulated considerable rethinking of the meaning of health and of the role of public health institutions in helping to achieve and maintain it (Breslow 1990). Whereas health had long been considered merely the absence of disease and infirmity, people were beginning to emphasize the positive aspects of health. This change in perspective was reflected in the influential definition of health offered by the World Health Organization (WHO) in its constitution in 1948. The WHO defined health as 'a complete state of physical, mental, and social well-being and not merely the absence of disease or infirmity' (WHO 1948).

There are two important aspects of this definition of health which set it apart from previous definitions (Kaplan *et al*. 1993). First, by emphasizing well-being as the criterion for health, the WHO definition abandoned the traditional perspective of defining health in negative terms, namely as the absence of disease. Second, by recognizing that health status can vary in terms of a number of different dimensions, namely physical, mental and social well-being, the definition abandons the exclusive emphasis on physical health which had been typical of previous definitions (Kaplan *et al*. 1993).

The growing interest in interventions designed to prevent diseases and promote health has led to a change in focus of public health strategies towards a greater emphasis on health promotion. *Health promotion* can be defined as 'any planned combination of educational, political, regulatory, and organizational supports for action and conditions of living conducive to the health of individuals, groups, or communities' (Green and Kreuter 1991: 432). Countries adopting health promotion as policy have directed it mainly at primary prevention through modification of lifestyle factors that account for the largest numbers of deaths (e.g. smoking, drinking too much alcohol, eating a fatty diet, leading a sedentary life). Health promotion influences lifestyles through two strategies, namely health education and fiscal and legislative measures. Education involves the transfer of knowledge or skills. Thus, health education provides individuals, groups or communities with the knowledge about the health consequences of certain lifestyles and with the skills to enable them to change their behaviour. Fiscal or legislative measures such as increasing the tax on tobacco or introducing seatbelt legislation are used to change the incentive structure that influences behaviour. Health promotion also uses strategies not directed at lifestyles such as environmental changes aimed at the protection of health (e.g. car safety measures).

The impact of behaviour on health

No single set of data can better illustrate the fact that our health is influenced by the way we live than the findings of a prospective study on the health impact of some rather innocuous health behaviours, conducted by Belloc, Breslow and their colleagues (Belloc and Breslow 1972; Belloc 1973; Breslow and Enstrom 1980).

In 1965, these researchers asked a representative probability sample of 6928 residents of Alameda county, California, whether they engaged in the following seven health practices:

1 Sleeping seven to eight hours daily.
2 Eating breakfast almost every day.
3 Never or rarely eating between meals.
4 Currently being at or near prescribed height-adjusted weight.
5 Never smoking cigarettes.
6 Moderate or no use of alcohol.
7 Regular physical activity.

At the time, it was found that good practices were associated with positive health status, those who followed all the good practices being in better health than those who failed to do so, and that this association was independent of age, sex, and economic status (Belloc and Breslow 1972).

Most striking, however, were the findings of two follow-up studies in which the relationship between these health habits and longevity was explored by using death records. At the first follow-up, conducted five and a half years later, 371 deaths had occurred (Belloc 1973). When the initial health practices in 1965 were then related to subsequent mortality, it was found that the more of these 'good' health practices a person engaged in, the greater was the probability that he or she would survive the next five and a half years (see Figure 1.2).

These findings were confirmed at a second follow-up investigation conducted nine and a half years after the initial inquiry, when again an inverse relationship between health practices and age-adjusted mortality rates was observed (Breslow and Enstrom 1980). Men who followed all seven health practices had a mortality rate which was only 28 per cent of that of men who followed zero to three practices; the comparable rate for women who followed all practices was 43 per cent of those who followed zero to three practices. The authors also observed a great stability in the health practices of each individual over the nine and a half year period.

The importance of lifestyle factors for the maintenance of health and the prevention of disease has also been underlined by the outcome of analyses of the contribution of lifestyle factors and other modifiable causes to mortality in the USA. These analyses were conducted by the Centers for Disease Control and Prevention in 1977 and 1990 (McGinnis and Foege 1993) and were more recently updated by Mokdad et al. (2004). Since all of these analyses reached very similar conclusions I will focus here on the most cited report of McGinnis and Foege (1993). These authors estimated that of the approximately 2,148,000 deaths that occurred in the USA in the year 1990, nearly 50 per cent were due to modifiable factors. More than 40 per cent of these premature deaths were due to lifestyle factors (e.g. smoking, eating the wrong diet, leading a sedentary lifestyle, consuming too much alcohol, sexual risk behaviour, illicit drug use, firearms, motor vehicle accidents). In addition, the list of modifiable causes includes preventable infectious diseases

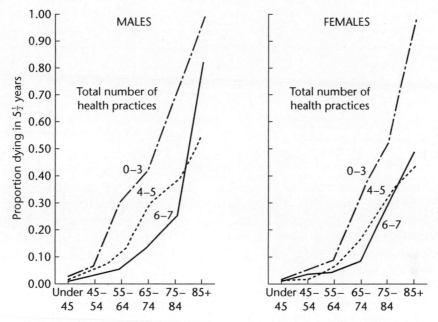

FIGURE 1.2 Age-specific mortality rates by number of health practices followed by sub-groups of males and females
Source: Matarazzo (1984)

(excluding HIV) and death caused by toxic agents which may pose a threat to human health as occupational hazards, environmental pollutants, contaminants of food and water supplies and components of commercial products. All these deaths were premature in the sense that they could have been postponed if individuals or communities had taken appropriate measures.

Findings such as these tend to support Becker's (1976) argument that most deaths are to some extent self-inflicted, at least in the sense that they could have been postponed if people had engaged in 'good' health practices like the ones listed by Belloc and Breslow (1972). The important implication of this research at the individual level is that the responsibility for health does not rest with the medical profession alone. Each of us can have a major impact on the state of our own health. At the institutional level, it emphasizes the potential effectiveness of preventive measures (i.e. primary prevention) that focus on persuading people to adopt good health habits and to change bad ones.

It is important to note, however, that life extension (i.e. mere quantity) is only one of the goals of health promotion, and perhaps not even the most important one. We may have to accept that we are unlikely to reach the age of 140, even with the healthiest of lifestyles (Fries *et al.* 1989). People are persuaded to engage in a healthy lifestyle not merely to lengthen their lives but to help them to stay fit longer and lead an active life right into old age without being plagued by pain, infirmity and chronic disease. Thus, the second major goal of health promotion is to increase the quality of life and to contribute to healthy and successful ageing by delaying the onset of chronic disease and extending the active lifespan (Fries *et al*. 1989). Low probability of disease and disease-related disability, and high cognitive and physical functional capacity in old age are two of the main components of successful ageing (Rowe and Kahn 1987).

The impact of stress on health

The concept of stress has become so much part of common culture that it does not seem to need definition. Reports about health consequences of everyday stress pervade the advice columns of popular magazines and even teenagers complain to their teachers that they are under undue stress due to an overload of homework. It has become public knowledge that stress, like smoking or drinking too much alcohol, can have adverse effects on physical as well as mental health.

As we will see later in this book (Chapter 6), there is now ample evidence that psychosocial stress results in health impairment. To some extent these health consequences of stressful life events are mediated by the same changes in endocrine, immune and autonomic nervous systems which have been described in the classic work of Selye (e.g. 1976) on the health impact of physical stressors. However, the experience of psychosocial stress also causes negative changes in health behaviour that contribute to the stress–illness relationship (e.g. irregular eating habits, increases in smoking, alcohol consumption and drug intake). Furthermore, stress is often also a result of people's lifestyles. Thus, research on stress and illness is closely related to our interest in the impact of behaviour on health.

From the biomedical to the biopsychosocial model of disease

That lifestyle factors and psychosocial stress are important determinants of health and illness is difficult to accept within the framework of the biomedical model which has been the dominant model of disease for several centuries (Engel 1977). This model assumes that for every disease there exists a primary biological cause that is objectively identifiable. Let us exemplify this approach with statements from a typical medical textbook, *Introduction to Human Disease* by Kent and Hart (1987). According to these authors, diseases are caused 'by injury which may be either external or internal in origin . . . External causes of disease are divided into physical, chemical and microbiologic . . . Internal causes of disease fall into three large categories' (vascular, immunologic, metabolic) (1987: 8, 9). Because behavioural factors are not considered to be potential causes of disease, they are also not assessed as part of the process of diagnosis.

By focusing only on biological causes of illness, the biomedical model disregards the fact that most illnesses are the result of an interaction of social, psychological and biological events. The logical inference of such a biological conception of disease is that physicians need not be concerned with psychosocial issues because they lie outside their responsibility and authority. Thus, the model has little to offer in guiding the kind of preventive efforts that are needed to reduce the incidence of chronic diseases by changing health beliefs, attitudes and behaviour.

In recognition of these problems, Engel (1977) proposed an expansion of the biomedical model which incorporates psychosocial factors into the scientific equation. The biopsychosocial model maintains that biological, psychological and social factors are all important determinants of health and illness. According to this approach, medical diagnosis should always consider the interaction of biological, psychological and social factors to assess health and make recommendations for treatment.

Social psychology and health

The growing recognition that lifestyle factors and psychosocial stress contribute substantially to morbidity and mortality from cardiovascular disease, cancer, injuries and other leading causes of death in industrialized countries was one of the factors which in the late 1970s led to the development of health psychology as a field which integrates psychological knowledge relevant to the maintenance of health, the prevention of illness and the adjustment to illness. Social psychology had, and still has, an important contribution to make to this endeavour, because lifestyles are likely to be determined by health attitudes and health beliefs. Effective prevention has to achieve large-scale changes in lifestyles and such attempts will have to rely on mass communication and thus on an application of social psychological techniques of attitude and behaviour change.

The interest of social psychologists in the study of stress developed more recently, because many of the most stressful life events (e.g. divorce, bereavement) involve a break-up of social relationships. Furthermore, the health impact of stressful events not only depends on the nature of these events but also on the individuals' ability to cope with the crisis and on the extent to which they receive social support from relatives, friends and other members of their social network. Finally, the impact of stress on health, although to some extent due to the brain's influence on physiological processes such as the body's immune response, is also mediated by the adoption of health-impairing habits as coping strategies (e.g. smoking, alcohol abuse). Thus, social factors are not only important in determining the stressful nature of many life events but also as moderators of the stress–health relationship.

Social psychologists have also made important contributions to another major area of health psychology, namely the analysis and improvement of health care systems. This involved issues such as physician–patient relationships, compliance with medical procedures, anxiety as related to medical procedures and burnout in the helping professions. Although a review of social psychological research on these topics would have been highly relevant in the context of this book, these issues will not be discussed. Due to space limitations any attempt at completely reviewing social psychological contributions to health psychology would have had to remain at a superficial level. Instead I decided to present an in-depth analysis of a number of selected areas. The reader interested in social psychological contributions to research into the health care system should consult the overview provided by Taylor (2011).

Plan of the book

Why do people engage in health-impairing behaviour and how can they be influenced? To answer these questions we need to know and understand the factors and processes that determine the adoption and maintenance of health behaviour. Chapter 2 presents the major models of behaviour from health and social psychology, to provide the theoretical framework for the analysis of determinants of health behaviour. All of these models assume that behaviour is deliberate and guided by people's outcome and normative beliefs. However, more recently there is increasing evidence that behaviour is often automatic and driven by impulses, of which people might not even be aware. This research is discussed and integration with models of deliberate action is suggested. Chapter 3 discusses strategies of behaviour change. I will argue that there are basically two stages to the modification of health behaviour. Individuals first have to be informed of the health hazards of certain behaviour patterns and persuaded to change. This can be achieved by public health interventions such as health education. Because people are often unable to change health-impairing behaviour patterns, a second stage may be necessary in which people are taught how to change and how to maintain this change. This second stage often relies on clinical intervention. Chapter 3 gives an overview of both the public health approach and the methods of clinical intervention.

The next two chapters discuss the major behavioural risk factors that have been linked to health. Chapter 4 focuses on health-impairing behaviour such as smoking, alcohol abuse and overeating. These behaviours are addictive in the sense that, once excessive, they are difficult to control. The self-protective behaviour covered in Chapter 5, such as eating a healthy diet, safeguarding oneself against accidents and avoiding behaviour associated with the risk of HIV infection, is in general somewhat more under the volitional control of the individual. In my discussion of these risk factors I will review both the empirical evidence that links these behaviours to negative health consequences and the effectiveness of public health strategies and/or therapy in modifying these behaviour patterns.

Chapter 6 discusses causes and consequences of psychosocial stress. Stressful life events have been related to an increased risk of morbidity and this health impact is not only mediated by the brain's influence on physiological processes but also by the adoption of health-impairing behaviours as coping strategies.

Chapter 7 reviews extra- and intrapersonal coping resources which help the individual cope with stressful life events. The review of extrapersonal coping resources focuses mainly on the beneficial effects of social support in moderating the impact of stress and discusses psychological and biological mechanisms assumed to mediate this relationship. The discussion of intrapersonal coping resources focuses on hardiness and dispositional optimism. Finally, hostility is discussed as a personality moderator of stress which does not reflect a coping resource.

In summarizing my overall perspective in Chapter 8, I reflect on the contribution of social psychologists to the public health effort through theories and strategies that help to change health-impairing behaviour patterns and reduce psychological stress. I argue for integrated public health interventions that use both persuasion and changes in incentives to influence health-impairing behaviour patterns. I also argue for a reorientation of research on behavioural risk factors, which focuses less on the extension of total life expectancy and more on the extension of *active* life expectancy and successful ageing. It is the reduction of morbidity rather than mortality which makes healthier lifestyles worthwhile for both the individual and society as a whole.

Further reading

McKeown, T. (1979) *The Role of Medicine*. Oxford: Blackwell. A fascinating analysis of the role of medical measures in the decline of mortality over the last few centuries in England and Wales. It shows that for practically all infectious diseases the major reduction in mortality occurred long before medical measures to cure them had been discovered.

Determinants of health behaviour: deliberate and automatic instigation of action

Why do people engage in health-impairing behaviour such as smoking or eating a poor diet, even if they know that they are damaging their health? Is there any way to influence them to change their behaviour? This chapter will present theoretical models from health and social psychology which will provide the framework for the analysis of the determinants of health behaviour. Knowledge of these determinants will help us to evaluate the potential effectiveness of the strategies of behaviour change that will be discussed in the following chapters.

There are several psychological models of behaviour which have either been developed specifically to predict health behaviour (health belief model, protection motivation theory) or as general models of behaviour (theory of reasoned action, theory of planned behaviour). These models, which will be reviewed in the first half of this chapter, emphasize processes of conscious information processing. They conceptualize behaviour as the endpoint of deliberate decision-making, with actors assumed to decide on a course of action after weighing the pros and cons of various behavioural alternatives.

Although these models do reasonably well in predicting health behaviour, they may paint a slightly unrealistic picture of how we go about engaging in health-relevant actions. We all know the saying that the road to hell is paved with good intentions. People decide to give up smoking and are convinced that they will succeed in doing so, and yet, sitting outside the pub with their friends, who all smoke, they find themselves lighting a cigarette. Or they go on a diet and decide to eat only a salad for lunch in a restaurant. And yet, after having read the menu listing some of their favourite dishes, they surprise themselves by ordering a three-course meal, including a dessert. In such cases self-control has broken down and impulsive behaviour appears to have taken over. By focusing exclusively on deliberate actions, classic theories neglect the fact that automatic and unconscious processes can exert a powerful impact on our behaviour. During the last few decades social psychologists (and some health psychologists) have become aware of this omission and there is now a great deal of theorizing and research on unconscious influences on behaviour. This work will be reviewed in the last part of this chapter.

The first section of this chapter will discuss attitudes, beliefs, goals and intentions as the major determinants of behaviour. Since the behaviour of interest in this book is health behaviour, I end this section by briefly defining this behaviour and reviewing its structure. In the second section, I review the classic theories of behaviour which have dominated research on health behaviour, such as the health belief model, protection motivation theory and the theories of reasoned action and planned behaviour. These are theories of deliberate action, which, with the exception of the health belief model, assume that the impact of attitudes and beliefs on behaviour is mediated by intentions. Since intentions account for less than half of the variance in measures of behaviour, I will end this part of the chapter by discussing implementation intentions as more specific intentions, which have been shown to improve behaviour predictions.

Although adding implementation intentions considerably improves the prediction of health behaviour, even the improved predictions account for less than half of the variance in behaviour. One major reason for this shortcoming of models of deliberate action is that our behaviour is often influenced by automatic processes, which operate outside conscious awareness. These processes will be reviewed in the last part of this chapter.

Attitudes, beliefs, goals, intentions and behaviour

Because most models of behaviour agree on the central role of attitudes, beliefs and intentions as determinants of behaviour, this section will define these central concepts and discuss the relationship between them.

The changing conception of attitudes

Attitudes reflect people's likes and dislikes, the way they evaluate the world around them. The traditional view conceived of attitudes as *dispositions* to evaluate an *attitude object* in a particular way (e.g. Eagly and Chaiken 1993). An attitude object can be any discriminable aspect of the physical or social environment, such as things (cars, drugs), people (doctors, the British), behaviour (jogging, drinking alcohol) and even abstract ideas (religion, health). Social psychologists have typically divided the evaluative tendencies that reflect an attitude into three classes, namely cognitive reactions, affective reactions and behaviour (e.g. Rosenberg and Hovland 1960; Ajzen 1988; Eagly and Chaiken 1993).

Evaluative responses of the cognitive type are thoughts or beliefs about the attitude object. For example, a positive attitude towards jogging might be associated with the belief that jogging helps one to keep one's weight down, increases fitness and decreases high blood pressure. Such beliefs are perceived linkages between the attitude object (i.e. jogging) and various attributes which are positively or negatively valued (i.e. low weight, high blood pressure).

Evaluative responses of the affective type consist of the emotions that people experience in relation to the attitude object. These evaluative responses also range from extremely positive to extremely negative reactions. For example, people may feel revulsion when they think of fatty foods or the smell of cigarette smoke, whereas the idea of physical exercise makes them feel good.

Evaluative responses of the behavioural type consist of overt actions towards the attitude object which imply positive or negative evaluations. Thus, people go jogging regularly regardless of weather conditions and ask smokers not to smoke in their presence. Behavioural responses can also consist of behavioural intentions. Thus, the experience of not fitting into ski pants that were too big last season might lead one to form the intention to start a weight loss programme next week. Similarly, a smoker who learns that a colleague and fellow smoker has just died from lung cancer might form the intention to stop smoking.

Implicit and explicit measures of attitude: challenging the unity of the attitude concept

The definition of attitude as an evaluative tendency that underlies the expression of attitudes in terms of cognitive, affective and behavioural responses implies a certain consistency between different types of evaluative responses: we should feel good about behaviours about which we hold positive beliefs and we should tend to engage in these behaviours. This conception, which had already come under pressure due to the discrepancy often observed between verbal expressions of attitudes and overt actions (e.g. LaPiére 1934; Wicker 1969) was further challenged by the research using implicit measures of attitudes. In contrast to explicit attitude measures, which are based on individuals' self-reports of their attitudes, implicit attitude measures are typically based on reaction times to unobtrusively assess people's attitudes. Research on implicit attitudes reopened the old controversy about the discrepancy between attitudes inferred from explicit self-reports and those derived from the way respondents behave.

Since there is some disagreement among attitude researchers whether it is the attitude or the procedure used to measure it which is implicit, we will start our discussion with the description of the two most frequently used implicit attitude measures, namely affective priming (Fazio *et al.* 1986) and the Implicit Association Test (IAT) (Greenwald *et al.* 1998). With the affective priming procedure, individuals are presented on each trial with a name or picture of an attitude object. Immediately afterwards they are presented with positive or negative adjectives (e.g. words such as 'useful', 'valuable' or 'disgusting') and are asked to decide as fast as possible whether the adjective is positive or negative. The time it takes people to make this judgement (i.e. their reaction time) constitutes the dependent measure. Thus the basic idea of the affective priming measure is that one can estimate the attitude towards the prime stimulus (i.e. the attitude object) by examining how the presence of the prime influences the speed of the affective categorization of the target stimulus (i.e. the adjective) that is presented subsequently (de Houwer *et al.* 2009). Exposure to the attitude object is assumed to automatically activate an evaluative response and this response should either facilitate or inhibit the evaluative response to the next stimulus (i.e. the adjective). Whether the evaluative response activated by the attitude object will facilitate or inhibit the subsequent response will depend on whether the attitude object and the adjective are evaluatively similar or dissimilar. Suppose that the attitude object is the picture of a cream cake and that respondents evaluate cream cakes negatively. Then presentation of the cream cake should automatically activate a negative evaluation. If the adjective that is presented immediately afterwards is also negative (e.g. the word 'failure'), respondents will be able to indicate the evaluative connotation of the target adjective relatively quickly. In contrast, if the adjective is positive (e.g. vacation), then the fact that the attitude prime has just activated a negative evaluative response might slow down the respondent's reaction.

Like the affective priming method, the IAT uses reaction times to infer implicit attitudes. In essence, the procedure assesses the strength of an association between two concepts with positive and negative evaluations. The reaction times are derived from the participants' use of two response keys which have been assigned a dual meaning. For example, in an application of the IAT to assess attitudes towards drinking beer, participants are asked to categorize stimuli from four categories, namely two target categories (e.g. pictures of beer and of water) and two attribute categories (e.g. pleasant and unpleasant words). In one set of trials, pictures of beer and positively evaluated words (e.g. vacation, joy) will be assigned to one key and pictures of water and negatively evaluated words (e.g. failure, accident) will be assigned to the other key. In a second set of trials beer and unpleasant words will share one key and water and pleasant words the other. The basic assumption underlying the IAT is that categorization performance should be a function of the degree to which categories that are assigned to the same key are associated in memory (de Houwer et al. 2009). For a beer drinker the task should be easier (i.e. shorter reaction times) when beer and positively evaluated words share one key and water and negatively evaluated words the other, whereas for somebody who dislikes beer, the other combination should be easier. Thus, the difference in the reaction times in these two sets of trials will be the implicit measure of attitudes to beer.

Both implicit attitude measurement procedures assess an individual's automatic attitudinal reaction to an attitude object. It is these spontaneous evaluative reactions which influence behaviour through automatic processes. Automatic processes are processes that occur without intention, effort or awareness and do not interfere with other concurrent cognitive processes. There is now a great deal of evidence that implicit attitude measures are better predictors than explicit attitude measures of behaviour that is outside individual control, particularly in contexts where there is a discrepancy between an individual's automatic reaction to an attitude object and how he or she would wish to respond. The less individuals have the opportunity or motivation to control their behaviour and the greater the discrepancy, the more superior will implicit attitude measures be over explicit measures in predicting this behaviour (Friese et al. 2008). For example, numerous studies have demonstrated that implicit racial attitudes are reliable predictors of subtle interracial behaviour (for reviews, see Dovidio et al. 2001; Fazio and Olson 2003; Friese et al. 2008).

Dovidio *et al.* (1997) reported a correspondence between attitude estimates based on a priming measure and nonverbal behaviours displayed while interacting with a black or white interviewer. Thus, the implicit measure of prejudice predicted lower levels of visual contact with the black interviewer and higher rates of blinking, both not predicted by the measure of modern racism. Wilson *et al.* (2000) found their affective priming measure of prejudice significantly related to the number of times white participants touched a black confederate's hand in a task where they had to share a pen. Finally, in a study of prejudice towards fat people, Bessenoff and Sherman (2000) found that an affective priming measure involving photos of fat and thin women correlated with the distance at which participants would later place their chair away from that of a fat woman.

In contrast to racial attitudes, where personal feelings may be in conflict with social norms, the most frequent conflict in the area of health behaviour is between personal likes and personal goals. For example, chronic dieters are in a conflict between their liking of the taste of palatable high calorie food and their knowledge that consumption of this food would endanger their goal of weight control. Similarly, smokers who are trying to stop are in a conflict between their urge to smoke a cigarette and their knowledge that keeping on smoking will shorten their life span.

Whenever there is a conflict between personal likes or dislikes and social norms or personal goals, explicit attitude measures are likely to reflect a compromise between the individuals' affective reaction to the attitude object and the expected consequences of a goal violation. For example, chronic dieters know that as much as they would enjoy an ice cream, eating ice cream would endanger their weight loss plans. Since both of these beliefs will influence their explicitly measured attitude towards ice cream (or eating ice cream), this attitude measure will be less positive than their implicitly measured attitude, which will be mainly determined by their affective experience while eating ice cream.

Are attitudes stable or context-dependent?

A further challenge to the dispositional definition of attitude comes from evidence that indicates that attitudes are often context dependent. The way we define the concept has implications for the stability we expect of people's attitudes. Eagly and Chaiken's (1993) proposal that evaluative responses reflect an inner tendency implies that people's attitudes should be relatively stable over time. With this assumption, Eagly and Chaiken are consistent with a tradition in attitude research which conceives of attitudes as learned structures that reside in long-term memory and are activated upon encountering the attitude object (e.g. Fazio and Williams 1986). This perspective has been termed the 'file-drawer model', because it conceives of attitudes as mental files which can be consulted for the evaluation of a given attitude object (Schwarz and Bohner 2001).

In recent decades, this view has been challenged by evidence that suggests that attitudes may be much less enduring and stable than has traditionally been assumed (for reviews, see Schwarz and Strack 1991; Erber *et al.* 1995; Schwarz and Bohner 2001; Schwarz 2007). According to this perspective, attitudes fluctuate over time and appear to 'depend on what people happen to be thinking about at any given moment' (Erber *et al.* 1995: 433). Proponents of this 'attitudes-as-constructions perspective' reject the view that people retrieve previously stored attitudes in making evaluative judgements. Instead, they assume that individuals make their judgements 'on-line', based on the information that is either presented or comes to mind in any given situation. This conception of attitudes as on-line judgements is inconsistent with the view that evaluative judgements are the expression of an underlying tendency (e.g. Schwarz 2007).

There is empirical support for both stability and malleability of attitudes. There is evidence that political attitudes can persist for many years or even a lifetime (e.g. Alwin *et al.* 1991; Marwell *et al.* 1987), but there is also evidence that attitudes change with changing context. For example, Wilson and his colleagues demonstrated that attitudes can change when people analyse their reasons for holding them and that this change can occur for a wide range of attitude objects, including political candidates (Wilson *et al.* 1989) and dating partners (Wilson and Kraft 1993).

How can these inconsistencies be reconciled? One potential solution suggested by theorists who subscribe to the attitude-as-construction perspective is to deny that their position implies that attitudes should be unstable and therefore not predictive of behaviour. They argue that even if attitudinal judgements are made on-line each time we encounter the attitude object, attitudes should remain stable to the extent that at each point in time respondents draw on similar sources of information (Erber *et al.* 1995; Schwarz and Bohner 2001). For example, since neither the taste of Coca-Cola nor its advertising campaigns are likely to change dramatically over the years, our attitude towards Coca-Cola is likely to remain stable, even if it were formed on a day-to-day basis.

Because it seems implausible and impractical that people construct their attitude anew each time they encounter an attitude object, we tend to subscribe to an alternative solution, namely that attitudes can be placed on a continuum of attitude strength. This continuum ranges from issues which are either so novel or irrelevant for individuals that they have not (yet) formed an attitude, to issues which are both familiar and important to individuals and towards which they have strong, well-developed attitudes. When people are asked to evaluate novel and unfamiliar stimuli they have no alternative but to form their evaluation on-line based on the information at hand. In contrast, when they are asked to evaluate an attitude object with which they have been familiar for many years and about which they have a great deal of information, they are likely to have made up their minds a long time ago and are therefore able to rely on this evaluative knowledge structure in making their judgement. We will discuss this question further in the context of my discussion of the relationship between attitudes and beliefs.

Implications for the definition of the attitude concept

The evidence discussed in this section presents problems for dispositional definitions of the attitude concept. Both the discrepancy often observed between implicit and explicit attitudes and the context dependence of attitudes are difficult to reconcile with the assumption that these different evaluative responses are the expression of an underlying tendency. Although such a reconciliation is not impossible and plausible explanations have been suggested (e.g. see Fazio 1990; Eagly and Chaiken 2007), I tend to favour the definition suggested by Zanna and Rempel (1988) of attitudes as 'the categorization of a stimulus object along an evaluative dimension' (p. 319). This definition does not imply that attitudinal judgements reflect some underlying disposition, and affective and behavioural responses are considered correlates of evaluative judgements. If one does not limit categorization to a cognitive process but includes positive and negative affective responses occurring below the level of awareness, the Zanna and Rempel definition would be more consistent with the evidence reviewed above than a definition of attitudes as a reflection of a tendency to evaluate.

The relationship between attitudes and beliefs

It is plausible that people's attitudes should be related to their beliefs about these attitude objects. And indeed, most cognitive theories of attitude share the assumption that the attitude towards some attitude object is a function of the attributes associated with that object and the evaluation of these attributes (e.g. Rosenberg 1960; Fishbein and Ajzen 1975; Sutton 1987). Similarly, a person's attitude towards performing a given behaviour is assumed to be a function of the perceived consequences of that behaviour and the evaluation of these consequences. However, since attitudes assessed with implicit measures reflect spontaneous evaluative responses, one would expect that the relationship between attitudes and beliefs should be stronger for attitudes measured with explicit rather than implicit measures.

The relationship between attitudes and beliefs can be expressed quantitatively in terms of expectancy–value models (e.g. Fishbein and Ajzen 1975). According to these models an individual's attitude towards some action depends on the subjective values or utilities attached to the possible outcomes of that action, each weighted by the subjective probabilities that the action will lead to these outcomes. Thus, one's attitude towards personally engaging in physical exercise would be a function of the *perceived likelihood* (i.e. expectancy) with which physical exercise is associated with certain consequences such as low blood pressure or physical fitness and the *evaluation* (i.e. value, subjective utility) of these consequences. The way such beliefs combine to produce an attitude can be expressed by the following equation:

$$A = \Sigma\, b_i\, e_i$$

As can be seen, the subjective probability with which the attitude object is associated with a particular attribute (b) is multiplied by the subjective evaluation (e) of this attribute. The resulting products are summed. With the hedonically relevant attitude objects that often form part of self-control dilemmas (e.g. food, drinks, cigarettes) one would expect that beliefs about the hedonic experience would weigh heavier with implicit than explicit attitude measures, whereas explicit measures should in turn be more heavily influenced by potential negative long-term effects of enjoying these attitude objects.

Fishbein and Ajzen (1975) have emphasized that a person's attitude towards an attitude object is not determined by all the beliefs the individual holds towards that object, but by a limited number of *salient* beliefs – (that is, beliefs which are cognitively highly accessible in this particular situation (e.g. Ajzen and Fishbein 2000). Since the accessibility of beliefs will depend on situational cues, Ajzen and Fishbein's expectancy x value conception of the relationship between beliefs and attitudes is consistent with the view that attitudes towards an attitude object will vary from situation to situation.

The relationship between attitudes, goals and intentions

Goals are conceptualized as cognitive representations of desired end-states. Thus, goals are states people evaluate positively and thus hold positive attitudes towards. However, being desirable is not a sufficient reason for people to adopt an end-state as a goal. For example, people might have a positive attitude towards jogging regularly and yet they might never jog. There could be several reasons for this. For example, if individuals play tennis three times per week and, in addition, go on extended bike tours at the weekend, they might see no need to jog, because they already engage in a great deal of physical exercise. In order to adopt a positively valued end-state as a goal, people must perceive a discrepancy between their present state and the goal. A second characteristic a desirable end-state must possess to be adopted as a goal is that it must be perceived as attainable. For example, even though most smokers in the USA report that they would like to quit smoking, many do not try to do so because after numerous failed attempts they have become convinced that for them the goal of quitting in unattainable. But even if a goal is desirable and attainable and even if there is a discrepancy between the present state and this end-state, the individual might still not adopt that goal, if moving towards that goal interferes with other even more desirable goals. For example, an overweight person might like to lose weight and might also believe that weight loss is possible. However, since abstention from eating palatable high-calorie food would interfere with eating enjoyment, the individual might not adopt weight loss as a goal or at least might not pursue this goal consistently.

Goals vary in abstractness. For example, the goal to become a better person is a very abstract one, whereas the goal of eating dinner at home at 6 p.m. is a very concrete goal. One major difference between goals which are more or less abstract is the difference in the number of means that are available to reach the goal. The more abstract the goal, the greater the number of potential means to reach it. Whereas there are numerous means possible to improve oneself and become a better person (from offering to clear the dinner table to donating money to good causes), eating dinner at home at 6 p.m. refers to a specific behaviour. Therefore, predicting specific behaviour from knowing a person's goals becomes easier the less abstract the goal.

Once people have adopted a goal, they have formed the intention to reach it. Like goals, intentions differ in abstractness and in the range of behaviours the individual can engage in to fulfil his or her intention. One important distinction is between goal intentions and implementation intentions. Whereas goal intentions (better known as behavioural intentions) only specify the intended behaviour to be executed in the near future, implementation intentions specify the precise time and the precise situational context of the execution of that behaviour (Gollwitzer 1999).

Measures of the strength of intentions indicate goal commitment. Goal commitment reflects the degree to which the individual is determined to pursue a particular goal. The models of deliberate behaviour to be reviewed later conceive of behavioural intentions (i.e. the intention to perform a specific behaviour) as the crucial mediating variable between attitudes and behaviour. More recently, the even more specific implementation intentions to perform a specific behaviour in a specific context at a specific time have become important in behaviour prediction (Gollwitzer 1999).

The relationship between attitude and behaviour

Social psychological research has often failed to find a substantial relationship between an attitude and a behaviour that would seem relevant to the attitude. This failure to find such a relationship was particularly likely in studies that related very general attitudes to much more specific behaviour (for reviews, see Ajzen and Fishbein 1977; Eagly and Chaiken 1993; Ajzen 2005). For example, a study of health attitudes and behaviour found that specific health behaviours, such as having regular dental check-ups or eating vitamin supplements, were largely unrelated to general attitudes towards health protection (Ajzen and Timko 1986).

The lack of correspondence that has frequently been observed in studies of the attitude–behaviour relationship does not imply, however, that we should abandon the idea that attitudes are predictors or determinants of behaviour. Since the early 1970s social psychologists have studied the conditions under which measures of attitude predict behaviour. In their extensive analyses of attitude–behaviour research, Fishbein and Ajzen (1975) and Ajzen and Fishbein (1977) identified two major conditions which needed to be fulfilled for studies to find attitude strongly related to behaviour: a relationship between attitude and behaviour was most likely to emerge if both attitude and behaviour had been assessed by measures which were (a) *reliable* and (b) *compatible*.

Reliability

Many of the classic studies of the attitude–behaviour literature which failed to observe a relationship between attitude and behaviour related attitudes to *single* instances of behaviour. As Ajzen and Fishbein (1977) and Epstein (1979) argued, single instances of behaviour are determined by a unique set of factors and are thus unreliable measures of behavioural tendencies (that is, the tendency to show a specific behaviour over time. For example, even a heavy smoker may refuse a cigarette offered on a particular occasion if he or she is suffering from a severe cold or does not like the particular brand of cigarettes. Only when one computes the average behavioural response over repeated occasions does the influence of factors that vary from one occasion to another tend to 'cancel out'. Thus, when one compares the number of cigarettes smoked on average by a heavy smoker with that smoked by a light smoker or a non-smoker, the cigarette consumption of the heavy smoker is likely to be higher. That aggregation across multiple instances of the same behaviour will increase the measure's temporal stability has been amply demonstrated (e.g. Epstein 1979).

Compatibility

The use of reliable measures is a necessary but not a sufficient condition to achieve high correlations between measures of attitudes and behaviour. To assure a strong relation between measures of attitudes and behaviour, these measures need to be not only reliable but also compatible. Measures of attitude and behaviour are compatible if both are assessed at the same level of abstractness. Ajzen and Fishbein (1977) developed some criteria which help to evaluate the degree of compatibility between measures of attitude and behaviour. Every instance of behaviour involves four specific elements: (a) a specific action; (b) performed with respect to a given target; (c) in a given context; and (d) at a given point in time. The principle of compatibility specifies that measures of attitude and behaviour are compatible to the extent that their target, action, context and time elements are assessed at identical levels of generality or specificity (Ajzen 1988).

For example, a person's attitude towards a 'healthful lifestyle' only specifies the goal (target), but leaves action, context and time elements unspecified by which this goal could be reached. There are numerous means to achieve the goal of healthfulness. A healthful lifestyle comprises numerous health practices that can be performed in many different contexts at many different times. A behavioural measure that would be compatible with this global attitude would have to aggregate a wide range of health behaviour across different contexts and times.

Consistent with this assumption, Ajzen and Timko (1986) reported that a measure of global attitudes towards health maintenance, which did not correlate significantly with the self-reported frequency with which respondents performed *specific* health protective behaviours, showed a substantial correlation with a behavioural index that aggregated the performance of a wide variety of different health protective behaviours. These behaviours related to different aspects of health and had been performed in a wide variety of contexts and times.

On the other hand, if we are interested in predicting *specific* behaviour, then an attitude measure would be compatible if it assessed the attitude towards performing the specific behaviour. Thus, Ajzen and Timko (1986) were able to predict specific health behaviours from equally specific attitudes towards these behaviours. For example, the reported frequency with which respondents had 'regular dental check-ups' correlated .46 with respondents' attitudes 'towards having regular dental checkups'.

The importance of compatibility between attitude and behaviour measures for establishing substantial attitude–behaviour relationships has been demonstrated in a meta-analysis of studies that varied in compatibility (Kraus 1995). Meta-analyses are a set of techniques for statistically integrating the results of independent studies. These techniques make it possible to quantify study outcomes of a comprehensive sample of studies on a given topic in terms of a common metric (effect size). This enables one to compare outcomes across studies and to examine the overall outcomes of findings of all studies combined. Kraus (1995) identified eight studies that manipulated levels of compatibility between attitude and behaviour measures while holding other factors constant. The behaviours studied ranged from participation in a particular psychology experiment to blood donations and self-reported use of birth control pills. Kraus reported a mean correlation of r = .13 at the lowest level of compatibility as compared to r = .54 when compatibility was high.

The principle of compatibility has implications for strategies of attitude and behaviour change. As with prediction, compatibility should be observed in attempts to change behaviour. Thus, mass media campaigns designed to change some specific health behaviour should use arguments mainly aimed at changing beliefs relating to that *specific* behaviour rather than focusing on more general health concerns. For example, to persuade people to lower the cholesterol content of their diet, it would not be very effective merely to point out that coronary heart disease is the major killer and/or that high cholesterol levels are bad for one's heart. To influence diets one would have to argue that very specific changes in one's diet, such as eating less animal fats and less red meat, would have a positive impact on blood cholesterol levels and that the reduction in serum cholesterol should in turn reduce the risk of developing coronary heart disease.

A number of meta-analyses of studies of the attitude–behaviour relationship reported substantial relationships between attitude and behaviour, suggesting that most studies use measures of these constructs which are reliable and compatible. Based on a meta-analysis of 88 attitude–behaviour studies, Kraus (1995) reported a mean correlation of r = .38. An even more extensive meta-analysis based on 644 independent studies found a similar mean correlation of r = .36 (Six 1996). However, with r = .23 (based on 69 studies), the mean correlation for the domain of health behaviour was somewhat lower than the overall mean for all behavioural domains taken together.

Health behaviour

Before discussing classic theories of behaviour in the next section, it might be useful briefly to consider the behaviour of interest in this book, namely health behaviour. Health behaviour is typically defined as behaviour undertaken by individuals to enhance or maintain their health (e.g. Kasl and Cobb 1970). Sometimes researchers further distinguish between health-impairing behaviours like smoking or drinking too much alcohol which have a negative effect on health, and health-protective or health-enhancing behaviours such as exercising or eating a healthy diet which may have a positive effect (Matarazzo 1984). However, even health-enhancing behaviours are frequently undertaken for reasons unrelated to health. For example, many people who diet deprive themselves to improve their looks rather than their health.

One could therefore argue for an alternative definition in terms of *objective* rather than intended consequences of health behaviour. Thus, we would use the term *health behaviour* to refer to behaviours which have been shown to have beneficial health consequences for those who practise them (e.g. exercising; eating sufficient fruit and vegetables). The term 'health-impairing behaviour' is then used for behaviour known to damage one's health. This health impairment can either be due to failure to engage in health-enhancing behaviours (e.g. lack of exercise) or to the performance of actions which are known to be unhealthy (e.g. smoking).

Based on a factor analytic study of ratings of 40 different health behaviours, Vickers *et al.* (1990) concluded that the domain of health behaviour is structured in terms of four correlated but empirically distinct dimensions:

- *wellness behaviour*, reflected by items such as 'I exercise to stay healthy', 'I limit my intake of food like coffee, sugar, fats, etc.', 'I take vitamins';
- *accident control*, consisting of items such as 'I have a first-aid kit at home', 'I fix broken things around my home immediately';
- *traffic risk-taking*, reflected by items such as 'I don't speed while driving', 'I carefully obey traffic rules to avoid accidents'; and
- *substance risk-taking*, which consists of items such as 'I do not drink' or 'I do not smoke or use smokeless tobacco'.

Wellness behaviour and accident control were positively correlated with each other and so were substance risk-taking and traffic risk-taking. Vickers *et al.* (1990) suggested therefore that, at the most general level, health behaviours could be considered to form two broad categories, namely *preventive behaviour* and *risk-taking behaviour*, with preventive behaviours being negatively correlated with risk-taking. Although these dimensions appear to map the way actors perceive their own behaviour, we will not use them in this book. Instead, as suggested earlier, we will use the terminology that reflects the objective consequences of health-relevant behaviour and distinguish between health-enhancing (or simply health behaviour) and health-impairing behaviour patterns.

Studies of the clustering of health-impairing behaviours report convergent patterns. These studies focus on the relationship of four major lifestyle risk factors (smoking, heavy drinking, lack of fruit and vegetable consumption and lack of physical exercise) and typically report a clustering of these behaviours. For example, a study based on the 2003 Health Survey for England found that 42 per cent of the sample had two lifestyle risk factors, 25 per cent had three or more risk factors and 5 per cent had all four lifestyle risk factors (Poortinga 2007). In the Dutch population, 20 per cent of the sample engaged in three or more risk behaviours (Schuit *et al.* 2002). In terms of the categorization suggested by Vickers *et al.* (1990), smoking and drinking reflect substance risk-taking, whereas lack of fruit and vegetable consumption and lack of physical exercise reflect reverse-coded wellness behaviours.

Models of deliberate behaviour

This section will discuss the four major models which guided research on health behaviour for many decades, namely the health belief model, protection motivation theory, the theory of reasoned action and the theory of planned behaviour. These models assume that individuals take account of information available to them and consider the likely consequences of behavioural alternatives that are available to them before engaging in action. In situations where there are no conflicting cognitions making decisions difficult, this deliberation might be over in a flash. Furthermore, people might often act according to intentions they have formed at some earlier time.

These models belong to the family of expectancy–value models. Expectancy–value models make the assumption that decisions between different courses of action are based on two types of cognition: subjective probabilities that a given action will lead to a set of expected outcomes, and evaluation of action outcomes. Individuals will choose among various alternative courses of action that action which will most likely lead to positive consequences or avoid negative consequences. With the exception of the health belief model, these theories assume that the impact of attitudes and beliefs on behaviour is mediated by (goal-) intentions. In the last part of this section, I will discuss implementation intentions as a more specific type of intention, which have been shown to improve behaviour prediction.

The health belief model

The health belief model was originally developed by social psychologists in the US Public Health Service in an attempt to understand why people failed to make use of disease prevention or screening tests for the early detection of diseases not associated with clear-cut symptoms, at least in the early stages. Later, the model was also applied to patients' responses to symptoms and compliance with or adherence to prescribed medical regimens. In the course of these applications, the model was considerably expanded (for reviews, see Janz and Becker 1984; Harrison *et al.* 1992; Sheeran and Abraham 2005).

The model
The health belief model assumes that the likelihood that an individual engages in a given health behaviour will be a function of the extent to which a person

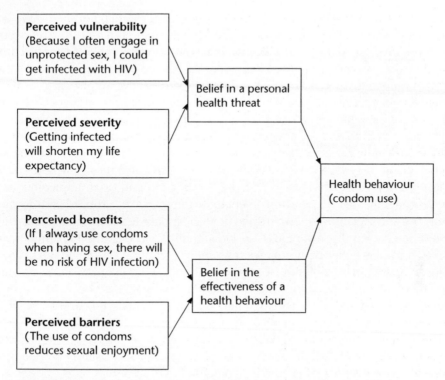

FIGURE 2.1 The health belief model applied to the reduction of sexual risk behaviour
Source: Adapted from Stroebe and de Wit (1996)

believes that he or she is personally *vulnerable* to contracting the particular illness
and of his or her perceptions of the *severity* of the consequences of becoming ill.
Vulnerability and severity jointly determine the *perceived threat* of the disease (see
Figure 2.1). For example, a sexually active student who frequently has unprotected
sex with a variety of partners might fear that he or she runs the risk of contracting
a sexually transmitted disease (perceived vulnerability). Obviously, getting such an
infection could have severe consequences (perceived severity).

Given some threat of contracting a disease, the likelihood of engaging in a particular health behaviour will further depend on the extent to which the individual
believes that the action yields *benefits* that outweigh *barriers* such as costs, incon-
venience or pain. For example, whether the student will decide to use condoms
will depend on his or her estimate of whether the benefits to health associated
with this action would really outweigh the costs in terms of the reduction of sexual
pleasure as a result of condom use or (in the case of women) the embarrassment of
having to negotiate with the partner.

Rosenstock (1974) further suggested that a *cue to action* might be necessary to
trigger appropriate health behaviour. This could be an internal cue like a bodily
symptom, or an external cue such as a mass media campaign, medical advice or
the death of a friend of similar age and lifestyle. For example, our sexually active

student might continue to hesitate about using condoms until he or she develops a skin condition following a sexual encounter, or until there is a report in the papers that the spread of AIDS among heterosexuals is accelerating. Thus, one reason cues to action might be effective is by increasing the personal relevance of a health threat. A second reason why cues to action might be effective is because they might increase the cognitive accessibility of relevant knowledge the individual already possesses. Thus, if the friend of a smoker develops serious coronary problems, this might bring to mind all the knowledge the individual has about smoking and heart disease, which he or she usually tries not to think about. As a result, the smoker might decide to have another attempt at quitting. A third reason why a cue to action might trigger behaviour is because it may form part of an implementation intention (Gollwitzer 1999). Implementation intentions are subordinate to goal intentions and specify when, where and how a response leading to goal attainment should be enacted. For example, if an individual had formed the implementation intention to phone her doctor as soon as she entered her office the next day to make an appointment, entering her office might act as a cue to action. By forming implementation intentions, people delegate the control of their behaviour over to anticipated situational cues which, when actually encountered, may elicit these responses automatically.

The relation between the variables of the health belief model has never been formalized or even explicitly spelled out. However, in most studies an additive combination is assumed. The additive combination of these variables implies that the influence of each of the variables on health behaviour is not moderated by any of the other factors. For example, the assumption that the threat of a disease is a function of the *sum* of the perceived *vulnerability* towards contracting a disease and the perceived *severity* of the disease implies that there is a moderate threat as long as one of these two variables is high, even if the other approaches zero. However, intuition suggests that the perceived threat of an illness would be very low if either of the two factors had a value of zero. For example, there may be many deadly diseases in the world (high severity) which do not worry us, because there is not the slightest chance that we could contract them (low vulnerability). With other diseases, the chance of contracting them might be high, but the consequences might be so minor that we would not really take preventive action.

A relationship in which the impact of each of the factors on health behaviour is dependent on the level of the other factor would be better represented by a model using some kind of multiplicative combination of vulnerability and severity. How-ever, even though a multiplicative combination of these components is intuitively more plausible than the additive combination, researchers in health have typically failed to demonstrate the multiplicative combination between severity and probabil-ity of threat (e.g. Rogers and Mewborn 1976; for a review, see de Hoog *et al.* 2007).

A further weakness of the health belief model is that a number of important determinants of health behaviour are not included. For example, the model does not consider potentially positive aspects of health-impairing behaviour patterns (e.g. the enjoyment of smoking) or that many health behaviours are popular for reasons totally unrelated to health (e.g. weight control and exercise behaviour is often motivated by the wish to look good rather than to be healthy). The model also fails to include self-efficacy (the individual's level of confidence that he or she is able to engage in the health protective action) as a factor influencing behaviour, even though there is a great deal of evidence that if people think they are unable to engage in a health-protective behaviour like keeping to a diet or stopping smoking, they are unlikely to do so (for a review, see Schwarzer and Fuchs 1996). A further weakness of the model is its failure to consider social influence variables such as the subjective norm component of the models of reasoned action and planned behaviour to be discussed later (see pp. 33–42). Finally, the model assumes that the belief in a personal health threat and in the effectiveness of a health behaviour have a direct influence on behaviour that is not mediated by behavioural intention. This assumption is inconsistent with evidence indicating that the influence of beliefs on behaviour is typically mediated by behavioural intentions (e.g. Wurtele *et al.* 1982; Wurtele 1988).

According to the health belief model there can be many reasons why individuals do not change their health behaviour even if their actual vulnerability is high. For example, people show a pervasive tendency to underestimate their own health risks compared to those of others (Weinstein 1987). Thus, even if they accept that eating a fatty diet increases the risk of heart disease, they might feel protected by a particularly hardy constitution. But even if individuals perceive a threat realistically, they are unlikely to engage in health-protective measures if they doubt their effectiveness or if they feel that the effort is just too great to make it worthwhile. Thus, any media campaign aimed at modifying health behaviour should contain arguments which persuade people that serious health consequences are likely to occur unless they change certain aspects of their lifestyle *and* that the adoption of a specific health behaviour would considerably reduce this risk.

Empirical evaluation of the model

Janz and Becker (1984) reviewed 46 studies based on the health belief model, of which 18 used prospective and 28 retrospective designs. In order to assess support for the model, they constructed a 'significance ratio' for each dimension, which divided the number of positive, statistically significant findings for a given dimension of the model by the total number of studies reporting significance levels for this dimension. The results were as follows: barriers (89 per cent), vulnerability (81 per cent), benefits (78 per cent) and severity (65 per cent). The authors interpret these results as providing substantial support for the model.

However, the fact that the association between two variables is statistically significant is not very informative concerning the strength of the relationship. To evaluate the strength of an association we would need information about 'effect sizes' which would allow us to estimate the variance in health behaviour that is accounted for by the various components of the model either separately or jointly. This information was provided by a meta-analytic review conducted by Harrison *et al.* (1992). Unfortunately, these authors were unusually restrictive in their selection of studies and based their analysis on only 16 studies (of which six had been included in the review of Janz and Becker 1984). Harrison *et al.* found overall that all four dimensions of the health belief model were significantly and positively related to health behaviours, but that less than 10 per cent of the variance in health behaviour could be accounted for by any one dimension. This would indicate a weak relationship compared to findings of meta-analyses of the models of reasoned action and planned behaviour which suggest that these models account for one third of the variance in behaviour (e.g. van den Putte 1991; Godin and Kok 1996; Six 1996; Armitage and Conner 2001). However, these results cannot easily be compared because Harrison *et al.* did not analyse the *joint* effect of the four dimensions of the model. The joint effect of all predictors taken together could be substantially greater than their independent effects.

Implications for the planning of interventions

According to this model, people are most likely to adopt some precautionary action if they can be persuaded that they are vulnerable to some disease, that developing that disease will have severe consequences, that adopting the preventive action will make them less vulnerable or reduce the severity of the illness, and that the perceived benefits of taking the precautionary action will outweigh the anticipated costs. In a meta-analysis of 105 studies of the impact of fear appeals on persuasion, de Hoog *et al.* (2007) found evidence that persuading individuals that they are vulnerable to a serious health risk has a strong impact on intentions to adopt the protective action and even on actual behaviour. Emphasizing response efficacy increased the persuasive impact of such communications at least as far as intention was concerned. There were no effects on behaviour.

These findings support the assumption that the health belief model identifies some of the central beliefs that underlie health behaviour. However, one has to remember that studies of the impact of fear-arousing communications typically select novel health problems about which the respondents have little information. Once individuals are well informed about a health risk, further emphasis of that threat in fear-arousing communication will have little effect. For example, most smokers who still smoke in the USA today would like to stop (e.g. USDHHS 1990). Providing them with further information about the health risk of smoking is therefore ineffective. They are unwilling to try to quit because they feel unable to do so. As we will see later, the individuals' perception of their ability to engage in a certain behaviour (i.e. self-efficacy; perceived behavioural control) is an important moderator of the impact of persuasive communications aimed at changing health behaviour. And this is one of the important variables which are not included in the health belief model.

Protection motivation theory

Although protection motivation theory has mainly been tested in the context of fear-arousing communications, the original version of the theory (e.g. Rogers and Mewborn 1976) constituted an attempt to specify the algebraic relationship between some of the components of the health belief model. According to the theory, protection motivation (i.e. the motivation to engage in some kind of health-protective behaviour) depends on three factors:

1 the perceived severity of the noxious event;
2 the perceived probability of the event's occurrence or perceived vulnerability; and
3 the efficacy of the recommended response in averting the noxious event.

The model does not include the costs of the recommended response as a variable.

According to this model, the response of a smoker exposed to a campaign that emphasizes the causal role of smoking in the development of lung cancer will depend on his or her answer to the following questions:

1 How bad is it to have lung cancer?
2 How likely is it that I will get lung cancer?
3 How much would stopping smoking reduce my risk of getting lung cancer?

The model assumes that the three factors combine multiplicatively to determine the intensity of protection motivation. More specifically, the intensity of protection motivation is assumed to be a monotonically increasing function of the algebraic product of these three variables.

An empirical test of the original model

Rogers and Mewborn (1976) tested the predictions of protection motivation theory in a series of three experiments, which used fear appeals on the topics of smoking, traffic safety and venereal diseases. In these experiments, fear-arousing communications manipulated each of the three crucial variables of the theory at two levels: high vs. low noxiousness of the depicted event, high vs. low probability of that event's occurrence and high vs. low efficacy of the recommended coping response. The results differed across the three studies and did not provide clear support for the model. In particular, in none of the three experiments was there any evidence of the three-way interaction (perceived vulnerability x perceived severity x perceived efficacy of coping) that would be expected on the basis of the multiplicative combination of the three factors of the model.

As Sutton (1982) pointed out, the failure of the study of Rogers and Mewborn (1976) to support the model could have been due to the fact that perceived efficacy and vulnerability are not independent of each other, as the model assumes. The recommended action is perceived as effective to the extent that it is thought to reduce the risk of occurrence of the noxious event. Therefore, perceived efficacy can never be greater than perceived vulnerability. This, Sutton argued, leads to inconsistencies in some conditions of the experiment. For example, under conditions of *high effectiveness and low vulnerability*, respondents are told that taking certain protective actions would considerably reduce their risk of contracting a certain disease, even though they had been informed beforehand that there was little chance of their getting this disease anyway. This kind of inconsistency may account for the fact that experimental tests failed to find many of the interactive effects predicted by the model.

The revised model

In a revision of protection motivation theory, Rogers (1983; Rippetoe and Rogers 1987; for a review, see Norman *et al.* 2005) abandoned the notion that the various factors combine multiplicatively and also expanded the theory by including additional determinants of protection motivation. Probably the most important variable added was self-efficacy. The concept of self-efficacy refers to a person's belief that he or she is able to perform a particular action (Bandura 1986). Because people might not be motivated to stop smoking or drinking alcohol, despite a negative attitude towards these behaviours, if they think that they would be too weak or too addicted to do so, the inclusion of self-efficacy in a model of health protective behaviour should improve predictions. The revision also incorporated the health belief model's perceived barrier construct (labelled 'response costs') and added a related one, the rewards associated with 'maladaptive' responses (e.g. the enjoyment of continuing to drink or smoke, the time and energy saved by not having health check-ups).

The revised model assumes that the motivation to protect oneself from danger is a positive function of four beliefs:

1 the threat is severe;
2 one is personally vulnerable;
3 one has the ability to perform the coping response; and
4 the coping response is effective in reducing the threat.

The motivation to perform the adaptive response is negatively influenced by the costs of that response and by potential rewards associated with maladaptive responses.

More specifically, Rogers divided these six variables into two classes, which he named threat appraisal and coping appraisal (see Figure 2.2). It is plausible that threat appraisal is based on a consideration of the factors of severity and vulnerability. After all, the threat experienced from continuing to smoke would be reflected by the severity of the likely health consequences and of the probability of contracting them. It is less plausible, however, also to include the intrinsic and extrinsic rewards of the maladaptive response (e.g. of continuing to smoke) under the concept of threat appraisal. These rewards would probably have been better subsumed under the category of response costs. After all, the adaptive response to the threat from the consequences of health-impairing behaviour is to stop and as a result to deprive oneself also of the rewarding qualities this behaviour may have had. The factors assumed to influence coping appraisal are the efficacy of the coping response, the individual's perception of his or her ability to execute the coping response (i.e. self-efficacy) and the costs of the recommended behaviour.

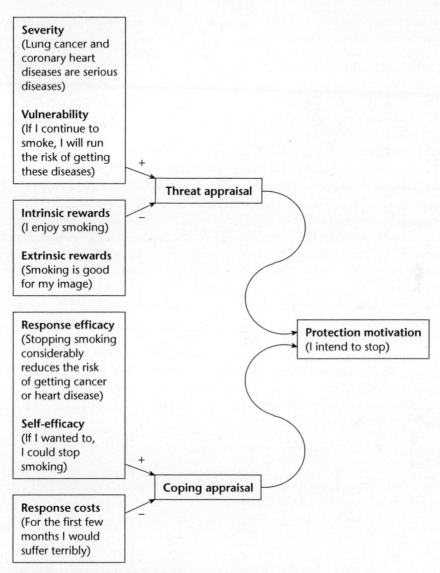

FIGURE 2.2 Protection motivation theory applied to the reduction of smoking
Source: Adapted from Stroebe and de Wit (1996)

Rogers postulated an additive combination of factors within a given class but a multiplicative influence between classes. Thus, severity and vulnerability are assumed to combine additively to determine threat appraisal. However, coping appraisal and threat appraisal are expected to combine multiplicatively. Thus, increases in threat appraisal should increase protection motivation only when coping appraisal is moderate to high. When coping appraisal is low, due, for example, due to low self-efficacy, then increased threat appraisal should not result in an increased intention to take protective action. Research assessing these assumptions has been reviewed by Rogers (1983).

Empirical tests of the revised model

Empirical comparisons of the revised protection motivation theory with the health belief model typically favour protection motivation. For example, Seydel *et al.* (1990) found a superiority of protection motivation theory due to the inclusion of self-efficacy. Wurtele and Maddux (1987) observed in a study on exercise behaviour that the predictors of the health belief model affected behaviour through behavioural intentions rather than directly, as assumed by the health belief model. Two meta-analytic assessments of protection motivation theory have also been quite supportive of model predictions (Floyd *et al.* 2000; Milne *et al.* 2000).

In support of protection motivation theory, both meta-analyses found intention and protective behaviour to be associated with the determinants assumed by the model. However, intention and behaviour were more strongly associated with coping appraisal (i.e. self-efficacy, response efficacy, response costs) than threat appraisal variables (i.e. vulnerability, severity, rewards). The meta-analysis of Milne *et al.* (2000) further separated studies according to whether the protective behaviour was measured concurrently with the protection motivation variables (i.e. cross-sectional studies) or at some later point in time (i.e. prospective studies). As one would expect, all associations between the variables of the model and behaviour were weaker in prospective than in cross-sectional studies. In fact, severity and response efficacy were no longer significantly associated with behaviour in prospective studies. Intention remained the strongest predictor of behaviour, even though the correlation was reduced from .80 to .40.

Implications for interventions

Unfortunately, neither of the two meta-analyses tested the assumption of protection motivation theory about the multiplicative combination of threat and coping appraisal variables. In particular, support for the multiplicative combination of threat appraisal and self-efficacy would have had important implications for the planning of interventions. For example, if self-efficacy for a given behaviour domain had been found to be relatively high in a target population (i.e. if most individuals feel competent to engage in a recommended health-protective action), the provision of information which increased vulnerability or severity would increase protection motivation and thus intention to act. Under these conditions individuals should be more likely to take action, the greater they perceive their individual risk. In contrast, when self-efficacy is low, that is when individuals feel that they are unable to engage in a given action (e.g. dieting to lose weight), increases in vulnerability should not result in increments in intentions. Under the latter conditions, rather than emphasizing risk, it might be more effective to provide individuals with information which increases their self-efficacy. However, even though there is no evidence for the multiplicative combination of threat and coping appraisal variables, the fact that coping appraisal variables have consistently been found to be more strongly associated with health-related behaviour than the threat appraisal variables suggests that intentions are likely to fail unless they also target coping appraisal. Since with health-impairing behaviours, such as smoking or unsafe sex, people know about the health risks involved in engaging in these behaviours, interventions may not even have to stress the health risks to be successful.

The theories of reasoned action and planned behaviour

Both the health belief model and protection motivation theory have generated a great deal of research in the health area. During the last decades, however, a number of more general models of behaviour have been developed which have also been applied to the health area. Obviously, it is not very economical to continue entertaining specific theories of health behaviour unless their predictive success is greater than that of general models of behaviour. The two most important general social psychological models of behaviour have been the theories of reasoned action (e.g. Fishbein and Ajzen 1975) and the theory of planned behaviour (Ajzen 2005). These theories have been tested extensively and have been successful in predicting a wide range of behaviours (for reviews, see Ajzen 1988, 2005; Conner and Sparks 2005). Since the theory of planned behaviour is merely an extension of the theory of reasoned action (adding perceived behavioural control as a further predictor of intention and behaviour), we will discuss both theories here.

The theory of reasoned action

The theory of reasoned action predicts behavioural intention and assumes that behaviour is a function of the intention to perform that behaviour. The intention to perform a given behaviour indicates the degree to which the individual is determined to pursue a behavioural goal and thus reflects goal commitment. According to the theory of reasoned action, a behavioural intention is determined by one's attitude towards performing the behaviour and by subjective norms (see Figure 2.3). For example, a person's attitude towards exercising will be a function of the perceived likelihood with which engaging in exercise is associated with certain consequences such as being healthier and fitter or reducing the risk of developing heart problems, and the evaluation of these perceived consequences.

Subjective norms combine two components, namely normative beliefs and motivation to comply. Normative beliefs are our beliefs about how people who are important to us expect us to behave. For example, a woman might believe that her husband does not want her to indulge in dangerous sports or that he would like her to lose some weight. However, whether such normative beliefs influence intentions will depend on one's willingness to comply with this norm. Thus, subjective norms are normative beliefs weighted by motivation to comply. The model quantifies these subjective norms by multiplying the subjective likelihood that a particular other (the referent) thinks the person should perform the behaviour by the person's motivation to comply with that referent's expectation. These products are analogous to the expectancy x value products computed for attitudes to the behaviour and are also summed over various salient referent persons. Although individuals have to engage in some kind of deliberation with novel behaviours or even with familiar actions that have to be performed in novel situations, the intention to perform a behaviour that has been executed repeatedly in that specific situation is activated automatically. However, since intentions involve some awareness of purpose, automatic activation of intentions does not imply that the behaviour is also initiated automatically. Thus, even though the intention to use my car will be activated automatically once I am ready to leave for work (i.e. I do not have to deliberate about the best means of transport to go there), I am usually conscious of this intention.

Situational factors can also influence the intention to perform a particular behaviour in a given situation by changing attitudes (Ajzen and Fishbein 2000). As I mentioned earlier, an individual's attitude towards performing a specific behaviour in a specific situation is based on a limited number of salient beliefs – that is, outcome beliefs – which are cognitively accessible at that particular moment. Thus, an individual's attitude towards eating a hamburger might have been strongly influenced by his belief that hamburgers have calories and that eating them would further aggravate his weight problem. However, on passing a hamburger stand and being exposed to the delicious smell of grilled meat and fried onions, the individual's attitude towards eating hamburgers might be more heavily influenced by the belief that eating a hamburger would be utterly enjoyable and that cutting down on food tomorrow would easily remedy today's overindulgence. Consistent with these assumptions, Ajzen et al. (2004) demonstrated that the fact that in hypothetical situations individuals typically overestimate their willingness to pay money for a good cause could be attributed to differences in beliefs and attitudes between these two situations, with individuals holding much more favourable beliefs and attitudes in the hypothetical situation.

Empirical evaluation of the theory of reasoned action
Empirical tests of the theory of reasoned action have assessed its success in predicting behavioural intentions and actual behaviour for a wide range of behavioural domains. The model has been applied to blood donation, family planning, eating at fast-food restaurants, smoking marijuana, mothers' infant feeding practices, dental hygiene behaviour and having an abortion (for a review, see Eagly and Chaiken 1993). In an extensive meta-analysis of research on the model based on 113 articles, van den Putte (1991) reported the following estimates of the various relations of the model based on 150 groups of respondents: the mean r for predicting intention from attitudes and subjective norms was .68, and the mean r for predicting behaviour from intention was .62. Thus, attitudes and subjective norms accounted for approximately 46 per cent of the variance in intentions and intentions for 38 per cent of the variance in behaviour. Other meta-analyses reported somewhat lower correlations between intentions and behaviour: based on 98 studies, Randall and Wolff (1994) computed an average correlation of r = .45. With a weighted mean correlation of r = .40 (n = 170 studies), Six (1996) found an even lower correlation between intention and behaviour.

Omissions from the theory

Despite being reasonably successful in predicting intention and behaviour, the theory of reasoned action has been criticized by researchers who have argued that intentions and actions are affected by a number of factors which are not included in the model of reasoned action. The most interesting of these additional determinants in the context of health behaviour is past behaviour. In a test of the theory of reasoned action that used self-reported consumption of alcohol, marijuana and hard drugs as dependent measures, Bentler and Speckart (1979) found that reported past behaviour added to the prediction of future behaviour even when intention was statistically controlled. This finding has been replicated in a number of further studies for exercise (Bentler and Speckart 1981), condom use (de Wit *et al.* 1990; Schaalma *et al.* 1993) and seat belt use (Sutton and Hallett 1989). In these later studies, multiple regression analyses showed that the prediction of behaviour was improved by the addition of past behaviour over and above the prediction achieved on the basis of intention.

The problem of volitional control

The finding that measures of past behaviour add to the prediction of future behaviour even when intentions are statistically controlled could represent the impact of any number of factors that influence behaviour but are not taken into account by the theory of reasoned action. In interpreting these findings, we have to remember that the theory of reasoned action offers a theoretical account of the factors that determine intentions. Intentions only reflect the motivation to act. Execution of an action not only depends on motivation but also on whether the behaviour is under volitional control of the individual (i.e. attainable). A behaviour is under volitional control if the individual can decide at will whether or not to perform it. Thus, past behaviour might reflect the influence of factors that are not under volitional control of the individual.

There are many factors which could lower the control individuals have over their actions. Some actions may have become so routinized and habitual that people perform them without thinking. For example, smokers might light a cigarette or pipe without intending to do so or without even realizing they are doing it. Because past behaviour would also have been influenced by their habit, using past behaviour to predict future behaviour would then improve predictions even when intentions are statistically controlled.

The control individuals have over their actions might also be lowered by the fact that these behaviours require skills, abilities, opportunities and the cooperation of others. As Eagly and Chaiken (1993) have pointed out, the great majority of studies that have supported the theory of reasoned action have involved relatively simple behaviours that do not require much in the way of resources and skills. Fishbein and Ajzen (1975) were not unaware of this issue, but they argued that people would take the need for resources or others' cooperation into account in forming their intentions. Changes in resources will then result in changes in intention. For example, if somebody who intended to play tennis with a friend on Monday evening learns that the friend has fallen ill, that person is likely to change his or her intention. Such unexpected changes in external conditions are one of the reasons why intentions predict behaviour better if the time lag between the assessment of intentions and behaviour is short.

Although this position is reasonable, the restriction of the model of reasoned action to behaviour that is under complete volitional control seriously limits the applicability of the model. Closer inspection reveals that very few behaviours are under the complete volitional control of the individual. Even the execution of such simple actions as brushing one's teeth depends on the availability of one's tooth-brush and toothpaste.

The theory of planned behaviour

This type of reasoning has led Ajzen to modify the theory of reasoned action and to develop the theory of planned behaviour (Ajzen 1988, 2005). The theory of planned behaviour incorporates perceived behavioural control over the behaviour to be predicted as an additional predictor (see Figure 2.3). Perceived controllability of a behaviour can be assessed directly by asking respondents to what extent performing a given behaviour was under their control, or by assessing the control beliefs assumed to determine perceived behavioural control. The theory of planned behaviour assumes that perceived behavioural control affects behaviour indirectly through intentions. Under certain conditions, it can also have a direct effect on behaviour that is not mediated by intentions (see Figure 2.3).

As we will see, there is a great deal of evidence to support the predictions of the theory with regard to perceived behavioural control. However, there has also been criticism that there has been a lack of congruence in the way perceived behavioural control has been operationalized in different studies. Kraft *et al.* (2005) and Rodgers *et al.* (2008) have argued that there are three different types of control that need to be distinguished in empirical studies, namely *perceived control* (reflecting the extent to which the individual feels that the behaviour is under his or her control), *perceived difficulty* (reflecting the extent to which the individual believes that performing the behaviour would be easy or difficult, and *self-efficacy* (reflecting people's judgements of their ability, or their confidence in their ability, to execute certain courses of action required to attain intended levels of performance). A meta-analysis of 15 studies of the theory of planned behaviour that included separate measures of the three types of control found self-efficacy to be most strongly associated with intentions and behaviour (Rodgers *et al.* 2008). Self-efficacy contributed substantial additional variance to the prediction of intention and behaviour after controlling for attitudes, subjective norms, perceived control and perceived difficulty. The contributions of perceived control and perceived difficulty were much more modest.

The assumption that perceived behavioural control affects intentions is consistent with expectancy–value theories of motivation. People who lack the ability or the opportunity to achieve some goal will adjust their intentions accordingly, because intentions are partly determined by people's perception of the probability that a goal can be reached by them (i.e. attainability of a goal). For example, stu-

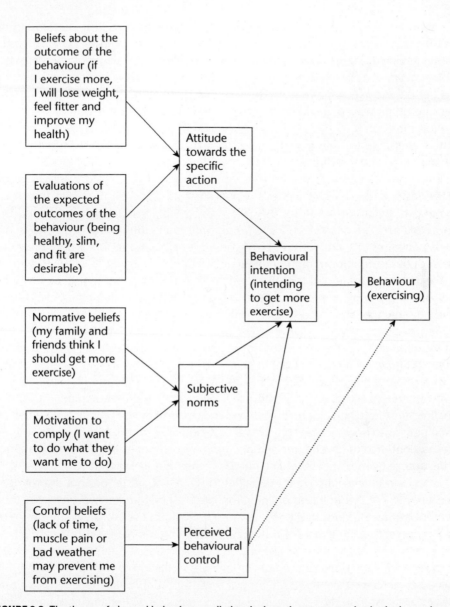

FIGURE 2.3 The theory of planned behaviour applied to the intention to engage in physical exercise

dents who have learnt from past performance that they lack the ability to achieve the kind of outstanding grades in their courses that they had hoped for are likely to adjust their intentions and aim for lower but more realistic grades.

The direct relationship between perceived behavioural control and behaviour which is not mediated by intentions (indicated by the broken line in Figure 2.3) is intuitively less plausible and depends on the accuracy of the individual's perception of actual control. For example, if a student has the firm intention to attend regularly a weekly lecture at 8 a.m. on Wednesday but knows that her old car might sometimes let her down and make her miss the class, she would perceive her control over attending as less than perfect. If her control perception were accurate and her car did break down from time to time preventing her from attending, the measure of perceived behavioural control would improve the prediction based only on intentions.

It is important to note that the direct link of perceived behavioural control to behaviour has a somewhat different theoretical status from the link that is mediated by intention. Whereas perceived behavioural control has a causal influence on intentions (e.g. the present author's fear of heights has prevented him from ever forming the intention to climb the Eiger Northface), it is not the perceived but the *actual* lack of control which *causally* influences behaviour. Thus, it is not the expectation that the car will break down, but the actual breakdowns, which prevents our student from regular attendance.

The latter example can also be used to illustrate that perceived behavioural control should only improve the prediction of behaviour (which is exclusively based on intentions) if it realistically reflects actual levels of control. Suppose the student decided to buy a new car and thus removed the impediment to regular class attendance, perceived behavioural control as assessed earlier would no longer improve predictions of behaviour.

In support of this assumption Ajzen and Madden (1986) found in a study of students' intentions to get an A in a course (best grade), and their actual grades, that the direct link between perceived behavioural control and behaviour only emerged when perceived behavioural control was assessed towards the end of their semester after students had received considerable information concerning their performance in the course by means of feedback on class projects and examinations. A measure of behavioural control taken at the beginning of the semester did not improve the prediction of behaviour based on intention. Supposedly, students' estimates of their own control over grades had become more realistic in the course of the semester. This suggests that students did not change their intentions, even if they realized that getting an A was rather unlikely. With a less important goal, they might have adjusted their intentions in the light of a more realistic perception of control. In that case, perceived behavioural control would probably not have improved on predictions based on the now more realistic intentions. Whether people are likely to adjust their intentions to a changed perception of control will probably depend on the importance of a goal.

Determinants of perceived behavioural control

The factors that influence perceived behavioural control can either be internal or external to the individual (Ajzen 1988). Examples of internal factors are information, skills, abilities, and also urges and compulsions. Our control over health behaviour is often threatened by those internal factors that are collectively referred to as 'willpower'. Thus, despite the firm intention to visit a doctor or to lose weight, a person with medical or weight problems may know from past experience that he or she is unlikely to execute these intentions. Examples of external factors are opportunity and dependence on others (Ajzen 1988). For example, we know that we can only go cross-country skiing tomorrow if the snow does not melt and if our boss allows us to leave the office on time.

Terry and O'Leary (1995) and Armitage and Conner (1999) have suggested that control over internal and external factors should be assessed separately. Belief in the control of internal factors (i.e. motivation or ability) would be reflected by self-efficacy. The measure of perceived behavioural control, on the other hand, would reflect the control over the more external factors influencing behaviour. In a study of exercise behaviour, Terry and O'Leary (1995) demonstrated that self-efficacy only influenced the intention but had no direct link to behaviour, whereas perceived behavioural control was only related to behaviour but not to intention. However, Armitage and Conner (1999) failed to replicate these findings in their study of eating a low-fat diet.

A related distinction is that between efficacy expectancy and outcome expectancy. An *efficacy* expectancy is the expectation that, if one tried to perform a certain behaviour, one would be able to do it. For example, an obese individual might be fairly confident that he or she could substantially reduce daily calorie consumption. However, a reduction in calorie intake does not necessarily result in substantial weight loss. Thus, whereas the perceived likelihood that one is able to reduce one's calorie intake is an *efficacy* expectancy, the expectation that this reduction will actually result in substantial weight loss is an *outcome* expectancy. The concept of perceived behavioural control as originally introduced by Ajzen and Madden (1986) refers to both outcome expectancy and efficacy expectancy.

Empirical evaluation of the model

The first published test of the model was a study of weight loss (Schifter and Ajzen 1985). Female college students were asked at the beginning of the study to express their attitudes, subjective norms, perceived behavioural control and intentions with respect to losing weight during a six-week period. In addition, the extent to which participants had made detailed weight reduction plans was assessed, as were a number of general attitudes and personality factors. Consistent with the theory, the intention to lose weight was predicted quite accurately on the basis of attitudes, subjective norms and perceived behavioural control. However, perceived behavioural control and intentions were only moderately successful in predicting the amount of weight that participants actually lost during the six weeks (i.e. an outcome), with perceived behavioural control being the better predictor. As expected, there was also an interaction between perceived behavioural control and intention on weight reduction: a strong intention to lose weight increased weight reduction only for those participants who believed that they would be able to control their calorie intake, if they wanted to. Respondents who had made a detailed plan at the beginning of the period also tended to lose more weight.

Since then a great number of empirical studies testing the model of planned behaviour have been published. The results of these studies tend to support the central predictions of the model that, unless a given behaviour in question is under complete volitional control of the individual, predictions of behaviour from the model of planned behaviour are superior to those based on the theory of reasoned action (e.g. Godin and Kok 1996; Armitage and Conner 2001). In a meta-analysis based on 142 independent tests of the theory of planned behaviour, Armitage and Conner (2001) reported an average multiple correlation of attitude, subjective norm and perceived behavioural control with intention of $r = .63$, accounting for 40 per cent of the variance. The average multiple correlation of perceived behavioural control and intention with behaviour was $r = .54$, accounting for 29 per cent of the variance in behaviour. Perceived behavioural control added an average of 6 per cent to the prediction of intention (controlling for attitude and norms) and 2 per cent to the prediction of behaviour, over and above intention.

A meta-analysis which focused only on applications of the theory of planned behaviour to the health domain reported similar findings. Based on 56 studies, Godin and Kok (1996) reported an average multiple correlation of $r = .64$ for the prediction of intentions. Attitudes towards the action and perceived behavioural control were most often significant contributors to the variation in intention. The prediction of behaviour yielded an average multiple correlation of $r = .58$. Thus, approximately one-third of the variation in the health behaviours studied can be explained by the combined effect of intention and perceived behavioural control. In half of the studies reviewed, perceived behavioural control added significantly to the prediction of behaviour, although intention remained the most important predictor. As one would expect, the contribution of perceived behavioural control to the prediction of behaviour was greatest for addictive behaviours, a behavioural domain where volitional control can be assumed to be weak.

Implications for interventions

The first step in designing a successful intervention according to the theory of planned behaviour is to specify the behaviour one wants to influence. For example, if one wanted to persuade homosexual men to avoid unsafe sex, one would first have to identify the different types of unsafe sex which these men might engage in and with whom they engage in unsafe sex. Whereas 'negotiated safety' would be a feasible and safe strategy with a long-term steady partner, it would not be with a casual partner. There is also evidence that whereas safe sexual behaviour with a steady partner is de-termined by intention, it is mainly predicted by perceived control for casual partners.

Once one has specified the behaviour one wants to influence, the second step is to assess empirically whether this behaviour is mainly determined by behavioural intentions or by perceived behavioural control. In the exceptional case where behaviour is mainly predicted by perceived behavioural control, one has to examine further the reasons for the lack of association between intention and behaviour. In the area of health behaviour, this is often due to the fact that there is little variance in intention. For example, most homosexual men intend to avoid engaging in unprotected anal sex with casual partners, but some do not succeed. Since those who do not succeed usually have low perceived behavioural control, the control variable becomes a better predictor of behaviour than intention. In this case, one might try to increase their control, for example through skill training.

In the more usual situation where behaviour is mainly determined by the relevant behavioural intention, one then has to assess the extent to which the intention to engage in this behaviour is determined by attitudes, norms or perceived behavioural control. If behaviour is primarily under attitudinal control, attempts to change that behaviour by influencing normative beliefs will not be very successful. Similarly, if the members of some group perform a given behaviour because they believe that people who are important to them expect them to perform this behaviour, trying to change their attitudes towards that behaviour will have little impact on their intentions. Finally, if behavioural intention is mainly determined by perceived control (e.g. I am not trying to quit smoking because I know from past experience that I will fail), influencing their attitude towards smoking (e.g. by pointing out the health risk) or telling them that their children would like them to stop is likely to have little impact on their intention.

Once one knows which of the determinants of intention (i.e. attitude, subjective norm, perceived behavioural control) is most important, one should identify the salient beliefs which underlie this factor. However, not all beliefs which are salient for a given behavioural domain are also strongly related to the relevant behaviour. For example, even though the negative health consequences of smoking are salient outcomes of this behaviour, the belief that smoking is unhealthy no longer discriminates between smokers and non-smokers (Leventhal and Cleary 1980). Thus, information about the negative health consequences of smoking is unlikely to persuade smokers to abandon their habit. Similarly, the perceived threat of contracting HIV infections has been found to have only a small association with heterosexual condom use in an extensive meta-analysis of the determinants of such use (Sheeran et al. 1999). Interventions which focus on the dangers of HIV and AIDS are therefore unlikely to be effective in increasing condom use. To be effective, interventions have to focus on those beliefs which most strongly discriminate between people who do and do not intend to perform the behaviour in question.

If interventions were always designed on the basis of this type of analysis, many costly failures could be avoided. This can be illustrated with the findings of a study of the effectiveness of a health education programme on AIDS developed by Dutch Educational Television (de Wit et al. 1990). Two groups of male and female students at secondary schools were assessed at two time points, using a questionnaire which measured AIDS-relevant knowledge as well as attitudes towards condom use, perceived norms regarding condom use, perceived behavioural control over condom use, and intention to use condoms. In the interval between the two assessments, half the respondents were exposed to the health education programme on AIDS whereas the other half were not exposed to the information.

Students reported that they learned a great deal of new information through the programme. Consistent with these self-reports, the intervention group showed a significant increase in relevant knowledge. However, despite its impact on AIDS knowledge, the intervention did not influence intentions to use condoms. Intentions were solely determined by attitudes towards condom use, perceived norms and perceived effectiveness. This finding is in line with the results of other studies indicating that neither knowledge nor perceived vulnerability seem to be related to behavioural risk reduction regarding HIV infection (e.g. Richard and van der Pligt 1991; Abraham *et al.* 1992). The obvious implication from such findings is that future AIDS campaigns should give less emphasis to AIDS knowledge and focus more on attitudes towards condom use, subjective norms and perceived effectiveness.

Narrowing the intention–behaviour gap: forming implementation intentions

Even though behavioural intentions are a good predictor of behaviour, there is certainly room for improvement. Based on a meta-analysis of meta-analyses, Sheeran (2002) estimated that 28 per cent of the variance in measures of behaviour is explained by intentions. With the amount of error variance due to less than perfect reliability and validity of measures used, even a perfect theory would never account for 100 per cent of the variance in behaviour. Thus, these estimates of variance accounted for in behaviour are likely to underestimate the strength of the association between intention and behaviour. However, even if we accept that numerous measurement artefacts attenuate the association observed between intention and behaviour, the gap between intention and behaviour remains large enough to have motivated researchers to develop techniques that would reduce it.

The most successful technique has been to persuade people to form more specific implementation intentions. Whereas behavioural intentions have the form, 'I intend to do X', implementation intentions involve the form, 'I intend to do X in situation Y' (i.e. if situation Y, then behaviour X). Thus, implementation intentions are the most concrete goals, goals that can only be reached by performing one specific behaviour, in one specific situation at one specific time. The efficacy of implementation intentions is typically assessed in studies in which implementation intentions are induced after intentions have been measured, by asking half of the participants to name the time and place in which they intended to perform a given behaviour.

For example, Sheeran and Orbell (2000) asked all the women in a medical practice in England, who were due for a cervical smear test, to indicate the strength of their intention to go for a smear test within the next three months. Half of these participants were then instructed to form implementation intentions by asking them to indicate when, where and how they would make an appointment to have the test. Asking individuals to form implementation intentions significantly increased attendance rates from 69 per cent of individuals without, to 92 per cent with an implementation intention. The two groups did not differ in the strength of their behavioural intention. Similar results have been reported in numerous studies and over a wide range of behaviours. In a recent meta-analysis of 94 independent studies, Gollwitzer and Sheeran (2006) reported an effect size of medium-to-large magnitude (d = .65) for the effect the induction of implementation intentions had in reducing the intention–behaviour gap.

How do implementation intentions work? One reason why people fail to act on their intentions is because they simply 'forget' to act when the opportunity arises. By specifying the time and situational context in which behaviour should be performed, the mental representation of the specified situational context cues becomes activated and highly accessible, making sure that people remember their intention when they encounter the situation in which they planned to act. Furthermore, the formation of an implementation intention will also create (or strengthen) the association between the situational cues and the response that is instrumental for obtaining the goal. As a result, the formation of an implementation intention increases the probability that people will remember the action intention when the specified situation arises (Webb and Sheeran 2007).

In support of these assumptions Sheeran (2002) found in a re-analysis of the data of the Sheeran and Orbell (2000) study that 74 per cent of participants made their appointment for the smear test on the date they had specified in their implementation intention. More direct evidence for the memory effect of implementation intentions comes from a study by Aarts *et al.* (1998). In this study, student participants were asked to go to the cafeteria (apparently to list the price of various food items), but to collect beforehand, on their way to the cafeteria, a consumption coupon at a departmental office. The location of the office was described as being 'down the corridor', 'directly after the first swing door' and 'near the red fire hose'. To induce implementation intentions, half of the participants were requested to plan the steps that were required to collect the coupon. Participants in the control condition were required to plan the steps necessary to *spend* the coupon (unrelated planning condition).

After an intervening task and before leaving for the cafeteria, participants were asked to perform a lexical decision task (which allows one to assess the cognitive accessibility of concepts). Among the words presented in the lexical decision task, the critical words were 'corridor', 'swing door', 'red' and 'fire hose'. As expected, participants who had formed an implementation intention had shorter recognition times for the critical words and were more likely to collect the consumption coupon on their way to the cafeteria. This pattern is consistent with the assumption that the greater cognitive accessibility of the situational cues (i.e. swing door and red fire hose) mediated the impact of the implementation intention on behaviour. In other words, individuals who had performed an implementation intention were more successful in collecting the coupon, because they were more likely to be reminded by the situational cues to perform this action.

With low effort actions such as phoning for an appointment or collecting a coupon, being reminded at a suitable moment to perform the action is probably sufficient to ensure that the action will be performed. If the action is well-learned and easy to perform, it might even be enacted automatically in response to the situational cue (Gollwitzer and Sheeran 2006). With more difficult behaviours such as stopping smoking or reducing one's chocolate consumption, it would seem less plausible that merely being reminded of an intention would also ensure action. However, communication of an implementation intention to the experimenter might increase an individual's commitment to perform that behaviour in studies where people have to record their implementation intentions during the experiment.

The importance of commitment was demonstrated in a study by Ajzen *et al.* (2009), who manipulated commitment and implementation intention in a factorial design. Participants, who had been asked to form the intention to rate local and national newscasts on a specific day in the month of April, were either asked to choose a specific day during that month to do the task (implementation intention) or were not asked to choose a day. Cross-cutting this manipulation, half the participants were asked to sign a commitment form promising to complete the study, while the other half were not asked to sign this form. Both commitment and the formation of an implementation intention increased compliance rates by approximately 20 per cent. However, a significant interaction between these two factors indicated that forming an implementation intention was only effective for individuals who had not committed themselves.

Forming an implementation intention also results in self-commitment which should increase the salience of a goal violation and thus of anticipated guilt feelings in the event that individuals fail to act on their intention. For example, if one forms the implementation intention to stop smoking at midnight on 31 December, any cigarette smoked on 1 January is in clear violation of this implementation intention. In contrast, if one violates the goal intention to stop smoking in the near future, one is unlikely to experience a clear goal violation effect because it remains unclear at which point continuing to smoke violates this intention.

Most research on implementation intentions has been conducted with approach goals, with individuals forming the intention to perform a specific action once a specific situation arose. In contrast to approach goals (where individuals at risk of failing to perform an intended action have to be reminded to get going), with avoidance goals people have to be reminded to suppress an unwanted response. Unfortunately, a great number of health behaviours involve avoidance goals such as resisting the temptation to smoke or to eat fatty food.

The difficulty with avoidance goals is that there are usually no clear-cut cues that can be used for the 'if part' of the implementation intention, as people typically do not know when and where temptation will overcome them. However, there are several strategies individuals can use to form implementation intentions that help them to resist a specific temptation. In each case, they first have to identify situations in which the risk of yielding to the targeted temptation is particularly high, second, think of a coping response that is likely to be effective in helping them to resist, and third, cognitively rehearse linking the coping response to the situation. The effectiveness of this type of implementation intention will not only depend on whether they remember the coping strategy at the right moment, but also on whether this coping strategy is effective in helping them to resist the temptation.

One possibility is to link the coping response to the tempting experience itself. For example, if we have a weakness for chocolate, we could recall the experience of temptation the last time just before we yielded and ate the chocolate. We could then form the implementation intention that whenever we experience this type of craving, we think of our diet and of the many reasons why we wanted to lose weight. Alternatively, we could intervene earlier in the sequence by avoiding buying chocolate. We could form the implementation intention to think of our diet (or of how good we would look with a few pounds less) whenever we saw chocolate on a supermarket shelf and were tempted to put it into our shopping trolley.

There are few empirical studies of the effectiveness of implementation intentions with avoidance goals. For example, Achtziger *et al.* (2008) had people form the implementation that whenever they thought about a particular snack food (identified earlier as tempting), they should ignore that thought. All participants reduced their consumption of the chosen snack food, but individuals who had formed an implementation intention showed significantly greater reduction. Adriaanse *et al.* (2009) had their participants identify specific situations in which they were particularly tempted to eat unhealthy snacks (e.g. feeling bored, acting social). Participants were then instructed to replace the unhealthy with a healthy snack in these situations. These implementation intentions resulted in a lower consumption of unhealthy and an increased consumption of healthy snacks. Finally, van Koningsbruggen *et al.* (in press) asked participants for each of a number of tempting snacks to remember when they were last time tempted to eat that snack. They were then instructed to form the implementation intention to think of dieting the next time they were tempted to eat the snack X or Y. Again, participants in the condition with implementation intentions were less likely to snack during the next two weeks. Thus, there can be no doubt that the formation of implementation intentions increases the likelihood that people will act on their intentions, even if the intention concerns avoiding temptations.

Beyond reasons and plans: when intentions are derailed

The last section of this chapter reviewed classic theories of behaviour, which all conceive of actions as the result of deliberation about the likely consequences of behavioural alternatives. These theories assume either implicitly or explicitly that the impact of beliefs and attitudes on behaviour is mediated by intention. It is this intention which is assumed to be the most direct cause of behaviour. However, as we discussed earlier, intentions only account for a limited amount of behaviour. There is a substantial intention–behaviour gap and it is individuals, who fail to act on their intentions, who are mainly responsible for this gap (Sheeran 2002). This section will discuss how external cues can automatically trigger behaviour without the intervention of conscious thought and thus succeed in derailing our good intentions.

The first part of this section will review research which challenges the assumption that goal pursuit always reflects a conscious process, with people being aware of a goal and of their intention to pursue that goal. There is increasing evidence that goals can be triggered by environmental cues without people's awareness (Kruglanski *et al.* 2002; Custers and Aarts 2005a, 2005b; Moskowitz and Ignarri 2009). As long as these goals that are primed by our environment are consistent with our consciously pursued goal intentions, no conflict arises. If our intention to diet is reinforced by a reflection in a shop window showing our bulging stomach, priming does not interfere with intentional behaviour.

Unfortunately, however, environmental primes often worsen our self-control dilemmas. The display of mouth-watering pastries in the window of a confectioner's shop or the delicious food smells wafting from the restaurant next door all prime the goal of eating enjoyment and undermine our firm intention to diet, endangering our plan to lose weight. As long as we are highly motivated to pursue our long-term goals of weight loss, alcohol abstinence or non-smoking and as long as we are able to fully concentrate on acting according to our intentions, we should be able to resist these temptations. However, when our motivational or cognitive resources are depleted, we might be unable to keep to our good intentions.

Automatic and deliberate influence of goals

There is suggestive evidence that goal-directed behaviour can be triggered by environmental cues without an intention having been formed (Custers and Aarts 2005a, 2005b; Moskowitz and Ignarri 2009). Theories of unconscious goal pursuit share with theories of conscious goal pursuit the basic assumption that goals are mentally represented as desired states relating to behaviour or outcomes (Custers and Aarts 2005b). Goals are attainable outcomes towards which individuals hold positive attitudes. Furthermore, for a goal to motivate goal-striving, there must also be a discrepancy between the actual state of the individual and the desired state. Unconscious goals are therefore as much determined by attitudes, social norms and perceived behavioural control as are conscious intentions. The main difference is that theories of unconscious goal pursuit make the assumption that goals can be unconsciously activated and pursued, without the individual having formed a conscious intention. Theories of unconscious goal pursuit assume that goals pre-exist in the actor's mind and form part of a knowledge structure that includes the goal itself, the context in which the goal can be enacted (opportunity) and the actions that need to be performed to reach the goal (means).

Cognitive accessibility refers to the ease and speed with which information stored in memory can be retrieved. The triggering stimuli that increase the accessibility of cognitive constructs are usually referred to as *primes*. Priming refers to the phenomenon that exposure to an object or a word in one context increases not only the accessibility of the mental representation of that object or concept in a person's mind but also the accessibility of related objects or concepts. As a result, the activated concept exerts for some time an unintended influence of the individual's behaviour in subsequent unrelated contexts without the individual being aware of this influence (Bargh and Chartrand 1999). Goals can be activated outside of awareness by exposing individuals to goal objects (e.g. a cake) or to situational cues that in the past have often been associated with the pursuit of a goal (e.g. pub opening time; dinner time).

Numerous studies have demonstrated that priming can activate goals without individuals being consciously aware of either the prime or the goal (for a review, see Custers and Aarts 2005b). For example, Holland *et al.* (2005) exposed half of their participants in an experiment to the smell of an all-purpose cleaner without them being consciously aware of the presence of the scent. When participants were asked to list five home activities which they wanted to perform during the rest of the day, significantly more individuals who had been exposed to the smell of the cleaner included cleaning as their goal than individuals who had not been so primed. This suggests that the smell of the cleaner increased the accessibility of the concept of cleaning, which was then used when participants were asked to retrieve plans and goals for home activities.

In this study goal priming was only shown to influence goal setting. However, there is also ample evidence that priming can influence goal enactment. For example, Bargh *et al.* (2001) unobtrusively exposed participants to words such as 'cooperative' and 'share' to prime the goal of cooperation. After that, participants took part in a resource dilemma task, in which they could either keep any profit for their own benefit or replenish the common pool. Participants who had been primed with the goal of cooperation were more likely to replenish the common pool than were the (unprimed) control group participants. The same effects were observed with participants who were given the explicit goal to cooperate. However, intentions to cooperate during the game (assessed afterwards) correlated with the extent of cooperative behaviour only for participants who had been explicitly instructed, but not for those who had formed the goal as a result of priming. Thus, people who were primed with words related to cooperation engaged in more cooperative behaviour, apparently without having formed a conscious intention to do so.

As discussed earlier, in order for behaviour to be adopted as a goal, the mental representation of the behaviour does not only have to be cognitively accessible, it also has to be associated with positive affect (Custers and Aarts 2005a, 2005b). Thus, priming people with words such as 'cooperate' and 'share' would not increase their cooperativeness unless they really liked acting cooperatively. That behavioural goals will not be adopted unless they are associated with positive affect was demonstrated in a series of studies by Custers and Aarts (2005a, 2007; see 2005b for a review). In most of these studies they used evaluative conditioning to associate previously neutral goals with positive affect. During these evaluative conditioning trials, the goals (CS) were presented subliminally, but the positive and neutral words used as unconditioned stimuli (US) were presented supraliminally. This procedure allowed not only the manipulation of participants' attitudes towards the goal (i.e. whether the goal was associated with positive or neutral affect), it also increased the cognitive accessibility of the behavioural goal.

Custers and Aarts (2005a) then demonstrated that positively conditioning the previously neutral behavioural goal did not only increase the wanting of this behaviour (assessed with a verbal choice task), it also influenced behaviour. In one of these studies, the relatively neutral behaviour of 'doing number sequence puzzles' was either associated with positive or neutral words in an evaluative conditioning task (Custers and Aarts 2005a, experiment 4). After that, participants were told that there was one more task before they could do number sequences puzzles, if there was still sufficient time. The task before the puzzles was a mouse-click task, in which participants had to work through five screens by clicking boxes according to a specified pattern. Since it can be assumed that the more individuals would like to do the puzzles, the faster they would work, the speed with which they worked on the mouse-click task was a measure of goal approach behaviour. As predicted, participants worked faster when the task of doing puzzles had previously been conditioned with positive rather than neutral words. Furthermore, they worked as fast when the positive goal had been adopted unconsciously as they did when the experimenter instructed them that it would be desirable if they could work on the puzzles.

In another study, Custers and Aarts (2007) used a goal with established positive value for students, namely 'socializing'. In the first part of what appeared to be three separate experiments, cognitive accessibility of socializing was manipulated by either priming participants subliminally to words referring to socializing or priming them with neutral words. Afterwards they had to do the mouse-click task and were told that if there was sufficient time they could participate in a lottery in which tickets could be won for a student 'dance fest' to take place later that week. Again, the speed with which participants worked on the mouse-click task was the dependent measure of interest. Participants' evaluation of socializing was assessed with an implicit attitude measure at the end of the experiment. In support of predictions, participants worked faster at the mouse-click task the more positive was their attitude towards socializing. However, this association only emerged for participants who had been subliminally primed with the goal of socializing. Thus, the goal of socializing affected behaviour only if it was an attractive goal and had been made cognitively accessible.

It is important to note, though, that goal priming in these studies only resulted in a modification of behaviour, which people initiated intentionally. Thus, the participation in the resource dilemma task by participants in the study of Bargh *et al.* (2001) was intentional, in response to instructions given by the experimenters. Unconscious priming only affected the *way* the game was played, not the *fact* that the game was played. Similarly, in the studies of Custers and Aarts (2005a, 2007), priming affected the speed with which the mouse-click task was performed and not the fact that participants performed the task. It seems therefore implausible that exposure to food primes will induce chronic dieters to indulge in high-calorie food without them being aware of their change in behaviour. However, since the goals involved in self-control dilemmas such as indulging in high-calorie food or relapsing on the intention to quit smoking are strongly associated with positive affect (otherwise there would be no dilemma), priming can easily shift the delicate balance in such dilemmas.

Self-control dilemmas and their resolution

As long as unconsciously primed goals are consistent with the intentions people pursue consciously, no goal conflict will arise. However, from the perspective of health psychology, the most important reason for the discrepancy between people's intentions and their behaviour is their inability to delay gratification in the face of temptations. And these temptations increase the cognitive accessibility of previously inhibited hedonic goals, which are inconsistent with long-term personal goals. The problem with long-term goals is that the image of a slimmer figure or a longer life-expectancy some time in the future is often not as rewarding as an ice-cream cone or a cool glass of wine in the immediate present. Thus, whether the temptation comes in the form of ice cream or chocolate derailing our dieting plans for the day or in the shape of a cool glass of wine ruining our intention to have an alcohol-free day or week, an important reason for the intention–behaviour gap is a breakdown of self-control. Self-control or self-regulation refers to the ability to regulate behaviour, attention and emotion in the service of personal standards or goals. This involves overriding or changing one's inner responses, as well as interrupting undesired behavioural tendencies and refraining from acting on them.

Several models in social psychology offer theoretical explanations for such losses of control (e.g. Fazio and Towles-Schwen 1999; Fazio and Olson 2003; Strack and Deutsch 2004; Stroebe *et al.* 2008a, 2008b). Some of these models distinguish between an experiential system that is passive, effortless, rapid and guided by intuition and affect, and a rational–analytic system that is intentional, effortful, logic-based and slow. The rational system is under conscious control and its operation is in line with the models described in the previous chapter. In contrast, the experiential system operates automatically, with little conscious input.

An excellent example for such a dual system theory and one that has frequently been applied to health behaviour (for a review, see Hofmann *et al.* 2009) is the Reflective–Impulsive Model (RIM) of Strack and Deutsch (2004). The RIM conceives of self-regulation as a conflict between an impulsive and a reflective system. Impulses are assumed to emerge from the activation of associative clusters in long-term memory (Hofmann *et al.* 2009). These associative clusters have been created by the joint activation of external stimuli, affective reactions to these stimuli and behavioural tendencies. For example, through repeated ice-cream consumption, the concept of ice cream, positive affective reactions to the ice-cream experience and the behaviour that has led to the positive affective reaction (i.e. licking an ice-cream cone) become associated. Once learnt, such associative clusters can be triggered by perceptual input (e.g. seeing an ice-cream stand) or internal stimuli (e.g. the thought of ice cream). When the person encounters such ice-cream stimuli in future, this 'ice-cream cluster' is likely to be reactivated, automatically triggering the corresponding impulse to buy and eat ice cream.

In contrast, the reflective system uses knowledge about the value and the probability of potential consequences. This information is weighed and integrated to reach a preference for one behavioural option. Whereas the reflective system requires a high amount of cognitive capacity, the impulsive system needs very few resources. Thus, individuals have to be motivated and able to engage the reflective system. If the issue is unimportant or if their cognitive resources are depleted or invested in other tasks, they will be unable to engage the reflective system. Since the impulsive system is always operating, factors that interfere with the reflective system lead to behaviour that is guided by impulse. Thus, the RIM would lead one to expect implicit measures of attitudes to predict behaviour better than explicit measures when individuals are either unmotivated or unable to exert control. In contrast, explicit measures of attitudes should do better when individuals are able and motivated to exert control over their behaviour.

Whereas the RIM assumes that intentions fail because of the automatic activation of attitudes or impulses, our goal conflict model proposes that even though goals will often be activated automatically, individuals who violate personal goals in the face of temptations are aware of what they are doing (e.g. Stroebe 2002, 2008; Papies *et al.* 2008a; Stroebe *et al.* 2008b). They experience a conflict and they usually do not give in without some fight. Our model was originally developed as an explanation of why chronic dieters often fail in their attempts to keep to a low-calorie diet, but it applies to any self-control dilemma where individuals have to choose between an immediate but short-lived reward and a long-term long lasting outcome.

To illustrate the goal conflict model for the case of dieting, chronic dieters experience a conflict between two motives or goals: the goal of eating enjoyment and the goal of weight control. At least for people who derive their eating enjoyment from high-calorie food, the two goals are incompatible. Due to their repeated attempts at weight control, their dieting goal is highly accessible for chronic dieters and dominates the goal of eating enjoyment. Thus, in the absence of palatable food stimuli, chronic dieters do not have to invest motivational or cognitive resources in keeping to their diet. However, since we live in a food-rich environment, people are permanently exposed to stimuli that represent palatable food and increase the accessibility of the eating enjoyment goal in chronic dieters. The window of a delicatessen, the smell of grilled meat from a hamburger stall or the picture of a chocolate-coated ice cream are all able to trigger the eating enjoyment goal and motivate the individual to approach these palatable food items. If chronic dieters are highly motivated and cognitively able to focus on their dieting goal, they are likely to succeed in fending off the temptation. However, if their motivational or cognitive resources are depleted, the eating enjoyment goal becomes dominant and the self-control conflict becomes acute. Unfortunately, chronic dieters are handicapped in their struggle by the fact that if repeatedly triggered by palatable food stimuli, the eating enjoyment goal may become the dominant goal and inhibit thoughts about eating control (Stroebe 2008; Stroebe *et al.* 2008a). Since the attractiveness of the temptation is reflected by the spontaneous evaluative responses elicited by implicit attitude measure, our model would also predict that under conditions of depletion of motivational or cognitive resources, implicit attitudes become better predictors of behaviour than explicit measures of attitudes or goals.

Automatic influence of attitudes on behaviour

As discussed earlier the attitudes as assessed by implicit attitude measures reflect the automatic, often preconscious evaluation of an attitude object, whereas attitude scores on explicit measures reflect evaluation that is based on beliefs and expected consequences of alternative actions. Although implicit and explicit measures of attitudes often converge, there are certain conditions under which they diverge and self-control dilemmas are one area of divergence. Self-control dilemmas arise when the immediate enjoyment of hedonically rewarding experience violates long-term personal goals such as weight loss, alcohol abstinence or marital faithfulness. Self-control will be more difficult the more desirable the hedonic experience and the lower our motivational and cognitive control resources. Because implicit measures are a direct reflection of the hedonic experience, whereas explicit measures are heavily influenced by beliefs about the potential negative consequences of violating one's personal goals, implicit measures will be better predictors of behaviour when self-control resources are depleted, whereas explicit measures will predict behaviour better when people are able and motivated to exert self-control.

Support for these assumptions comes from studies which assessed people's attitude towards tempting food items with explicit as well as implicit measures of attitudes towards these food items and then measured consumption of these foods under conditions of full or depleted control resources. For example, in a study of Friese *et al.* (2008, experiment 1) participants' attitudes towards chocolate and fruits was measured with an IAT as well as an explicit attitude measure. Fruit versus chocolate consumption was assessed by offering participants a choice of five items from a box that contained a variety of five small fruits and a variety of five small chocolate bars. Cognitive resources were manipulated by putting half of the participants under high cognitive load (having to remember an eight-digit number) while making the choice, whereas the other half made their choice under low cognitive load (one-digit number). The dependent measure was the number of chocolate bars chosen. In line with predictions, the cognitive load manipulation interacted significantly with type of attitude measure in predicting choice. Simple slope analysis indicated that with low cognitive load the explicit and not the implicit measure predicted the number of chocolate bars chosen, whereas effects were reversed under high cognitive load.

In a second study, Friese *et al.* (2008) manipulated motivational resources using an ego-depletion manipulation. According to the influential model of self-regulation by Baumeister *et al.* (e.g. 1998) the ability to exert self-control relies on a limited resource and any exertion of self-control depletes this resource. Baumeister *et al.* used the analogy of a muscle to describe this depletion of self-control resources: as the exertion of a muscle would tire the muscle, the exertion of self-control depletes self-control resources, leading to a reduction in people's ability to exert self-control. And there are several studies which demonstrate that ego depletion reduces the impact of restraint standards on health-related outcomes (e.g. Vohs and Heatherton 2000). However, these studies did not include measures of implicit attitude. As we argued earlier, the likelihood of yielding to a temptation is determined by the relative magnitude of our control resources (motivation and ability) on the one hand and the attractiveness of the temptation on the other. The greater the temptation and the lower our control resources, the greater is the probability that we will yield to the temptation.

Friese *et al.* (2008) measured their participants' attitude towards potato chips with an implicit and an explicit attitude measure. Ego depletion was manipulated by having participants watch an emotion-arousing film. Whereas participants in the ego depletion condition were told to suppress their emotions, participants in the control condition were told to let their emotions flow. After watching the film, participants had to rate the taste of a sample of potato chips on a number of dimensions. The amount of chips eaten was the dependent measure. As in the previous study, there was a significant condition by type of attitude measure interaction. Simple slope analysis indicated that implicit measures predicted consumption under ego depletion but not control conditions, whereas explicit measures predicted in the control but not the ego depletion condition. There was also a marginally significant main effect of ego depletion on the amount of chips eaten, with more chips eaten by participants in the ego depletion condition. Thus, once motivation was depleted, behaviour was governed by automatic responses rather than controlled action.

Drinking alcohol probably reduces cognitive as well as motivational resources and thus frequently leads people to violate their self-control goals. One would therefore expect that under the influence of alcohol behaviour in a self-control dilemma would be better predicted by implicit than explicit attitudes. Support for this assumption comes from a study by Hofmann and Friese (2008), who had their participants test and rate chocolate candies. Whereas half the participants were given orange juice 30 minutes before the taste test, the other half were given orange juice mixed with vodka. Findings with the alcohol manipulation fully replicated results with ego depletion. Under the influence of alcohol, implicit attitude was the better predictor of consumption, whereas without alcohol the explicit measure predicted better. There was also a main effect of alcohol on eating behaviour, confirming that alcohol led to more eating at the group level.

A somewhat different paradigm was used in a study by Ostafin *et al.* (2008), who assessed the impact of ego depletion on alcohol consumption in individuals who habitually consumed large amounts of alcohol (at-risk drinkers). Drinking motivation was either measured with an explicit or an implicit (IAT) measure. Alcohol consumption was assessed in a test in which participants had to rate the taste of three different types of beer. To motivate participants to control their drinking, they were told that after the beer tasting a reaction time test would be conducted and that they would win a prize if their reaction time was fast enough. As in previous studies, the implicit measure predicted consumption better under ego depletion than control conditions and ego depletion also resulted in a general increase in consumption. However, in contrast to previous research, the explicit measure did not predict consumption under either condition.

It is plausible to assume that failure of the explicit measure to predict consumption under low ego depletion was due to the fact that the experimenters induced additional restraint with their promise of a prize in the reaction time task. Support for this assumption comes from a study by Friese *et al.* (2008, experiment 3), which with the exception of the restraint manipulation is identical to that of Ostafin *et al.* (2008). Friese *et al.* replicated the pattern of their previous studies: that the implicit measure predicted beer consumption under ego depletion but not control condition and the explicit measure predicted under control but not ego depletion conditions. Furthermore, there was again a main effect, with everybody drinking more when ego-depleted.

These studies show that the outcome of self-control conflicts between immediate rewards and long-term personal goals is determined by two sets of factors, namely the attraction of the immediate reward (reflected by the implicit attitude) and the motivational and cognitive resources available to individuals to resist the temptation. Depletion of these resources increases the risk of a breakdown of self-control. Therefore, people on a diet should not watch TV while eating, should not drink alcohol and should not deplete their self-control resources by engaging in another self-control battle such as trying to quit smoking at the same time (but see p. 118).

Automatic influence of habits on behaviour

Much of the behaviour of interest to health psychology is enacted on a regular basis. It is therefore likely to have become habitual. Habits are 'learned sequences of acts that have become automatic responses to specific cues and are functional in obtaining certain goals or end states' (Verplanken and Aarts 1999: 104). Habits are unproblematic, as long as our habitual behaviour is consistent with our health goals. Unfortunately, however, this is often not the case. Smokers who want to kick their habit or fast-food addicts who want to adopt healthier eating habits are all confronted with environmental cues that in the past have been associated with their habit and might cue an unwanted behaviour sequence.

Most habit theorists agree that habits are the residue of past goal pursuits. They develop when people repeatedly use a particular behavioural means in a particular context to reach their goals. Behaviour becomes habitual if it is performed frequently, regularly and under environmental conditions which are stable. Habits are cognitively represented as associations between goals and behavioural responses that allow an automatic behavioural response upon activation of a goal (Aarts and Dijksterhuis 2000). Thus, if we always drive to work, the goal of 'going to our office' will automatically trigger the behavioural response of 'taking the car'. We might walk to our car unthinkingly, even if we have to take the bus because the car is at a garage for some extensive repairs.

Behaviour is unlikely to become habitual if it is only performed once a year or under unstable environmental conditions. Thus, whereas much of our grocery shopping (e.g. choice of supermarket, choice of brands of washing powder, oil, margarine, toothpaste, etc.) is habitual and automatic (in the sense that we do not have to deliberate where to go, once we have decided to go grocery shopping, nor what brands of oil, margarine or toothpaste to buy), buying Christmas presents will need a great deal of deliberation. Similarly, if we move to a different town, where parking is a problem and people take the bus or bike, the goal of 'going to our office' is unlikely to automatically trigger the response of taking the car. Or, if our fast-food habit is strongly associated with the Chinese takeaway in our neighbourhood, living in a different neighbourhood will make it easier to break the habit (Wood *et al.* 2005).

By being performed automatically and without the need of deliberation, habitual behaviour has the great advantage of allowing us to use our (limited) cognitive resources for other purposes. Thus, if we always drive to work, we do not have to ponder over a choice of transport means on planning to go to the office. And while driving to work, we can leisurely plan our day rather than concentrating on performing the multitude of acts required when driving a car or on planning the route we have to take in order to reach our office. The great disadvantage of the automaticity of habitual behaviour is that it is difficult to change if we have formed the intention to do so. Even deviation from one's usual way home to pick up some shopping can prove a challenge. We might have promised to stop at the supermarket to pick up some supplies needed for dinner and yet we might find ourselves arriving home, having totally forgotten about the planned deviation from our customary route.

Why are habits difficult to break? One reason is memory. Since habits are represented in memory as associations between a goal and a behavioural response, the habitual behavioural response is the one most likely remembered when the goal is activated. This explains why one would walk to one's car, even if it is being repaired and not parked outside. In this case, all one needs to break the habit and choose another mode of transport is a reminder that the car is being repaired. Taking the bus or the bike is probably more effortful than taking the car (otherwise one would not normally go by car), but the difference might be less than expected. After having had to take the bus a few times, one might even decide to make this the habitual means of getting to the office.

The problem with many of the habits involving health-impairing behaviour is that the habitual behaviour is associated with a more positive affect than the behavioural alternatives. Thus, for the smoker trying to quit, the immediate shot of nicotine is more rewarding than the years added to life expectancy some time in the distant future, and for the dieter the immediate enjoyment of a hamburger is more rewarding that the slim figure to be achieved some time in the future. Furthermore, the environment in which the habitual response is usually performed acts as a cue to make the whole knowledge structure cognitively available. For example, for the smoker who is trying to stop, drinking beer in the pub with his friends (exactly the context in which he used to enjoy smoking), will not only remind him of the taste of a cigarette, but also of the pleasure he used to derive from smoking. Similarly, the person who thrice weekly stopped on his way home to enjoy a pizza in his neighbourhood pizzeria, but denies himself this pleasure due to the need to shed some pounds, will salivate when remembering the enjoyment of eating, each time he passes the pizzeria on his way home. In each case, the risk of relapse is great. Smokers have only a 5 per cent chance of succeeding each time they try to quit (Hughes *et al.* 2004) and restrained eaters are better known for their relapses than their restraint (Herman and Polivy 1984). And since it is the context in which we usually engage in a particular habit which reminds us of the habitual response and the affective consequences associated with this response, it is plausible that the risk of relapse is greatest in the context in which the habitual behaviour is usually performed.

For this reason, behaviour that we perform regularly and under stable environmental conditions is often better predicted by our past behaviour in these situations than by our intentions assessed at some other occasion. In contrast, intentions will be a better predictor of behaviour that is performed infrequently and under conditions that vary a great deal. Support for these assumptions comes from a meta-analysis of studies that included measures of past behaviour in tests of theories of reasoned action and planned behaviour (Oulette and Wood 1998). In line with predictions, intentions were a much better predictor than measures of past behaviour for actions that were only performed once or twice a year and in unstable contexts. In contrast, measures of past behaviour were better predictors than intentions of actions that were performed regularly and in stable contexts. These findings are indeed consistent with the assumption that habitual behaviour is automatic in the sense that it is triggered by situational cues rather than guided by conscious intentions.

Further support comes from a study by Danner *et al.* (2008) of the role of habits in snacking or drinking alcohol. In the first phase of their study, the frequency and context stability of past behaviour was measured for three behaviours, namely snacking, drinking milk and drinking alcohol. These two measures were combined into an index of habit strength. In addition, participants' intention to perform these behaviours in the next four weeks was assessed. Four weeks later, participants had to report how frequently they had engaged in each of these behaviours over the period. There were significant main effects for intentions (marginal for snacking) as well as habit strength for each of the behaviours. For snacking and drinking milk (but not for drinking alcohol), there was also the predicted interaction between habit strength and intention: intentions predicted snacking and milk drinking when habits were weak, but not when habits were strong. The pattern of findings was similar with regard to drinking alcohol, but the interaction did not reach statistical significance. That habits predict behaviour better than intentions when habits are calculated as frequent performance of a behaviour in stable contexts was also demonstrated for buying fast food, taking the bus and watching TV news (Ji and Wood 2007) and for eating fruit and vegetables (de Bruijn *et al.* 2007).

If habits are mentally represented as associations between goals and actions which are instrumental for attaining these goals, activation of the goal should also activate the behaviour representation. Thus, if a student always uses her bicycle to travel to the university, activation of the goal to act (having to attend a lecture) should automatically trigger the habitual response (bicycle). This hypothesis was supported in a study with student participants, who varied in the extent to which they were habitual bicycle users (Aarts and Dijksterhuis 2000). In a pre-test, the researchers established five locations in the university town which could be reached by bicycle (e.g. shopping mall, university) and also the major reason why students wanted to go to these locations (e.g. shopping, attending classes). Half the participants were then given sentences to read which primed the five travel goals without mentioning locations (e.g. attending a lecture). The assumption was that reading these sentences would cognitively activate the five travel goals. Then, in an apparently unrelated task, all participants were presented with the five locations and a word presenting a travel mode, and had to decide as quickly as possible whether the presented mode of transport was a reasonable way to get to that location. The dependent measure was the time taken to answer this question. In support of predictions, habitual bicycle users responded faster than non-habitual bicycle users when 'bicycle' was offered as a travel mode, but only if they had been primed with the relevant travel goals. Without goal priming, they did not respond faster to 'bicycle' offered as a travel mode than did the non-habitual bicycle users. This rules out the explanation that habitual bicycle users responded faster because they were more familiar with the concept of 'bicycle'. The activation of a relevant travel goal was necessary to activate bicycling as a travel mode in habitual bicycle users.

If habits are cognitively represented as links between goals and actions that are instrumental for attaining these goals, then forming implementation intentions should operate through the same processes as the formation of habits. After all, in forming an implementation intention, individuals create a mental link between a situational cue and a specific action. Whereas with habits the association between the relevant situation and the behaviour is learnt through repeated performance of the behaviour, with implementation intentions the association is learnt through repeated mental simulation of performing that action in that specific situation. Support for this assumption comes from the study by Aarts and Dijksterhuis (2000), who used the travel goal paradigm described above. This time, they exposed all participants to the goal prime, but added an implementation intention condition as a factor, cross-cutting the extent to which individuals were (or were not) habitual bicycle users. Implementation intentions were formed by asking individuals to write down each of the travel goals and plan precisely how to reach these goals. Again, the dependent measure was the time it would take individuals to recognize 'bicycle' as a word in a lexical decision task. In support of predictions that the formation of implementation intentions would operate the same way as the formation of a habit, non-habitual bicycle users recognized 'bicycle' faster after they had formed an implementation intention than without such an intention. In fact, non-habitual bicycle users who had formed an implementation intention recognized the word 'bicycle' as quickly as habitual bicycle users without an implementation intention. Forming an implementation intention had no effect on habitual bicycle users.

The breaking of habits: implications for interventions

The fact that habitual behaviours are instigated and executed more or less automatically, without the individual consciously intending or choosing the behaviour, has implications for interventions aimed at changing such behaviour. First, there is some evidence to suggest that the existence of strong habits makes individuals less interested in attending to information relevant to the habitual behaviour (Verplanken and Aarts 1999). But even if a persuasive communication succeeds in inducing individuals to form the intention to change a habitual behaviour, they are likely to experience difficulties in acting on this decision. These difficulties might merely be due to the fact that the individual has to remember consciously to control the behaviour sequences which have previously been enacted automatically. Even though the joke of the bus driver who stops at every bus stop when she takes her family shopping in the family car is probably exaggerated, most of us will have experienced situations where we walked to the old address of friends even though we knew they had moved, or dialled an old telephone number even though we were well aware of the new number.

In these cases we merely have to remember to replace a habitual sequence of behaviour by an alternative sequence. However, breaking habits is likely to be even more difficult if there is no alternative sequence to replace the old one. For example, individuals who want to stop smoking, to reduce their alcohol consumption or to eat less have to interrupt a given sequence of behaviour without being able to replace it by an alternative set of responses. According to Mandler (1975), the interruption of an integrated response sequence produces a state of arousal that, in the absence of certain alternative responses (completion or substitution), develops into an emotional expression which could often be anxiety. Furthermore, in the case of appetitive behaviours, attempts at consciously interrupting the habitual sequence of events might give rise to urges and cravings (Tiffany 1990). Dieters might be unable to ban the thought of food, just as smokers cannot avoid thinking about cigarettes. Furthermore, in cases of addictive behaviour such as smoking or drinking too much alcohol, nicotine or alcohol deprivation is likely to result in physiological reactions which impair normal functioning. Thus, for interventions to be successful, we not only have to persuade individuals to stop smoking, or to reduce their consumption of alcohol, we also have to teach them to break the link that associates their behaviour with the environmental and internal stimulus conditions which trigger and support it.

Deliberate and automatic instigation of action: an attempt at integration

While reading the last section you might have wondered what to believe: is behaviour automatically instigated or the result of deliberation? And you were right to raise this question. It is a highly controversial issue that has been hotly debated between those who believe that much of human action is unconscious and unintentional (e.g. Bargh 2002) and those who believe that it is informed by cognitions and is intentional (e.g. Ajzen and Fishbein 2000). And between these two extreme positions are explanations in terms of two system theories such as the RIM of Strack and Deutsch (2004) that assumes that some behaviours are deliberate and others (namely impulses) are automatic. My own position is that most behaviour of importance is performed deliberately, but that the reasons *why* it is performed are often triggered outside our awareness by internal or external stimuli. We usually know *what* we are doing, but not *why* we are doing it (Nisbett and Wilson 1977). Since this might sound cryptic, let me explain it in more detail.

An important distinction in studying behaviour is between the instigation and the execution of behaviour. While I am usually aware that I am driving to my office (rather than going by bus or bike), I might be so deeply in thought that I may not be aware of the route I am taking and how fast I am going. There is consensus that the regulation of the execution of well-learnt behaviour occurs outside our awareness. Thus, it would be undisputed that the students who had been primed by Bargh *et al.* (1996) with the stereotype of old people, and as a result walked more slowly down a corridor than those who had not been primed, were unaware of having slowed down. But then, unless people are in a rush, they are usually not aware of how fast they are going. It would overload our cognitive system if we had to consciously monitor the execution of all our behaviours. As far as I am aware, all studies that demonstrated effects of priming on behaviour assessed the execution of behaviour and not its instigation. Since theories of deliberate action attempt to explain the instigation rather than the execution of behaviour, research that demonstrates that the execution of behaviour is influenced by priming effects outside the individual's awareness would not be inconsistent with these theories.

As Ajzen and Fishbein (2000: 18) pointed out, their theories have no difficulty in accounting for the impact environmental or internal stimuli might have on individual beliefs and attitudes outside individual awareness: 'Attitudes, subjective norms, and perceived behavioral control are assumed to be available automatically as performance of a behavior is being considered'. It has been a central feature of the reasoned action approach that people's attitude towards performing a given action is determined by their *salient* beliefs – that is, by the few outcome expectancies that are highly accessible at that particular moment. And the accessibility of outcome expectancies can fluctuate over time, influenced by environmental and internal cues. The person who expresses the firm intention to keep to a calorie-reduced diet when filling out some questionnaire is probably envisioning the pleasures of looking great after having lost a great deal of weight. Thus, the salient beliefs at that particular time will be beliefs about the positive outcome of dieting. But when the same person is deciding to eat a hamburger in the evening, the decision is probably guided by the anticipated pleasure of biting into a juicy hamburger. And this person would be unaware that this change of expectancies was primed by the sight of a hamburger advertisement or the delicious smell of meat being grilled in the garden next door.

Environmental and internal cues might also influence the reference person or reference group that is most important to us at that particular moment and thus shapes our subjective norms with regard to a specific behaviour. For example, a student might have thought of her father, who expects her to get top grades, when stating her intentions to study hard over the weekend. However, at the weekend, her lover might become the most important person, and he might expect her to spend her time with him. The impact of environmental cues on the accessibility of significant others and on the goals associated with these others has been demonstrated in a series of experiment by Shah (2003). He showed that priming a person subliminally with a close reference individual (e.g. a parent, best friend) not only increased commitment to the goals which were important to the primed reference person, but also influenced goal-directed performance.

We have already discussed that environmental or internal stimuli can trigger chronic goals (e.g. eating enjoyment) outside the individual's awareness. Similarly, such stimuli can also trigger goal or behavioural intentions formed at some earlier time. The reasoned action approach does not assume that intentions are always newly-formed, each time a person decides to act. Once we have formed an intention in a particular situation, this intention is likely to become accessible whenever we are confronted with the same or a similar situation. This in turn increases the probability that such intentions become accessible at the moment that is right for action. If there are no conflicting reasons, we will probably act on the activated intention without much further thought. This is particularly likely in situations involving habitual behaviour such as driving to work or brushing one's teeth. If we always drive to work or brush our teeth in the morning, we do not have to deliberate what to do, but just do it. There can be doubt, however, whether in these types of routine situation people really form an intention or whether the behaviour is directly activated by situational cues. I am certainly not aware of forming an intention to take my car in the morning, because these days I always go by car. But when I am walking out of the house I am certainly aware that I am intending to take my car as I begin to wonder where I parked it the night before.

There is scarce evidence to support the arguments presented in this section, because most studies on automatic behaviour have not assessed whether the primes used to trigger the behaviour might also have changed people's beliefs, subjective norms or intentions. But the evidence that is available tends to be consistent with the position presented here. For example, Ajzen et al. (2004) demonstrated that the change in behaviour evidenced by students who either voted in a hypothetical or a real referendum to donate money to a scholarship fund was accompanied by a change in beliefs, attitudes and intentions, which became significantly less favourable. The study Holland et al. (2005), who exposed students to the smell of a household cleaner, nicely demonstrated that external cues can influence people's intentions. Finally, Karremans et al. (2006) found that subliminally priming individuals with the brand name of a soft drink increased their intention to order that drink next time they had the opportunity to do so.

Research that illustrates that implicit attitudes are better predictors of behaviour in self-control dilemmas when motivational resources are impaired, whereas explicit measures are better predictors when people are in full control of their resources. This may reflect an extension of the compatibility principle of Ajzen and Fishbein (1977) discussed earlier (p. 21). According to this principle, measures of attitudes predict measures of behaviour best when both have been assessed under the same conditions. Whereas Ajzen and Fishbein were concerned about the compatibility of measures in terms of target, action, context and time, one would have to add level of control over the behavioural and attitudinal response to this list. Because implicit attitude measures are taken under conditions of low control, it is plausible that they should be better predictors of people's reactions in self-control dilemma situations under conditions where control resources are also impaired.

The fact that people are continually exposed to a stream of external cues which influence the cognitive accessibility of outcome and normative beliefs, and that changes in internal states (e.g. hunger) continually influence the valence attached to different outcomes, explains the modest association between intentions and behaviour assessed at different points in time, particularly with regard to situations that involve some kind of conflict. This association would be substantially increased if we were able to measure intentions moments before people take action. But while this would be interesting for theoretical reasons, it would not be very helpful for people who are interested in predicting the behaviour of others.

Summary and conclusions

The first section of this chapter introduced the concepts of attitudes, beliefs, goals and intentions as major determinants of health behaviour. We then discussed the conditions under which attitudes are related to behaviour and stressed the need for measures of attitude and behaviour which are both reliable and compatible. Attitudes will only be related to behaviour if the measures of attitude and behaviour are specified at the same level of generality.

The next part of the chapter reviewed classic models of behaviour from health and social psychology. These models assume that behaviour is the result of deliberation about likely consequences of actions. The health belief model and protection motivation theory identify five determinants of health behaviour. According to these theories, individuals are likely to engage in health protective behaviour if they perceive a *health threat* which appears *serious*, and if they feel able to *perform some action* that is likely to *alleviate* the health threat and that is *not too effortful or costly*. The theory of reasoned action assumes that the intention to perform a particular behaviour is determined by one's attitude towards performing the behaviour and by subjective norms. Thus, the beliefs that losing weight would lead to a number of consequences which are positively valued (attitude) and that friends, family members and/or one's partner would prefer one to lose weight (subjective norms) are likely to result in the intention to lose weight. All other factors that influence behaviour must do so through one of these two components.

These four models are theories of motivation that describe the factors influencing the formation of behavioural intentions. However, even though intentions are important determinants of behaviour, actual performance depends also on other factors, such as ability, skills, information, opportunity and strength to maintain one's motivation during the execution of an intention. The concept of perceived behavioural control is used as a summary index of all internal and external factors that might thwart our intentions. According to the model of planned behaviour, our intention to lose weight will be a function of perceived behavioural control over weight loss as well as of our attitude towards losing weight and our beliefs about the shape important others want us to have. Perceived lack of control with regard to weight loss could be due to perceived low self-efficacy (e.g. 'I will never be able to control myself'), low outcome expectancy (e.g. 'Even if I eat less, I will never lose any weight') and external influences (e.g. 'How can I lose weight when I have to attend several business lunches every week?').

It is uneconomical to entertain specific theories of health behaviour such as the health belief model or protection motivation theory unless the predictive success of these specific models is greater than that of general models such as the theory of planned behaviour. It is unlikely that these specific models will do better in predicting behaviour than the theory of planned behaviour, because all the components of the specific model can be integrated into the more general theory of planned behaviour. Thus, an individual's attitude towards continuing to smoke will be the sum of the products of the positive (e.g. weight control, pleasure) and negative consequences of smoking, each weighted by its valence. Individual perceptions of vulnerability to lung cancer as well as the severity of lung cancer would therefore enter into this attitude. The attitude towards stopping, on the other hand, would reflect the perceived costs of stopping as well as beliefs about the efficacy of smoking cessation in preventing lung cancer. The concept of perceived behavioural control, as one of three determinants of intention in the theory of planned behaviour, incorporates perceived self-efficacy as well as outcome expectancies. Finally, the model also considers subjective norms which have no place in the health belief model but might be important determinants of health behaviour such as smoking or weight loss.

But even though the theory of planned behaviour is superior to the earlier models in predicting behavioural intentions, the fact remains that intentions account for less than 30 per cent of the variance in measures of behaviour and even with the more specific implementation intentions, more than half of the variance in behaviour remains unexplained. Furthermore, adding perceived behavioural control does not substantially improve the predictive validity of this model. Even if we accept that part of this unexplained variance is due to the less than perfect reliability of our measurement instruments, there remains a substantial gap between intention and behaviour and this gap is mainly due to individuals failing to act according to their intentions.

There are many reasons why people might not act according to their intentions. For example, the situation might have changed between the time when they stated their intention and the time when they were expected to act. But even if the situation did not change, people might have made unrealistic assumptions about the situation which they had to correct when they were finally expected to act. Most academics are familiar with the phenomenon that they accept deadlines for the not too distant future, somehow assuming that by then they will have ample time to write the promised chapter or article. Since these types of discrepancy are usually due to a change in intention, they are not really inconsistent with models of deliberate behaviour.

In the last section, automatic influences on behaviour were discussed, which seem less easily reconciled with the theories of deliberate action reviewed earlier. The fact that the belief-based explicit measures of attitudes do not predict the resolution of self-control dilemmas when cognitive or motivational resources are depleted, or that intentions fail to predict behaviour when strong habits exist, appears to be inconsistent with these theories. Although this is true for the health belief and protection motivation models, it is not true for the theories of reasoned action and planned behaviour. According to those theories, an individual's attitude towards a specific action is determined by a small number of salient beliefs. And the beliefs that are salient on responding to a questionnaire will often differ from the beliefs that are salient when the intended behaviour is being performed. Furthermore, situational cues might change the accessibility of the people important to actors and thus the subjective norms, which influence their behaviour in a given situation.

Finally, people often have many conflicting intentions that they could apply to any given situation, and situational cues might determine which intention becomes salient and thus also the behaviour that is enacted. Therefore the reasoned action approach is not inconsistent with the assumption that situational cues influence behaviour and that there is likely to be an intention–behaviour gap. However, the one point where the two approaches are different is that the reasoned action approach would assume that people are aware of their intentions when they act, whereas the automatic behaviour theorist would assume that they are not.

Further reading

Ajzen, I. (2005) *Attitudes, Personality and Behaviour*, 2nd edn. Maidenhead: Open University Press. A very readable account of the conditions under which attitudes predict behaviour. Discusses the principles of aggregation and compatibility as well as the theories of reasoned action and planned behaviour.

Ajzen, I. and Fishbein, M. (2000) Attitudes and the attitude–behavior relation: reasoned action and automatic processes, in W. Stroebe and M. Hewstone (eds) *European Review of Social Psychology*, 11. Chichester: Wiley. In this chapter Ajzen and Fishbein discuss the relationship between their models and the assumptions made by theories of automatic behaviour.

Conner, M. and Norman, P. (eds) (2005) *Predicting Health Behaviour*, 2nd edn. Maidenhead: Open University Press. Contains excellent and detailed descriptions of the different models of health behaviour, and comprehensive reviews of health psychological research conducted to test these models. Particularly relevant are the chapters on the health belief model, protection motivation theory and the theory of planned behaviour.

Custers, R. and Aarts, R. (2005) Beyond priming effects: the role of positive affect and discrepancies in implicit processes of motivation and goal pursuit, in W. Stroebe and M. Hewstone (eds) *European Review of Social Psychology*, 16: 257–300. The chapter reviews the literature on automatic behaviour and presents a framework within which the non-conscious activation of goal-directed behaviour can be understood.

Beyond persuasion: the modification of health behaviour

If we accept estimates like those of McGinnis and Foege (1993) and Mokdad *et al.* (2004) that more than 40 per cent of the mortality from the 10 leading causes of death in the USA is due to modifiable lifestyle factors, health promotion offers challenging opportunities to social psychologists. During the last decades there has been great progress in social psychological understanding of processes of persuasion, attitude and behaviour change, and health promotion would constitute a worthwhile field of application of this knowledge (for reviews, see Chaiken *et al.* 1996b; Petty *et al.* 1997; Bohner and Wänke 2002; Rothman and Salovey 2007). Social psychologists should help to design mass media campaigns to inform people of the health hazards involved in smoking, drinking too much alcohol, eating a fatty diet, failing to exercise and other behaviours that are detrimental to their health, and to persuade them to change their lifestyles.

Unfortunately, persuasion is often not enough to achieve lasting changes in health behaviour. For example, even though the first report in which the US Surgeon General pointed out the health hazards of smoking had a considerable impact on smoking behaviour, particularly among males, many of the people who still smoke would like to give it up but do not succeed in doing so. Survey data show that about one-third of all current smokers make an attempt to stop at least once per year and that only one-fifth of these succeed in any single attempt (CDC 1994). Although there is probably no harm in reminding these smokers of the damage they are continuing to do to their health, what most of them need is help not only in quitting but also in staying off cigarettes.

The nature of change

Before we approach the main topic of this chapter, namely strategies of attitude and behaviour change, we have to clarify whether to conceive of change as movement along a continuum or a progression through qualitatively different stages. The models discussed so far view the process of health behaviour change as movement along a continuum. To predict behaviour, these theories combine the assumed determinants of behaviour in an algebraic equation assuming that the numerical value of the equation locates the individual on a single continuum that indicates the probability of action. Any intervention that increases the value of the prediction equation is presumed to enhance the prospects for behaviour change (Weinstein and Sandman 1992).

The example of smoking presented earlier is more in line with stage theories of change. These theories propose that health behaviour change involves progression through discernible stages from ignorance of a health threat to completed preventive action. The different stages are assumed to represent qualitatively different patterns of behaviour, beliefs and experience, and factors which produce transitions between stages vary, depending on the specific stage transitions being considered. Consistent with this view, our example of smoking implied that there are at least two qualitatively different stages in the modification of health behaviour. The first involves the *formation of an intention* to change. Individuals have to be informed of the health hazards of certain behaviours and to be persuaded to change. However, even if people accept a health recommendation and form the firm intention to change, they are likely to experience difficulty in *acting* on these intentions over any length of time. Thus, a second stage involves teaching people how to change and how to maintain this change. Whereas the first stage of this process can be most effectively achieved through persuasion or other social psychological procedures of social influence, with behaviour such as substance abuse or excessive eating, clinical intervention may sometimes be needed at the second stage.

This simple stage model allows one also to illustrate the important characteristics of stage models, namely that people at different points in the process of changing their behaviour are confronted with different problems, that they use different strategies to deal with these problems, and that different types of interventions are therefore needed to influence them. Stage models offer a systematic analysis of the different problems which confront individuals as they move from being unaware of a health problem to taking action and maintaining it. Two stage theories will be presented, namely the precaution adoption process model of Weinstein (1988; Weinstein and Sandman 1992) and the transtheoretical model of behaviour change (e.g. Prochaska *et al.* 1992).

Precaution adoption process model

The precaution adoption process model of Weinstein (1988; Weinstein and Sandman 1992) was originally developed as a dynamic version of the health belief model and of protection motivation theory. I will present here the most recent version of the model (Weinstein and Sandman 1992).

The model
The starting point for this model is the individual who is unaware of a given health risk, either out of personal ignorance or because the risk is as yet generally unknown (Stage 1). Examples for the latter are the risk of HIV infection before

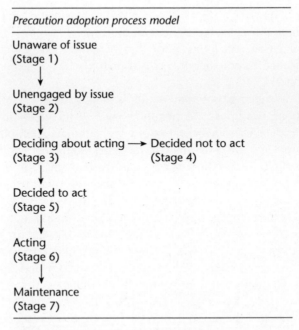

FIGURE 3.1 Stages of the precaution adoption process model

1980, but also the dangers involved in smoking before anti-smoking campaigns started in 1964. When people first learn about some issue, they are no longer unaware of the risk, but they may not really be concerned by this knowledge either (Stage 2). However, further communication from friends or the mass media may convince them that the risk is really a serious one and that they are personally at risk. This would move them to Stage 3 of the precaution adoption process, the stage at which decisions are being considered. This decision-making process can result in the decision either not to take action or to take action. If the individual decides not to take action, the precaution adoption process ends, or at least it ends for this particular point in time. This outcome represents a separate stage (Stage 4), although not a stage along the route to action. If people have decided to adopt a precaution (Stage 5), the following step is to initiate action (Stage 6). Stimulated by the transtheoretical model of behaviour change, Weinstein and colleagues added a 'maintenance' stage (Stage 7) to indicate repetitions that may be required after a preventive action has first been performed. Whereas with lifestyle change – such as adopting physical exercise or stopping smoking – maintaining the new behaviour is essential, there are other precautions, such as buying a burglar alarm or having asbestos removed from one's home where actions need not be continued.

Evaluation of the model
One strength of the model is that it offers a systematic analysis of the factors which influence people as they move from stage to stage. For example, reading about some

previously unknown risk factor should be important in moving people through the first two stages, but information which makes personal vulnerability salient (e.g. a health scare) and outlines some effective remedy should be most important in determining whether someone will adopt the precautionary action (move from Stage 3 to 5). Finally, the presence of situational obstacles and constraints should be most important when intentions have to be translated into action (Stages 5 and 6).

However, the precaution adoption process model has not stimulated a great deal of published research (Weinstein and Sandman 1992; Blalock *et al.* 1996). In one of the few applications to health issues, Blalock *et al.* (1996) studied stages in the adoption of health behaviours that protect individuals against the risk of developing osteoporosis, a disorder characterized by decreased bone mass and increased susceptibility to fracture from which women are most at risk. Two behaviours are recommended to reduce the risk of developing osteoporosis, namely calcium consumption and weight-bearing exercise. Participants in this cross-sectional study were 620 women between the ages of 35 and 45 years. They were sent a questionnaire assessing their precaution adoption stage with regard to both calcium consumption and exercise, and measuring the variables assumed by the model as predictors for the various stages. Examples of these predictor variables were health motivation, barriers against exercising or eating calcium-rich food, self-efficacy and osteoporosis knowledge.

Findings indicated that most of these predictor variables significantly discriminated between respondents in the relevant stages. For example, in line with theoretical expectations, the level of individual self-efficacy with regard to exercising was highest for individuals in Stages 6 and 7 who were currently exercising, lower in Stages 4 and 5 for those who were contemplating action, and lowest in Stages 1 to 3. Similar patterns were observed for most predictors and both kinds of health precautions.

Although findings like this are consistent with the stage model suggested by Weinstein and his colleagues, they are not actually inconsistent with the assumptions underlying continuum models such as the models of planned behaviour and reasoned action (Ajzen 2005). For example, since self-efficacy is one of the determinants of the intention to act and of actual behaviour in the model of planned behaviour, this model would also predict that individuals who hold very weak intentions should differ significantly in their self-efficacy regarding this particular behaviour from those who hold strong intentions or those who are actually engaged in this particular behaviour (Weinstein *et al.* 1998).

The transtheoretical model of behaviour change

The model
At present, the transtheoretical model (TTM) is undoubtedly the most popular stage theory of health behaviour change. It distinguishes five stages of change through which individuals are assumed to move when they change a given problem behaviour. Prochaska *et al.* (e.g. 1992) originally considered change as a

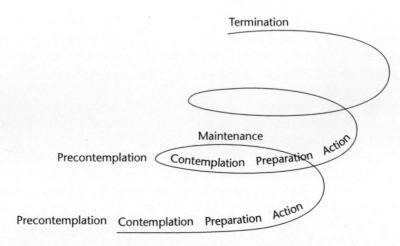

FIGURE 3.2 A spiral pattern of the stages of change of the TTM
Source: Prochaska *et al.* (1992)

linear progression through these stages. Because relapse is the rule rather than the exception, they changed the original conception to assume a spiral pattern. During relapse individuals regress to some earlier stage such as contemplation or even precontemplation. However, it is still assumed that these stages form a simplex pattern in which adjacent stages are more highly correlated with each other than any other stage. The following description of these stages will be based on Prochaska *et al.* (1992).

Precontemplation is the stage at which there is no intention to change behaviour in the foreseeable future. Individuals at this stage are typically not even aware that they have a problem, even though their family or friends might feel that there is a need for them to change. They can be identified by their negative answer to a question about whether they are intending to change the problem behaviour within the next six months. In terms of the precaution adoption process model of Weinstein and Sandman (1992), the precontemplation stage includes both people who have never thought about the desirability of changing and those who have thought about it, but arrived at the conclusion that they do not need or wish to change. For example, there will be few smokers who have never thought about stopping. Some smokers may have even stopped for some time and then decided that the benefits of not smoking were not worth their deprivation. It seems plausible that such people may need different types of arguments and will be more difficult to influence than individuals who never thought about a given health risk.

Contemplation is the stage in which people are aware that a problem exists and are considering doing something about it without having reached a definite decision. There is no commitment to act. A smoker who is at this stage may feel some unease about the potential health damage due to smoking or the impact smoking may have on their family, but he or she will not yet have made the decision to stop.

Individuals at this stage weigh the 'pros' and 'cons' of changing their behaviour. Individuals can remain in this stage for long periods of time. Contemplators will indicate that they are seriously considering changing the health-impairing behaviour in the next six months.

Preparation is a stage at which individuals have not only formed a firm intention to change, but have also begun to make small behavioural changes. An example would be a smoker who has formed the intention to stop and has already begun to reduce his or her cigarette consumption, or to delay smoking the first cigarette of the day. Although they have made some reductions in their problem behaviour, they have not yet reached the criterion for effective action such as stopping smoking, or abstaining from drinking alcohol. They usually score high on measures of both contemplation and action.

Action is the stage at which individuals change their behaviour and/or their environment in order to overcome their problem. Operationally, individuals are classified in the action stage if they have successfully altered their addictive behaviour for a period ranging from one day to six months. Successfully altering addictive behaviour means reaching a particular criterion such as abstinence.

Maintenance is the stage at which individuals expend great effort to prevent relapse and to consolidate the gains made during action. In the case of addictive behaviour, this stage begins at six months following the initial action and continues for an indeterminate period. For some behaviours maintenance can be considered to last for a lifetime.

The movement through these stages is assumed to be caused by the processes of change, decisional balance (i.e. the benefits and costs of changing) and self-efficacy/temptations. The TTM specifies different types of cognitions that are assumed to change and different strategies of change which individuals are assumed to employ when moving through different stages. With regard to types of cognitions, the TTM borrowed concepts from Janis and Mann (1977) and Bandura (1986). Based on the theoretical ideas of Janis and Mann, it was assumed that individual perceptions of the 'pros' and 'cons' of engaging in a given problem behaviour (decisional balance) would change as individuals moved through the stages (e.g. Velicer *et al.* 1985; Prochaska *et al.* 1994). Following Bandura (1986) it was further assumed that the level of the individual's self-efficacy would be important in the change process. Self-efficacy represents the individual's level of confidence that they are able to change a given problem behaviour and to maintain this change.

The processes of change reflect the behavioural or cognitive techniques employed by individuals to modify a particular problem behaviour. A list of 10 change processes has been developed inductively from a scrutiny of recommended change techniques in systems of psychotherapy (Prochaska *et al.* 1992). The 10 strategies of change can be divided into two broad categories, namely cognitive-affective and behavioural processes. The cognitive-affective processes include activities related to thinking and experiencing emotion about changing a health-impairing behaviour such as smoking, namely:

- consciousness-raising (gathering information);
- dramatic relief (experiencing and expressing affect about smoking/non-smoking);
- environmental re-evaluation (considering the consequences for others);
- self-re-evaluation (realization that behaviour change is important);
- social liberation (attending to changing social norms regarding smoking).

Behavioural processes are categories of behaviour which are assumed to be helpful for changing this behaviour:

- counter conditioning (substitution of health behaviour for smoking);
- stimulus control (avoiding cues to smoking);
- reinforcement management (being rewarded by self or others);
- self-liberation (commitment to action);
- helping relationships (obtaining social support).

The model does not state precisely how these variables relate to stages of change beyond describing them as 'intertwined and interacting variables in the modification of mental and health behaviours'. As Sutton (2005) criticized, it is not clear whether the processes of change influence the pros, cons, self-efficacy and temptations, which in turn influence the stage transitions, or whether some other causal model is assumed. This is a major theoretical deficit, which is probably due to the way the model was developed as a collection of processes and strategies that had been found useful in psychotherapy.

Evaluation of the model
There are three lines of evidence used to support the TTM. The first line claims support for the hypothesis that individuals move through *each* of the various stages. With the development of questionnaires measuring individual stages of change, it has become possible to assess this assumption. Thus McConnaughy *et al.* (1983, 1989) claim to have demonstrated that scores of adjacent stages of change were more highly correlated than were scores for stages that were non-adjacent. However, this conclusion has been challenged by Sutton (1996) who argued that the correlation between non-adjacent stages was often *nearly* as high as that for adjacent stages. Further evidence inconsistent with the assumption that there is an 'orderly' progression through each of the stages has been reported by Budd and Rollnick (1996). Using a newly constructed 'Readiness to Change Questionnaire' on a sample of men with drinking problems, the authors found that adding a direct path in their structural equation model between precontemplation and action fitted their data better than the structure assumed by the stage model. This finding is inconsistent with the assumption that individuals can only move to action via the contemplation stage.

The second line of argument offered in support of the TTM claims that in different stages individuals employ different processes of change. This assumption was tested in a meta-analysis of 34 studies that reported cross-sectional data on the use of change processes by stage (Rosen 2000). Consistent with predictions, the use of change processes varied substantially across stages. However, no sequence of change processes was common to all health behaviours. For smoking, the sequence was in line with the model, with affective–cognitive processes used most frequently before deciding and behavioural processes used most frequently during abstinence. However, the sequence was inconsistent with the model for diet change and exercise. In diet change, people used affective–cognitive processes as much during action and maintenance as during earlier stages, and in exercise adoption people used cognitive–affective processes most frequently during action and maintenance, when they should have used them least often according to the model.

Whereas Rosen's (2000) meta-analytic findings supported the process of change assumptions of the TTM at least for smoking cessation, a prospective cohort study of approximately 1000 adolescents, who were current or former smokers at baseline, found little support for the predicted associations of specific processes of change with stage transitions (Guo et al. 2009). Processes of change were assessed with a standard questionnaire developed for smoking cessation by members of the Prochaska research team. Stages of change and processes of change were assessed three times in intervals of three months to examine whether higher processes of change scores in stage-appropriate processes were associated with stage progress in the different three-month periods. The theoretically appropriate process of change scores predicted few transitions from each stage and the researchers concluded that use of processes of change 'was not associated generally with stage transitions . . . giving no support to the central tenet of the TTM' (Guo et al. 2009: 828).

Similarly negative findings had been reported earlier by Herzog et al. (1999) in a longitudinal study of smoking cessation. This study used data collected as part of a larger study of worksite cancer prevention from 600 smokers who completed a baseline and two annual follow-up surveys. When strategies of change at baseline were used to predict stage movement prospectively, no support was found for the TTM. None of the strategies of change measured at baseline was significantly related to progressive change out of the precontemplation or contemplation stages at the follow-up measurements, one and two years later.

Decisional balance has also been related to stages of change (Velicer et al. 1985). In a cross-sectional study of the relationship between stages of change and decisional balance across 12 problem behaviours Prochaska et al. (1994) reported clear commonalities. Thus, for all 12 problem behaviours the 'cons' of changing the behaviour were higher than the 'pros' for respondents in the precontemplation stage, whereas the reverse was true for respondents in the action stage. Similarly, in a prospective study of a sample of smokers, decisional balance scores allowed the prediction of movements from contemplation to other stages (Velicer et al. 1985). Contemplators who saw the advantages of stopping smoking outweighing the disadvantages were most likely to move to action and were found to be more likely to have given up smoking six months later, whereas contemplators with the reverse balance were more likely to have moved back to precontemplation status. However, these findings were not replicated by Herzog et al. (1999).

Because the pro and con statements reflect beliefs about the perceived advantages and disadvantages of changing the problem behaviour, the difference between the number of pro and con statements endorsed by individuals forms a crude measure of their attitude. Thus the relationship observed between stages and change and decisional balance may merely indicate a positive relationship between individuals' attitudes towards changing a given problem behaviour and their intention to do so. In line with this assumption, Kraft et al. (1999) reported from a study of a sample of smokers that intention to try to stop smoking increased linearly with an increase in cons and decreased linearly with an increase in pros. Furthermore, although the measure of stages was significantly related to the measure of pros and cons when entered individually, this effect disappeared when intention was entered first into the regression analysis.

The third line of argument concerns the most central prediction of the TTM, namely that persuasive communications aimed at health behaviour change will be most effective if they match the stage of change occupied by an individual at that moment. The model would thus predict that information matched to the individual's present stage location would facilitate change, whereas information that is mismatched would not facilitate (or even inhibit) stage transition (Weinstein et al. 1998).

There is not a great deal of empirical support for these hypotheses. One of the earliest studies was conducted by Dijkstra et al. (1996), who tested some of these predictions in a longitudinal field experiment with a sample of just over 1000 smokers who were given information matched to their stage of change. In a pre-test, these smokers had to assign themselves to one of four stages of change on the basis of descriptions of these stages. The authors added a stage to the original stage model, by dividing precontemplators into 'immotives' who were not considering changing within the next five years, and 'precontemplators' who were considering stopping in less than five years. Smokers in each of the four stages of change were then randomly assigned to one of four information conditions:

- information about the health consequences of smoking;
- self-efficacy enhancing information about how to stop smoking;
- both types of information combined; and
- a control condition with no information.

The post-test questionnaire sent 12 weeks after these communications assessed intentions to stop, changes in stage, attempts to stop for 24 hours, and refraining for more than seven days from smoking. Dijkstra et al. reported the appropriate analysis in which they compared smokers who received communications that matched the stage they had reached with smokers who received a communication that did not match their stage of change only in a later publication (1998b). For immotives and precontemplators the matched communications were no more effective than the mismatched ones. However, for the contemplators and preparers combined, the matched communications proved to be marginally more effective with regard to stage transitions than the messages which were mismatched.

More consistent support for matching was reported by Dijkstra *et al.* (2006), who randomized 481 smokers and ex-smokers to receive an intervention that was either matched or mismatched to their stage. Smokers in the precontemplation stage, the contemplation stage and the preparation stage, and ex-smokers in the action stage, were randomly assigned to conditions in which they received one of three types of information: (1) information that increased the positive outcome expectations of stopping; (2) information that decreased the negative outcome expectations of quitting; or (3) information that increased self-efficacy. The main dependent variable was forward stage transition, assessed two months after receipt of the information. In line with predictions, smokers who were in a precontemplation stage at baseline benefited significantly more from information emphasizing the advantages of stopping (in terms of forward stage movement at follow-up) than did those who received information designed to reduce the disadvantages of stopping or self-efficacy information. By contrast, those who were in the contemplation stage benefited most from information that decreased negative outcome expectations regarding stopping. As Dijkstra *et al.* (2006) argued, it is plausible that for individuals who have no intention of stopping (precontemplation), information about the positive effects of stopping is more effective than information that stopping is not as bad as people think, whereas the latter information should be most useful for people who have made up their mind to stop in the near future (contemplation). The pattern of effects in the preparation and action stages was in the right direction, but did not reach acceptable levels of significance. Although these findings are partially supportive of the assumption that matching information to stages increases the impact of persuasive communication, the conditions of this study mainly manipulated pros and cons rather than the processes of change specified by the TTM.

Three studies that were modelled more closely after the TTM did not find any evidence for the superiority of matched over mismatched communications (Quinlan and McCaul 2000; Blissmer and McAuley 2002; de Vet *et al.* 2008). In a test of the TTM with regard to fruit intake, De Vet *et al.* (2008) randomly assigned precontemplators and contemplators to receive web-based individualized communications that were either appropriate for precontemplation, contemplation or action. The information was tailored to emphasize the processes of change that were appropriate for each of the stages. Post-test measures were obtained one week after receipt of the communication. Although fruit intake increased significantly between pre- and post-test in contemplators, but not in precontemplators, there were no differences between conditions in fruit intake or stage progression.

Quinlan and McCaul (2000) compared stage-matched and stage-mismatched communications to an assessment-only condition in 92 smokers who were in the precontemplation stage. The stage-matched interventions consisted of six activities deemed theoretically appropriate for smokers thinking about stopping (e.g. 'why I smoke', 'how much it costs to smoke', 'effects of smoking', 'reasons to quit smoking'). The stage mismatched information consisted of action-oriented information (e.g. plan of actions; setting a quit date, identifying triggers). There were no differences in the impact of stage-matched and stage-mismatched communications on attempts to decrease smoking at follow-up one month later, but both communications were more effective than no communication. Significantly more individuals tried to stop in the mismatched than the matched condition.

Finally, Blissmer and McAuley (2002) conducted a study that was similar to that of Quinlan and McCaul, comparing the impact of a stage-matched to a stage-mismatched communication. Although 40.4 per cent of participants in the stage-matched communication had progressed one or more stages as compared to 31.8 per cent in the mismatched group, this difference was not significant (according to a test conducted by Sutton 2005).

In conclusion, the TTM of behaviour change focuses on a number of interesting variables. However, with the exception of processes of change, these variables have also been included in other approaches to health behaviour. The weakness of the model is that it does not allow the derivation of theoretically based predictions about the relationship between the different variables. Furthermore, research guided *by* this model has not yet resulted in a great deal of support *for* the model. This leaves one wondering how the model has managed to remain so popular over the years. One reason is probably that scientific process in psychology does not always follow the Popperian principles of falsified theories being supplanted by better ones. Some theories are so inherently plausible that they can survive in spite of contradicting evidence. However, a second reason is that many of the assumptions included in the TTM are also part of other models that are empirically better supported.

Implications of stage models for interventions

The major implication for interventions derived from stage models of change is that the nature of the interventions has to be matched to the stage of change of the target individuals. And it makes a great deal of sense that a smoker, who is unconcerned about the dangers of smoking, needs different information than somebody who wants to quit but does not know how. But as Heckhausen (1980) suggested three decades ago, it is probably sufficient to distinguish a volitional phase of intention formation from an action stage of behaving according to that intention.

Conclusions

Stage models describe the different tasks assumed to confront individuals at different stages of behaviour change and the types of intervention which would induce these individuals to move to the next stage. They thus could offer a heuristic framework for the design of interventions and for the tailoring of interventions to particular target populations. However, at present there is so little empirical support, particularly for the wildly popular TTM, that one might be ill-advised using the model for matching communications to stages of change.

Our discussion in the remainder of this chapter will therefore be structured in terms of two stages of change, namely the formation of intentions and their realization. This distinction is not being proposed here as a stage theory, but is used as a heuristic device to structure the discussion of change. Whereas the processes that motivate change and aim at the formation of an intention to change a given health behaviour can be subsumed under the public health model which relies on strategies of health promotion, clinical interventions may be needed to help individuals to change health-impairing behaviours such as excessive eating, smoking or alcohol abuse. Thus, sometimes it may be necessary to employ therapy to teach individuals the skills they need to act on their intentions.

The public health model

The term 'public health model' is used here to refer to interventions that rely on health promotion and are designed to change the behaviour of large groups, such as the members of an industrial organization, or the citizens of a state or country (Leventhal and Cleary 1980). The objective of this type of health promotion is primary prevention, that is, to induce people to adopt good health habits and to change bad ones. There are basically two ways to effect this change, namely through *persuasion* and through *modification of relevant incentives*.

Persuasion is used in health promotion to influence individual health beliefs and behaviour. People are exposed to more or less complex messages that reflect a position advocated by a source and arguments designed to support that position. The source may be a medical expert or a public health institute and the message may point out that a specific unhealthy practice such as overeating or leading a sedentary life is likely to result in a number of very unpleasant health consequences.

Modification of relevant incentives is often employed as a health promotion strategy to increase the effort or costs of engaging in certain unhealthy practices or to decrease the costs of healthful practices. Thus governments may use fiscal and legal measures to alter the contingencies affecting individuals as they drink, smoke or engage in other health-damaging behaviour. Often persuasion and incentive modification strategies are combined. Thus a health promotion campaign aimed at preventing alcoholism might involve mass media messages pointing out the dangers of alcoholism, worksite health promotion programmes, and changes in incentives such as an increase in the tax on alcohol or a legal restriction on the sale of alcoholic beverages.

A third health promotion strategy relies on passive protection through the regulation of product designs or the engineering of the physical environment to make it safer. However, this strategy is of less interest in the context of a book on social psychology and health and will therefore only be mentioned briefly. The main focus of our discussion in this section on the public health model will be on persuasion and modification of incentives.

Persuasion

Persuasion can be defined as the effects of exposure to relatively complex messages from other persons on the attitudes and beliefs of the recipients. Research has studied the impact of characteristics of the communicator, the message or the recipient on influencing attitude change. Before highlighting empirical research on persuasion in laboratory and field settings, a brief theoretical analysis of persuasion will be presented. This should improve understanding of the processes or variables which mediate the impact of communications on beliefs and attitudes.

Theories of persuasion

Although theories of persuasion typically incorporate motivational and affective principles, most of the more recent theories have been based on a cognitive analysis of persuasion processes. In the decades following World War II persuasion research was dominated by an information-processing paradigm that emphasized reception and learning of the arguments contained in persuasive messages (e.g. Hovland *et al.* 1959; McGuire 1985). This perspective stimulated a great deal of interest in the relationship between recipients' retention of the message content and the extent to which they were influenced by a message (see Eagly and Chaiken 1993). However, the findings that emerged from this type of research seemed to be inconsistent with the notion that attitude change was a function of the reception and learning of the arguments contained in the persuasive message (although see Eagly and Chaiken 1993: 264).

This confronted researchers with a puzzling problem. If it was not the actual content of the arguments which resulted in persuasion, how then do persuasive communications influence beliefs and change attitudes? One answer to this question was provided by the *cognitive response theory* developed by Greenwald (1968) and refined by Petty, Cacioppo and others (see Petty *et al.* 1981b; Petty and Wegener 1999). The cognitive response approach stresses the mediating role of the thoughts or 'cognitive responses' which recipients generate as they reflect upon persuasive communications. According to this model, listening to a communication is like a mental discussion in which the listener responds to the arguments presented in the communication. Cognitive responses reflect the content of this internal communication. The model assumes that these cognitive responses mediate the effect of persuasive messages on attitude change. Since cognitive responding is assumed to vary both in magnitude and favourableness, persuasion should be a function of the *extent* of cognitive responding that occurs as well as its *favourableness*.

The extent to which individuals engage in argument-relevant thinking is determined by their processing motivation and ability. The more motivated and able individuals are to think about the arguments contained in a communication, the more they will engage in argument-relevant thinking. Whether increases in processing ability or motivation increase or decrease the persuasive impact of a communication will depend on the favourableness of individual responses to that communication. The favourableness of cognitive responses depends mainly on the quality of the arguments contained in a communication. A persuasive communication which contains many strong arguments will stimulate predominantly positive thoughts whereas a communication containing weak arguments will elicit unfavourable cognitive responses. With strong arguments stimulating favourable thoughts, increases in processing motivation and/or ability should result in an increased persuasion. With weak arguments eliciting unfavourable thoughts, increased motivation or ability to engage in argument-relevant thinking will decrease the persuasive impact of the communication.

These predictions have been tested in numerous experiments (see Petty and Wegener 1999). The impact of processing motivation on persuasion has typically been studied by manipulating the personal relevance of the topic of the communication. Consistent with prediction, increasing the personal relevance of a communication resulted in decreased persuasion for communications containing mainly weak arguments, but increased persuasion for messages which consisted of strong arguments (Chaiken 1980; Petty *et al.* 1981a).

The impact of processing ability or capacity has often been studied through the use of distraction. Distracting individuals while they are listening to a message should decrease their ability to process the message. Petty *et al.* (1976) manipulated distraction by having respondents record visual stimuli while listening to a message. The degree of distraction was varied by the frequency with which the stimuli flashed on a screen. The favourableness of respondents' cognitive responses was manipulated by using either very strong or very weak arguments. In line with expectations from cognitive response theory, distraction increased persuasion for weak messages and decreased persuasion for strong messages. Furthermore, an analysis of the thoughts which respondents reported having had during the communication indicated that distraction inhibited the number of counter-arguments to the message which contained weak arguments and reduced the number of favourable thoughts for the version consisting of strong arguments. Capacity may also be low because the individual possesses little knowledge about the topic in question (Wood *et al.* 1985) or is under time pressure (Ratneshwar and Chaiken 1991).

The cognitive response model shares with the earlier information processing theories the assumption that individuals who listen to a communication systematically evaluate the arguments contained in the communication to arrive at a decision about the validity of any conclusions or recommendations given. However, individuals sometimes may not be motivated or able to evaluate an argument and still want to form an opinion on the validity of a recommended action.

The *dual-process models* of persuasion which have more recently dominated persuasion research, namely the *elaboration likelihood model* (e.g. Petty and Cacioppo 1986; Petty and Wegener 1999) and the *heuristic-systematic model* (Chaiken *et al.* 1996b; Chen and Chaiken 1999), suggest that the kind of systematic processing implied by the cognitive response model is only one of two different modes of information processing that mediate persuasion. If individuals are either unwilling or unable to engage in this extensive and effortful process of assessing arguments, they might base their decision to accept or reject the message on some peripheral aspect such as the credibility of the source, the length of the message or other non-content cues. This has been called *heuristic processing* (Chaiken 1980; Eagly and Chaiken 1993).

In heuristic processing people often use simple schemas or decision rules to assess the validity of an argument. For example, people may have learned from previous experience that health recommendations from physicians tend to be more valid than those from lay persons. They may therefore apply the rule that 'doctors can be trusted with regard to health issues' in response to indications that the communicator is a medical doctor, and agree with the health message. Because the individual agrees with the message without extensive thinking about the content of the arguments, dual-process theories assume that attitudes formed or changed on the basis of heuristic processing will be less stable, less resistant to counter-arguments and less predictive of subsequent behaviour than those based on systematic processing. In support of these assumptions a number of studies show that attitude changes accompanied by high levels of issue-relevant cognitive activity are more persistent than changes that are accompanied by little issue-relevant thought (e.g. Haugvedt and Petty 1992).

A central prediction of dual-process models is that heuristic cues have a greater impact on attitudes than argument quality when motivation or ability to engage in issue-relevant thinking is low, whereas argument quality has a greater impact when motivation or ability to process is high. Experiments manipulating variables which were assumed to affect processing motivation or ability, such as personal relevance, time pressure, message comprehensibility or prior knowledge, have also yielded results supportive of the theory. As one would expect, the influence of peripheral cues on attitudes is low when processing ability and motivation is high, but increases substantially when recipients lack the motivation or ability to process the message extensively (e.g. Petty *et al.* 1981a; Wood and Kallgren 1988).

This pattern of finding has typically been explained by assuming that systematic and heuristic processing are mutually exclusive processing modes, with systematic processing being employed when processing motivation and ability are high, and heuristic processing being used when motivation and ability are low (Chaiken 1980; Petty and Cacioppo 1986). However, disregarding peripheral cues because processing motivation is high seems wasteful, given that these cues may contain valid and easily accessible information. Chaiken *et al.* (e.g. 1996a) developed an alternative conception which implies that heuristic processing is the default option which is always employed in assessing the validity of a persuasive argumentation. Like earlier theoreticians, they argued that individuals need to be economical with their limited processing capacity. Individuals will therefore invest only as much effort into processing a given set of arguments as is warranted by the importance of the issue at hand. Chaiken *et al.* introduced the notion of a 'sufficiency principle' which reflects a trade-off between minimizing effort and reaching an adequate level of confidence in one's judgement. If an issue is of no great importance (e.g. low personal relevance), individuals will require much less confidence. They will invest little effort and rely solely on heuristic processing, even though heuristic processing is not very effective in creating subjective confidence in the validity of an attitude. With increasing importance of a particular issue the level of subjective confidence desired by the individual will also increase. Therefore individuals will increasingly rely on systematic processing. Even though systematic processing requires greater processing capacity, it is generally more effective in increasing subjective confidence because it provides the individual with more judgement-relevant information than does heuristic processing. Conclusions based on systematic processing typically override the judgemental impact of heuristic processing and, as a result, the impact of heuristic cues is attenuated.

There are two conditions, however, under which individuals will rely on heuristic processing even when highly motivated to process a persuasive message systematically – namely, if their processing capacity is limited or if the information is ambiguous. The impact of processing motivation on systematic processing is limited by processing capacity. Even if individuals are highly motivated to engage in systematic processing of persuasive arguments, they may have to rely on heuristic processing due to low processing capacity. Second, individuals may rely on heuristic cues in their assessment of the validity of a position, even after extensive systematic processing, if the persuasive arguments are so ambiguous that systematic processing does not result in clear-cut conclusions (Chaiken and Maheswaran 1994).

Implicit in our discussion so far has been the assumption that individual information processing is motivated by the desire to hold attitudes and beliefs that are objectively valid. Chaiken *et al.* (e.g. 1996a) have modified the heuristic-systematic model and added motives other than the need to be accurate. Of particular interest for health psychology is *defence motivation*, which reflects the desire to hold attitudes and beliefs that are consistent with existing central attitudes and values – for example, the belief that one is healthy and safe. Defence motivation leads to a directional bias in accepting a given attitudinal position. For example, heavy drinkers, who have been told that alcohol will damage their health and that they should cut down, might look for information on the positive effects of alcohol. Both systematic and heuristic processing might be employed in a biased way. Within the systematic mode, selective processing involves the biased evaluation of evidence and arguments. Material that is congruent with existing self-relevant beliefs – for example, that moderate alcohol consumption can be good for coronary heart disease (CHD) – will be more easily accepted than incongruent material. Individuals are likely to read incongruent evidence more carefully and spend more time disproving it than they will with arguments that are congruent with the position they wish to defend. Within the heuristic mode, biased processing might be achieved by questioning the reliability or validity of an heuristic if it leads to conclusions that challenge the validity of a preferred position. For example, even if a patient usually follows the heuristic that 'doctors can be trusted with regard to health issues', when receiving a particular threatening diagnosis the patient may introduce an additional heuristic, namely that one should always consult several experts before making important decisions.

To summarize, over the years dual-process models have undergone a theoretical evolution which has dramatically changed the assumptions underlying these models. Thus, the assumption that the two modes of information processing are alternatives, with one (heuristic processing) being employed when individuals are unmotivated or unable to engage in issue-relevant thinking and the other (systematic processing) being employed when motivation and ability are high, has been replaced by the assumption that the two modes co-occur. Heuristic processing is assumed to serve as a default option. When individuals are motivated to use systematic processing because an issue is important, systematic processing typically overrides the impact of heuristic processing, unless individuals are unable to process systematically (due to capacity limitations or lack of knowledge) or the evidence is so ambiguous that they have to base their conclusions on heuristic cues. Second, the assumption that individuals always strive for accurate judgements has been replaced by the assumption that communications can arouse different processing motives (e.g. defence motivation rather than accuracy motivation).

The impact of persuasion

The major difficulty in persuading people to engage in healthful behaviour patterns is that they involve immediate effort or renunciation of gratification in the here and now in order to achieve greater rewards or to avoid worse punishment in the remote future. As religious leaders discovered centuries ago, when facing similar (or even worse) problems, fear appeals can be an effective way of achieving compliance. Today, fear or threat appeals are the mainstay of most mass media health promotion campaigns. These appeals frequently combine information that is fear-arousing with information that provokes a sense of personal vulnerability to the illness threat, because in order to arouse fear a health risk must not only have serious consequences but the individual must also feel personally at risk. For example, even though HIV infection has very serious consequences, these consequences will not be fear-arousing to those heterosexuals who consider AIDS to be a disease which only affects homosexuals and drug users. Fear appeals are usually followed by some recommendation that, if accepted, would reduce or avoid the danger. The effectiveness of fear appeals has been studied extensively (for a review, see de Hoog *et al.* 2007). Because much of persuasion-based health promotion employs fear appeals, the following section about laboratory research on persuasion will discuss the effectiveness of this kind of persuasive appeal.

Persuasion in the laboratory: the case of fear appeals

In a typical early study of the impact of fear appeals smokers would be exposed to factual information about the danger of smoking in a low-threat condition. In a high-threat condition, they would in addition be exposed to a film which would make the nature of lung cancer more vivid by including a section on a lung cancer operation, showing the initial incision, the forcing apart of the ribs, and the removal of the black and diseased lung. Under both conditions, a recommendation would be given that these consequences could be avoided if respondents gave up smoking.

Early research on fear arousal has been guided theoretically by the assumption that fear is a drive or motivator of attitude change (for a review of early studies, see Leventhal 1970). The risk information arouses fear which is reduced by the rehearsal of the communicator's recommendations. When a response reduces fear, it is reinforced and becomes part of one's permanent response repertory. The drive model therefore suggests that greater fear should result in greater persuasion, but only if the recommended action appears effective in avoiding the danger. If this is not the case, fear may be reduced by other means such as denying or ignoring the danger or derogating the communicator.

Because part of the empirical evidence was inconsistent with the drive model, Leventhal (1970) introduced a more cognitive theory, the 'parallel response model', which no longer assumed that emotional arousal was a necessary antecedent of the adaptation to danger. According to this model, a threat is cognitively evaluated and this appraisal can give rise to two parallel or independent responses, namely danger control and fear control. Danger control involves the decision to act as well as actions taken to reduce the danger. Fear control involves actions taken to control emotional responses (e.g. use of tranquillizers or alcohol) as well as strategies to reduce fear (e.g. defensive avoidance). These responses typically have no effect on the actual danger. Witte (1992) later extended the parallel response model by adding the plausible assumption that the perceived efficacy of the recommended response determines whether individuals engage mainly in danger or in fear control. If a recommendation seems effective in averting a threat, individuals will engage in danger control; if it appears ineffective, they will mainly focus on fear control.

The important contribution of the parallel response model, which, as we shall see later, is structurally similar to stress-coping theory (Chapter 6), is the central role given to cognitive appraisal processes and the differentiation of emotional from cognitive responses to fear-arousing communications. Its weakness is that it does not specify the processes of cognitive evaluation which precede the action tendencies. This task was completed by later models which focused exclusively on cognitive processes. According to the health belief model (e.g. Rosenstock 1974) and to protection motivation theory (e.g. Rogers and Mewborn 1976; Rogers 1983), individuals accept a recommendation if they perceive it as *effective* (effectiveness) in averting *negative* consequences (severity) which would otherwise be *likely to happen to them* (vulnerability). In terms of these models, fear influences attitudes and behaviour not directly, but only indirectly through the appraisal of the severity of the threat. These models suggest that even the most vulnerable individuals would not adopt protective actions which they perceive as ineffective in averting the negative consequences. In addition to response efficacy, the revised version of protection motivation theory also emphasized self-efficacy, that is the person's confidence in his or her ability to enact the protective response. The effect of low self-efficacy should be similar to that of low response efficacy.

There are two problems with all of these models: first, there is no empirical evidence for the predicted interaction between threat and response efficacy (Witte and Allen 2000; de Hoog *et al.* 2007). Second, even though the two parallel response models assume that cognitive appraisal mediates the impact of persuasion on attitude and behaviour change, they make no predictions about these processes of information processing. The stage model of processing of fear-arousing communications was developed to address these deficiencies (Stroebe 2000; Das *et al.* 2003; de Hoog *et al.* 2005, 2007). According to this model, the important determinants of the intensity of processing are the perceived severity of a health threat and personal vulnerability (i.e. personal relevance of the threat). If both severity and vulnerability are low, individuals are unlikely to invest much effort into processing information about this threat and will rely on heuristic processing. But even at low severity, individuals who feel vulnerable will begin to pay some attention and process information about the risk systematically, though at low intensity. If a health threat is severe, individuals are likely to systematically process information about this threat, even if they do not feel vulnerable. The reason for this deviation from dual process predictions is that severe health threats can always become personally relevant, even if one does not feel vulnerable at the moment. Thus, an epidemic that is only prevalent in some distant continent might suddenly spread to Europe and a virus, which mainly endangers gay men, might suddenly enter the heterosexual population.

Most interesting, according to the stage model, is the situation where individuals feel vulnerable to a health threat that is also severe. Since the threat is severe, individuals will be motivated to engage in systematic processing. However, since feeling at grave risk is also very unpleasant, individuals will be motivated to engage in systematic processing that is defensive (i.e. biased systematic processing). In appraising the fear appeals, they will be highly motivated to minimize the risk. They will engage in a biased search for inconsistencies and assess the evidence with a bias in the direction of their preferred conclusion (e.g. Sherman *et al.* 2000). However, if the arguments in the appeal are strong and persuasive, individuals may not succeed in minimizing the threat. Their main hope now is that the recommended action will really protect them against the impending risk to their health. They will engage in biased processing of the recommended action which will involve attempts to make the recommendation appear highly effective, because only then will individuals feel safe. Thus, defence motivation will lead to a *positive* bias in the processing of the action recommendation and will heighten the motivation to engage in the protective action regardless of the quality of the arguments supporting this action.

A meta-analysis based on 95 published studies of the efficacy of fear appeals supported most of the predictions of the stage model (de Hoog *et al.* 2007). As predicted, the attitudes towards the health recommendation were only affected by severity of the health threat and argument quality, but not by personal vulnerability. A person's attitude towards an action recommended as protection against a serious health threat should depend only on the strength of the arguments in favour of that action and not on whether the individual himself or herself is at risk. In contrast, both vulnerability and severity influenced intention to perform a protective action and even actual behaviour and these effects were not moderated by the efficacy of the recommended protective action. Finally, it made no difference whether the health risk information was accompanied by pictorial material. Thus, adding pictures of diseased lungs to the health warning on cigarette packs is unlikely to increase the efficacy of these messages.

An analysis of the cognitive and affective responses triggered by these communications was also consistent with predictions of the stage model. Both vulnerability and severity induced fear and negative affect in respondents. More importantly, however, analyses of cognitive responses supported the hypotheses of the model about differences in biased processing of fear appeals as compared to action recommendations. Feeling vulnerable to a severe health threat triggered thoughts attempting to minimize the threat (i.e. denying, downgrading or criticizing the fear appeal) and at the same time stimulating positive thoughts about the value of the action recommendation. This last finding does not only explain the consistent failure to find an interaction between the efficacy of the recommended action and the seriousness and personal relevance of the health threat, it also explains why anxious or desperate individuals often take recourse to all kinds of treatments of totally unproven efficacy.

It is important to note that fear appeals are unlikely to be effective when they warn of risks that are well known to the individuals engaging in risky behaviour. For this reason, most of the studies of the efficacy of fear appeals described earlier have used relatively novel health threats with which the participants in these studies were relatively unfamiliar. For example, de Hoog et al. (2005) used the threat of repetitive strain injury (RSI) (e.g. 'mouse arm'). Since some individuals have problems with RSI, which can be severe enough to prevent them using their computer for example, the threat is plausible, and yet student respondents are not very familiar with the risk behaviour. People who still smoke or homosexual men who still engage in unprotected anal intercourse know about the risk they are taking and pointing it out to them is unlikely to be effective. It is therefore not surprising that fear appeals have typically been found to be ineffective or even counterproductive in HIV-prevention interventions (Albarracin et al. 2006; Earl and Albarracin 2007).

Conclusions and implications from these studies

It is difficult to draw conclusions from these studies with regard to designing health promotion interventions. Even though there was evidence of defensive processing, the overwhelming majority of studies on fear appeals has found that higher levels of threat resulted in greater persuasion than did lower levels. However, the effectiveness of high-fear messages appeared to be somewhat reduced for respondents who feel highly vulnerable to the threat. There is some evidence, however, that unless individuals feel vulnerable to a threat, they are unlikely to form the intention to act on the recommendation given. Thus, if a man believes that only homosexual men run the risk of HIV infection during intercourse but he is himself heterosexual, then he might readily accept the recommendation that homosexual men should always use condoms during intercourse and his readiness to accept this recommendation should be the greater, the greater the risk that is described. However, these beliefs will have no impact on his own sexual risk behaviour. Thus, unless the communication also stresses the risk to heterosexual men and thus makes him feel vulnerable, it will affect his attitudes but have no impact on his intentions.

There may also be limitations to the effectiveness of fear appeals which are not revealed by experimental studies that often use *novel* threats to influence behaviour which is completely under the *voluntary control* of the research participants. Fear appeals are most likely to be effective for individuals who are in a precontemplation stage because they are unfamiliar with a given health risk. For example, when the dangers involved in unprotected anal intercourse among men became known in the early 1980s, this information appeared to result in a tremendous reduction of individuals engaging in this activity. However, there was a hard core of men who continued to engage in this high-risk activity and, as the intervention studies to be reviewed later illustrate, simply reiterating the dangers of HIV infection did not achieve risk reduction with these individuals. The extent to which they engaged in risk behaviour was also unrelated to self-perceived vulnerability (Gerrard *et al.* 1996). They knew the risk but continued because they were unable or unwilling to use condoms. To induce behaviour change in these individuals, one would have to persuade them that condoms do not necessarily reduce sexual pleasure and/or one would have to teach them the technical and social skills involved in condom use.

Persuasion in the field
Although laboratory studies can tell us a great deal about how to develop persuasive appeals that have maximum impact on individuals who are exposed to them, they provide only limited information about the effectiveness of persuasion in a mass media context. In real life, audiences can actively or passively avoid exposure to health messages. There can be little doubt, however, that an extensive national campaign can produce meaningful behavioural changes in attitudes and behaviour. The data on changes in per capita cigarette consumption in the USA during the latter half of the twentieth century certainly suggest that the anti-smoking campaign, which began with *Smoking and Health: A Report of the Surgeon General* (USDHEW 1964), had great impact (see Figure 3.3). Yet, even with such apparently clear-cut data, it is difficult to decide how much of the decline in smoking behaviour should be attributed to the media campaign, and how much to other causes. For example, as a result of the changing attitude towards smoking, there were large increases in local excise taxes on cigarettes between 1964 and 1978. Between 1965 and 1994 the average price of a pack of cigarettes increased from 27.9 cents to 169.3 cents (Sorensen *et al.* 1998). The increased cost of cigarettes is likely to have contributed to the decrease in cigarette consumption. Therefore, to assess the impact of the media campaign on smoking behaviour, one would need a control group which is comparable in every respect to the US population but which was not exposed to the campaign. Without such a comparison, we will never be certain whether smoking behaviour would have changed even without the anti-smoking campaign.

The evidence from controlled studies suggests that mass media communications often result only in modest attitude change and even more modest behaviour change (for reviews, see McGuire 1985; Sorensen *et al.* 1998). For example, mass

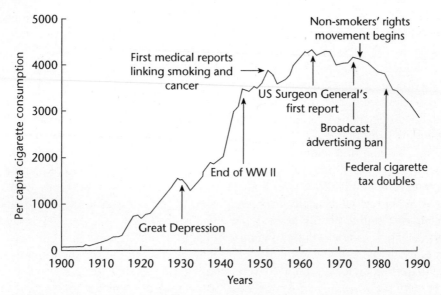

FIGURE 3.3 Per capita cigarette consumption among adults and major smoking and health events in the USA, 1900
Source: Novotny *et al.* (1992)

media campaigns persuading individuals to wear seat belts have not been terribly effective, resulting in a mere 4.4 per cent increase in seat belt use according to one meta-analysis (Johnston *et al.* 1994). Similarly, a mass media campaign to encourage family planning had no detectable effect on relevant indicators such as the sale of contraceptives, the number of unwanted pregnancies and the birth rate (Udry *et al.* 1972). Finally, the impact of the large community-based intervention trials conducted during the 1980s was rather disappointing (for a review, see Sorensen *et al.* 1998).

Limits to persuasion

Why is it so difficult to motivate people at least to *try* changing their poor health habits? The present discussion of the reasons why persuasive appeals used in health promotion campaigns often have rather modest effects on attitudes or intentions will focus on two issues:

1 The choice of the domains of health behaviour targeted by public health interventions.
2 The content of the persuasive communications used in those interventions.

Jeffery (1989) has attributed the failure of many public health campaigns to persuade people to adopt healthful lifestyles to a discrepancy between individual and population perspectives of health risk. He argued that people are not persuaded to change because engaging in the kind of health-impairing behaviour patterns targeted by health promotion campaigns may not be all that risky. There is a discrepancy between individual and population perspectives of health risks. Public health policies are guided by the *population attributable risk*, that is, the number of excess cases of disease in a population that can be attributed to a given risk factor. Individual decision-making, on the other hand, is determined by individual rather than population gain. Highest personal gain, however, is achieved when absolute risk to the individual and relative risk are both high. The problem with many health-impairing behaviour patterns is that the *relative risk*, that is the ratio of chance of the disease for individuals who engage in a risky behaviour and those who do not, is rather low (statistically expressed as *odds ratio*). For example, a sedentary lifestyle is related to heart disease, but the relative risk is modest. And yet, because heart disease is the most common cause of death in most countries and because a sedentary lifestyle is very common, the excess burden in the population attributable to this risk factor is high. But even if the relative risk for a behavioural risk factor is high, the *absolute risk*, that is the probability of becoming ill or dying within a given period of time, may still be so low as to make it not seem worthwhile for the individual to change. For example, even though a smoker runs a much higher risk of developing lung cancer than a non-smoker, the 10-year absolute risk of lung cancer for a 35-year-old man who is a heavy smoker is only about 0.3 per cent, and the risk of heart disease is only 0.9 per cent (Jeffery 1989). And yet, these small numbers have a tremendous significance from a population perspective. In a group of 1 million heavy smokers aged 35, nearly 10,000 will die (prematurely) before age 45 because of the smoking habit. From the perspective of the individual, however, the odds are heavily in favour of survival with or without behaviour change.

But do people really know this? The few studies which have assessed individuals' perceptions of behavioural risks suggest that people vastly overestimate these risks. For example, when a national sample of Americans was asked to estimate how many of 100 smokers 'would die of lung cancer because they smoke', the average response was 42.6 (Viscusi 1990) which is far above the actual risk. It is doubtful, however, whether individuals would apply these risk estimates also to themselves. There is considerable evidence that individuals are much more optimistic about their own chances than they are about those of others, and this tendency has become known as the false optimism bias (Weinstein 1987). Thus, van der Velde *et al.* (1994), who asked a small random sample of citizens of Amsterdam to estimate both 'their chances of becoming infected with the AIDS virus within the next two years because of their sexual behaviour' and that of 'a man/woman of your age', reported that own risk was given at 5 per cent, other risk at 19 per cent. It is worth noting that, although these citizens estimated their own risk as much lower than that of their fellow men and women, their estimate was still above the (likely) 'true risk'.

A second question is whether individuals really use information about prevalence or base rates in making decisions about changes in their lifestyle. Information campaigns typically emphasize relative risks (i.e. the increase in risk due to a given health-impairing behaviour) and rarely mention base rates (i.e. absolute risk). They may be justified in doing this. There is ample evidence from other areas of judgement (e.g. attribution theory; Borgida and Brekke 1981) that people under-use prior probabilities derived from base rates. It would actually seem reasonable for people to take precautionary measures against risk factors which double or triple the risk of some terrible consequence occurring to them, even if the absolute risk of such an incidence is rather low. Thus, even though the evidence is not yet conclusive, we would expect that as long as the relative risk due to some behavioural risk factor was high, people may be persuaded to adopt precautionary measures even if the absolute health risk was rather modest.

Another reason for the modest impact of many public health interventions is that they use communications which have been developed on the basis of common sense and without the benefit of social psychological theorizing. More specifically, many of the community interventions use a 'one-size-fits-all' intervention (Sorensen et al. 1998), even though attitude theories suggest that the most important determinants of attitude change vary across different segments of the population. Because we discussed the implications of these theories for interventions earlier, we will focus here on a few examples to illustrate this point.

The most specific guidelines for the design of a successful intervention can be derived from the models of reasoned action and planned behaviour (Fishbein et al. 1994). According to these theories, persuasive arguments will only be effective if they influence the attitudes, norms and control perceptions which are relevant for the behaviour in question. Thus, to design an intervention, one will have to establish empirically the relative importance of attitudes, subjective norms and perceived behavioural control as determinants of the intention to engage in the targeted health behaviour. It makes little sense to try to change individuals' attitude towards a given health-impairing behaviour, when the reason they engage in this behaviour is that they feel unable to stop (i.e. perceived behavioural control) or that they think that their partner expects them to engage in this behaviour (subjective norms). Once one has determined which of the components of the model of planned behaviour exerts influence on the behaviour to be influenced, one has to conduct empirical studies to 'elicit' from members of the target population the salient beliefs which underlie these determinants. Because most of these factors vary across different sub-groups of the population, one will have to design different communications for these different groups.

For example, not everybody is interested in health issues and thus motivated to change as a result of health information. Adolescents are often not very concerned about their health. They are likely to feel that health warnings are not (yet) relevant to them and will therefore not be motivated to attend to health communications (Thompson 1978). Rather than trying to convince them of the importance of health issues, their lack of interest in health should be taken into account in the design of communications. Arguments should focus on those beliefs which are related to the targeted health behaviour in that particular age group. For example, Abraham *et al.* (1992) concluded from a study of young Scottish teenagers that, since young people's intentions to use condoms were mainly affected by perceived barriers to condom use, educational programmes should focus on acceptability barriers rather than emphasizing young people's vulnerability to infection, the severity of infections and condom effectiveness.

Health communications are also less effective for individuals of lower socio-economic status. An analysis of 20 years of Belgian studies of the impact of health communications suggested that these programmes were most effective for individuals of high socio-economic status (Kittel *et al.* 1993). Similarly, in a study of the association of sexual risk behaviour and exposure to HIV health promotion folders, Janssen *et al.* (1998a) found that risk perception with regard to unprotected sex increased with exposure to health promotion materials only for gay men who were well educated. Among the uneducated there was even a negative relationship: higher exposure rates were related to lower perceived risk of unprotected intercourse.

One potential explanation for such differences is that many of these health communications have been designed by the well educated for the well educated. Thus, the less educated audiences might have been less able to understand the arguments or, even if they understood them, might have found them less convincing. There is a great deal of evidence which is consistent with these assumptions:

1 There is a strong relationship between socio-economic status (SES) and ill health. High SES individuals are also healthier and this gap has been widening over the years (for reviews, see Kenkel 1991; Adler *et al.* 1994; Williams and Collins 1995).
2 Socio-economic status is negatively related to knowledge about health risks (e.g. Kenkel 1991; Janssen *et al.* 1998b).
3 The lower individuals' socio-economic status, the more they are likely to live unhealthily by smoking, eating a poor diet, drinking too much alcohol and being physically inactive (e.g. Kenkel 1991; Adler *et al.* 1994; Williams and Collins 1995).
4 The more people know about adverse health consequences, the less they are likely to engage in health-impairing behaviour patterns (e.g. Kenkel 1991).
5 Finally, for smoking there is even evidence that the relationship with level of education only emerged after the health consequences of smoking became widely established (Farrell and Fuchs 1982).

However, there is evidence to suggest that the differential impact of health education and promotion on individuals of different socio-economic levels is not exclusively mediated by health knowledge. Thus, the impact of level of education on health behaviour is only partially reduced when health knowledge is controlled for (Kenkel 1991). Similarly, the impact of educational level on health is also only partly reduced if health behaviour is controlled for. This is consistent with earlier findings that health knowledge is neither the only, nor even the most important, factor mediating the relationship between socio-economic status and health outcome.

Beyond persuasion: changing the incentive structure

In view of the uncertain effects of health promotion via mass media persuasion, it is hardly surprising that governments often decide to influence behaviour by changing the rewards and costs associated with alternative courses of action rather than relying on persuasion. Thus, government policies can be introduced that alter the set of contingencies affecting individuals as they engage in health-damaging behaviour (Moore and Gerstein 1981). For example, governments can increase the costs of smoking or drinking by increasing the tax on tobacco and alcohol products, they can institute stricter age limits, or they can reduce availability by limiting sales.

Legal age restrictions

In most countries a large segment of the population (as defined by a minimum drinking or driving age) is not permitted to buy alcohol or drive a car. Although the value of such age limitations in reducing drinking problems or accident rates among the young has been doubted, the evidence from studies of changes in age limitations suggests that age limits do exercise a restraining effect. For example, evaluations of the impact of changes in minimum drinking age on alcohol problems and alcohol-related problems in the relevant age groups have indicated that raising the drinking age reduces both alcohol consumption and motor vehicle accidents (e.g. Ashley and Rankin 1988).

Price and taxation

One of the basic assumptions of economic theory states that, everything else being equal, the demand for a good should decrease if the price of that good is increased. The relation between changing prices and changing consumption can be expressed by price elasticities. Price elasticity reflects the way in which consumption responds to changes in price. It is defined as the percentage change in the quantity of a good demanded divided by the percentage change in the price associated with the change in demand. Thus, an elasticity of -0.7 means that a 10 per cent increase (decrease) in price would reduce (increase) the quantity of the good demanded by 7 per cent. A commodity is said to have high price elasticity if the demand reacts to changes in price, that is, if demand goes up when prices go down, or goes down when prices go up. Similarly, income elasticity reflects the way the demand for a commodity reacts to changes in income.

There is ample evidence to demonstrate that the demand for alcoholic beverages, like the demand for most other commodities, responds to changes in price and income. In a review of econometric studies that estimated the values of price and income elasticities of alcoholic beverages for Australia, Canada, Finland, Ireland, Sweden, Great Britain and the USA, Bruun and colleagues (1975) concluded that, with everything else remaining equal, a rise in alcohol prices generally led to a drop in the consumption of alcohol, whereas an increase in the income of consumers generally led to a rise in alcohol consumption. A recent meta-analysis confirmed these conclusions (Wagenaar et al. 2009). There is similar evidence for smoking, although less research seems to have been conducted on this issue (for reviews, see Warner 1981, 1986; Walsh and Gordon 1986).

Conclusions

If one compares the effectiveness of public health strategies that use persuasion with those that change the contingencies associated with a given behaviour (e.g. price), the latter strategy often seems more effective. However, there are limitations to the use of monetary incentives or legal sanctions to influence health behaviour which do not apply to persuasion. First, these strategies cannot be applied to all health behaviours. Whereas it is widely accepted that governments should control the price of tobacco products and alcohol, a law forcing people to jog daily would be unacceptable and difficult to enforce. Second, the use of monetary incentives or legal sanctions to control behaviour might weaken internal control mechanisms that may have existed beforehand. Research on the effects of extrinsic incentives on intrinsic motivation and performance has demonstrated that performance of an intrinsically enjoyable task will decrease once people have been given some reward for performing that task (e.g. Lepper and Greene 1978). For example, if health insurance companies decided to offer lower rates to people who engage in regular physical exercise, such financial incentives might undermine the intrinsic motivation of people who exercise because they enjoy doing it.

Mass media communications can alert people to health risks that they might not otherwise learn about. Thus, public health education through the mass media has already resulted in a major change in health attitudes, which in turn may have increased popular acceptance of legal actions curbing health-impairing behaviour. For example, Warner (1981) attributed the large growth in state and local excise taxes for cigarettes between 1964 to 1972 to the anti-smoking campaign. The anti-smoking campaign in the USA is also an illustration of the fact that persuasion and incentive-related strategies do not preclude each other and are probably most effective when used in combination. Thus, the anti-smoking campaign resulted in a non-smoking ethos which was probably responsible for the legislative successes of the non-smokers' rights movements during the 1970s and 1980s.

Settings for health promotion

Following the review of public health approaches to health promotion, this section will give a few examples of the settings in which the strategies discussed in the preceding sections have been applied. We will begin this discussion with a somewhat unusual setting for a *public* health measure, namely the physician's office.

The physician's office

Although prevention has not been a strong component of traditional medical practice, medical school curricula are increasingly emphasizing the value of diagnosing health-impairing habits in healthy people and of advising them to change (Taylor 2011). As health experts who usually have a relationship of trust with their patients, physicians are particularly credible agents for inducing changes in health behaviour. Health advice is therefore more likely to be followed if it is issued by one's personal physician rather than some anonymous mass media source. Thus, physicians can become influential in health promotion by merely advising patients to change health-impairing behaviour. For example, there is evidence from 39 controlled trials of smoking interventions in medical practices that advice given to patients to stop smoking resulted in a moderate though significant reduction in the number of people who smoked (Kottke *et al.* 1988).

Physicians are likely to be even more effective in their traditional role of making health recommendations if they act on the basis of medical tests and examinations. For example, the advice to eat a low-cholesterol diet is more likely to be followed by a patient who has just received feedback that his serum cholesterol values are high, than without such feedback. To increase adherence in these situations it is important, however, that the information is made understandable to the patient and that specific recommendations are given. Instead of merely telling patients that they should lower their cholesterol intake, specific goals should be set. Furthermore, the physician (or a dietician working with the physician) should give specific information on the cholesterol content of various foods to help patients reach these goals. Finally, doctors and patients should agree on a date for new tests to be conducted to allow feedback on the success of these measures.

Schools

The school system is an ideal place for health promotion because, potentially, one can reach the total population and reach them early enough to prevent health-impairing habits from developing. For example, schools have been particularly active in instituting anti-smoking programmes (for reviews see Rooney and Murray 1996; Wiehe *et al.* 2005). These programmes vary from lectures by school principals or physicians to fear-arousing films, teacher participation (e.g. introducing material on smoking into science and hygiene classes) and student participation (e.g. anti-smoking essays, group discussion). Evaluations of these programmes suggest that only moderate reductions in the number of students who start smoking have so far been achieved (Rooney and Murray 1996). Furthermore, these effects appear to dissipate over time so that there seems to be no long-term impact (Wiehe *et al.* 2005). Alcohol prevention programmes appear to have been more effective (Perry *et al.* 1996).

Worksite

The worksite is an advantageous setting for conducting health promotion activities because a very large number of people can be reached on a regular basis. This allows the use of strategies that combine the public health approach with some of the clinical approaches to be discussed later. There is also a potential for manipulation of the social and physical environments in order to create positive incentives for healthy behaviour. Furthermore, the possibility of reduced health care costs and absenteeism make such interventions attractive for organizations (Cataldo and Coates 1986; Terborg 1988). The advantages of instituting such worksite health promotion programmes seem to have been recognized by many industrial organizations (Fielding and Piserchia 1989).

There are three ways in which companies have dealt with poor health habits of their employees. The first is through on-the-job programmes that help employees to practise better health behaviour. Thus, the most commonly offered health promotion activities consist of advice on exercise, stress management, smoking cessation, weight loss, nutrition and hypertension detection and control (Fielding 1986; Terborg 1988). A second way in which industry has promoted good health habits is by structuring the working environment in ways that help employees to engage in healthy activities. For example, companies might provide on-site health clubs, or restaurants that provide a balanced diet, low in fat, sugar and cholesterol. Very few industries use a third approach, namely offering monetary incentives for health behaviour (Terborg 1988). Although there is great enthusiasm about the efficacy of these programmes, results of large trials conducted to evaluate the effectiveness of such worksite health promotion programmes have been mixed (e.g. Salina *et al.* 1994; Byers *et al.* 1995; Glasgow *et al.* 1995, 1997; Sorensen *et al.* 1996; Maes *et al.* 1998). There is evidence, however, that more intensive interventions can be effective (e.g. Salina *et al.* 1994; Byers *et al.* 1995).

Community

This type of intervention incorporates a variety of different approaches, ranging from door-to-door or mass media information campaigns telling people about the availability of a breast cancer screening programme to a diet modification programme that recruits participants through community institutions. Evaluation of community-based interventions using quasi-experimental control group designs which compare intervention communities to matched control communities suggests that these interventions can be effective although results are rather variable (Sorensen *et al.* 1998).

Two early community studies targeting cardiovascular disease prevention were the North Karelia Project and the Stanford Three Community Study. The North Karelia Project, a large-scale community intervention conducted in northern Finland, resulted in a substantial reduction in coronary risk factors (Puska *et al.* 1985). An intensive educational campaign was implemented using the news services, physicians and public health nurses who staffed community health centres. An assessment of the effectiveness of these programmes based on self-report data showed that, compared to a neighbouring province used as a control group and not exposed to the campaign, there was a considerable improvement in several dietary habits in North Karelia (especially concerning fat intake). There was also a net re-duction in smoking in North Karelia, as well as small but significant net reductions in serum cholesterol levels and blood pressure. Most importantly, however, there was a 24 per cent decline in cardiovascular deaths in North Karelia, compared with a 12 per cent decline nationwide in Finland. Although the generalizability of these results is limited by the fact that the project was instituted in response to con-cerns among the North Karelia population about the extremely high heart disease rate in the area, findings such as these suggest that community-based interventions can be effective in changing health-impairing behaviour patterns.

The Stanford Three Community Study exposed several communities to a massive media campaign concerning smoking, diet and exercise through television, radio, newspapers, posters and printed material sent by mail (Farquhar et al. 1977; Meyer et al. 1980). In one of the communities, the media campaign was even supplemented by face-to-face counselling for a small subset of high-risk individuals. A control community was not exposed to the campaign. The media campaign increased people's knowledge about cardiac risk and resulted in modest improvements in dietary preferences and other cardiac risk factors.

In the late 1970s three large community-based intervention trials were started, the Stanford Five-City Project, the Minnesota Heart Health Project and the Pawtucket Heart Health Project. These trials, which varied in length from five to seven years, were aimed at reducing coronary risk factors, including high blood pressure, elevated serum cholesterol levels, cigarette smoking and obesity. In two of the projects (Five-City, Minnesota) impact was assessed both by repeated measures taken in a cohort and independent cross-sectional surveys conducted periodically over the period of the intervention. In Pawtucket only cross-sectional surveys were employed. The overall results of these studies have been somewhat disappointing. Analyses of the differences for the cohort between measurements at baseline and at the end of the six-year intervention in the Five-City Project, which was the most successful of these trials, showed that the treatment cities produced significantly greater improvement in cardiovascular disease knowledge as well as greater reductions in blood pressure and smoking than the control cities (Farquhar et al. 1990). These findings could not be replicated with the cross-sectional samples. In the Minnesota Heart Health Project, the only treatment effect that could be detected was a small reduction in smoking among women (Luepker et al. 1994). There was also some indication of treatment effects on physical activity. But this effect could only be demonstrated for a one-item measure and not when a more extensive and reliable physical activity questionnaire was used. The intervention did not have any significant effects on blood cholesterol levels, blood pressure or weight. Finally in Pawtucket, only a slowing down of secular weight increases could be observed. Whereas the average weight (related to height) increased in the control city, it remained relatively stable in Pawtucket (Carleton et al. 1995). The community intervention had no detectable impact on smoking, blood cholesterol or blood pressure. In none of these studies has there been any impact on incidence or prevalence of CHD or mortality.

There has been much speculation about the reasons for the rather modest impact of these interventions. One plausible reason is that these studies were conducted during a time when major efforts were made by governmental institutions all over the USA to change health-impairing lifestyle patterns in the population. These efforts included information campaigns as well as changes in taxation and legislation. That these efforts were successful is demonstrated by the pervasive health improvements which were observed in the non-intervention, control cities in all three studies. Since the community interventions in these studies also appeared to rely heavily on education about health risks, the added effect of these treatments was probably too weak to be demonstrated reliably. Thus the failure of these interventions to have pervasive effects on coronary risk factors and coronary health in these communities may yet be another demonstration that information about the negative consequences of health-impairing behaviour patterns is ineffective with populations who are already well informed about these consequences but do not know how to change. These interventions might have been more effective if they had provided the citizens of these communities with more information about how to go about changing their health-impairing behaviour.

Web

More than 60 per cent of individuals in Great Britain and 70 per cent in the USA use the internet (Strecher *et al.* 2005). In developed countries more that 263 million people are internet users (Portnoy *et al.* 2008). Thus, the internet can play an important role in health communication. According to some estimates 79 per cent of Americans who have an internet connection have used it to search for health information (Suggs and McIntyre 2009).

In addition to reaching a large number of people, another advantage of the internet is that it is interactive. This advantage can be used in interventions by *tailoring* a persuasive communication on the basis of the responses of a questionnaire filled in by respondents earlier. This makes it possible to provide individuals with precisely the information they might need to be willing to change their behaviour and once they are willing, to provide the information that might help them to change. For example, in the case of a campaign for the promotion of safer sex practices, one can examine the individual's beliefs about the safety of different practices and then correct those beliefs that are held erroneously. Or, in the case of alcohol consumption, one can assess people's knowledge of health consequences and their perception of consumption norms. This would allow one to give personalized feedback about the individual's consumption.

This type of tailoring can be done automatically by a computer-based expert system, a computer program that mimics the reasoning and problem-solving of an expert and, on receiving the information provided by the respondents automatically delivers the type of information that is most effective in helping respondents to change their health behaviour. Tailoring can either be static or dynamic. Static tailoring is based on one assessment, typically performed at the start of an intervention. Dynamically tailored interventions are based on assessments that are continued during the course of an intervention. For example, in interventions based on the TTM, dynamically tailored intervention make it possible to provide respondents with precisely the type of information that is appropriate for the state they are in at any given moment.

Not all computer-delivered interventions for health promotion and behavioural risk reduction are web-based. When people do not have access to the internet but possess a computer, non-tailored as well as tailored interventions can be delivered via a CD-ROM.

These possibilities have been used in numerous studies and there is evidence that computer-assisted interventions can be effective. Participants for such interventions can be recruited via internet advertisements, but also through flyers, community centres or schools and universities. A recent meta-analysis based on 75 randomized controlled trials of computer-assisted interventions published between 1988 and 2007 and involving more than 35,000 participants, found significant improvements in nutrition and in disordered eating (binge/purging), increases in safer sexual behaviour and reductions in tobacco use and use of other substances (Portnoy et al. 2008). These effects were of small to medium size. No improvements were observed for physical activity or weight loss/weight management. Unfortunately, this meta-analysis 'could not fully evaluate the efficacy of tailoring, because there was no variability for tailoring in these studies' (Portnoy et al. 2008: 12). More than 80 per cent of the interventions were tailored. These findings were replicated in a more recent meta-analysis that focused exclusively on computer-tailored interventions and found not only significant effects on dietary improvement (fat reduction, increased fruit and vegetable consumption, prolonged smoking abstinence), but also on physical activity (Krebs et al. 2010).

Conclusions

Drawing on different settings for health promotion allows one to reach different sections of the population. Therefore there are good reasons for pursuing each of the venues of health habit change. Community interventions and school pro-grammes can be used to educate the population about unhealthy lifestyles and to motivate people either not to adopt health-impairing behaviours or to change such behaviours if they have already been adopted. Physicians can also play an impor-tant part in this endeavour. Schools are potentially able to play a role in informing students about the health risks of unhealthy behaviours such as smoking, drug use and excessive drinking. Industrial organizations, on the other hand, can become important sources of motivation for individuals to change health-impairing habits. Because large industrial organizations can often also afford to employ profes-sional counsellors in their health promotion classes, they can effectively combine the public health and clinical therapy approach. In recent years, the internet has opened whole new possibilities of reaching large sections of the population in a very cost-effective manner. Finally, it should be remembered that the efficacy of health interventions is a function both of their *impact* in producing individual behaviour change and their *reach*, defined as the number of individuals who are affected in the population (Sorensen *et al.* 1998). Whereas the individual impact of public health interventions is likely to be smaller than that of clinical treatments, their efficacy could be larger because of their more extensive reach.

The therapy model: changing and maintaining change

Even if people have formed the strong intention to change some problematic health behaviour, they are unlikely to succeed at their first attempt. Most people who seek therapy for problematic health behaviour will first have attempted to achieve the desired change on their own. Thus 90 per cent of an estimated 37 million people who stopped smoking in the two decades following the US Surgeon General's first report linking smoking to cancer did so unaided (American Cancer Society 1986). After all, therapy is expensive and most people believe that they are quite capable of giving up smoking or losing weight on their own, at least until they try to do so.

Unlike the public health model, most therapy programmes involve a one-to-one relationship where 'patients' and therapists are in dyadic interaction, although group treatments and self-therapy programmes are also used (Leventhal and Cleary 1980). With the advent of the internet, therapy programmes can also be delivered on-line. Because people who come to therapy programmes have already decided to change and are motivated to act on their decision, the function of therapy programmes is not to *persuade* people to change but to help them to *achieve* and *maintain* the desired change.

Cognitive–behavioural treatment procedures

Early therapy directed at changing problematic health behaviour has mainly relied on behavioural techniques. Behavioural treatment procedures can be distinguished from other therapeutic orientations in that they involve one or a number of specific techniques that use learning-based principles to change behaviour (e.g. classical and operant conditioning). More recently techniques designed to impact specifically on cognitive variables have been increasingly included in behavioural treatment programmes (e.g. self-management procedures, skill training and cognitive restructuring). In therapy that aims for health behaviour change, classic behavioural techniques such as classic conditioning and operant procedures have become less popular and are increasingly replaced by cognitive behavioural techniques that rely on self-monitoring, cognitive restructuring and skill training. This section will outline the theoretical principles underlying these therapeutic procedures. A more detailed description of specific therapies (e.g. for alcoholism, obesity, smoking), as well as an evaluation of their effectiveness, will be given in Chapter 4.

Classical conditioning

Classical conditioning was first described in 1927 by the Russian physiologist Pavlov who, in research on the digestive system of dogs observed that many of these animals already began to salivate when they heard the footsteps of the assistant who normally fed them. Pavlov reasoned that the normal response to food (salivating) had become linked to the assistant's footsteps. Thus, by regularly preceding the stimulus that normally elicits salivation (i.e. the food), the assistant's footsteps had gained the power to elicit this response. Expressed more technically, salivation had become conditioned to the sound of the steps.

The first study which demonstrated that classical conditioning can be used to condition aversive reactions in humans was an experiment by Watson and Raynor (1920) in which they used a loud noise to instil fear of laboratory rats in a little boy. The noise was a very loud bang that was known to make the child cry and to display all signs of fear. Watson and Raynor demonstrated that the fear reaction which had initially been elicited by the noise now became linked to (i.e. conditioned to) the rat. Thus, through classical conditioning, the child's fear of the loud noise developed into a fear of a laboratory rat. Following this principle, Watson and Raynor developed the model for aversion therapy.

Early attempts at aversion therapy relied on electric shock (e.g. McGuire and Vallance 1964). However, although shocks are quite effective with laboratory animals, they do not seem to work well with humans. Modern behaviour therapies therefore employ aversive reactions that are *relevant* to the response that needs to be changed. Thus, aversion therapy with smokers induces them to smoke continually, inhaling every six to eight seconds until they cannot stand it any longer (Lichtenstein and Danaher 1975). Aversion therapy with alcoholics has used vomit-inducing drugs (e.g. disulfiram). Aversion therapy increasingly uses imaginary rather than real stimuli to arouse aversion (e.g. Elkins 1980). In this procedure, both the target behaviour and the aversive stimulus are presented through imagination. For example, whereas originally one had alcoholics experience the effects by giving them alcohol after intake of disulfiram, one now relies on having alcoholics imagine these effects.

Operant conditioning

Operant procedures modify behaviour by manipulating the consequences of such behaviour. They involve the contingent presentation (or withdrawal) of rewards and punishments in order to increase desirable or decrease undesirable behaviour. Behavioural theorists assume that health behaviours, like any other behaviour, have been learned through processes of operant conditioning. For example, a widely accepted theory of alcohol abuse, the Tension Reduction Hypothesis, assumes that alcohol is consumed because it reduces tension. By lowering tension, and thus reducing an aversive drive state, alcohol consumption has reinforcing properties. Cigarette smoking may have similar tension-reducing functions.

Like the early forms of aversive conditioning, operant procedures initially used electric shocks to change behaviour. Because these procedures did not prove to have lasting effects, present-day operant procedures frequently employ some form of contingency management. For example, smokers or alcoholics may agree with their therapist on some set of rewards or punishments that will be enacted, contingent on their behaviour.

Self-management procedures

Classical and operant conditioning procedures are based on the assumption that the forces shaping a person's life lie primarily in the external environment. In contrast, self-management procedures are based on the assumption that individuals can organize their environment in ways which make certain behaviours more likely (e.g. Miller and Munoz 1976). For example, individuals can reward themselves for reaching certain behavioural goals (e.g. for losing a certain amount of weight) or punish themselves for transgressing a predetermined rule (i.e. not to drink before the evening).

Self-monitoring and goal-setting are probably the most effective components of self-management. Through self-monitoring, the individual identifies problem areas (e.g. high risk situations) and problem behaviours (e.g. snacking). This then allows the setting of goals in order to achieve change. The application of self-reinforcement always involves some goal that has to be reached for the reinforcement to be applied. That this is an important determinant of the effectiveness of such procedures is suggested by research on goal-setting in the context of task performance in industry. This work has consistently demonstrated that setting specific and challenging goals and providing relevant feedback leads to substantial increases in performance (for a review, see Locke and Latham 1990). Specific goals are likely to result in specific behavioural intentions. The greater effectiveness of specific over more global goals would therefore also be consistent with predictions derived from the models of reasoned action or planned behaviour. Because self-reinforcements are usually made dependent on reaching very specific goals, and because individuals provide themselves with relevant feedback through self-monitoring, these procedures are comparable to those used in goal-setting research.

Skill training

Skill training procedures are a core component of cognitive behaviour therapy for substance abuse (e.g. Kadden et al. 2004), The main assumption underlying skill training techniques is that people engage in health-impairing behaviour because they lack certain skills. For example, people might become alcoholics because they lack the appropriate strategy to cope with stress (Riley et al. 1987; Kadden et al. 2004). Relapsed addicts frequently report that stress and negative emotional states often immediately preceded their return to drug use (e.g. Baer and Lichtenstein 1988; Bliss et al. 1989). By providing individuals with the skills for coping with such stressful situations, there will be an alternative response to cope with the problem. This should reduce the need to turn to cigarettes or alcohol in order to be able to cope. People with substance abuse problems typically also lack the skills to resist temptations, when exposed to high-risk situations (e.g. walking past their local bar; being offered a cigarette). A second important area of skill training is therefore to teach substance abusers how to recognize high-risk situations and how to cope with them successfully.

Cognitive restructuring

These techniques help patients to identify and correct the self-defeating thoughts which are frequently associated with emotional upset and relapse experiences. For example, Mahoney and Mahoney (1976) described the irrational and maladaptive cognitions that dieters often experience. These include thoughts about the impossibility of weight loss, the adoption of unrealistic goals which are soon disappointed, and self-disparaging statements. Using the methods of Beck (1976) and Meichenbaum (1977), patients are taught to discredit these arguments.

Relapse and relapse prevention

One distressing aspect of changing problematic health behaviour either through therapy or unaided is that people are often unable to maintain their changed habits. Thus relapse rates for addictions range from 50 to 90 per cent with approximately two-thirds of the relapses occurring within the first 90 days (Marlatt 1985; Brownell *et al.* 1986). Similarly, in the field of weight control, few of the dieters who succeed in losing substantial amounts of weight are able to maintain their losses for any significant period of time (Sternberg 1985).

Despite the high probability that clients who undergo therapy to change some health-impairing habit will experience a relapse soon after the end of their therapy, this possibility used not to be discussed (or even acknowledged) during therapy. Thus, when it happened, clients were unprepared to cope with relapse. This attitude has changed and specific relapse prevention approaches have been developed (e.g. Marlatt 1985; Brownell *et al.* 1986). Relapse prevention is a cognitive-behavioural approach that aims at identifying and preventing high-risk situations for relapse (Witkiewitz and Marlatt 2004).

The most comprehensive theory of the relapse process has been developed by Marlatt and colleagues (Marlatt and Gordon 1980; Marlatt 1985). The model was later revised by Witkiewitz and Marlatt (2004). The original model of relapse (see Figure 3.4) integrates elements from social psychological theories such as social learning, attribution and dissonance theory to account for the relapse process.

Treatment approaches based on relapse prevention begin with the assessment of high-risk situations for relapse (that is, the situations in which the individual's attempts to refrain from using a substance are threatened. For example, individuals with alcohol problems will be tempted whenever they pass their favourite bar and perhaps even see their friends having drinks. Or the temptation might arise whenever they are watching TV in the evening. If individuals are able to cope effectively with the high-risk situation their self-efficacy regarding their ability to resist temptation will increase and the probability that they relapse in future will decrease. It is assumed that individuals who manage to maintain abstinence or to comply with

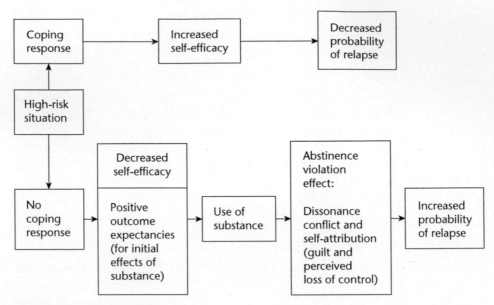

FIGURE 3.4 The original model of relapse
Source: Adapted from Marlatt (1985)

some other rule regarding the target behaviour (e.g. controlled drinking, smoking reduction, dieting) experience a sense of control. This sense of control, which will become stronger the longer the period of abstinence maintenance or successful rule-following, will be threatened when individuals encounter a high-risk situation. On the other hand, if individuals fail to cope with the high-risk situation and cannot resist the temptation, their self-efficacy will decrease and they will have positive expectancies regarding the effects of using the substance. This will result in substance use and an abstinence violation effect.

The main difference between the original and the revised model is that in the revised model a number of additional variables have been added, namely distal risk factors (e.g. family history, social support and substance dependence), physical withdrawal symptoms, affective states (e.g. depressive mood), craving and motivation. And whereas the original model specified clear causal paths, the extended model assumes that most causal paths are reciprocal. Thus, coping skills influence drinking behaviour and, in turn, drinking behaviour influences coping skills. On the positive side, these changes appeared to bring the model in line with empirical findings that were inconsistent with the original model (Witkiewitz and Marlatt 2004). On the negative side, it is difficult to see how the revised model can be empirically refuted.

If individuals manage to cope effectively with the high-risk situation, the probability of relapse will decrease significantly. One reason for this emphasized by Marlatt and Gordon (1980) is that individuals who cope successfully will have validated their sense of control. They will therefore expect to cope with future high-risk situations. This expectancy is closely associated with the notions of self-efficacy (Bandura 1986) and perceived behavioural control (Ajzen 1988). High self-efficacy or high perceived behavioural control are positively related to behavioural intentions. Individuals are more motivated to engage in a behaviour, if they perceive their ability to perform that behaviour successfully as high rather than low.

In contrast, failure to cope with the high-risk situation should decrease the sense of control or self-efficacy. The risk of failure should be particularly high if the situation also involves the temptation to engage in the prohibited behaviour as a means of coping with the stress. For example, if an individual is very anxious about the outcome of some examination and also feels that smoking a cigarette or having a drink would calm him or her down, the risk of relapse is very high. Thus, the sense of being unable to cope effectively in a high-risk situation combined with the positive outcome expectancies for the effects of the old habitual coping behaviour greatly increases the probability of an initial relapse.

Most people who attempt to change a health-impairing habit such as smoking or drinking perceive 'stopping' in a 'once and for all' manner. Thus, the transgression of an absolute rule will result in what Marlatt and Gordon (1980) termed the *abstinence violation effect* (i.e. the inference that the failure to remain abstinent is an indication of one's complete lack of willpower and self-control). However, because similar effects can be observed in dieters who have violated their diet norm, one should perhaps use the more general concept of a *'goal violation effect'* (Polivy and Herman 1987).

One major reason for the abstinence or goal violation effect is *self-attribution*. The concept of attribution refers to the processes by which individuals arrive at causal explanations for their own or other people's actions (Heider 1958). These explanations can vary on a continuum that ranges from attributions to internal causes to attributions to external causes. Examples of internal causes would be personality, ability or motivation. Examples of external causes would be task difficulty or social pressure. Individuals who relapse are likely to make internal attributions. They tend to blame the relapse on personal weakness or failure and to interpret it as evidence of their lack of willpower and their inability to resist temptation. This self-attribution will further decrease the individual's sense of self-efficacy and control.

A second reason for the abstinence or goal violation effect is *dissonance*. The flagrant violation of a dietary goal or abstinence rule would also be inconsistent with the individual's self-concept (as a dieter or abstainer) and therefore arouse dissonance. Dissonance is an aversive internal state, as unpleasant as, for example, anxiety. Thus, whenever dissonance is aroused, individuals are motivated to reduce it (Festinger 1957). In the case of violations of abstention rules, dissonance can either be reduced by changing one's self-image or by changing one's attitude towards abstention. Thus, ex-smokers who relapse could reduce their dissonance either by deciding that they have no willpower or by persuading themselves that smoking is not so bad after all. Obviously, both mechanisms of dissonance reduction would increase the risk of future relapse.

According to this analysis, the first step to take in the prevention of relapse is to teach clients to recognize high-risk situations that are likely to trigger a relapse (Marlatt 1985). The second step involves teaching them the coping skills that are necessary to master the high-risk situation. Such relapse prevention techniques have now been tested with a variety of health behaviours including alcohol abstinence (e.g. Chaney *et al.* 1978), smoking (e.g. Shiffman *et al.* 1985) and weight control (Sternberg 1985). Empirical tests of relapse prevention, which have mainly been guided by the original model, have led to conflicting results, and these discrepancies appear to be mainly dependent on the substance involved in the study. A meta-analysis of 26 studies that applied relapse prevention techniques found treatment effects of moderate size for alcohol use, but much weaker effects for smoking (Irvin *et al.* 1999). Furthermore, a recent meta-analysis of relapse prevention treatments of smokers detected no long-term benefits from skills-based intervention to prevent relapse (Hajek *et al.* 2009). The authors concluded that their 'review failed to detect a clinically significant effect of existing behavioural relapse prevention methods for people quitting smoking' (p. 12).

Changing automatic response tendencies

It is ironic that at a time when therapy for alcohol abuse, smoking and obesity has shifted more and more towards using cognitive techniques, there is increasing evidence that these health-impairing behaviour patterns are strongly influenced by implicit attitudes, which express the automatic, often preconscious evaluation of an attitude object. Because it is a defining characteristic of implicit attitudes that individuals have little control over their expression, cognitive techniques may be less effective in changing them. This may be one of the reasons why the skills cognitive behaviour therapists teach people with health-impairing behaviour problems (e.g. alcohol abuse, smoking, obesity) to improve their ability to resist temptations in high-risk situations proved to have so little effect. The recognition of implicit attitudes as powerful risk factors for substance abuse will therefore necessitate a reorientation of therapy approaches towards a greater emphasis of behavioural techniques.

There are already several techniques that have proved to be effective in changing implicit attitudes with regard to alcohol and unhealthy eating. More importantly, it could even be demonstrated that changing these implicit attitudes also influenced relevant behaviour (for a review, see Friese *et al.* 2010). For example, Houben *et al.* (2010a) used a classical conditioning paradigm to unobtrusively change the alcohol-related attitudes and drinking behaviour of their participants. For participants in the experimental group, alcohol-related words (e.g. wine, beer, whisky) were repeatedly paired with negative pictures, while soft drink-related words were paired with positive pictures. In the control condition, alcohol-related words were paired with neutral pictures. The repeated association of alcohol-related words with negative pictures in the experimental condition resulted in a change in alcohol-related implicit attitudes (measured with an IAT) in the experimental compared to the control condition. Furthermore, participants in the experimental condition also reported less alcohol consumption in the following week, compared to their drinking at baseline.

In a replication of this study, participants in the experimental condition were repeatedly exposed to beer-related pictures paired with negative words and negative pictures (Houben *et al.* 2010b). In the control condition, participants were shown the same pictures, but without the critical pairing of beer-related pictures with negative stimuli. This conditioning procedure resulted in significant change in explicit attitudes in the experimental compared to the control condition. Furthermore, participants in the experimental condition also drank less beer in a subsequent bogus taste test. And most importantly, these participants also reduced their beer consumption in the following week (measured with a drinking diary, controlling for average weekly alcohol use). Thus, these studies demonstrate that classical conditioning procedures can significantly change alcohol-related attitudes and drinking behaviour.

Houben *et al.* (2010c) used *response inhibition training* to change drinking behaviour. Participants in this study completed a so-called 'Go/No-Go' task on exposure to beer or water stimuli. The Go/No-Go task requires participants to withhold their behaviour in response to a specific stimulus (e.g. alcohol, unhealthy food). Because impulse-evoking stimuli automatically elicit a preparation to act, a stop signal associated with such a stimulus results in behavioural inhibition (Veling and Aarts 2009). Using this technique, Houben *et al.* (2010c) had participants in the experimental condition press a key when a water stimulus appeared (Go) but to *inhibit* a response when shown a beer stimulus (No-Go). In the control condition, this contingency was reversed. In a subsequent bogus taste test of beers, participants in the experimental condition drank less beer than participants in the control condition. This effect appeared to generalize to self-reported beer consumption in the following week.

Another procedure, which has proved effective in influencing health-impairing behaviour relies on changing approach–avoidance tendencies with regard to unhealthy food or alcohol. Approach–avoidance tendencies are often assessed by having participants pull or push a joystick on exposure to a stimulus of a certain category, with pulling the joystick towards them reflecting approach and pushing it away reflecting avoidance (Chen and Bargh 1999). In an attempt to change unhealthy eating patterns, Fishbach and Shah (2006) presented their participants with a series of food-related words reflecting either healthy (e.g. apple, broccoli) or tasty, but unhealthy, options (e.g. cookie, cake, fries). Participants in the experimental condition were instructed to pull the joystick towards them whenever pictures of healthy food items were shown and push the joystick away from them on exposure to unhealthy but tasty food items. In the control group, the contingency was reversed. When participants were afterwards offered a choice of healthy and unhealthy food items as a reward for taking part, participants in the experimental group were more likely than those in the control group to choose healthy food.

In a conceptual replication of this study, Wiers *et al.* (2010b) used somewhat modified avoidance training with heavy social drinkers, who had to push away a joystick on exposure to alcohol pictures. They found that the training procedure changed implicit attitudes towards alcohol in an approach–avoidance IAT. The avoid-alcohol training procedure also resulted in less drinking in a sub-sample of participants, who had become faster and faster in pushing the joystick away and thus avoiding the alcohol pictures.

Although these findings are promising, all of the studies reviewed so far have been conducted with individuals who did not have a serious alcohol or eating problem. Furthermore, the follow-up periods have been rather short. However, evidence is emerging that such methods can work with clinical patients. In a study with alcohol dependent clinic patients, Wiers *et al.* (2010b) demonstrated that the avoidance training they had developed for their earlier study did not only change implicit attitudes towards alcohol (IAT) but also had long-term effects on drinking behaviour. When contacted one year later, a significantly larger percentage of patients in the experimental group (58 per cent) than in the control group (43 per cent) had not relapsed during this period. The study of Wiers *et al.* is very important, because it is the first demonstration that these methods can have long-term effects with clinical patients. Nevertheless, replications with other patient groups will be needed before these procedures can become standard components of clinical treatment.

Summary and conclusions

This chapter presented and discussed two types of approaches to the modification of health behaviour, the public health model and the therapy model. The public health model involves health promotion programmes that are designed to change the behaviour of large groups (e.g. members of industrial organizations, students of a school, citizens of a community or even the population of a country). Three major strategies are used to achieve this objective: persuasive appeals, economic incentives and legal measures.

Mass media health appeals are quite effective in increasing people's knowledge of certain health hazards but they are often less effective in changing their behaviour. As I have tried to point out, the impact of many of these communications on attitudes and behaviour could have been increased if their design had been based on social psychological theory and methodology. However, it would be misleading to assess the impact of public health interventions solely on the evidence of their efficacy in producing individual behaviour change. The impact of an intervention is a function of both efficacy and reach. Thus, even when the impact on individual behaviour is relatively small, the overall impact of public health interventions on the population can still be substantial. Furthermore, the effects of continuous public health campaigns are likely to accumulate.

As the anti-smoking campaign of the 1960s and 1970s illustrated, public health approaches can achieve significant behaviour change if extensive media campaigns are combined with economic and legal measures. Thus, the mass media campaign that was initiated by the report of the US Surgeon General (USDHEW 1964) is likely to have played a causal role in the global change of attitudes towards smoking. This general change in climate was probably responsible for the increases in local and state taxation during the late 1960s and for the legislative successes of the non-smokers' rights movements during the 1970s.

However, the example of smoking can also serve to illustrate the weaknesses of the public health approach. It has been very successful in conveying information about the health risk of smoking in the USA. Most smokers now believe that cigarette smoking is hazardous. It has been less successful in changing behaviour. Nearly one-third of the US population continues to smoke, despite the considerable reduction in the prevalence of smoking during recent decades.

The fact that many of the people who smoke today would like to stop suggests that a sizeable proportion of those individuals have been unable to stop on their own and would profit from some form of therapy. Thus, even though educational campaigns can be effective in motivating individuals to change, good intentions are often not enough in the case of health-impairing behaviour such as substance abuse or excessive eating. By teaching people strategies (including techniques aimed at changing automatic response tendencies) that help them to maintain the motivation and to execute their intention to change, clinical therapy can make an important contribution to changing these sorts of behaviours. Thus, public health strategies and clinical therapy are complementary rather than contradictory approaches. To decide to undergo therapy, individuals must first be aware of having a problem and be willing to do something about it.

Further reading

Bohner, G. and Wänke, M. (2002) *Attitudes and Attitude Change*. Hove: Psychology Press. A brief and very readable introduction to theories of attitude and attitude change.

Fishbein, M. and Ajzen, I. (2010) *Predicting and Changing Behavior: The Reasoned Action Approach*. New York: Psychology Press. This book presents the most recent summary of the reasoned action and planned behaviour approach.

Hofmann, W., Friese, M. and Wiers, R. (2008) Impulsive versus reflective influences on health behavior: a theoretical framework and empirical review. *Health Psychology Review*, 2: 111–37. A very readable discussion of research on self-control dilemmas from the theoretical perspective of the impulsive–reflective model of Strack and Deutsch (2004).

Jeffery, R.W. (1989) Risk behaviors and health: contrasting individual and population perspectives. *American Psychologist*, 44: 1194–202. This article argues that the discrepancy between individual and population perspectives of health risk is responsible for the failure of many public health campaigns to influence health behaviour.

Rothman, A. and Salovey, P. (2007) The reciprocal relation between principles and practice, in A. Kruglanksi and T. Higgins (eds) *Social Psychology: Handbook of Principles*, pp. 826–49. New York: Guilford. An excellent discussion of all aspects of the process of health behaviour change.

Sutton, S. (2005) Stage theories of health behaviour, in M. Conner and P. Norman (eds) *Predicting Health Behaviour*, 2nd edn, pp. 223–75. Maidenhead: Open University Press. An excellent critical review of stage theories of health behaviour.

CHAPTER 4

Behaviour and health: excessive appetites

The two previous chapters examined determinants of health behaviour and the effectiveness of strategies of change. The present chapter and the next one will discuss the major behavioural risk factors that have been linked to health. The discussion of behaviour and health will be divided into two sections. This chapter covers health-impairing behaviour related to excessive appetites such as smoking, drinking too much alcohol and overeating. These are appetitive behaviours that, once they have become excessive, are exceedingly difficult to control. People who want to change often enter counselling or therapy programmes to help them to act according to their intentions.

In contrast, the self-protective behaviours such as eating a healthy diet, exercising, safeguarding oneself against the risk of injury from accidents (e.g. wearing a seat belt) and avoiding behaviour associated with contracting AIDS (e.g. needle sharing, unprotected sex) that are discussed in Chapter 5 are generally somewhat more under the voluntary control of the individual.

The structure of our discussion of behavioural risk factors is similar in both chapters. Each section will begin with a critical review of the empirical evidence that links these behaviours to negative health consequences. After a discussion of theories of the development and maintenance of these behaviours, the effectiveness of strategies of attitude and behaviour change in modifying the risk of health impairment will be discussed.

Smoking

The health consequences of smoking

Since the US Surgeon General, in his first report on smoking (USDHEW 1964), identified cigarette smoking as the single most important source of preventable mortality and morbidity, smoking rates among adults in the USA have dropped from 42.4 per cent in 1965 to 19.8 per cent in 2007 (CDC 2008a). Similar trends have been observed in Great Britain, where rates were down to 24 per cent in 2005, and in Germany where rates were down to 24.3 per cent in 2003

(OECD Health Data 2007). Other countries did slightly less well. For example, in Denmark, 26 per cent of individuals still smoked in 2004 (OECD Health Data 2008a). In the Netherlands, the percentage of people who still smoked in 2006 was even higher (31 per cent; OECD Health Data 2008b). The most successful developed country with regard to smoking reduction is undoubtedly Sweden, where smoking rates are down to 17.5 per cent (OECD Health Data 2005). In all of these countries, fewer women smoke than men, but the gender difference has decreased considerably over the years.

In view of this widespread reduction in smoking rates, it seems paradoxical that the number of cigarettes sold in the world has increased by 950 billion since 1980. In 1995 5422 billion cigarettes were smoked worldwide, more than 100 billion cigarettes a week, a pack a week for every man, woman and child in the world. The reason is that even though smoking rates have declined in all developed countries, they have increased in many developing countries. China gets through a quarter of all cigarettes smoked, but Latin America and the former communist countries also account for large parts of worldwide consumption (*Independent*, 7 March 1996).

Morbidity and mortality

The negative health effects of smoking are appalling. It has been estimated that between 2000 and 2004, 443,000 people died prematurely each year of smoking-related diseases in the USA alone (CDC 2008b). The WHO estimates that tobacco use is the primary cause of 5 million deaths worldwide each year (Davis *et al.* 2007). The difference in life expectancy at birth between smokers and non-smokers has been estimated as 7.3 years (Barendregt *et al.* 1997). Furthermore, there is evidence that eliminating smoking will not only extend life expectancy and result in an increase in the number of years lived without disability, but it will also compress end-of-life disability into a shorter period (Nusselder *et al.* 2000).

Of the deaths each year due to CHD (the leading cause of death in industrialized countries), 30 to 40 per cent can be attributed to cigarette smoking (Fielding 1985). Cigarette smokers are two to four times more likely to develop CHDs than non-smokers. Overall, the mortality from heart disease in the USA is 70 per cent greater for smokers than non-smokers (USDHHS 1985). Similar excess rates have been reported for Canada, the UK, Scandinavia and Japan (Pooling Project Research Group 1978).

The second leading cause of death in the USA and other affluent industrial nations is cancer. Smoking is responsible for approximately 30 per cent of all deaths from cancer (CDC 2008b) and for approximately 90 per cent of lung cancer deaths in men and almost 80 per cent of lung cancer deaths in women. The risk of dying from lung cancer is more than 23 times higher among men who smoke cigarettes and 13 times higher among women who smoke cigarettes than in individuals who never smoked (USDHHS 2004). Smoking also doubles the risk of dying from stroke, the third leading cause of death in the USA (USDHHS 1990). Finally, smoking is responsible for at least 75 per cent of deaths from chronic obstructive pulmonary disease, a heterogeneous group disease that is characterized by an obstruction of airflow that interferes with normal breathing.

There is a strong dose-response relationship between cigarette consumption and severe disease. Thus, even infrequent smokers are at risk. Smoking one to four cigarettes a day results in a 50 per cent increase in mortality risk from all causes. The risk of dying from heart disease is nearly three times higher than that of non-smokers (Bjartveit and Tverdal 2005). For pipe and cigar smokers who do not inhale deeply the risk of morbidity and mortality is somewhat smaller than that for cigarette smokers but still considerably higher than that for non-smokers (Fielding 1985). It is less clear whether smokers of filter cigarettes run a lower risk of morbidity and mortality than smokers of non-filter cigarettes (Fielding 1985).

Because people who smoke live unhealthily in other respects as well (see e.g. Schuit *et al*. 2002; Chiolero *et al*. 2006; Poortinga 2007), smokers are at even greater risk of ill health than indicated by the increase in relative risk due to smoking. Furthermore, it is particularly the heavy smokers who are most likely to engage in other health-risk behaviour (Chiolero *et al*. 2006). A national survey of behavioural risk factors conducted in the USA indicated that, compared to non-smokers, smokers had higher age-adjusted rates of 'acute drinking' (five or more alcoholic drinks per occasion at least once a month) and 'chronic drinking' (averaging two or more alcoholic drinks per day), more episodes of driving while intoxicated, and lower use of seat belts (Remington *et al*. 1985). This association between smoking and alcohol consumption might have contributed to the finding that smokers have a 50 per cent greater risk of accident deaths than people who never smoked (Leistikow *et al*. 2000). Current smokers also differ from former and 'never' smokers in their dietary intake and physical activity. For example, a study of 3250 working adults found that current smokers consumed more calories per day from high-fat and high-calorie foods, including dairy products, meat, eggs, French fries and fats, and reported less frequent leisure time physical activity than former and never smokers (French *et al*. 1996). Clustering of health-impairing behaviour factors has also been reported in large-scale studies conducted in Great Britain (Poortinga 2007), Switzerland (Chiolero *et al*. 2006) and the Netherlands (Schuit *et al*. 2002). And all these risk behaviours may independently or synergistically contribute to higher chronic disease risk in smokers.

The health benefits of stopping
Smoking cessation has major immediate health benefits for men and women of all ages (USDHHS 1990). Former smokers live longer than continuing smokers. Only one year after stopping smoking, the risk of coronary heart disease is reduced by half. After 15 years it is the same as that of people who never smoked. The risk of lung cancer also declines steadily in people who quit smoking and after 10 years is less than half of that of continuing smokers.

Smoking and weight
Smoking has one effect that may be considered positive, particularly by women: it appears to lower body weight. Middle-aged smokers weigh less than non-smokers, and smokers who quit smoking tend to gain weight, women more so than men (for a review, see French and Jeffery 1995). However, there is no evidence that *young*

people who start smoking reduce their body weight and no weight differences have been observed in a large sample of young men and women (Klesges *et al.* 1998). This suggests that the weight control benefits of smoking take years to accrue and are probably due to a slight attenuation of the commonly observed weight increase as people age. In contrast to the weight control benefits of smoking, the costs of stopping appear to be immediate. Smokers who stop smoking gain between 2.3kg (USDHHS 1990) and 6kg (Klesges *et al.* 1997) within one year, the higher gains being observed in those who manage to stop completely. Although this weight gain is unlikely to reduce the health benefits gained from stopping smoking, it can act as a deterrent for cosmetic reasons. There is persuasive evidence that weight gain following smoking cessation is mainly due to the removal of the stimulating effect of nicotine on metabolic rate: weight gain can be suppressed through nicotine replacement, and there appears to be a linear relationship between nicotine dose during replacement and the extent to which weight gain is suppressed, and weight gain occurs once nicotine replacement is stopped (e.g. Doherty *et al.* 1996). However, there is also evidence to suggest that people eat more after they stop smoking (USDHHS 1990), probably to replace smoking enjoyment with eating enjoyment.

Passive smoking
In addition to the impact on their own health, smokers also endanger the health of others. In the past decades there has been increasing awareness of the health hazards due to exposure to *environmental tobacco smoke* (Brownson *et al.* 1997; USDHHS 2006). On an involuntary basis, spouses or colleagues of smokers are exposed to second-hand tobacco smoke and thus to the same toxic materials with which smokers endanger their health.

There is now convincing evidence that second-hand smoke is associated with increased risk of lung cancer and deaths from CHD in non-smoking partners or colleagues of smokers (USDHHS 2006). More than 50 epidemiologic studies have addressed the association between second-hand smoke exposure and the risk of lung cancer in lifelong non-smokers and estimate a 30 per cent increase in disease risk. The increase in risk of CHD among non-smokers due to passive smoking has been estimated to be 25 per cent in a large meta-analysis (He *et al.* 1999). An update of this meta-analysis with nine cohort and seven case control studies conducted up to the spring of 2003 arrived at practically the same estimate of relative risk (USDHHS 2006).

Epidemiological data also indicate that maternal smoking during pregnancy and after birth is a major risk factor for sudden, unexplained, unexpected death of an infant before one year of age, commonly referred to as Sudden Infant Death Syndrome (SIDS), with the relative risk estimates ranging from 1.4 to 3.5 (USDHHS 2006). There is also evidence that fathers who smoke in the same room as the infant considerably increase the risk of the infant dying of SIDS (USDHHS 20006). The evidence of the health impact of environmental smoking has led to the introduction of much more stringent restrictions in the places where tobacco can be smoked in the USA (USDHHS 1986, 2006) and Europe.

The economic costs of smoking

While the cost of smoking in terms of human lives is beyond question, the argument that smoking also imposes a financial burden on society (as advanced by several US state governments in court cases against the tobacco industry in 1996) can be challenged. Although smokers impose considerable costs through hospitalization, medical costs and higher absenteeism rates, they also produce extra tax income via tobacco taxes. Furthermore, with their early death they subsidize the collectively financed retirement plans of non-smokers, and contribute less to the high health costs of an ageing population. Economic analyses have repeatedly indicated that these financial benefits outweigh the costs imposed by smoking (Manning et al. 1989; Barendregt et al. 1997). However, there is still debate about whether all the relevant health costs have been considered in these analyses (e.g. the picture might change if the effects of environmental tobacco smoke were included) (Warner 2000).

Determinants of smoking

In attempting to explain why people smoke, one has to distinguish between becoming a smoker and maintaining the habit. Social pressure from peers or older siblings is probably the prime factor in experimenting with smoking (Leventhal and Cleary 1980; Spielberger 1986). For example, a prospective study of the initiation of smoking which followed two cohorts of teenagers for several years from ninth grade (14–15 years old) found that the number of friends who smoked at the beginning of the study was strongly associated with experimenting with cigarettes during the study (Killen et al. 1997). This initial experimentation is a crucial step and is one of the reasons why the prevention of smoking should begin in school and target young people before they have experimented with it (Best et al. 1988).

The reasons smokers give for why they maintain the habit, once initiated, have been extensively analysed (Ikard et al. 1969; Leventhal and Avis 1976; Spielberger 1986). Factor analyses of self-report data collected from samples of smokers have led to very similar factor structures (Shiffman 1993). For example, a study conducted by Leventhal and Avis (1976) resulted in the following factors: pleasure–taste (e.g. 'I like the taste of tobacco'); addiction (e.g. 'I get a real gnawing hunger for a cigarette when I haven't smoked for a while'); habit (e.g. 'I smoke cigarettes automatically without even being aware of it'); anxiety (e.g. 'When I am nervous in social situations, I smoke'); stimulation (e.g. 'Smoking makes me feel more awake'); social rewards (e.g. 'I smoke to be sociable'); and 'fiddle' (e.g. 'Handling a cigarette is part of the enjoyment of smoking').

Leventhal and Avis (1976) and Ikard and Tomkins (1973) examined the validity of these reports by dividing respondents on the basis of their responses to such questionnaires into high and low scorers on a particular dimension. When the actual smoking behaviour of these respondents was examined under experimentally manipulated conditions, respondents' behaviour validated their reported reasons for smoking. For example, when smokers were given cigarettes adulterated with vinegar, those high on the pleasure–taste factor showed a sharp drop in the number of cigarettes smoked, but those low on the factor did not (Leventhal and Avis 1976). When asked to monitor their smoking by filling out a card for each cigarette smoked, habit smokers significantly reduced their smoking, whereas pleasure–taste smokers did not (Leventhal and Avis 1976). Finally, there was more smoking during and after a fear-arousing film for smokers who used smoking for anxiety reduction (Ikard and Tomkins 1973). Both studies also found that addicts suffered the most during periods of deprivation.

Findings such as these could have important implications for clinical therapy. For example, therapy aimed at a smoker whose main motive in smoking is to reduce anxiety would have to differ from that aimed at someone who smokes out of habit. However, in a review of studies that related individual smoking motives to cessation processes, Shiffman (1993: 736) found little evidence 'that smoking typology classifications substantially affect cessation processes or inform treatment decisions'.

Smoking attitudes and intentions

According to the theories of reasoned action and planned behaviour, attitudes, subjective norms, perceived control and intentions are important determinants of smoking behaviour (Ajzen 2005). These models further assume that attitudes, subjective norms and perceived control are all based on beliefs. Consistent with expectations from these models, numerous studies have indicated that smoking intentions are closely linked to positive attitudes towards smoking, and subjective norms (e.g. Sutton 1989). That intention is a good predictor even of the onset of smoking behaviour has been demonstrated in prospective studies in the USA and Europe (e.g. Chassin et al. 1984; de Vries et al. 1995; Conner et al. 2006). Attitudes and behavioural norms are also good predictors of smokers' intention to stop smoking (Rise et al. 2008). However, as one would expect with addictive behaviour, intentions are not a very strong predictor of actual behaviour (Norman et al. 1999; Rise et al. 2008), but an even poorer predictor of length of abstinence (e.g. Borland et al. 1991; Norman et al. 1999).

That individuals who have a positive attitude towards stopping smoking and would thus like to quit are often unable to act on their intention is consistent with the finding that smokers typically hold neutral to negative global attitudes towards smoking on explicit and even implicit measures of attitudes in most studies (e.g. Swanson et al. 2001; Huijding et al. 2005). Whereas the former finding is hardly surprising in view of the fact that most smokers would like to quit, it would have been plausible that smokers indicate positive attitudes towards smoking on implicit measures. After all, these measures reflect the automatic affective reactions that stimuli evoke and are assumed to play an important role in smoking and other addictive behaviours. It is interesting to note, however, that these implicit measures have been found to be correlated with measures of nicotine dependence and craving for cigarettes (e.g. Payne et al. 2007; Waters et al. 2007).

Addiction

According to the nicotine regulation model developed by Schachter and his colleagues, individuals smoke to regulate the level of nicotine in the internal milieu (Schachter 1977, 1978; Schachter *et al.* 1977b). Smoking is stimulated when the nicotine level falls below a certain set point. Thus, Schachter (who was a lifelong smoker himself) conceptualized smoking essentially as an escape–avoidance response. Smokers smoked to escape the aversive consequences of nicotine withdrawal.

Schachter tested this hypothesis in a series of innovative studies (Schachter 1977; Schachter *et al.* 1977a, 1977b). In the first study, they lowered the level of nicotine in cigarettes and found that long-time, heavy smokers increased their smoking by 25 per cent, but light smokers only by 18 per cent (Schachter 1977).[1] To examine whether these changes reflected a need to maintain an optimal level of nicotine in the blood, Schachter *et al.* (1977a) compared smoking levels in respondents who were chemically induced to excrete nicotine either at a very high or a very low rate. Most of the nicotine absorbed by an individual is chemically broken down, but a fraction of nicotine which escapes this process is eliminated as such in the urine. The rate of excretion of unchanged nicotine (an alkaloid) in the urine depends on the acidity of the individual's urine. During different weeks, respondents in this experiment took either substantial doses of placebo or of drugs that acidify the urine (e.g. vitamin C – ascorbic acid). The fact that respondents who took vitamin C increased their average cigarette smoking by roughly 15 to 20 per cent supported Schachter's hypothesis.

Smokers are not only convinced that smoking reduces stress, they also smoke more in stressful situations like examinations, colloquia, stressful seminar presentations or when being administered painful electric shocks (Schachter *et al.* 1977b). Schachter reasoned that this behaviour is induced by the fact that stress makes the urine more acidic and thus lowers the blood-nicotine level. Thus, cigarette smoking under stress serves the function of regulating serum nicotine. To test this assumption, Schachter *et al.* (1977b) conducted an experiment which independently manipulated level of stress and acidity of urine. Consistent with the nicotine regulation model, exposure to a painful rather than a weak electric shock increased smoking in respondents who had been given a placebo, but not in respondents who had been given a pill that prevented their urine from acidifying.

Does smoking help smokers to reduce stress, to calm down or to improve their performance? It does indeed, but only if they are compared to smokers who are deprived of nicotine. Thus, smokers who are smoking high-nicotine rather than low-nicotine cigarettes can take more painful electric shocks, are less irritated by aeroplane noise and do better at motor performance tasks (Schachter 1978). However, when the mood or performance of smokers who are permitted to smoke as much as they want is compared with the mood or performance of control groups of non-smokers,

---

[1] This effect has not been consistently replicated in more recent studies (for a review, see Rose 2006).

a remarkable fact emerges: smoking only improves the mood of smokers or their performance to the level customary for non-smokers (Schachter 1978).

More recently, a very similar model has been developed by Parrott (e.g. 1999, 2005), who argued that during the period between one cigarette and the next smokers experience acute nicotine deprivation with abstinence symptoms such as tension, anger and anxiety. When these symptoms increase, smoking is initiated, replenishing the nicotine level and thus reducing tension and stress. Thus, like Schachter, Parrott argues that smokers smoke to regulate their level of plasma nicotine. As a result, smokers are probably correct in reporting that smoking helps them to relax and to reduce stress, but the tension they reduce is a consequence of nicotine withdrawal. Consistent with this assumption, smokers' stress levels are only similar to those of non-smokers if they have just smoked a cigarette and thus raised their level of plasma nicotine. During periods of nicotine deprivation, their stress level is worse than that of non-smokers (Parrott and Garnham 1998). Thus, like Schachter, Parrott suggests that smoking only reduces the stress and negative mood that is caused by the smokers' nicotine dependence. Regular smokers need nicotine to maintain normal moods and become irritable and stressed when plasma nicotine levels are falling. Thus, as Schachter has phrased it aptly, 'the heavy smoker gets nothing out of smoking. He smokes only to prevent withdrawal' (Schachter 1978).

If smokers were smoking primarily to obtain nicotine, a therapy where the nicotine smokers miss when stopping smoking is replaced by other means should be extremely successful. As we will see later (p. 119), while nicotine replacement therapy considerably reduces the probability of relapse in smokers who stop, its effectiveness is far from perfect. Furthermore, studies of symptoms of smokers, who were either abstinent for several days, smoked normal cigarettes or denicotinized cigarettes that were similar to normal cigarettes except for the removal of nicotine, demonstrated that smoking denicotinized cigarettes avoided some of the typical symptoms of abstinence (e.g. Buchhalter et al. 2005; Donny et al. 2006). Smoking denicotinized cigarettes eliminated such abstinence symptoms as 'desire for sweets', 'hunger' and 'urges to smoke'. Here no difference was observed between groups that smoked nicotinized and those that smoked denicotinized cigarettes. In contrast, for symptoms such as 'difficulty concentrating', 'increased eating', 'feeling restless' and 'impatience', smokers of denicotinized cigarettes showed the same level of symptoms as smokers who were abstinent (e.g. Buchhalter et al. 2005).

Although these findings support the conclusion that smoke components other than nicotine play a role in cigarette addiction, they are not necessarily inconsistent with the Schachter/Parrott theory. For example, through their repeated association with the delivery of nicotine, the constellation of sensory (e.g. aroma, sensation when inhaling smoke) and motoric (e.g. handling, puffing, inhaling) components of smoking may have required reward value (i.e. classical conditioning). Their absence in tobacco abstinence might therefore contribute the abstinence effects. By providing smokers with these sensory and motoric components of smoking, denicotinized cigarettes might therefore reduce some of the psychological consequences of tobacco abstinence.

Genetics and smoking

The first scientific evidence on the heritability of smoking was reported by Fisher (1958), who found that monozygotic (i.e. identical) twins had higher concordance rates than dizygotic (i.e. non-identical) twins. Greater concordance of a trait or behaviour among monozygotic twins is an indication of a genetic influence, because monozygotic and dizygotic twin pairs are exposed to the same social environment, but differ in the extent to which they share genetic material (i.e. monozygotic twins share all, dizygotic half). These findings have been frequently replicated in large studies of twins, with the magnitude of the genetic influence estimated around 50 per cent of the total variance in smoking behaviour (for a review, see Heath and Madden 1994). It has also been established that genetic factors contribute not only to the initiation but also to the maintenance of smoking habit (Heath and Martin 1993).

It is important to note that a strong genetic influence on behaviour such as smoking does not have the same meaning as the genetic determination of eye colour or blood type. Whereas we cannot change our eye colour or blood type, we have control over whether we smoke. Genetic influence in this case simply means that some people are more likely to take up smoking, if exposed to tobacco products, and will also find it more difficult to stop. Given that smoking is an addiction, it is interesting to note that the magnitude of the genetic influence on smoking is comparable to that of alcoholism (Heath and Martin 1993).

Stopping smoking unaided

According to a survey of US smokers conducted by the Centers for Disease Control (CDC 2002), 70 per cent of current smokers reported that they wanted to stop smoking completely, and 41 per cent reported trying to stop for at least one day in the past few years. The majority of smokers who try to stop do so without any form of help (even nicotine replacement). Early studies of unaided smoking cessation based on interviews with smokers who had stopped reported that 60 per cent had done so without outside help (Schachter 1982; Rzewnicki and Forgays 1987). More recently it has been estimated that 90 per cent of the 44 million Americans who had stopped smoking at that time had done so without professional help (Fiore et al. 1990). Even as late at 1996, the majority of smokers gave up without either professional help or use of pharmacological therapy (Chapman 2009).

Unfortunately, only a few of those who try are really successful. According to a study by Cohen et al. (1989), abstinence rates of smokers at 12 months after the attempt to stop unaided are 13 per cent if one uses the standard criterion for abstinence, namely that individuals are not smoking around the time when the follow-up measurement is taken (*point prevalence abstinence*). Abstinence rates are reduced to just over 4 per cent if *continuous abstinence* since the stop attempt is used as the criterion. A review of more recent studies arrived at a similar estimate of abstinence rates after unaided quit attempts of 3 per cent to 5 per cent, 6 to 12 months after a given quit attempt (Hughes et al. 2004). These data are similar to those of a survey conducted in 2000 according to which 4.7 per cent of current smokers who tried to quit were able to stop for at least three months (CDC 2002).

The success rates of individuals who try to stop without any help usually form the baseline against which to compare the efficacy of all types of interventions. However, such a comparison would only be valid if one could assume that the two groups were identical at the outset. This is unlikely to be the case. It seems plausible that smokers try at first to stop by themselves and will only seek professional help or use anti-smoking medication if they cannot manage to stop on their own. Such comparisons are therefore likely to underestimate the efficacy of interventions.

Predictors of success

Who tries to stop smoking and who is ultimately successful? These are questions which can best be addressed in longitudinal studies of the natural history of smoking in which smokers are assessed before and after their attempts at giving up smoking. One such study followed a young community sample from 1987 to 1994 (Rose *et al.* 1996). A second study involved a smaller sample of adult smokers assessed before and six months after the introduction of a mandated smoking ban at their workplace (Borland *et al.* 1991). A third longitudinal study by Carey *et al.* (1993), for which respondents were recruited on the basis of their intention to stop, only provides information on the predictors of success.

According to stage theories of behaviour change discussed earlier (pp. 65–75), one would expect that the factors which motivate individuals to stop may no longer be helpful in attempts at maintaining abstinence. In line with this assumption, Borland *et al.* (1991) found that the desire to stop smoking was the best predictor of making an attempt, but was unrelated to success. Similarly, the belief that smoking was damaging to their own health was strongly related to attempts to stop but not to success in doing so in the young sample of Rose *et al.* (1996). However, this differential pattern could also be a methodological artefact reflecting reduced variance: if most of the individuals who stop smoking believe that smoking is dangerous, this factor can no longer differentiate between successful and unsuccessful quitters.

It is interesting to note that whereas the fear of the negative health consequences of smoking only motivated individuals to stop smoking but did not appear to help them to maintain abstinence, strongly valuing a healthy lifestyle increased the likelihood of both stopping and abstaining (Rose *et al.* 1996). The differential effect of such apparently similar constructs could be due to the fact that maintaining a healthy lifestyle involves much more than the mere avoidance of illness. Whereas the fear of smoking-related illnesses will have abated once people have stopped, the wish to keep fit and to feel healthy is likely to be a continuing concern which should help individuals not only to maintain abstinence but also to engage in health-enhancing activities such as eating a healthy diet and exercising.

With regard to social support, one has to distinguish between support for stopping and support for continuing to smoke. Experiencing support for stopping from family and friends increased the motivation to stop as well as the success in stopping in the Borland's sample of workers (Borland *et al.* 1991). However, the study of the young adolescents suggests that if social support for stopping is perceived as social pressure, it can become negatively associated with successful cessation (Rose *et al.* 1996). This finding may indicate that behaviour change that can be attributed to external causes by the individual is less likely to be maintained than change attributed to internal causes (Harackiewicz *et al.* 1987). In the course of this study these young individuals moved out of the sphere of influence of their parents who may have exerted the social pressure, and this could also have contributed to this finding. Surprisingly, support for continuing to smoke, such as having close friends who smoke, was no barrier to making attempts to quit. However, it did increase the opportunity for relapse for those who attempted to stop.

Self-efficacy with regard to stopping smoking should be related to both the motivation to stop and the success rate. Smokers who feel that they have no control over their smoking behaviour should be less likely to try to stop than smokers who feel very much in control. Given that their perception of control is somewhat realistic, smoking self-efficacy should also be a predictor of success rate. Support for this last assumption comes from a longitudinal study by Carey *et al.* (1993). These authors reported that smokers who had stopped successfully and were abstinent at the end of the 12-month period had significantly higher smoking self-efficacy at intake than those who had failed to stop.

The extent to which smokers are addicted is also likely to affect success in maintaining abstinence. Cohen *et al.* (1989) found lighter smokers to be approximately twice as likely as heavy smokers to succeed in their cessation attempts. Other studies support this association (e.g. Borland *et al.* 1991; Carey *et al.* 1993). How long people smoked, on the other hand, was unrelated to success in stopping (Carey *et al.* 1993; Rose *et al.* 1996). Educational status was positively associated with motivation to stop as well as to success (Rose *et al.* 1996; Jeffery *et al.* 1997).

Weight concerns have typically been considered as a factor that negatively affects both the decision to give up smoking and the success rate in doing so (Perkins 1993; Meyers *et al.* 1997). And yet, studies of the association of weight concerns and smoking cessation report conflicting results. In two prospective studies of unaided smoking cessation no association was observed between weight concerns and either serious attempts to quit or the likelihood of smoking cessation (French *et al.* 1995; Jeffery *et al.* 1997). In contrast, a study of participants in community-based smoking cessation intervention found that weight-concerned smokers were significantly less likely to be abstinent after 12 months than smokers who were not concerned about their weight (Meyers *et al.* 1997). The reasons for these inconsistencies remain unclear.

One promising way to address the problem of weight concerns in smoking cessation interventions would be to combine smoking treatment with weight gain prevention programmes. However, two early studies which followed this line found that the weight gain programmes included in smoking treatment programmes were not only ineffective in preventing weight gain, but that they also appeared to interfere with the success of the smoking treatment (Hall *et al.* 1992; Pierie *et al.* 1992). One reason for this finding could have been that smokers who seek clinical treatment for their smoking might find it difficult enough to cope with stopping smoking without being distracted by having to pay attention to strategies that prevent weight gain. Although plausible in terms of research on ego depletion (e.g. Baumeister 2002), more recent studies did not support this assumption. A meta-analysis of the findings of 10 randomized controlled trials that compared combined smoking treatment and behavioural weight control to smoking treatment alone for adult smokers found no evidence that adding weight control treatment to behavioural smoking cessation treatment undermined tobacco abstinence (Spring *et al.* 2009). In fact, in the short term (less than three months), participants in the combined treatment were even more successful in stopping smoking than were individuals whose treatment focused on smoking alone. However, after six months the differences between treatments had disappeared. Thus, adding weight control to smoking treatment certainly does no harm. But it does not appear to add any long-term benefits either.

Helping smokers to stop

Treatment strategies to help smokers stop can be divided into pharmacological and psychosocial. The earliest pharmacologic options for smoking cessation consisted of nicotine replacement therapies. More recently two non-nicotine agents have become available (bupropion and varenicline). Psychosocial interventions include clinical therapy, counselling and also mass media health education. Interventions vary with regard to the stage of the stop-smoking process at which they are most effective. Health education and counselling are probably most effective in helping smokers to *decide* to stop. In contrast, nicotine replacement helps to reduce the craving in the early phases of stopping. Clinical therapies try to help smokers who decided to stop throughout the process of stopping including long-term maintenance. Outcome is usually measured with one or both standard criteria, namely that individuals are not smoking around the time when the follow-up measurement is taken (*point prevalence abstinence*) or that they have not smoked since their stop attempt (*continuous abstinence*).

Many clinics in the USA offer intensive smoking cessation programmes for inpatients as well as outpatients. For example, the Nicotine Dependence Center at the famous Mayo Clinic in Rochester, Minnesota has provided treatment services to over 37,000 patients since 1988. In Great Britain, the government has set up comprehensive stop smoking services within the National Health Service (NHS). These services are now available across the NHS in England, providing counselling and support to smokers wanting to quit. Services are provided in group sessions or one to one, depending on local circumstances and clients' preferences. For example, the Maudsley Clinic in south London offers smoking cessation treatment that varies from individual advice to multi-session supportive group programmes comprising seven weekly sessions with optional monthly follow-up to one year.

Pharmacotherapy

Only first-line medication will be considered here, that is medication that is considered to be safe and effective for the treatment of tobacco dependence, except in the presence of contraindications (e.g. pregnancy) or specific populations for which there is insufficient evidence of effectiveness (e.g. light smokers, smokeless tobacco users). In view of the important role of nicotine dependence in smoking, it would seem useful to provide nicotine replacement therapies to abate withdrawal symptoms. Once people have overcome the initial withdrawal symptoms and managed to stop smoking, the nicotine replacement can be gradually tapered off to avoid further withdrawal. The first type of nicotine replacement which became widely available was nicotine chewing gum. Since then, nicotine patches, nasal sprays, inhalers and lozenges have become available (Cummings and Hyland 2005). A review of studies evaluating these commercially available forms of nicotine replacement concluded that these treatments increase quit rates approximately one and half to twofold regardless of clinical setting or use of other treatment (Cummings and Hyland 2005). A combination of long-term use of nicotine patches (more than 14 weeks) and ad lib use of nicotine gum or spray has been shown to nearly double the effectiveness of each of these treatments used separately (USDHHS 2008).

In addition to nicotine replacement, two non-nicotine agents have been effective in the treatment of tobacco dependency. One of these agents, bupropion, was originally developed as an antidepressant. Bupropion is formulated as a 150mg sustained release (SR) tablet to be taken twice daily. The most recent and probably most effective non-nicotine agent recommended as a first-line treatment of tobacco dependence is varenicline.

Cognitive-behaviour therapy

Most clinical approaches to smoking cessation are based on a mixture of behavioural and cognitive-behavioural approaches. The techniques used include classical conditioning (aversion therapy), operant procedures (stimulus control, contingency management), self-management procedures and nicotine 'fading'. Recent work relies on multi-component programmes that combine several of these techniques, with the emphasis on more cognitive therapy techniques and away from aversive and other behavioural techniques (for a review, see USDHHS 2008).

Three kinds of stimuli have been used in *aversion therapies*: electric shock, imaginal stimuli and cigarette smoke itself. *Shock aversion* has been consistently ineffective and the efficacy of imaginal aversion or *covert sensitization* has also been fairly low (Schwartz 1987). In this latter procedure, smokers have first to imagine themselves preparing to smoke and then to experience nausea. As an escape–relief dimension, they then imagine themselves feeling better as they turn away and reject their cigarettes.

Cigarette smoke as an aversive stimulus is used in *rapid smoking*, a clinical procedure in which individuals are instructed to smoke continually, inhaling every six to eight seconds, until tolerance is reached. This results in a nicotine satiation and an irritation of the mucous membrane and throat passages which reduces smoking pleasure. It is expected that this unpleasant experience will be cognitively rehearsed and thus have a long-term effect. A meta-analysis of 19 studies conducted in 2000, which compared the effectiveness of rapid smoking to an untreated control group estimated the relative odds ratio at 2 (USDHHS 2000). That is, compared to the untreated group, approximately twice as many smokers in the treated group became abstinent. In terms of estimated abstinence rates, the treatment will increase the percentage of smokers who quit by nearly 9 per cent over the untreated control group. It is interesting that this method is relatively effective. Because it relies on classical conditioning, it is one of the few techniques likely to influence directly the more automatic reactions reflected by implicit measures. However, because rapid smoking affects the heart–lung system and results in increases in heart rate, carboxyhaemoglobin and blood-nicotine levels, the health of the patients should be carefully assessed before rapid smoking is selected as a treatment procedure (Lichtenstein 1982). It is partly due to the side-effects of this treatment that the clinical practice guidelines on smoking cessation written by a panel of experts for the USDHHS (2008) no longer recommend rapid smoking.

Operant procedures are designed to detect the environmental stimuli that control the smoking response (stimulus control) or to manipulate the consequences of this response (e.g. contingency contracting). Stimulus control techniques are based on the assumption that smoking has become linked to environmental and internal events which trigger the smoking response (e.g. finishing a meal and drinking coffee or alcohol). The effectiveness of traditional stimulus control approaches to smoking cessation has not been impressive (Lichtenstein and Danaher 1975; Schwartz 1987). However, a novel method of reducing stimulus control called 'scheduled smoking' has been found effective in studies conducted by Cinciripini *et al.* (e.g. 1995). All smokers in these studies received behaviour therapy. In addition, smoking schedules and smoking reduction were manipulated in a factorial design during a period of three weeks before the agreed-upon stop date (Cinciripini *et al.* 1995). Scheduled smokers who were only allowed to smoke at specific times of the day were more likely still to be abstinent one year later than smokers who had been allowed to smoke freely before they stopped.

A recent field study which manipulated smokers' control over their smoking shed light on the mechanism responsible for the effectiveness of scheduled smoking (Cately and Grobe 2008). This study used hand-held computers to measure timing of smoking occasions and rewardingness of these occasions for three days. This was followed by a three-day scheduled or uncontrollable smoking phase in which participants were prompted by the hand-held computer to smoke on the same schedule that they had previously recorded. During both phases, smokers had to rate reward from smoking and other subjective responses (e.g. craving, mood) immediately after having finished smoking. During the scheduled or uncontrollable phase, smokers experienced smoking as significantly less rewarding, had less reduction in craving and poorer mood. The authors suggest that the reduction in

TABLE 4.1 Percentage of smokers abstinent after one year

		Smoking reduction	
		Reduced (%)	Non-reduced (%)
Smoking	Yes	44	32
Schedule	No	18	22

Source: Adapted from Cinciripini *et al.* (1995).

reward associated with the loss of control over smoking might be responsible for the effectiveness of scheduled smoking.

It is interesting to note that in the study of Cinciripini *et al.* (1995), smoking schedules were most effective when combined with a planned progressive reduction in smoking frequency (see Table 4.1), but that non-scheduled progressive reductions, where smokers could decide when to smoke the reduced number of cigarettes were least effective. This latter finding is in line with the results of a meta-analysis of 18 studies on monitored nicotine fading, a procedure by which smokers are asked to monitor their daily tar and nicotine intake and try a progressive reduction, which found little evidence that the procedure was effective (USDHHS 1996a).

In *contingency contracting*, smokers agree with some agency (usually the therapist) on a set of rewards/punishments that will be enacted contingent on their behaviour. For example, smokers may pay a sum of money to the therapist and have it returned when they succeed in cutting down. Although there is some evidence that contracting is quite effective until the deposit is returned (Schwartz 1987), a meta-analysis of 22 contingency contracting schemes conducted as part of the Clinical Practice Guidelines of the USDHHS (2000) found no evidence for the long-term effectiveness of the technique. The failure of these contracts to have long-term effects could be due to the fact that individuals who abstain from smoking because they feel bound by a contract attribute their *not* smoking to this agreement. They may therefore be less likely to develop the sense of self-efficacy and feeling of control over their smoking behaviour that is necessary to maintain their abstinence at the end of therapy (Bandura 1986). They might also not be motivated to engage in the kind of negative re-evaluation of smoking that is likely in people who have to justify the stopping to themselves.

Examples of the *cognitive techniques* recommended as efficacious by the Clinical Guidelines of the USDHHS (2008) are general problem-solving skills and social support. The category of general problem-solving and skills training consists of three components: smokers are taught to identify events, internal states or activities that place them at high risk of relapse. Examples are negative affect and stress, being around other smokers, drinking alcohol, experiencing craving, the presence of smoking cues and the availability of cigarettes. Second, smokers are trained to avoid these situations and to develop and practise coping or problem-solving skills which help them to cope with these danger situations. Examples are learning to anticipate and avoid temptation and trigger situations, learning cognitive strategies that will reduce negative moods, learning cognitive and behavioural activities to cope with smoking urges (e.g. distracting attention, changing routines) and changing one's lifestyle to reduce stress and/or exposure to smoking cues. The third component consists of provision of basic information about smoking (e.g. the addictive nature of smoking) and successful quitting. Based on 104 studies, a meta-analysis conducted as part of the Clinical Guideline of the USDHHS (2000) estimated the odds ratio of success with these techniques at 1.5. That is, 50 per cent more smokers will become abstinent in the treatment compared to the control group. Given the low success rate in an untreated control group, this translates into a 5 per cent increase in smokers who reach abstinence. Social support should consist of a supportive environment as part of the treatment (access to counsellors, helpful and accessible clinical staff). Whereas the recommendations of the year 2000 also recommended strategies to increase social support for stopping in the smoker's social environment, this recommendation was dropped in 2008, apparently because of lack of empirical support on efficacy. One suspects that this lack of supportive evidence is more likely to be due to a failure of therapy to have an impact on the social network of smokers (i.e. reduction in the number of friends who smoke) rather than due to social support for stopping being ineffective.

Community interventions for smoking cessation

In spite of the substantial decline in cigarette smoking observed in the years after the US Surgeon General's report which received wide coverage in the mass media, one cannot be confident that this decrease in rates was caused by this communication, rather than some other reason. To demonstrate the effectiveness of mass communication in inducing smoking cessation, one needs experimental or quasi-experimental *intervention* studies, in which one group of people is exposed to the communication while an otherwise comparable group is not. If it can be shown that the experimental group has an advantage in cessation rates over the control group, this difference can be attributed to the communication.

Probably the most successful community intervention was achieved in the North Karelia project described in the preceding chapter (e.g. Puska *et al.* 1985). As part of this project, an intensive educational campaign was implemented for the reduction of cigarette smoking. The neighbouring province of Kuopio was selected as a control group not exposed to the campaign. Self-reported numbers of cigarettes smoked per day fell by more than one-third among the men in North Karelia, compared to only a 10 per cent reduction among men in the control community. The campaign had no effect on smoking rates of women. Because self-reports of smoking rates could be distorted by social desirability effects, it is encouraging that a 24 per cent decline in cardiovascular deaths among men was observed in North Karelia as compared with a 12 per cent decline in other parts of the country (Puska *et al.* 1985). Similar effects on smoking reduction have been observed in two community studies conducted in Australia (Egger *et al.* 1983) and Switzerland (Autorengruppe Nationales Forschungsprogramm 1984). On the basis of these studies, the US Surgeon General (USDHHS 1984) concluded that the absolute reduction in smoking prevalence in intervention sites was about 12 per cent greater than the reduction in comparison communities.

Later community studies conducted in the USA have reported more moderate effects (e.g. Farquhar et al. 1990), or no effect at all (e.g. Carleton et al. 1995). Typical of these modest effects are the findings of the COMMIT study, the largest community trial for smoking intervention to date, launched in 1989 (COMMIT Research Group 1995). In this study one of each of 11 matched community pairs was randomly assigned to the intervention. The four-year community-based intervention used methods similar to those of earlier community trials (e.g. Farquhar et al. 1990) to encourage smokers, particularly heavy smokers, to achieve and maintain abstention. It was therefore disappointing that the intervention had no effect on heavy smokers (those who smoked more than 25 cigarettes per day). However, for the group of light-to-moderate smokers a small but significant difference emerged. The proportion of light-to-moderate smokers who stopped in the intervention communities (30.6 per cent) was 3 per cent higher than the proportion of smokers who stopped in the control communities (27.5 per cent).

One can only speculate about the reasons for this apparent reduction in the impact of more recent interventions. A likely reason is the vast improvement in knowledge about the health-impairing nature of smoking that occurred during the previous four decades. Community interventions still rely heavily on the dissemination of information about the deleterious consequences of smoking and thus have little impact on the large proportion of smokers who are well aware of the damage they are doing to their health. These smokers need help to stop and this help is less easily provided in community settings. However, the fact that the impact of health education could not be demonstrated in these community studies should not be taken as evidence that health education is no longer important. Data from the 1985 National Health Interview Survey (Kenkel 1991) demonstrate that while smoking knowledge is fairly widespread, the remaining differences in knowledge are still significantly related to smoking.

Web-based interventions

These interventions have the potential to reach a large percentage of the smoking population. More than 60 per cent of individuals in Great Britain and 70 per cent in the United States use the internet (Strecher et al. 2005). Furthermore, there is evidence from a survey conducted in 2002 that 6 per cent of US internet users search the web for smoking cessation information. However, while the reach of internet programmes is large, one can doubt that merely sending people information about the dangers of smoking and informing them of ways to quit would be effective. A meta-analysis conducted as part of the Clinical Guideline Report in 2000 concluded that self-help manuals about smoking cessation do not increase the cessation rates relative to no self-help materials and the same seems to be true for video- and audiotapes when used alone (USDHHS 2000). However, that web-based interventions that go beyond the provision of self-help booklets can be effective has been demonstrated in a recent meta-analysis that reported a small effect of such interventions (Rooke *et al.* 2010).

In addition to reaching a large number of people, another advantage of the web is that it can be interactive. This advantage can be used in interventions by tailoring a persuasive communication on the basis of the responses of a questionnaire filled in by respondents earlier. This procedure was used by Strecher *et al.* (2005), who had 3971 participants respond to an enrolment questionnaire that asked about smoking history, motives for quitting, expected difficulties in quitting and situations that were expected to present challenges. In the intervention condition, this information was used to tailor a cessation guide and three sequential tailored newsletters. The content of the tailored information was based on the behavioural and cognitive therapy principles described earlier, including stimulus control, self-efficacy enhancement and suggestions for coping. In addition, participants were encouraged to use nicotine replacement therapy. This tailoring was achieved by a computer program. Participants in the control group received similar information, the main difference being that this information was not tailored. (A second difference, however, was that these participants also did not receive three follow-up newsletters.) Of the 3971 participants enrolled in the study, 470 individuals never logged on to the website. The outcome measures consisted of questionnaires after 6 and 10 weeks. After 6 weeks continuous abstinence was defined as not smoking for the previous 28 days and after 12 weeks as at least 10 weeks of abstinence. Results indicated that the tailored version was significantly more effective than the untailored version. In the tailored version 29 per cent of participants who had logged on were abstinent after 6 weeks and 22.8 per cent after 12 weeks, compared to 23.9 per cent and 18.1 per cent in the non-tailored control condition (odds ratios: 1.30 and 1.34). The effect sizes of the internet intervention are comparable to those found in comparisons of tailored vs. untailored printed materials. A meta-analytic comparison of the effectiveness of tailored vs. non-tailored printed self-help smoking material based on 10 studies yielded an average odds ratio of 1.36 (Lancaster and Stead 2002).

Interventions at the worksite

These interventions make use of the fact that the place of work is an excellent setting for health promotion programmes because large numbers of people can be reached on a regular basis. Therefore, many large firms have introduced health promotion programmes. A meta-analysis of 19 studies reported abstinence rates at six months of 16.7 per cent in the intervention and 8.5 per cent in the control condition (odds ratio: 2.03; Smedslund *et al.* 2004). At 12 months, the difference had narrowed (odds ratio: 1.56) and at more than 12 months it was no longer significant. However, at a time when most smokers are well aware of the health consequences of smoking and are also likely to have failed already in attempts to stop smoking, merely providing participants with information about health consequences no longer appears to be sufficient (e.g. Glasgow *et al.* 1995, 1997; Sorensen *et al.* 1996).

Hotlines and helplines

This is another setting available to smokers who want to stop. In the USA all states run some type of free telephone-based programme, such as the American Cancer Society's Quitline tobacco cessation programme that links callers with trained counsellors who can help plan methods to stop smoking that fit each person's unique smoking pattern. A meta-analysis of nine studies comparing Quitline counselling to minimal or no counselling or self-help found that such hotlines significantly increased abstinence rates (USDHHS 2008).

Physician's advice

This is probably the most cost-effective anti-smoking intervention. The Clinical Guidelines of the USDHHS (2008) recommend that all physicians should strongly advise every patient who smokes to quit. Based on 10 studies, the USDHHS (1996a) estimates the odds ratio for physician's advice to stop, which took no more than three minutes of the physician's time, at 1.3. A more recent meta-analyses based on 41 studies conducted between 1972 and 2007 arrived at a somewhat higher odds ratio of 1.66 (Stead et al. 2008).

It is interesting that the advice to stop smoking appears to have much greater impact when given by physicians than when provided as part of a community intervention. This is probably due to the fact that physicians are health experts and that the advice is personalized. Because individuals who visit their physician often seek remedy for some health problem, they may also be in a particularly receptive mood on such occasions. Thus, although the effects of smoking interventions in medical practice are modest, their advantage is that they are cost-effective and reach smokers who might not be reached by any other programme.

Primary prevention

School-based health education

In view of the serious difficulties smokers experience when they try to stop smoking, school-based anti-smoking programmes aimed at preventing young adolescents from starting the habit would appear most promising. After all, teenagers are most at risk of starting to smoke. A survey in the USA indicated that the probability of starting to smoke at a given age for individuals who have not started previously (the hazard rate of starting smoking) increases to a peak of 15 per cent at age 19, then declines quickly to 2 per cent at age 24 (Douglas and Hariharan 1993 – see Figure 4.1). Furthermore, a longitudinal study of the natural history of cigarette smoking by Chassin et al. (1990) suggested that even infrequent experimentation in adolescence was associated with a substantial increase in the probability that the individual would smoke as an adult. Regular adolescent smoking appeared to raise the risk of adult smoking by a factor of 16 compared to non-smoking adolescents. Furthermore, there was a positive linear relationship between the grade in which adolescents began to smoke and adult smoking. These findings underline the importance of primary prevention programmes directed at adolescent populations.

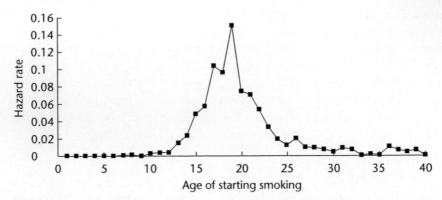

FIGURE 4.1 The probability of starting to smoke at any given age (US sample)
Source: Douglas and Hariharan (1994)

Unfortunately, most of the early programmes which were conducted in health education courses and emphasized the long-term health risks of smoking were ineffective in persuading children not to smoke. The likely reason for this failure is that children are already familiar with the health consequences of smoking and in any case are not at that age yet very much concerned about health issues. The programmes developed later by Evans and his collaborators therefore avoided the health and threat-oriented approach (e.g. Evans *et al.* 1978). Instead, they emphasized the socially undesirable aspects of smoking to motivate individuals not to smoke (e.g. cigarettes smell bad). They also included the development of specific action plans and social skills to resist pressures to try cigarettes. Thus, individuals were trained in skills needed to reject offers of cigarettes without alienating peers.

In a review of four generations of school-based anti-smoking studies, only moderate reductions in the number of students who start smoking have been found. Based on a meta-analysis of 90 studies published from 1974 to 1991, Rooney and Murray (1996) estimated that on average 5 to 8 per cent of students who might otherwise have started to smoke were prevented from doing so. Similar intervention effects have been reported in the Netherlands (Dijkstra *et al.* 1992). Although most of these programmes included information about the health consequences of smoking, they mainly focused on providing training, modelling, rehearsal and reinforcement of techniques to resist social pressure to smoke, and to resist smoking messages in advertisements and the media.

Given the serious health consequences of smoking and the difficulty smokers have in stopping once they have become addicted, interventions which reduce the number of young people who start the habit by 5 per cent would still be regarded as quite effective. However, most of these studies only assessed *short-term* effects of interventions. A systematic review of school-based randomized controlled trials of smoking prevention with follow-up evaluation to age 18 (and at least one year after intervention ended) that had current smoking prevalence as primary outcome found little to no evidence of long-term effectiveness (Wiehe *et al.* 2005). Of the eight studies (published between 1989 and 2001) included in this review only one reported statistically significant results, suggesting that school-based intervention effects resulted in decreased monthly smoking prevalence at age 18 (Botvin *et al.* 1995). And this latter study has been criticized for using a one-tailed analysis and for failing to account for the multiplicity of outcome variables that were measured (Glantz and Mandel 2005). A more recent meta-analytic review of studies published between 2001 and 2006 also concluded that there was 'no evidence for the long-term effectiveness of school-based interventions' (Müller-Riemenschneider *et al.* 2008: 302).

It is interesting to speculate why school-based programmes appear to have so little impact in the long run. One contributory factor could be that there is now so much information on social pressures and the negative health effects of smoking that school-based programmes cannot not add a great deal to the information, advice and training received by adolescents in the control conditions. Another possibility is that schools and teachers are not the optimal sources for health education. While adolescents might be willing to accept information from teachers about all areas of knowledge taught in schools, they might be less willing to take advice on issues that go beyond these topics and could be perceived as interfering with their social lives.

Legal and economic measures

A second strategy of primary prevention could involve further restrictions in the sales of cigarettes (e.g. stricter age limits) as well as increases in taxation. On average, teenagers have less disposable income than adults and are therefore more likely to be deterred from smoking by marked increases in the price of cigarettes, particularly if they have not yet started the habit or are still in a period of experimentation. A 10 per cent increase in price has been estimated to result in a 7 to 14 per cent reduction in demand of adolescents, but only a 3 to 5 per cent reduction in adults (Brownson *et al.* 2006).

Recent economic models distinguish addictive consumption from other consumption by recognizing that for addictive goods such as cigarettes or heroin, current consumption depends on past consumption. Such models predict that the impact of price increases would increase over time (e.g. Becker *et al.* 1994). Heavy smokers are likely to continue smoking heavily and will not respond readily to increases in price. However, they might be able to reduce their smoking slowly in response to price increases. Furthermore, price increases will also reduce the probability of adolescents picking up the habit. The combined impact of such effects should result in a reduction in smoking in the long run.

Smoking restrictions at the workplace have not only succeeded in reducing exposure to second-hand smoke for non-smokers, they have also been effective in influencing smokers. Smokers who are employed at workplaces where smoking is banned are likely to consume fewer cigarettes per day, are more likely to consider stopping and also are more successful in stopping attempts than are smokers in workplaces with weaker policies (Brownson *et al.* 2002).

These analyses suggest that legal and economic measures can be effective means of reducing consumption among current smokers as well as smoking initiation. Tax increases would seem a promising strategy to prevent young people from being recruited into smoking, particularly if these are combined with the various educational programmes. Another promising strategy would be restrictions on tobacco advertising. However, there has been little evidence that partial restriction of advertising has any effect on youth or adult smoking. However, there is some evidence that countries that adopt comprehensive advertising bans can expect substantial reduction in tobacco use (Brownson *et al.* 2006).

Conclusions

Smoking has been identified as the single most important source of preventable morbidity and mortality and nowadays this fact is accepted by smokers and non-smokers alike. Most smokers admit that they would like to stop. However, only about 13 per cent of smokers who try to stop by themselves manage to be abstinent a year later, and this rate is further reduced if one takes continuous abstinence as the criterion. Despite this, the majority of smokers who stop smoking do so without professional help. Those smokers who seek therapy are likely to be the most problematic cases.

With the war against smoking having been waged continuously since the mid-1960s, most smokers in western industrialized nations are now aware of the negative health consequences associated with smoking. This may be the reason why community or worksite interventions which rely mainly on informing smokers about health consequences are less and less likely to have a measurable impact. However, more intensive interventions which provide social support and skill training are still effective. Furthermore, nicotine replacement therapies have also been demonstrated to be effective even when not accompanied by therapy.

Giving up a long-established habit like smoking is difficult. The most promising strategy for smoking prevention therefore involves inducing people not to start smoking. Because school-based programmes do not appear to be effective in the long term, other approaches to influence adolescents are needed. It could be that schools are not the most optimal agents for health change and that adolescents might be more receptive if approached by health care providers (e.g. Fidler and Lambert 2001; Hollis *et al.* 2005). Additionally, measures which increase the price and reduce the availability of tobacco products have also been shown to be effective. These measures should be complemented by a restriction on tobacco advertising. Finally, the fact that the large educational components of community anti-smoking interventions do not appear to have a demonstrable impact should not be taken as evidence that health education is no longer important. It merely demonstrates that education is not effective for people who are already well informed. However, to keep children and young people well informed of the dangers of smoking, the war against smoking has to be continued.

Alcohol and alcohol abuse

Alcohol and health

There is widespread consensus among health professionals that the inappropriate or excessive use of alcohol leads to an increased risk of morbidity and mortality (Ashley and Rankin 1988; Hurley and Horowitz 1990; Mokdad *et al.* 2004). Mokdad *et al.* (2004) estimated for the year 2000 that 85,000 deaths in the USA could be attributed to alcohol consumption. In recognition of these health risks, any alcoholic beverage that is bottled for sale in the USA now has to carry the following health warning:

> Government Warning: According to the Surgeon General, women should not drink alcoholic beverages during pregnancy because of the risk of birth defects. Consumption of alcoholic beverages impairs your ability to drive a car or operate machinery, and may cause health problems.

However, although not undisputed (e.g. Shaper *et al.* 1988), there is also evidence that the relationship between alcohol consumption and mortality is J-shaped, with light drinkers having a longer life expectancy than abstainers, mainly due to a reduction in the risk of CHD and stroke (Rehm *et al.* 2001; Corrao *et al.* 2004; Klatsky and Udaltsova 2007). As far as pregnant women are concerned, there is increasing evidence suggesting that they should totally refrain from alcohol consumption.

Morbidity and mortality

With a curvilinear relationship between levels of alcohol consumption and morbidity and mortality, the criteria according to which light, moderate and heavy consumption levels are defined becomes important. Unfortunately, different studies use different criteria (e.g. Hurley and Horowitz 1990; Williams and DeBakey 1992; Klatsky and Udaltsova 2007). One problem is that studies which define consumption levels in terms of number of drinks per day often fail to state clearly whether they are referring to the US standardized measure containing 15g of pure alcohol (i.e. ethanol). However, even if authors are clear about the size of the units they are referring to, there is a lack of consensus about the level of consumption that should be considered heavy drinking. Some authors appear to define heavier drinking as consumption of two or more standard drinks (i.e. more than 28.34g of pure alcohol per day; see Hurley and Horowitz 1990); others use three standard drinks (45g) as the criterion for heavy drinking (e.g. Klatsky and Udaltsova 2007). Finally, Corrao *et al.* (2004), a European team, define light drinking as 25g per day, moderate drinking as 50g per day and heavy drinking as 100g per day. Thus, a moderate drinker according to Corrao *et al.* would be considered a heavy drinker according to Klatsky and Udaltsova (2007).

Based on 156 studies (116,702 participants), a meta-analysis of the association between alcohol consumption and the risk of diseases conducted by Corrao *et al.* (2004) reported a direct relationship between level of alcohol consumption and various cancers (oral cavity and pharynx, oesophagus, larynx, breast, colon, rectum, liver). With regard to non-neoplastic conditions, strong direct trends in risk were found for liver cirrhosis, chronic pancreatitis and injuries and violence, with liver cirrhosis associated with the greatest risk. Surprisingly, significant risk increases were already observed for all these conditions at the lowest dose of alcohol considered (25g/day, corresponding to approximately two drinks). For CHD the association was curvilinear, with significant protective effects being observed up to 72g/day of alcohol, while an increased risk was obtained starting from 89g/day. This curvilinear relationship between levels of alcohol consumption and health also emerges in studies of mortality, where light to moderate drinking has a protective effect, which is particularly marked for death due to CHD (e.g. Rehm *et al.* 2001; Klatsky and Udalltsova 2007). However, occasional heavy drinking substantially increases the mortality risk even for individuals who on average are very light drinkers (Rehm *et al.* 2001).

In the USA about 3.5 per cent of recorded deaths are officially attributed to causes directly linked to alcohol (Mokdad *et al.* 2004). However, some epidemiologists suspect that there is a substantial under-reporting of alcohol-related conditions, particularly as contributing causes of death, and that the actual number is much higher (Hurley and Horowitz 1990). One strategy to trace the relationship between mortality and excess alcohol consumption has been to demonstrate that the mortality rate of heavy drinkers for a given cause is in excess of that for moderate drinkers or abstainers. However, in order to attribute a difference in mortality between these groups to the difference in alcohol consumption, one has to be certain that differential consumption was the only risk factor in which the two groups differ. This assumption is often unfounded, because people who are heavy drinkers or alcoholics usually engage in other habits that are deleterious to their health. For example, a review of studies on the relationship between alcoholism and smoking found that an average of 90 per cent of men and women in the alcoholic groups were smokers, a proportion that is much higher than that in the general population (Istvan and Matarazzo 1984). In interpreting findings that heavy drinkers suffer from an excess mortality from certain forms of cancer, one has therefore to separate the impact of alcohol from that of smoking. For example, the excess in the development of cancer of the oral cavity, pharynx, larynx and oesophagus among heavy drinkers could be attributed to the combined effects of both alcohol consumption and smoking (Corrao *et al.* 2004).

Alcohol and liver cirrhosis
A second strategy for investigating the health risk of alcohol abuse has been to focus on mortality from specific causes that are likely to be related to excess alcohol consumption. Not surprisingly, the most clear-cut evidence comes from mortality due to cirrhosis of the liver. Cirrhosis is a disorder of the liver in which

healthy liver tissue has been damaged and replaced by fibrous scar tissue. In 2001 cirrhosis of the liver was the tenth leading cause of death in the USA for men and the eleventh leading cause for women, killing about 27,000 people each year (Anderson and Smith 2003). The meta-analysis of Corrao et al. (2004) estimated that heavy drinking results in a relative risk of 26.52 over non-drinkers. This means that heavy drinkers are more than 26 times more likely to develop liver cirrhosis than are light drinkers.

A longitudinal analysis of the association of per capita alcohol consumption and liver cirrhosis deaths in 14 European countries for the period from 1960 to 1995 found a substantial association both between and within countries (Ramstedt 2001). In general, countries with a high level of per capita consumption also have a high level of liver cirrhosis deaths among both men and women. According to the cross-national correlation, a 1-litre increase in per capita consumption is associated with an 18 per cent higher cirrhosis mortality rate among men and a 14 per cent higher mortality rate among women. The pooled effects for all 14 countries over time, though somewhat weaker, were still substantial: a 1-litre increase in per capita consumption resulted in a 14 per cent increase in cirrhosis deaths for men and a 8 per cent increase for women.

There is also evidence that imposed restrictions on alcohol consumption are accompanied by a drop in death due to liver cirrhosis (Ledermann 1964). For example, in Paris there was a sharp drop in cirrhosis death rates coincidental with the two world wars. The data for World War II are particularly instructive, because cirrhosis deaths dropped from 35 in 1941 to a low of 6 in 1945 and 1946. They began to rise again in 1948, the year when wine rationing was discontinued. Obviously, there were other factors present during this period that are likely to have at least contributed to the drop in liver cirrhosis mortality.

Alcohol and traffic deaths
Alcohol has also been implicated in death from injuries. According to some estimates, a third to a half of adult Americans involved in accidents, crimes and suicides had been drinking alcohol prior to the event (Hurley and Horowitz 1990). In 1982 the US National Highway Transportation Safety Administration estimated that 57 per cent of all fatal car crashes were alcohol-related and even though the estimated proportion had dropped substantially by 1996, it was still high at 41 per cent (DeJong and Hingson 1998). However, from 1982 to 2004 alcohol-related traffic crash death rates in the USA declined by 50 per cent even though traffic fatalities that did not involve alcohol increased by 15 per cent over the same period (Bloss 2006).

The fact that a high percentage of persons causing accidents were under the influence of alcohol is suggestive, but it is not sufficient to infer that alcohol increases the risk of accidents. For example, the finding that 52 per cent of drivers killed in car accidents in New York between the years 1974 and 1975 had previously consumed alcohol (Haberman and Baden 1978) is difficult to interpret unless one knows the percentage of drivers of the same age and sex and with the same amount of alcohol at the same time and weekday who were *not* involved in accidents. If 52 per cent of those drivers had also consumed alcohol, there would be no case to argue that alcohol consumption increases the risk of traffic accidents.

Evidence from studies that employed adequate control groups suggests that alcohol consumption significantly increases the risk of injuries from all types of accident. In a study of drivers who were killed in car accidents in New York City, McCarroll and Haddon (1962) found that 50 per cent of these drivers had a blood alcohol concentration (BAC) at or above the 0.10 per cent level (i.e. were fairly intoxicated), as compared to less than 5 per cent of drivers tested at the site of the accident a few weeks later. These tests were conducted on the same day of the week and at the same time of day at which the accident had occurred, with drivers who moved in the same direction.

More indirect evidence comes from studies that demonstrate that the involvement of alcohol varies with type and severity of accident as well as the time of day when these accidents occurred. For example, based on an analysis of 500,961 accidents with casualties that involved less than three vehicles recorded in France between 1995 and 1999, Figure 4.2 presents the number of single-vehicle accidents with positive blood alcohol tests by number of fatalities per accident and time of day (Reynaud *et al.* 2002). Single-vehicle accidents are particularly suspicious, because with no other car involved there is a high probability of driver error. As we can see, alcohol involvement increased with accidents that occurred at night time, particularly at the weekend, and it also increased with increasing number of fatalities.

Further indirect evidence comes from studies that relate changes in the per capita consumption of pure alcohol in a given country to changes in traffic fatalities. A time series analysis conducted on data from the USA for the period from 1950 to 2002 estimated that a 1-litre increase in per capita consumption was associated with an increase of four male car accident fatalities per 100,000 inhabitants (Ramstedt 2008). With 5.7 deaths, the association was strongest for younger men in the age group 15 to 34 years. For women the overall relationship was not significant.

Foetal alcohol syndrome

Aristotle was probably the first to observe that drunken women often bore children who were feeble-minded. The advice of the US Surgeon General that women should not drink alcohol during pregnancy is based on more recent observations suggesting that prenatal exposure to alcohol is associated with a distinct pattern of birth defects that have been termed 'foetal alcohol syndrome' (FAS). A number of physical malformations have been reported, for example, head circumference and nose are smaller, the nasal bridge is lower and there is a growth deficiency. However, the most serious aspect of FAS is mental retardation. The incidence of FAS is estimated at .097 cases per 1000 live births in the general obstetric population and 4.3 per cent among heavy drinkers (Abel 1995). The general incidence is more than 20 times higher in the USA (1.95 per 1000) than in Europe (Abel 1995). The incidence is also much higher in individuals from lower socio-economic backgrounds.

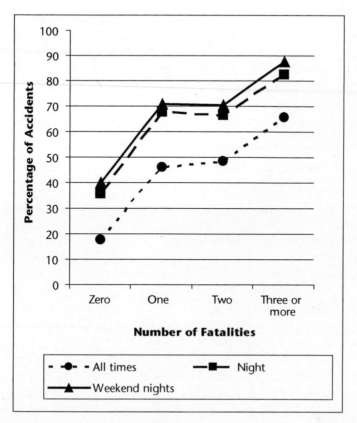

FIGURE 4.2 The involvement of alcohol in single-vehicle accidents by number of fatalities and time of day

Although the description of FAS is non-controversial, its causes, and particularly the level of alcohol consumption during pregnancy that is considered safe, are highly disputed. Current estimates place the foetus at risk if maternal drinking during pregnancy is six glasses of wine per day (450ml of wine or approximately 60ml of absolute alcohol) (Abel 1980). However, the frequency of alcohol-related birth defects is much lower than the frequency of abusive drinking among pregnant women (Hurley and Horowitz 1990). This suggests that other factors may modify the impact of alcohol on prenatal development. Women who drink excessively during pregnancy are also likely to do a number of other things that are unhealthy to the foetus, such as smoking, not eating properly and taking drugs. For example, nutritional deficiencies during pregnancy may be responsible for the low birth weight of children born with FAS. One extensive study of factors which increase the risk of FAS for women who abuse alcohol during pregnancy has identified four variables, namely number of previous births, history of alcohol problems, greater proportion of drinking days and race (Sokol et al. 1986). However, even though being of African American or Native American descent has been found to be associated with an increase in the risk of FAS in the USA (Abel 1995), studies around the globe have shown that no racial group is immune. Furthermore, FAS represents only the most severe type of foetal damage that can be produced by prenatal alcohol exposure. Lower levels of maternal drinking also have measurable effects on the foetus (Hurley and Horowitz 1990). It is therefore advisable for pregnant women to abstain from alcohol consumption during pregnancy and probably also during breastfeeding.

Behavioural and cognitive consequences of alcohol consumption

According to popular belief, alcohol consumption (or more precisely alcohol intoxication) impairs people's motor and cognitive performance and also reduces social inhibitions. All of this is true. However, while popular belief would attribute these effects to the pharmacological properties of alcohol, there is evidence that they are to some extent due to non-pharmacological factors. *Alcohol outcome expectancy theory* has been suggested to account for non-pharmacological effects of alcohol (e.g. Goldman *et al.* 1987; Jones *et al.* 2001).

According to alcohol outcome expectancy theory (Goldman *et al.* 1987; Jones *et al.* 2001), people have formed beliefs about the effects of drinking alcohol and these beliefs do not only influence their drinking behaviour (as discussed later), they also act as self-fulfilling hypotheses, bringing about the consequences that are being expected. Studies of alcohol outcome expectancies have found that people believe that alcohol relaxes them, makes them feel better and enhances their social, physical and sexual pleasure (e.g. Brown *et al.* 1980; George *et al.* 1995).

In the normal drinking situation pharmacological and outcome expectancy effects are confounded. People who drink alcohol usually know that they do. Therefore researchers had to develop balanced placebo designs to separate the pharmacological effects of alcohol from outcome expectancy effects. In these designs the content of drinks (alcohol, no alcohol) and people's beliefs about the content of these drinks (alcohol, no alcohol) are manipulated factorially: people are given a drink (e.g. orange juice), which either contains or does not contain alcohol (e.g. vodka). Cross-cutting this manipulation they are either told that their drink does or does not contain alcohol. Thus, in the condition where people drink an alcoholic drink but think they do not, the pharmacological effects of alcohol should emerge (unmitigated by expectations). In contrast, in the condition where people drink pure orange juice but think it contains alcohol, the effect of expectations should emerge (unmitigated by the pharmacological effects of alcohol).

An early meta-analysis of these balanced placebo studies suggested that the impact of alcohol on memory and motor performance was mainly due to the pharmacological effects of alcohol, whereas the impact of alcohol on sexual arousal was mainly due to people's expectations (Hull and Bond 1986). However, later research revealed that even non-social behaviours were influenced by expectancies (Fillmore and Vogel-Sprott 1995; Fillmore *et al.* 1998). These studies further demonstrated that expectancy effects were stronger the more individuals believed that alcohol would impair their performance (Fillmore and Vogel-Sprott 1995; Fillmore et al. 1998). Although the way such expectations influence cognitive or motor performance is not well understood, studies of the influence of stereotypes on motor (Bargh et al. 1996) and cognitive performance (Dijksterhuis and van Knippenberg 1998) have demonstrated similar effects. Bargh et al. (1996) demonstrated that participants who had been primed with the stereotype of 'the elderly' walked more slowly down a corridor leading away from the experiment and Dijksterhuis and van Knippenberg (1998) demonstrated that participants primed with the stereotype of 'professor' performed better on a trivial pursuit task than those primed with the stereotype of 'secretary'.

If alcohol expectations can even influence people's performance on cognitive and motor tasks, it is hardly surprising if they can also modify social behaviour. The case of sexual behaviour is particularly interesting in this context, because unlike cognitive and motor performance, where the pharmacological and expectancy effects operate in the same direction (i.e. impairment), with sexual behaviour pharmacological and expectancy effects work in opposite directions. While men expect that alcohol makes them sexually more responsive, studies of male sexual response reveal that increasing alcohol doses are related to a decrease in penile tumescence. And yet, when alcohol and expectancy effects are pitted against each other in studies using the balanced placebo design, the expectation to drink alcohol results in increased tumescence and increased arousal even in the cell where the drink actually contains alcohol, at least as long as the alcohol dose was not large enough to counteract the effect of expectations (Goldman et al. 1987).

Two studies by Friedman et al. (2005) examined the processes that underlie these expectancy effects. Male participants in these studies, who were subliminally primed with either alcohol or non alcohol-related words, were shown photographs of young women and had to rate either their attractiveness or their intelligence. Results indicated that males primed with alcohol words rated the women more attractive than men who had been primed with non-alcohol words. The effects were stronger the more these men believed that alcohol would increase their sexual desire.

However, alcohol-fuelled expectations may not be the only explanation for the positive association between the use of alcohol and having sex that has so frequently been reported. Steele and colleagues (e.g. Steele and Josephs 1990) have suggested an alternative explanation, based on the fact that consumption of alcohol decreases cognitive capacity (i.e. working memory) and thereby limits the amount of information to which one can attend. As a consequence, intoxicated individuals are particularly impaired when cues simultaneously activate and inhibit behaviour. This will be problematic in situations that involve response competition between two responses, one of which is dominant in the sense that there is an essentially automatic inclination to select that response option over another. Examples of dominant responses are those that are habitual or impulsive.

As we discussed earlier (Chapter 2), self-control dilemmas involve conflicts between the impulse to go for immediate gratification (e.g. tasty food, sexual pleasure) and some higher-order goal or personal standard (e.g. dieting, staying faithful). By impairing working memory and thus reducing the ability to pay attention to any but the most salient aspects of a situation, alcohol makes it more difficult for the individual to override such impulses. This 'alcohol myopia' will prevent individuals who deliberate under alcohol influence about potential courses of action from considering the more subtle or remote consequences of their alternatives. As a result, the impact of the most salient immediate aspects of experience on emotions and behaviour will increase, whereas the effect of the more remote and subtle aspects will decrease.

MacDonald *et al.* (2000) tested alcohol myopia theory with regard to the decision to have sexual intercourse without using condoms. There is a great deal of evidence from survey data that alcohol use is a risk factor for unplanned and unsafe sexual intercourse. For example, a representative survey of students in Canada conducted in 1998 found that students were more likely to engage in unplanned and often unsafe sexual intercourse when under the influence of alcohol. However, quite apart from the fact that alcohol inebriation might be used as an excuse rather than being causal, such questionnaire studies do not allow us to differentiate between different psychological explanations for the disinhibiting effect of alcohol.

MacDonald *et al.* (2000) argued that in a sexual situation, sexual arousal acts as a salient cue, which dominates the perception of individuals under alcohol myopia. Whereas individuals who are not under the influence of alcohol would be able to also consider the likely negative consequences of unsafe sex, alcohol myopic individuals would be unduly affected by the salient cue and disregard other cues. To test this hypothesis, male participants, who had either been given no drink, an alcoholic drink or a placebo drink, watched a sexually arousing film of a couple engaging in heavy petting who then discovered that they had no condom available. Participants were asked whether they would engage in sex without condoms, if they were in the situation shown in the film. After indicating their intention participants had to list the thoughts that influenced their decision. They were then divided into two groups on the basis of their reported sexual arousal. In support of hypotheses, the intentions of the alcohol group did not differ for participants who reported low arousal. In contrast, highly aroused participants were more likely to intend to have sex without condoms, when they had drunk alcohol rather than a non-alcoholic drink (placebo) or no drink at all. Furthermore, the sexually aroused participants listed more thoughts in favour of having sex without condoms if they had drunk alcohol than without alcohol. Finally, controlling for these thoughts eliminated the impact of the interaction between alcohol and sexual arousal on intention.

The application of alcohol myopia theory to sexual behaviour is an example of the interaction of the physiological and non-physiological effects of alcohol. By impairing the individual's working memory capacity, the pharmacological effects of alcohol reduce the individual's capacity to control the impulsive reaction to go for pleasure even if this behaviour could have very deleterious consequences in the long run. The fact that alcohol outcome expectations made the sexual option even more attractive increased the dominance of the impulsive response.

Self-control dilemmas are not the only dilemmas affected by alcohol consumption. In an earlier study, MacDonald *et al.* (1995) applied alcohol myopia theory to the factors which affect decisions to drive under the influence of alcohol. When people are deciding whether to drink and drive, they are likely to be confronted with inhibiting cues which discourage them from drinking and driving and instigating cues that encourage this behaviour. Inhibiting cues are the knowledge that one might be involved in an accident or caught by the police, whereas instigating cues may include the fact that one is tired, does not want to leave one's car, or that public transport is very cumbersome. Whereas a sober person is able to weigh all these pros and cons in arriving at a decision, an intoxicated person might be disproportionately influenced by the most salient cues, such as that one is tired, and that using the train would take hours.

MacDonald *et al.* (1995) reasoned that intoxicated individuals might decide to drive in situations in which cues that tend to instigate driving are more salient than cues which normally inhibit driving under the influence. They tested this hypothesis in a series of laboratory and field studies in which individuals who were either intoxicated or sober were asked questions about drinking and driving. For half the respondents, these questions were straightforward: they were simply asked whether they would drive after having consumed alcohol. For the other half, the questions were formulated in a conditional way so that an impelling reason to drive was made salient. Thus, half of the respondents were merely asked whether they would drink and drive the next time they were out at a party, whereas the other half were asked whether they would drink and drive if they were out at a party and 'only had a short distance to drive home', or 'had promised their friends that they would drive'. In line with predictions derived from alcohol myopia theory, respondents who had ingested alcohol before responding to the questionnaire were equally (or even more) negative about drinking and driving than sober individuals when the questions were unconditional, but much less negative when the questions were formulated in a conditional way. These effects occurred even though intoxicated individuals realistically perceived their ability to drive as rather poor.

Hazardous consumption levels and alcoholism

What level of consumption is hazardous to the health of men or non-pregnant women? This is largely a matter of conjecture and as we have seen definitions of heavy drinking vary widely, ranging from 30g of pure alcohol per day (e.g. Hurley and Horowitz 1990) to 100g per day (Corrao *et al.* 2004). It should be noted that three to four glasses of wine per day already constitute heavy drinking according to the stricter definitions.

Approaching the problem from the standpoint of the lower limit of consumption of clinical alcoholics, Schmidt and de Lint (1970) found that the reported consumption of 96 per cent of the alcoholics in their sample was a daily intake at or above 150ml of pure alcohol, the quantity of alcohol contained in 1 litre of average strength red wine. There is reason to doubt the accuracy of such self-reports, however, because representative surveys done in the USA, Finland and Canada on self-reported consumption account for only 40 to 50 per cent of total alcohol sales when projected to the whole population (Furst 1983).

However, even if accurate, measures of the quantity of drinking are of little help in diagnosing alcoholism. As Vaillant (1983: 21–2) pointed out, 'a yearly intake of absolute alcohol that would have represented social drinking for the vigorous 100-kilogram Winston Churchill with his abundant stores of fat would spell medical and social disaster for an epileptic woman of 60-kilograms or for an airline pilot with an ulcer'. Thus the percentage of pure alcohol in an individual's blood (blood alcohol concentration) which is used by governments all over the world to determine safe driving limits, depends very much on body weight (see Figure 4.3).

A more promising approach to the definition of alcohol abuse, and one that is also more in line with the common view of alcoholism, is to combine reported consumption and reported problems related to drinking. Thus, the *Diagnostic and Statistical Manual of Mental Disorders* (DSM-IV; APA 1994) defines *alcohol abuse* as a maladaptive pattern of alcohol use leading to clinically significant impairment

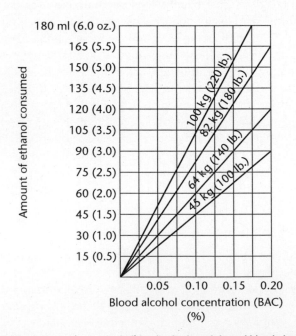

FIGURE 4.3 Nomogram of ethanol (pure alcohol) intake, body weight and blood alcohol concentration
Note: To approximate the BAC, trace horizontally to the right to intercept the diagonal line representing body weight. Then trace downward to find the peak BAC. This process can be reversed to estimate the amount of alcohol consumed. The BAC falls consistently at 0.015 per cent per hour.
Source: Mooney (1982)

or distress, as manifested by one (or more) of the following problems occurring within a 12-month period:

1 Failure to fulfil major role obligations at work, in school, or home due to recurrent alcohol use (e.g. repeated absence, poor performance, neglect of children or household).
2 Recurrent alcohol use in situations in which it is physically hazardous (e.g. driving).
3 Legal problems due to recurrent alcohol use.
4 Recurrent alcohol use despite having persistent social or interpersonal problems caused by drinking (e.g. arguments with spouse about drinking, physical fights).

The DSM-IV also distinguishes alcohol abuse from *alcohol dependence*, the latter being the more serious form of alcoholism. The alcohol dependent person is one who, in addition to some of the above symptoms of alcohol abuse, shows evidence that he or she has tolerance to the effects of alcohol or has experienced withdrawal symptoms. Using the similar DSM-III criteria, a community study conducted from 1981 to 1985 in the USA indicated that about 5 per cent of the population had alcohol abuse and 8 per cent had alcohol dependence at some time in their lives. Approximately 6 per cent had alcohol abuse or dependence during the preceding year (APA 1994: 202).

A number of screening instruments have been developed which can be used in health care and community settings to detect individuals with drinking problems (for a review, see Cooney et al. 1995). One of the screening interviews for clinical practice, CAGE (Ewing 1984) assesses the following four areas related to lifetime alcohol use:

1 Have you ever felt a need to cut down on your drinking?
2 Have you ever felt annoyed by someone criticizing your drinking?
3 Have you ever felt bad or guilty about your drinking?
4 Have you ever had a drink first thing in the morning to steady your nerves and get rid of a hangover?

Two positive responses are considered sufficient indication for the existence of an alcohol problem. The weakness of the CAGE is that it does not include questions about the frequency of drinking and intensity of drinking. It is therefore preferable to use the Alcohol Use Disorders Identification Test (AUDIT) developed by Babor et al. (2001) for the WHO, which includes questions that identify current problems, levels of alcohol consumption or binge drinking. If determination of a formal clinical diagnosis is necessary, individuals identified through screening should undergo a structured clinical interview to determine whether the DSM diagnostic criteria are met.

There are also biological indicators of alcohol abuse based on laboratory analyses of blood samples. The best known indicators are plasma gamma glutamyl tranferase (GGT) and mean corpuscular volume (MCV). Both reflect cellular injury to the liver (Cooney et al. 1995).

Theories of alcohol abuse

Theories of alcohol abuse can be divided into two groups: those that view it as an identifiable unitary disease process, and those that conceive of it in terms of behavioural models. This section will discuss both these approaches.

The disease concept of alcohol abuse

Of the various disease conceptualizations of alcoholism which have appeared in the literature over the past 40 years (e.g. Alcoholics Anonymous 1955; Jellinek 1960), the one developed by Jellinek has become most widely known. Jellinek presented a typology of alcoholism, specifying two types of alcoholic disease which he called the 'gamma' and the 'delta' syndromes. Gamma alcoholism, which is said to be the predominant type in North America, is characterized by:

- acquired increased tissue tolerance to alcohol;
- adaptive cell metabolism;
- physical dependence on alcohol (craving); and
- loss of control.

Once a person with gamma alcoholism begins to drink, he or she is unable to stop. The social damage is general and severe. In delta alcoholism, which is said to be the predominant type of alcoholism in France and other wine-drinking countries, the gamma alcoholic's inability to stop is replaced by inability to abstain. Delta alcoholics drink great amounts of alcohol on a regular basis. There is little social or psychological damage, but there may be physical damage, such as liver cirrhosis.

It has been hypothesized that the difference between alcoholics and non-alcoholics is based on a psychological predisposition, an allergic reaction to alcohol, or some nutritional deficits which may or may not be genetically influenced. One major implication of this approach is that treatment must emphasize the permanent nature of the alcoholic's problem and that the disease can only be arrested by lifelong abstinence.

Despite a great deal of research, there is no reliable empirical evidence for a psychological predisposition (Vaillant 1983) or for the physiological processes assumed by the disease model to lead to alcoholism (George and Marlatt 1983). Furthermore, there is now evidence that, rather than having to give up alcohol altogether, some alcoholics (the less severely dependent ones) can be taught to return to controlled social drinking through therapy (Heather and Robertson 1983; Rosenberg 1993). Definitions of controlled drinking have varied but have usually included some limit on the amount and frequency of consumption (e.g. a maximum of 30ml alcohol per day) and the condition that drinking results in neither signs of dependence nor social, legal or health problems (Rosenberg 1993).

Most damaging to Jellinek's conception, however, have been studies examining the 'loss of control' hypothesis using balanced placebo designs (Marlatt *et al.* 1973; Maisto *et al.* 1977; Berg *et al.* 1981). These studies examined the hypothesis that the apparent 'loss of control' after alcohol consumption is due to the *knowledge* that one has consumed alcohol rather than to the pharmacological effects of alcohol. The knowledge that they have drunk alcohol probably provides individuals with an excuse to consume more alcohol. The balanced placebo design allows one to manipulate independently expected and actual beverage content.

For example, social drinkers and alcoholics who participated in a study by Marlatt *et al.* (1973) were either led to believe that their drinks would contain vodka and tonic, or that they would contain only tonic. In fact half the respondents in each of those conditions received a drink containing vodka, and the other half received tonic water only. Following this drink, participants had to engage in a taste-rating of alcoholic beverages. Those who believed that their 'primer' drink had contained alcohol drank significantly more than those who thought that they only drank tonic. The amount consumed was unaffected by the actual alcohol content of these drinks, thus disconfirming the loss of control hypothesis.

Furthermore, studies using the balanced placebo design suggest that many of the behavioural consequences of alcohol are due to expectations about the effects of alcohol rather than its pharmacological impact (Marlatt *et al.* 1973; Marlatt and Rohsenow 1980; Hull and Bond 1986; Fillmore *et al.* 1998). In particular, the knowledge that one has consumed alcohol appears to disinhibit enjoyable but illicit behaviour (such as sexual behaviour, or further alcohol consumption) by providing an excuse for what would otherwise be considered inappropriate acts (Hull and Bond 1986).

Genetics and alcoholism

Although it has long been known that susceptibility to alcoholism runs in families, it is unclear whether this relationship should be attributed to socialization or heredity. However, twin and adoption studies have made it possible to disentangle the influence of genetic and environmental factors on alcoholism. For example, if *adopted* children whose biological parents have alcohol problems also have a higher risk of alcoholism than do adopted children whose biological parents have no alcohol problem, this increase in risk is likely to be due to genetic factors. In line with this assumption, studies have shown that biological sons of alcoholics adopted away at birth were several times more likely to become alcoholics than were the sons of non-alcoholics (e.g. Goodwin *et al.* 1973, 1974; Cloninger *et al.* 1981; Sigvardsson *et al.* 1996).

Twin studies have also been used to assess the extent to which alcoholism is determined by genetic factors. Because twins share the same family environment, regardless of whether they are monozygotic or dizygotic, a greater similarity in alcohol problems among monozygotic than dizygotic twin pairs would be an indication of a genetic influence on alcoholism. Most twin studies of individuals with alcohol dependence found concordance in the alcohol dependence of twin pairs to be greater for monozygotic twins than for dizygotic twins (Walters 2002).

Although there is now general consensus that there is a genetic disposition towards alcohol abuse, there is less agreement about the magnitude of the genetic influence. Most authors (e.g. Higuchi *et al.* 2006) seem to follow McGue (1999), who suggested that 50 to 60 per cent of the variability in alcohol liability was associated with genetic factors. However, whereas McGue's estimate was based on only a few studies, a meta-analytic summary of 50 genetic behaviour studies arrived at a much lower estimate of 20 to 26 per cent heritability (Walters 2002).

Walters (2002) also found evidence that the severity of alcohol abuse might moderate the gene–alcohol misuse relationship. This would be in line with the assumption that there are two types of alcoholism which differ in the extent to which they are influenced by genetic factors (Cloninger *et al.* 1981). One is more severe, sets in early, and is genetically influenced. The other is less severe and mediated primarily by environmental factors. Unfortunately, there is a great deal of overlap in confidence intervals in the Walters meta-analysis so that his findings do not allow a clear rejection of the continuum view of alcohol misuse.

Walters' meta-analysis is also somewhat equivocal with regard to gender differences in the heritability of alcoholism. There is a gender difference, with heritability estimates being lower for women than men, but this difference is attenuated when only studies with large sample sizes are considered. Thus, it seems increasingly likely that the tendency towards alcohol abuse is equally heritable for men and women (e.g. Kendler *et al.* 1992; Heath *et al.* 1997).

In assessing the impact of environmental factors, genetic studies allow us to distinguish two types, namely those shared by all the family members and those which are non-shared. Examples of shared conditions are social class, modelling by parents, and child-rearing practices. Examples of unshared environmental influences are damage to the embryo before birth, accidents or peer relations. Twin studies have suggested that the predominant source of non-genetic variance in alcoholism risk can be attributed to non-shared rather than shared environmental factors (e.g. Heath *et al.* 1997). Similarly, most studies of adoptive families have not found that non-biologically related (adoptive) children of alcoholic parents had an increased risk of alcoholism (e.g. McGue 1999). However, studies that assessed the similarity in alcohol involvement of non-biologically related (adoptive) sibling pairs found some resemblance between like-sexed siblings who were within two years of age (McGue 1999). This suggests some influence of shared environmental factors, but implicates siblings as a more likely source of environmental influence than parents. Since same-sex siblings, who are similar in age, might move in the same peer group, it would still be possible that the peer group is the environmental factor that is responsible.

Behavioural and cognitive models of alcohol use and abuse
Psychological approaches to understanding the causes and development of alcohol use and abuse subsume a number of diverse conceptual models that range from theories that emphasize learning through reinforcement to more cognitive models that emphasize expectations. According to the learning approaches, alcoholism is fundamentally a manner of drinking alcohol that has been learned either through conditioning (classical, operant) or through observational learning. In contrast,

cognitive models such as alcohol outcome expectancy theory assume that people drink alcohol because of the expected consequences of drinking. In the following, I will first present a classic learning theory of alcohol use and abuse, namely the tension reduction hypothesis of alcohol consumption (e.g. Cappell and Greeley 1987), and then review three cognitive approaches that explore different causes of alcohol use and abuse, namely alcohol outcome expectancies (e.g. Jones *et al.* 2001), reasons and motives (e.g. Farber *et al.* 1980; Cooper *et al.* 1995) and finally attitudes and the relationship between automatic and controlled processes in alcohol use and abuse (e.g. Wiers *et al.* 2002).

The tension reduction hypothesis of alcohol consumption

The basic assumption of the tension reduction hypothesis is that alcohol is consumed because it reduces tension. According to this model:

- increased tension constitutes a heightened drive state;
- by lowering tension and thus reducing this drive state, alcohol consumption has reinforcing properties; and
- such drive-reducing reinforcement strengthens the alcohol consumption response.

Research conducted with animals and humans to test the original model has produced rather inconclusive findings (for reviews, see George and Marlatt 1983; Cappell and Greeley 1987). The major problem with the tension reduction hypothesis is the assumption of a linear relationship between alcohol consumption and tension reduction. Contrary to this assumption, experimental evidence indicates that alcohol produces a biphasic response, with small amounts leading to a state of arousal that is experienced by the drinker as a euphoric high. With continued consumption, this phase gives way to a suppressive effect accompanied by tension and depression. George and Marlatt (1983) argued that because the relaxing and euphoric effect associated with small amounts of alcohol immediately follows the initiation of drinking, it has a much more potent associative tie to drinking behaviour than the delayed negative effect. Thus, people may drink to have this positive effect. George and Marlatt suggested that it is the expected rather than the actual tension-reducing properties of alcohol that are most influential in determining alcohol consumption. People drink because they expect that it will relax them.

Alcohol outcome expectancy theory

Alcohol outcome expectancy theory assumes that drinking is motivated by the expected consequences of alcohol. Whether these expectations are valid or not is unimportant (Jones *et al.* 2001). The positive expectation that if one drinks one will be more sociable and relaxed motivates people to drink, whereas the negative expectation that if one drinks one will end up having a hangover will motivate restraint.

The most widely used measure of alcohol expectancies is the Alcohol Expectancy Questionnaire (e.g. Brown *et al.* 1980; George *et al.* 1995). In developing this questionnaire, interviews were conducted with a broad spectrum of people and their expectations about the positive and negative consequences of alcohol were elicited. On the basis of these responses a questionnaire was developed in which people were asked to indicate their agreement or disagreement with statements such as 'Drinking makes the future seem brighter'; 'After a few drinks I am more sexually responsive' or 'If I have a couple of drinks, it is easier to express my feelings' (Brown *et al.* 1980). Agreement indicates that respondents expected alcohol to have these effects. Questionnaire responses from a large sample were then factor analysed. Whereas the study by Brown *et al.* (1980), which had focused only on positive experiences with moderate drinking, resulted in six correlated factors, all reflecting positive expectancies, later studies added negative factors to this model (e.g. George *et al.* 1995). The individual's overall outcome expectancy is reflected by the sum of the expectancy endorsements. More fine-grained assessment can be achieved by analysing the individual's responses to the different sub-scales of the questionnaire.

Numerous studies have found alcohol outcome expectancies to predict various aspects of drinking behaviour (for a review, see Jones *et al.* 2001). Thus, positive alcohol expectancies have been found to be significantly and positively related to drinking behaviour and negative alcohol expectancies to be inversely related to drinking behaviour. Prospective analyses have also shown that expectancies predict the initiation and maintenance of drinking behaviour as well as the onset of drinking behaviour. However, expectancies are more strongly associated with quantity than with frequency of drinking.

In terms of the theories of reasoned action and planned behaviour (e.g. Fishbein and Ajzen 1975; Ajzen 2005), alcohol outcome expectancies reflect one aspect of behavioural outcome beliefs that form the cognitive underpinning of a person's attitude towards drinking alcohol. According to the expectancy-value conception of attitudes proposed by Fishbein and Ajzen (1975), a person's attitude towards drinking alcohol should be the product of the subjective probability that alcohol results in certain consequences and the value attached to these consequences. As Leigh (1989) criticized in her insightful evaluation of alcohol expectancy research, alcohol expectancies reflect perceived consequences, but not the evaluation of these consequences. Although we know which expectancies have been considered positive (or negative) during the construction of the questionnaire, the fact that an item is on average rated as positive does not preclude the possibility that some individuals diverge in their evaluation. Thus, without knowledge of the individual evaluations of the respondents who fill in the Alcohol Expectancy Questionnaire in a particular study, the possibility cannot be excluded that some of the expected consequences are considered negative by some of the respondents but positive by others. For example, the fact that respondents expect to feel sexier after a few drinks might be attractive to a bachelor; however, it might be a reason to stay away from alcohol for a married executive who has to spend a great deal of time away from home.

This leads to a second shortcoming of alcohol expectancy theory in comparison to the theory of planned behaviour – namely that behavioural outcome beliefs are the only determinant of behaviour that is being considered. The approach thus neglects other important determinants of behaviour such as the individual's normative beliefs about the expectations of others. The fact that important others expect one not to drink might motivate one to refrain from drinking, even if one held positive expectations about the likely consequences of alcohol consumption.

Motivation for alcohol use

The fact that people hold particular expectations about the consequences of drinking alcohol does not necessarily mean that people drink to attain these outcomes. As we discussed earlier, people might hold outcome expectancies without necessarily wanting to attain these outcomes. This is obvious for negative outcomes such as having a hangover or falling off one's bike while riding home; it is less obvious for outcomes that are considered positive by some but negative by others.

Alcohol motivation theories assume that alcohol is drunk to enhance positive emotions and to alleviate negative ones. One of the earliest surveys of reasons for drinking, conducted by Farber *et al.* (1980) resulted in two factors. One factor reflected the need to drink to alleviate some unpleasant state. These individuals agreed with statements such as 'drinking helps me to forget some of my problems'; 'I drink when I am sad'; 'I need a drink to help me relax'. This factor can be considered as an escape drinking or negative reinforcement dimension. The second factor reflected social drinking. Participants scoring high on this factor were individuals who drink to reach some social goal such as peer acceptance or approval. They would agree with statements such as 'I drink because the people I know drink', 'I drink because I want to belong to a group of people who usually drink' or 'I drink to be sociable'.

Cooper *et al.* (1995) extended and specified this motivational model. They proposed that drinking to enhance positive emotions and to cope with negative ones were the proximal motivational determinants of alcohol use and abuse through which the influence of alcohol-related positive and negative expectancies, emotions and other individual difference variables is mediated. They tested this model in a cross-sectional study of two random samples of adolescents and adults. In support of their assumptions, they found that both motives predicted alcohol use and that alcohol-related expectancies of positive and negative reinforcement were the main predictors of these motives.

Automatic and controlled processes in alcohol use and abuse

Alcohol is an addictive substance and heavy drinking can interfere with daily functioning. It is therefore likely that many people with alcohol problems try to reduce their alcohol consumption. As a result, they might frequently experience self-control dilemmas between the temptation to enjoy another drink and the conflicting goal of reducing their alcohol consumption. Problem drinkers are characterized by their inability to resist such temptations. As I discussed in Chapter 2, several social psychological models offer theoretical explanations for this type of self-control dilemma. For example, the Reflective-Impulsive Model (RIM) of Strack and Deutsch (2004) conceives of self-regulation as a tug of war between an impulsive and a reflective system. According to this model, people in self-control dilemma situations are likely to follow their impulses unless they are motivated and able to control them. Unfortunately, alcohol consumption reduces people's ability to control their impulses.

Although developed as an explanation of the problems chronic dieters have in controlling their food intake (e.g. Stroebe 2008; Stroebe *et al.* 2008a, b), our goal conflict model could also be applied to the control of alcohol consumption. According to the goal conflict model, individuals with alcohol problems experience a conflict between two goals, the goal of alcohol enjoyment and the goal of cutting down on their drinking. Unless they are alcohol dependent, heavy drinkers should be able to maintain their alcohol control intention as their dominant goal, as long as they are not exposed to cues signalling drinking enjoyment. However, once they enter high risk situations full of cues signalling drinking enjoyment (e.g. their local pub) or once they begin to drink alcohol, the delicate balance between these two goals is likely to shift for two reasons: alcohol cues or alcohol consumption increases the cognitive accessibility of the alcohol enjoyment goal, which could lead to the alcohol enjoyment goal becoming the dominant goal; and alcohol undermines the individual's ability to control their drinking.

Implicit in both explanations is the assumption that heavy drinkers have a more positive attitude towards drinking than people who do not have an alcohol problem. As discussed earlier, this assumption has been supported for explicit measures of alcohol outcome beliefs (Jones 2001). Surprisingly, however, early studies using the IAT as the implicit measure of alcohol attitudes suggested that implicit attitudes did not discriminate between light and heavy drinkers (Wiers *et al.* 2002). However, this negative finding appears to have been due to problems with the IAT and more recent studies with a modified IAT found support for the assumption that implicit attitudes predicted drinking behaviour (e.g. Houben and Wiers 2008).

Attempts to demonstrate that priming with alcohol cues activates alcohol approach tendencies in heavy drinkers have so far had mixed success. A study by Ostafin *et al.* (2003), who used a modified evaluative priming task (Fazio *et al.* 1995) with college students, who were either problem or normal drinkers, failed to find evidence that alcohol cues primed approach motivation. The primes used in this study were either alcohol-related (e.g. liquor, six pack) or neutral words (e.g. table, tenfold). The targets consisted of 10 approach motivation-related words (e.g. advance, forward) or 10 avoidance motivation-related words (e.g. withdraw, escape). Participants were instructed to categorize each of the target words as being related to approach or avoidance by pressing one of two computer keys. Facilitation scores were computed by deducting the alcohol primed reaction time for a given target from the neutral primed reaction time to the same target. Findings indicated that although alcohol primes slowed down the reaction of problem (but not of normal) drinkers to avoidance responses, alcohol primes did not facilitate reactions to approach responses. A possible reason for the failure of this study to find effects on approach behaviour could have been that the student sample did not really contain people with serious alcohol problems.

A more recent study that specifically selected heavy drinkers into the sample reported suggestive evidence that heavy drinkers have stronger approach tendencies towards alcohol cues (Field *et al.* 2007). This study used a stimulus-response compatibility task to assess approach responses. Participants were either shown alcohol-related pictures or control pictures on a computer screen and had to move a manikin either towards the pictures or away. Compared to light drinkers, heavy drinkers were significantly faster in approaching rather than avoiding alcohol pictures, whereas no such difference occurred for light drinkers. Although a visual comparison with the control means suggests that this difference was due to heavy drinkers being faster in their approach (rather than being slower in their avoidance response), the authors did not statistically assess this contrast. Thus, one cannot totally exclude the possibility that the effects were due to a slowing of avoidance response to alcohol in heavy drinkers.

More successful were studies that tested the assumption that alcohol consumption reduces people's ability to resist temptations. In a study of candy consumption described in Chapter 2 Hoffmann and Friese (2008) assessed the influence of alcohol consumption on eating restraint. Whereas without alcohol candy consumption was mainly predicted by an (explicit) measure of eating restraint, under the influence of alcohol implicit attitudes towards candy became the main predictors. Furthermore, participants in the alcohol condition consumed more candy than did participants in the control condition. Evidence that reducing drinkers' self-control resources increases the association between implicit alcohol attitudes and drinking behaviour comes from a study conducted by Ostafin *et al.* (2008) with problem drinkers. These authors used an ego-depletion task to reduce drinkers' self-control resources (Baumeister *et al.* 1998). As predicted, participants whose self-control resources had been depleted did not only drink more alcohol in a taste test of different beers, but the ego-depletion manipulation also increased the association between their implicit alcohol attitudes and their drinking behaviour.

Clinical treatment of alcohol problems

Virtually all approaches to the treatment of alcoholism include some cognitive–behavioural treatment procedures. Since excellent reviews of behavioural treatment procedures are available (e.g. Hurley and Horowitz 1990; Hester and Miller 1995; Miller 2002; Kadden *et al.* 2004), only a brief overview will be given here.

Treatment goals
With the increased acceptance of behavioural approaches to alcoholism, the goals of treatment have also changed. Although the proponents of Jellinek's disease concept believed that the only cure for alcoholism is complete abstinence, some

behaviour therapists believe that at least the less severely dependent alcoholics can be taught to drink moderately. Several factors seem to be important in predicting which problem drinkers may succeed at controlled drinking rather than complete abstinence (for reviews, see Miller and Hester 1986; Rosenberg 1993). Individuals who have the best prospects are relatively young, married, employed, have had a relatively brief history of alcohol abuse and believe that the goal of controlled drinking is attainable. Controlled drinking training does not seem to be an effective method for chronic alcoholics who are severely dependent. Once severe dependence has occurred, the alcoholic no longer has the option of returning to social drinking (Hurley and Horowitz 1990). Thus complete abstinence still appears to be the preferred goal for most patients who need clinical treatment.

Detoxification

Before the initiation of therapy, alcoholics frequently have to be 'dried out'. In severe cases they may need medication to counteract alcohol withdrawal symptoms, which include anxiety, tremors and hallucinations. There are basically two approaches to detoxification. One method employs the substitution of alcohol with another more easily controlled drug in this category (usually barbiturates or benzodiazepines). Slow reduction of the medication minimizes withdrawal symptoms (Mooney and Cross 1988). An alternative approach uses minimal medication in the hope that severe withdrawal symptoms will help patients to recognize the severity of their condition. Obviously, the second approach requires very close medical supervision.

Clinical therapies

Motivation enhancement therapy

Motivation enhancement therapy (MET) has been developed specifically for the Project MATCH, a large U.S. intervention trial (Miller 1995; Project MATCH Research Group 1998). The technique is based on the plausible assumption, derived from the processes of change model of Prochaska and DiClemente (1983), that patients need to be motivated to change their behaviour, before therapists can be successful in teaching them how to change. The aim of the MET is to produce rapid and internally motivated change. Therefore, the contemplation and preparation stages are the most crucial for the MET therapist. The patients have to consider the consequences of their alcohol consumption. They will only move from contemplation to preparation if they realize that the serious negative consequences of their drinking outweigh all the positive aspects it may have. In the preparation stage, patients firmly resolve to take action and to change their behaviour. Only once they have reached this stage is the type of skills training involved in cognitive behaviour therapy (CBT) likely to be effective. The MET does not attempt to teach patients specific coping skills, but employs motivational strategies to mobilize the patients' own resources by eliciting ideas from them on how the change might occur.

It would follow from the perspective of the processes of change that MET should be most effective with less motivated patients. However, the evidence for this assumption is not conclusive (e.g. Heather *et al.* 1996; Project MATCH Research

Group 1998; UKATT Research Team 2007). Some support comes from a randomized trial of a brief intervention with problem drinkers in a primary care setting (Heather et al. 1996). Heather et al. found that MET was significantly more effective than behaviour change skills training for patients who were still in the contemplation stage. For the more motivated patients, the two approaches were equally effective. However, neither the Project MATCH Research Group (1998) nor the UKATT Research Team (2007), which conducted large multi-centre studies in the USA (Project MATCH) and the UK (UKATT), found support for the assumption. Given that the plausibility of the assumption that teaching individuals changing skills will not be effective unless they are willing to change, the scarcity of evidence in support of this hypothesis is puzzling.

Cognitive behaviour therapy
This therapy is based on social cognitive learning theory and assumes that people start drinking because they lack the skills to cope with major problems in their lives and they use alcohol as an alternative coping strategy. Once they have started drinking, they are unable to stop because they lack the skills to cope with high-risk situations that cue drinking. To be effective, a therapeutic technique has to address this broad spectrum of problems rather than focusing on drinking behaviour per se. The major aim of therapy is to teach alcoholics to identify high-risk situations that precipitate relapse and to teach them coping skills to deal with such situations (Kadden et al. 2004).

The first task in a CBT programme is therefore the identification of high-risk situations. The second major task consists of teaching patients the skills that are necessary to cope with these situations, without touching alcohol. The *Cognitive-behavioural Coping Skills Therapy Manual* developed for the Project MATCH devotes separate sessions to teaching patients to cope with cravings and urges to drink, to manage thoughts about alcohol and drinking, to cope with high-risk situations in which one has been drinking in the past, to be able to refuse drinks, and to cope with lapses (Kadden et al. 2004).

It is difficult to evaluate the effectiveness of CBT because most studies compare CBT to other therapy methods with the frequent outcome that all methods are equally effective. An excellent example of such a study is the Project MATCH, probably the most expensive and most carefully executed trial in the history of research on alcoholism. The Project MATCH was a large multi-centre US trial designed to match the most effective treatment to individual patient characteristics. The three treatments compared in this study were CBT, MET and a 12-step facilitation therapy to be described later (see pp. 153–4). Detailed therapy manuals were developed for each of these therapies. The therapies were provided to 1726 volunteers by trained therapists. The findings were an anticlimax. Very few of the matching hypotheses were supported and there were hardly any differences between treatments. Since many alcoholics also recover without therapy (e.g. Kendell and Staton 1966; Imber et al. 1976; Polich et al. 1981), it is difficult to judge whether the lack of differences is due to equal effectiveness or equal ineffectiveness.

Some arguments in support for the latter explanation were recently provided by Cutler and Fishbain (2005), who reanalysed the MATCH data set and raised two interesting and related points. First, the treatment effects on drinking behaviour occurred after the first week of treatment and did not change much afterwards. Second, the correlation between the number of treatment sessions a patient attended and outcome, particularly long-term outcome, was rather low. If a treatment was effective, particularly one based on learning a different set of skills during each session, one would expect some kind of dose–response effect, with patients who attended more treatments being better off.

Another disturbing feature of CBT research is that it has failed to demonstrate mediation – that is, to empirically identify the processes which are assumed to be responsible for the impact of CBT on alcohol consumption (Morgenstern and Longabaugh 2000). Because the aim of CBT is the teaching of specific coping skills, improvement in these coping skills should mediate the effect of CBT on alcohol consumption. From a review of 10 studies assessing mediating mechanisms, Morgenstern and Longabaugh (2000: 1475) concluded that 'the results indicate little support for the hypothesized mechanisms of action of CBT'.

Finally, the few recent studies that allow one to compare CBT against no treatment controls suggest that CBT effects are at best marginal. The evidence comes from studies of the effectiveness of pharmacological treatments which included control groups that received only CBT or a placebo pill. I will discuss the pharmacological effects later and focus here on these control groups. For example, the COMBINE study, a large assessment of pharmacological treatment, allows one to assess the impact of CBT against a control group without CBT one year after treatment (Anton et al. 2006). In the year after treatment, the CBT intervention group had three more days abstinent than the control group without CBT, a difference that was marginally significant. In the CBT intervention group there were also seven fewer individuals with more than one heavy drinking day during the one-year post-treatment period, a difference that was not even marginally significant. Another pharmacological study that allowed the comparison of a CBT control group against a group that received 'treatment as usual' (a psychosocial intervention that did not teach any coping skills) found no difference for percentage of days without heavy drinking and percentage of days with drinking over a six-month period (Balldin et al. 2003). However, CBT significantly reduced the amount of alcohol drunk per drinking day and the time to first relapse. Finally, a pharmacological study that allowed the comparison of CBT with a supportive group intervention that was considered a placebo psychosocial treatment found no difference a year later (Hautzinger et al. 2005). Thus, even though CBT appears to have some effects sometimes, these effect are rather weak.

Behavioural couples therapy
One way to increase the effectiveness of CBT is to combine it with behavioural couples therapy (BCT). The basic assumption underlying BCT is that alcohol abuse and relationship problems are reciprocal and that to be effective a therapy has

to involve the partner to address these problems. Studies show that patients with alcohol problems often have higher relationship distress and that these relationship problems are associated with relapse (Powers et al. 2008). The interactions of distressed couples are frequently characterized by negative rather than positive reciprocity. Actively involving the spouse does not only make it possible to address causes of relationship distress during the therapy, it can involve the partner as a coach. BCT combines the skill training of CBT with relationship therapy aimed at improving relationship functioning. A recent meta-analysis of BCT for alcohol and drug use disorders (with the majority of studies targeting individuals with an alcohol problem) that compared BCT to individual-based treatments found a clear superiority at follow-up for frequency of alcohol use as well as relationship satisfaction (Powers et al. 2008).

Pharmacotherapy
Disulfiram, the oldest pharmacological treatment for alcohol abuse, interferes with the degradation of alcohol and induces nausea and vomiting if one drinks alcohol in the days following ingestion of the drug. When disulfiram was first introduced, the practice was to have the patient experience the disulfiram–alcohol reaction. This practice has now been replaced by vividly describing this reaction. Fuller (1995) recommends the use of disulfiram only as part of a multi-component treatment and, because of its numerous side-effects, only for alcohol dependent patients who have relapsed. Because the effectiveness of disulfiram is dependent on patients taking the drug, this type of treatment is mainly effective if the drug is administered by someone at the clinic or by a family member (Fuller 1995).

The two medications for which there is the greatest evidence of efficacy in alcoholism are Naltrexone and Acamprosate (Kranzler and van Kirk 2001), both approved by the US Food and Drug Administration in 1994. Naltrexone blocks opoid receptors that are involved in the rewarding effects of drinking and craving alcohol. Acamprosate acts on the GABA and glutamate neurotransmitter system and is assumed to reduce symptoms of abstinence such as insomnia, restlessness and anxiety. These drugs should be taken for at least three months, a period that can be extended for a year or longer USDHHS (2005).

Nalextrone has moderate but statistically significant effects on drinking outcome measures such as drinking frequency and relapse to heavy drinking, but not necessarily abstinence (e.g. Kranzler and van Kirk 2001; Balldin et al. 2003; Anton et al. 2006; for a review, see Ross and Peselow 2009). Acamprosate increases the proportion of dependent drinkers who are successful in maintaining abstinence for several weeks or months (USDHHS 2004). This has been demonstrated in several trials conducted in Europe (Ross and Peselow 2009). It has been suggested that mainly patients with greater severity of alcohol dependence benefit from acamprosate.

As with all pharmacological treatments for health behaviour change discussed in this book, the main problem with these drugs is maintenance of change after the medication has been stopped. For example, in the COMBINE study, arguably the most extensive study of pharmacological alcohol treatment today, the differences between the drug and the placebo groups had disappeared one year after the end of treatment (Anton *et al.* 2003)

Predictors of treatment success

Who profits most from treatment? Research on patient characteristics has demonstrated that patients who are married, in stable employment, free of severe psychological problems, with less severe alcohol dependence and of higher socio-economic status respond most favourably to treatment (Hurley and Horowitz 1990; Adamson *et al.* 2009). In one of the few studies of social psychological predictors of treatment success, Jonas (1995) assessed the extent to which the determinants of the model of planned behaviour measured during therapy predicted relapse one year later in a sample of alcoholics undergoing therapy. When intention and perceived control were used as predictors of behaviour, only perceived control emerged as an independent predictor, accounting for 16 per cent of the variance in relapse behaviour. Thus, whether or not these alcoholics managed to abstain from drinking was unrelated to the strength of their intentions to abstain. It was solely related to their own estimate of how much control they perceived over their drinking. In line with this finding, self-efficacy (a component of perceived behavioural control) also emerged as the most consistent predictor variable of treatment outcome in the review of Adamson *et al.* (2009). This suggests that, once people have agreed to undergo therapy, it might be more effective to work on the factors which determine the patients' perceived control rather than further strengthening their intention to abstain. This may be one of the reasons for the failure of motivational therapy to have the expected effects.

Community-based interventions for alcohol problems

Brief interventions by health care providers

General hospitals or medical practices offer convenient settings in which to screen individuals for alcohol problems and to apply short interventions. One way to reduce alcohol consumption in a community is to provide a brief intervention in primary care (i.e. the doctor's office) or in hospital settings involving physicians, nurses or psychologists. In general practice as well as hospitals, patients are routinely asked about alcohol consumption during registration, general health checks and as part of health screening. Individuals identified as excessive drinkers on the basis of screening are then given brief interventions that include feedback on alcohol use and harms, identification of high-risk situations for drinking and coping strategies, and the development of a personal plan to reduce drinking. In general practice, these interventions take place within the time of a standard consultation: 5 to 15 minutes for a general physician, longer for a nurse (Kaner *et al.* 2007). In hospitals, brief interventions sometimes take up to three sessions (McQueen *et al.* 2009).

Research has demonstrated that advice from a general practitioner can be effective in reducing drinking among clients with a drinking problem. A recent meta-analysis of 21 random controlled trials conducted in primary care settings and involving more than 7000 patients, which compared the alcohol consumption of patients exposed to brief interventions to that of untreated control groups found a significant reduction in consumption for men (average difference, 57g/w of ethanol), reflecting about six standard drinks per week (Kaner *et al.* 2007). The reduction for women was smaller (mean difference 10g/w) and did not reach statistical significance. Results of a meta-analysis of brief interventions provided to heavy alcohol users admitted to general hospital wards were less conclusive (McQueen *et al.* 2009).

These findings raise two questions, namely why brief interventions are effective at all, and why they seem more effective in primary care settings. I would assume that being labelled a problem drinker is probably the most important aspect of these brief interventions. Unlike smokers, people who drink alcohol are often unaware that the level of their drinking is unusual and problematic, and identifying them as problem drinkers will already have a beneficial effect. There is evidence that merely providing people with data that indicate that their alcohol consumption is above the norm results in a reduction in alcohol consumption (e.g. Bewick *et al.* 2008). However, being labelled a problem drinker is probably more surprising for social drinkers warned off by their physicians than for heavy drinkers given brief interventions in general hospitals. Furthermore, these heavy drinkers are likely to have been more alcohol dependent and would therefore have experienced greater difficulties in reducing their alcohol consumption.

Self-help groups

No discussion of alcohol problems would be complete without a consideration of self-help groups, in particular the largest network of self-help groups in the world, namely Alcoholics Anonymous (AA). This network has approximately 87,000 groups in 150 countries, and over 1.7 million members (McCrady and Delaney 1995). The AA approach to alcohol problems is guided by the disease concept and outlined in 12 consecutive activities or steps that alcoholics should achieve during the recovery process (NIAAA 2000). This 12-step process involves the following:

- admitting that one is powerless and cannot control one's addiction;
- recognizing a greater power that can give one strength;
- examining past errors with the help of a sponsor, who is one of the experienced members;
- making amends for these errors (e.g. by apologizing to people one harmed or hurt);
- learning to live a new life with a new code of behaviour;
- helping others who suffer from the same addiction.

Individuals receiving the 12-step treatment are encouraged to accept that their affliction is the result of an underlying biological or psychological vulnerability that leads to loss of control over alcohol consumption. They have to accept that they are and will always be vulnerable and that the only solution for them is complete abstinence. However, 12-step programmes that accept the disease model but not the spiritual assumption of acceptance of a greater power are also conducted outside the AA (e.g. Ouimetter *et al.* 1997). These latter programmes have been labelled 'Twelve-Step Facilitation' (TSF).

Given the lack of scientific basis for the disease model on which the 12-step pro-gramme is based, it is surprising that it performs as well (or as poorly) as scientifi-cally based therapies such as CBT or MET. A meta-analysis of eight trials involving 3417 people that compared either AA or TSF programmes to other techniques (e.g. CBT, MET) concluded that the 'available experimental studies did not demonstrate the effectiveness of AA or other 12-step approaches in reducing alcohol use and achieving abstinence compared with other treatments' (Ferri *et al.* 2009: 2). This conclusion is surprising, as there is some evidence that 12-step approaches outper-form other therapies on one important variable, namely the percentage of patients maintaining complete abstinence. For example, an observational study involving 3000 patients in US Department of Veterans Affairs hospitals, which compared predominantly 12-step programmes with predominantly cognitive–behavioural programmes found that a significantly greater percentage of patients in the 12-step programmes (25.12 per cent) achieved total abstinence after one year compared to 17.9 per cent in the CBT treatment group (Ouimetter *et al.* 1997). While interpreta-tion of these results is complicated by the non-experimental nature of this study, similar problems do not arise in the Project MATCH. In this study, patients with alcohol abuse problems were randomly assigned to either a TSF procedure or two other treatment techniques (CBT and MET). Again, the only significant difference between these three groups was in terms of patients maintaining complete absti-nence: 'Among TSF clients, 36% were abstinent during months 37 to 39, compared with 24% of CBT and 27% of MET clients' (Project MATCH Research Group 1998: 1307). The argument that numerous studies have demonstrated that good clinical outcomes are significantly correlated with the frequency of attendance at AA meet-ings is less persuasive (Emrick *et al.* 1993), because this correlation could be due to the decision of those who relapse to stop attending AA meetings.

There are a number of factors that could contribute to the effectiveness of the 12-step approach, particularly if it is augmented by attendance at AA meetings. Attending AA meetings and adopting a sponsor institutes some degree of external control. Furthermore, replacing the old social network of pub-crawling friends with new friends from among fellow AA members is likely to provide social support for the new habit of abstinence. Maintaining abstinence should also be facilitated by the belief that even the smallest taste of alcohol will, with absolute certainly, result in total loss of control. Finally, abstinence might be an easier goal for many problem drinkers than controlled drinking, because with time they will forget how good alcohol can taste, whereas every sip with controlled drinking will remind them of that.

Web-based interventions
These interventions are not only cost-effective and can reach a great number of people, they also seem reasonably effective. A recent meta-analysis of computer-

delivered intervention for alcohol and tobacco use, which also included web-based interventions with participants with alcohol problems, concluded that such interventions can be moderately successful (Rooke *et al.* 2010).

Primary prevention

Since the late 1960s the attention of those concerned with public health aspects of alcohol has shifted from individuals suffering from alcoholism to the general overall consumption of alcohol in a given society and the factors that affect this consumption (Ashley and Rankin 1988). This change of approach was motivated by research conducted by Ledermann (1956, 1964). According to Ledermann, the frequency distribution of drinkers in a population is continuous, unimodal and positively skewed (see Figure 4.4). The fact that there is no separate peak at the high end of the distribution for alcoholics suggests that:

- the proportion of heavy drinkers in a given population can be estimated from knowledge of the mean per capita consumption; and
- that this proportion can be decreased by reducing the mean per capita consumption by means of fiscal and legal measures.

Consistent with Ledermann's position, there is convincing evidence that per capita consumption and excessive drinking (inferred from the rates for death from liver cirrhosis) are closely related. Although one cannot infer causality on the basis of purely correlational evidence, the finding described earlier, that restrictions imposed on alcohol consumption led to a drop in deaths from liver cirrhosis, suggests that measures reducing the per capita consumption are likely to result in a decrease in alcohol problems. There are two main strategies of primary prevention which have been employed to reduce drinking problems, namely health education to persuade people not to engage in harmful drinking, and health protection measures aimed at controlling the availability of alcohol.

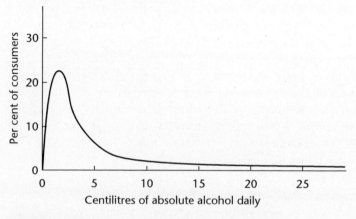

FIGURE 4.4 Frequency distribution of alcohol consumption
Source: de Lint (1976)

Health education

Health education programmes have been shown to affect public knowledge about, and attitudes towards, alcohol, but it has not been demonstrated convincingly that such programmes have resulted in behaviour change leading to a reduction in per capita consumption (Ashley and Rankin 1988). Such education programmes are likely to be counteracted by the pervasive efforts of the alcohol industry in promoting alcohol consumption. There is some evidence that alcohol advertising not only affects brand choice, but increases overall alcohol consumption. In an analysis of data from 17 countries for the period 1970 to 1983, Saffer (1991) demonstrated that countries with bans on the advertising of spirits (i.e. hard liquor) have about 16 per cent lower alcohol consumption than countries with no bans.

However, the success of brief interventions by primary care provides described above tends to suggest that interventions which target problem drinkers could be effective. Such interventions should provide information which helps to identify problem drinkers and which recommends sensible drinking goals. After all, unlike most smokers, many problem drinkers are unaware that they have a drinking problem and that they are damaging their health. Making them aware of these facts might motivate them to change their behaviour. In view of the widespread desire of people to diet and lose weight, such anti-alcohol campaigns might also stress the fact that the consumption of alcoholic beverages results in weight gain.

That school-based health education can be effective has been demonstrated in a major alcohol use prevention programme that was conducted in 24 school districts in north-eastern Minnesota using random assignment to the intervention or control conditions (Perry *et al.* 1996). The intervention programmes were implemented during sixth, seventh and eighth grade for three school years. The intervention consisted of social–behavioural curricula in schools, peer leadership and parental involvement. Students were trained in skills to communicate with their parents about alcohol and to deal with peer influence and normative expectations. The project was more successful with students who had not used alcohol at the beginning of sixth grade than among students who had begun drinking. Students who had not used alcohol at the beginning of the study showed lower onset rates in the intervention than the control groups and also reported lower alcohol use for the past year and past month at eighth grade. There were no significant differences in the alcohol use between intervention and control groups for those students who had already begun to drink alcohol at the start of the study. This might indicate that alcohol use is difficult to reverse, even as early as the beginning of sixth grade. But it would also seem plausible that adolescents who begin drinking alcohol early live in a social context that supports drinking and thus dampens the effect of educational programmes.

Health protection

Health protection measures include legislative and regulatory controls of the price of beverages, numbers and locations of outlets, hours and days of sale, and minimum legal drinking age. Studies spanning several decades have indicated that price control via taxation can be effective in reducing alcohol consumption (Ashley and Rankin 1988; Hurley and Horowitz 1990).

It has been demonstrated that the demand for alcoholic beverages responds to changes in price and income. In a meta-analysis of 112 studies of alcohol tax or price effects, Wagenaar et al. (2009) estimated elasticities for beer at –0.17, for wine at –0.69 and for spirits at –0.80. Thus, a 10 per cent increase in price should result in a 1.7 per cent decrease in beer consumption, a 6.9 per cent decrease in the consumption of wine and an 8 per cent decrease in the consumption of spirits.

It is interesting to note that price increases are likely to affect even heavy drinkers. Summarizing elasticities reported in 10 individual-level studies of heavy drinking, Wagenaar et al. (2009) arrived at an estimate of –0.28. This effect is smaller than the price-tax effect found for overall drinking (–0.44). Thus, even though price increases are likely to reduce alcohol consumption even among heavy drinkers, this effect is smaller than that on average alcohol consumption.

The most striking evidence for the impact of price changes on alcohol consumption comes from Finland, where alcohol taxes were reduced by 33 per cent in March 2004, resulting in an estimated increase in per capita consumption of 10 per cent in 2004 and a further 2 per cent in 2005 (Herttua et al. 2008). A time series analysis comparing the rate of weekly alcohol-related deaths in 2003 to that in 2004 estimated that the decrease in the price of alcoholic beverages resulted in an additional eight alcohol-related deaths per week, a 17 per cent increase over 2003 (Koski et al. 2007)

Minimum legal drinking age laws which forbid the sale of alcohol to individuals below a certain age are key measures for reducing alcohol availability among youth. States in the USA which increased the minimum drinking age to 21 in the late 1970s and early 1980s experienced a 10 to 15 per cent decline in alcohol-related traffic death among drivers in the targeted age groups, compared with states that did not adopt such laws. Furthermore, there is evidence that people aged 21 to 25 who grew up in states with an 'age 21 law' drink less alcohol compared to those who grew up in other states (DeJong and Hingson 1998). It is not surprising therefore that in 1984 the federal government passed a law which forced all states to increase the minimum drinking age to 21.

Conclusions

Alcohol abuse and dependence are widely recognized to be a serious public health problem. Alcohol abuse is characterized by a long-standing pathological pattern of daily alcohol consumption, and an impairment of social or occupational functioning. Alcohol dependence is in addition characterized by increased tolerance to alcohol and the experience of withdrawal symptoms. Although there is a biological vulnerability to alcohol, drinking patterns are learnt and can be influenced by learning processes. However, given the damage that alcohol abuse can do to the lives of alcoholics, and given the high costs and moderate success rates of treatment techniques, strategies of health protection and health education that aim to prevent alcoholism would appear to be a necessary additional approach to reduce alcohol problems in society.

Eating control, overweight and obesity

Obesity, like alcoholism, carries a social stigma. Society has a strong bias against people who are obese, a bias that can even be found in young children (Maddox *et al.* 1968). It is therefore not surprising that the majority of individuals with obesity try to lose weight. But results of treatment outcome studies suggest that they have great difficulty in reducing their weight even if they want to do so, and only very few manage to maintain their weight loss in the long term (e.g. Mann *et al.* 2007).

Overweight, obesity and body weight standards

The concepts of 'overweight' and 'obesity' imply a standard of normal or 'ideal' weight against which a given weight is judged. Because height and weight are highly correlated, such a standard has to be height-specific. One way to do this would be to define ranges of normal or ideal weight for each height. A more convenient strategy, and one that has now been generally accepted, is to use an index of body weight, which is corrected for height. One can then define the range of normal and ideal weight for this index. The body mass index (BMI) provides such a tool. It is obtained by dividing weight in kilograms by height in metres squared (kg/m^2). This index has a very high correlation with body fat (as estimated from body density), particularly when age is taken into account (Simopoulos 1986). It has also been shown to correlate highly with excess fat mass and abdominal obesity as evaluated by waist girth (Bouchard 2007). In terms of this index, 'overweight' has been defined as a BMI of 25 to 30 kg/m^2. A BMI above 30 kg/m^2 constitutes obesity (WHO 2000). Figure 4.5 presents the percentages of obese men and women in selected countries.

As Figure 4.5 shows, in most countries obesity rates are higher for women than for men. Obesity also varies by social class. In most western industrialized countries, obesity has been more prevalent among the lower socio-economic groups and these effects are most prominent among women (Stroebe 2008). Since 1980, there has been an alarming increase in obesity rates. In 1976, 15.1 per cent of the American population was obese; in 2003 to 2004, the average obesity rate was 32.3 per cent (Ogden *et al.* 2006). In Britain, rates have risen from 6 per cent for men and 8 per cent for women in 1980 to 23 per cent and 25 per cent respectively in 2002 (Rennie and Jebb 2005).

Obesity and health

The association between obesity and ill health has been well documented. Sources of evidence have been studies conducted by life insurance companies (Society of

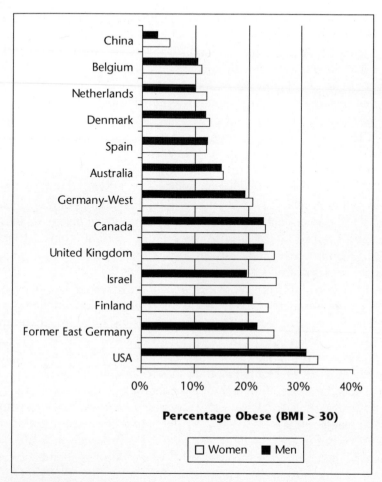

FIGURE 4.5 Percentage of obese persons in selected countries
Source: Stroebe (2008)

Actuaries 1960; Society of Actuaries and Association of Life Insurance Medical Directors of America 1979) and longitudinal studies (for a review, see Stroebe 2008). It is less clear whether overweight is also associated with health impairment. There is evidence emerging to suggest that this is not the case (e.g. McGee 2005). The causes of excess death associated with obesity are cardiovascular disease, stroke, diabetes mellitus (Willett and Manson 1996) and some forms of cancer (Renehan *et al.* 2008).

There is evidence from prospective studies that the health risk associated with obesity is affected by the distribution of body fat (e.g. Larsson *et al.* 1989; Lapidus 1990). It was found that carrying excess abdominal fat increased one's risk of ill health and mortality even with BMI held constant (Després and Kraus 1998). According to clinical guidelines published in 1998, men and women with waist circumferences greater than 102 centimetres and 88 centimetres respectively are considered at risk (National Heart, Lung, and Blood Institute 1998).

By now there can be no doubt about the negative association between obesity and longevity. It is less clear, however, whether being overweight (BMI 25 to 29.9) is also associated with increased mortality risk. Although many studies report a continuous increase in risk from normal weight through overweight to obesity (e.g. Manson *et al.* 1995), a recent meta-analysis based on data from 26 studies conducted in the USA and other countries found a significant increase for obesity but not for overweight (McGee 2005).

Another controversial issue about the association between BMI and mortality is whether it is steadily increasing or whether underweight is also unhealthy. Supporters of the monotonous relationship argue that findings of curvilinearity are the result of two confounding variables, namely cigarette smoking and undetected illnesses. First, smokers weigh less than non-smokers and also have a higher mortality rate. Second, undetected illnesses at the time of entry into a longitudinal study might have similar effects.

The explanation in terms of smoking has been tested by analysing data separately for smokers and non-smokers, or more elegantly, by including smoking as a factor in the analysis. Although smoking had substantial impact on mortality risk, it had very little impact on the outcome of these analyses. The potential impact of undetected illnesses at baseline measurement has been minimized by two procedures: medical examination of all respondents at baseline (in order to detect and exclude cases of illness), or by excluding all cases of mortality in the first two to five years after baseline measurement (assuming that these may have been due to illnesses that were already present at baseline). Again, the use of these procedures has not altered the U-shaped association between BMI and mortality. Two extensive meta-analyses of prospective cohort studies found mortality risk to increase with low as well as high BMI (Troiano *et al.* 1996; McGee 2005). Furthermore, the increased mortality risk for low BMI remained even after smoking had been controlled. That low BMI is associated with increased mortality had also been accepted in an expert statement of the National Task Force on the Prevention and Treatment of Obesity (2000).

Social and psychological consequences of obesity

Individuals with obesity, and particularly obese women, are likely to be the target of prejudice and discrimination (for a review, see Brownell *et al.* 2005). Prejudice, as a negative attitude towards a particular group, is based on the stereotypical beliefs which society shares about the members of that group. The stereotypes that exist in western societies about those who are overweight or obese are rather unflattering. They are perceived as less intelligent, less hardworking, less attractive, less popular, less successful and more weak-willed and self-indulgent than individuals of normal weight (e.g. Hebl and Mannix 2003). Although the stereotypical view of individuals who are overweight or obese also contains positive traits such as that they are caring, friendly and humorous, the overall attitude towards them tends to be negative. Weight discrimination against peers can already be found in children and adolescents (Puhl and Latner 2007).

The negative attitude towards obesity prevalent in western society has behavioural implications that pervade all walks of life. Obesity seriously lowers women's chances of marrying. Gortmaker et al. (1993) found that young obese women were far less likely to marry during a seven-year period than were non-obese women who differed from them only in body weight. If obese women did finally marry they were far more likely to drop in social class than were non-obese women. However, the discrimination against individuals with obesity is not restricted to the interpersonal domain. A study conducted in 1964 and 1965 found that obese high-school students were less frequently accepted into prestigious 'Ivy League' colleges than were non-obese students (Canning and Mayer 1966). Again, the effects were more marked for women than for men.

That these effects are not limited to elite colleges in the USA has been demonstrated by a large-scale Swedish study that followed a cohort of more than 700,000 men for more than 30 years (Karnehead et al. 2006). Men who were obese at age 18 had been doing worse in the educational system than their peers who were of normal weight, even when adjustments were made for intelligence and parental education.

Discrimination is likely to continue when obese individuals enter the job market. In one study, 16 per cent of the employers surveyed said that they would not hire obese women under any circumstances (Stunkard and Sobal 1995). When individuals with obesity do get jobs, their salaries are often lower than those of colleagues of normal weight. Register and Williams (1990) found that overweight women earned on average 12 per cent less than did women of normal weight, a difference that was not observed for men. A more recent review of studies on inequity in pay according to body weight indicated that this pattern is not unusual (Fikkan and Rothblum 2005). Although weight discrimination in pay does occur for men (e.g. Frieze et al. 1990), the evidence with regard to women is much more consistent.

In view of the extent of their stigmatization, it is not surprising that individuals who are overweight or obese have lower levels of self-esteem. A meta-analysis of 71 studies of the association between body weight and self-esteem reported correlations of −.12 between actual weight and self-esteem, and of −.33 for self-perceived weight (Miller and Downey 1999). The association was somewhat higher for women than for men and for individuals with high rather than low SES. There is also evidence that individuals who are obese are at higher risk of depression (Roberts et al. 2000; Onyike et al. 2003). In a cross-sectional analysis based on the NHANES data and using the DSM III/R criteria for major clinical depression, Onyike et al. (2003) found obesity to be associated with a significant increase in past month major depression. In a longitudinal study, Roberts et al. (2000) used data from the 1994 and 1995 waves of the Alameda County Study. Excluding all participants who were diagnosed as having had a major depressive episode at baseline in 1994, individuals who were obese in 1994 had twice the risk of normal weight individuals of developing a major depressive episode in 1995.

Genetics and weight

There is ample evidence from twin and adoption studies that body weight is strongly influenced by genetic factors. For example, based on data of the Virginia 30,000, a huge study that included twins and their parents, siblings, spouses and children, Maes *et al.* (1998) estimated genetic variance in BMI at 67 per cent. This estimate is only slightly higher than that of an extensive review of behaviour-genetic studies of weight and obesity, which suggested heritability of BMI to be approximately 60 per cent (Grilo and Pogue-Geile 1991). These estimates are similar in magnitude to those for intelligence.

It is important to realize, however, that even though body weight is largely determined by genetic factors, this does not mean that individuals are powerless to change it. Whereas people cannot change their blood type or eye colour, they can influence several of the processes which affect body weight. For example, the extent to which individuals are physically active is strongly determined by genetic factors (Frederiksen and Christensen 2003), as is their daily calorie intake (Rankinen and Bouchard 2006), both of which are under individual control. However, individuals with a genetic tendency towards weight gain are likely to find it more difficult to control their weight than individuals who lack this genetic vulnerability.

Because the food one eats and the extent to which one exercises are the most important environmental influences on weight and because meals are typically shared within a family, it would appear plausible to expect the shared family influences to be more important than the non-shared effects. It is therefore surprising that Grilo and Pogue-Geile (1991: 534) concluded on the basis of their review that 'experiences which are shared within a family do not play an important role in determining individual differences in weight, fatness, and obesity'. This conclusion was based on convincing evidence from different types of study. First, there was no correlation between the weight of adoptive siblings living in the same family. Second, the correlation between the weight of children and their biological parents was the same for those who lived with these parents and those adopted away. Third, monozygotic twins who were reared together were as similar in their weight as monozygotic twins who were reared apart. Fourth, spouses who lived together were no more similar in their weight than engaged couples who did not yet live together. These data suggest that practically all the environmental influences on weight are due to experiences which are not shared by family members.

The physiological regulation of eating behaviour

Many of our physiological systems are regulated by set points familiar from the thermostats used in central heating systems, refrigerators or air conditioning. If one adjusts the thermostat of one's central heating system to a given temperature, the system will switch on whenever the sensors register that the temperature has dropped below this set point. Whereas it is plausible that body temperature is regulated according to a set point, the fact that there is such a wide variation in body weight seems to rule out such regulation. However, it has been argued that even though there is wide interpersonal variability, the body weight of most adults remains remarkably stable over time (Keesey 1986).

The most important derivation of the set point theory is that the organism will defend its body weight against pressure to change. Thus, weight reduction and maintenance of a lowered body weight (i.e. weight suppression) is assumed to result in a compensatory decrease in metabolic rate. The physiological pressures produced by attempts to maintain weight loss below one's set point is also assumed to be accompanied by significant psychological and behavioural changes (e.g. Keys *et al.* 1950). Thus, weight suppression is expected to be associated with increased irritability and depression, increased hunger and a preoccupation with food. Finally, it is thought likely that organisms will increase calorie intake to re-establish their original weight (Keys *et al.* 1950).

Support for these predictions comes from studies conducted during World War II, when a group of conscientious objectors was maintained on a starvation diet for several months (Keys *et al.* 1950). Their body weight fell at first, but eventually stabilized at 75 per cent of the previous values. This equilibrium was reached partly by a decrease in basal metabolic rate and partly by a comparable decrease in the amount of metabolically active tissue. Furthermore, most returned to their previous weight once food restrictions had been removed. Similarly, when Vermont prisoners agreed to a considerable increase of their daily caloric intake, they achieved weight gains of 15 to 25 per cent during a half-year period. When the experiment terminated, these respondents soon returned to their normal weight (Sims and Horton 1968).

However, evidence based on individuals observed under more normal conditions is much less supportive of set-point theory. For example, there is little support for the assumption that weight is tightly controlled. First, longitudinal studies that follow samples of people over extended periods of time report a great deal of weight variation (e.g. Gordon and Kannel 1973). Second, the dramatic weight increase observed in most developed countries during the last three decades would be difficult to reconcile with set-point theory. Finally, the fact that individuals appear to be unable to compensate for the calories they add to their meals when drinking soft drinks or alcohol (Mattes 1996) would be difficult to reconcile with the notion that body weight is tightly regulated.

The outcomes of studies that assess whether weight suppression reduces metabolic rate have been mixed. Although there is evidence of a decrease in metabolic rate during periods of active fasting and calorie reduction (e.g. Ravussin *et al.* 1985), this appears to be a short-term effect. If the body were defending its body weight against pressure to change, one would expect such defensive processes to continue, even after the weight reduction has stopped, as long as the weight loss is maintained. However, most of the evidence suggests that once people have stabilized their weight at the lower level, metabolic rate increases again.

Finally, there is little evidence for the assumption that long-term weight suppression is associated with psychological distress. That individuals might be preoccupied with thoughts about food while actively reducing their calorie intake is beyond dispute, but there is no support for the assumption that normal dieting is associated with increased distress (French and Jeffery 1994). There is also no evidence for the assumption that individuals who lose a great deal of weight and try to maintain their weight loss experience distress (Klem *et al.* 1998).

If there is no set point and no defence of the organism against weight loss, why do people find it so difficult to lose weight and to maintain their weight loss? I will discuss the psychological reasons in the next section. In the context of this section, three reasons are relevant: first, the body does seem to go into an energy-saving mode during a calorie-reducing diet. Although this is a temporary phenomenon that was very useful during evolutionary times, when our forefathers and mothers had to last through extended periods of food scarcity and starvation, it is not very helpful when one is trying to lose weight. Second, the lower body weight resulting from weight loss is associated with a lower resting metabolic rate (due to tissue loss) and a lower energy expenditure during physical activity, due to the decrease in body weight. Thus, after a certain amount of weight loss, dieting individuals are likely to reach a new balance, where their calorie reduced diet no longer results in weight loss but matches their reduced calorie needs. The third and probably most important reason is that body weight is determined by lifestyle. People are creatures of habit and have routines that determine when they eat, what they eat, how much they eat and when they exercise. Thus, one's lifestyle supports a stable weight and one's weight is unlikely to change unless we also change our lifestyle. While people are usually willing to change while actively dieting, they often slide back into their old habits once they have reached their target weight or for other reasons have stopped actively trying to lose weight. Because their old lifestyle was associated with a higher weight, reverting to their old routines is likely to result in weight gain.

The regulation of food intake and energy homeostasis is accomplished by a variety of integrated neurohumoral systems which I cannot even attempt to discuss adequately in the context of this book. However, it is interesting to note that there is evidence for the existence of hormones which regulate food intake in inverse proportion to fat mass. Of particular importance in this regulatory process appears to be the hormone leptin. It is secreted by fat cells and direct administration of leptin into the central nervous system potently reduces food intake.

Psychological theories of eating

Psychosomatic theory

In 1957 Kaplan and Kaplan published an important theoretical article on the psychosomatic concept of obesity, in which they rejected the then widely-held position that obesity was caused by an organic disorder in metabolism and suggested that it was due to overeating. Based on learning theory principles, they proposed two hypotheses to explain why some people have a tendency to overeat. One cause of abnormal overeating was a 'disturbance in hunger or appetite' (Kaplan and Kaplan 1957: 197) due to hunger or appetite having become classically conditioned to non-nutritional stimuli that in the past had been regularly associated with hunger or eating (e.g. one's dinner time). A second cause of abnormal overeating was due to the fact that (according to the Kaplans) eating reduced fear and anxiety. Fear and anxiety are negative drive states and any behaviour that reduces these negative states will be reinforced. Individuals who have learned this association will be tempted to eat whenever they experience fear or anxiety, even though they experience no conscious increase in hunger or appetite. With these hypotheses, the Kaplans offered a persuasive and theory-based explanation of overeating. However, they failed to explain why stimuli that are regularly associated with eating should induce eating only in overweight and obese individuals and why only overweight and obese individuals should experience eating as fear-reducing.

In another pioneering article, Hilde Bruch (1961), a psychiatrist with a psychoanalytic background, offered an explanation for the assumed tendency of obese individuals to overeat when experiencing anxiety or strong emotions. She suggested that these individuals were unable to distinguish sensations of hunger from other forms of strong bodily arousal. She attributed this to experiences in childhood, with the ultimate cause being the failure of parents to teach their children to recognize hunger signals. If parents use food as an expression of love or to pacify their children whenever they show signs of upset rather than in response to nutritional needs, children cannot learn to recognize internal hunger signals and to distinguish them from other states of bodily arousal.

Empirical support for the assumed insensitivity of obese individuals to hunger signals comes from a study by Stunkard and Koch (1964) who found gastric motility to correlate with self-reports of hunger in normal but not in overweight individuals. A more direct test of this hypothesis was conducted by Schachter et al. (1968) in a classic experiment that became the model for much of the later research on eating. Overweight and normal weight student participants were led to believe that they would take part in a taste test, in which they had to rate the taste of different types of crackers. This cover story allowed the researchers to study the amount people would eat under different experimental conditions. Before the taste test, the state of satiety was manipulated by asking half the participants to eat roast beef sandwiches at the start of the experiment (a so-called 'preload'). Cross-cutting this, anxiety was manipulated by letting half the participants expect that they would receive painful electric shocks, whereas the other half expected only mild shocks. Consistent with the insensitivity hypothesis, the preload affected the amount eaten by normal weight but not by overweight individuals. However, there was no support for Bruch's second hypothesis that obese individuals overeat because they misinterpret anxiety as hunger. Anxiety did not significantly influence the number of crackers eaten by overweight participants. Later research did not replicate these anxiety findings but reported that obese people increased their eating under high anxiety (for a review, see Stroebe 2008).

Externality theory

The development of externality theory was strongly influenced by the findings of the Stunkard and Koch (1964) and the Schachter *et al.* (1968) studies. Both studies seemed to indicate that the eating behaviour of overweight or obese individuals was unaffected by internal hunger and satiety stimuli. This led Schachter *et al.* to conclude 'that internal state is irrelevant to eating by obese, and that external, food-relevant cues trigger eating for such people' (p. 97). Such food-relevant cues could be any non-caloric properties of food (e.g. taste) or any aspect of the environment that had been regularly associated with eating (e.g. dinner time) or signalled palatable food (e.g. sight or smell of food). The assumption that the food intake of over-weight or obese individuals is regulated by these external cues rather than internal cues signalling hunger or satiety would explain why these individuals often overeat in food-rich environments. Although the environmental influence on eating could have been explained in terms of one of the Kaplans' learning theory principles, Schachter (1971) did not incorporate learning theory assumptions into his theory.

Schachter *et al.* tested this hypothesis in numerous innovative laboratory and field experiments (for reviews, see Schachter 1971; Stroebe 2008). For example, in one experiment in which the food-relevant cue 'dinner time' was manipulated with a wall clock that ran either fast or slow, Schachter and Gross (1968) found that overweight (but not normal weight) participants ate more crackers if they thought it was past their dinner time rather than before. Thus dinner time appeared to serve as a food-relevant external cue that triggered eating. In a field study conducted during Jom Kippur (a day of fasting in the Jewish religion), Goldman *et al.* (1968) showed that religious Jews, who were overweight, found it less difficult to keep to their fast the more time they spent in the synagogue. This relationship could not be observed for normal weight religious Jews. Apparently the absence of food cues made it easier for overweight individuals to abstain from eating, but had no effect on normal weight individuals, presumably because their eating behaviour was not influenced by external food-relevant cues. Despite the plausibility of this 'externality hypothesis', and wide experimental support, the fact that some studies failed to demonstrate these effects finally led to the demise of the theory (for a review, see Rodin 1981). It is now widely accepted that across all weight groups there is only a weak relationship between the degree of overweight and the degree of external responsiveness (Nisbett 1972; Rodin *et al.* 1977).

Eating restraint and the boundary model of eating

The construct of 'dietary restraint' was originally developed by Herman and Polivy (1984) to offer an explanation for why there was only a weak relationship between obesity and externality. They argued:

- that obese people frequently try to diet in an attempt to conform to social prescriptions regarding body weight; and

- that it was the conscious restraint of eating that was responsible for the relationship between externality and obesity (e.g. Herman and Mack 1975).

When restrained individuals force themselves to ignore or override internal demands in their attempt to diet, an insensitivity to internal hunger cues and an over-reliance on external cues is likely to develop. Although overweight is one of the determinants of dietary restraint, the fact that many individuals of normal weight are also restrained eaters may explain why the relationship between externality and overweight is weak. Herman and Mack (1975) developed the Restraint Scale to assess the degree of self-imposed restriction of food intake and weight fluctuations. However, because people can be chronically concerned about their weight without permanently starving themselves, Herman later abandoned the claim that individuals with high restraint scores were essentially food-deprived (see Heatherton *et al.* 1988).

Herman and Polivy (1984) incorporated the concept of eating restraint into a 'boundary model' of the regulation of eating which became the dominant psychological theory of eating behaviour for decades (see Figure 4.6). They proposed that biological pressures work to maintain food intake within a certain range. The aversive qualities of hunger keep consumption above a minimum level and the aversive qualities of satiety keep it below some maximum. Between these two zones, there is a zone of biological indifference, where eating is regulated by non-physiological,

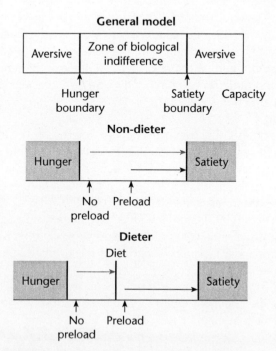

FIGURE 4.6 The boundary model of eating regulation
Source: Herman and Polivy (1984: 149)

social and environmental influences. Restrained eaters or dieters are assumed to differ from normal eaters (or non-dieters) in two respects: first, restrained eaters impose a 'diet boundary' within their zone of biological indifference. This boundary consists of a set of cognitive rules construed to limit food intake in order to maintain or achieve a desirable weight. Thus, in contrast to normal eaters whose eating is regulated via bodily feedback, restrained eaters are assumed to regulate their food intake cognitively. Second, restrained eaters are assumed to have a larger zone of biological indifference. Due to their frequent dieting and overeating, they have become somewhat insensitive to hunger and satiation cues: they can take much more food deprivation than unrestrained eaters before they experience hunger, and they can eat much more before feeling really full.

According to the boundary model, the diet boundary is both the strength and the Achilles heel of restrained eaters' attempts to achieve or maintain a desirable weight. It allows restrained eaters to keep their weight down if they monitor it. But if they cross this boundary, due either to circumstances outside their control or to lapses in attention, then a goal violation effect sets in, and they eat until they are full. This disinhibited reaction, termed 'counter-regulation', has been attributed to the 'all or none' thinking of restrained eaters. Once they have crossed their diet boundary, they see no point in further restraint.

There are two sets of factors assumed to induce overeating in restrained eaters, namely the impairment of cognitive resources and actual or perceived dietary violations. Factors that interfere with cognitive control are assumed to disturb the regulation of food intake in restrained eaters because they impair the ability of restrained eaters to monitor their food intake. Thus, the experience of emotional distress should result in overeating either because individuals need cognitive resources to cope with their emotions or because the goal of achieving a desirable weight loses its importance when compared to the problems which induce distress.

Empirical evidence
The 'emotion hypothesis' has been tested in experiments which compared the eating behaviour of restrained and normal eaters after the induction of negative mood or in a neutral situation. Most of these studies found that the induction of negative emotions in the laboratory (e.g. via a film or a failure experience) led to overeating among restrained eaters (e.g. Baucom and Aiken 1981; Schotte et al. 1990; Heatherton et al. 1991). Similar effects have been observed for the induction of stress on eating (for a review, see Greeno and Wing 1994). The consumption of alcoholic beverages under laboratory conditions has resulted in less reliable effects (e.g. Polivy and Herman 1976).

A second set of factors which disturbs dietary restraint is actual or perceived dietary violation. The effects of dietary violation on subsequent eating behaviour of restrained and normal eaters have been examined by inducing respondents to 'preload' with some rich (and therefore normally forbidden) food at the beginning of what was apparently a food-tasting experiment (e.g. Herman and Mack 1975; Hibscher and Herman 1977). In the first study on the effects of preload by Herman

TABLE 4.2 Number of grams of ice cream consumed by restrained and normal eaters under different preload conditions

	Preload (number of milkshakes)		
	0	*1*	*2*
High restraint (> 8.5)	97.17 (9)	161.09 (11)	165.90 (10)
Low restraint (< 8.5)	205.20 (10)	130.12 (8)	108.22 (9)

Source: Herman and Mack (1975: 656)

and Mack (1975), normal weight female respondents were asked to taste different flavours of ice cream after having been given either no preload or a preload of one or two milkshakes. Respondents were divided into restrained and normal eaters on the basis of the Restraint Scale. It was expected that normal eaters would eat less ice cream after a large rather than no preload. Restrained eaters, on the other hand, would 'binge', once they realized that their calorie intake already exceeded their daily ration. Consistent with these expectations, the intake of non-restrained respondents varied inversely with preload size (counter-regulation), whereas that of restrained respondents showed a direct relationship (see Table 4.2). Studies that demonstrated that it was not the actual number of calories in the preload but the (manipulated) beliefs about the calorie content that determined whether restrained eaters overeat, indicate that the preload effect was mediated by cognitive rather than physiological mechanisms (e.g. Polivy 1976; Spencer and Fremouw 1979).

Critique of the boundary model
Although the boundary model still dominates psychological research on eating, it has attracted a great deal of criticism on both empirical and theoretical grounds (e.g. Heatherton and Baumeister 1991; Lowe 1993). Instead of giving a comprehensive review of these criticisms, I will describe our own concerns which motivated my colleagues and me to develop our goal-conflict model of eating to be described in the next section.

One of our concerns is meta-theoretical and relates to the fact that Herman and colleagues abandoned the claim that individuals with high restraint scores were food-deprived (Heatherton *et al.* 1988). As a result, the boundary model no longer offered an explanation for the over-responsiveness of overweight and obese individuals to food-relevant external cues. The boundary model takes the existence of eating restraint as given and offers no explanation about its development. Due to its suspected role in the development of eating disorders, eating restraint is seen as dysfunctional or even dangerous. I have suggested the alternative explanation that restrained eaters are likely to be individuals who are (a) genetically disposed to weight gain and (b) have developed the concern for dieting to counteract this disposition (Stroebe 2002, 2008; Stroebe *et al.* 2008a). They are not starving themselves, but they monitor carefully what they eat and how much they eat. The positive correlation between BMI and restraint indicates that these attempts are not always successful. However, without restricting their food intake, these individuals might have gained even more weight.

Our major concern, however, was about the assumed mediating role of cognitions in inducing overeating in restrained eaters. Herman and Polivy (1984) attributed the tendency of restrained eaters to overeat, once they have breached their diet boundary, to so-called 'what-the-hell' cognitions. Having violated their diet boundary, dieters give up all attempts at eating control and eat until the satiety boundary is reached. Jansen *et al.* (1988) examined this hypothesis in a study in which respondents' 'self-talk' (of preloaded and non-preloaded restrained and non-restrained eaters) was taped during and after a standard ice-cream 'taste test'. There was no indication of an increase in disinhibitory thoughts in restrained eaters. Furthermore, a number of studies have reported disinhibition effects under conditions that did not involve violation of a diet boundary. For example, Jansen and van der Hout (1991) found that restrained eaters who merely smelled a preload counter-regulated in a subsequent taste test in which they were asked to taste various food items. Similarly, Fedoroff *et al.* (1997) reported that exposure to the smell of pizza baking induced overeating in restrained (but not normal) eaters in a subsequent pizza taste test. Both these findings are problematic for the boundary model, because no transgression had occurred that could have induced overeating.

Why should the smell of palatable food undermine the dieting intentions of chronic dieters? There is no empirical support for the assumption that these disinhibition effects result from 'what-the-hell' cognitions combined with a decreased sensitivity to internal cues of satiation in restrained eaters. Instead, we would suggest that the smell of palatable food triggers the anticipation of eating enjoyment in restrained eaters and that it is this anticipation that is responsible for overeating. This assumption would also explain why all successful empirical demonstration of disinhibition effects among restrained eaters used ice cream or some other highly palatable food (e.g. cookies, candies or nuts). There is also evidence from humans (for a review see, Yeomans *et al.* 2004) and even from rats (Rogers and Blundell 1980) that palatability is associated with greater food intake. And yet, palatability and eating enjoyment are not considered major determinants of eating by the boundary model. These concerns motivated us to develop our goal conflict model of eating which assumes that the anticipation of the pleasure of enjoying tasty food is the major force that motivates restrained eaters to violate their diet.

The goal conflict model of eating

According to the goal conflict model of eating, the difficulty restrained eaters experience in resisting the attraction of tasty food is due to a conflict between two incompatible goals, namely the goal of eating palatable food (i.e. eating enjoyment) and the goal of weight control (Stroebe 2002, 2008; Stroebe *et al.* 2008a, b). Restrained eaters would like to enjoy eating palatable food, but as chronic dieters they do not want to gain weight (or may even be trying to lose weight). Their difficulty, and one that is characteristic of all self-control dilemmas, is that eating enjoyment is immediately rewarding, whereas the rewards of weight control are in the future and can only be enjoyed in the long term. Restrained eaters therefore need to shield their goal of weight control by inhibiting thoughts about eating.

This may not be necessary when working on some engrossing task at their place of work, because, being busy in an environment without food cues, even restrained eaters are unlikely to think of eating enjoyment. Unfortunately (at least from the perspective of restrained eaters) most of us live in food-rich environments where we are surrounded by cues signalling or symbolizing palatable food and where such food is widely available. These food cues are likely to prime the goal of eating enjoyment and increase its cognitive accessibility, triggering hedonic thoughts about the pleasure of eating. This would be no problem if restrained eaters were able to easily ban these thoughts from their minds. However, food not only 'grabs' their attention, they also find it difficult to withdraw it. Although they are successful in shielding their weight control goal against brief exposure to a single food cue, more continuous priming is likely to increase the accessibility of the eating enjoyment goal to such an extent that it becomes the focal goal. Since eating enjoyment and eating control are incompatible goals, at least for chronic dieters who tend to have a weakness for high-calorie food, the increased accessibility of eating enjoyment will result in inhibited access to the mental representation of the goal of eating control (i.e. dieting thoughts). Figure 4.7 depicts this process.

There is a great deal of empirical support for the processes assumed by the goal conflict model (for reviews, see Papies *et al.* 2008a; Stroebe 2008; Stroebe *et al.* 2008). We demonstrated that exposure to descriptions of people eating palatable food (e.g. Jim eats a piece of pizza) triggers hedonic thoughts in restrained but not in normal eaters (Papies *et al.* 2007). Thus, whereas restrained eaters think how tasty a pizza would be and how enjoyable it would be to eat it, normal eaters do not appear to engage in these hedonic thoughts. Restrained eaters also respond with increased salivation to food cues (e.g. Brunstrom *et al.* 2004) and the smell of palatable food produces food cravings (Fedoroff *et al.* 1997). In a study in which

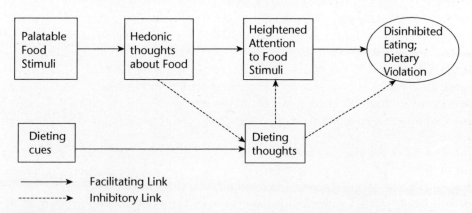

FIGURE 4.7 Why restrained eaters fail: a process model of unsuccessful eating restraint

we first exposed restrained and normal eaters to attractive food items and then measured their visual attention for food, we could also demonstrate that restrained eaters find it difficult to withdraw their attention from these food cues (Papies *et al.* 2008b).

Finally, and most importantly, we could further demonstrate that the activation of hedonic thoughts about food in restrained eaters makes the mental representation of their dieting goal temporarily less accessible (Stroebe *et al.* 2008). We used a lexical decision task to assess the cognitive accessibility of eating control words. In a lexical decision task, participants are presented with either words or non-word letter strings and must decide as quickly as possible whether they have seen a word or a letter string. The idea behind this procedure is that the more accessible these words are in the individuals' minds, the faster they recognize them. We then primed individuals subliminally with words either representing tasty food items or with neutral words. These primes appeared for less than 30ms on the screen and participants would see no more than a flash of light. And yet, when restrained eaters were primed with words representing palatable food items, they took longer to recognize dieting words than when they had been primed with non-food words. In contrast, such food primes did not influence the recognition of dieting words in normal eaters.

Those of us who are chronic dieters have probably experienced this process of mental inhibition when they entered a restaurant with the firm intention to eat a salad, but after consulting the menu listing all the tasty alternatives ended up ordering a three-course meal. The study by Fedoroff *et al.* (1997), described earlier, provides an experimental demonstration of this process. In terms of our theory, the delicious smell of baking pizza would be an eating enjoyment prime, and the increased pizza consumption would be the result of an inhibition of dieting thoughts in restrained eaters.

However, not all restrained eaters are unsuccessful in their dieting attempts. Fishbach *et al.* (2003) suggested that with repeated and successful attempts at self-control in a given domain, facilitative associative links can be formed in some individuals between specific temptations and the overriding goal with which they interfere. For these individuals, the activation of a temptation, even if it occurs without their awareness, might suffice to activate the higher-order goal. The fact that, as we reported earlier, a multitude of studies have demonstrated that restrained eaters are usually not very good at resisting temptation would suggest that these successful restrained eaters are in the minority. However, Fishbach *et al.* (2003) presented empirical evidence that chronic dieters who perceived themselves as successful in controlling their weight (measured with a brief scale) did indeed react with increased accessibility of dieting thoughts to exposure to palatable food words.

In terms of the paradigm used in the Stroebe *et al.* (2008) study, this would mean that for a sub-group of successful restrained eaters, priming the eating enjoyment goal with tempting food stimuli would not result in the suppression of dieting thoughts but in a slight increase in their accessibility. Papies *et al.* (2008c) therefore replicated the Stroebe *et al.* (2008) study and found indeed

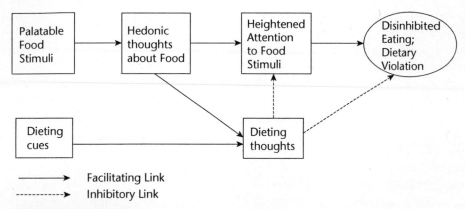

FIGURE 4.8 A process model of successful eating restraint

that self-perceived success moderated the impact of palatable food primes on response times to dieting words. Whereas subliminal exposure to palatable food primes slowed down the recognition of dieting words in unsuccessful restrained eaters, it actually speeded up recognition (i.e. increased their accessibility) in successful restrained eaters. Papies *et al.* (2008c) further demonstrated that the self-perception of these successful restrained eaters is indeed justified. Compared to unsuccessful restrained eaters, successful restrained eaters have a lower BMI and are also more likely to act in line with their intention to resist eating tempting food items.

Since successful restrained eaters activated rather than inhibited dieting thoughts on exposure to tasty food items, it seemed plausible that they would also suppress hedonic thoughts about this food. To our great surprise, there was no support for this assumption. Several studies indicated that successful restrained eaters reacted as hedonically to tasty food as did their unsuccessful counterparts. Thus, successful restrained eaters appear to be no less tempted by palatable food. But while exposure to palatable food increases dieting thoughts in successful restrained eaters, it inhibits dieting thoughts in unsuccessful restrained eaters. This suggests that if we could somehow remind unsuccessful restrained eaters in tempting situations of their dieting goal, they might become successful in controlling their eating.

We conducted two studies to test this hypothesis (van Koningsbruggen *et al.* in press) in which we used implementation intentions to remind participants to think of dieting whenever they were tempted by several palatable but calorific food items (chocolate, pizza, cookies, French fries or chips). All participants were first asked to recall the last time they had been tempted to eat chocolate. They were then asked to indicate briefly why it was important for them to resist the temptation to eat chocolate. Participants in the implementation intention condition were then asked: 'Please tell yourself: the next time I am tempted to eat chocolate I will think of dieting.' This procedure was repeated for all five foods. Participants in the control condition did not form implementation intentions after they had indicated why it was important for them not to eat the food items.

Our first study was conducted to test whether implementation intentions would indeed increase the accessibility of dieting thoughts in unsuccessful restrained eaters when exposed to any of these food temptations. For successful restrained eaters the induction of implementation intention should make no difference, because exposure to temptation food should increase the accessibility of dieting thoughts automatically without the need of reminders. In this first experiment, accessibility of dieting thoughts was assessed with a word completion task that was apparently part of a separate study in which participants had to complete word fragments that could either be seen as a dieting word or a word unrelated to dieting. These word fragments were presented as part of a list that also contained many complete words, and some of those were our palatable food words. In line with predictions, the induction of implementation intentions increased the accessibility of dieting thoughts in unsuccessful restrained eaters. Unsuccessful restrained eaters under implementation intentions were much more likely than those without implementation intentions to complete critical word fragments in terms of dieting-related meanings, if the fragment followed one of the palatable food words. For successful restrained eaters, dieting accessibility was always high, with or without implementation intentions.

To test whether the induction of implementation intentions was also effective in enhancing the self-control of dieters in real-life eating situations, we again induced 'think-of-dieting' implementation intentions in some of our participants. The study was conducted on the internet and participants were (unexpectedly) asked two weeks later how much of each of the palatable food items they had eaten. Consistent with predictions and also replicating the pattern of findings on accessibility of dieting thoughts, the induction of implementation intentions reduced consumption among unsuccessful restrained eaters, compared to the condition where no implementation intentions had been formed. In contrast, successful restrained eaters already ate very little without having formed an implementation intention. For them the formation of implementation intentions had no additional effect.

Conclusions

According to Popper, a new theory is superior to an earlier one, if it cannot only explain all the findings that were consistent with the old theory, but also findings which the old theory was unable to explain. In this sense, our goal conflict model is superior to the boundary model, because it can not only explain all of the research findings that support the boundary model of eating, but also those findings which are inconsistent with that model. If one assumes that preloads of tasty food constitute eating enjoyment primes rather than perceived violations of a dieting goal, our theory can account for the findings of all the preload studies. Given that restrained eaters usually eat only 30g more ice cream than normal eaters (e.g. Herman and Mack 1975), the priming explanation seems also more plausible than the assumption that these chronic dieters abandoned all eating restraint and ate until they reached their satiety boundary. And unlike the boundary model, our theory can also explain why exposure to sight and smell of palatable food should result in overeating. Finally, our theory can also account for the findings of research conducted to test Schachter's (1971) externality theory, because external food-relevant cues are likely to act as eating enjoyment primes.

Clinical treatment of obesity

Cognitive-behavioural approaches

The basic assumption underlying cognitive–behavioural treatment of obesity is that eating and exercise are learned behaviours and, like any other learned behaviour, can be modified. It should therefore be possible to reduce body weight by achieving a reduction in the quantity of food eaten and by increasing exercise behaviour (Wing 2004). The goal of most cognitive–behavioural programmes is to achieve a weight loss of 0.5 to 1 kg per week. To reach this goal, participants have to change their calorie intake, their level of physical activity, or both.

As for any cognitive–behavioural treatment, the starting point for the treatment of obesity is the diagnosis of the high-risk situations or behaviours for the individual. The key strategy for such a diagnosis is self-monitoring. Patients are asked to monitor their eating and exercise behaviours with the goal of identifying particular problem areas that can be targeted by treatment. Once patients have learned how to keep a food diary, they also have to self-monitor their physical activity to identify problems in this area. Feedback is the second function of self-monitoring. Dieters are instructed to regularly weigh themselves to gain some idea of the effectiveness of their diet.

The next important step is goal-setting. To achieve the intended weight loss, patients usually set goals for intended calorie intake (1000 to 1500 kilocalories per day) and for physical activity (activity that uses at least 1000 kilocalories per week). Typically, substantial behaviour change is required to achieve these goals. For example, if individuals report that they eat little at meals, but snack while they are working and also in the evening when watching TV, a specific sub-goal might be to reduce snacking or to replace high-calorie snacks with fruit. With regard to exercise, the goal could be walking half an hour on five days of the week. This might be achieved by walking to work instead of driving or parking the car further away from one's place of work and walking at least part of the way.

Training patients in the skills required to achieve weight loss is another important aspect of cognitive–behavioural programmes. Patients have to acquire the skills to self-monitor their eating and to provide themselves with a low-calorie diet. They are taught to read food labels, to recognize the fat content of different types of food and to prepare low-calorie alternatives.

The cognitive–behavioural approach assumes that environmental cues are important in eliciting behaviour. Patients are therefore taught to restructure their home environment in order to elicit the desired behaviour. Thus, they may be asked to stop buying high-calorie desserts, to store high-calorie foods in difficult-to-reach places, and to buy more fruit and vegetables. Therapists also try to provide new reinforcers to replace the reinforcement value of the forbidden foods. Weight loss would constitute one such potent reinforcer. Therapists also use reinforcers such as praise and positive feedback.

In line with the relapse process theory of Marlatt (e.g. 1985; Witkiewitz and Marlatt 2004) and to avoid patients abandoning the programme after some minor violation of their diet or exercise rules, cognitive–behavioural weight control programmes now emphasize that lapses are a natural part of the weight loss process. Based on information from the self-monitoring diaries, patients are taught to identify situations which tempt them into overeating and to develop strategies that help them to cope with these situations.

Cognitive–behavioural programmes can result in substantial weight loss during treatment. In a review of the effectiveness of cognitive–behavioural weight loss programmes, Wing (2004) summarized the results of 12 trials that had been conducted since 1990. She selected only trials which (a) prescribed diet plus exercise and which (b) she considered the largest and the longest. The initial treatment in these studies lasted for an average of 23 weeks and resulted in a weight loss of 10.4kg. A review of studies with particularly long follow-up periods arrived at an even higher estimate lost at the end of treatment (14kg; Mann et al. 2007). Unfortunately, most of the lost weight was regained in the years following the treatment. Four to seven years after treatment, participants in the studies reviewed by Mann et al. had regained 7.4kg, leaving them with an actual weight loss of only 3kg.

In contrast to the outcomes with adults, cognitive–behavioural treatment of childhood obesity has yielded promising results. In a report of 10-year treatment outcomes for obese children in four randomized treatment studies, Epstein et al. (1994) reported that 30 per cent of these children were not obese 10 years after the treatment. These changes were substantially greater than those of various control groups included in these studies. The children had been between 20 and 100 per cent overweight when 6 to 12 years old at intake. Treatment was family-based and included weekly meetings for 8 to 12 weeks, with monthly meetings continuing for 6 to 12 months from the start of the programme. Consistent with findings reported earlier, the obese parents who were treated in the same programme showed initial weight loss, followed by relapse. After five years all had regained their baseline weight and after 10 years parents in all groups were more heavily overweight than they had been at the beginning of the study.

Why is cognitive–behavioural treatment so much more effective with children than with adults? One reason could be that children are not yet as fixed in their eating habits as adults. Furthermore, the eating of children is very much under the control of adults who may be more effective in controlling the diets of their children than they are in controlling their own. By the time these children grow up to manage their own diets, they may have internalized the pattern of eating learned at home.

Pharmacotherapy

Before the widespread acceptance of behaviour therapy, appetite suppressant (anorectic) drugs were the most popular treatment for obesity. These drugs were widely used because they led to substantial and effortless weight loss. Neverthe-less, this type of pharmacotherapy had two major disadvantages: some of these drugs (especially the amphetamines) were likely to be abused, and the weight loss achieved with drug therapy was rarely maintained.

Anorectic drugs have now become safer (though not really safe). Pharmaco-therapy would therefore be useful in cases of severe obesity, if the problem of the maintenance of weight loss could be solved. Because the maintenance of drug-induced weight loss requires some change in lifestyle, the combination of anorectic drugs with behaviour therapy would seem to constitute an optimal approach: the use of drugs would achieve a fast and effortless weight loss while the techniques of behaviour therapy would lead to the required changes in lifestyle.

To test this hypothesis, Craighead (Craighead *et al.* 1981; Craighead 1984) conducted two studies to compare the combined effects of drug and behaviour therapy with the impact of drug or behaviour therapy used alone (see Figure 4.9). Although participants who received pharmacotherapy alone or in combination with behaviour therapy had significantly greater weight losses than those under only behaviour therapy, a one-year follow-up showed a striking reversal in the relative efficacy of treatments. Behaviour therapy patients regained significantly less weight than respondents under pharmacotherapy or the combined treatment conditions. The resulting trend in net weight loss now favoured the behaviour therapy alone (net

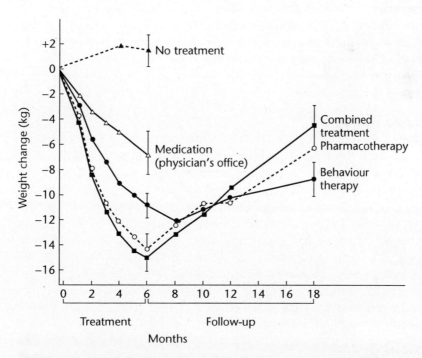

FIGURE 4.9 Weight change during six months of treatment and one-year follow-up
Source: Craighead *et al.* (1981)

loss: 9.0kg) over the other two conditions (net loss pharmacotherapy alone: 6.3kg; net loss combined treatment: 4.6kg). Thus, somewhat surprisingly, therapy was not only ineffective in helping to maintain the weight losses due to pharmacotherapy, but the long-term effects of behaviour therapy were actually poorer if patients had also received pharmacotherapy than if they had not.

It is interesting to speculate how the addition of medication could compromise the effectiveness of behaviour therapy. It seems possible that the reduction in appetite caused by the anorectic drug prevented individuals from learning the cognitive–behavioural techniques in the presence of competing hunger cues. Thus, when the drug was stopped, they might have been unprepared to cope with the resulting increase in hunger. However, this interpretation was not supported by findings of a second study conducted by Craighead (1984) in which she used pharmacotherapy during either the first or the second half of a 16-week behaviour therapy programme. Long-term results of these two sequences were no different from those of a combined treatment in which medication was administered for the total 16 weeks of behaviour therapy.

A second interpretation could be derived from theories of cognitive control (e.g. Bandura 1997). Patients who received the combined treatment may have attributed their weight loss to medication and may thus have failed to develop the feeling of control over their weight that is important for the maintenance of weight loss. The validity of this explanation could have been tested if Craighead and colleagues had included a condition in their studies that combined placebo medication with behaviour therapy. Even though some doubt may remain about the theoretical interpretation of these results, the practical implications are obvious: the long-term effects of behaviour therapy are not improved by pharmacotherapy. Thus, not only does pharmacotherapy carry a potential health risk (for a review, see Berg 1999), it also seems to be ineffective.

Very low-calorie diets

Very low-calorie diets (VLCDs) are supplemented fasts that are designed to spare lean body mass through the provision of 70 to 100g of protein a day in a total of 300 to 600 calories. VLCDs produce average weight losses of 20kg in 12 weeks (Blackburn *et al.* 1986). They produce greater weight loss initially than do low-calorie diets (LCDs) that provide 800 to 1200 kilocalories per day (Anderson *et al.* 2001; Tsai and Wadden 2006). However, according to a meta-analysis of randomized controlled trials, the initial advantage of VLCDs over LCDs is lost in the long run, because of greater weight regain (Tsai and Wadden 2006). Thus, VLCDs are not only expensive (approximately $2500 for 26 weeks; Wadden 1995) and potentially unhealthy (Berg 1999), but also ineffective. Therefore these diets should be replaced by LCDs which provide at least 800 kilocalories per day and may produce less of a maintenance problem.

Meal replacements

If dieters succeed in preparing low-calorie meals that are tasty, they still have to resist the temptation to eat more than their daily calorie allowance would permit. Meal replacements reduce this risk, because patients are provided with pre-packaged meals in exactly the portion size they should consume. Meal replacements consist of a wide range of food products that include beverages, pre-packaged shelf-stable and frozen entrées and meal/snack bars. These foods can either be used as the sole diet or in combination with other foods.

In a study with overweight or obese men and women, Jeffery *et al.* (1993) combined behaviour therapy with a condition in which patients in addition received pre-packaged meals for five breakfasts and five frozen dinners each week for an 18-month programme. The pre-packaged breakfasts contained cereal, milk, juice and fruit; dinners consisted of lean meat, potatoes or rice, and vegetables. Adding meal replacements to standard cognitive–behavioural therapy led to greater weight loss than standard therapy alone during the 18-month treatment period. A meta-analysis of six randomized controlled studies that compared the effects of partial meal replacements during a one-year period with those of a traditional calorie-reduced diet also showed superior effects of partial meal replacements (Heymsfield *et al.* 2003).

The problem with these diets is again weight maintenance. A follow-up of the Jeffery *et al.* (1993) study conducted one year later found that patients had regained most of the weight they had lost, and that the advantage of the meal replacement treatment had disappeared (Jeffery and Wing 1995). The likely reason is that after stopping their pre-packaged meals, patients returned to their old eating habits, increasing the portion size and the fat content of their food.

Since meal replacements are sold commercially, patients would be able to remain on them indefinitely. In a study conducted in Germany, participants who stayed on a meal replacement diet for four years were able to maintain a weight loss of 8.4 per cent of their body weight (Flechtner-Mors *et al.* 2000). Good weight loss maintenance with meal replacements over a five-year period was also reported by Rothacker (2000). However, in both studies replacement meals were provided free of charge by the researchers. When participants have to pay for these meals themselves, the costs can be quite prohibitive. There is evidence to suggest that if researchers merely provide patients with the 'opportunity' to purchase and use portion-controlled meals as a maintenance strategy but do not pay for them, patients will choose not to buy them and consequently fail in their attempt at weight loss maintenance (Wing *et al.* 1996).

Exercise

Most of the weight reduction techniques described earlier aim at the input side of the energy equation. But because overweight individuals consume more energy than they expend, increasing energy expenditure would offer an alternative or additional means of reduction. The neglect of exercise, particularly in the early weight control programmes, has been justified by the belief that exercise does not use up many calories (e.g. two miles of walking uses only about 200 calories) and that this minor effect is likely to be outweighed by the increase in appetite resulting from such exercise.

In contrast, studies that examined the impact of exercise alone and in combination with cognitive–behavioural techniques have found that a combination of diet

TABLE 4.3 Duration of various activities to expend 150 kilocalories for an average 70kg adult

Intensity	Activity	Approximate duration in minutes
Moderate	Volleyball, non-competitive	43
Moderate	Walking, moderate pace (3mph, 20 min/mile)	37
Moderate	Walking, brisk pace (4mph, 15 min/mile)	32
Moderate	Table tennis	32
Moderate	Raking leaves	32
Moderate	Social dancing	29
Moderate	Lawn-mowing (powered push mower)	29
Hard	Jogging (5mph, 12 min/mile)	18
Hard	Field hockey	16
Very hard	Running (6mph, 10 min/mile)	13

Source: USDHHS (1996b)

plus supervised group exercise (vs. diet alone) has resulted in greater weight losses in most cases (e.g. Stalonas *et al.* 1978; Dahlkoetter *et al.* 1979). There is therefore no longer doubt that the likelihood of long-term weight loss is increased in people who exercise. There is still discussion, however, about the different ways in which exercise contributes to weight control. The biological link between exercise and weight is relatively straightforward (USDHHS 1996b). Increases in fat mass and the development of obesity occur when energy intake exceeds daily energy expenditure for a long period of time. Theoretically, approximately 1 kilo of fat is stored for each 7700 kilocalories of excess energy intake. Unfortunately for weight control, the human body is a very efficient machine. Table 4.3 lists the duration of various activities to expend 150 kilocalories. As one can see, to work off the equivalent of eating a 150g serving of creamy fruit yoghurt, 30g of salami or 200ml white wine, an adult who weighs 70kg has to walk at moderate pace for 37 minutes, jog for 18 minutes or dance for 29 minutes.

There may be a second way by which exercise increases energy expenditure. There is evidence that the increase in metabolic rate produced by exercise is maintained for some time after a person has stopped exercising. Thus, exercise may use more calories than are needed for the physical movement per se. A meta-analysis of 22 studies examining the effects of diet and diet-plus-exercise on resting metabolic rate showed that exercise reduced but did not eliminate the drop in resting metabolic rate resulting from the diet (Thompson *et al.* 1996).

Most researchers in this area doubt, however, whether these metabolic effects can fully account for the substantial effects that have been observed in studies that assessed the added impact of exercise on weight control (Brownell 1995). They suggest that psychological mechanisms may contribute to the impact of regular exercise on weight loss. It would seem plausible, for example, that adherence to an exercise regimen increases people's feelings of self-efficacy. Such an increase in the sense of self-efficacy and the feeling of control over their weight might lead those who exercise to be more motivated in following a dietary instruction. This interpretation would also explain the finding that the impact of exercise on weight was even stronger at the long-term follow-up.

The assumption that the effect of exercise on weight control is mainly mediated by psychological rather than physiological or metabolic effects has implications for the type of exercise regimen one prescribes for obese individuals (Brownell 1995). Designs for exercise programmes have traditionally been guided by considerations of improving coronary fitness. For this purpose, exercise has to be done with sufficient frequency (three times a week) and at sufficient intensity to bring the heart rate to at least 70 per cent of maximum and of sufficient duration (i.e. 20 minutes per occasion). As Brownell (1995) has argued, these considerations, which may have discouraged generations of obese individuals from trying to exercise, are probably irrelevant for the type of exercise that should be recommended as part of weight loss diets. Dropping these requirements would allow us to prescribe exercise regimens which are more easily integrated into people's lifestyles (e.g. Perri *et al.* 1997).

Conclusions

According to Wing (2004), state of the art cognitive–behavioural treatments take five to six months and result in an average weight loss of 10.4kg. Since most of the lost weight will be regained, one wonders whether this is really worth the deprivation it involves. After all, individuals who were moderately obese at the beginning of their diet would still be obese at the end. But even if people regained all their weight five years after their diet, they might still be better off than they would have been without dieting. The average American aged 20 to 50 years typically gains 0.5 to 1kg per year (Williamson 1991) and participants in weight loss programmes are likely to gain even more. Thus, the untreated control group in a recent study by Rothacker (2000) gained 6.5kg over the five-year period of the follow-up. If we take this as a baseline, participants in weight loss programmes would be nearly 10kg lighter five years after the programme ended than they would have been without such a programme.

Commercial weight loss programmes

Commercial weight loss programmes are big business in Europe as well as in the USA. Although there are differences between these programmes, their common feature is that they focus on diet, exercise and lifestyle modifications and apply some of the same techniques that are used in clinical programmes. Weight Watchers International is the world's largest commercial weight loss programme and also the one that has been most thoroughly evaluated.

The efficacy of the Weight Watchers programme has been evaluated in six randomized controlled studies (Rippe *et al.* 1998; Lowe *et al.* 1999; Djuric *et al.* 2002; Heshka *et al.* 2003; Dansinger *et al.* 2005; Truby *et al.* 2006). For example, Heshka *et al.* randomly assigned 423 overweight and obese men and women either to

Weight Watchers or to a self-help programme. Participants in the self-help programme received a 20-minute consultation with a dietician at intake and were given publicly available printed material about dieting and exercise. Participants assigned to Weight Watchers were given vouchers that entitled them to attend sessions. At two years, approximately 25 per cent of the original participants had dropped out in either condition. Analyses were conducted on an intention-to-treat basis (last available value for drop-outs carried forward).[2] Throughout the two years, participants in the commercial group lost significantly more weight than the self-help group.

A six-month randomized controlled trial conducted in the UK compared Weight Watchers to three other programmes, namely Slim-Fast, Rosemary Conley and the Atkins Diet (Truby *et al.* 2006). Participants were 292 overweight and obese men and women who applied after a BBC advertising campaign. This study also included a waiting list control group. Rosemary Conley is a group-based programme similar to Weight Watchers. Slim-Fast provides a programme of replacement meals and the Atkins diet is a well-known low carbohydrate diet, described in a diet book. For the group-based programmes, participants were reimbursed for participation in regular meetings. For Slim-Fast, two meal replacements per day were paid for. Participants in the Atkins condition received a copy of *Dr Atkins' New Diet Revolution* (1999). After six months, 82 participants had dropped out of the study (17 Atkins; 11 Weight Watchers; 16 Slim-Fast; 17 Rosemary Conley; 21 control group). An analysis on an intention-to-treat basis, with baseline values carried forward to replace missing values, did not yield significant differences between the different treatment conditions. However, weight loss in all treatment conditions differed significantly from that in the control group.

What can we conclude from these studies? Participants in commercial programmes manage to lose moderate amounts of weight, and the weight loss is greater the longer they participate. Admittedly, the magnitude of weight loss and weight loss maintained is minimal, compared to the weight obese individuals would need to lose in order to reach normal weight. However, if one takes into account that without the intervention these individuals would probably have continued to *gain* weight, even a relatively small weight loss is definitely worthwhile.

Trying to lose weight without help

Most people who try to diet to lose weight do not join an organized weight loss programme. A national survey conducted in the USA in 1966 estimated that 46 per cent of all men and 70 per cent of all women had been on diets to lose weight at some time during their lives. Current dieting was estimated at 7 per cent for men

---

[2] The intention-to-treat analysis is based on all participants, even those who dropped out of the study. Estimates are used for the missing values of individuals who did not finish the study. One popular method is the 'last observation carried forward', whereby the last known observation is used to fill in observations that are missing.

and 15 per cent for women (reported in Jeffery *et al*. 1991). There is also evidence that dieting is strongly related to per cent overweight, with heavier individuals making more attempts to lose weight (Jeffery *et al*. 1991).

Unfortunately, the evidence on the effectiveness of these do-it-yourself diets is scarce. However, data on weight loss from a telephone survey of a large sample of individuals who tried to lose weight do not compare unfavourably with the effectiveness of clinical programmes. Average achieved weight loss was 0.634kg per week for men and 0.5kg per week for women, which is approximately the weekly weight loss achieved in clinical therapies. However, the authors of this study warned that these averages may reflect only the experience of those most successful at losing weight (Williamson *et al*. 1992). What is needed is long-term follow-up data on the success rate of a sizeable sample of obese men and women who are dieting to lose weight.

Is long-term weight loss possible?

It is a common dictum in weight loss research that the main problem is not losing weight, but maintaining the weight loss. However, there are reasons to argue that data from clinical studies might paint too gloomy a picture. First, as mentioned before, conclusions that are based on a comparison of the weight-outcome of an intervention with initial weight are likely to underestimate the effectiveness of weight loss programmes, because patients might have gained even more weight had they remained untreated. Second, as Schachter (1982) pointed out many years ago, these conclusions are based on *single* attempts at weight loss and individuals with weight problems typically make multiple attempts to lose weight. Whereas any single attempt at weight loss might have a low probability of success, the cumulative probability of repeated attempts could be considerably higher. Third, there is consistent evidence that those who enrol in weight loss programmes may represent the most severe cases and may be more resistant to successful treatment (e.g. Fitzgibbon *et al*. 1994).

Information on weight loss and weight loss maintenance in the general population allows one to be slightly more optimistic. McGuire *et al*. (1999) found that of a random sample of 474 individuals, 145 (30.6 per cent) reported to have at some time during adulthood intentionally lost at least 10 per cent of their weight. Weight loss maintainers were defined as individuals who had maintained a weight loss of 10 per cent from their maximum weight for at least one year. Of the 145 individuals who reported to have intentionally lost 10 per cent of their maximum weight, 48 per cent were successful weight loss maintainers for one year. Twenty five per cent had even maintained this weight loss for more than five years and were still 10 per cent below their maximum weight at the time of the survey.

Further information on a non-clinical sample is available from the 3000 members of the National Weight Control Registry (NWCR) in the USA (Wing and Hill 2001). Although the NWCR cannot provide information about the prevalence of successful weight loss or weight loss maintenance in the general population, it allows one to study the strategies used by individuals who were successful in maintaining substantial amounts of weight loss. To enrol in the Registry, participants must have lost at least 13.6kg and maintained this loss for at least one year. Members of the Registry had been considerably overweight before they engaged in their weight loss attempt (maximum lifetime BMI: 35) and nearly 90 per cent reported to have experienced previous weight loss attempts that had been unsuccessful.

Members used many different strategies to lose weight, but the one commonality is that 89 per cent combined diet with exercise to achieve weight loss (Hill *et al.* 2005). The most popular weight loss practices were to restrict certain foods (88 per cent), limit quantities (44 per cent) and count calories or fat grams (25 per cent). More than half of these members reported receiving some type of help with their weight loss (commercial programme, physician, nutritionist), a percentage that is considerably higher than that in the general population (Wing and Phelan 2005). They now maintain a body weight that is on average 10 BMI units lower than their pre-weight loss BMI (Wing and Hill 2001). On average, members reported consuming 1381 kilocalories per day, with 24 per cent of calories from fat, 19 per cent from protein and 56 per cent from carbohydrates. They also engage in high levels of physical activity comparable to approximately one hour of brisk walking per day.

Can dieting be harmful?

It is a reflection of the changing attitude towards dieting that this question is being asked at all. However, concern has risen that dieting, aside from the possibility of being ineffective, may also have potentially harmful effects (e.g. Brownell and Rodin 1994). There are two issues which have been discussed in this context, namely that 'weight cycling' or 'yo-yo dieting' has negative consequences for the health of the dieter, and that weight concerns and dieting contribute to the development of eating disorders.

Because obesity appears to be unhealthy, it would seem plausible that losing weight should improve the health of obese individuals. However, a review of studies on the association between weight loss and mortality by Williamson (1995) found only one study, the 1950 Metropolitan Life Insurance Study, reporting beneficial effects of weight loss. In this study, the life expectancy of individuals who had initially received substandard insurance because they were overweight, but who had subsequently lost weight, improved to that of insured people with standard risk. More recent epidemiological studies have typically found that weight fluctuation was associated with increased mortality (for reviews, see Brownell 1995; Williamson 1995). However, none of these studies allows one to separate the effects of intentional from unintentional weight loss. Unintentional weight loss can be due to factors such as severe illness, poverty or certain eating disorders which could also result in health impairment. One therefore has to concur with both Brownell (1995) and Williamson (1995) who concluded that this evidence does not allow any firm conclusions to be drawn about the health consequences of intentional weight loss in the obese.

Do unsuccessful dieters get depressed? It appears plausible that individuals who chastise themselves into losing weight, only to regain it a few years later, react with depression. However, in a review of the findings of several cross-sectional studies of weight cycling, as well as of their own longitudinal study, Foster *et al.* (1996) found no evidence that individuals who had regained the weight they had lost reacted with increased depression.

There is consistent support from observational studies that weight concerns contribute to the development of eating disorders. Prospective studies that followed samples of young girls found evidence for an association between weight concerns and shape concerns at the outset of the research and the development of partial syndromes of eating disorders later (e.g. Killen *et al.* 1996). In contrast to findings from observational studies, results of randomized controlled trials testing cognitive–behavioural weight loss interventions consistently show substantial weight loss and either improvement or no change in symptoms of eating disorders. A review of five paediatric behaviour modification programmes concluded that 'professionally administered weight loss programs for overweight children did not increase symptoms of eating disorders and were associated with significant improvements in psychosocial status' (Butryn and Wadden 2005: 289–90). All of these treatments also resulted in substantial weight loss and follow-up periods had varied from six months to 10 years. There is also ample evidence for adults that professionally administered weight control programmes do not increase (and sometimes even decrease) the risk of eating disorders (for reviews, see National Task Force on the Prevention and Treatment of Obesity 2000; Stice 2002; Butryn and Wadden 2005).

Three potential explanations for the contradictory findings of prospective and intervention studies have been discussed (e.g. Stice *et al.* 2005). First, the inconsistency might have occurred because measures of dietary restraint do not assess dieting behaviour but weight concern. Studies have repeatedly demonstrated that measures of dietary restraint are at best weakly related to observational measures of dietary behaviour. A second explanation for these contradictory findings which suggests that behavioural interventions promote healthy dieting behaviour whereas eating restraint scales might reflect unhealthy dieting behaviour is therefore more consistent with existing evidence. The fact that eating disorder prevention programmes with adolescents do not only reduce eating pathology but also reduce the risk of weight gain would be consistent with this assumption (Stice and Shaw 2004). A third explanation could be that the association between dieting and binge eating in observational studies is due to a third factor which increased the risk of both variables. As Stice (2002: 836) suggested, 'a tendency toward caloric overconsumption may lead to both self-reported dieting and eventual onset of binge eating and bulimic pathology'. If this were the case, 'dieting would be a proxy risk factor for binge eating and bulimic symptoms solely because it is a marker for overconsumption'.

Although it would be *scientifically* satisfying if we had sufficient data to resolve the inconsistency between the findings of longitudinal and prospective studies, we can draw *practical* conclusions without such a resolution. The findings of intervention studies have demonstrated conclusively that if adolescents engage in healthy dieting practices, they can not only lose weight without the risk of developing eating disorders, but their dieting might even improve their disordered eating (Stice 2002). There is also evidence that obese children can reach and maintain normal weight if they change their eating habits (e.g. Epstein *et al.* 1994). Children and adolescents are therefore an important target group for weight loss interventions. However, given the magnitude of the obesity problem, there is no hope of solving it with clinical interventions alone. We need to develop public health interventions that persuade people to change poor eating habits and help them to develop healthy weight loss and weight maintenance practices.

Prevention of overweight and obesity

Probably the most consistent and least disputed finding of the weight loss studies reviewed in this chapter has been that weight loss is difficult and that maintaining weight loss is even more difficult. Furthermore, the difficulty of weight loss and of weight loss maintenance increases steeply with the amount of weight that needs to be lost. This leads one to the inescapable conclusion that the war against obesity can only be won with effective primary prevention: people should be prevented from becoming overweight or obese in the first place.

There are two strategies to achieve this, namely health education and environmental changes. To be effective, health education campaigns need to use the whole range of persuasive techniques that have been developed by social and health psychologists during the last few decades, since simply warning people of the negative health impact of their lifestyle has proven insufficient in most areas of health behaviour change. The aim of environmental changes is to reduce or eliminate those factors in our 'toxic environment' which facilitate unhealthy eating and exercising behaviours. This can be achieved by changing the costs associated with alternative courses of action – for example, by increasing the price or reducing the availability of unhealthy options or by reducing the price or increasing the availability of healthy options. Children and adolescents are the most promising targets for such interventions, not only because their obesity rates are increasing at an alarming rate in most industrialized countries, but also because in countries where children eat some of their meals in schools, their food environment can be influenced. In the USA and the UK, schoolchildren not only spend a large amount of their time at school, they also eat a large share of their daily food while they are there.

Health education

A recent meta-analysis of 64 school-based prevention programmes found that only 13 produced significant effects (Stice *et al.* 2006). All studies had control groups and assignment to intervention or control group was either random or based on matching. With r = .04, the average effect size for all prevention programmes was very small, but still significantly different from zero. As in the Planet Health study, interventions were typically more effective with girls than boys. For the

13 interventions that were successful the effect size was r = .22, which would be considered a medium effect size of clinical significance. Since few of these programmes included long-term follow-up periods, it is unclear whether these weight gain prevention effects persisted after the end of the intervention. These effects may seem disappointing, but the average effect size for these interventions is very similar to that observed from prevention programmes for other public health problems (Stice *et al.* 2006). The few weight-gain prevention programmes that have been conducted with adults had even more modest results (for a review, see Stroebe 2008).

Environmental changes

Given the modest effects of interventions based on health education, our main hope of stemming the obesity epidemic appears to rest with interventions aimed at changing the 'toxic' environment. Reducing portion sizes in restaurants, forbidding food advertising during children's hours, restriction of the sale of soft drinks, candy bars and other minimally nutritious foods in schools, a tax on soft drinks and fast food, with the tax income used to subsidize healthy food and to finance health education programmes, and providing incentives for communities to develop parks and public sports facilities to encourage physical activity are all measures worthy of consideration. The possibilities are endless, however most changes would be difficult to implement for political reasons, not only because they interfere with powerful economic interests but also because many of these measures would have very limited popular support.

There is some evidence from the USA that taxing soft drinks and fast food can be effective in reducing the obesity risk (Kim and Kawachi 2006). Some of the states in the USA level such taxes, some do not, and some states did, but have repealed them. Analysing data between 1991 and 1998 Kim and Kawachi (2006) found that states without a soft drink or snack food tax were more than four times as likely to undergo a high relative increase in obesity prevalence (defined as at or above the 75th percentile in the relative increase) than states that taxed soft drinks and snack food. States that had repealed the tax were 13 times more likely than states with a tax to experience a relative high increase. These findings are compatible with the assumption that taxes on unhealthy food can influence obesity prevalence.

Pricing strategies would probably be most easily implemented in specific settings such as schools and worksites. In their excellent review of obesity prevention interventions, Schmitz and Jeffery (2002) describe several studies that tested the impact of pricing strategies to increase the sales of low-fat food in cafeterias and through venting machines. For example, lowering fresh fruit and salad bar prices by 50 per cent in worksite cafeteria resulted in a three-fold increase in sales (Jeffery *et al.* 1994). Since snack food is frequently sold through vending machines, these machines could be used to implement pricing strategies effectively. Several studies have demonstrated that sales of low-fat snacks at vending machines increase when prices for these snacks are reduced (French *et al.* 1997, 2001).

Although more information is needed on the elasticity of fast food, soft drinks and snack foods, using taxes and pricing would appear to be an effective strategy in battling the obesity epidemic. Although these strategies lack popular support at present, opinions might change as the obesity epidemic takes its inevitable course. Once people have become convinced of the health damage of obesity and of the fact that non-nutritious foods are major contributor to the obesity epidemic, they might be more willing to support such changes, particularly if some of the tax income were used to subsidize healthier options.

Conclusions

Obesity is associated with an increased risk of CHD, stroke and adult-onset diabetes. Willett and Manson (1996: 399) therefore concluded that for most adults, 'optimal health will be experienced if a lean body weight is maintained throughout life by means of regular physical activity and, if needed, modest dietary restraint'. It is less clear, however, what course of action one should recommend to those who become overweight or even obese. Although clinical weight loss therapies appear to be effective in the short run, the available evidence suggests that most of the weight which obese individuals manage to lose is regained within a few years after the end of these therapies. One of the reasons why attempts at dieting to lose weight often fail is that individuals who want to lose weight live mentally 'all day in the refrigerator' as Wegner (1994) once aptly put it. Therefore, instead of focusing individuals on trying to reduce the calorie content of their diets, one should persuade them to focus less on calories and instead change the *composition* of their diet. There is evidence that overweight persons who eat a low-fat diet lose weight gradually over a long period even if they are allowed to consume as many carbohydrates as they want. Thus, recommendations aimed at lowering the fat content of a diet and increasing the consumption of fruit and vegetables are likely not only to have a positive health impact but also to result in slow weight loss in overweight individuals. This weight loss could be accelerated, at further benefit to their health, if overweight individuals could be persuaded to become physically more active, or even to engage in regular exercise.

Summary and conclusions

This chapter has presented evidence on the impact of smoking, alcohol abuse and excessive eating on health. Without doubt, the findings on health deterioration are strongest for cigarette smoking, which has been identified as the single most important source of preventable mortality and morbidity in each of the reports of the US Surgeon General produced since 1964. There can be no doubt that alcohol *abuse* is also a very serious public health problem which impairs social and occupational functioning in addition to health. Finally, obesity is linked to increases in the risk of serious diseases such as diabetes and hypertension, and to increased mortality.

Once people smoke, drink too much alcohol or have a weight problem, these appetitive behaviours are difficult to change. Even though therapy might help individuals to act on their intentions to adopt more healthy habits, the strength of their intentions may be at least as important as the therapy for the eventual outcome. Because of the difficulties in changing these health-impairing habits, I argued that primary prevention is a more effective health strategy than behaviour change. I further suggested that programmes of primary prevention should rely not only on persuasion and health education but also on planned changes in the rewards and costs associated with these health behaviours. These latter strategies may be less applicable for weight control. However, there is evidence that cigarette consumption and alcohol abuse can be influenced by increases in the tax on tobacco and alcohol products, by instituting stricter age limits or by a reduction of availability through limiting sales.

Further reading

Hester, R.K. and Miller, W.R. (eds) (2002) *Handbook of Alcoholism Treatment Approaches: Effective Alternatives*, 2nd edn. Boston, MA: Allyn & Bacon. Provides excellent reviews of a wide range of psychological treatment approaches. This book is an important source for anybody interested in issues of treatment of alcoholism.

Macdonald, T.K., Zanna, M.P. and Fong, G.T. (1995) Decision making in altered states: effects of alcohol on attitudes towards drinking and driving. *Journal of Personality and Social Psychology*, 68: 973–85. Presents laboratory experiments and field studies which demonstrated the effects of alcohol myopia, the notion that alcohol intoxication decreases cognitive capacity so that people are more likely to attend only to the most salient cues.

Stroebe, W. (2008) *Dieting, Overweight and Obesity: Self-regulation in a Food-rich Environment*. Washington, DC: American Psychological Association. This book reviews the health consequences as well as psychological theories and research on determinants of overweight and obesity.

US Department of Health and Human Services (2000) *Clinical Practice Guidelines: Smoking Cessation*, www.surgeongeneral.gov/tobacco/treating_tobacco_use.pdf (accessed February 2009). An authoritative evaluation of the effectiveness of clinical techniques for smoking cessation by a panel of experts. Their evaluation is based on an extensive review and analysis (using meta-analysis wherever possible) of the scientific literature on outcomes of clinical smoking cessation interventions. In 2008 a short update became available.

CHAPTER

5

Behaviour and health: self-protection

This chapter will focus on health-enhancing or self-protective behaviours, such as eating a healthy diet, exercising, avoiding behaviours that are essential to the transmission of AIDS (unprotected sex, needle sharing) and protecting oneself against accidental injuries. The division of health behaviours into excessive appetites and self-protection is somewhat arbitrary. However, there is a difference between these two types of behaviour with regard to the extent to which they are under volitional control. Although people frequently need therapy to enable them to stop smoking, to give up alcohol or to lose weight, it would be rather unusual if people required therapy to reduce the salt content of their food, take up jogging, to practise safe sex or to fasten their seat belts.

Healthy diet

Obesity is not the only health risk that is related to diet. There is growing evidence that important ingredients of our diet, when taken in excess, may have a deleterious effect on our health. Thus, an excessive consumption of (saturated) fats has been linked to an elevated morbidity and mortality from atherosclerotic heart disease and even cancer, and a high intake of salt (sodium chloride) has been related to the development of hypertension and ultimately cardiovascular disease (Committee on Diet and Health 1989).

Fats, cholesterol and coronary heart disease

Of all the dietary risk factors, the relation between excessive of consumption of saturated fats and CHD has been studied most extensively. The hypothesis specifying the role of dietary fat in the development of CHD has been modified over the years with the emergence of new empirical evidence. This indicates that there are good and bad fats, just as there are good and bad cholesterols. Food fats can be divided into two categories, vegetable and animal fats. The latter may be further divided into three sub-categories: dairy fats, land animal fats and marine fats, including the fats of fish and of marine mammals such as whales or seals. The properties of the fatty acid composition of these types of food fats are very different. Vegetable and marine fats are unsaturated and contain substantial amounts of polyunsaturated fatty acids, mainly linoleic acid. Dairy and meat fats are much more saturated and contain only small amounts of linoleic acid.

Cholesterol is a fat-like substance mainly produced by the liver. Contained in most tissues, it is also the main component of deposits in the lining of arteries. It is carried in the blood mainly by two proteins, namely low-density lipoproteins (LDLs) and high-density lipoproteins (HDLs). These proteins are packages that allow lipids like cholesterol to be transported within the water-based bloodstream. Low-density cholesterol (LDLc) is actually a building block that is used for the construction of cell membranes. The problem is that if there is too much LDLc, it starts to be deposited on the walls of the blood vessels thereby helping the formation of 'plaques'. Plaque formation leads to a narrowing of the arteries and thus to atherosclerosis. As will be discussed below, there is evidence to suggest that excessive ingestion of saturated fats is a major cause of the elevation of LDLc. In contrast, high-density cholesterol (HDLc) is believed to be good cholesterol which protects against atherosclerosis. It serves as 'lipid scavengers', a means of transporting cholesterol from parts of the body where there is an excess to the liver where it can be disposed of (MAFF 1995). These modifications of the hypothesis were only made during the last few decades of the twentieth century. Therefore most of the early data available on population serum cholesterol or on food fats cannot be related to these distinctions. However, this poses no major problems because levels of LDLc are highly correlated with levels of total cholesterol, at least in population studies (Pasternak *et al.* 1996). Thus, averaged over groups, total cholesterol levels are a good indicator of levels of low-density cholesterol.

There is now wide consensus that, in industrial societies, the risk of CHD rises as serum cholesterol increases over most of the serum cholesterol range. This consensus is based on population studies which compared dietary habits and serum cholesterol across different nationalities. These studies have consistently reported a strong relationship between dietary cholesterol and serum cholesterol (Blackburn 1983). For example, the so-called 'Seven Country Study' (Keys 1980), which was carried out in the USA, Japan and five European countries, found a very high correlation between the ingestion of saturated fats and serum cholesterol levels (r = .89) and between the fat content of the diet and the incidence of CHD (r = .84).

Epidemiological studies which assessed the relationship between dietary cholesterol and serum cholesterol *within* a given culture at the individual level have typically failed to find an association. For example, 24-hour dietary recall interviews were conducted with a sample of approximately 2000 men and women residents in the community of Tecumseh (Michigan, USA) to determine the influence of diet on serum cholesterol levels. No relationship could be found between dietary variables and levels of serum cholesterol concentration for men or women. There is also little evidence of a relationship between diet and CHD from these studies (Stallones 1983).

The failure of these studies to demonstrate a relationship between dietary cholesterol and serum cholesterol on an individual level has been used by proponents of a genetic perspective to argue that serum cholesterol levels are mainly determined by genetic levels and that diet has very little impact (e.g. Kaplan 1988). However, this claim would not only be difficult to reconcile with the outcomes of the population studies described earlier (e.g. Keys 1980), but would also be inconsistent with the evidence from dietary intervention studies which demonstrate that substantial reductions in dietary fat content result in reduction in serum cholesterol (e.g. Schuler *et al*. 1992; Hunninghake *et al*. 1993; Byers *et al*. 1995). I will therefore review these studies before discussing whether cholesterol-lowering interventions actually reduce mortality.

The effectiveness of dietary interventions in improving healthy eating

Dietary interventions aimed at changing people's eating behaviour (i.e. lower saturated fat consumption; increased consumption of fruits and vegetables) appear overall to have a small but significant effect. A recent meta-analysis of 53 experimental or quasi-experimental intervention studies based on 26,417 individuals resulted in an overall effect size of d = 0.31 (Michie *et al*. 2009). According to Cohen (1992) this is a small effect. However, the effect is comparable to effects usually observed in psychological intervention studies. Interestingly, neither the delivery format (individual vs. group) nor the setting (e.g. workplace vs. community) moderate the efficacy of these interventions.

This meta-analysis is particularly important, because these researchers attempted to identify the behaviour change techniques that contributed most to intervention efficacy. Their analysis identified 'prompting self-monitoring of behaviour' as the one technique that contributed most to efficacy. Thus, interventions that prompted participants to monitor their behaviour (e.g. with a food diary) were more effective than those that did not induce self-monitoring. This technique proved particularly effective when combined with techniques such as prompting goal-setting, prompting reviewing and reconsidering previously set goals, and giving participants feedback on their performance (Michie *et al*. 2009). The effect size of interventions that combined prompting self-monitoring with one of the other three techniques was significantly greater (0.54) than effect sizes of interventions that did not include self-monitoring and one of the other techniques (0.24).

One limitation of this type of analysis needs to be noted: even effective techniques are unlikely to be identified in a survey of the literature, if there are insufficient studies in which they have been applied. Given the overwhelming evidence of the effectiveness of planning and the formation of implementation intentions in narrowing the intention–behaviour gap, the scarcity of studies applying this technique in the area of eating and exercising might have been responsible for the failure of this meta-analysis to identify implementation intentions as effective. For example, in a study in which people were instructed to plan to eat a low-fat diet during the next month, half of the participants were additionally asked to formulate their plans as much as possible and to write them down (Armitage 2004).

Compared to participants who were not asked to form plans, those who had formed plans significantly reduced their fat intake one month later (measured with a validated food frequency questionnaire).

Another limitation is that most of these studies recruited individuals who were already motivated to change their diets. The effects of these studies are therefore likely to overestimate the impact of dietary interventions at the population level. Dietary interventions face the major obstacle that individuals are often unaware of deficiencies in their diets. For example, a nationwide campaign in the Netherlands to reduce fat intake identified the fact that the Dutch underestimate their fat consumption as a major barrier to a reduction in that consumption (Van Wechem *et al.* 1998).

The effectiveness of dietary interventions in reducing cholesterol levels

The impact of dietary interventions in community, worksite or primary health care settings in reducing cholesterol levels varies from 0 to 10 per cent. For example, in the large-scale community intervention conducted in Northern Finland described earlier (see pp. 92–3), Puska *et al.* (1985) reported an average reduction in serum cholesterol of 4 per cent in men and of 1 per cent in women in the intervention as compared to the control communities during the period 1972–7. In contrast, none of the three community studies undertaken in the USA to reduce cardiovascular disease risks during the 1980s reported significant intervention effects on cholesterol levels (Luepker *et al.* 1994; Carleton *et al.* 1995; Winkleby *et al.* 1996).

Similar variability can be observed in the effects of worksite dietary intervention studies. Whereas two major dietary worksite interventions failed to have any impact on cholesterol levels (Glasgow *et al.* 1995, 1997), a worksite intervention on workers with cholesterol levels above 5.2mmol or higher who had volunteered to participate in a screening and intervention study showed modest but significant effects (Byers *et al.* 1995). The control group received approximately five minutes of dietary education. The intervention group received in addition a total of two hours of nutrition education delivered in multiple sessions over the next month. Whereas the control group showed a reduction in their cholesterol level of 3 per cent 12 months later, the intervention group showed a reduction of 6.5 per cent. One potential reason for the greater effectiveness of the intervention by Byers *et al.* (1995) is the fact that they focused on risk groups who should be more motivated to reduce their cholesterol levels.

That this is the level of change to be expected from dietary interventions conducted outside hospital wards is indicated by a meta-analysis based on 19 randomized controlled trials of dietary interventions with free-living individuals (Tang *et al.* 1998). This review reported a mean percentage reduction in blood total cholesterol after at least six months of intervention of just over 5 per cent. The authors suggested as a reason for these modest effects that according to food intake reports the targets for dietary change were seldom achieved. In fact, the observed reductions in blood total cholesterol were consistent with those one would have predicted on the basis of the reported dietary intake. A meta-analysis of intervention studies published a year later and based on 37 interventions found a somewhat larger reduction of total cholesterol and even in LDLc (Yu-Poth *et al.* 1999). However, whereas the study by Tang *et al.* (1998) was restricted to dietary interventions to lower cholesterol, the study of Yu-Poth *et al.* also included trials which focused on weight loss and other cardiovascular disease-preventive interventions (e.g. exercise). For dietary change alone the estimate of Tang *et al.* is probably more appropriate.

Studies of dietary counselling in primary medical care settings often show more powerful effects, particularly with patient samples who suffer from CHD. For example, in a 12-month study conducted in Germany, angina patients were randomly assigned to an intervention and a control group (Schuler *et al.* 1992). The control group was given the usual medical care. The intervention comprised intensive physical exercise in group training sessions (minimum two hours per week), home exercise periods (20 minutes daily) and a low-fat, low-cholesterol diet. Patients assigned to the intervention group stayed on a metabolic ward for the first three weeks of the programme. During this period they were taught how to lower the fat content of their regular diet to less than 20 per cent of total calories. Information sessions were conducted five times a year giving an opportunity for patients and their spouses to discuss dietary and exercise-related problems.

According to 24-hour dietary protocols, patients in the intervention group made considerable changes in their dietary schedule, reducing their total fat consumption by 53 per cent. This should have resulted in reduction in cholesterol levels of more than 20 per cent. However, the actual reduction was only 10 per cent. A similar discrepancy, and even less reduction in cholesterol, was reported by Hunninghake *et al.* (1993) who prescribed a lipid-lowering diet to more than 100 patients suffering from moderate hypercholesterolemia. These authors reported that the 5 per cent average reduction in the mean levels of total and LDL cholesterol produced by the low-fat diet was much less than the reduction anticipated. Again, dietary protocols completed by patients suggested good dietary adherence.

Additional information from the German study suggests that the discrepancy between reported fat reduction and the actual reduction in levels of cholesterol may have been due to the low reliability of the self-report data (Schuler *et al.* 1993). First, during the strict supervision of the metabolic ward in the first phase of the study, the fat-reduced diet resulted in the expected decrease of cholesterol levels of 23 per cent. Second, whereas patients' compliance in attending the supervised group exercise sessions was significantly correlated with average total cholesterol ($r = -.51$), the 24-hour dietary protocols were uncorrelated with any of the cholesterol measures. Although the low reliability of the dietary protocols could have been due to lapses in memory, or to the fact that patients show more adherence to their diets on days when they are completing their diaries, the most plausible explanation is that patients' dietary reports were influenced by the wish to be 'good patients'.

The main components of these interventions were nutritional education, combined with information about the health risk involved in eating diets high in saturated fats. Because information on health risks appears to be mainly effective for individuals who are unaware of these risks, one wonders whether persuasive messages which also increase eating-related self-efficacy or perceived control over eating behaviour would not have been more effective. This would suggest that an intervention which, in addition to giving nutritional education, targeted respondents' confidence in being able to eat healthily would be more effective than these standard interventions.

The effectiveness of cholesterol-lowering drug interventions

The most important issue from a public health perspective is, however, whether these types of intervention lower the risk of CHD and, even more importantly, decrease all-cause mortality. By early 1990, approximately 50 randomized clinical trials of cholesterol-lowering regimens by diet, drug or surgical methods (i.e. ileal bypass; a bypass of the end of the small intestines) had been conducted. A review of several meta-analyses of the outcomes of these trials concluded that despite substantial reductions in cholesterol levels and even coronary mortality, none 'of the seven published meta-analyses reported an overall statistically significant effect of lipid lowering on all-cause mortality' (Furberg 1994: 1307).

None of these meta-analyses included trials of 'statins', a new generation of lipid-lowering drugs which block the endogenous synthesis of cholesterol in the liver to reduce the levels of low-density lipoprotein cholesterol. Recent large clinical primary and secondary prevention trials have shown these statins to be safe, well tolerated and effective. A meta-analysis based on prospective data from more than 90,000 participants (half of whom suffered from CHD at intake) in 14 randomized trials of statins reported a 12 per cent proportional reduction in all-cause mortality per mmol/L reduction in LDLc (Cholesterol Treatment Trialists' Collaborators 2005). This reflected a 19 per cent reduction in coronary mortality and a non-significant reduction in non-coronary mortality. Similar results were reported from a meta-analysis of nearly 70,000 patients, who all suffered from CHD. Statin therapy reduced all-cause mortality by 16 per cent and coronary mortality by 23 per cent.

These studies indicate that statins achieve reductions in low-density cholesterol which in turn result in a substantial reduction in mortality from CHD and from all causes. That these drugs not only reduce coronary mortality, but also all-cause mortality, can be attributed to two factors, namely their increased effectiveness in lowering cholesterol levels and the absence of the kinds of side-effects of the early drugs which resulted in increases in non-coronary mortality (Jacobs 1993).

Beyond cholesterol: the Mediterranean diet

There is increasing evidence that a 'Mediterranean diet', representing an (idealized) dietary pattern usually consumed among the populations bordering the Mediterranean sea (but probably most typical for the food consumed on the island of Crete), confers health advantages that go beyond that of mere cholesterol-lowering diets. This diet is characterized by high consumption of olive oil, unrefined cereals, fruits, vegetables, fish and low to moderate consumption of dairy products (mostly as cheese and yoghurt), low consumption of meat and meat products, and moderate wine consumption with meals.

Most of the research on the health-protective effects of the Mediterranean diet consists of prospective cohort studies, in which the extent to which participants' diet adhered to the Mediterranean ideal was assessed. A recent meta-analysis of this type of research, based on 12 prospective studies with a total of more than 1.5 million participants, concluded that greater adherence to the Mediterranean diet was associated with significant health benefits, such as a significant reduction in all-cause mortality, mainly attributable to a reduction in mortality due to cardiovascular diseases and cancer (Sofi *et al.* 2008). There was also an overall reduction in the incidence of Parkinson's and Alzheimer's disease.

Even prospective cohort studies share the shortcoming of all non-experimental research, in that they cannot exclude the possibility that adherence to a Mediterranean diet was associated with other lifestyle factors that could have been responsible for the observed effects. Even though researchers tried to control for all obvious risk factors (e.g. BMI, exercising, smoking, etc.) one can never be sure whether some non-obvious (and therefore uncontrolled) factor that covaried with this particular lifestyle could not have been responsible for the findings. It is therefore important that these benefits of the Mediterranean diet have also been demonstrated in experimental studies (randomized controlled trials). The most extensive of these is probably the Lyon Diet Heart Study conducted with individuals who had suffered heart attacks (De Lorgeril *et al.* 1999). Whereas the patients assigned to the experimental group were asked to comply with a Mediterranean-type diet, the patients in the control group received no dietary advice from the investigators beyond being told to follow a prudent diet suggested by their physicians. Four years after the initiation of the study, there was a significant reduction in all-cause and cardiovascular mortality and in the recurrence of myocardial infarction in the group that received the Mediterranean diet compared to the control group. Whereas in the Lyon Diet Heart Study the observed health effects were not accompanied by changes in cholesterol, blood pressure or other traditional risk factors, other intervention studies have reported changes in traditional risk factors for participants in the group exposed to the Mediterranean diet (e.g. Singh *et al.* 1992; Estruch *et al.* 2006).

Salt intake and hypertension

Hypertension (i.e. high blood pressure) is a major risk factor for strokes and CHD. There may be many causes of hypertension but the one that has most frequently been cited is intake of salt. Thus, the WHO Expert Committee on Prevention of Coronary Heart Disease felt sufficiently confident of the link to advocate a general reduction in the consumption of salt (WHO 1982). These recommendations have been reiterated by other expert panels. For example, the Committee on Diet and Health of the National Research Council in the USA recommended that the total daily intake of salt be limited to 6g or less (Committee on Diet and Health 1989). The same recommendation was given in the manual of nutrition of the British Ministry of Agriculture, Fisheries and Food (MAFF 1995).

Although a heated debate between proponents and opponents of salt reduction is still ongoing, there is reason to believe that this recommendation may be overstating the case. As Taubes (1998: 906) commented in an article in *Science*, two conspicuous trends have characterized the salt dispute: 'On the one hand, the data are becoming increasingly consistent – suggesting at most a small benefit from salt reduction – while on the other, the interpretations of the data, and the field itself, have remained polarized'. The anti-salt lobby continues to maintain its recommendation of a general reduction in daily salt intake.

As observers of these 'salt skirmishes' have noted, the results from the advocates of strict salt restriction and those from authors with more liberal views are fairly similar: salt reduction would decrease blood pressure among normotensive persons by approximately 2mm Hg, and in the hypertensive patients about 5mm Hg (e.g. Luft 1997). Furthermore, as Hooper *et al.* (2002: 631) concluded from a systematic review and meta-analysis of randomized controlled trials, even 'intensive interventions, unsuited to primary care or population prevention programs produce uncertain effects on mortality and cardiovascular events and only small reductions in blood pressure'.

These findings support researchers who have argued that salt restriction is only beneficial for *some* individuals, namely those who are particularly salt-sensitive, because of a decreased capacity of the kidney to excrete sodium (e.g. Haddy 1991). Therefore the benefits of a reduction in dietary salt intake are likely to be clinically meaningless to individuals with normal blood pressure, even though there may be a public health impact on the population level. In contrast, individuals who suffer from mild hypertension may benefit from a moderate reduction in daily salt intake. It is essentially without side-effects, and even if drug therapy is finally required to lower blood pressure, dietary sodium restriction may reduce the effective dose of the drug and thereby also reduce potential side-effects (Haddy 1991).

At the same time, other dietary changes should be recommended which may be even more effective in lowering blood pressure. As a randomized controlled study demonstrated, a diet rich in fruits, vegetables and low-fat dairy foods, and reduced in saturated fats and total fat content can lower systolic blood pressure in both hypertensive (11.4mm Hg) and normotensive (3.5mm Hg) participants, even though it had the same salt content as the control diet (Svetkey *et al.* 1999). This diet has the additional advantage that it is likely to reduce cholesterol levels and thus another factor contributing to high blood pressure in the long term.

Conclusions

There can be no doubt that high serum cholesterol levels and high blood pressure are risk factors for CHD. There is also consensus that dietary changes can reduce both of these risk factors. Thus, a decrease in the consumption of saturated fats and an increased consumption of fruit and vegetables should not only lower levels of serum cholesterol (e.g. Michie *et al.* 2009), it might also lower blood pressure (e.g. Svetkey *et al.* 1999). Decreasing the salt content of one's diet should have further beneficial effects on blood pressure, particularly for individuals who are salt sensitive.

Thus, although it would be unrealistic at present to expect more than a 5 to 10 per cent reduction in cholesterol levels as a result of normal public health interventions involving dietary education delivered via mass media, at the worksite or in primary care settings, there are other important reasons why dietary education via the mass media (as well as legal measures relating to disclosure of the fat content of food products) are important and likely to have a major public health benefit. First, like all cut-off points, the cut-off point for what constitutes dangerous vs. non-dangerous levels of cholesterol is somewhat arbitrary. Therefore, the effects on the cardiovascular system of a diet low in saturated fats should be beneficial for many people, even if their cholesterol levels are not especially high. Second, a healthier diet is also likely to have beneficial effects on people's blood pressure. Third, fat-rich diets are one of the major risk factors for overweight. Persuading people to lower the (saturated) fat content of their diets might therefore help them to control their weight without needing to restrict their calories. Thus, public health campaigns directed at healthy eating might help to reduce the negative health consequences of both overweight and calorie-restrictive diets. Finally, since the Mediterranean diet is likely to be more acceptable than the typical low-fat, calorie restricted diet, the evidence of the protective effects of the Mediterranean diet might pave the way for more effective dietary interventions.

Physical activity

If one were to conduct a survey of beliefs about what people should do to improve their health, regular exercise would probably be mentioned by most respondents. However, such beliefs do not always translate into action. Even in the USA, where health consciousness appears to be much higher than in Europe, only 15 per cent of the adult population exercise regularly and intensively enough in their leisure time to meet current guidelines for fitness (three times a week for at least 20 minutes) and this percentage has changed very little during the last decade. The percentage is much higher for adolescents but declines strikingly as age or grade in school increases (USDHHS 1996b).

There is strong evidence that regular vigorous dynamic physical activity decreases the risk of hypertension, cardiovascular disease, colon cancer, non-insulin dependent diabetes mellitus and mortality from all causes. Regular physical activity also appears to relieve symptoms of depression and anxiety and improve mood (USDHHS 1996b). Such *aerobic* or *endurance exercises*, intended to increase oxygen consumption, include jogging, bicycling and swimming. All these are marked by their high intensity, long duration and need for high endurance. *Strength* or *resistance training* (e.g. weight-lifting) increases the size and strength of muscles without improving endurance. The importance of resistance training is increasingly being recognized as a means to preserve and enhance muscular strength and to prevent falls and improve mobility in the elderly (USDHHS 1996b). However, because most research has been conducted on the health consequences of aerobic exercise, our discussion of exercise in this section will focus nearly exclusively on this type.

Physical activity and physical health

Physical activity is usually defined as any bodily movements produced by skeletal muscles that result in energy expenditure beyond resting expenditure (e.g. Thompson *et al.* 2003). Physical activity has frequently been categorized, according to the context in which it occurs, into occupational, household and leisure-time activities. Leisure-time activities refer to exercise people do for recreational purposes such as sports or walking. However, in a typical day, most people engage in activities that would not easily be subsumed under any of these categories, such as walking to their place of work, climbing steps, carrying luggage or working in the garden. I will therefore use a simpler categorization here and divide activities into leisure and non-leisure time activities, with leisure-time activities reflecting the activities that are typically considered exercise (e.g. sports, jogging, hiking) and non-leisure time activities including occupational and household activities as well as those activities that are not directly occupational or household but are also not performed for recreational purposes.

Leisure-time activities
In a study conducted in the Netherlands, Magnus *et al.* (1979) reported that habitual walking, cycling and gardening during more than eight months of the year was associated with fewer acute coronary events. The amount of these activities did not appear to matter, but it was important that they were performed throughout most of the year. Similarly, Morris *et al.* (1980) reported from their study of middle-aged male office workers that men who kept fit and engaged in vigorous sports during an initial survey between 1968 and 1970 had an incidence of CHD in the next eight and a half years that was somewhat less than half that of their colleagues who engaged in no vigorous exercise.

A more extensive study was conducted in the USA with a large sample of male graduates of Harvard University (Paffenbarger *et al.* 1978, 1986). In this study 16,936 male alumni who had entered Harvard between 1916 and 1950 returned a questionnaire concerning their physical activities (e.g. walking, stair climbing, sports) either in 1962 or in 1966. A second questionnaire in 1972 identified the non-fatal heart attacks that had occurred in the meantime. Records of fatal heart attacks were obtained for a period of 12 to 16 years.

During the first 6 to 10 years there were 572 first heart attacks. Age-specific rates of CHD declined consistently with increasing energy expended per week on exercise. Energy expenditure was aggregated into a composite index of physical activity and expressed in terms of kilocalories per week. Men with an index below 2000 kcal/week were at 64 per cent higher risk than peers with a higher index.

Heart attack risk was clearly related to present-day activity rather than activity during student days. Thus, the fact that an alumnus had engaged in competitive sports as a student was unrelated to heart attack risk in later life. Furthermore, as Figure 5.1 indicates, the inverse relationship between activity and heart attack risk

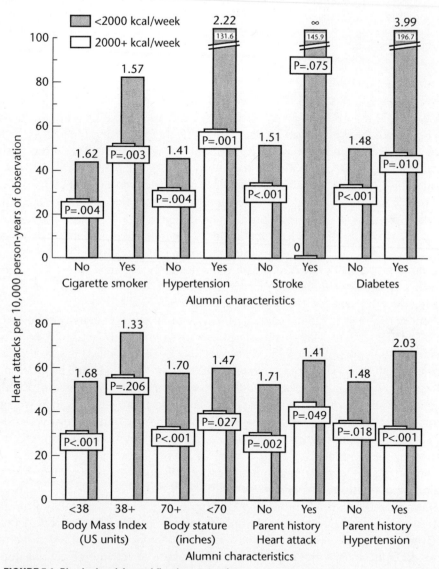

FIGURE 5.1 Physical activity and first heart attack

Note: Given here are paired combinations of the physical activity index and other characteristics of Harvard male alumni.

Relative risk is calculated as follows:

rates for alumni with low physical activity index
rates for alumni with high physical activity index

Source: Paffenbarger *et al.* (1978)

could be demonstrated even when other risk factors were controlled for. This is very important since risk factors such as body weight or smoking are strongly and negatively related to exercise adherence. Exercise was also negatively related to mortality. Death rates from coronary heart disease and from all causes declined steadily as energy expenditure increased from less than 500 to 3500 kcal/week. Beyond this point there was only a slight increase in rates. Men who expended less than 2000 kcal/week were at a 31 per cent higher risk of death than more active men.

Non-leisure-time activity

With their classic study of 3975 longshoremen (i.e. wharf labourers who load and unload cargo) aged 35 to 75 years, who were followed for a 22-year period from 1951 to 1973, Paffenbarger and his colleagues (Paffenbarger and Hale 1975; Brand et al. 1979) continued the pioneering work of Morris et al. (1953) on the health-protective effects of occupational activity. It was found that the relative risk of dying from CHD of individuals engaged in moderate and light physical activity was nearly twice that of workers doing the heavy jobs. The negative relationship between physical activity and coronary mortality remained when other known factors that contribute to CHD, such as heavy cigarette smoking and high systolic blood pressure, were controlled for. Similar findings were reported in other studies relating work activity to mortality from CHD (for a review, see Powell et al. 1987). While most of these studies used all-male samples, some have replicated these findings for both sexes (e.g. Brunner et al. 1974; Salonen et al. 1982).

A more recent longitudinal study based on data on physical activity collected by the US National Center for Health Statistics in the period 1971 to 1975 (NHANES 1) is interesting because it compared the relative health effects of leisure time and non-leisure time activity for more than 10,000 adults ranging in age from 35 to 74 at baseline (Arrieta and Russell 2008). Leisure-time activity was assessed with a question about how much exercise participants had from activities they engaged in for recreation. With regard to non-leisure time activity, participants were asked about how physically active they were on a typical day, aside from recreation. Responses were coded into three categories: low, moderate or high. Vital status information (i.e. mortality) about members of this cohort was obtained from the beginning of the study to the year 2000.

Data for the group of 35- to 59-year-olds were analysed separately from that of individuals aged 60 to 74. I will only report the analysis for participants who survived the first five years following the measurement of their physical activity levels, because in that group the likelihood of physical activity restrictions due to an illness is reduced (i.e. reverse causality). Compared to low levels of non-leisure activity, there was a reduction in mortality risk of 26 per cent for moderate and 37 per cent for high non-leisure activity for the younger age group. For the older age group, both leisure and non-leisure-time activities had a health-protective effect. Compared to low levels of activity, moderate leisure-time activity resulted in a reduction of 12 per cent, while moderate non-leisure-time activity resulted in a reduction of 18 per cent. For high levels, the risk reduction was 34 per cent and 38 per cent respectively.

Although this study would suggest that non-leisure-time activity is more important than leisure-time activity, most other research indicates that it is the actual amount of energy expended, rather than the context in which it is expended, that is important for health benefits. Furthermore, these health benefits appear to increase linearly with increasing levels of physical activity. In a review of 44 observational studies conducted in Canada, Denmark, Finland, Germany, Israel, the Netherlands, Norway, Sweden, Great Britain and the USA, Lee and Skerett (2001) concluded that the risk of dying during a particular period declines with increasing levels of physical activity. This inverse relation has been found for men and women and younger and older individuals.

Most of the research on the health impact of physical activity relies on self-report measures of activity levels. One exception is a study by Manini *et al.* (2006), who assessed energy expenditure objectively (doubly labelled water method) in a small sample of 302 healthy men and women, aged 70 to 82 years, who lived in the community. These individuals were followed for just over six years after the measure of energy expenditure had been taken. The absolute risk of mortality was 12.1 per cent in the highest tertile of activity energy expenditure, 17.6 per cent in the middle and 24.7 per cent in the lowest tertile. Thus, the mortality risk over the six-year period was twice as high with the lowest as compared to the highest level of energy expenditure. These results changed little after adjusting for smoking status, educational level or prevalent health conditions. The authors estimated that for every 287kcal per day of activity expenditure, there is approximately a 30 per cent lower risk of mortality.

Physical fitness

In most of the studies reviewed here, some screening was used to exclude individuals who were already suffering from some diagnosed illness. However, the most extensive clinical screening was probably done in a study by Blair *et al.* (1989), in which male and female participants received a preventive medical examination at a clinic at the outset of the study. All individuals who had a personal history of heart attack, hypertension, stroke or diabetes were excluded, as were respondents who had abnormal responses to a resting or exercise electrocardiograph.

Physical fitness, which can be considered an objective indicator of habitual physical exercise, was measured directly by a treadmill exercise test assessing treadmill test endurance. The average follow-up of the participants (10,224 men and 3120 women) was slightly more than eight years. Fitness was negatively related to mortality. This inverse relationship was significant for mortality from all causes and for mortality from CHD. It remained significant even after statistical adjustment for age, smoking habits, cholesterol level, systolic blood pressure, fasting glucose level and parental history of CHD.

Extended follow-up of this sample provided the opportunity to evaluate the relationship of changes in physical fitness with mortality in a cohort of 9777 men (Blair *et al.* 1995). The average interval between the two examinations was 4.9 years and follow-up for mortality after the second examination was an average of 5.1 years. Results indicated that improvements in fitness were associated with a substantial reduction in mortality risk. Thus, men who were unfit at their initial examination but who became fit by the time of their subsequent examination had a 44 per cent reduction in mortality.

Control of confounding variables

Since none of the studies on the impact of exercise used random assignment of respondents to levels of physical activity, the issue of temporal priority (i.e. whether the assumed cause really preceded the assumed effect) is difficult to establish. When individuals are free to determine their own level of physical activity, it is likely that they choose to become less active with the onset of some disease process. Health screening of participants at the beginning of a study enables exclusion of individuals who already suffer from CHD or some other serious illness. However, with medical diagnoses being less than perfectly reliable, even careful medical screening could not rule out the possibility that the lowering of activity levels was due to some undiagnosed illness. However, as Powell *et al.* (1987) argued, if self-selection by illness were an important factor, studies with medical screening before the observation period should show smaller and less consistent associations between activity and health than those without prior screening. In their extensive review of studies on physical activity and CHD, Powell *et al.* (1987) failed to find evidence for such a difference.

A second strategy to safeguard against self-selection by illness is to omit all deaths or illnesses that occurred during the first two or three years of follow-up after exercise assessment. This was done in the studies of Paffenbarger *et al.* (1986), Blair *et al.* (1989) and Arrieta and Russell (2008). A strong negative relationship still pertained between exercise and mortality risk. Since one would expect the strength of the inverse relationship to weaken considerably over time if individuals with sub-clinical heart disease were overrepresented in the inactive group, the persistence of a strong relationship makes an interpretation in terms of this type of self-selection less plausible.

There is a second type of self-selection, however, that cannot be controlled by these procedures – namely, self-selection by risk factors. There is evidence that people who are older, of lower socio-economic status (SES), overweight or smokers are more likely to drop out of voluntary exercise programmes than younger, middle- or upper-class, normal weight, non-smoking individuals. Since all these variables are also related to increased risk of morbidity and mortality, this type of selection could account for the health difference. However, in many of the studies reported earlier, the health benefit of exercise could be demonstrated even when these risk factors were statistically controlled.

Even though a controlled intervention study is still needed in this area, the studies described earlier have been very thorough in controlling for all suspected confounding variables. Studies of leisure-time activity suggested that a weekly energy expenditure in excess of 1500 to 2000kcal is sufficient to reduce the risk of mortality from heart disease. It is left to the reader to judge whether one can, as most writers in this area appear to do, consider a vigorous daily half-hour run or daily walk of an hour to be a moderate level of physical activity that is attainable by most adults. Fortunately for those who are satisfied with less than maximal health benefits, the relationship between activity level and health appears to be monotonic, at least for leisure-time activity. In other words, there is a consistent association between exercise and health benefits: every increase in exercise will benefit our health.

Mediating processes

A number of biological mechanisms have been proposed to explain how physical activity might prevent the development of CHD (Powell et al. 1987; Thompson et al. 2003). It has been suggested that muscular activity may directly protect the cardiovascular system by stimulating the development of collateral vessels that support the heart muscle. There is evidence from animal studies that physical activity increases the diameter of epicardial coronary arteries (e.g. Kramsch et al. 1981) and enhances coronary collateral development (Neil and Oxendine 1979).

Exercise could also prevent sudden cardiac death by enhancing myocardial electrical stability. This could be responsible for the lower rate of sudden deaths reported for the more active participants in several studies. There is some evidence that physical training increases cardiac parasympathetic tone in humans (Kenney 1985). Parasympathetic stimulation reduces ventricular fibrillation that can be caused by insufficient blood supply to the heart muscle (Kent et al. 1973). There is also evidence from animal studies of a heightened resistance to ventricular fibrillation after exercise training (e.g. Billman et al. 1984).

Finally, physical exercise may have beneficial effects on factors that contribute to the development of CHD, such as overweight, high blood pressure and atherosclerosis. Evidence has shown that exercise has positive effects on weight control and reduces the risk of hypertension. More than 40 randomized controlled trials conducted to determine the effect of exercise on blood pressure indicated that regular exercise lowers both systolic and diastolic blood pressure by 2.6 and 1.8 mm Hg in normotensive and 7.4 and 5.8 mm Hg in hypertensive individuals (for a review, see Thompson et al. 2003). However, since the positive effects of exercise on health have been demonstrated in studies that controlled for weight and hypertension (e.g. Paffenbarger et al. 1978), these factors are unlikely to be the major mediators of the exercise–health relationship. Regular exercise may also lower the risk of atherosclerosis. A meta-analysis of more than 50 exercise training trials with a duration of more than 12 weeks demonstrated an increase in HDLc levels of 4.6 per cent and reductions in LDLc levels of 5 per cent (Thompson et al. 2003). Finally, there is also evidence that physical activity reduces insulin resistance and glucose intolerance (Thomson et al. 2003).

How much physical activity is needed to maintain physical health?

According to the updated recommendations of the American Heart Association, all healthy adults between the ages of 18 and 65 should engage in moderate-intensity aerobic physical activity (e.g. brisk walking at 3 to 4mph) for a minimum of 30 minutes on five day per week or in vigorous-intensity exercise such as jogging for a minimum of 20 minutes on three days per week (Haskell *et al.* 2007). There is some evidence that splitting exercise into shorter bouts (e.g. three times 10 minutes instead of 30 minutes a day) results in similar health benefits (Dunn *et al.* 1998). In addition to aerobic exercise, exercise that maintains or increases muscular strength is also recommended.

Physical activity and psychological health

It is widely believed that aerobic exercise has a beneficial effect on mental health. Aerobic fitness programmes such as jogging, dancing or swimming have come to be frequent prescriptions for treating depression. There is indeed empirical evidence from correlational and intervention studies that physical activity relieves symptoms of depression and anxiety and improves mood (McDonald and Hodgdon 1991; USDHHS 1996b; Martinsen and Morgan 1997).

Exercise and depression

Depression refers to a mental health problem that is characterized by depressed mood, a markedly reduced interest or pleasure in almost all activities and a number of other symptoms such as insomnia, agitation and weight loss. According to some estimates, depression affects one in five people during their lifetime. Evidence from community studies among men and women indicates that physical activity is associated with substantially reduced symptoms of depression and reduced occurrence of clinical depression (USDHHS 1996b). For example, data from a telephone survey conducted in the state of Illinois indicated that adults who spent more time participating in regular exercise, sports or other physical activities had fewer symptoms of depression than people reporting no physical activity (Ross and Hayes 1988). Similar results were reported in a community study conducted in the German state of Bavaria (Weyerer 1992). However, this kind of correlational evidence is ambiguous with regard to causality. Although participants may be depressed *because* they are unfit and inactive, they may also be inactive because they are depressed. There could also be a third factor (e.g. some physical illness) that is responsible for both reduced activity and depression.

Support for the hypothesis that physical activity reduces depressive symptoms in individuals who are mildly to moderately depressed comes from experimental intervention studies (e.g. Dunn *et al.* 2005; Blumenthal *et al.* 2007). The 80 participants in the study by Dunn *et al.* (2005), who had all been diagnosed with mild to moderate depression, were randomly assigned to one of four exercise groups or an exercise placebo group. The exercise groups differed in the amount of supervised exercise and in the number of occasions per week in which they performed their exercise. The group with the high exercise dose conducted an amount of exercise that complied with the recommendations of the American Heart Association described earlier. The low dose group performed only half as much exercise. The exercise placebo control group met three times per week for stretching exercises. The primary outcome measure was the change in depressive symptoms from baseline to 12 weeks. Depressive symptoms were assessed with the Hamilton Rating Scale for Depression, a multiple-choice questionnaire that physicians use to rate patients' symptoms. The high dose of exercise resulted in a significant drop in depression scores. The improvement in this group was also significantly greater than that in the low dose or the placebo group. These latter groups did not differ from each other. The number of occasions over which the weekly exercise dose was distributed did not appear to make a difference.

Somewhat weaker findings were reported by Blumenthal et al. (2007) from one of the most carefully conducted experimental intervention studies to date. Participants were 202 men and women, diagnosed with major depression, who participated in the study between October 2000 and November 2005. Participants were assigned randomly to one of four conditions: supervised aerobic exercise; home-based aerobic exercise; antidepressant medication; or placebo. Patients in the supervised aerobic exercise condition attended three supervised group exercise sessions per week for a 16-week period. Patients in the home-based exercise programme received the same instructions but exercised at home. Patients in the pill condition received either an antidepressant or a placebo pill. At post-treatment, the two exercise groups displayed significantly higher aerobic capacity than the pill groups, with the patients in the supervised programmes scoring highest. The main outcome measures were remission rate of major depressive illness and a reduction in scores on a self-report measure of depressive symptoms. Planned contrasts demonstrated that supervised exercise, home-based and medication resulted in higher remission rates compared to placebo, with no difference between the two treatment groups. However, the contrasts just failed to reach conventional significance and effects on the self-report measure were non-significant. The second outcome measure (changes in Hamilton ratings) did not result in significant differences.

Based on the outcomes of 23 randomized controlled trials in which an exercise condition was compared to a no-treatment or control intervention, a recent meta-analysis resulted in a large effect (Mead et al. 2009). However, this effect was considerably reduced and only borderline significant when only trials that used intention-to-treat methodology were included. Since both the intervention trials of Blumenthal et al. (2007) and of Dunn et al. (2005), which are two of the methodologically soundest studies in this area, resulted in some significant exercise effects, I tend to conclude that exercise does have a positive (albeit weak) effect on depressive symptoms in individuals who are mildly to moderately depressed.

Exercise may even protect individuals against developing depression. A prospective study of 10,201 Harvard male alumni found an inverse relationship between the level of physical activity assessed in 1961 or 1966 and the incidence of depression during the following 23 to 27 years (Paffenbarger et al. 1994). Respondents were asked in 1988 whether any health problems had ever been diagnosed by a physician and to indicate the year of onset. They were given a list which included depression (among other health problems, e.g. CHD, emphysema). Incidence of depression was determined by an attack first experienced during the follow-up period. Results indicated an inverse relationship between physical activity reported at intake and the incidence of depression during the follow-up period. The relative risk of depression was 27 per cent lower for men who had reported playing three or more hours of sport each week than for men who had reported playing no sports.

Mediating processes

A number of physiological and psychosocial mechanisms have been suggested to account for the impact of exercise on depression (for a review, see Morgan 1997). It has been suggested that aerobic exercise may facilitate the production of brain norepinephrine. Low norepinephrine levels in the central nervous system have been suspected as a cause of some depressions. Another hypothesis is that improved mood states following exercise are stimulated by the release of endorphins, which are opium-like substances produced by the body. At the more psychological level it has been argued that exercise may reduce anxiety and depression because it distracts individuals and prevents them from focusing on their problems (Bahrke and Morgan 1978). Although this could account for some immediate effects of exercise on anxiety and mood, it is difficult to see how it could explain long-term effects.

A better explanation of such long-term effects is the assumption that exercise may increase individual feelings of self-efficacy. The fact that one is regularly exercising or participating in an exercise group may increase one's feeling of being disciplined, effective and competent. Some of the positive effects of exercise may also stem from factors associated with exercise, such as social activity and a feeling of involvement with others. Thus, for example, bicycling with friends, swimming with a companion or running with others may improve mood because of the companionship provided.

Physical activity and healthy ageing

Physical activity can play an important role in slowing down the decline in physical fitness associated with advancing age, in preventing disability and in helping the elderly to preserve their independence (for reviews, see Buchner et al. 1992; Wagner et al. 1992). Ageing is characterized by a diffuse loss of physiologic capacity and reserve. The older we become, the less physically fit we become. This decline in physical fitness with advancing age does not develop suddenly at age 65, but begins at middle age and progresses steadily thereafter. Data from cross-sectional studies suggest that between the ages of 30 and 80, we lose approximately 50 per cent of aerobic capacity (i.e. the ability of the body to produce energy by using oxygen) and between 30 and 40 per cent in the strength of back, leg and arm muscles (Buchner et al. 1992). For many years it was generally accepted that such decline was genetically programmed and, as a result, inevitable.

Replicating a development which took place in the study of ageing and intelligence more than a decade earlier (e.g. Baltes and Schaie 1976), researchers have recently noted that the effect of age on physical fitness appears to differ widely between individuals. Whereas some older individuals show substantial physical decline, for others the decline with age is minimal. This suggests that the steep mean decline in physical fitness which appeared to be the 'normal' or 'usual' consequence of ageing may not be inevitable. Rowe and Kahn (1987, 1997) coined the term 'successful ageing' to refer to this type of preservation of function. Successful ageing is characterized by three components, namely low probability of disease and disease-related disability, high cognitive and physical functional capacity, and active engagement with life. Successful ageing is thus more than the absence of disease, and more than the maintenance of functional capacities. It is their combination with active engagement with life that reflects successful ageing most fully.

Evidence from epidemiological studies strongly supports the role of regular physical activity in successful ageing by preserving muscle performance, promoting mobility and reducing fall risk. Several large-scale longitudinal studies observed that for men and women (aged 65 and older) who were functionally intact (e.g. were able to climb stairs and walk half a mile) at baselines measurement, inactivity was associated with a markedly increased risk of losing mobility during the following few years (Wagner et al. 1992). Intervention studies have also demonstrated that aerobic and strength exercise can improve aerobic capacity and muscle strength in older adults (Buchner et al. 1992). Two more recent meta-analyses of the impact of exercise interventions on the functional status of older adults reported modest but significant effects on measures of functional status (e.g. walk speed, walk endurance and balance; Gu and Conn 2008; Kelley et al. 2008). That the benefits of physical activity can extend beyond the improvement of functional status has been demonstrated by a meta-analysis of the impact of physical activity on the psychological well-being of older adults. Netz et al. (2005) reported small but significant improvements in psychological well-being in the treatment as compared to the control groups.

The preservation of physical fitness alone would not enable elderly individuals to 'actively engage with life' unless their cognitive functional capacity was also maintained at a high level. There is evidence from non-intervention studies that physically active seniors have better cognitive functions than inactive ones (Wagner et al. 1992). Further support comes from a longitudinal study which followed a sample of more than 1000 high-functioning elderly (70 to 79) for a two-year period (Albert et al. 1995). This study identified 'strenuous activity in and around the house' as one of four predictors of maintenance of cognitive functions over a two-year interval. In contrast, the evidence from intervention studies, which would be less ambiguous with regard to causal interpretations, is inconsistent. But most of these programmes have been of short duration, and small sample sizes have limited their statistical power (Buchner et al. 1992; Wagner et al. 1992).

The determinants of physical activity

Determinants of regular exercise

Who are the people who keep fit, and how can we persuade those who do not do so to engage in regular exercise? Unfortunately, from a perspective of health education, many of the variables which have been found to be related to exercise participation and adherence, such as age, socio-economic status, education, smoking and proximity to the exercise facility are difficult to influence (Dishman 1982; Sonstroem 1988). Among the *physical variables*, body fat and body weight appear to be major determinants of adherence to exercise programmes (e.g. Dishman and Gettman 1980).

Research on the *attitudes* which characterize participants in exercise programmes has often relied on rather global measures of attitudes towards physical activity and sports such as the Physical Estimation and Attraction Scales (Sonstroem 1978; Sonstroem and Kampper 1980). These global measures have been only moderately successful as predictors of recruitment into exercise programmes (for reviews, see Dishman 1982; Sonstroem 1988). This is not surprising because global attitudes are notoriously poor predictors of specific behaviour (see Chapter 2).

According to the model of reasoned action, the best predictor of a specific behaviour is people's intentions to engage in that behaviour, which in turn is predicted by their attitude towards that specific behaviour and their perceptions of how important others expect them to behave (weighted by their motivation to comply; subjective norms). The model of planned behaviour adds perceived behavioural control as a third determinant of intention and as a potential predictor of behaviour. These two models have been used successfully to study a range of physical activities, including various leisure-time activities. In a meta-analytic review of 72 studies based on these models, Hagger *et al.* (2002) found support for both. Attitudes, subjective norms and perceived behavioural control explained 45 per cent of the variance in intentions, with attitudes and perceived behavioural control being stronger predictors than subjective norms. Intention and perceived behavioural control jointly accounted for an average of 27 per cent of the variance in physical activity measures across studies.

According to these models, intention and perceived behavioural control are the only variables that directly influence behaviour. This implies that the impact of social structural variables should be mediated by intention and perceived behavioural control. Godin *et al.* (2010) tested this assumption in a longitudinal study with a sample 1483 Canadian men and women between the ages of 18 and 80. Attitudes towards leisure-time physical activity, subjective norms, perceived behavioural control and intentions were assessed at intake. Past behaviour was measured by asking participants to indicate how active they had been in their leisure time during the preceding three months. In addition several social structural factors were assessed such as level of education, family income, gender, age and material deprivation. Material deprivation was measured at neighbourhood level through an index that reflected levels of education, employment and income in a given neighbourhood. Three months later at Time 2, participants were contacted again and asked to indicate the extent to which they engaged in leisure-time physical activity during the last three months.

The measures of intention, perceived behavioural control and of the social structural variables were significantly correlated with behaviour at Time 2.

However, hierarchical regressions computed to test whether the effects of social structural variables on behaviour were indeed mediated by intention and perceived behavioural control indicated only partial mediation. Statistically controlling for the effects of intention and perceived behavioural control on behaviour (by entering them first into the hierarchical regressions) resulted in a significant reduction of the effects of education, income, age, gender and material deprivation on behaviour. However, these reduced effects were still significant (or marginally significant in the case of gender and material deprivation). This indicates that, in addition to an indirect effect that is mediated by intention and perceived behavioural control, structural factors also had a direct effect on behaviour.

Determinants of exercise maintenance

So far I have only reviewed studies which assessed the determinants of the intensity and frequency with which people engaged in regular exercise. However, there is also research on individuals who plan to increase their level of physical activity and who typically have signed up for exercise programmes at their university or at a sports centre. Since few people manage to attend such courses regularly and some people even drop out completely, such studies enable researchers to assess the determinants of exercise maintenance over time (e.g. Jonas 1995; Armitage 2005; Williams *et al.* 2008).

According to the theories of reasoned action and planned behaviour, *continued participation* in exercise programmes (i.e. adherence) should be predicted from attitudes towards continued participation in an exercise programme rather than from attitudes towards exercise in general. Since only individuals with positive attitudes towards physical activity are likely to be recruited into the group of exercisers, programme adherence should only be weakly related to general attitudes towards physical exercise. In line with this argument, global measures of attitudes towards physical activity have typically been unsuccessful in predicting adherence, even in cases where they were reasonable predictors of recruitment into the exercise programme (e.g. Sonstroem and Kampper 1980).

Studies that assessed attitudes and behavioural intentions towards continued programme participation have been fairly successful in predicting programme adherence or exercise maintenance (e.g. Jonas 1995; Armitage 2005). In a prospective study of a sample of more than 100 men and women who had registered for a four-month fitness course at the University of Tübingen (Germany), Jonas predicted intention to participate ($R^2 = .45$) during the second half of the semester on the basis of attitudes towards participation and perceived control (but not subjective norm). Attitudes towards the fitness course – that is, whether participants liked or disliked the course – was a further determinant of intention. Intention accounted for 25 per cent of the variance of actual participation (measured objectively). Perceived behavioural control did not make a significant contribution to the prediction of behaviour over and above intention, but participants' affective reactions towards participation did. The more participants enjoyed participation, the more likely they were to continue.

It is interesting that the influence of perceived behavioural control on intention in this study only became significant in the second half of the semester and that, probably as a result, intentions became a significantly better predictor of behaviour during this second half of the course. It seems that during the first part of the course, participants learned to become more realistic about the constraints on their behaviour. However, in contrast to the participants in the study of Ajzen and Madden (1986) described earlier (see p. 38), who did not weaken in their intention to get a top grade in their course, even if they realized that this goal had become rather unrealistic, participants in the Jonas study adjusted their intentions in the light of their more realistic perception of behavioural control. As a result, their intentions became a better predictor of their behaviour during the second half of the course. Although these findings are different from those of Ajzen and Madden they are not inconsistent with the model of planned behaviour that allows for perceived behavioural control to influence behavioural intentions without specifying the conditions under which this is likely to happen.

There are probably two conditions that are necessary to produce the pattern reported by Jonas (1995): first, intention has to be measured halfway through a course to allow adjustment. If initial intention is used as predictor, the type of adjustment found by Jonas cannot emerge. This explains why a similar longitudinal study conducted by Armitage (2005), whose participants enrolled in a 12-week course of physical exercise, did not replicate the findings of the Jonas study. When Armitage regressed mean attendance on intention and behavioural control, only perceived behavioural control emerged as a significant predictor. Since he used intention assessed at the beginning of the 12-week course as a predictor, participants were unable to adjust their intentions in the light of a more realistic perception of perceived behavioural control. A second factor is probably the importance of the behavioural goal that is being assessed. Whereas it is easy to adjust one's intentions with regard to physical exercise to a more realistic level, giving up the hope to get an A in a course may be much more difficult, even in the light of this goal becoming highly unlikely (Ajzen and Madden 1986).

Despite inconsistencies in the pattern of results reported by Jonas and Armitage, both studies agree in identifying perceived behavioural control as an important determinant of behaviour maintenance. This conclusion, which is also supported by the studies of Rhodes *et al.* (2008) and Williams *et al.* (2008), is inconsistent with the theoretical ideas about the determinants of behaviour maintenance developed by Rothman *et al.* (2004). These researchers argued that self-efficacy (which is one component of perceived behavioural control) should only influence the initiation of health behaviour but play no role in its maintenance. At this stage, self-efficacy should no longer be important, because 'having demonstrated that they can successfully perform the behavior over an extended period of time, people feel less need to question or verify their ability to engage in the behavior' (Rothman *et al.* 2004: 137).

What conclusions can we draw about how to persuade people to exercise and how to increase adherence to exercise programmes? Researchers in this area seem to agree that people join exercise programmes to obtain some health-related benefits (e.g. improvement in cardiovascular fitness, weight loss), but that they stay because the programme is convenient and enjoyable, which suggests a two-step procedure. Since convenience is likely to be a predictor of initiation as well as adherence, mass media campaigns should not only emphasize the health-related benefits of specific exercise, but should also point out that it takes less effort to stay healthy than most people might anticipate. Furthermore, whereas it is difficult to persuade people to join a health club or even to take a daily half-hour walk, it may be much easier to persuade them to rearrange their daily lives and become more physically active.

That individuals can be persuaded to change minor routines has been demonstrated by Brownell *et al.* (1980). These authors observed that only 6 per cent of the people in shopping malls, railway stations and bus stations tended to use stairs rather than escalators. When a simple sign pointing out the benefits of exercise was placed at the bottom of the stairs and escalators, stair use was nearly tripled. Similarly, one might be able to persuade people to walk to work instead of driving or, at least, to park their cars further away from their place of work. Who knows? People who enjoy these small activities and who have become more physically fit as a result may even decide to take up jogging or join an exercise class.

The efficacy of interventions to promote physical activity

The review of studies of the impact of individual-level interventions in the Surgeon General's Report concluded that:

> behavioral management approaches have been employed with mixed results. Where an effect has been demonstrated, it has often been small. Evidence of the effectiveness of techniques like self-monitoring, frequent follow-up telephone calls, and incentives appear to be generally positive over the short run, but not over long intervals. Evidence on the relative effectiveness of interventions on adherence to moderate or vigorous activity is limited and unclear.
>
> (USDHHS 1996b: 226)

Since then, matters have become clearer and a recent meta-analysis of 69 interventions using experimental or quasi-experimental designs and aimed at improving physical activity levels of more than 18,000 individuals reported a significant effect with an overall effect size of d = 0.32 (Michie *et al.* 2009). This is a small effect according to the classification of Cohen (1992), but in the typical range for psychological interventions. The findings for physical activity interventions actually closely paralleled those reported on interventions aimed at improving healthy eating: the one behaviour change technique that accounted for most variance in efficacy was asking the respondents to keep a record of their physical activity (e.g. a diary). Other change techniques that were effective in combination with the prompt to self-monitor were prompts to induce specific goal-setting and to provide feedback on behaviour. Neither the delivery format (e.g. individual vs. group) nor the setting in which the interventions was executed (e.g. workplace or community) appeared to moderate the impact of these interventions (Michie *et al.* 2009).

One important limitation of these studies is that they only inform us about the efficacy of strategies to increase the activity level of individuals who want their activity level increased, but not about effective methods to persuade sedentary people to become more active. The usual procedure by which participants in these studies were recruited appears to be to inform people by e-mail, website or mass media that volunteers are invited to participate in some physical activity programme that claims to help them increase their level of physical activity (e.g. Spittaels *et al.* 2007). This suggests that the people who participate in these studies are already dissatisfied with their present level of physical activity and decide to participate in the hope of becoming more physically active.

So how do we persuade sedentary individuals to become more active? One source of information about the efficacy of campaigns aimed at persuading people to increase their level of physical activity is provided by the community-wide interventions described earlier. And this information is not terribly encouraging. Of the three community interventions which included a component that promoted physical exercise, the Minnesota Heart Health Program (Luepker *et al.* 1994), the Pawtucket Heart Health Program (Carleton *et al.* 1995) and the Stanford Five-City Project (Farquhar *et al.* 1990), only one, the Minnesota Heart Health Program (MHHP) had a significant, albeit small, effect on levels of physical activity. The MHHP advocated regular physical activity as part of its effort to reduce risk factors for CHD. Three intervention communities received a five- to six-year programme designed to reduce smoking, influence diet and increase physical activity levels. Mass media were used to educate the public about the relationship between regular physical exercise and reduced risk for CHD, and health professionals promoted physical activity through their local organizations. Three other communities which received no intervention served as comparison sites. Leisure-time physical activity was assessed as the percentage of participants who described themselves as regularly active. Cross-sectional comparisons between intervention and control communities indicated small but significant increases in levels of physical activity in the intervention communities during the first three years. This effect was no longer significant after the third year when activity levels increased also in the control communities. The Surgeon General's Report therefore concludes that the results of community-based interventions to increase physical activity have been generally disappointing.

The success of the community-wide mass media campaigns reported since then to improve physical activity levels has also been mixed. For example, the national mass media 'ACTIVE for LIFE' campaign promoted moderate-intensity physical activity such as walking, cycling, swimming, dancing and heavy gardening via television ads, posters, leaflets and a website in England (Hillsdon *et al.* 2001). Although people were aware of the campaign and became significantly more knowledgeable about the health recommendation for physical activity, there was no evidence that the campaign improved physical activity, either overall or in any sub-group.

A mass media campaign targeting physical activity in the Australian state of New South Wales was only slightly more effective (Bauman *et al.* 2001). The campaign tag line was 'Exercise, you have to take it regularly, not seriously', and components included paid television advertising and paid advertisements in the print media. Although the campaign had an impact on awareness and knowledge, it had no significant effects on activity levels of the total sample. However, a sub-group of individuals, who at baseline were 'motivated but insufficiently active' showed some improvement in activity level.

The VERB campaign launched in 2002 by the US Centers for Disease Control is one of the few mass media campaigns that appears to have been effective in increasing physical activity levels in the targeted group (Huhman *et al.* 2007). The campaign combined national advertising with school and community promotions and internet activities to persuade US children of 9 to 13 years to become physically more active. The campaign used professionally produced television, radio and print advertisements that, according to the published reports, were based on theories of planned behaviour. The messages were aimed at improving children's beliefs about the positive effects of physical activity and their self-efficacy in overcoming the barriers related to participation. The campaign ran from 2002 to 2004 and was evaluated through a longitudinal study of a nationally representative cohort of children and their parents interviewed annually, with the first interview being conducted in the months before the start of the campaign. After two years a dose-response effect could be demonstrated: controlling for physical activity levels at baseline, there was a clear association between the extent of campaign awareness and physical activity levels after two years. The more children reported seeing the campaign messages, the more physical activity they reported and the more positive their attitudes were towards the benefits of physical activity.

Conclusions

Next to stopping smoking and eating healthily, exercising regularly is important for maintaining health and increasing one's life expectancy. The research reviewed in this section demonstrated an inverse relationship between physical activity and morbidity and mortality. Furthermore, consistent with the models of reasoned action and planned behaviour, attitudes towards engaging in a specific form of exercise and perceived control are good predictors of physical exercise. Although physical activity is also determined by social structural variables such as age, income or educational level, these effects are partly mediated by intention and perceived behavioural control.

There is also evidence that interventions aimed at helping people to increase their level of physical activity are reasonably effective. However, participants in these interventions are usually individuals who already are motivated to increase their level of physical exercise. The effects of campaigns aimed at persuading people to increase physical activity levels have not been impressive. Although it is difficult to judge from the brief descriptions of the interventions given in many of these reports, one of the reasons for their moderate impact could have been their reliance on health education and health appeals. If one wants to persuade people to change health-impairing behaviour patterns and to adopt healthy behaviour, one has to analyse the belief structure underlying each of these lifestyles. The a priori assumption implicit in the design of many health promotion campaigns – that people engage in health-impairing behaviour patterns out of ignorance of the negative health consequences – is often wrong. Although some people may engage in health-impairing behaviour patterns out of ignorance, more often there are other reasons. In order for a campaign to be effective, these other reasons need to be identified and persuasive arguments developed to focus on them.

Prevention of HIV infections and AIDS

By December 2008 33.4 million people worldwide were infected with HIV (Human Immunodeficiency Virus), the virus that causes AIDS (Acquired Immune Deficiency Syndrome). In 2008 alone, 2.7 million people were newly infected and 2 million people died of AIDS-related causes in that year. Since 1981, more than 25 million people have died of AIDS (UNAIDS 2009). There is still neither a vaccine nor a cure, but with the introduction of highly active antiretroviral therapy (HAART) in 1996, there appears to be an effective means to suppress the infection. With the introduction of HAART, HIV/AIDS has become a chronic disease and the life expectancy of HIV-infected individuals has been greatly extended, at least in those countries were this therapy is available and where people can afford it (e.g. Fang *et al.* 2007; McDavid Harrison *et al.* 2010). But HAART does not eliminate the infection, it only suppresses it. And life expectancy for HIV-infected individuals remains still shorter than that of the general population, even in the USA (Hill and Pozniak 2010; McDavid Harrison *et al.* 2010). The only means by which people can escape the infection is by avoiding behaviours that are essential to the transmission of HIV. Thus, programmes aimed at changing behaviour are still the only strategy to stop the AIDS epidemic.

The cause of AIDS

AIDS is caused by infection with HIV which attacks the immune system. The immune system reacts with the formation of antibodies. Although these antibodies do not play a protective role as they do in more familiar virus infections, they can be used as indicators of the presence of the virus. These antibodies can be detected in the blood serum by tests two weeks to three months after the infection. Individuals who have developed antibodies are said to be seropositive. But even before the development of antibodies, the individual can be infectious to others through sexual intercourse or blood donations. The HIV virus responsible for the AIDS epidemic in the western world is the HIV-1 virus. More recently, it has been discovered that a second HIV virus exists (HIV-2) which is mainly restricted to parts of West Africa (Adler *et al*. 1997). Although this virus has also been known to induce AIDS in some cases, it appears to do so more slowly than the original virus (HIV-1). When referring to HIV in this book, I will be referring to the HIV-1 virus, which accounts for most of the HIV infections worldwide.

According to a study based on national HIV surveillance data from 25 states of the USA, average life expectancy after an HIV diagnosis increased from 10.5 to 22.5 years from 1996 to 2005. There was some evidence that life expectancy was worse for individuals diagnosed at a later stage of the disease (McDavid Harrison *et al*. 2010). An even larger study is the Antiretroviral Therapy Cohort Collaboration Study, based on more than 43,000 patients who initiated combination antiretroviral therapy between 1996 and 2005 in Canada, Europe and the USA (Antiretroviral Therapy Cohort Collaboration 2008). During this period, life expectancy at age 20 increased from 36.1 to 49.4 years and thus reached two-thirds of the life expectancy of the general population in these countries. However, there were substantial differences between sub-groups. Women had higher life expectancy than men. Patients who were presumably infected through injecting drug use had lower life expectancies. Finally, patients with lower baseline CD4 cell counts had lower life expectancy than those with higher baseline counts. Thus, death rates for people with HIV/AIDS are still somewhat higher than in the general population, despite the substantial improvement in survival after the introduction of HAART (Hill and Pozniak 2010).

Infection with HIV damages the immune system by infecting and killing one type of white blood cell, the CD4+ T-helper cells. These cells serve an important function in the regulation of the immune system. They stimulate other cells to mount an attack on invading germs. By infecting and ultimately killing the T-helper cells, the HIV stops the process of responding to invading germs at the beginning any thus severely reduces a person's ability to fight other diseases. Without a functioning immune system to ward off other germs, the individual is vulnerable to becoming infected by bacteria, protozoa, fungi and other viruses, along with any malignancies, which would ordinarily not have been able to gain a foothold. Usually AIDS is diagnosed through the presence of unusual opportunistic infections (i.e. infections that use the opportunity of lowered resistance) or unusual forms of cancer (e.g. Kaposi's sarcoma, a cancer of the skin and connective tissues). The AIDS virus also appears to attack the nervous system, causing damage to the brain.

Modes of transmission

The virus is transmitted by the exchange of cell-containing bodily fluids. For transmission to occur, these bodily fluids must contain a sufficient concentration of the virus. Only three bodily fluids pose an infection risk, namely blood, semen and vaginal secretions. Other bodily fluids such as saliva, urine and faeces (in the absence of blood) do not contain sufficient concentrations of the virus to pose a risk of infection (Kalichman 1998).

One common route of HIV transmission is sexual intercourse. Anal intercourse is a high-risk activity for both partners, but the risk of infection is greater for the receptive than the insertive partner. The risk of HIV infection through vaginal intercourse is lower than through anal intercourse, because there is less likelihood of lesions. As with anal intercourse, both partners run the risk of infection but the risk is two to four times higher for the receptive (female) partner (Kalichman 1998). Although oral genital sex is also a biologically plausible route of transmission, the amounts of virus in the saliva are so small that there appears to be little risk of infection. However, there may be some risk involved in oral–penile sex when ejaculation occurs into the mouth. Exposure of semen to the oral cavity has been reported to be the sole risk factor in a number of cases (Kalichman 1998).

Among injection drug users, the risk of infection is not caused by the drug use per se, but by the sharing of injection equipment. The HIV is carried in contaminated blood left in the needle or syringe and the virus is transmitted to another individual when dirty syringes or needles are reused. In general, the risk of contracting AIDS through contact with infected blood is very high. Thus, blood transfusions from infected donors carry an extremely high risk of infection (Friedland and Klein 1987).

There is no evidence that HIV can be transmitted through casual contact. It does not seem to enter the body across skin that is intact, and thus is not transmitted by touching, hand-shaking, sharing eating utensils, sneezing or living in the same household (Curran *et al.* 1988). Thus, in studies of households where one person was HIV infected, none of over 400 family members was infected except for sex partners or children born to infected mothers (Curran *et al.* 1988).

The epidemiology

The first report of AIDS in the USA involved fewer than a dozen men in summer 1981. By 1990, the number of people living with HIV/AIDS worldwide had risen to around 8 million and was 33.4 million in 2008. The majority (67 per cent) live in sub-Saharan Africa, where people living with HIV/AIDS constitute 5.1 per cent of adults aged 15–49 (UNAIDS 2009). The prevalence is much lower in North America (1.4 million people; 0.4 per cent) and western and central Europe (850,000 people; 0.3 per cent). Racial and ethnic minorities are often more affected by the epidemic than other populations. For example, in the USA, African-Americans account for 46 per cent of HIV prevalence but only 12 per cent of the population (UNAIDS 2009).

The risk of infection due to behaviours that allow viral transmission is determined by three factors, namely the frequency of these behaviours, the risk of infection attached to these behaviours (i.e. the likelihood that a given interaction between individuals differing in serostatus results in infection), and the prevalence of HIV in the population (or the particular sub-population with whom the individual engages in the risk behaviour). In the USA and western Europe sexual intercourse between men has been the dominant mode of transmission, with the risk increasing since the advent of HAART (UNAIDS 2009). Heterosexual transmission accounted for less than a third of new infections in North America and western Europe 2006. However, in sub-Saharan Africa, heterosexual contact is the prime mode of transmission. For example, in Swaziland, heterosexual contact is estimated to account for more than 90 per cent of the new infections (UNAIDS 2009). But even in central Europe heterosexual transmission is responsible for more than half of the new infections (UNAIDS 2009).

In the western world, where injecting drug use was a substantial source of infection, its role has declined dramatically since the late 1980s. For example, in Switzerland, where injecting drug users accounted for the majority of new infections in the late 1980s, this mode of transmission is only responsible for 4 per cent of infections today (UNAIDS 2009). In North America and western Europe, it was responsible for less than 15 per cent and 8 per cent of new infections respectively in 2006 (UNAIDS 2009).

The risk of transmission of HIV infection from mother to child has nearly been eliminated in wealthy countries through universal HIV testing for pregnant women, provision of antiretroviral, elective caesarean delivery and avoidance of breastfeeding (e.g. Mofenson 2010). However, in poor countries, this mode of transmission is still responsible for a large number of new infections. It has been estimated that worldwide more than 1000 children are newly infected with HIV each day, most of them in sub-Saharan Africa (Mofenson 2010).

Prior to the institution of protective measures to make the blood supply secure, haemophiliacs and other blood recipients could contract AIDS through blood transfusions. It has been estimated that 12,000 persons in the USA were infected with HIV through transfusions before screening of donated blood and plasma for antibodies to HIV begun in 1985. By that time, 70 to 80 per cent of persons with haemophilia had already been infected with HIV (Friedland and Klein 1987).

Diagnosis of HIV infection

After infection with the HIV virus, the body produces antibodies that can be used to diagnose the infection. Most individuals produce antibodies within six to eight weeks of exposure and nearly 100 per cent will have antibodies within six months (Sax *et al.* 2010). These antibodies can be identified with HIV tests. For individuals who are at high risk (e.g. men who have unsafe sex with men) such tests should be performed regularly, at least once a year, probably even more often. In addition to the conventional HIV tests which require that blood samples are sent to a laboratory and results have to be communicated at a second meeting days or even weeks later, there are now rapid tests available which give results while one waits. While rapid tests provide reliable negative results, false positives are possible. Therefore, in cases of positive results, blood samples have to be taken and sent to an approved laboratory for conventional testing. However, even with traditional tests, positive results will usually have to be confirmed by conducting a second test.

There are several reasons why it is important that people who are infected with HIV are aware of their HIV status. First, awareness is likely to reduce sexual risk behaviour. According to a meta-analysis based on studies conducted in several metropolitan areas in the USA, HIV-positive individuals who were aware of their serostatus were much less likely to engage in risky sexual behaviour (unprotected anal or vaginal intercourse) than HIV-positive individuals who were not aware of their infection (Marks *et al*. 2005). Second, infected individuals who are aware of their serostatus can benefit from antiretroviral treatment. There is some indication that this treatment is more effective if the infection is treated in a relatively early stage (UNAIDS 2009). Furthermore, such antiretroviral treatment decreases the viral load, which reduces the likelihood of HIV transmission. However, even in a high-income country such as the USA, approximately a quarter of the individuals infected with HIV were unaware of their infection in 2004 (Pinkerton *et al*. 2008). In middle- to low-income countries, awareness is likely to be much lower (Adam *et al*. 2009). Pinkerton *et al*. (2008) estimated that the 4 per cent increase in serostatus awareness that occurred in the USA between 2001 and 2004 could be credited with preventing nearly 6000 new HIV infections during that period. This effect is likely to be less in low-income countries where antiretroviral drugs are less widely available.

Treatment of HIV and AIDS

Since 1996 antiretroviral drugs have been available for treatment of HIV/AIDS. When three or four of such drugs are taken in combination, the approach is known as HAART (see above). Different antiretroviral drugs inhibit the retrovirus at different phases of its life cycle. Whereas the nucleoside and non-nucleoside reverse transcriptase inhibitors function by interfering with the ability of HIV to produce DNA early in the HIV replication cycle, protease inhibitors block the maturation of viral particles ('virions') released by a mature HIV cell into the bloodstream, an event that occurs late in the replication cycle. Integrase inhibitors inhibit the integration of viral DNA into the DNA of the infected cell and maturation inhibitors inhibit the last step of the process. These agents must be taken in combination, because no single antiretroviral drug is likely to suppress the infection for long.

The use of antiretroviral drugs has not only increased the life expectancy of people living with AIDS and helped to prevent the mother-to-child transmission of the virus, it has done so by increasing CD4 level and reducing viral load (i.e. quantity of virus copies in an individual's blood). By lowering viral load, antiretroviral treatment also lowers the risk of the treated individual being infectious when having sexual intercourse with a seronegative partner (Attia *et al*. 2009). However, these positive effects can only be achieved if individuals are conscientious in taking their drugs (i.e. high adherence), because successful treatment of HIV infection requires nearly perfect adherence. Since these drugs can have serious side-effects including fatigue, diarrhoea, nausea, stomach pain and lipodystrophy (i.e. maldistribution of fat tissue), and since these regimens can be complicated (requiring patients to take several pills per day), adherence has been a major problem. However, adherence to the prescribed treatment is fundamental for achieving viral suppression, for increasing the levels of CD4 cells and for minimizing the risk of the development of drug resistance (Cambiano *et al.* 2010). In fact, non-adherence has been found to be associated with a significantly increased risk of death (Chesney 2003).

Studies of social cognitive determinants of adherence to antiretroviral medication regimes have typically found that medication-taking self-efficacy and negative affect or depression were direct predictors of adherence, with social support and spirituality having more indirect effects (see e.g. Simoni *et al.* 2006; Dilorio *et al.* 2009). Beliefs about the relationship of adherence, viral load and disease progression were also found to be related to non-adherence (Chesney 2003). A study by Wroe and Thomas (2003) distinguished further between intentional and non-intentional non-adherence. Intentional non-adherence is characterized by intentionally not taking one's medication or the altering of doses to suit one's needs. In contrast, unintentional non-adherence reflects simple forgetting to take the medication. Intentional non-adherence has been related to the balance of reasons for and against taking the medication: the more reasons a person could think of why they should not take the medication, the more likely it was that they would decide not to adhere. In contrast, these reasons did not differentiate the high and low unintentional non-adherence groups. There was a trend such that the high unintentional non-adherence group was younger, more depressed and more anxious than the high intentional non-adherence group.

The advent of HAART and the knowledge that AIDS had changed from a terminal to a treatable, albeit chronic, disease reduced the threat of an HIV infection and increased the rate of unsafe sex among men who have sex with men. As a result, both the amount of HIV-related sexual risk behaviour among homosexual men (Stolte *et al.* 2004) and the incidence of new HIV infections (Sullivan *et al.* 2009) have increased in recent years. Thus, in a cross-sectional study of two convenience samples surveyed at the Atlanta Gay Pride Festival in 1997 and 2005, Kalichman *et al.* (2007) found that the proportion of men who reported engaging in unprotected anal intercourse with two or more partners increased from 9 per cent in 1997 to 21 per cent in 2005. Similarly, a longitudinal study based on the Amsterdam cohort study of HIV-positive homosexual men reported that risky sex with casual partners increased from 10.5 per cent in 2000 to 27.8 per cent in 2003 (Stolte *et al.* 2004).

Even though the initial optimism about antiretroviral drugs has been replaced by realism among homosexual men, there is evidence that the availability of these drugs reduced the threat of HIV infection. Thus, Stolte *et al.* (2004) reported that even though the homosexual men in their sample seemed quite realistic about the effectiveness and consequences of HAART, those who inclined towards perceiving HIV/AIDS as less threatening since HAART were more likely to change from protected to unprotected anal intercourse. Similar findings were reported from a longitudinal study conducted with homosexual men in Rotterdam (Van der Snoek *et al.* 2005). Again, less perceived need for safe sex since HAART availability was associated with greater incidence of sexually transmitted diseases and with HIV seroconversion, even though the great majority of participants strongly disagreed with statements that HAART availability had reduced the threat from HIV/AIDS. Similarly, a meta-analytic review of the relationship between beliefs about HAART and unprotected sexual intercourse reported that the likelihood of unprotected sexual behaviour was significantly higher in homosexual as well as heterosexual individuals who were less concerned about engaging in unprotected sex given the availability of HAART (Crepaz *et al.* 2004).

Prevention of HIV infection through safe(r) sex

Abstention from penetrative sex

Sex is considered totally safe only if there is no risk of the partners being exposed to HIV – that is, if sex partners do not engage in any activities which result, or can result, in an exchange of blood, semen or vaginal secretions. Because condoms sometimes fail, penetrative sex cannot be considered totally safe, even when condoms are being used. Only non-penetrative sexual behaviours such as hugging, holding, kissing or massaging qualify as totally safe sex practices (Kalichman 1998). Because individuals often find it difficult to abstain from penetration once they begin a sexual encounter, safe sex is not a very viable goal for prevention interventions. Most interventions therefore aim at persuading individuals to engage in sex which is *safer* rather than safe. Safer sex is defined by activities which substantially reduce, but do not totally eliminate, the risk of infection (Kalichman 1998).

Condom use

Condom use is the most common way to practise safer sex. The use of latex condoms substantially reduces the risk of HIV infection. This has been demonstrated in research with heterosexual couples in which one partner is HIV infected and the other is not (for a review, see Kalichman 1998). For example, in a prospective study of HIV-seronegative women who were in a stable monogamous relationship with a seropositive man, Saracco *et al.* (1993) found that 2 per cent of the spouses of men who consistently used condoms during sexual intercourse contracted AIDS, as compared to 15 per cent of the partners of men who used condoms inconsistently. Similarly, gay men who used condoms only some of the time were six times more likely to become infected with HIV than those who used condoms all the time (Detels *et al.* 1989).

Condoms can slip or break and this is more likely during anal than vaginal intercourse (Kalichman 1998). In a survey of homosexual men from the Amsterdam Cohort Study who used condoms regularly, condoms were reported to have slid off or become torn during anogenital sex in 3.7 per cent of the cases. However, the magnitude of the failure rate depended on the type of lubricant used by these men. Condoms used with water-based lubricants failed less frequently (1.7 per cent) than condoms used with no lubricants (5.9 per cent) or with oil-based lubricants (10.3 per cent) (de Wit *et al.* 1993).

Not all condoms are made of latex. Some condoms are made of natural membranes, most commonly lambs' intestines. Although these condoms are durable, effective against unwanted pregnancies, and increase the sensation of sexual stimulation during intercourse, they also have larger pores. Because viruses are much smaller than sperms, these condoms offer little protection against HIV (Kalichman 1998). Another option, namely condoms made from polyurethane, appears to offer a safe alternative to latex condoms (Kalichman 1998).

Strategies aimed at reducing the risk of unprotected anal intercourse

Since condom use can lower sexual intimacy and enjoyment, homosexual men who wanted to continue engaging in unprotected anal intercourse (UAI) have developed a number of strategies with which they try to lower the risk involved (Kippax *et al.* 1997; Jin *et al.* 2009). First there is serosorting, a strategy to practise UAI only with a partner whom one believes to be HIV negative. If both sexual partners are seronegative, there is no risk of exposure to HIV, even during unprotected penetrative sex. However, this strategy would only be safe if one could be certain that the partner was really seronegative. This is presumably the case with UAI within a *monogamous* relationship where both partners have had their serostatus *tested* and found that they are seronegative. Kippax *et al.* (1997) suggested the term 'negotiated safety' to refer to agreements between partners to abstain from unprotected sex outside their relationship. Another strategy is 'strategic positioning' where the HIV-negative man takes only the insertive role in UAI. Finally, in 'withdrawal', the HIV-negative man engages in receptive UAI only when ejaculation inside his rectum does not occur.

Although all these strategies are likely to result in some reduction of the risk involved in UAI, 'negotiated safety' is the only one that can really be safe. But even with this strategy, safety depends on the extent to which both partners keep to their agreements. In the Australian sample of homosexual men studied by Kippax *et al.* (1997), 9 of the 181 seronegative men in seroconcordant steady relationships reported unprotected anal intercourse with a casual partner even though they had an agreement with their steady partner not to have unsafe sex outside their relationship. Data collected in the Amsterdam Cohort Study of homosexual men indicated that of 47 seronegative men with a concordant partner who engaged in unprotected sex within their steady partner, 8 violated a safe sex agreement and engaged in unprotected sex with casual partners (de Vroome *et al.* 2000). This type of evidence suggests that even negotiated safety does not totally exclude the infection risk.

Jin *et al.* (2009) conducted a longitudinal study to assess the risk of HIV infection in a sample of homosexual men, some of whom used one of the risk reduction strategies. There were 53 HIV seroconversions among the sample of just over 1000 participants. The researchers concluded that only negotiated safety and strategic positioning were not associated with significantly increased HIV incidence, compared with no UAI. Unfortunately, with such a small sample, a null finding could easily be due to lack of power. Thus, even though these strategies are likely to result in some risk reduction compared to UAI without any safeguards, there is still considerable risk attached.

Psychosocial determinants of sexual risk behaviour

Because abstention from penetrative sex is a rather unattractive option for most sexually active individuals, research on the factors assumed to influence strategies of AIDS risk reduction has mainly focused on psychosocial determinants of condom use for heterosexual individuals (e.g. Sheeran *et al.* 1999; Albarracin *et al.* 2001) and homosexual men (e.g. de Wit *et al.* 2000).

Condom use among heterosexuals

Meta-analyses of factors influencing heterosexual condom use report some support for the theories of reasoned action and planned behaviour (Sheeran *et al.* 1999; Albarracin *et al.* 2001). The three variables specified by the theory of reasoned action, namely attitudes towards condom use, social norms regarding condom use and intentions to use condoms, were found to be strongly related to condom use in both meta-analyses. Perceived behavioural control was also related to behaviour, but this association disappeared once the influence of intention on behaviour was being controlled for (Albarracin *et al.* 2001).

The health belief model fared less well than the theories of reasoned action and planned behaviour (Sheeran *et al.* 1999). According to the health belief model, condom use should be determined by the perceived threat of an HIV infection (i.e. severity x vulnerability) and the perceived costs and benefits of condom use. Surprisingly, perceived threat appears to play a rather minor role in motivating precautionary behaviour. Thus, the association between perceived severity of an HIV infection and condom use did not reach acceptable levels of significance. Because AIDS is generally regarded as a deadly disease, this could be a 'ceiling effect'. However, no 'ceiling effect' occurred for the measures of vulnerability. And yet, perceived vulnerability also showed a low correlation, albeit significant, with condom use in this meta-analysis. An even weaker and non-significant association between vulnerability and condom use was reported in a meta-analysis of samples of heterosexuals and gay men by Gerrard *et al.* (1996).

I can only suggest two potential explanations for these puzzling findings. One reason for the weak association between measures of perceived susceptibility and protective behaviour could be that most people believe that they are not at risk of HIV infection through sexual contact (Sheeran *et al.* 1999). Although this perception may not be unrealistic for some groups at this point in time, it could also be a reflection of a denial process for others. The latter assumption is supported by the findings of the meta-analysis of sexual risk behaviour by Gerrard *et al.* (1996), who reported that even though perceptions of vulnerability were related to past risk and precautionary behaviours, this association was much stronger for low-risk than for high-risk groups. A second factor which might have reduced the relationship between perceived vulnerability and precautionary behaviour could be that the threat of HIV has now been known for many years and individuals who were willing and able to adopt precautionary behaviour have already done so. This latter explanation may also account for the finding that HIV/AIDS knowledge was only weakly related to condom use. This should not be misinterpreted as an indication that information about this type of health risk is unimportant. Health education has to be continued to maintain this level of knowledge, especially among adolescents who are particularly at risk.

Measures of the other determinants of behaviour of the health belief model, namely perceived benefits of, and barriers to, condom use fared marginally better. Perceived benefits such as the efficacy of condom use, the belief that condoms are attractive to use and do not interfere with sexual pleasure, and perceived barriers such as embarrassment when buying condoms, were weakly but significantly related to condom use. It is interesting to note that beliefs related to condom attractiveness (e.g. make sex less spontaneous, make sex less enjoyable, reduce partner's sexual pleasure) also showed the highest correlation with the intention to use condoms in a young sample studied by Sutton et al. (1999).

Two variables which do not form part of any of these theoretical models have also demonstrated a strong association with condom use (Sheeran et al. 1999). This is interesting, because they are likely to be amenable to modification through interventions. One of these variables was 'carrying a condom' or 'condom availability'. The close association of this variable with condom use is hardly surprising since condom availability is one of the preconditions for condom use. Furthermore, carrying a condom is likely to reflect a strong intention to use condoms. Nevertheless, this finding is important in view of the fact that few interventions have focused on this type of preparatory behaviour.

The other variable which showed a strong association with condom use was communication about condom use. Whereas talking about the risk of contracting AIDS had only a small positive association with condom use, discussions with the partner about whether condoms should be used were strongly associated with using a condom during sexual intercourse. This finding is consistent with the results of intervention studies discussed below (see pp. 228–9), showing that training in sexual negotiation skills increases safe sex behaviour among homosexual men.

Condom use among homosexuals
Findings of studies which apply the models of reasoned action and planned behaviour to condom use among homosexual men are less consistent, though still supportive of the models of reasoned action and planned behaviour. Whereas a study by Fisher et al. (1995) supported all the specified relations of the model of reasoned action and suggested few differences between their samples of homosexual men and heterosexual men and women, Gallois et al. (1994) found substantial differences. They reported that the determinants from the theory of reasoned action were useful in predicting safe and unsafe sexual behaviour in their heterosexual, but not their homosexual, sample. Kelly and Kalichman (1998) reported that the variables of the model of reasoned action accounted for 7 to 12 per cent of the variance in condom use among their sample of self-identified sexually active homosexual men. In this study substantial additional variance was accounted for by a variable not included in the theories of reasoned action

and planned behaviour, namely the reported pleasure individuals derived from unprotected anal sex.

The results of a prospective study by de Wit *et al.* (2000) suggest that the differential impact of the variables of the models of reasoned action and planned behaviour observed in the various studies of condom use by homosexual men may be due to differences between samples in the type of relationships in which the sexual behaviour was enacted. De Wit *et al.* found that the value of the theories of reasoned action and planned behaviour in predicting safe sex behaviour (i.e. condom use and abstention from anal sex) depended very much on the relationship with the partner. Whereas the intention to engage in safe sex with a steady partner was strongly related to attitudes, subjective norms and perceived behavioural control, only perceived behavioural control emerged as a significant predictor of safe sex intentions with a casual partner (see Table 5.1). The same pattern emerged with regard to the prediction of actual behaviour: safe sex with a steady partner was only predicted by intentions, whereas safe sex with a casual partner was only predicted by perceived behavioural control. Finally, the model accounted for 64 per cent of the variance in safe sex behaviour with steady partners, compared to only 21 per cent in safe sex with casual partners. Thus, whether these homosexual men engaged in safe sex with their steady partner depended to a large extent on their intentions, but their safe sex behaviour with casual partners depended on their assertiveness and their social skills in persuading their casual partner to keep it safe. It is interesting to note that in a meta-analytic summary of three studies of heterosexual individuals, Sheeran and Orbell (1998) found intention to be much less strongly related to condom use with a casual rather than a steady partner.

Because a substantial proportion of the men in this sample had casual relationships in addition to their steady partner, we wondered whether the quality of their steady relationship would influence whether or not they would also have sex with a

TABLE 5.1 Determinants of safe sex intentions and safe sex behaviour of homosexual men by type of relationship

	Casual partners	**Steady partners**
Intentions		
Attitude	.05	.41*
Subjective norm	~.12	.31*
Perceived behavioural control	.52*	.06
R square	.54*	.79*
Behaviour		
Intention	~.09	.85*
Perceived behavioural control	.52*	~.06
R square	.21*	.64*

Note: Displayed are standardized multiple regression coefficients (β).
* significant at p < .001.
Source: de Wit *et al.* (2000)

casual partner. Bakker *et al.* (1994) had found with a heterosexual sample that the quality of their relationship and their 'relational commitment' was negatively related to the intention of these individuals to engage in extra-relational sex. A prospective study with homosexual men of the impact of the quality of a steady relationship on sexual behaviour outside that relationship revealed an unexpected pattern (de Vroome *et al.* 2000). Whether these homosexual men had extra-relational sex was unrelated to the quality of the relationship with their steady partner. However, relationship quality had a strong impact on whether they engaged in *safe* sex with a casual partner. The better their relationship with their steady partner, the more likely they were to take protective measures when having sex with a casual partner. It is interesting to note that these relational measures improved the prediction of behaviour even when intention to engage in safe sex and perceived behavioural control were statistically controlled.

Implications for interventions

Three major conclusions can be drawn from these findings with regard to the design of interventions: first, interventions which rely on epidemiological information to emphasize the severity of AIDS and the vulnerability of the target population are likely to fail, because none of these factors appears to be a major determinant of condom use. Instead communications should aim at eroticizing condom use (see e.g. Tanner and Pollack 1988; Kyes 1990). Second, persuasive communications should not only target the beliefs underlying attitudes, subjective norms and perceived control, but also persuade people to be prepared and to discuss condom use with their prospective partners. Third, persuasive communications aimed at increasing condom use among homosexual men have to differentiate clearly between condom use in steady as compared to casual relationships. Whereas condom use in steady relationships is mainly determined by attitudes and subjective norms, condom use in casual relationships appears to be mainly controlled by perceived behavioural control. Thus, whereas persuasion should be effective in influencing condom use in steady relationships, some kind of negotiation skill training would probably be more effective with regard to condom use in casual encounters.

The efficacy of interventions

The early interventions were rarely derived from social psychological theories of attitude and behaviour change but based on an 'informal blend of logic and practical experience' (Fisher and Fisher 1992: 463). However, these interventions were probably quite effective despite such shortcomings. Providing individuals with information about the risk of HIV infection and the development of AIDS *and* motivating them to avoid unsafe sexual behaviour was probably sufficient to achieve behaviour change in the early stages of the epidemic. Risk behaviour cohort studies conducted in San Francisco and New York, both epicentres of the AIDS epidemic, reported 60 per cent reductions in unprotected anal intercourse in the late 1980s, with less than 20 per cent of the participants reporting having had unprotected anal intercourse during the previous year. There was also a substantial decline in average number of sexual partners during this period (McKusick *et al.* 1985; Winkelstein *et al.* 1987; Coates *et al.* 1989). Studies conducted in less affected areas typically reported higher levels of risk behaviour among homosexual men, even though substantial reductions in risk behaviour had occurred even there (e.g. de Wit *et al.* 1992).

With the dangers of HIV widely known today, people who still engage in sexual risk behaviour either believe that they are not at risk or are unwilling or unable to avoid unsafe sex. Therefore to be effective now, interventions have to do more than provide information and motivate individuals. They also have to incorporate behavioural skill training, teaching individuals the ability to communicate with, and be assertive with, a potential sexual partner.

In recent years numerous meta-analyses assessing the efficacy of interventions to reduce the risk of transmission of HIV have been published (for a review, see Noar 2008; Vergidis and Falagas 2009). Practically all these analyses found significant reductions of condom use and unprotected sex (Noar 2008). A meta-analysis of the impact of HIV interventions on sexual risk behaviour among homosexual men by Johnson *et al.* (2008) reported a reduction in self-reported unprotected anal intercourse by 27 per cent. This represents a decrease from 10.1 unprotected occasions per six-month period to 7.4.

The most extensive meta-analysis of HIV interventions has been conducted by Albarracin *et al.* (2006), based on 254 HIV intervention trials and 99 control groups spanning the period from 1985 to 2003. Participants in these trials included heterosexual men and women as well as homosexual men. The meta-analysis compared the impact of passive as well as active interventions. Passive interventions are characterized by the presentation of material to audiences that have minimal opportunity to participate. They include messages to induce attitudes and norms favourable to condoms, to increase perceived threat about, and relevant knowledge of, HIV and finally, messages to model skills that promote condom use. Although active interventions typically also include this type of message, their main distinguishing feature is the inclusion of client-tailored counselling, activities to increase behavioural skills and the administration of HIV counselling and testing. The behavioural skills training includes condom use skills (practice with unwrapping and applying condoms), interpersonal skills (e.g. role-playing of interpersonal conflict about condom use) and self-management skills (e.g. practice in decision-making while intoxicated; avoidance of high risk situations).

The main conclusions from this meta-analysis were as follows:

- Overall, interventions resulted in significant increases in pro-condom use attitudes, control perceptions, norms about condom use, intentions to use condoms, HIV knowledge, behavioural skills and condom use.
- Active interventions had greater impact on condom use than passive interventions.

- Interventions were most effective in clinical settings and least effective in community settings.
- The presentation of behavioural skills arguments as well as condom use training had positive effects for men but not women. In contrast, attitudinal arguments, information, self-management skills training, and HIV counselling and testing had a greater positive effect on women than men.

Because schools provide an obvious access point for intervening with adolescents, a population which is both at risk and difficult to reach in any other way, it is interesting to discuss the special problem involved in this type of programme. School-based programmes face a problem which is less salient in the development of programmes for other settings, namely the degree to which such programmes can address condom use in addition to providing information about sexual abstinence. Abstinence-based programmes favoured in the USA focus on the importance of refraining from sexual intercourse until after marriage. These programmes either exclude discussion of contraceptive measures such as condoms or focus on contraceptive failure in preventing pregnancies or infections. These programmes have typically proved to be ineffective (for reviews, see Kirby and DiClemente 1994; Kalichman 1998).

In contrast to abstinence-based interventions, programmes which emphasize that students should avoid *unprotected* intercourse by either abstaining from intercourse or by using condoms have proved to be more effective. Successful programmes include behavioural skill-building activities that enhance self-efficacy for performing risk-reducing and safer sex negotiation strategies. While behavioural skills training appeared to have less impact in schools than in other settings, condom use skill training and normative arguments were more effective (Albarracin *et al.* 2006). It is important to note that none of the programmes accelerated the onset of sexual activity or increased its frequency (Kalichman 1998). These findings are important because concerns about reckless sexual behaviour are the most frequent reason why people oppose programmes that target avoidance of unprotected intercourse rather than promotion of sexual abstinence.

No review of HIV intervention would be complete without mentioning interventions delivered through the internet. Such interventions allow one to reach a wide range of people, who would be difficult to reach through normal channels. Since these interventions can be set up to be interactive, they allow one to tailor the information for the specific needs and risk characteristics of the respondent. A recent meta-analytic review of 12 HIV prevention interventions, which included all computer-based interventions (i.e. not only those delivered via the internet), concluded that 'computer-based interventions have been efficacious in increasing condom use and reducing sexual activity, numbers of sexual partners, and incident of STD. Results also suggested that these types of interventions have been as efficacious as many commonly utilized human-delivered interventions in HIV prevention' (Noar *et al.* 2009: 113). Surprisingly, only a minority of studies reviewed by Noar used the internet to deliver the intervention. It is easy to predict, however, that internet-delivered intervention will become the standard type in the near future.

Conclusions

It is evident that there has been a substantial reduction of behaviours that are known to be involved in the transmission of HIV. There can be little doubt that the marked behaviour change that has occurred since the advent of the AIDS epidemic has been a reaction to the diffusion of information about AIDS. Although this type of risk education has to be continued in order to maintain the level of knowledge, it also has to be recognized that risk education is not enough. To be effective, any intervention aimed at reducing sexual risk behaviour should complement sexual risk information with some form of training in the skills which people need to engage in safer sex.

Prevention and control of unintentional injuries

One consequence of the dramatic change in causes of death during the twentieth century is that unintentional injuries became the major cause of death during the first four decades of a person's life. Whereas previously the greatest threat to the health and welfare of children came from infectious diseases, inadequate nutrition and sanitation, injuries became the cause of more deaths to children in the USA and most western countries than the next six most frequent causes combined (Christophersen 1989). Therefore, the loss of potential years of life before age 65 due to injury-caused death now is far greater than the loss due to any of the other leading causes (Waller 1987). Thus, a decrease in the death rate due to injuries would save more person-years of life than a decrease in any of the other causes of death.

The epidemiology

In the USA, unintentional injuries continued to be the fifth leading cause of death in 2006, exceeded only by heart disease, cancer, stroke and lower respiratory diseases (*Injury Facts* 2010). Among US adolescents aged 10 to 19, unintentional injuries are the leading cause of death and motor vehicle crashes account for the majority of these deaths (57.9 per cent among the ages 10 to 14 and 72.3 per cent among the ages 15 to 19) (Sleet *et al.* 2010). Road traffic accidents are also a leading cause of death for youth worldwide (Sleet *et al.* 2010). In the USA, drowning and poisoning are the next frequent causes of unintentional injury deaths, but with rates below 10 per cent (Sleet *et al.* 2010). However, deaths are only part of the picture. It is estimated that for every injury death there are approximately 12 injury hospitalizations and 641 emergency department visits (Sleet *et al.* 2010).

The control of unintentional injury

Injury is usually defined as bodily 'damage resulting from acute exposure to physical and chemical agents' (Haddon and Baker 1981: 109). Injury occurs when these agents impinge on the body at a level which the body cannot resist. There are three public health strategies for injury control: *persuasion*, *legal requirements* and *structural change*. While the first two strategies rely on inducing people to change their behaviour, the third approach reduces the risk of injuries by changing the design of equipment, vehicles or the environment.

Strategies of injury protection can be placed on an active–passive continuum, according to the effort they require from the person implementing that strategy. For example, the most *active* strategy to lower the risk that children get scalded by hot tap water would be to prevent children from running hot water. This would involve forbidding them to approach the hot water tap and monitoring them whenever they are near any taps. A less active strategy would involve lowering the setting of the water heater to a level where the water is no longer scaldingly hot. This would require *only one action*, the adjustment of the thermostat. The least active strategy would be a legal requirement for manufacturers of water heaters to fix settings at a level that does not allow water heaters to discharge water that is scaldingly hot (Wilson and Baker 1987). This would make water heaters safe for children without any actions from their caretakers. There is consensus among experts in the area of injury control that protecting people through environmental changes or changes in vehicles or equipment used, whenever possible, is more effective than mass education or the introduction of legal requirements to induce self-protective behaviour.

Persuasion

As with other areas of health behaviour, it is very difficult to persuade people to take actions that protect them against accidental injuries. The use of seat belts provides a good example. In most countries, only 10 to 20 per cent of drivers used their belts before the introduction of laws requiring their use, even though their use requires very little effort and although they reduce mortality risk to wearers involved in accidents by 60 per cent according to some estimates (e.g. Robertson 1986). It should therefore have been easy to persuade people to use their belts.

Despite this, media campaigns persuading drivers to use seat belts have been notoriously ineffective (Robertson 1986, 1987). In one study, radio and television advertisements urging seat belt use were employed extensively in one community, moderately in a second and not at all in a third. In the five weeks of the study no significant change in seat belt use occurred that could be attributed to the campaign (Fleischer 1972, reported by Robertson 1987). Equally disappointing were the results of a nine-month seat belt use campaign on one cable of a dual-cable television system used for marketing studies. Observation of seat belt use did not show any differences between the households on the experimental cable and those on the control cable or the community at large, even though the advertisements were shown nearly 1000 times, often during prime time (Robertson et al. 1974).

Why are people so resistant to persuasion, even when it is in their own self-interest to take action? One reason is that persuasive strategies usually focus on knowledge and motivation, and thus affect only two of the factors that are involved in self-protection. Obviously, knowledge of both the risk and the protective action is a prerequisite to self-protection. But even if individuals know that a certain action will protect them against some danger, they might forget to implement it at the relevant moment. This is particularly likely to happen when the necessity for the protective behaviour arises infrequently and is also not consistently related to a sequence of action.

But even if people are reminded of the self-protective action, they might not be motivated to engage in that action because it is effortful and/or because the likelihood of an accident seems remote. For example, the reminder systems installed in most US cars in the early 1970s did little to increase seat belt use (Robertson 1987). In such cases, compliance with protection recommendations can often be increased by linking additional incentives to the behaviour and/or by making the behaviour less effortful. For example, if children's car seats could be made to fasten in more easily, or even be permanently installed from underneath the regular seat such that they could be unfolded when needed, people would probably be more likely to use them every time they have small children as passengers in their cars.

Finally, people might fail to take a self-protective action if they have insufficient control over the behaviour that is required. For example, parents have only limited control over the behaviour of small children. Thus, whenever the safety of small children is involved, structural changes to make the child's environment safer will be particularly effective. Similarly, people convicted of drunken driving are often people with alcohol problems who may be unable to control their drinking (Robertson 1987). In such cases, a withdrawal of their driving licence until they have overcome their alcohol problem would be more effective than education concerning the dangers of drunken driving.

Legal requirements

Legal requirements are effective to the extent that they succeed in linking new incentives to a given behaviour. Thus, seat belt laws introduce a new incentive for seat belt use, namely, the avoidance of paying a fine. There is ample evidence for the success of legal requirements in inducing behaviour change. For example, when the Swedish government made seat belt use compulsory for front seat passengers in private cars, seat belt use increased from 30 to 85 per cent within a few months (Fhanér and Hane 1979). In the USA, with the exception of New Hampshire, all states now have laws requiring seat belt use. However, these laws vary in terms of enforcement. Primary seat belt laws allow police to ticket drivers for non use of seat belts, even if there has been no other traffic infraction. Secondary seat belt laws allow ticketing for non use of seat belts only if there has been another traffic violation. National seat belt use rates were approximately 17 per cent in 1983 and rose to 75 per cent in 2002 (Houston and Richardson 2005). However, the reinforcement provision matters. According to an analysis of annual state safety belt use over the period 1991 to 2001, states with primary seat belt laws had seat belt use that was 9.1 percentage points higher than their secondary counterparts (Houston and Richardson 2005).

Laws requiring parents to restrain their infants or toddlers during motor vehicle travel, which have been adopted by all US states, have also been very effective. According to observational surveys at shopping centres in 19 cities, the rate of child restraint use increased from roughly 20 per cent in 1980 to 80 per cent in 1990 (Graham 1993). Estimates suggest that the number of infant and toddler fatalities in motor vehicle crashes are 25 to 40 per cent less than they might have been if child restraint laws had not been adopted (Graham 1993).

Laws requiring the use of helmets by motorcyclists have been similarly successful (Houston and Richardson 2008). Based on cross-sectional time series data for the 50 US states and Washington, DC, for the period 1975 to 2004, Houston and Richardson estimated that states requiring all motorcyclists to wear helmets have motorcyclist fatality rates that are 22 to 33 per cent lower than those of states that do not require the use of helmets.

For legal requirements to be effective, the behaviour that is enforced has to be easily monitored. Thus, the law limiting blood alcohol concentration in drivers is difficult to enforce. According to some earlier estimates, only 1 in 2000 drivers illegally impaired by alcohol is actually arrested for the offence (Robertson 1984). However, roadside sobriety checkpoints are increasingly being employed to enhance the probability that drunk drivers will be detected and apprehended. Furthermore, swiftness of punishment has been enhanced by state legislation that authorizes police to suspend a driver's licence before conviction on the basis of evidence that the driver has exceeded the legal blood alcohol limit (Graham 1993).

Even though laws offer additional incentives to encourage self-protective behaviour, they still have to rely on the motivation of the individuals at risk to be effective. This also limits their usefulness. Thus, they often have least impact on those sub-groups that are at greatest risk, because those likely to be most reckless are least likely to comply with legal requirements. For example, seat belt laws seem to be least observed by the young and the alcohol-impaired (Robertson 1978).

Structural changes

The great advantage of the structural approach to injury control, which changes the environment to make it safer, is that it protects people without requiring any effort on their part. An example of a successful structural change was the introduction of smaller containers for children's aspirin. The number of children dying after the ingestion of bottles of flavoured aspirin decreased substantially after bottle sizes were reduced to contain only sub-lethal doses, even when all the tablets in a bottle were consumed. This strategy was more effective than the introduction of childproof caps that had to be replaced after every use and that some children were able to circumvent (Wilson and Baker 1987).

In the area of traffic safety, the introduction of federal standards in the USA in 1968 that required new cars to meet performance criteria for crash worthiness and crash avoidance resulted in an estimated reduction of 14,000 traffic deaths per year by 1982 (Robertson 1986). Substantial further reductions in traffic fatalities have been achieved by electronic stability control systems, a computerized technology that improves the safety of vehicle stability by detecting and minimizing skids and advanced airbag systems that distinguish between adult and child passengers and tailor deployment to occupant size, belt status, position and crash severity (Braver *et al.* 2010).

Conclusions

The opinion of experts in the area of injury control that passive strategies are preferable to active strategies is compelling, since any active strategy for controlling injury depends on convincing a large number of people to change their behaviour in a way that protects them against injury, which has proved very difficult to do. Persuasion is particularly liable to fail when the behaviour is effortful, inconvenient, costly, difficult to control and/or when the risk of injury seems rather remote. However, the application of passive strategies is not always possible and even the safest vehicles, agents etc. can be dangerous in the hands of individuals who behave without regard for their own safety or that of other people. Legal requirements can help in such situations, but again, their application is limited. Thus, there is no substitute for mass education, in addition to the passive strategies outlined above, in the area of injury control.

Summary and conclusions

The second half of the twentieth century witnessed an unprecedented change in health attitudes. It is hard to imagine today that until the early 1960s people believed that they could smoke, eat and drink excessively with nothing worse to fear than a smoker's cough, a degree of overweight and a hangover. This era of happy ignorance ended in 1964 with the first Surgeon General's Report on the dangers of cigarette smoking and the condemnation of food high in cholesterol (USDHEW 1964).

For some time, sex appeared be the one behaviour that could be enjoyed with impunity, especially after the invention of the pill. This happy state of affairs was first marred by the genital herpes scare (a sexually transmitted viral infection which received wide publicity in the mid-1980s) and ended with the news of the sexual transmission of the AIDS virus. Exercise had always been considered healthy (like eating an apple a day) but only recently has this belief been supported by scientific evidence.

As the proponents of health promotion like to emphasize, the dissemination of the evidence from epidemiological research on the health impact of various health behaviours to the public resulted in substantial attitude and behaviour change. Gluttony went out of fashion. Perrier-drinking, vegetarian, monogamous non-smokers who jog regularly and never drive without wearing their seat belts have become almost the modal men and women of the postmodern age.

As we have seen, however, there are two ways to evaluate the evidence of the impact of health promotion on health behaviour. We can be elated about the 20 per cent decrease in the number of smokers in the USA in the 20 years after the first report on smoking by the Surgeon General, but we can also be disenchanted by the fact that 20 per cent of the population in the USA still smokes cigarettes, in spite of all the research findings establishing smoking as a health hazard.

How can we explain the apparent lack of response to health warnings? Are they suicidal? Does their resistance to persuasion suggest that health promotion is ineffective and should be abandoned? It seems to me that the dramatic changes in health attitudes and behaviours that have occurred over the last 45 years are sufficient evidence that health education can be effective. One has to keep in mind that, even though good health and long life are important goals for most people, they are not the *only* goals. As Becker (1976) succinctly stated, a person may be a heavy smoker or so committed to work as to omit all exercise, not out of ignorance, but because the lifespan forfeited does not seem worth the cost of giving up smoking or changing his or her diet. And for many others the goal of being healthy may seem difficult to reach because they feel unable to give up smoking or change their diet, even if they wanted to.

For those of us who, in our ambition to squeeze the last minute out of our potential lifespan, have had to forfeit many of life's pleasures, it is hard to understand (and to accept) that there are still people around who smoke, drink like fish and eat greasy food as if there were no tomorrow. It is difficult to resist the temptation to point out to them what damage they are doing to their health. However, in all likelihood they will have heard these arguments before, and hearing them once more will not change their minds or influence their behaviour. If we really want to 'help' them, we have to find out the reasons why they continue to engage in behaviours which they know to be deleterious to their health.

Further reading

Albarracin, D., Gillette, J.C., Earl, A.N., Glasman, L.R., Durantini, M.R. and Ho, M-H. (2006) A test of major assumptions about behavior change: a comprehensive look at the effects of passive and active HIV-Prevention Interventions since the beginning of the epidemic. *Psychological Bulletin*, 131: 856–97. A comprehensive meta-analytic review that synthesizes research on the effects of a large number of interventions conducted since the beginning of the HIV epidemic among a variety of populations, and compares the reality of intervention effectiveness with theoretical proposals about the nature of effective interventions.

CDC AIDS Community Demonstration Projects Research Group (1999) Community level HIV intervention in 5 cities: final outcome data from the CDC AIDS community demonstration. *American Journal of Public Health*, 89: 336–45. This Community AIDS intervention has been designed by a panel of behavioural experts (including M. Fishbein). The study demonstrates that community interventions can work well, if they are designed in line with social psychological theories.

Michie, S., Abraham, C., Wittington, C., McAteer, J. and Gupta, S. (2009) Effective techniques in healthy eating and physical activity interventions: a meta-regression. *Health Psychology*, 28: 690–701.

Taubes, G. (1998) The (political) science of salt. *Science*, 281: 898–907. Entertaining discussion of the scientific controversy about the health consequences of salt consumption. Supports the impression that public health research is sometimes motivated by missionary zeal rather than scientific objectivity.

US Department of Health and Human Services (1996) *Physical Activity and Health: A Report of the Surgeon General*. McLean, VA: International Medical Publishing, www.cdc.gov/nccdphp/sgr/pdf/sgrfull.pdf. This is still the most comprehensive review of research on the health consequences of physical activity. The chapters are written by experts and provide comprehensive reviews of research findings.

6

Stress
and health

The present chapter and Chapter 7 focus on stress as a risk factor for ill health and on social and personality variables as moderators of the stress–health relationship. There is ample evidence that stress results in health impairment. Although these health consequences are to some extent mediated by changes in the endocrine, immune and autonomic nervous systems, the experience of stress also causes negative changes in health behaviour that contribute to the stress–illness relationship. This chapter examines the evidence for the assumption that stress increases the risk of ill health and discusses some of the processes that might mediate the stress–illness relationship. Chapter 7 considers social and personality variables that moderate the impact of stress on health.

Physiological stress and the breakdown of adaptation

The stress concept has been made popular by Selye's seminal work on a pattern of bodily responses that occurs when an organism is exposed to a stressor such as intensive heat or infection. Although much of the theoretical foundation for this work had been prepared by Cannon (1929), Selye's research advanced our understanding of physiological reactions to noxious stimuli and served as a paradigm for later conceptions of stress.

In his highly readable book, *The Stress of Life*, Selye (1976) described how, as a young medical student at the University of Prague, he was impressed by the fact that, apart from the small number of symptoms characteristic of a given illness (and important for the clinical diagnosis of that illness), there appeared to be many signs of bodily distress which were common to most, if not all, diseases (e.g. loss of weight and appetite, diminished muscular strength and motivational deficits). But it was not until 10 years later, while doing physiological work on animals, that Selye discovered a set of apparently non-specific bodily responses which seemed to occur whenever an organism was exposed to a stressor, whether this stressor was surgical injury, extreme cold or non-lethal injections of toxic fluids. These bodily reactions consisted of a considerable enlargement of the adrenal cortex, shrinkage of the thymus and lymph glands, and ulceration of the stomach and duodenum.

The adrenals are two small endocrine glands situated above the kidneys. They consist of two portions: a central part, the medulla, and an outer rind, the cortex. Both synthesize hormones that are involved in mobilizing the organism for action. The thymicolymphatic system, on the other hand, plays an important role in the immune defence of the body. Using these morphological changes as indices of adrenal cortical activity including an involvement of the immune system, Selye suggested that these endocrine responses helped the organism to cope physiologically with the stressor agent. If one assumes that bodily injuries frequently occur in a context in which the animal has to fight or run, physiological responses that mobilize the organism for action are indeed adaptive. Selye defined these non-specific responses as 'stress'.

No organism can stay in a heightened state of arousal indefinitely. Reactions to stressors therefore change over time. Selye argued that with repeated exposure to the stressor, the defence reaction of the organism passes through three identifiable stages. Together these stages represent the General Adaptation Syndrome. First, in the 'alarm' phase, the organism becomes mobilized to meet the threat. In the second stage of 'resistance', the organism seems to have adapted to the stressor and the general activation subsides. However, an extended exposure to the same stressor can 'exhaust' the adaptive energy of the body. Thus, the third stage of 'exhaustion' occurs if the organism fails to overcome the threat and depletes its physiological resources in the process.

There are therefore two ways in which the stressor can harm an organism: it can either cause damage directly if it exceeds the power of adaptation of an organism or indirectly as a result of the processes marshalled in defence against the stressor. Selye termed the diseases in whose development the stress responses of the organism played a major role 'diseases of adaptation'. For example, the ulcers which are typical of the third stage of the General Adaptation Syndrome would be considered to be a disease of adaptation. Similarly, the various illnesses which seem to be related to the accumulation of stressful life events would also belong in this category. Thus, illness is the price the organism has to pay for the defence against extended exposure to stressor agents.

Over the years Selye's model has been criticized for a number of reasons. One major point of criticism has been that it assigns a very limited role to *psychological* factors. In contrast to Selye, researchers now believe that psychological appraisal is important in the determination of stress (Lazarus and Folkman 1984). It is possible that even with the stressors used by Selye, the stress response was mediated by the emotional disturbance, discomfort and pain rather than being a direct physiological response to the tissue damage caused by these noxious stimuli. Thus Mason (1975: 24) noted that 'conventional laboratory situations designed for the study of physical stressors, such as exercise, heat, cold, etc. very often also elicit an appreciable degree of emotional disturbance, discomfort, and even pain'. If precautions are taken to minimize psychological reactions, there is no activation of the adrenal system. A related criticism concerned Selye's 'non-specificity assumption' that all stressors produce the same bodily response. There is increasing evidence that specific stressors produce distinct endocrinological responses and that individuals' responses to stress may be influenced by their personalities, perception and biological constitution (e.g. Dickerson and Kemeny 2004; Segerstrom and Miller 2004). These arguments challenge Selye's assumption of the uniform response to stress. But this critique should not detract from the fact that Selye's ideas have had a lasting impact on stress research.

Psychosocial stress and health

A second major impetus in the advancement of stress theory came from psychiatrists, who began to study life events as factors contributing to the development of a variety of psychosomatic and psychiatric illnesses (e.g. Cobb and Lindemann 1943; Holmes and Masuda 1974). Basic to this work is the assumption that psychosocial stress leads to the same bodily changes which Selye observed as a result of tissue damage. This essentially psychosomatic tradition generated clinical and epidemiological research which tends to support the assumption that the experience of stressful life events increases the risk of morbidity and even mortality.

The assumption that psychosocial stress has a negative impact on health was first studied in the context of major life events. Major life events range from cataclysmic events such as the death of a spouse or being fired from a job to more mundane but still problematic events such as having trouble with one's boss. While some research examined the impact of *specific* life events such as bereavement or unemployment, the majority of studies use self-report lists or interview-based measures of critical life events to investigate the *cumulative* health impact of the number or total severity of stressful life events which subjects reported having experienced during a given period of time. Because the accumulation of minor irritations may also be stressful, attention has also been focused on the cumulative health effects of the more minor stressful events that occur from day to day. Such daily stresses might include having too many meetings or not enough time for one's family. The following section will evaluate the evidence from this research with regard to the health-impairing nature of psychosocial stress.

The health impact of cumulative life stress

Major life events

Although in more recent years a number of interview-based measures of critical life events have been developed (Wethington et al. 1995), early research on the health impact of stressful life events relied almost exclusively on self-report 'checklists' (Turner and Wheaton 1995) pioneered by Holmes and Rahe (1967) with their development of the Schedule of Recent Experiences (SRE) and the Social Readjustment Rating Scale (SRRS).

Self-report measures typically consist of lists of life events and require respondents to indicate which of these events they have experienced during a given time period.

The checklist developed by Holmes and Rahe (1967) lists 43 items which describe 'life change events'. Life change events were defined as those events that require a certain amount of social readjustment from the individual (see Table 6.1). Since it was assumed that any event which forced an individual to deviate from his or her habitual pattern would be stressful, the list included pleasant as well as unpleasant events. The inclusion of positive as well as negative changes is reasonable if, true to the Selye tradition, stress is assumed to be caused by the need to adapt to new situations. However, there is now evidence that only negative events are related to indicators of ill health (e.g. Ross and Mirowsky 1979).

TABLE 6.1 The Social Readjustment Rating Scale (SRSS)

Rank	Life event	Mean value
1	Death of spouse	100
2	Divorce	73
3	Marital separation	65
4	Jail term	63
5	Death of close family member	63
6	Personal injury or illness	53
7	Marriage	50
8	Fired at work	47
9	Marital reconciliation	45
10	Retirement	45
11	Change in health of family member	44
12	Pregnancy	40
13	Sex difficulties	39
14	Gain of new family member	39
15	Business readjustment	39
16	Change in financial state	38
17	Death of close friend	37
18	Change to different line of work	36
19	Change in number of arguments with spouse	35
20	Mortgage over US$10,000	31
21	Foreclosure of mortgage or loan	30
22	Change in responsibilities at work	29
23	Son or daughter leaving home	29
24	Trouble with in-laws	29
25	Outstanding personal achievement	28
26	Wife begins or stops work	26
27	Begin or end school	26
28	Change in living conditions	25

Rank	Life event	Mean value
29	Revision of personal habits	24
30	Trouble with boss	23
31	Change in work hours or conditions	20
32	Change in residence	20
33	Change in schools	20
34	Change in recreation	19
35	Change in church activities	19
36	Change in social activities	18
37	Mortgage or loan less than US$10,000	17
38	Change in sleeping habits	16
39	Change in number of family get-togethers	15
40	Change in eating habits	15
41	Vacation	13
42	Christmas	12
43	Minor violations of the law	11

Source: Holmes and Rahe (1967)

In answering the checklist, respondents are requested to indicate all the life events they have experienced during a given time period. The measure of cumulative life stress can either consist of the number of life events experienced during a given period of time (SRE) or of a weighted score that also takes account of the severity of these events (SSRS). Thus the two scales differ only in the weight assigned to life events. The SSRS provides scale values based on a rating of the magnitude of social readjustment such an event would require (Holmes and Rahe 1967). The unweighted scores (reflecting merely the number of stressful events experienced) or the life change unit scores (reflecting the summed intensity of these events) can then be related to subsequent periods of illness. Surprisingly, weighting scores by the severity of life events rather than using the mere frequency of events does not seem to improve the power of these scales to predict health problems (Turner and Wheaton 1995).

Although the checklist was also used in a great number of studies in which life events were only assessed retrospectively after the onset of some illness (e.g. Rahe and Lind 1971; Rahe and Paasikivi 1971), the ease with which it could be administered made it feasible to screen large numbers of people and thus encouraged investigators to conduct prospective studies (i.e. studies in which life events were assessed before the onset of illness). In one of the most impressive projects of this kind, Rahe (1968) assessed the changes that occurred in the lives of 2500 Navy officers and enlisted men in the six months prior to tours of duty aboard three Navy cruisers. These life change unit scores were then related to shipboard medical records at the end of the six-month tour of duty. Individuals with life change unit scores in the top 30 per cent of the distribution were categorized as a high-risk group, those with the lowest 30 per cent as a low-risk group. Rahe found that in the first few months of the tour the high-risk group had nearly 90 per cent more first illnesses than the low-risk group. Furthermore, the high-risk group consistently reported more illnesses each month for the period of the tour than did the low-risk group.

However, other prospective studies were less supportive of the stress–illness relationship. For example, Theorell *et al.* (1975), who studied a sample of over 4000 Swedish construction workers, found no relationship between stressful life events for a given year and mortality, hospitalization or days off work during the following year. Goldberg and Comstock (1976) were similarly unsuccessful in a prospective study relating life events to death and hospitalization in two American communities. Furthermore, as Rabkin and Struening (1976) pointed out, the correlations between life stress and illness are typically below .30, suggesting that life events account for less than 9 per cent of the variance in illness.

The initial excitement with which the development of these measures had been greeted was soon followed by a period of critical re-evaluation. One line of argument has raised the possibility that the relationship between life stress and health could be due to a reporting bias (e.g. Mechanic 1978). After all, studies that rely on life event scales do not assess the amount of stress and the number of illnesses directly, but relate self-reported life stress to treatment-seeking behaviour. Thus, individuals with low treatment-seeking thresholds, who consult their doctors for even the most minor health problems, may also be more likely to report any upheaval as a major life event. This assumption could account for most of the results of the Navy study of Rahe (1968) described earlier.

Along similar lines, Watson and Pennebaker (1989) argued that self-report measures of both stressful life events and health complaints reflect a pervasive mood disposition of negative affectivity, which represents a stable personality disposition to experience negative mood and is closely related to the dimension of neuroticism. While negative affectivity correlates highly with measures of symptom reporting, it seems to be unrelated to objective health indicators (e.g. blood pressure levels, serum risk factors, immune system functions). Watson and Pennebaker (1989) suggest that individuals who score high on negative affectivity are hypervigilant and are therefore more likely to notice and attend to normal body sensations. Since their scanning is fraught with anxiety and uncertainty, they tend to interpret normal symptoms as painful and pathological.

Negative affectivity could not account for outcomes of studies where life event measures are related to physical health measures. For example, Sibai *et al.* (1989) investigated the association of wartime stress variables and coronary artery disease in the war-torn Lebanon of 1986. Participants were patients undergoing angiography because of clinical evidence of heart disease. Patients filled out a questionnaire before they came to know the results of the arteriogram. In the questionnaire they had to indicate whether they or their nuclear family had recently experienced any of a range of war-time stressors (e.g. injury, kidnapping, assault, serious threats, displacement from home, damage to home). Patients who had more than a 70 per cent narrowing of their arteries were nearly three times as likely than patients whose arteries showed no evidence of atherosclerosis to have experienced exposure to war events. This finding would be difficult to explain in terms of negative affectivity, because it compared two groups of patients. Since report of angina symptoms is one of the reasons why patients have to undergo coronary angiography, one would expect negative affectivity to be higher among the healthy patients for whom no physical basis could be found for those complaints.

That war stress may not only accelerate the development of atherosclerosis but may also induce myocardial infarction has been demonstrated in a study of effects of Iraqi missile attacks on the incidence of myocardial infarction and sudden deaths among Israeli civilians (Meisel *et al.* 1991). This study is also interesting from a methodological point of view, because it relates an objectifiable stressor (the missile attacks) to an objectifiable health measure (myocardial infarction). The authors reported a sharp increase in the incidence of acute myocardial infarctions during the first days of the Gulf War when compared to a number of control periods (e.g. same period one year earlier; the weeks directly before the attacks). There is similar evidence that after the September 11 terrorist attacks in New York there was a significant increase in New York of patients with acute myocardial infarctions and a somewhat smaller increase in patients with unstable angina (Feng *et al.* 2006).

A second line of argument against the use of self-report measures of life events has been that of the contamination of stress and illness measures (e.g. Schroeder and Costa 1984). Life event scales may be confounded with measures of health in at least two ways: first, life event scales frequently include items that may reflect the physical and psychological conditions of the respondent. If items such as 'Personal injury or illness' or 'Pregnancy' are used as measures of stressful life events, then the event score is directly contaminated with concurrent physical health. Second, life event scales often include items that could reflect the result rather than the cause of psychological problems (e.g. troubles with in-laws, fired at work, separation). Consistent with these assumptions, Schroeder and Costa (1984) demonstrated that the correlation obtained between standard measures of life events and physical illness disappeared when 'contaminated items' were eliminated from the life event scale. However, these findings could not be replicated by Maddi *et al.* (1987).

A third line of argument has been that the checklist approach treats all life events of a given type as equivalent (Kessler 1997). Death of a spouse, for example, is assigned a life change score of 100, irrespective of the suddenness of the death or any other circumstance surrounding the death which might have made it more stressful. There is evidence from studies of individual events such as bereavement that the strength of the relationship between life events and depression increases substantially when these sorts of distinctions are made (Stroebe and Stroebe 1987).

One strategy to solve this problem has been the 'contextual' approach to using information about the person and his or her life situation to construct an independent judgement of how stressful the event would be for a typical person in such a situation (Wethington *et al.* 1995). This approach, pioneered by Brown and Harris (1978, 1989), involves two stages. The first stage uses a semi-structured interview, the Life Events and Difficulties Schedule (LEDS) (Brown and Harris 1989). This interview consists of a series of questions asking whether certain types of events have occurred over the past 12 months and a set of guidelines for probing positive responses. The aim of the interviewing method is to enable the interviewer to construct a narrative of each event. The LEDS uses strict criteria about what constitutes a stressful life event, and allows a classification of each event on the basis of severity of threat, emotional significance and domain of life experience in which it occurred. The second stage consists of expert evaluations of the event descriptions developed on the basis of the interviews. These are presented to a panel of raters, blind to the illness status of the respondent, who discuss the appropriate ratings of threat. Thus, the death of a partner would be assigned different scores depending on the circumstances surrounding the death. For example, a sudden loss might be rated as more threatening than a loss following an extended illness. Although this method is in many ways superior to the checklist method, the resulting rating of severity incorporates already some of the psychological assumptions about the severity of an event (i.e. that a sudden loss is more severe than anticipated loss) which the researcher wanted to test in the first place.

Minor life events

Methodological problems increase in severity as one moves from self-report measures of major life events to scales that assess minor events such as 'daily hassles'. Hassles are 'irritating, frustrating, distressing demands that to some degree characterize everyday transactions with the environment' (Kanner et al. 1981: 3). Kanner et al. (1981) developed the Hassles Scale that consists of a list of 117 potential hassles. Examples of such hassles are 'misplacing or losing things', 'troublesome neighbours', 'thoughts about death', 'concerns about owing money', 'trouble relaxing' and 'concerns about job security'. Subjects are asked to mark each hassle that happened to them during a given period of time and then to indicate how severe each of the hassles had been during this time (somewhat severe, moderately severe, extremely severe). From this information two summary scores can be computed: frequency, reflecting the number of items checked; and intensity, reflecting the mean severity of the items checked. Although developed as a measure of daily stresses, the scale was originally intended for once-a-month administration for several consecutive months.

In one study, the Hassles Scale was given to 100 middle-aged adults for nine consecutive months and related to reported psychological symptoms, including depression and anxiety (Kanner et al. 1981). Hassles were found to be a better predictor of concurrent and subsequent psychological symptoms than were more major life events. Furthermore, while major life events had little impact on symptoms independent of the effect of hassles, hassles continued to predict symptoms even after the impact of major life events had been statistically controlled. That hassles predicted health outcome as well as or better than major life events was also reported by DeLongis et al. (1982), Monroe (1983), Zarski (1984) and Weinberger et al. (1987).

Research using the Hassles Scale was soon subjected to the same criticism that had been levelled against studies that relied on measures of major life events. Specifically the Dohrenwends and their colleagues raised the issue of contamination (Dohrenwend *et al.* 1984; Dohrenwend and Shrout 1985). They first argued that the Hassles Scale contained many items that may well reflect psychological symptoms (e.g. 'You have had sexual problems other than those resulting from physical problems'; 'You are concerned about your use of alcohol'; 'You have had a fear of rejection'). When Lazarus *et al.* (1985) demonstrated that a hassles sub-scale consisting only of items that were not confounded showed as high a correlation with psychological symptoms as a sub-scale that consisted mainly of confounded items, Dohrenwend and Shrout (1985) changed their argument to suggest that all hassles reflected symptoms, due to the response format of the Hassles Scale. They argued that the fact that the lowest intensity permitted by the response scale is 'somewhat severe' could be interpreted by subjects as implying that an event had to be at least 'somewhat severe' to be reported as a hassle. Thus, only subjects who experienced difficulties in coping with a given hassle would feel that they should report it.

In response to these criticisms, DeLongis *et al.* (1988) modified the Daily Hassles Scale, eliminating contaminated items, changing the response format by having the subject only rate the extent to which an event constituted a hassle, and asking research participants to respond to the scale on a *daily* basis for several consecutive days. This last change made it more plausible that the scale really assessed daily events and was also in line with methodological trends towards the development of measures which assess stressful experiences at the daily level (for a review, see Eckenrode and Bolger 1995). Consistent with the assumption that daily hassles result in health impairment, DeLongis *et al.* (1988) reported a significant relationship between daily stress and the occurrence of both concurrent and subsequent health problems such as flu, sore throats, headaches and backaches. However, this study does not rule out the possibility raised by Watson and Pennebaker (1989) that the association between daily hassles and reported symptoms is at least partly due to the influence of negative affectivity.

Conclusions

There is evidence that measures of cumulative stress, reflecting both major and minor stressors, are significantly related to psychological and physical health problems. However, with regard to studies based on self-report measures of stress, there is now considerable doubt about how justifiable it is to interpret this relationship in terms of a causal impact of stress on health. There are not only problems of reporting bias and item contamination, but there is also increasing evidence that self-report measures of both stress and health complaints reflect a stable personality disposition of negative affectivity, or neuroticism, that could at least be partly responsible for the relationship observed between these measures. Some of these problems can be addressed by the use of personal interviews, but the costs of administering interviews are high. Because negative affectivity is unrelated to objective health measures, the use of such a measure may constitute a more effective safeguard against this type of criticism.

A final shortcoming of these lists is that they distinguish stressors only in terms of severity or the extent of readjustment they might require. Other important aspects of stressors such as the *duration* of the stressor or the extent to which it can be *controlled* are not considered. For example, stressors might be acute and time limited (e.g. public speaking; examination) or chronic (e.g. bereavement, refugees). Chronic stressors reflect both situations that persist for an extended period of time and situations that last for a short period but are likely to be seen as threatening for a long period of time (e.g. being the victim of a sexual assault). Controllability of a stressor refers to the ability of the individual to end the stress when desired (Miller *et al.* 2007). Controllability is correlated with chronicity: whereas acute stressors can vary in controllability, chronic stressors usually do not. There is evidence that these aspects of stress events modulate the physiological response to stress (e.g. Miller *et al.* 2007).

The health impact of specific life events: the case of partner loss

Most of the ambiguities involved in using cumulative life event measures can be avoided by studying the health consequences of specific stressful life events. The loss of a partner through death combines a number of features which make it particularly suited to the study of the health impact of stressful life events. Partner loss is not only one of the most severely stressful life events, but is also objectifiable (thereby eliminating the risk of reporting biases affecting the measure of stress). Since the loss of a marital partner is also reflected in census and health records, large bodies of data are available which permit the analysis of excess risk in terms of specific illnesses and even mortality. Finally, with the possible exception of loss due to suicide of the partner (persons might have been driven to it by the illness of their spouse), there can be no doubt that the stressful life event (i.e. the loss) preceded the health problems. Thus, while many of the life events such as 'divorce' or 'separation' listed in life event inventories could be consequences rather than the cause of personality problems or depression, this is unlikely in the case of bereavement. A brief overview of the major findings of research on the health consequences of partner loss will therefore be presented.

The loss of a partner through death can indeed adversely affect the health of the surviving partner. This has been shown both in epidemiological surveys comparing marital status groups on various health measures, and in longitudinal cohort studies that examine the health status of bereaved (compared with non-bereaved) persons for a period of time following loss (for reviews, see Archer 1999; Stroebe *et al.* 2007).

Consequences can be so direct that the life of the bereaved person is itself threatened. As cross-sectional surveys in many different countries have shown, the widowed have higher mortality rates than their married counterparts. Furthermore,

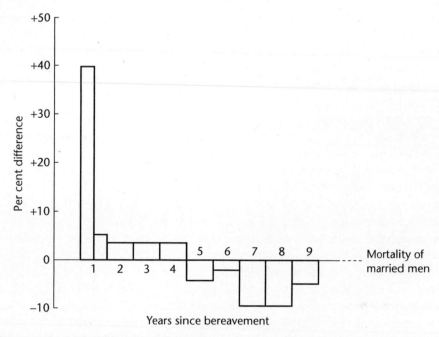

FIGURE 6.1 Percentage difference between the mortality rates of widowers over age 54 and those of married men of the same age by number of years since bereavement
Source: Parkes *et al.* (1969)

the greatest risk to life appears to be in the first few weeks and months following loss. The classic study by Parkes *et al.* (1969) clearly illustrates this phenomenon. As Figure 6.1 shows, in their longitudinal study of a sample of widowers over the age of 54, there was a 40 per cent increase in mortality during the first half year of bereavement, compared with married controls over an equivalent period. Although there are some variations between studies in patterns of excess mortality rates for the widowed, certain regularities have emerged (for a review, see M. Stroebe and Stroebe 1993). Thus, excesses for widowers are relatively higher than those for widows, as are the excesses for younger as compared with older bereaved spouses. Other studies have confirmed this pattern (Siegel and Kuykendall 1990; Umberson *et al.* 1992).

Despite the excess risk of mortality, expressed in absolute numbers, there are very few bereaved persons who do actually die prematurely. However, for a much larger proportion bereavement is associated not only with intense suffering over an extended period of time, but also with an increased risk of succumbing to a variety of psychological and somatic complaints and illnesses. Thus, depression rates are higher for widowed than non-widowed persons. Visits to physicians are more frequent among the former than the latter, and the physical illness rates of the bereaved are elevated.

Studies are beginning to identify those bereaved individuals who are at particular risk of suffering from the various adverse consequences of loss. There is some evidence that health consequences are affected by such factors as the mode of death (more severe consequences after a sudden rather than an expected loss), gender (men suffering more severe consequences) and the extent of social support the individual receives after the loss (more severe consequences for people who do not receive much social support) (for reviews, see Stroebe and Schut 2001; Stroebe *et al.* 2007).

While the relationship between bereavement and various mental and physical health debilities has been reasonably well established, this alone is not convincing evidence that it is the stress of bereavement that is the mediating factor. There are a number of alternative explanations. Depression models would tend to look instead to such factors as loneliness consequent upon losing a loved person, or to reactions of helplessness and 'giving up'. Others have argued in terms of artefacts, such as homogamy between spouses (i.e. the similarity of marital partners in sociological, psychological and physical traits), or the fact that partners had joint unfavourable environments (e.g. they breathed the same unhealthy air or both had poor diets).

However, there also seems very little doubt that bereavement is stressful. Longitudinal studies have consistently identified a variety of strains associated with the loss of a spouse, ranging from financial hardships, to social constraints, to problems in the care of bereaved children (Stroebe *et al.* 2007). Systematic analysis of types of stressors encountered by bereaved people has been provided by Stroebe and Schut (1999). Criticizing traditional theoretical approaches, these investigators argued that coming to terms with the death of a close person necessitates confrontation with two types of stressor, which they define as *loss-oriented* and *restoration oriented* coping. Bereaved people have to attend not only to loss of the person him- or herself (going over the events of death, reminiscing, tending the grave etc.), defined as loss orientation, but also to the changes that come about as a result of loss (taking on the tasks that the deceased had performed; finding new roles and identity etc.), defined as restoration orientation. A process of oscillation in confronting vs. avoiding these two stressors was postulated as critical to successful adaptation.

The results outlined above in relation to risk factors for poor bereavement outcome (low self-esteem, lack of social support, a sudden loss etc.) can easily be interpreted within a more general stress framework. Thus, traumatic deaths are particularly difficult for survivors to come to terms with, and are associated with high rates of debility (Jacobs 1999). That such circumstances are more stressful for survivors than the peaceful death of an elderly person 'in the fullness of time' seems self-evident. Moreover, such results suggest that it is persons with inadequate coping resources – for example, those people who hold the belief that they have little control over events – who feel particularly unable to cope with the stressful circumstances of bereavement.

What makes critical life events stressful?

By relating the incidence of illness to specific stressful events, research on the health impact of critical life events evaded the thorny issue of specifying why certain psychological experiences are stressful, how the organism recognizes stressful events and distinguishes them from positive events, and how inter-individual differences in reactions to stress can be explained. Thus, while it appears quite plausible that the physical stressors used by Selye, such as extreme cold or the injection of non-lethal amounts of toxic fluids, should challenge the defence systems of an organism, it is less obvious why the death of a partner or the loss of a job should have a similar impact.

These issues have been addressed by psychological approaches to stress which analyse the cognitive processes that mediate between life events and stress. Interactional approaches take the general view that stress is the result of a perceived mismatch between environmental demands and the resources available to the individual in dealing with these demands (e.g. French and Kahn 1962; Lazarus and Folkman 1984). A more specific theory developed by Seligman and his collaborators (Seligman 1975; Abramson et al. 1978; Peterson and Seligman 1987) identified perceived lack of control as a key characteristic of stressful situations.

Stress as a person–environment interaction

For several decades, Lazarus (e.g. Lazarus and Folkman 1984) has been the chief proponent of the interactional view of stress. According to Lazarus and Folkman's widely accepted definition, 'Psychological stress is a particular relationship between the person and the environment that is appraised by the individual as taxing or exceeding his or her resources and endangering his or her well-being' (1984: 19). Thus the extent of the stress experienced in a given situation does not depend solely on the demands of the situation or on the resources of the person, but on the relationship between demands and resources as perceived (appraised) by the individual. This is not meant to imply, however, that situations do not differ in the extent to which they are likely to be experienced as stressful.

The two central processes in Lazarus's theory that determine the extent of stress experiences in a given situation are cognitive appraisal and coping. *Cognitive appraisal* is an evaluative process which determines why and to what extent a particular situation is perceived as stressful by a given individual. Lazarus distinguishes three basic forms of appraisal, 'primary appraisal', 'secondary appraisal' and 'reappraisal'. In primary appraisal, individuals categorize a given situation with respect to its significance for their well-being and decide whether the situation is irrelevant, positive or potentially harmful. In secondary appraisal they evaluate the potential threat in terms of their coping resources and also decide on coping options.

Lazarus and Folkman (1984) emphasize that primary and secondary appraisal processes typically occur concurrently. Thus, when confronted with environmental demands individuals evaluate whether the demands pose a potential threat and whether sufficient coping resources are available to cope with them. If they find the environmental demands taxing or threatening, and at the same time view their coping resources as inadequate, they perceive themselves to be under stress, an experience which usually results in negative emotions. Thus, both the evaluation of a situation as stressful, and the intensity of the stress experience, depend to some extent on the individual's evaluation of relevant coping resources.

The notion of reappraisal was introduced to emphasize that cognitive appraisal processes are in a permanent state of flux, due to new inputs. Thus the original appraisal of a situation may change as new information about the situation or about the impact of one's own behaviour is received. The realization that what one took to be symptoms of angina pectoris turned out to be only a bad case of heartburn will lead to a reappraisal of the threat signalled by the symptoms.

When a situation has been appraised as stressful, individuals have to do something to master the situation and/or to control their emotional reactions to the situation. These processes of responding to stressful demands have been called *coping processes*. Lazarus and Folkman (1984) distinguish two basic forms of coping: problem-focused coping and emotion-focused coping. Coping is problem-focused when it is directed at managing and altering the problem that is causing distress. For example, a student who is worried about an impending exam will do everything to be well prepared (e.g. attend classes, join a work group). However, the student might also be so anxious that he or she begins to have trouble sleeping or is unable to concentrate. In order to reduce this emotional distress, the student may engage in a range of emotion-focused forms of coping. These could include cognitive operations such as attempts to reappraise the situation as less threatening. But they may also include actions such as taking sleeping pills, smoking or drinking alcohol in order to cope with the emotional distress and calm his or her nerves.

The extent to which the situation is experienced as stressful, as well as the individual's success in mastering it, will depend on his or her *coping resources*. Lazarus and Folkman (1984) distinguish resources that are primarily properties of the person and resources that are primarily environmental. Person resources include physical resources such as health and energy, psychological resources such as positive beliefs (e.g. positive self-concept, belief in control) and competencies such as problem-solving and social skills. Examples of environmental resources are material resources (e.g. money) and social support.

It is worth noting that there are important similarities between the cognitive stress model of Lazarus and Folkman (1984) and models of health behaviour such as the health belief model (see pp. 24–8) and protection motivation theory (see pp. 28–33). This overlap is hardly surprising because both types of theory have been developed to explain how individuals evaluate threats, and how these evaluations determine the way in which people deal with threatening situations. Thus the process of primary appraisal in cognitive stress theory, though much broader (i.e. not restricted to health threats), is structurally similar to the process of threat appraisal as conceptualized for health threats by the health belief model or protection motivation theory discussed earlier. According to models of health behaviour, the probability that an individual engages in a given behaviour to avoid some health threat will depend on the individual's assessment of whether he or she is susceptible to the particular illness and on his or her perception of the severity of the consequences of getting the disease.

The concept of secondary appraisal in cognitive stress theory shares some similarities with the construct of coping appraisal in the revised version of protection motivation theory (see pp. 30–3). Like secondary appraisal, coping appraisal involves both the assessment of whether one has the ability to perform a coping response and of whether the coping response is effective in reducing the threat. However, the inventory of coping strategies incorporated in the cognitive stress model is much broader than the actions assumed by models of health behaviour. Models of health behaviour focus on one coping strategy only, namely problem-oriented coping behaviour designed to reduce or avoid the health threat. Emotion-focused coping, at least if used exclusively, would be considered dysfunctional from the perspective of health behaviour models, because it would not directly contribute to the reduction in health risk. In fact one of the rationales which motivated the development of models of health behaviour was to investigate strategies of persuasion which would motivate problem-oriented coping rather than emotion-focused coping or problem avoidance.

The cognitive stress model developed by Lazarus and colleagues offers a general framework for the analysis of psychological stress. Although the model identifies many important general principles of stress and coping, its high level of generality can be a disadvantage in research that attempts to use the model to derive testable predictions for specific stressful life events. Therefore a number of more specific stress theories have been developed that either apply the interactive approach to specific life events (e.g. the Deficit Model of Bereavement; Stroebe and Stroebe 1987, or the Person–Environment Fit Model of Work Stress; Caplan 1983) and/or specify more accurately those aspects of a situation that determine the intensity and persistence of the stress experience (e.g. theory of learned helplessness; Seligman 1975). I will focus on the theory of learned helplessness because it has rivalled the model of Lazarus as a major influence on stress research.

Stress as learned helplessness

Although Seligman's (1975; Peterson et al. 1993) original interest was in the causes of depression rather than stress ('stress' does not appear as a term in the subject index of his 1975 book), his analysis of the conditions under which life events can result in depression identified perceived lack of control as an essential characteristic of situations that are stressful. The original formulation of the learned helplessness model was derived from escape–avoidance research conducted with animals. These experiments showed that while normal animals, exposed to electric shocks that they can escape from, learn to escape after a few shocks, animals that had previously experienced unavoidable shock do not seem to learn the escape response. Later research demonstrated that repeated experiences of uncontrollability had similar effects on humans (e.g. Hiroto 1974; Hiroto and Seligman 1975).

Seligman developed the learned helplessness model as a unified theoretical framework which integrated the data from animal and human research. The basic assumption is that when people or animals experience an event that they cannot control, they develop an expectation of lack of control in similar future situations. This learning results in the helplessness syndrome consisting of motivational, cognitive and emotional deficits: if the persons or animals have learned that the escape from aversive stimulation occurs independent of responses, they will not try very hard to initiate a response that can produce relief; they will also fail to learn new responses that would help them to avoid aversive outcomes and they will react to the traumatic experience first with fear and then depression. On the basis of the similarity of the symptoms of learned helplessness and depression, Seligman proposed that learned helplessness was a major cause of reactive depression.

The extension of the learned helplessness model to depression raised a number of problems. Seligman had originally emphasized that it was the uncontrollability rather than the aversiveness of outcomes which was responsible for the motivational and emotional deficits. It seemed implausible, however, that people would get depressed because uncontrollable good things tended to happen to them. Furthermore, the view that depressive persons feel helpless is inconsistent with their tendency towards self-blame. If individuals believe that their outcomes are independent of their responses, how could depressed individuals feel responsible for these outcomes? Another inadequacy of the old helplessness model concerned the generality of helplessness across situations and duration over time (Abramson *et al.* 1978). The model does not permit predictions about the conditions under which uncontrollability leads to long-term and broadly generalized helplessness symptoms rather than temporary helplessness that may only concern in a very restricted sphere of life (Försterling 1988).

To solve these problems, a cognitive revision of the model was suggested by Abramson *et al.* (1978). According to the revised model, the relation between the experience of uncontrollability and depressive symptoms is mediated by individuals' causal attributions, that is, their interpretations of the reasons for their failure to control a given situation which implies aversive outcomes. Three attributional dimensions are assumed to be important in producing helplessness: internality, stability and globality. For example, a person who loses his or her job might have reasons to attribute this either internally (e.g. personal incompetence) or externally (bankruptcy of the firm he or she worked for). While he or she might feel depressed in either situation, the attribution to personal incompetence is most likely to result in loss of self-esteem. Personal incompetence would also be a more stable cause than a bankruptcy. While it is relatively unlikely that a future employer would also have to close down, personal incompetence is a stable condition that would also be a problem with the next employer. Globality refers to the extent to which helplessness is confined to specific areas. For example, if an individual merely felt incompetent with regard to a very specific line of work, and that he or she would do much better by changing to another line, helplessness would be much less pervasive than if the individual felt generally incompetent to work in his or her chosen occupation. Finally, the severity and intensity of depressive symptoms will be greater the more important and potentially aversive the situation is in which helplessness is experienced.

Thus, according to the attributional theory of learned helplessness, it is not the aversiveness of a negative life event that results in stress and depression, but rather the experience of lack of control induced by negative events that are attributed to internal, stable and global causes. The pre-helplessness phase, in which the individual expends effort to bring the situation under control, is characterized by ongoing stress. During this phase individuals will try to cope with the threat, either by problem-focused coping or by emotion-focused coping. Learned helplessness, when the individual stops trying to cope, is analogous to the phase of exhaustion of resources described by Selye. People often do recover and manage to re-establish control, but the more the individual attributes the helplessness to internal, stable and global causes, the more the stressful experience will result in enduring depressive reactions with the associated cognitive and emotional consequences.

The attributional model further suggested that a characteristic *attributional style* may exist that disposes individuals towards reacting with depression to stressful life events. Seligman and colleagues (e.g. Abramson *et al.* 1978) argued that depression-prone individuals should tend to attribute aversive events to internal, global and stable causes. Two measures of this pessimistic explanatory style were developed: a self-report questionnaire called the Attributional Style Questionnaire (ASQ) and a content analysis procedure called the CAVE (Content Analysis of Verbatim Explanations) technique.

The ASQ presents respondents with six bad events (e.g. you meet a friend who acts hostilely towards you) and six good events (e.g. you did a project which is highly praised). Respondents are asked to imagine themselves in these situations and to provide causal explanations for these events. They are then required to rate each cause in terms of internality, stability and globality. Explanatory style is inferred from the respondents' scores across the three attributional dimensions, computing separate averages for good and bad events. With the CAVE technique, verbatim quotes of causal attributions for good or bad events of the sample of interest are rated by judges in terms of their internality, stability and globality. This technique allows researchers to assess attributional style on the basis of interview material collected for a completely different purpose.

The relationship between attributional style and depression has been observed in numerous studies. A meta-analysis of more than 100 studies found moderate correlations between the predicted attributional pattern and depression (Sweeney *et al.* 1986). However, critics of the revised theory of learned helplessness doubt the importance of attributions as mediators of depression. In particular, Brewin (1988) argued that some events may have such a major impact on their own account that causal cognitions are relatively unimportant in mediating the emotional response. Thus, there are life events which are so far beyond the range of usual human experience that they would be markedly distressing to almost anyone; examples would be extreme situations as the result of acts of war, collective disasters and accidents, crimes of violence or the violent loss of a loved one. And yet, while powerful events such as the loss of a child or spouse are stressful and saddening for nearly everybody, only a minority of those affected by loss react with enduring depression and health deterioration. It seems plausible that the depressive pattern of attributions is associated with a weakened resistance to, and poorer recovery from, depression. Unfortunately, the theory is somewhat vague about the precise nature of these other factors. Some of these concerns have been addressed in yet another reformulation of the helplessness theory, called the hopelessness theory of depression (Abramson *et al.* 1989).

In their later research, Seligman and colleagues began to relate the pessimistic attributional style to physical illness and even mortality using the CAVE technique to assess attributional style (e.g. Peterson and Seligman 1987; Peterson *et al.* 1988; for a review, see Peterson *et al.* 1993). In doing so, Seligman addressed an important claim made in his 1975 book, namely that learned helplessness would result in an impairment of physical as well as mental health.

In one study the age at death of members of the Baseball Hall of Fame whose playing career occurred between 1900 and 1950 was related to their characteristic attributional style (Peterson and Seligman 1987). Attributional style could be assessed for 24 players on the basis of verbatim quotes reported in sports pages. Peterson and Seligman found a marginally significant correlation (r = .26) between the extent to which players offered internal, stable and global explanations for bad events and life expectancy. Players who offered external, unstable and specific explanations for good events also lived shorter lives (r = .45).

In another study, attributional style was assessed from interviews completed at the age of 25 years by 99 graduates of Harvard University from the classes of 1942 to 1944, who were mentally and physically fit at the time of the interview. Men who at age 25 explained bad events by referring to their own internal, stable and global negative qualities had significantly poorer health some 20 to 35 years later. Thus, health status assessed by the individual's personal physician at age 45 showed a significant correlation of .37 with pessimistic explanatory style measured at age 25. Health status measured at age 60 correlated .25 with the same attributional style scores. These findings suggest that pessimistic attributional style in early adulthood is a risk factor for poor physical health in middle and late adulthood. However, although Peterson and Seligman (1987) discuss various pathways between explanatory style and physical well-being, there is little empirical evidence concerning the processes which might mediate this relationship.

Conclusions

Both Lazarus and Seligman have developed theories that identify the cognitive processes underlying the stress experience and make predictions with regard to the initiation of coping behaviours. According to the cognitive stress theory of Lazarus, a situation is stressful if it is potentially harmful and if the individual perceives that his or her resources are insufficient to prevent the aversive outcome. While the original theory of learned helplessness conceived of stress as resulting from uncontrollability regardless of whether the event implied harmful or positive outcomes, the stress definition of the revised model is consistent with that of Lazarus and his colleagues in perceiving stress as resulting from the risk of encountering aversive consequences. The revised version of learned helplessness theory further specifies the conditions under which such *aversive* situations are likely to result in persistent feelings of hopelessness and depression. The theory suggests that perceived lack of control over aversive events that is attributed to internal, stable and global causes is likely to result in anxiety and depression. The model further assumes that a characteristic attributional style exists which constitutes a risk factor for depression as well as poor physical health.

With regard to coping, both theories imply that when individuals are exposed to potentially threatening situations, they will initiate coping strategies to contain the threat. These strategies might consist of problem-oriented coping behaviours but they could also involve emotion-oriented coping behaviours. In addition, the learned helplessness model makes the prediction that in chronic stress situations coping activities will essentially be abandoned if the causes of uncontrollability are perceived as internal, stable and global.

How does psychosocial stress affect health?

Stressful life events like the loss of a job or the death of a spouse do not operate on one's bodily system in the same manner as the noxious physical or chemical stimuli studied by Selye. And yet, as we saw earlier, there can be little doubt that the experience of stressful life events is associated with an increased risk of a wide range of physical and mental disorders. There are two types of mechanisms which mediate the impact of psychosocial stress on health: first, stress can affect health directly through changes in the body's physiology. Second, stress can affect health indirectly through changes in individual behaviour.

Physiological responses to stress

Acute stress

In evolutionary terms, the function of physiological reactions to an acute stress was to prepare the organism for action. If one assumes that bodily injuries frequently occur in a context in which an animal has to fight or flee, it makes sense that the stress responses consist mainly of catabolic processes, that is, processes involved in the expenditure of energy from reserves stored in the body. It is therefore not surprising that the sympathetic–adrenal–medullary system and the hypothalamic–pituitary–adrenocortical system are the two major neuroendocrine systems that are responsible for many of the physiological changes associated with stress. 'Endocrine' refers to the internal secretion of biologically active substances or hormones. Hormones are chemical substances which are released from an endocrine gland (e.g. pituitary) into the bloodstream and act on a distant target site.

Activation of the *sympathetic–adrenal–medullary system* (SAM) leads to an increase in the secretion of two hormones, norepinephrine and epinephrine. The release of these catecholamines stimulates cardiovascular activity and raises blood pressure. The heart beats faster, increasing the amount of blood pumped with each beat. By constricting peripheral blood vessels and those leading to the gastrointestinal tract, blood pressure is raised. At the same time, the arteries serving muscles (including the coronary arteries of the heart muscle) are dilated, thus increasing their blood supply. Catecholamines also relax air passages. Breathing becomes faster and deeper, the bronchioles of the lungs dilate and the secretion of mucus in the air passages decreases. Thus more oxygen is available for the metabolism. Catecholamines also cause the liberation of glucose (one of the major sources of usable energy) from the liver, thus availing the muscles of large energy resources. One further effect, which is quite advantageous in the case of physical injury, is that catecholamines increase the tendency of the blood to coagulate.

The activation of the *hypothalamic–pituitary–adrenocortical system* (HPA) leads to increases in the secretion and release of corticosteroids from the adrenal cortex. For the physiology of stress reactions, the most interesting corticosteroid is cortisol. Cortisol is important for energy mobilization of the body. It promotes the synthesis of glucose from the liver. Cortisol also mobilizes the fat stores from adipose tissues and increases the level of serum lipids, that is, fat-like substances in the blood such as triglycerides and cholesterol, which also provide energy for skeletal and heart muscles. Finally, cortisol down-regulates the inflammatory action of the immune system.

The hormones released by the SAM and the HPA play an important role in the modulation of the immune system. Whereas Selye's (1976) research originally led to the assumption that stress was broadly immunosuppressive, it has more recently been argued that a broad decrease in immune function would not have been evolutionary-adaptive in life-threatening situations (Dhabar and McEwen 1997; for reviews, see Segerstrom and Miller 2004; Schneiderman *et al.* 2005). There is now evidence that acute stress actually activates the immune system. Cells of the immune system (i.e. natural immunity) migrate into the tissue that is most likely to suffer damage during physical confrontation, such as the skin. Once positioned there, these cells are able to contain microbes that may enter the body through wounds and thereby facilitate healing (Dhabar and McEwen 1997; Segerstrom and Miller 2004).

The activation of these physiological stress systems prepares the organism for combat or escape. However, the vigorous physical activity which the stress response prepares us for is rarely an appropriate response to cope with the typical stressful life events encountered today. Instead, in many stressful situations the stress response is likely to hinder rather than help coping and adjustment. Furthermore, while stress responses in the distant past were typically activated by transitory stressors, today many stressors are chronic rather than acute, resulting in more extended elevations of arousal levels. This can impair the functioning of various organ systems, including the immune system, leaving the organism open to infections.

Chronic stress

As Selye (1976) argued, the acute stress response becomes maladaptive if it is repeatedly or continuously activated. For example, the chronic stimulation of the cardiovascular system through hormones secreted by the SAM system in response to stress leads to a sustained increase in blood pressure. Chronically elevated blood pressure forces the heart to work harder and can lead to damaged arteries and plaque formation (Schneiderman *et al.* 2005). The elevation of basal levels of stress hormones as a result of chronic stress also suppresses immunity and might diminish the immune system's capacity to react to the anti-inflammatory action of cortisol (Miller *et al.* 2002). Chronic stress is particularly problematic for elderly individuals, because of the age-related deterioration of the immune system (Schneiderman *et al.* 2005).

Cognitive responses to stress

Brosschot *et al.* and others have recently suggested that it is not the stressful events themselves that are responsible for most of the stress-related physiological activity in daily life, but the thoughts and worries that these events stimulate (e.g. Broschot *et al.* 2006, 2007; Pieper *et al.* 2010; Thayer and Brosschot 2010). These cognitions are caused by the perceived uncontrollability of a stressor (if the stressor is controllable, there is no need to worry or ruminate about it). Such perseverative cognitions prolong the experience of uncontrollability and finally also the physiological activation resulting from the cognitive representation of the stressor's uncontrollability. Thus, perseverative cognitions are assumed to play an important role in converting the immediate physiological concomitants of life events and daily stressors into the prolonged activation of physiological responses to the stressor, which over time will lead to disease. In support of the theoretical assumption that perseverative cognition acts directly on somatic disease via the cardiovascular, immune and endocrine systems, Brosschot *et al.* (2006) review evidence that worry, rumination and even the anticipation of stressful events are associated with enhanced cardiovascular, endocrinological and immunological activity.

Behavioural responses to stress

The experience of stress motivates individuals to engage in a variety of behavioural strategies which aim to reduce the threat or to cope with the emotions aroused by the potentially aversive experience. For example, an executive who is competing for an important promotion will attempt to enhance chances of success by working longer hours and by generally increasing the quality of his or her performance. When the workload becomes so extreme that people abandon regular meals and just 'grab a quick bite' whenever there is time, when they resort to tranquillizers, cigarettes or alcohol to calm down or go to sleep, coping behaviour can become deleterious to their health.

The assumption that individuals who are under stress are more likely to engage in these kinds of unhealthy behaviour patterns is supported by findings from a survey of a probability sample reported by Cohen and Williamson (1988). In this study, small but statistically significant correlations were observed between perceived stress and shorter periods of sleep, infrequent consumption of breakfast, increased quantity of alcohol consumption and greater frequency of illicit drug use. Marginally significant relations were also found between stress and (a) smoking and (b) lack of physical exercise.

Similarly, the widows and widowers who participated in the Tübingen Longitudinal Study of Bereavement reported changes in tranquillizer use, smoking and alcohol consumption (see Table 6.2). While widows mainly increased their use of tranquillizers and sleeping pills, widowers reported increases in alcohol consumption and smoking. This pattern is consistent with epidemiological data showing that liver cirrhosis is one of the causes of death in which widowers show the greatest excess over married men (M. Stroebe and Stroebe 1993). It is also consistent with reports from relapsed addicts that stress often immediately preceded their return to drug use (e.g. Condiotte and Lichtenstein 1981; Shiffman 1982; Baer and Lichtenstein 1988; Bliss *et al.* 1989). Behavioural factors such as alcohol use and carelessness probably play a role in the relatively high accident rates of people under stress.

Finally, individuals under stress are also likely to draw on their social resources and seek out social support (e.g. Amirkhan 1990). Increased interaction with others results in greater probability of exposure to infectious agents and consequent infection. However, the need to seek out social support under stress is to some extent also influenced by individual differences in affiliative tendencies and the nature of the stressor. Under some conditions, stress could therefore also lead to social withdrawal and decreased risk of exposure to infections.

Stress and disease

Stress has been associated both with impairments in psychological and physical health. With regard to psychological health there is extensive evidence from

TABLE 6.2 Percentage of men and women interviewed who specified an increase in their use of tranquillizers, sleeping tablets, alcoholic beverages or cigarettes[a]

	Women		Men	
	Married *(n = 30)*	*Widowed* *(n = 30)*	*Married* *(n = 30)*	*Widowed* *(n = 30)*
Tranquillizers	0.0	24.1	0.0	10.0
Sleeping tablets	3.3	13.3	3.3	6.9
Alcoholic beverages	3.3	6.7	3.3	17.2
Smoking	10.0	17.2	10.0	30.0

[a] Data from the first interviews of the Tübingen Longitudinal Study of Bereavement. Widowed respondents were asked for an increase in use since the death of their partner. Married respondents were asked for increases during the comparable time period.

studies using life stress inventories and assessments of specific life events that chronic stress predicts subsequent depression (for a review, see Kessler 1997). With regard to physical health, the disorders which have attracted most attention are infections, coronary heart disease (CHD), alimentary conditions such as dyspepsia and ulcers and psychopathological problems such as depression. Stress has also been suspected to be important for many other diseases including diabetes mellitus, asthma and even cancer. However, there is still debate about the causal role of stress in the development of various diseases and the mechanisms that mediate this relationship. I will therefore merely illustrate these stress effects using the role of stress in CHD, infections, autoimmune disorders and depression as examples.

Stress and CHD

There are two major forms of CHD, namely angina pectoris and myocardial infarction. The symptoms of angina pectoris (literally, 'strangling of the chest') are periodic attacks of distinctive chest pain, usually situated behind the sternum and radiating to the chest and left shoulder. Patients suffering from angina pectoris complain of tightening, or pressure, or a 'band' around the chest. Attacks of angina pectoris are typically brought on by physical exercise and emotional exertion and usually disappear within 1 to 2 minutes or, at most, 5 to 10 minutes of stopping exertion. They are quickly relieved by rest or medication aimed at dilating blood vessels and reducing blood pressure. The major cause of angina pectoris is an insufficient supply of oxygen to the heart due to atherosclerosis. Attacks of angina pectoris rarely involve permanent damage to the heart muscle.

If plaque grows at a rate exceeding the blood supply available for the nutrition of its cells, it is likely to rupture and form the basis for a thrombosis, which will then completely block an already narrow passage. Such ruptures may also be the result of haemodynamic factors such as high levels of arterial blood pressure (Herd 1978). The formation of blood clots which obstruct the artery and diminish the blood supply to the left ventricle of the heart is the most frequent cause of myocardial infarction, a necrosis (death) of the heart tissue caused by a long-lasting insufficiency of the oxygen supply. Myocardial infarction is one of the major causes of death in most industrialized nations.

Much of the evidence for the relationship between stress and CHD derives from retrospective studies that use life event scales and are therefore open to methodological criticism (e.g. Rahe and Lind 1971; Rahe and Paasikivi 1971; Theorell and Rahe 1971; Rahe *et al.* 1974). For example, Rahe *et al.* (1974) gathered life change data on more than 200 survivors of myocardial infarctions and a similar number of cases of abrupt coronary death in Helsinki. Next of kin, most of whom were spouses, provided the life change data for the victims of sudden deaths. Results indicated marked elevation in the magnitude of total life changes during the months prior to infarction compared to the same time period one year earlier. The major problem with this type of study is that the retrospective assessment of life events is likely to be influenced by the respondent's knowledge of the occurrence of an illness. Since the belief that stress is bad for coronary health is part of common culture, respondents inclined to search for explanations for their own or their partner's illness are likely to remember more stressful life events as having occurred just prior to the event.

There are, however, also many studies on the impact of stress on heart disease which used prospective designs on individuals who were already at high risk (e.g. Byrne *et al.* 1981; Ruberman *et al.* 1984). For example, Byrne *et al.* (1981) examined a cohort of 120 men and women who survived heart attacks. At the first interview, which took place 10 to 14 days following their admission into a coronary care unit, these patients responded to an extensive questionnaire that also contained questions about personal, social and financial worries prior to the heart attack which, in the judgement of the patients, may have contributed to the attack. Of the 102 members of the original sample who could be located eight months later, 20 had a recurrence of the heart disease, and seven had died as a direct consequence of the heart attack. The individuals who had a recurrence of the disease, whether fatal or non-fatal, had reported significantly more worries at the first interview than people who had not suffered a recurrence. Somewhat similar findings were obtained in a large study reported by Ruberman *et al.* (1984). Thus, even though the evidence from retrospective studies of the impact of cumulative life stress on CHD is somewhat problematic, results from studies of the impact of bereavement and from prospective studies with high-risk groups provide consistent evidence on the relationship between psychosocial stress and heart disease.

These findings from human studies are complemented by results from animal experiments which provide evidence of the importance of experimentally manipulated psychological stress in the development of atherosclerosis. In a series of studies Clarkson *et al.* (1987) subjected cynomolgus monkey colonies to stress by repeatedly reshuffling groups and breaking up stable social structures. Dominant monkeys in unstable and therefore stressful social situations developed increased coronary atherosclerosis in comparison with both subordinates, who probably did not struggle very hard to achieve dominance, and dominant monkeys in socially stable groups. The administration of beta-blockers reduced the tendency to develop atherosclerosis.

There are several *mechanisms* by which stress can contribute to CHD. Stress is likely to accelerate the development of atherosclerosis, by increasing the secretion of catecholamines and cortisol (both involved in mobilizing fat stores) and thus increasing the level of serum lipids. An extensive review of research on the impact of stress on the level of serum lipids found that the majority of studies showed significant increases in cholesterol (and especially free fatty acid levels) in response to emotional arousal induced by a variety of stressors (Dimsdale and Herd 1982). Catecholamines also increase the tendency of blood to coagulate, which may contribute to the formation of blood clots and consequent blocking of arteries, especially arteries already narrowed due to the formation of atherosclerotic plaque.

Another line of argument has proposed that an exaggerated *psychophysiological reactivity* to behavioural challenge may be implicated in the development of major cardiovascular disorders such as CHD and essential hypertension (Manuck and

Krantz 1986; Blascovich and Katkin 1995). According to this hypothesis, repeated physiological reactions involving excessive heart rate and/or pressor responses to behavioural stressors promote arterial 'injury' through haemodynamic forces such as turbulence and sheer stress. Cardiovascular reactivity is measured in terms of heart rate, blood pressure or other cardiovascular changes in response to stress, as opposed to measuring only resting levels of these variables.

Evidence for the involvement of physiological reactivity in the development of atherosclerosis comes from animal as well as human studies. Clarkson *et al.* (1986) measured cardiac reactivity in two cohorts of male and female cynomolgus monkeys who were fed a moderately atherogenic diet (i.e. likely to result in atherosclerosis) for approximately two years. These monkeys are particularly suitable for this kind of study because they are known to be highly susceptible to the development of diet-induced atherosclerosis. Heart rate measurements were obtained on each animal under both resting and stressful conditions. 'High' and 'low' heart rate reactors only differed in their responsiveness to the stress situation. They did not differ in average heart rate during baseline measurement. When the coronary arteries of 'high' and 'low' heart-rate reactive animals were investigated at the end of the two-year period, the 'high' heart rate reactors had roughly twice the coronary artery atherosclerosis of the 'low' reactors.

Since physiological reactivity is typically not assessed in epidemiological studies, there is little evidence on the reactivity–CHD relationship in human beings. Probably the only prospective study in which haemodynamic reactivity to stress was assessed and later related to the development of CHD was reported by Keys *et al.* (1971). These authors reported that the magnitude of participants' diastolic blood pressure response to cold immersion (the cold pressor test) was significantly associated with development of CHD at a 23-year follow up.

In a more recent cross-sectional study reported by Blascovich and Katkin (1995), patients who were referred for coronary angiography underwent psychological stress testing before the medical assessment. Cardiovascular reactivity assessed in terms of changes in blood pressure was a significant predictor of various indicators of the progression of atherosclerosis in these men even when traditional predictors had been controlled for. According to Brosschot *et al.* and Pieper *et al.*, perseverative cognitions offer a more plausible explanation than exaggerated psychophysiological reactivity for the extended effects of stressful events on physiological responses. As discussed earlier, these reasearchers hypothesized that worry might be the primary mechanism by which a person prolongs a stressor's cognitive representation, along with its physiological effects. Brosschot *et al.* tested this assumption in two studies in which participants were fitted with an ambulatory monitoring system that measured heart rate and heart rate variability throughout the day (Brosschot *et al.* 2007; Pieper *et al.* 2010). Chronically enhanced heart rate is a risk factor for all-cause mortality (Palatini and Julius 1997) and reduced heart rate variability is also an all-cause mortality risk factor (Tsuji *et al.* 1994). In the study by Brosschot *et al.* (2007), the ambulatory monitoring system signalled to participants with a short 'beep' approximately every hour that they needed to fill in a diary.

In the study by Pieper *et al.* (2010), a hand-held computer was used for the diary. Each diary asked for the presence of one or more worry period and one or more stressor during the preceding period. Stressful events were defined as all minor or major events which made participants feel irritated, angry or depressed. Worry episodes were described to participants as instances when they felt worried for a certain period, were agitated about something or kept on about some problems. In support of their hypothesis, both studies showed that worry had more impact on heart rate and heart rate variability than did stressful events. Brosschot *et al.* found that stressors and prolonged worrying were associated with high heart rate and low heart rate variability, not only during waking, but also during sleeping hours. More importantly, however, worry duration mediated the effects of stressors. When the effects of worry duration on heart rate and heart rate variability were statistically controlled for, the effects of stressors were essentially eliminated. Pieper *et al.* found only marginal effects of stressful events on heart rate. However, there were substantial, independent and prolonged effects of worry episodes on heart rate and heart rate variability. These findings provide strong support for the hypothesis that perseverative cognitions play an important role in prolonging the physiological impact of stressful life experiences.

In addition to these physiological pathways, there are also behavioural pathways that might mediate the impact of stress on coronary health. As discussed earlier, stress is associated with a number of poor health practices which can accelerate the development of atherosclerosis. Individuals under stress are likely to increase their consumption of cigarettes and alcohol, adopt poor eating habits and engage in very little physical exercise (e.g. Cohen and Williamson 1988).

Stress, immune functioning, and infectious disease

Infections are caused by some infectious agent, but exposure to such agents does not always cause infection. Whether the individual exposed to an infectious agent actually develops an infection depends on his or her susceptibility to infections, which is primarily mediated by the immune system. There are numerous factors which affect an individual's susceptibility to disease (e.g. prior exposure to the micro-organism and the development of immunity, nutritional status of the host, a wide range of genetic factors). Since Selye's classic work on the effect of stress on the immune system, exposure to stress has to be included among the determinants of individual susceptibility. The three major pathways through which stress influences the immune system are direct innervation of the central nervous system and immune system (nerves ending at immune organs such as the thymus, bone marrow, spleen and even lymph nodes), the release of hormones (e.g. epinephrine, norepinephrine, cortisol, growth hormones, prolactin), and behaviour (health behaviour).

Research on the impact of stress on susceptibility to immune system-mediated disease such as infections has assessed the effects of stress *either* on indicators of the functioning of the immune system *or* on disease outcome. There are very few studies which have attempted to assess both the impact of stress on disease and the role of immunological changes in mediating this relationship (e.g. Kemeny *et al.* 1989; Cohen *et al.* 1998). I will first discuss studies of the relation between stress and immune functioning, and then go on to consider stress effects on the onset and progression of infectious disease.

Psychoneuroimmunological research on humans has focused on the study of immune processes occurring in circulating peripheral blood which transports the immune components between organs of the immune system and sites of inflammation. The general function of the immune system is to protect the body from damage by invading micro-organisms. These foreign substances are called antigens and include bacteria, viruses, tumour cells and toxins. The identification and elimination of antigens is accomplished by several types of lymphocytes (white blood cells).

To understand the influence of psychosocial stressors on the immune system, it is important to distinguish between *natural* and *specific* immunity (for a review, see Segerstrom and Miller 2004). *Natural immunity* is an unspecific, fast and all-purpose immune reaction that provides defence against any pathogen and does not require prior exposure to that pathogen. The largest group of cells involved in natural immunity is the granulocytes, which include phagocytic cells (e.g. neutrophil and macrophages) that eat their targets. The generalized response initiated by these cells is *inflammation*. Macrophages also release communication molecules or *cytokines*, which have a broad effect on the organism, including fever and inflammation, but also promote wound healing (Segerstrom and Miller 2004). Natural killer cells are another form of cells involved in natural immunity. They recognize and destroy non-self cells. *Specific immunity* depends on specific recognition of the pathogen and is the usual outcome of infection or prophylactic immunization. It is more specific and acts against one specific antigen only. Although specific immunity is extremely efficient, it takes several days for a full defence to be mounted and the body has to rely on natural immunity to contain the infection in the meantime.

To measure the functioning of the immune system, researchers use either quantitative or functional measures. *Quantitative* or *enumerative* tests of the immune system involve counting the number or percentages of different types of immune cells such as T-helper cells, suppressor/cytotoxic T-helper cells and natural killer (NK) cells in the peripheral blood (Cohen and Herbert 1996). Quantifying the number of circulating cells is important for two reasons: first, the body needs a minimum number of each type of immune cell to respond adequately to antigenic response, and second, an optimal response requires a balance of the various cell types. Since these different sub-groups perform specialized functions, it is not possible to use a single measure to determine global immunological competence (Cohen and Williamson 1991; Cohen and Herbert 1996).

Functional measures examine the performance of certain immune cells. The ability of lymphocytes to proliferate rapidly in the face of antigenic challenge is essential to an adequate immune response. Lymphocytic proliferation is a test of cellular immunity that examines how effectively lymphocytes divide when stimulated through incubation with mitogens such as phytohemagglutinin (PHA) or concanavalin A (Con A). Mitogens are substances which are capable of inducing lymphocytes to divide. It is assumed that greater proliferation indicates more effective cell function. The ability of natural killer cells to destroy tumour cells is assessed by incubating natural killer cells with tumour cells. These tests are *in vitro* tests. Cells are removed from the body and their function is studied in the laboratory (Cohen and Herbert 1996; Uchino *et al.* 1996).

There is ample empirical support for the assumption that chronic psychosocial stress is associated with an impairment of the functioning of the immune system (Kiecolt-Glaser and Glaser 1991; Glaser and Kiecolt-Glaser 1994; Cohen and Herbert 1996; Segerstrom and Miller 2004). Studies of such diverse groups as bereaved spouses, separated and divorced men and women, psychiatric patients with major depression and family care-givers of Alzheimer's disease victims have demonstrated that members of such groups are more distressed and show relatively poorer immune functions than well-matched community counterparts (e.g. Stein *et al.* 1985; Kiecolt-Glaser *et al.* 1987, 1988). Other researchers have observed modest suppression of immune function in medical students during examinations, compared to similar measures taken one month previously when students were less distressed (e.g. Glaser *et al.* 1985). There is also increasing evidence that changes in immune response occur as a function of prolonged and repeated exposure to stress (e.g. Kiecolt-Glaser *et al.* 1987; McKinnon *et al.* 1989). For example, McKinnon *et al.* (1989) found impairment in immune functions (relative to a matched control group) in people who lived near the nuclear power station at Three Mile Island and had been exposed to more than six years of stressful uncertainty associated with the accident at this station.

These findings demonstrate the effects of psychological stress on the immune system. It is less clear, however, whether these changes in immune functions really lead to the development of illness (Cohen and Williamson 1991; Segerstrom and Miller 2004). Although we know that gross alterations in immunity can be associated with greater morbidity and mortality (e.g. AIDS), little is known about the actual health consequences of these more modest changes in immune functions. It is therefore important to show that psychological stress is related to disease outcome.

Some evidence for this association comes from experimental studies of the role of stress in increasing susceptibility to infection. In these experiments, volunteers whose exposure to stressful life events had been assessed beforehand were exposed to some unpleasant but not dangerous virus, typically a cold virus (Cohen *et al.* 1993, 1998). In one of these studies, Cohen *et al.* (1993) exposed 420 male and female volunteers through a nasal drip to either a cold virus or a saline solution (i.e. placebo group). These volunteers entered quarantine for two days before and seven days after the viral challenge or saline exposure. Psychological stress was measured by self-reported number of major stressful life events during the previous 12 months, perceptions of current demands exceeding capabilities to cope, and current negative affect. There were two health outcomes in this study, namely infection and clinical disease. Infections result from the multiplication of the invading micro-organism. However, it is possible for a person to be infected without developing clinical symptoms. Whereas none of the individuals in the saline control group developed an infection, there was a clear association between level of stress and health outcome for those who were exposed to the virus: highly stressed individuals had a significantly higher risk of infection and of developing a cold than persons who were less stressed. Controlling for health practices did not reduce the association between stress and susceptibility to illness.

Cohen *et al.* (1998) replicated this study with 276 volunteers who entered quarantine for six days, one day before being exposed to the virus and five days following the viral challenge. Life stressors were assessed by a standardized semi-structured interview, the Life Events and Difficulties Schedule (LEDS) (Brown and Harris 1989) which allows one to make a reliable classification of stressors in terms of severity and chronicity. Eighty-four per cent of the participants developed an infection but only 40 per cent actually developed colds. With regard to the influence of stress on susceptibility to disease, an interesting difference emerged between acute and chronic stressors. Whereas there was no association between acute events and susceptibility, the experience of chronic stressors lasting one month or longer was associated with increased risk of infection. Furthermore, the risk of infection increased significantly with the duration of the life stressor (see Figure 6.2).

This study is also exemplary in that it assessed the role of a range of potential mediating variables in accounting for the association between stress and risk of infection. To qualify as a potential mediator of the stress–infection–susceptibility relationship, a variable has to be associated with stress and with risk of infection. Thus, one has to demonstrate that the assumed mediator is influenced by stress and

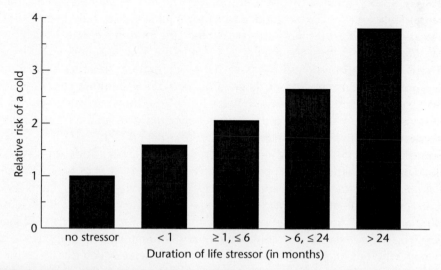

FIGURE 6.2 Relative risk of developing a cold contrasting persons with stressors of varying duration with those without any stressor
Source: Cohen *et al.* (1998)

that it in turn influences the individual's susceptibility to stress. Finally, it has to be demonstrated that if one statistically controls for this variable in tests of the stress–infection relationship, this reduces or even eliminates this relationship.

Many of the health practices measured (e.g. smoking, exercising, sleep efficiency) were significantly associated with both chronic stress and increased risk of infection. And yet, statistically controlling for these health practices resulted in only minor reductions of the association between chronic stress and susceptibility to infection. Thus, as in their previous study, the authors concluded that the association between stress and susceptibility to colds was not 'primarily mediated by health practices' (Cohen *et al.* 1998: 222). More puzzling was the finding that chronic stressors in this study were not found to be associated with elevated levels of stress hormones such as epinephrine, norepinephrine or cortisol. Changes in these stress hormones therefore could not have mediated the relationship between stress and health, even though elevated levels in these hormones were associated with greater risks of colds.

This leaves us with a puzzle. There is now convincing evidence that stress, and particularly chronic stress experiences, are associated with an increased susceptibility to infectious disease. However, despite some support for the assumed impact of stress on endocrine, immune and behavioural variables, there is so far little direct evidence that any of these variables mediate the association between stress and infection.

Stress, immune functioning, and autoimmune disorders

There is also a second puzzle. The immunosuppressive model does not explain how stress might affect those diseases whose central feature is excessive inflammation. Excessive inflammation is involved in the development of allergic, autoimmune, rheumatologic and cardiovascular disease, all conditions which have been found to be aggravated by stress (Miller *et al.* 2002). Since the immunosuppressive action of stress would also suppress the inflammatory immune response, one would expect that stress would improve these diseases. This is not, however, what is usually found.

Inflammation is a first line of defence of the natural immune system against pathogens. The immune system's inflammatory response can be triggered by infections and trauma and the mechanisms associated with inflammation initially promote healing by facilitating the migration of immune cells into the wound or site of inflammation. Inflammation is driven largely by certain cytokines (known collectively as pro-inflammatory cytokines). These include tumour necrosis factor-alpha and several interleukins, specifically IL-1-beta and IL-6 (Penwell and Larkin 2010). Cytokines are protein substances released by cells that serve as intercellular signals to regulate immune responses to injury and infection (Kiecolt-Glaser *et al.* 2002). The primary action of these cytokines is to attract immune cells to the site of infection or injury and to cause them to become activated and to respond. Although the mechanisms associated with inflammation are initially helpful for the immune defence against infections and injury, chronic or recurring infections can provoke pathological changes.

To explain the impact of stress on inflammatory conditions, Miller *et al.* (2002) suggested that chronic stress diminished the immune system's sensitivity to glucocorticoid hormones (e.g. cortisol) that normally down-regulate the inflammatory response of the immune system. This insensitivity develops in response to overexposure to the hormones, which the HPA and SAM systems secrete in response to chronic stress. As a result, the immune system's capacity to respond to the anti-inflammatory action of cortisol is diminished and inflammatory processes flourish uncontrolled. There is increasing evidence that inflammation is not only associated with progression of autoimmune diseases, but also cardiovascular disease and certain cancers (for reviews, see Kiecolt-Glaser *et al.* 2002; Penwell and Larkin 2010).

Miller *et al.* (2002) tested their model with a group of severely chronically stressed individuals, namely parents whose children were undergoing active treatment for cancer. The control group consisted of parents of medically healthy children. The reactivity of pro-inflammatory cytokines to a (synthetic) glucocortoid was assessed *in vitro* by incubating a blood sample with the hormone. In support of their model, the capacity of a synthetic glucocortoid hormone to suppress the *in vitro* production of the pro-inflammatory cytokine inteleukin-6 was diminished among parents of cancer patients but not among parents of healthy children.

Stress and depression
There is ample evidence that stress experiences can trigger episodes of depression. According to some estimates between 60 and 80 per cent of cases of depression are preceded by major life events (e.g. Hammen 2005; Monroe and Harkness 2005). However, these estimates only apply to first lifetime episodes of depression. Major depression is typically characterized by recurrent episodes over the life course and there is a great deal of evidence from cross-sectional as well as longitudinal studies that first lifetime episodes of depression are more strongly associated with major life stress than are successive recurrences (for a review, see Monroe and Harkness 2005). For example, in one longitudinal study, Kendler *et al.* (2000) found that the strength of the association between stressful life events and onset of a depressive episode declined approximately 13 per cent with each recurrence. Whereas the odds ratio for an individual's first major episode of depression to be preceded by a stressful life event was 9.38, it was only 6.74 for individuals who had one, 5.22 for individuals who had two and 3.63 for individuals who had three prior episodes of depression.

There are two conflicting theoretical explanations for these findings. On the one hand, individuals might get habituated to major life events or become better able to cope with them. Therefore, the association between serious life events and major depressive episodes weakens with each depressive episode and it becomes less likely that a major life event will trigger a depressive episode. This has become known as the autonomy hypothesis (Monroe and Harkness 2005). Alternatively, it is also possible that with each successive episode of depression individuals become more *sensitized* to life stress. As a result, less and less serious life events begin to trigger depressive episodes. Because depressive episodes are now triggered by minor life events, the association between major life events and depressive episodes becomes weakened. At present there is insufficient evidence to decide between these two hypotheses. However, the evidence that is available is more supportive of sensitization rather than habituation (Ormel *et al.* 2001; Morris *et al.* 2010).

Depression is not only a mental illness, it is also a risk factor for physical diseases. Evidence from several prospective studies links depressive symptoms to CHD (for reviews, see Kiecolt-Glaser 2002; Suls and Bunde 2005). Kiecolt-Glaser *et al.* (2002) review evidence to suggest that depression is also a risk factor for several other medical problems. Given the association between chronic stress and depression, this raises the question whether depression has a causal influence on these health outcomes. Such a causal influence could be due to the association of depression with health-impairing behaviour patterns. People who are depressed do not expend a great deal of effort on taking care of themselves. They engage in less exercise, have poorer nutrition and a greater propensity for alcohol and drug abuse (Kiecolt-Glaser *et al.* 2002). Alternatively, it is possible that the effect of depression on CHD is not causal, but due to the impact stress has on this condition. So far, there is insufficient evidence to distinguish between these two explanations.

Summary and conclusions

The stress concept was made popular by Selye's work on the bodily responses of organisms exposed to stressors such as intensive heat or cold, non-lethal injections of toxic substances and infections. Selye suggested that these bodily reactions to stress were non-specific and helped the organism to cope with the stressor. Diseases of adaptation characteristic of the stage of exhaustion are the price the organism has to pay for the defence against extended exposure to stressor agents.

The psychosocial approach to stress is based on the assumption that psychosocial stress results in the same kind of bodily changes which Selye observed as a consequence of tissue damage. In this tradition, evidence was generated to demonstrate that specific life events or cumulative life stress are associated with an increased risk of morbidity or even mortality.

This research related stressful life events to the incidence of illness, but did not address the question of why certain psychological experiences are stressful and how the organism distinguishes stressful from positive events. This issue was later addressed by psychological theories of stress which focus on the cognitive processes that mediate between life events and stress. Two approaches were described, the cognitive stress theory of Lazarus *et al.* and the theory of learned helplessness from Seligman *et al.* Both theories conceive of stress as resulting whenever events are appraised as potentially harmful and when individuals perceive their resources to be insufficient to prevent the aversive outcome.

The last section of the chapter addressed the question of how stressful events can be detrimental to psychological and physical health. The impact of psychosocial stress is mediated by two pathways, a direct route via the body's physiology and an indirect route, affecting health through the person's behaviour. The joint impact of these reactions to stress contributes to the development of ill health either by interacting with other causes of disease or by affecting the body's ability to resist infection. This research resulted in a substantial modification and extension of Selye's original model. We also know a great deal more about the pathways by which stress affects health. The puzzle is nearly solved, but not quite. We have been able to identify many of the physiological and behavioural pathways through which stress could impact on physical and mental health. But even though we have been able to demonstrate that stress results in these physiological and behavioural changes and even though we have been able to demonstrate that some of these changes have a negative health impact, to my knowledge there are no prospective studies that demonstrate that specific stress-induced behavioural or physiological changes mediated the impact of stress on the development of specific diseases.

Further reading

Blascovich, J. and Katkin, E.S. (eds) (1995) *Cardiovascular Reactivity to Psychological Stress and Disease*. Washington, DC: American Psychological Association. This book evaluates the evidence concerning the cardiovascular reactivity hypothesis. This hypothesis suggests that exaggerated psychophysiological reactivity to stress may be implicated in the development of major cardiovascular disorder.

Brosschot, J.F., Gerin, W. and Thayer, J.F. (2006) The perseverative cognition hypothesis: a review of worry, prolonged stress-related physiological activation, and health. *Journal of Psychosomatic Research*, 60: 113–24. This article reviews evidence in support of the assumption that it is not cardiovascular reactivity but perseverative cognitions such as worry and rumination that are responsible for most of the stress-related physiological activity in daily life.

Cohen, S. and Williamson, G.M. (1991) Stress and infectious disease in humans. *Psychological Bulletin*, 109: 5–24. Comprehensive review of research on the relationship between stress and infectious disease in humans.

Lazarus, R.S. and Folkman, S. (1984) *Stress, Appraisal, and Coping*. New York, NY: Springer. In this classic monograph the authors review the literature on stress as it related to the cognitive stress theory of Lazarus, Folkman and their colleagues.

Schneiderman, N., Ironson, G. and Siegel, S.D. (2005) Stress and health: psychological, behavioral and biological determinants. *Annual Review of Clinical Psychology*, 1: 607–28. A comprehensive review of the factors that are assumed to be responsible for the effect of acute and chronic stress on health.

Stroebe, M., Schut, H. and Stroebe, W. (2007) Health outcomes of bereavement. *Lancet*, 370: 1960–73. A comprehensive review of research on the health consequences of losing a marital partner.

Watson, D. and Pennebaker, J.W. (1989) Health complaints, stress, and distress. Exploring the central role of negative affectivity. *Psychological Review*, 96: 234–54. Argues that self-report measures of both stressful life events and health complaints reflect a pervasive mood disposition to experience negative mood. While negative affectivity correlates highly with measures of symptom reporting, it seems to be unrelated to objective health indicators.

Moderators of the stress– health relationship

I n interviews with bereaved individuals to assess the health consequences of their loss experience, I have been impressed by the tremendous differences in the way these people coped with the event, differences that were often quite unrelated to situational indicators of the severity of the event (e.g. Stroebe *et al.* 1988). Such differences in adjustment are of course consistent with the interactional concept of stress, according to which individual differences in coping styles and coping resources are as important as variations in situational demands in determining the extent to which stress is experienced. This chapter will present a more detailed discussion of coping processes and of the major coping resources which moderate the relationship between stress and ill health.

Strategies of coping

Coping strategies or styles play an important role in an individual's physical and psychological well-being when he or she is confronted with negative or stressful life events (Endler and Parker 1990). Coping has typically been defined as 'the person's cognitive and behavioural efforts to manage (reduce, minimize, master, or tolerate) the internal and external demands of the person–environment transaction that is appraised as taxing or exceeding the resources of the person' (Folkman *et al.* 1986b: 572). Thus coping encompasses the cognitive and behavioural strategies which individuals use to manage both the stressful situation and the negative emotional reactions elicited by that event.

The most striking feature of this definition of coping is its breadth. Coping processes are not only assumed to include all the decisions and actions taken by an individual faced with a stressful life event, but also the attendant negative emotions. The only limiting condition is that to constitute 'coping', these cognitive and behavioural strategies should have the function of 'managing' the stressful situation. This implies that to constitute coping, strategies should *aim* at lowering the probability of harm resulting from the stressful encounter and/or at reducing negative emotional reactions. Whether or not these strategies are successful in reaching the goal of managing the stressful situation is not part of the definition of coping.

Dimensions of coping

A great deal of research effort has been invested in the identification of basic dimensions of coping. This is not surprising, because analyses of the literature on coping or of self-reports of cognitive or behavioural coping strategies employed by samples of respondents in stressful encounters have suggested an immense variety of coping strategies. In these investigations respondents were presented with lists of coping strategies and asked to indicate which of these they used in coping with a recent stress experience. Responses were then factor-analysed. Factor analysis is a statistical procedure which allows one to identify from the intercorrelations of a set of items a smaller number of basic dimensions assumed to be responsible for these correlations.

Studies which followed such a procedure have uncovered a variety of different basic dimensions (e.g. Folkman and Lazarus 1980; Folkman *et al.* 1986a, 1986b; Amirkhan 1990; Endler and Parker 1990). In a study which resulted in the construction of one of the most widely used coping scales, the Ways of Coping Questionnaire, Folkman *et al.* (1986a) identified eight distinct coping strategies (see Table 7.1). Endler and Parker (1990), on the other hand, who used a comparable procedure in the development of their Multidimensional Coping Inventory, arrived at three dimensions, namely task-oriented coping, emotion-oriented coping and avoidance-oriented coping. The factor analytic study of Amirkhan (1990) also led to the identification of three dimensions, but these were somewhat different from those identified by Endler and Parker. Amirkhan labelled his dimensions problem solving, seeking social support and avoidance.

There are a number of reasons for these inconsistencies. Far from being an objective procedure, the outcomes of factor analyses are dependent on numerous aspects of a study, such as the composition of the item pool or of the sample of respondents, and the method of factor analysis used. Finally, researchers have great freedom in the labels they attach to their scales, so that even apparent similarities between studies are often more the result of consistencies in labelling than in the items which underlie a dimension.

And yet it is possible to infer some consensus between these studies. There seem to be a number of basic dimensions which emerge in all this research (for a review, see Parker and Endler 1992). Most studies suggest that coping has two major functions, namely to reduce the risk of harmful consequences that might result from a stressful event (i.e. problem-focused coping) and to regulate the distressing emotional reactions to the event (i.e. emotion-focused coping). These two types of coping do not reflect mutually exclusive alternatives but are processes that often co-occur. While problem-focused coping is usually reflected by one or two factors, there is often a wide array of emotion-focused factors. Thus, two of the strategies identified by Folkman *et al.* (1986a) appear to be clearly problem-focused (confrontive coping, planful problem solving), five are clearly emotion-focused (distancing, self-controlling, accepting responsibility, positive reappraisal, escape avoidance), and one focuses on both functions (seeking social support).

TABLE 7.1 The coping strategies identified by Folkman

Scale 1: confrontive coping	Scale 5: accepting responsibility
Stood my ground and fought for what I wanted	Criticized or lectured myself
Tried to get the person responsible to change his or her mind	Realized I brought the problem on myself
I expressed anger to the person(s) who caused the problem	I made a promise to myself that things would be different next time
I let my feelings out somehow	
Scale 2: distancing	**Scale 6: escape–avoidance**
Made light of the situation; refused to get too serious about it	Wished that the situation would go away or somehow be over with
Went on as if nothing had happened	Hoped a miracle would happen
Didn't let it get to me; refused to think about it too much	Had fantasies about how things might turn out
Tried to forget the whole thing	Tried to make myself feel better by eating, drinking, smoking, using drugs or medication, and so forth
Scale 3: self-controlling	**Scale 7: planful problem-solving**
I tried to keep my feelings to myself. Kept others from knowing how bad things were	I knew what had to be done, so I doubled my efforts to make things work
I tried to keep my feelings from interfering with other things too much	I made a plan of action and followed it
	Changed something so things would turn out all right
	Drew on my past experiences; I was in a similar position before
Scale 4: seeking social support	**Scale 8: positive reappraisal**
Talked to someone to find out more about the situation	Changed or grew as a person in a good way
Talked to someone who could do something concrete about the problem	I came out of the experience better than when I went in
I asked a relative or friend I respected for advice	Found new faith
Talked to someone about how I was feeling	Rediscovered what is important in life

Source: Adapted from Folkman *et al*. (1986a)

A second dimension which frequently emerges from this research is approach vs. avoidance (Roth and Cohen 1986). Avoidant coping is related to several constructs with a long research history (e.g. repression-sensitization; Byrne 1961 and monitoring vs. blunting; Miller 1980). An individual can confront his or her emotions (e.g. by reappraising the situation or confiding in a friend) but he or she can also avoid this confrontation using strategies such as denial, distraction or wishful thinking. Similarly, the individual can confront a health threat by undergoing some extensive diagnostic procedure or a recommended operation, but he or she might also decide that it would be better to avoid seeking a diagnosis or having an operation. The Ways of Coping Questionnaire dimensions of distancing and escape–avoidance reflect avoidance strategies, whereas confrontative coping, seeking social support, accepting responsibility and planful problem-solving would seem to involve approach-based coping.

A third dimension which has typically emerged in these studies is the seeking of social support. Individuals might cope with a stressful experience alone or seek social support to help reduce the stress. As a social psychologist I would naturally like to add this social dimension to coping. However, Endler and Parker (1990) were probably right when they argued that social support should be considered a *resource* for coping strategies rather than a specific coping dimension.

This leaves us with a two-dimensional classification implying four categories of coping, namely problem-focused approach, problem-focused avoidance, emotion-focused approach and emotion-focused avoidance. Table 7.2 presents examples of these coping strategies to illustrate that these two dimensions are indeed independent. Whereas approach and avoidance are the endpoint of a continuum, emotion-focused vs. problem-focused coping represent two independent dimensions. Stressful situations almost by definition arouse strong emotions which are likely to impair the ability of the individual to proceed through the decision-making and action sequence. Therefore individuals typically have to deal with problems and emotions at the same time. Whether a stress situation elicits predominantly emotion-focused or problem-focused coping will to some extent depend on the controllability of the situation. Some stress situations are characterized by the fact that there is very little the individual can do to change the situation, whereas others are controllable and elicit the full choice of coping alternatives. Moreover, it is important to note that controllability, like stress, is a person–environment interaction. Although some stress experiences may be universally uncontrollable, others may be uncontrollable only for individuals who lack some specific ability that is necessary in order to control the situation.

TABLE 7.2 Examples of coping strategies

	Problem-focused coping	**Emotion-focused coping**
Approach coping	Planning Seeking instrumental support Task-oriented coping Confrontive coping	Cognitive restructuring Seeking emotional support Turning to religion Acceptance Positive or negative reinterpretation
Avoidance coping	Problem avoidance Behavioural disengagement	Denial Distancing Mental disengagement Wishful thinking Social withdrawal

Source: Solberg and Segerstrom (2006)

The differential effectiveness of strategies of coping

Given the extensive research devoted to the identification of basic dimensions of coping, it is disappointing how little is known about the differential effectiveness of these coping strategies. Even though numerous studies have related coping strategies to physical and psychological well-being following stressful encounters, few general conclusions can be drawn from this research. There are a number of conceptual and methodological reasons for the failure of this outcome research to produce clear-cut results.

A major problem with much of the early research on coping is that it assessed coping effectiveness in relation to a range of *different* stressful encounters (e.g. Aldwin and Revenson 1986; Folkman *et al.* 1986a; McCrae and Costa 1986). Participants in these studies were asked to indicate the most stressful event they experienced during a specified period. This may have included financial problems, health problems, interpersonal disputes and difficulties at work. In view of the general consensus in the literature that the effectiveness of a given coping strategy is dependent on the nature of the stressful encounter, the decision to adopt a procedure which aggregates measures of coping effectiveness across *different* encounters and thus essentially disregards the nature of the stressful encounter is surprising.

This problem has been recognized in more recent studies of coping effectiveness which were explicitly based on the assumption that the degree to which individuals have control over a stress situation moderates the effectiveness of their coping strategies. More specifically, it was predicted that in situations over which the individual has a great deal of control, problem-focused coping strategies should be more effective than emotion-focused strategies, whereas emotion-focused coping strategies should be most effective in stress situations over which the individual has very little control. However, despite the plausibility of this hypothesis, empirical support has been rather mixed (for a review, see Terry and Hynes 1998).

One potential reason for these inconsistencies could be psychometric problems with the measures used to assess emotion-focused coping. As Stanton and her colleagues (1994; Austenfeld and Stanton 2004) have argued, some of the scales used to assess emotion-focused coping contain items which confound coping strategy with coping outcome. For example, the coping scale developed by Endler and Parker (1990) contains emotion-focused coping items which solely reflect distress (e.g. 'become very tense'). Other items reflect low self-esteem (e.g. 'focus on my inadequacies').

To address these problems, Stanton *et al.* (2000) developed a new measure of emotional approach coping that yielded two distinct factors, namely emotional processing and emotional expression. Items measuring emotional expression included 'I acknowledge my emotions' or 'I take time to figure out what I'm really feeling'. Emotional expression was reflected by items such as 'I take time to express my emotions' or 'I allow myself to express my emotions'. Longitudinal and experimental studies using these scales indicated the adaptive potential of emotional approach coping for a range of stressors, including infertility, breast cancer and chronic pain (for a review, see Austenfeld and Stanton 2004).

Evidence that confrontation of one's emotions is associated with better adjustment than avoidance is consistent with research by Pennebaker on the positive health impact of disclosure of previously undisclosed traumatic events. Pennebaker consistently found that subjects who had been instructed to write about past traumatic events (Pennebaker *et al.* 1988) or recent upsetting experiences (Pennebaker *et al.* 1990) reported fewer health centre visits following the experiment when compared with controls who wrote about trivial events (for a review, see Pennebaker 1989). A meta-analysis based on 146 randomized studies of experimental disclosure resulted in a small but significant effect of d = .151 (Frattaroli 2006).

Originally Pennebaker accounted for the ameliorative effects of expressive writing in terms of a theory of inhibition, which outlines the processes by which failure to confront traumatic events results in poorer health. The central assumption of this theory is that inhibition of thoughts, feelings and behaviour is an active process requiring physiological work. When individuals inhibit their desire to talk or think about traumatic experiences over long periods of time, cumulative stress is placed on the body resulting in increased vulnerability to stress-related disease. Later, Pennebaker (1997) changed the focus of his explanation from potential negative effects of suppression to positive effects of disclosure. He argued that disclosure helps the individual to organize the experience, to clarify psychological states to others and to translate emotional experiences into the medium of language. However, Frattaroli (2006) found little support for that theory. She concluded that the data offered most support for 'exposure theory'. This theory assumes that when a person repeatedly confronts, describes and in essence relives the thoughts and feelings about a negative experience, this repetition and exposure leads to an extinction of those thoughts and feelings.

But even though confrontational varieties of emotion-focused coping appear to be more effective than avoidance coping, this association may be curvilinear. There is evidence to suggest that thinking too much about one's emotions is also associated with poor outcome. Nolen-Hoeksema and her colleagues have identified rumination as an ineffective coping strategy (e.g. Nolen-Hoeksema *et al.* 1997; Nolen-Hoeksema and Larson 1999). Ruminators tend to focus passively on their symptoms of distress and the meaning and consequences of these symptoms, instead of actively working through their emotions. Ruminative response styles may prolong depression by enhancing the effects of negative mood on cognition and by interfering with instrumental behaviour. The difference between good and bad emotion confrontation may be that ruminators engage in wishful thinking and passively reiterating their emotions. In contrast, non-ruminators actively engage in positive reappraisal, trying to reconstruct the meaning of the stress situation in a new and positive way. However, it is possible that the goal of rumination may not be confrontation of emotions but avoidance. In ruminating about peripheral issues such as the causes of the loss and the events that led up to it, the grieving individual might try to avoid confronting the one terrible truth, namely that the loved person has been lost for ever.

In general, most of the empirical literature suggests that chronic reliance on avoidant coping is associated with poorer adjustment than are coping strategies in which individuals confront their emotions (e.g. Carver *et al.* 1993; Stanton and Snider 1993; Nolen-Hoeksema and Larson 1999). In one study, avoidance was even found to be associated with cancer progression (Epping-Jordan *et al.* 1994). Use of avoidant coping is also associated with lower medical regimen adherence in HIV-positive individuals (Weaver *et al.* 2005), greater risk-taking among HIV-positive injection drug users (Avants *et al.* 2001) and compromised recovery of functions following surgical procedures (Stephens *et al.* 2002).

There may be one exception to this general pattern. Limited evidence suggests that emotional avoidance could be useful in some very specific situations, namely when confronting a stressor that is short-term and uncontrollable. When one cannot do anything to solve a problem that may be resolved shortly and in due course, the best strategy might be to put it out of one's mind. Support for this assumption comes from a study by Heckman *et al.* (2004) of women who had to repeat a mammography because the initial result had been questionable. Heckman found that women who had used cognitive avoidance regarding the outcome were less anxious after they had been informed of a beneficial outcome.

Finally, there are two conceptual issues which have so far been neglected in research on coping effectiveness, namely the choice of the criterion used to define 'effectiveness' and the time frame during which effectiveness is assessed. In most of these studies, effectiveness has been defined in terms of the level of distress individuals experienced at some arbitrarily chosen point in time following the stressful encounter. A coping strategy was considered effective if individuals who used this coping strategy experienced less distress, mood disturbance or depressive symptoms than individuals who used other coping strategies. It can easily be demonstrated that this choice of criterion is problematic. Although psychological health and physical health are often correlated, there are many instances in which they are not. For example, a man who uses denial to cope with symptoms of an acute coronary illness may have less distress in the short run, but risks serious physical consequences in the long run. Similarly, Pennebaker *et al.* (1990) found that individuals who expressed their emotions about some undisclosed trauma had increased levels of psychological distress but also fewer health centre visits.

The second conceptual issue concerns the time frame. This refers both to the time elapsed between the stress experience and the use of a coping strategy, and to the interval between the assessment of the coping strategy and the measurement of outcome. For example, despite the overwhelming support for the superiority of approach over avoidance coping, there is evidence to suggest that avoidant coping strategies such as denial may be quite effective in the initial stages of coping with severely traumatic events. Such strategies can reduce stress and anxiety and allow for a gradual recognition of threat. If one deals oneself with threatening material in a way that prevents it from becoming overwhelming, one is provided with the time needed for assimilation of stressful information and for mobilization of efforts to change the environment or provide protection (e.g. Roth and Cohen 1986; Stroebe 1992). Because individuals eventually have to assimilate even the most painful experience, the chronic use of denial is likely to impair the likelihood of adjustment. A related issue concerns the time between the assessment of a coping strategy and the measurement of outcome. It seems plausible that some coping strategies may have a positive impact in the short run but be counterproductive in the long run. For example, most researchers report that the use of alcohol and drugs in coping with the loss of a loved person is associated with increased distress in the long run (e.g. Nolen-Hoeksema and Larson 1999). And yet, it is quite conceivable that the immediate effect of alcohol and drugs is a positive one.

Conclusions

Much of the early work on effectiveness of coping styles was stimulated by the interactional stress theory of Lazarus, Folkman and their colleagues, a theory which does not make predictions about the choice of coping strategies or effectiveness in coping. As a consequence of the lack of a guiding theory and, at the same time, the ready availability of instruments to measure coping styles, researchers have often adopted an atheoretical research strategy of asking individuals to report (retrospectively) the coping styles they used in stress situations, and then relating these reports to some measure of distress. The methodological weaknesses of this type of research were aggravated by using cross-sectional designs and aggregating findings across different stress situations.

More recently, these problems have been recognized and approaches to coping research have been improved. There are more studies which use a prospective methodology to study individual coping with a specific stress situation. For example, several studies have examined the impact of coping with breast cancer on outcomes assessed at a one-year follow-up. These have shown that avoidant coping was related to higher levels of distress (e.g. Carver *et al.* 1993; Stanton and Snider 1993) and to poorer disease outcome (Epping-Jordan *et al.* 1994). More recently, momentary reports of coping have been used to avoid problems related to the retrospective nature of coping reports (Stone *et al.* 1998). Finally, and probably most importantly, these methodological advances have been paralleled by the development of theories which allow one to derive predictions about effective coping (e.g. Carver and Scheier 1990). As a result, the number of studies which use theoretical perspectives to derive predictions about effective or ineffective coping with a particular stressor is increasing. The coming years should bring major advances in our knowledge about the relative effectiveness of different coping styles.

Coping resources as moderators of the stress–health relationship

According to cognitive stress theories, the impact of stress on health is also dependent on the coping resources which are available to the individual confronted with the stressful life event. In analysing coping resources, researchers distinguish between extrapersonal and intrapersonal resources (e.g. Lazarus and Folkman 1984; Stroebe and Stroebe 1987; Cohen and Edwards 1989). *Extrapersonal coping resources* are resources external to the individual which are potentially helpful in alleviating the stress. Examples of extrapersonal resources likely to help the individual in coping with stressful life experiences are financial resources and social support. *Intrapersonal coping resources* consist of the personality traits, abilities and skills which enable people to cope with the stress experience. Coping resources are sometimes referred to as 'stress-buffering' resources because they are presumed to protect or buffer people against the negative impact of stressful events (e.g. Cohen and Edwards 1989).

Coping resources can moderate the impact of stressful life events by influencing stress appraisal or by affecting the coping process (Cohen and Wills 1985). Most resources intervene at both of these stages. For example, the pessimistic attribution style conceptualized as part of the revised model of learned helplessness is assumed to moderate both appraisal and recovery (e.g. Peterson and Seligman 1987). Similarly, the extent to which individuals perceive that supportive others are available will affect the appraisal as well as the coping process (Cohen and Wills 1985). Much of the empirical research on coping resources investigates whether a person's health status is related to the extent to which he or she possesses a given resource. For example, as will be demonstrated below, there is evidence that individuals who have a great deal of social support suffer a lower risk of mental and physical impairment and even mortality than individuals who have little social support.

Extrapersonal coping resources

Two major extrapersonal coping resources are material resources and social support. Whereas there is an extensive literature on social support as a coping resource (for reviews, see House 1981; Cohen and Wills 1985), economic resources are rarely discussed in this context (Lazarus and Folkman 1984). The role of economic resources will therefore be considered only briefly and most of this section will be devoted to the discussion of the impact of social support on health and well-being.

Material resources

In view of the strong negative relationship which has been observed between social class and illness and between social class and mortality (Adler *et al.* 1994), it is surprising that material resources are so infrequently discussed as a coping resource. It seems plausible that the coping function of economic resources contributes to the negative association between socio-economic status and morbidity or mortality. After all, people with money, especially if they have the skills to use it effectively, should have more coping options in most stressful situations than people without money. Money can provide easier access to legal, medical and other professional assistance.

The problem in using data on the association between socio-economic status and health as evidence in this context is that the relationship itself is not very well understood. However, in addition to the factors discussed earlier (p. 88), namely deficits in knowledge about health risks and poor health habits, differential exposure to stressful life events could also be responsible for the higher morbidity and mortality associated with low socio-economic status. Moderate but significant positive correlations between socio-economic status and life-change scores indicate that stressful life events are over-represented in the lower classes. There is also evidence that exposure to undesirable life events is more likely to evoke mental health problems in low rather than high socio-economic status individuals (e.g. Dohrenwend 1973). The greater vulnerability of lower-class individuals seems to some extent to be due to a differential availability of social support (Brown and Harris 1978). However, it is plausible that restricted access to other coping resources due to limited economic means could also contribute to this relationship.

If economic resources form an important coping resource, they should buffer the individual against the deleterious impact of stress. However, at least in bereavement research – the one area in which socio-economic status has been studied as a stress moderator – there does not seem to be any evidence that high socio-economic status buffers individuals against the health-impairing impact of the loss experience. While most studies show that widowed individuals of low socio-economic status are less healthy than those of high socio-economic status, the comparison with non-bereaved control groups indicates that the health differential due to socio-economic status is the same for bereaved and non-bereaved groups (for a review, see Stroebe and Stroebe 1987). However, the fact that economic resources do not appear to buffer the individual against the health impact of bereavement does not preclude the possibility that such resources could not protect against other types of stressful events.

Social support

Over the past few decades, much research effort has been invested in the examination of the beneficial effects of social support on health and well-being. There is now a great deal of evidence that the availability of social support is associated with a reduced risk of mental illness and physical illness, and even mortality (for reviews, see Cohen and Wills 1985; House et al. 1988; Stroebe and Stroebe 1996; Berkman et al. 2000; Cohen 2004; Barth et al. 2010; Pinquart and Duberstein 2010). 'Social support' has been defined as information from others that one is loved and cared for, esteemed and valued, and part of a network of communication and mutual obligation (Cobb 1976). Such information can come from a spouse, a lover, children, friends or social and community contacts such as churches or clubs.

Conceptualization and measurement of social support

The measurement of social support has been approached from two perspectives which differ in the way they conceptualize social support: one conceives of it in terms of the *structure* of the target person's interpersonal relationships or social network, the other in terms of the *functions* that these relationships or networks serve for him or her (for a discussion see Cohen and Wills 1985; House and Kahn 1985; Stroebe and Stroebe 1996).

Structural measures reflect the social integration or embeddedness of the individuals by assessing the existence or quantity of social relationships for those individuals. This information is relatively objective, reliable and easy to obtain. It can sometimes be gathered by observation or from behavioural records (e.g. marriage records, organizational memberships). But even if it is based on self-reports, information about whether a person is married, lives alone or belongs to some church is simple to collect, and usually fairly accurate (House and Kahn 1985). A standardized procedure for measuring various social network characteristics (e.g. size, density) has been developed by Stokes (1983) and is known as the Social Network List. There is consistent evidence that low levels of social relationship are associated with an increased risk of mortality (Berkman and Syme 1979; Blazer 1982; House *et al.* 1982; Berkman *et al.* 2000).

Functional measures of social support assess whether interpersonal relationships serve particular functions. Various topologies of support functions have been proposed (e.g. House 1981; Cohen and McKay 1984; Stroebe and Stroebe 1987). Most distinguish between emotional, instrumental, informational and appraisal support. *Emotional support* involves providing empathy, care, love and trust. *Instrumental support* consists of behaviours that directly help the person in need; for example, individuals give instrumental support when they help other people to do their work, take care of their children or help them with transportation. *Informational support* involves providing people with information which they can use in coping with their problems. *Appraisal support* is closely related to informational support. It also involves the transmission of information, but in this case it is information that is relevant for the person's self-evaluation. Thus, by comparing oneself to another person, one may use the other as a source of information in evaluating oneself.

The measurement of social support functions has been based on measures assessing the individual's perception of either the availability of others who provide these functions or the actual receipt of these support functions during a given time period (for a discussion of this distinction, see Dunkel-Schetter and Bennett 1990). Examples of measures of the *perceived availability* of social support are the Interpersonal Support Evaluation List (ISEL) (Cohen *et al.* 1985) and the Social Support Questionnaire (SSQ) (Sarason *et al.* 1983). The ISEL assesses the perceived availability of four types of social support (tangible, appraisal, self-esteem, belonging). For example, respondents have to indicate whether there are people with whom they can talk about intimate personal problems or who would help them with advice. The items of the SSQ consist of two parts, one assessing the number of available others whom individuals feel they can 'count on' for a particular type of support, and another measuring the individual's degree of satisfaction with the perceived support available in that particular situation. The number of available support providers is more similar to structural measures of social network size than to measures of functional support and is only moderately related to the satisfaction with the social support that is available.

A widely used scale to assess *received* social support is the Inventory of Socially Supportive Behaviors (ISSB) (Barrera *et al.* 1981). The items of the ISSB describe specific supportive behaviours that represent emotional, tangible, cognitive–informational and direct guidance support. Respondents are asked to indicate how often during the past four weeks each supportive behaviour occurred. The individual's score thus represents the average frequency of receipt of these supportive behaviours.

Relationship between measures
It seems plausible that the number of social relationships a person has established is strongly related to the functional support the person perceives as available or actually receives. However, the different types of measures of social support show only weak relationships with each other. For example, Sarason *et al.* (1987), who examined the relationship between the Social Network List and measures of perceived and received social support (SSQ; ISSB) found only modest correlations between network size and satisfaction with perceived or received social support. These findings are reasonable if one considers that adequate functional support might be derived from *one* very good relationship but may not be available from several superficial ones.

The relationship between measures of the perceived availability of social support and received social support is also typically very modest. That low correlations are quite typical can be seen from Dunkel-Schetter and Bennett's (1990) survey of studies of the relationship between these two types of measure. Newcomb (1990), who examined the relationship between these two types of functional measure using structural equation modelling, found strong support for the existence of two latent constructs representing perceived and received social support, as well as evidence for a moderate degree of overlap.

Many researchers have argued that, in view of the modest correlations between these different measures, social support should be regarded as a complex construct consisting of three components, namely social embeddedness or integration, perceived availability of social support and received social support (e.g. Dunkel-Schetter and Bennett 1990). Measures of social integration conceptualize social support in terms of the size and structure of an individual's interpersonal network. They describe the channels through which supportive resources can, but need not, flow and are thus only indirect measures of social support. Perceived availability and the actual receipt of social support conceptualize social support in terms of the support functions served by the individual's interpersonal network. They thus reduce the richness of group interactions in that they reflect only those actions of group members that can be considered positive and helpful. Although from a social psychological perspective the actual exchange of resources would appear to be more central to the concept of social support than their perceived availability, measures of the perceived availability of support have been found to be more closely related to health than measures of received support (e.g. Schwarzer and

Leppin 1992). One reason for the weak association of received social support and health outcome is that the supportive behaviour of others is not only a function of who is available but also of the instances in which help might have been needed during the period in question. It is therefore not surprising that, unlike measures of the perceived availability of support, measures of received support have often been found to be positively related to negative life events and symptoms (Sarason *et al.* 1990).

The impact of social support on health

Much of the impetus for the research on social support and health came from the field of epidemiology. In an impressive early survey, Berkman and Syme (1979) were able to demonstrate a relationship between social support and mortality. These investigators studied social and community ties among a random sample of 6928 women and men whose age varied from 30 to 69 when first interviewed in 1965 in Alameda County, California. Each of the four types of social relationship that was assessed at that time (marriage, contacts with extended family and friends, church membership, membership of other organizations) independently predicted the rate of mortality over the succeeding nine years. Individuals who were low on an overall social network index which weighted the intimate ties more heavily had approximately twice the mortality risk of individuals who were high on this index over the nine-year period.

Do these findings really show that the availability of social networks extends one's lifespan? One obvious alternative explanation is that the relationship between networks and mortality could have been due to the fact that isolated people were ill at the time of the survey and unable to maintain their social contacts. However, this appeared not to be the case, because the social network index continued to predict mortality after health status at the time of the baseline survey was statistically controlled.

Berkman and Syme (1979) had to rely on self-reports of physical health, cigarette smoking, alcohol consumption, obesity and level of physical activity. Since self-report health measures are not the most reliable or valid indicator of a person's health status, it was important to replicate these findings with more objective indicators of health status. This was done in a large-scale prospective study which was part of the Tecumseh Community Health Study (House *et al.* 1982). The sample consisted of 2754 men and women who were aged 39 to 69 at the outset of the study in 1967. In addition to an assessment of several classes of social relationships and activities, a wide range of health indicators were biomedically measured (e.g. levels of blood pressure, cholesterol, respiratory functions, electrocardiograms). Again, composite indices of these relationships were inversely related to mortality over the 10- to 12-year follow-up period even after adjustment for initial health status. People with low levels of social relationship had approximately twice the mortality risk of those with high levels.

This basic pattern has been replicated in other studies in the USA (see Schoenbach *et al.* 1986) and in Sweden (e.g. Welin *et al.* 1985). Of the American

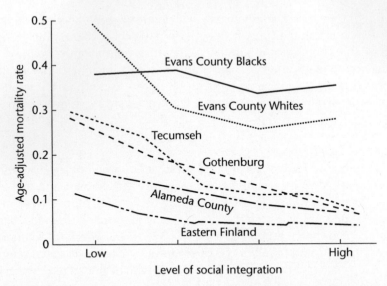

FIGURE 7.1 Level of social integration and age-adjusted mortality for males in five prospective studies
Source: Adapted from House *et al.* (1988)

studies only the Evans County study (Schoenbach *et al.* 1986) also provided data on blacks. Although the levels of mortality vary greatly across studies, and even though the social support effects are weaker for women than for men, the patterns of prospective association between social integration and mortality are remarkably similar. This can be seen from Figures 7.1 and 7.2, which show the age-adjusted

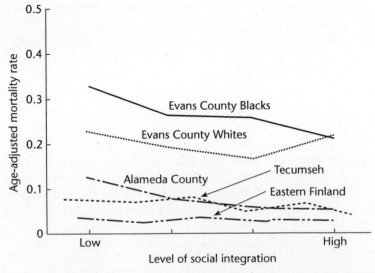

FIGURE 7.2 Level of social integration and age-adjusted mortality for females in five prospective studies
Source: Adapted from House *et al.* (1988)

mortality rates for males and females, respectively, from those five studies for which parallel data could be extracted (House *et al.* 1988).

Less dire consequences of the lack of social support have also been established. There is evidence that social support is inversely related to the prevalence and incidence of a number of physical diseases. There is also empirical evidence that social support facilitates recovery from coronary heart disease (CHD). Early evidence for the health-protective effect of social support for patients with established coronary artery disease came from a prospective study of 1368 symptomatic patients with more than 75 per cent closure of at least one major coronary artery (Williams *et al.* 1992). These patients had undergone coronary angiography at the beginning of the study between 1974 and 1980, and at the same time had responded to a measure of perceived social support. Marital status was also recorded as a structural measure of social support. By the end of the study in 1989, 781 patients had undergone surgery and 237 had died of cardiovascular causes. When survival was assessed over a five-year period, controlling for the extent of cardiac disease at the time of intake, married patients were found to have better survival rates than unmarried patients. There was also a significant interaction between marital status and confidant(e) availability. Unmarried patients without a confidant(e) had a more than threefold increase in the risk of death within five years compared with patients who were either married or had a close confidant(e).

In the meantime, the positive association between social support and survival of patients with CHD has been established in numerous studies (for a review, see Barth *et al.* 2010). In a meta-analysis based on 20 studies of patients suffering from CHD, Barth *et al.* (2010) found that functional support significantly reduced the risk of cardiac as well as all-cause mortality. Structural social support significantly reduced all-cause mortality, but the reduction in cardiac mortality was not significant. However, only mixed support could be found for the assumption that social support would also reduce the risk of *developing* CHD.

Next to cardiovascular diseases, cancers are the second leading cause of deaths in industrialized countries, accounting for 22 per cent of all deaths in the USA (Kung *et al.* 2008). There is a great deal of evidence that structural and functional social support reduce the risk of cancer mortality (Nausheen *et al.* 2009; Pinquart and Duberstein 2010). A meta-analysis based on 87 studies of the association of measures of structural and functional social support with cancer mortality both in initially healthy samples and in cancer patients found the association significant for both groups (Pinquart and Duberstein 2010).

Because levels of stress were not assessed in these studies, it is unclear whether these findings merely reflect a generalized beneficial effect of social support, independent of stress, or whether social support buffered individuals against the deleterious impact of stress. Both hypotheses are discussed in the literature. Figure 7.3 illustrates the two ways in which social support can benefit health and well-being.

A *direct effect* of social support on health – independent of the amount of stress individuals experience – could occur because large social networks provide people

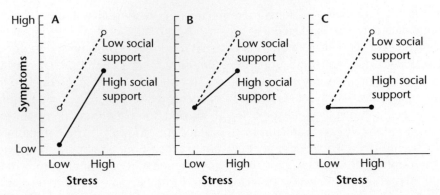

FIGURE 7.3 An illustration of the two ways in which social support is assumed to benefit health: the direct effect hypothesis (Panel A) proposes that the health benefits of social support occur irrespective of the level of stress; the buffering effect hypothesis proposes that social support protects the individuals to some extent (Panel B) or totally (Panel C) against the negative impact of stress on health

with regular positive experiences and a set of stable, socially rewarded roles in the community (Cohen and Wills 1985). For example, individuals with high levels of social support may have a greater feeling of being liked and cared for, which will positively affect their feeling of self-worth and self-efficacy. Interaction with others is also likely to increase positive affect and limit the intensity of duration of negative affect (Cohen 2004). The positive outlook this provides could be beneficial to health independent of stress experience. A high level of social support may also encourage people to lead a more healthful lifestyle.

According to the *buffering hypothesis*, social support affects health by protecting the individual against the negative impact of high levels of stress (Figure 7.3). This protective effect can best be understood by means of analogy with the effects of an inoculation. Just as a difference in the health of individuals who are or are not inoculated should emerge only when they are exposed to the infectious agent, the protective function of social support is only effective when the person encounters a strong stressor. Under low-stress conditions, little or no buffering occurs. Thus, under low-stress conditions, no differences would be expected in the health and well-being of groups enjoying differential levels of social support.

Buffering could operate through two types of process: first, individuals who experience a high level of social support may *appraise* a stressful event such as a financial crisis or the loss of a job as less stressful than people with little social support, because they know that there are people to whom they can turn for advice or who would even be willing to support them financially. A second way in which social support might buffer the negative impact of stress is by improving people's ability to cope with the stressor. Thus somebody who is experiencing a crisis might be better able to cope if he or she knows people who can give advice or perhaps even provide a solution to the problem.

To differentiate between the direct effect and the buffering effect of social support, studies have to assess the impact of differential levels of social support under differential levels of stress on health and well-being. The pattern that has emerged from this type of research is less than clear cut. Some studies reported only main effects while others found interactions between stress and social support. In a review of this literature, Cohen and Wills (1985) examined the hypothesis that these differences in findings are related to the type of measure that was used in a given study. They reasoned that for a buffering effect to occur, the type of social support that is available should be closely linked to the specific coping needs elicited by a stressful event. Since only functional measures assess different types of social support, only studies using functional measures should yield evidence of buffering effects. The use of structural measures of social integration, which assess the existence or number of relationships but not the functions actually provided by those relationships, should only result in main effects. Their review supported this hypothesis.

The role of personality dispositions in research on social support and health
A thorny issue that so far has not been satisfactorily addressed in research on social support and health is the possibility that personality dispositions contribute to the observed relationship between measures of social support and health. There are two different routes by which personality could influence the relationship between social support and health:

1 Personality characteristics could increase an individual's chance of finding social support and at the same time contribute positively to his or her coping ability. For example, it seems plausible that individuals who are socially competent are also more likely to develop strong support networks and to stay healthy by effectively coping with stressful events or by performing health-enhancing behaviours (Cohen and Wills 1985).
2 Personality characteristics might also bias individual reports of levels of social support and of health symptoms. This issue is particularly problematic where functional measures of social support and self-report measures of stress have been related to self-reports of psychological and physical symptoms. For example, in our Tübingen study of bereavement a significant correlation ($r = .32$) was observed between a scale measuring perceived availability of social support and the neuroticism scale of the Eysenck Personality Inventory. Individuals who had high scores on neuroticism tended to report lower levels of perceived social support. Since, according to Watson and Pennebaker (1989), these individuals are also more likely to report higher levels of stressful life events and higher levels of psychological and somatic symptoms, neuroticism could be partly responsible for relationships observed between measures of perceived social support, perceived stress and perceived symptoms.

There are various strategies for dealing with these problems in research on perceived social support and health. One is to reduce the influence of reporting biases by using objectifiable life events (e.g. unemployment, death of a partner) and biomedical health measures. A second safeguard is to use prospective designs which allow one to assess the impact of stress and social support measured at Time 1 on symptoms at Time 2, while statistically controlling for differences in symptoms at Time 1. A third strategy involves the inclusion of measures of personality dispositions that are known correlates of social support (e.g. neuroticism, social competence) and using such measures as control variables.

This last strategy was used by Cohen *et al.* (2003) in one of their studies in which volunteers were infected with a cold virus. They found that the personality dimension of sociability appeared to give infected people some protection against developing a cold. Increases in sociability were associated in an approximately linear manner with decreases in the rate of illness. Since sociability is also positively related to measures of social support, with more sociable individuals enjoying higher levels of social support, these results could offer an alternative explanation for the many findings of associations between social support and health. However, surprisingly, level of social support was not associated with the likelihood of developing a cold in this study. Furthermore, statistical control for measures of social support did not reduce the association between sociability and likelihood of developing a cold in the present study.

The potential confounding influence of personality dispositions is less problematic in prospective epidemiological studies which relate measures of social integration to mortality. First, personality variables are less likely to influence the simple network measures typically used in these studies (e.g. reports about marriage, membership of organizations) than reports about the perceived availability of social support. Second, mortality is a dependent measure that is uninfluenced by this type of reporting bias. Finally, the alternative possibility that personality influences both the *actual* size of a person's social network (e.g. neurotics may be less likely to find partners or friends) and his or her health can be controlled by using prospective designs that demonstrate the impact of social support on change in health over time.

How does social support affect health?

There are a number of psychological and biological processes through which social support might influence individual health. It is interesting to note that whereas the behavioural processes would mainly account for main effects of social support, the biological processes would be more consistent with stress buffering. For example, a person who is integrated into a large social network of family and friends is subject to social controls and peer pressures that influence normative health behaviours. Depending on whether these pressures promote healthy or unhealthy behaviour patterns, social integration could have a positive or negative impact on health. There is some evidence, however, that social support is positively associated with behaviours that are promotive of health (e.g. non-smoking, adequate sleep, prudent diet and moderate drinking behaviour). Thus Berkman and Syme (1979) reported a positive relationship between their structural measure of support and various health practices.

Strong support for the association of social support and health practices comes from studies of patient adherence to medical treatment (DiMatteo 2004).

Adherence to medical treatment recommendation is an important determinant of treatment success and studies have shown that an appreciable number of patients (as many as 25–40 per cent) are non-adherent (DiMatteo 2004). Assistance and support from family and friends can have great influence on adherence by encouraging optimism and self-esteem, and giving practical assistance (e.g. helping to monitor drug intake). In a meta-analysis based on 122 studies that correlated structural and functional social support with patient adherence to medical regimens, Di Matteo (2004) found practical and emotional social support to be significantly correlated, with practical social support being more highly correlated (r = .31) than emotional social support (r = .15). The social support–adherence relationship was also stronger for measures of functional social support than for marital status (r = .06). Finally, patient adherence was significantly affected by family conflict. The odds of non-adherence were more than twice as high in families with high rather than low conflict.

Many of the *psychological* processes that link social support to psychological well-being and health may be mediated by self-esteem, that is, the positive or negative beliefs and evaluations that the individual holds towards him- or herself. It is widely accepted among clinical, personality and social psychologists that a positive and stable self-esteem is important for individual well-being. As Tajfel (1978) emphasized, the social groups to which we belong are major determinants of our definition of 'self' and form the basis of social identity. Social identity refers to that part of people's self-concepts which derives from their knowledge of their memberships of various social groups together with the emotional significance attached to these memberships. Thus, embeddedness in a large interpersonal and social network may positively contribute to social identity and self-esteem.

Social relationships may also fulfil a number of support functions which are beneficial for individual self-esteem. There is broad agreement among the helping professions concerning the central role of emotional support for self-esteem and psychological well-being. As Bernard (1968: 137) has described: 'One of the major functions of positive, expressive talk is to raise the status of the other, to give help, to reward; in ordinary human relations it performs the stroking function. As infants need physical caressing or stroking in order to live and grow, and even to survive, so do adults need emotional or psychological stroking or caressing to remain normal'.

Group members also serve validational functions which are important for an individual's interpretation of reality. Success or failure in responding to situational demands depends not merely on one's skills but also on whether one is able to assess these abilities and the environmental demands realistically. People often fail because they overestimate their ability or underestimate the difficulty of the task. According to Festinger (1954), the assessment of the validity of one's beliefs about 'reality' and about one's own level of ability frequently depends on social comparison processes, particularly when objective criteria are lacking. Social comparison processes are also important for the evaluation of the appropriateness of one's emotional reactions, particularly in novel, emotion-arousing situations (Schachter 1959). Such processes are therefore likely to play an important role in the perception and evaluation of bodily symptoms.

Ultimately, the impact of social and psychological variables on physical health must be transmitted through *biological* processes. In reviews of the relationship between social support and physiological processes, Uchino and colleagues (Uchino *et al.* 1996; Uchino 2006; Reblin and Uchino 2008) focused particularly on mechanisms underlying the association between social support and physical health. Uchino *et al.* (1996) reported that of the 81 studies which examined social support and physiological processes, 57 focused on aspects of cardiovascular function. The most commonly used cardiovascular measures include heart rate, systolic blood pressure and diastolic blood pressure. In general, the results of correlational studies relating social support to blood pressure are consistent with the assumption that higher social support is associated with better cardiovascular regulation (e.g. lower blood pressure), although the mean effect size ($r = .08$) was rather modest. Because drawing causal conclusions from correlational findings is always problematic, it is important to note that there is also fairly consistent support from prospective intervention studies on normotensive and hypertensive individuals which suggest a positive effect of social support on cardiovascular regulation (Uchino *et al.* 1996). Finally, there is even evidence from experimental laboratory studies to identify one of the mechanisms by which social support influences cardiovascular regulation: social support reduces cardiovascular reactivity in acute stress situations (effect size: $r = .28$; Uchino *et al.* 1996). These positive effects may not even require the actual presence of others in acutely stressful situations. Cardiovascular reactivity to stress may even be reduced by the perceived availability of social support (Uchino and Garvey 1997).

Uchino *et al.* (1996; Uchino 2006) also reviewed the rather small number of studies of the association between social support and endocrine function. An examination of the endocrine function is important because it is associated with both the cardiovascular and the immune systems. A consistent association was found between low social support and higher levels of catecholamines (i.e. epinephrine and norepinephrine). In their earlier review, there was little evidence for a relationship between social support and cortisol levels. However, more recently, studies that have measured salivary cortisol over several time points have more consistently found an inverse relationship between cortisol levels and social support (Uchino 2006). Consistent with these findings and in line with the immuno-suppressive effects of cortisol, a meta-analysis of nine studies which examined the association between social support and functional immune measures revealed a moderately strong association ($r = .21$), indicating that higher levels of social support are associated with better immune functioning (Uchino *et al.* 1996).

More recently, limited evidence has emerged to suggest that inflammatory mechanisms of the immune system might play a role in the association between social support and disease processes. Support for this assumption comes from the study of parents of children with cancer by Miller *et al.* (2002) reported in the last chapter (see pp. 290–1). Social support was found to be unrelated to glucocorticoid sensitivity among parents of healthy children. However, among parents of children with cancer, glucocortoid sensitivity declined to the extent that parents reported low tangible support. These results suggest that tangible social support buffered these parents against the effect stress had in deregulating the inflammatory response of their immune system. However, the evidence is mixed. A recent review of this evidence therefore concluded that although 'social support and inflammation may be linked . . . it is premature to claim that inflammation is the mechanism through which social support exerts salubrious effects on health' (Penwell and Larkin 2010).

Can we improve health by improving social support?

The positive association between social support and health observed in numerous studies would suggest that interventions aimed at providing people with social support should result in significant health improvements, at least in individuals with low levels of social support. In addition to being of practical importance, such interventions would also be theoretically important, because they would finally demonstrate a causal relationship between social support and health. This would be important, because all studies on the association between social support and health reviewed earlier were observational. And even though prospective observational studies can rule out reverse causation (i.e. that health improvements caused improvements in social support) they cannot rule out the possibility that the covariation of social support and health was due to some third variable. This could be a personality factor such as sociability, but it could also be some genetic factor that determines that people who have high levels of social support also enjoy better health.

Unfortunately, the few randomized controlled trials conducted to assess social support interventions have been unsuccessful. Social support interventions have typically been offered to patients with a serious life-threatening illness (e.g. heart attack, cancer) and have consisted of some type of group therapy. One of the largest social support interventions was the multi-site ENRICHD (Enhancing Recovery in Coronary Heart Disease) trial (ENRICHD Investigators 2003). This was a randomized controlled clinical trial with 2481 patients, who had suffered myocardial infarction and had low social support and/or depression. Patients were assigned randomly either to an intervention or a usual care group. The intervention group received cognitive behaviour therapy (CBT) that addressed problems related to depression and/or lack of social support. After six months there was a significant improvement in levels of social support in the intervention group compared to controls. However, after 29 months there was no difference in survival between the intervention and the control group. Similarly negative results were reported in a study with metastatic breast cancer patients, who were randomly assigned to either an expressive group therapy or a no intervention control group (Goodwin *et al.* 2001). Although women in the intervention group reported less distress and less pain, the intervention did not prolong survival. Similar results were reported in other studies with breast cancer patients (see Cohen 2004).

Although one can conclude from these findings that provision of group therapy to individuals suffering from serious medical ailments is unlikely to increase survival, one can question whether other forms of social support provision might not have been more effective. After all, the positive effects of social support observed in observational studies was due to people's social network of friends, relatives or marital partners, all people to whom one was close and who cared for one. In contrast, therapy support groups consist of people who, at least initially, are strangers and with whom one might never develop a close relationship. And even though the therapy in the ENRICHD study appeared to have helped people to improve their social support network, these effects were weak and did not persist over time.

Intrapersonal coping resources

Numerous personality variables have been suggested as moderators of the impact of stress on health, and the list of variables keeps on being extended. Because it would be too ambitious in the context of this chapter to attempt an exhaustive review of this rich but complex body of literature, the discussion will be restricted to two personality variables that have been extensively studied as coping resources which moderate the relationship between stress and health, namely hardiness (e.g. Kobasa *et al.* 1982) and dispositional optimism (e.g. Scheier and Carver 1987), both coping resources that increase the individual's resilience towards stress. In a subsequent section, hostility and anxiety will be discussed as a personality variables which moderate the stress–health relationship without constituting coping resources (Siegman and Smith 1994; Miller *et al.* 1996; Brosschot *et al.* 2005; Shen *et al.* 2008).

The hardy personality

Hardiness has been proposed by Kobasa (1979) as a constellation of personality characteristics that protects individuals against the health-impairing impact of stress. There are three components of the hardy personality:

1 *Control*, which refers to people's belief that they can influence events in their lives.
2 *Commitment*, which refers to people's sense of purpose and involvement in the events and activities in their lives.
3 *Challenge*, which refers to the expectation that change rather than stability is normal in life and that change in the form of life events can be a positive phenomenon providing an opportunity for growth, rather than a threat to security.

Hardy individuals would score high on all three dimensions and would thus possess a life philosophy which buffers them against the debilitating impact of stressful life events.

The measurement of hardiness

In the course of the development of the concept of hardiness, the scales used to measure it have changed. The most frequently used instrument to measure hardiness in recent research seems to be a composite of five scales. Control is measured by the Powerlessness Scale of the Alienation Test (Maddi *et al.* 1979), and the External Locus of Control Scale (Rotter *et al.* 1962). Commitment is measured by the Alienation from Self Scale and the Alienation from Work Scale of the Alienation Test (Maddi *et al.* 1979). Challenge is measured by the Security Scale of the California Life Goals Evaluation Schedule (Hahn 1966). For each of these scales a high score reflects a relative lack of hardiness.

The practice of combining the various scales used to measure hardiness into one overall score is based on the assumption that individual differences on these measures reflect a common dimension of hardiness. If this assumption were correct, correlations between individual scores on pairs of scales should be high and factor analyses of the five scales should yield a single factor. But this assumption has been questioned (e.g. Funk and Houston 1987; Hull *et al.* 1987; Cohen and Edwards 1989). In fact, Kobasa *et al.* (1981) reported surprisingly low correlations between pairs of scales used to measure hardiness.

Hardiness and health
The concept of hardiness was developed and tested in a study which tried to differentiate people who reacted to stress with illness from those who stayed healthy on the basis of their personality (Kobasa 1979). Suggestive evidence for a buffering effect comes from a prospective study of executives of a utility company, in which Kobasa *et al.* (1981, 1982) collected three sets of data at one-year intervals. Using reported illness summed over Years 2 and 3 as the dependent variable, and Year 1 stressful events, hardiness and constitutional predisposition (a measure of parents' illness) as predictors, they found significant main effects for stressful life events, hardiness and constitutional predisposition. Although the pattern of means was consistent with a buffering effect for hardiness, no interactions were significant. However, Kobasa *et al.* (1982) reported that an analysis of the same data set controlling for illness at Year 1 and dropping constitutional predisposition from the analysis revealed a significant buffering effect.

A retrospective study of a sample of female former students of a small liberal arts college provided further evidence for a stress-buffering effect of hardiness (Rhodewalt and Zone 1989). Life stress was measured with an adapted form of the Schedule of Recent Life Events. Subjects had to indicate which of the events they had experienced during the last 12 months. Participants also had to rate whether the event was desirable or undesirable, controllable or uncontrollable, and the amount of adjustment that was necessary for them to cope with the event. Health was assessed with the Beck Depression Inventory (a self-report scale of common symptoms of depression) and the same illness rating scale as the one used by Kobasa (1979). The authors found a buffering effect of hardiness for both depression and self-reported physical illness (see Figure 7.4). Thus, hardiness seemed to protect these women somewhat against the negative impact of stress on psychological and physical health.

This study is particularly interesting because it also assessed hardiness-related differences in appraisal of stress. Although hardy and non-hardy women did not

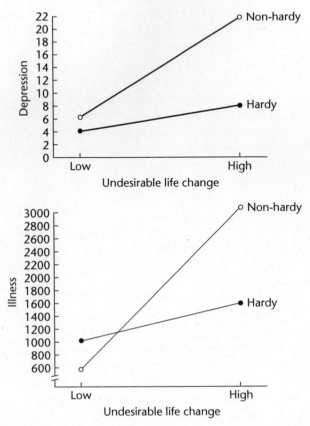

FIGURE 7.4 Predicted values of depression and illness for the interaction of hardiness with undesirable life change
Source: Rhodewalt and Zone (1989)

differ in the absolute number of stressful events reported, non-hardy women reported significantly greater numbers of undesirable life changes. Thus, non-hardy women declared that roughly 40 per cent of their life experiences were undesirable, whereas their hardy counterparts appraised only 27 per cent of their experiences in this manner. In addition to appraising a greater number of events as negative, non-hardy women also reported that the negative events required more adjustment than did hardy women. These findings suggest that the buffering effect of hardiness is at least partly mediated by differences in appraisal processes.

However, there are also several reports of studies which either failed to find any evidence for a buffering effect (e.g. Schmied and Lawler 1986; Funk and Houston 1987), only observed buffering effects for one of the components of the Hardiness Scale (e.g. Ganellen and Blaney 1984) or found it only for men but not women (Klag and Bradley 2004). Furthermore, there is evidence that hardiness is highly correlated with negative affectivity or neuroticism (Funk and Houston

1987; Hull *et al.* 1987; Allred and Smith 1989). As Watson and Pennebaker (1989) have shown, self-report measures both of stress and of health complaints reflect a pervasive mood disposition of negative affectivity or neuroticism. Thus, it may not be the hardy individuals who are particularly stress-resistant, but the non-hardy individuals who are neurotic and psychologically maladjusted and who therefore view their lives as more negative and stressful and also report higher levels of health complaints. As the findings of Watson and Pennebaker further suggest, these complaints could be *unrelated* to physical health problems. It would therefore be important in future research to test whether the buffering effect of hardiness can be replicated with objective stress situations using biological or other objective indicators of health status.

Dispositional optimism

Dispositional optimism is a second personality variable which has been suggested as a moderator of the stress–health relationship. It has been proposed that an optimistic nature can motivate people to cope more effectively with stress and consequently reduce the risk of illness (Scheier and Carver 1985, 1987). The crucial factor in optimism, according to Scheier and Carver, is that optimists will be more likely than pessimists to see desired outcomes as within their reach. People who see desired outcomes as attainable should continue to exert effort at reaching these outcomes, even when doing so is difficult. On the other hand, when outcomes are sufficiently unattainable, people will reduce their efforts and eventually abandon their pursuit of a given goal. Since optimists are assumed to see desired outcomes as more attainable than pessimists, and should therefore be more persistent in their attempts to attain these outcomes, they should also be more likely than pessimists to employ approach rather than avoidance coping (Solberg and Segerstrom 2006).

Evidence for the greater persistence of optimists comes from a prospective study of college retention, in which dispositional optimism measured at college entry was significantly associated with college retention one year later (Solberg Nes *et al.* 2009). The more optimistic students were when they entered college, the less likely it was that they dropped out (odds ratio 1.40). This effect remained significant, even after academic aptitude and high school grade point average had been controlled for. Optimists were also more highly motivated and better adjusted or less distressed than pessimists. Further (structural equation) analyses indicated that the effect of optimism on retention was mediated by motivation and adjustment/distress. Thus, because optimists were more motivated and adjusted better to college life they were less likely to drop out.

The measurement of optimism

Scheier and Carver (1985) began their research by developing a measure of dispositional optimism, the Life Orientation Test (LOT) which has since been revised (Scheier *et al.* 1994). The LOT has been designed to measure the extent to which individuals hold the general expectation that good things are likely to happen to them. The revised LOT consists of 10 items, of which 6 reflect optimism and 4 are irrelevant filler items. Three of the optimism items are phrased in a positive way (e.g. 'In uncertain times, I usually expect the best'), and three are phrased in a negative way (e.g. 'If something can go wrong for me, it will'). The irrelevant filler items are included to distract respondents from the purpose of the scale. Respondents answer each item by indicating the extent of their agreement on a five-point scale.

Optimism and health

Evidence for optimism-related differences in coping has been reported in numerous studies (e.g. Scheier et al. 1986, 1989; Aspinwall and Taylor 1992; Chang 1998; Segerstrom et al. 1998; for a meta-analytic review, see Solberg et al. 2006). For example, Scheier et al. (1986), who administered both the LOT and the Ways of Coping Questionnaire to a sample of undergraduates, found that optimism was associated with more use of problem-focused coping, seeking of social support and emphasizing the positive aspects of a stressful situation. In contrast, pessimism was associated with denial and distancing, and with focusing on the goal with which the stressor was interfering.

The association between optimism and coping styles has been further clarified in a meta-analysis 50 studies (involving 11,629 participants) that related the LOT to measures of coping (Solberg et al. 2006). Optimism correlated positively with approach coping ($r = .17$) and negatively with avoidance coping ($r = -.21$). The correlations with problem- and emotion-focused coping were somewhat lower ($r = .13$ and $r = -.08$ respectively). However, when problem-focused coping was separated into problem approach and problem avoidance categories, optimism was positively correlated with approach ($r = .17$) and negatively with problem avoidance ($r = -.29$). A similar distinction for emotion-focused coping resulted in a correlation of $r = .13$ with emotion approach and $r = -.21$ with emotion avoidance. The authors concluded that optimism is more predictive of approach versus avoidance coping than problem-focused versus emotion-focused coping.

That the impact of optimism on differences in adjustment to life stress is at least partially mediated by differences in coping styles has also been demonstrated in several studies (e.g. Aspinwall and Taylor 1992; Chang 1998; Segerstrom et al. 1998). For example, a longitudinal study of college students who were interviewed twice, once shortly after entering college and again three months later, found that optimists made less use of avoidant coping (Aspinwall and Taylor 1992). Avoidant coping in turn predicted less successful adjustment to college life three months later. Greater optimism was also related to greater use of active coping. This in turn predicted better adjustment to college.

The fact that the impact of optimism on adjustment is only *partially* mediated by differences in coping strategies indicates that differences in coping style are not the only reason why optimists adjust better to stressful situations. A recent twin study suggests the possibility that part of the association between optimism and adjustment could be due to a genetic covariation between these variables (Mosing et al. 2009). This study was based on a large sample of older monozygotic and dizygotic twins for whom scores on the LOT, on a test of psychological disorder, and on self-rated health were available. The authors report that 20 per cent of the variance in mental health and 14 per cent of the variance in self-rated health was explained by genetic factors shared with optimism. This implies that a substantial proportion of the correlation between the LOT and measures of adjustment is likely to be determined genetically.

Optimism not only reduces the distress associated with stressful life experiences, but also appears to buffer individuals against the physical effects of life stress. Support for this assumption comes from a prospective study of the impact of what is claimed to be a major stressor, namely the first year of law school at a top American university (Segerstrom et al. 1998). Pre-test data were collected during the two weeks preceding law school, and post-test data were collected halfway through the first semester. Optimism was measured with the LOT, supplemented by a situation-specific optimism scale at the pre-test. Dependent measures were mood changes and various measures of the immune system. In support of predictions, dispositional and situational optimism were associated with less mood disturbance and fewer negative effects on the immune system at the post-test taken halfway through the first semester.

This study also examined whether the relationship between optimism and measures of mood and immune functioning was mediated by optimism-related differences in coping styles. As in previous studies, optimism was found to be related to less avoidant coping. Although controlling for difference in coping styles reduced the association between optimism and mood, it did not affect the link between optimism and immune parameters. Since mood disturbances are in turn related to immune measures, the pattern of findings would be consistent with the assumption that coping styles partially mediate the optimism–mood relationship and that the mood disturbances are in turn at the root of the impairment of immune functioning.

That optimists recover more quickly from major surgery has been shown in studies of coronary bypass patients and of women who underwent surgery for breast cancer (Scheier et al. 1989). Optimists recovered faster from the effects of the bypass surgery and there was also a positive relationship between optimism and post-surgical quality of life six months later, with optimists doing substantially better than pessimists. Comparable findings were reported from a longitudinal study of women with early stage breast cancer. These women were interviewed before surgery and several times after surgery. Optimists reported less distress at each point of measurement than pessimists and this effect was mediated by aspects of subjects' coping reactions, particularly the tendency of optimists to make less use of denial and behavioural disengagement.

However, like hardiness research, the research based on the optimism scale has been criticized for its overlap with negative affectivity and neuroticism (Smith et al. 1989). In a replication of the study of Scheier and Carver (1985) on undergraduate stress, Smith et al. administered a measure of negative affectivity in addition to the LOT. Their findings for the LOT were comparable to those reported by Scheier and Carver: optimists tended to engage more in problem-focused coping and less in avoidant coping than pessimists and they also reported fewer symptoms at the second assessment. However, these relationships disappeared when level of neuroticism was statistically controlled. In contrast, statistical control of optimism scores did not eliminate the relationship between neuroticism and these same symptoms. As Smith *et al.* (1989: 645) concluded, 'at the very least, these findings suggest that optimism as defined by the LOT is not related to coping and symptom report independently of the influence of neuroticism'. Scheier *et al.* (1994) countered this criticism by arguing that since pessimism formed part of the concept of neuroticism, it was to be expected that controlling for neuroticism would reduce the association between optimism and health measures. They further presented data which indicated that control for neuroticism reduced but did not eliminate the association between optimism and depression. Furthermore, since neuroticism is mainly related to symptom reporting but not to actual physical change (Watson and Pennebaker 1989), findings such as the immune changes reported by Segerstrom *et al.* (1998) could not be accounted for in terms of neuroticism.

Other moderators of the stress–health relationship

Not all personality characteristics which moderate the stress–health relationship are coping resources. There are some personality characteristics which, rather than helping the individual to alleviate the impact of stress experiences, appear to have the opposite effect: they increase vulnerability. This section will discuss hostility and anxiety as cases in point.

Hostility

Anger and hostility have long been suspected as risk factors of health impairment, in particular coronary heart disease (CHD). However, much of the recent research on the association between hostility and CHD has been stimulated by attempts to resolve inconsistencies in findings of research on the Type A Behaviour Pattern (Siegman 1994). The Type A 'coronary-prone' behaviour pattern had been identified during the 1950s as a risk factor for the development of CHD. The Type A individual was described as a person 'who is *aggressively* involved in a *chronic, incessant* struggle to achieve more and more in less and less time, and, if required to do so, against the opposing efforts of other things or other persons' (Friedman and Rosenman 1974: 67).

Although there was quite a bit of positive support for Type A as an independent risk factor in CHD (e.g. Rosenman *et al.* 1975) there was sufficient negative evidence (e.g. Shekelle *et al.* 1985) to stimulate a search for explanations of these inconsistencies. One of the potential causes suggested was the multidimensional nature of the Type A construct (Siegman 1994). The Type A Behaviour Pattern encompasses behaviours reflecting such diverse motives as ambition, hostility, time urgency and aggressiveness, and it seemed likely that not all these factors were associated with CHD. More specifically, it was suggested that the 'potential for hostility' was the most likely candidate as the 'toxic' component in the Type A Behaviour Pattern (Siegman 1994).

Hostility has been defined as an enduring, negative attitude towards others involving cognitive, affective and behavioural components (Siegman and Smith 1994). The cognitive component reflects negative beliefs about others, including cynicism and mistrust. The affective component consists of a variety of negative emotions, ranging from anger and rage to resentment and contempt. The behavioural component includes aggression and a variety of more subtle forms of antagonism. Thus, 'hostility connotes a devaluation of the worth and motives of others, and expectation that others are likely sources of wrong doing, a relational view of being in opposition to others, and a desire to inflict harm or see others harmed' (Smith 1994: 24).

The measurement of hostility

There are a number of different measures of hostility which are based on either the structured interview originally developed to assess Type A behaviour, or on self-report questionnaires. The structured interview (SI) consists of a series of questions about an individual's characteristic responses to a variety of situations. These interviews are tape-recorded and rated for hostile content (e.g. self-reported annoyance), hostile intensity (report or display of intense feelings), hostile style (i.e. behaviour displayed during the interview) and overall potential for hostility (based on clinical judgement). Measures of hostility based on SIs show the highest association with CHD (Miller et al. 1996).

The most frequently used questionnaire measure of hostility is the Cook–Medley Ho Scale. The Ho scale was originally derived empirically on the basis of those items from the Minnesota Teacher Attitude Inventory that discriminated teachers with good vs. poor rapport with students (Cook and Medley 1954). Although the Ho scale is used as an indicator of general hostility, there is evidence that it is multidimensional (e.g. Barefoot et al. 1989). The major dimensions measured by this scale are cynicism (negative beliefs about others), hostile affect (negative emotions in relation to others), aggressive responding (a tendency to use aggression as a means of coping with problems) and hostile attribution (reflecting beliefs that others intend to harm the respondent). The popularity of the Ho scale stems from empirical findings that link it to a number of physical health outcomes, including CHD and premature mortality from all causes, even though the association is less strong and less consistent than that found with the SI (Miller et al. 1996).

Hostility and CHD

Much of the research on hostility and physical health assessed the association with CHD. The different endpoints used as indicative of CHD were angina, myocardial infarction, sudden cardiac death and the extent of occlusion in coronary arteries. The most persuasive evidence that hostility is a risk factor in the development of CHD comes from prospective studies of initially healthy individuals. Probably the earliest prospective study was conducted on sub-samples of a larger study of the development of CHD, namely the Western Collaborative Group Study (Matthews *et al.* 1977). The sub-samples consisted of 62 men who had developed various forms of CHD over the course of 4.5 years and an age-matched control group of 124 healthy men. The SIs had been taken prior to the development of symptoms of CHD and were rated blindly on a number of aspects of the Type A coronary-prone behaviour patterns reflecting hostility. The variables providing the best discrimination between men who had developed heart disease and the healthy controls were ratings of potential of hostility, anger directed outwards, frequent experience of anger and irritation at waiting in lines. Even more convincing evidence was reported by Barefoot *et al.* (1983) in a 22-year follow-up of a sample of 225 medical students from the University of North Carolina who had filled in the Ho scale when they were students. Subjects who had low hostility scores (below the median) experienced significantly fewer coronary events during the 22-year period than subjects with hostility scores above the median of Cook–Medley scores.

Although the evidence from prospective studies has not been totally consistent, it provides strong support for a hostility–heart disease association. Miller *et al.* (1996: 344) concluded from their meta-analytic review of the empirical research that 'evidence from both cross-sectional and prospective studies suggests that hostility is a robust risk factor'. Although the magnitude of this association varied as a function of the measurement device used, the 'effect sizes for the structured interview measures of hostility are equal or greater in magnitude to those reported for traditional risk factors for CHD, such as elevated serum cholesterol, blood pressure and cigarette smoking' (Miller *et al.* 1996: 341).

Similar conclusions were reached in a more recent meta-analysis of prospective studies of the association between anger and hostility and CHD in initially healthy individuals as well as individuals with existing CHD (Chida and Steptoe 2009). Anger and hostility were associated with a 19 per cent increased risk in CHD events in the initially healthy population and with a 24 per cent increased risk of poor prognosis in the population with already existing CHD. The authors argue that their findings suggest the desirability of psychological management of anger and hostility in addition to pharmacological treatment of CHD.

Mechanisms linking hostility and health
Having accepted that hostility is a risk factor for CHD one now has to address the issue of whether it impairs health by contributing to, or more specifically by moderating, the stress–health relationship. To demonstrate that hostility is a (stress-) moderator variable, one has to demonstrate that stressful events have a stronger health impact on individuals who are high rather than low on hostility. A link is provided by one of the theoretical explanations offered for the association between hostility and health, namely the explanation in terms of physiological reactivity (Williams *et al.* 1985). Williams *et al.* argued that hostile people are likely to display two

psychological responses that are associated with increased physiological arousal: they are prone to experience anger and to engage in vigilant observation of their social environment, scanning for signs of hostile behaviour. Anger and vigilance are associated with increases in blood pressure, heart rate and stress-related hormones in response. Given their anger-proneness, hostile people experience anger more frequently and intensely than individuals who are less hostile. More frequent episodes of anger produce elevated levels of cardiovascular and neuroendocrine responses that contribute to CHD. In support of this model, there is evidence from laboratory studies that hostile individuals respond to potential stressors with larger and more prolonged increases in heart rate, blood pressure and neuroendocrine (e.g. cortisol, catecholamines) secretion (for a review, see Smith and MacKenzie 2006). In recent studies, hostility has also been found to be positively associated with inflammatory markers (e.g. plasma interleukin-6 concentration), another potential mediator of the stress–health relationship (Suarez 2003).

A second explanation, the psychosocial vulnerability model, suggests that although hostility itself is not a moderator of the stress–health relationship, it is associated with a powerful moderator variable, namely social support. Their mistrust of others and their expectation that others will behave in a hostile manner towards them induces hostile individuals to behave in an antagonistic and aggressive way towards others. This behaviour pattern is likely to reduce the willingness of others to be supportive, and to evoke interpersonal conflict and hostility from others. However, hostile attitudes towards the social environment not only lower the availability of social support, but also heighten their risk of getting involved in social conflicts and interpersonal stress (Miller et al. 1996).

A third explanation suggests that hostile individuals are more likely to engage in health-impairing behaviour patterns and that these behaviours mediate the relationship between hostility and illness (Leiker and Hailey 1988). There is evidence that hostile individuals report more health-impairing behaviours. In a study of undergraduates, Leiker and Hailey (1988) found that high Ho scores were associated with reports of less physical exercise, less self-care and more alcohol use (including drinking and driving). Similar results were reported by Houston and Vavak (1991). This pattern is also in line with findings from a recent study of a sample of Dutch adolescents in which criminal behaviour was found to be associated with both a tendency to adopt health-impairing behaviour patterns and with ill health (Junger et al. 1999). However, Miller et al. (1996) found that the association between hostility and CHD could even be demonstrated when health behaviour variables were statistically controlled. Similarly, Junger et al. (1999) found that the relationship between criminal behaviour and health remained significant even after controlling for associated differences in health behaviour. Thus, even though the association between hostility and health-impairing behaviour patterns is likely to contribute to the health problems of hostile individuals, the health behaviour model does not provide a complete account of the mechanisms underlying the association between hostility and physical health.

Anxiety

Anxiety has been characterized as a strong negative emotion with worry as one of the core aspects (Kubzansky et al. 1997). There is a great deal of evidence from epidemiological studies that establishes chronic anxiety as an independent risk factor for CHD (e.g. Haines et al. 1987; Eaker et al. 1992; Kawachi et al. 1994a, 1994b; Shen et al. 2008). The most persuasive evidence comes from a recent longitudinal study by Shen et al. (2008). These researchers assessed whether anxiety characteristics predicted the onset of myocardial infarction independently of other known psychological risk factors (e.g. hostility, Type A behaviour). This investigation was part of the Normative Ageing Study, a longitudinal study focusing on the biomedical and psychological changes associated with ageing in a group of initially healthy men, who in this instance were followed up for a period of more than 12 years. In addition to anxiety (assessed with several standard anxiety measures), Type A behaviour, hostility and depression were assessed. All anxiety measures prospectively predicted the occurrence of myocardial infarctions with relative risks varying between 1.36 and 1.47. Most importantly, however, control for hostility, Type A behaviour, depression and even alcohol consumption and smoking did not reduce this association.

Worry is a core component of anxiety and there is suggestive evidence that it might be responsible for the increased incidence in CHD among anxious individuals. For example, a three-year national study following the September 11 terrorist attacks found increased cardiovascular ailments in the years following the attacks among individuals who reported acute stress responses (Holman et al. 2008). However, these effects were exacerbated in individuals who reported ongoing worries about terrorism at both two and three years after the attacks. Further evidence comes from a prospective study by Kubzansky et al. (1997) based on the sample of the Normative Ageing Study (e.g. Shen et al. 2008). Worry was measured at baseline in 1975 with a 20-item worry scale that asked participants to rate how much they worried about five domains (social conditions, health, finances, self-definition and ageing). The study then assessed all CHD problems that occurred among participants in the 20-year period between 1975 and 1995. There was a significant relationship between the total worry score and all instances of CHD and specifically with instances of myocardial infarction.

Although I am not aware of any study that assessed whether anxiety and chronic worrying exacerbated the impact of stressful life events on health, such a moderator role is highly plausible. It is nearly a truism to assume that individuals who are anxious and worry about things are most likely to be strongly affected by stressful life events. In fact, highly anxious individuals are likely to experience all kinds of events as stressful that would not bother more robust people. That anxiety and worry moderate the impact of stressful life events is also suggested by the theoretical and empirical work of Brosschot and others described in Chapter 6 (e.g. Brosschot et al. 2007; Pieper et al. 2010). According to their perseverative cognitions hypothesis, worry is the primary mechanism by which a person prolongs a stressor's cognitive representation, along with its physiological effects. In support of this assumption, the findings of the studies of Brosschot Pieper indicated that the effects of stressful events on heart rate and heart rate variability were mainly due to people's worry rather than the stressful experience itself.

Summary and conclusions

This chapter has focused on the impact of coping strategies and coping resources as moderators of the impact of stress on health. Even though research on basic dimensions of coping and on the differential effectiveness of coping strategies in alleviating the health-impairing impact of stress has been marked by inconsistencies, some generalizeable findings are beginning to emerge. First, avoidance vs. approach and emotion-focused vs. problem-focused coping are emerging as the two major dimensions of coping. Second, even though avoidant coping strategies such as denial, distancing or escape are sometimes effective in the early stages of coping with some traumatic events, they may be a risk factor for adverse responses to stressful events if used chronically. Third, once conceptual problems with measures of emotion-focused coping had been addressed, there is increasing evidence that emotional approach coping can be effective in coping with a range of stressors. And research on optimism suggests that emotional and behavioural approach coping can be effective, if individuals have the ability to cope with a stressor.

The discussion of extrapersonal coping resources focused on the beneficial effect of social support on health and the role of social support as a stress-buffering resource. There is consistent evidence from epidemiological studies that individuals with low levels of social support have higher risks of morbidity and mortality. There is also evidence that the perceived availability of social support buffers individuals against the impact of stressful life events. I discussed biological, behavioural and psychological processes which are assumed to mediate the positive impact of social support on health.

The section on intrapersonal coping resources reviewed research on personality characteristics that help to protect individuals from the negative impact of stressful life events. The discussion focused on two personality dimensions which have specifically been developed in the health context, and seem to convey some degree of resilience on individuals, namely the hardy personality and dispositional optimism. Hardiness consists of three components, namely control, commitment and challenge. It is believed that individuals who are high on these dimensions are better able to withstand the impact of stress and that this relationship is mediated by differences in appraisal processes. Hardy individuals are thought to evaluate stressful events as less stressful and threatening than non-hardy individuals. There is evidence both for the buffering effect of hardiness and for the mediating role of appraisal processes. However, due to the high correlation between hardiness and negative affectivity or neuroticism, it is somewhat unclear whether the buffering effect of hardiness should be interpreted in terms of a protective effect of hardiness on health, or in terms of differences in the way neurotic individuals perceive or report stress and health symptoms.

Dispositional optimism was discussed as a second personality variable which is assumed to moderate the impact of stress on health and well-being. It has been assumed that the greater stress resistance of optimists is mediated by differences in coping strategies. In particular, optimists should be more likely to engage in problem-focused coping whereas pessimists should use denial and distancing as preferred ways of coping. Evidence was presented to support this assumption. However, like hardiness, optimism is correlated with neuroticism, and it is not yet clear to what extent neuroticism may be responsible for the relationship between optimism and health and well-being.

Finally, hostility and anxiety were discussed as examples of potential moderators of the stress–health relationship which do not constitute coping resources. There is strong evidence linking hostility and anxiety to CHD. It is less clear, however, whether they constitute independent risk factors (i.e. affect health even in the absence of stress) or moderators between stress and health. However, in both cases there is strong evidence to suggest that, even if they might constitute independent risk factors, they also play a role as moderators of the stress–health relationship.

The body of research reviewed in this chapter has identified important extrapersonal and interpersonal resources which appear to protect individuals against the deleterious impact of stressful life events, and/or help to reduce exposure to stressful situations. Since the health impact of most of the intrapersonal resources seems to be either mediated by cognitive appraisal or coping processes, this research raises the possibility that one could direct intervention towards the modification of styles of appraisal or coping. Furthermore, since both appraisal and coping are affected by social support, it might also be helpful to provide people with extrapersonal resources such as social support, and thereby improve their capacity to deal with stress.

Further reading

Cohen, S. (2004) Social relationships and health. *American Psychologist*, 59: 676–84. This is a very readable discussion of the relationship between social relationships (social support, social networks and negative interactions) and health.

Segerstrom, S.C., Taylor, S.E., Kemeny, M.E. and Fahey, J.L. (1998) Optimism is associated with mood, coping, and immune change in response to stress. *Journal of Personality and Social Psychology*, 74: 1646–65. A prospective study which demonstrated that dispositional optimism to some extent protected individuals undergoing a stressful experience from the negative impact of stress on mood and the immune system.

Smith, T.W. and MacKenzie, J. (2006) Personality and risk of physical illness. *Annual Review of Clinical Psychology*: 435–67. This is a readable and comprehensive discussion of the evidence linking personality characteristics to health as well as of explanations of this association in terms of biological and behavioural mechanisms.

Taylor, S.E. and Stanton, A.L. (2007) Coping resources, coping processes and mental health. *Annual Review of Clinical Psychology*, 3: 377–401. This is an excellent review of the role of coping resources and coping processes as moderators of the impact of stress.

Urchino, B.N. (2006) Social support and health: a review of physiological processes potentially underlying links to disease outcomes. *Journal of Behavioral Medicine*, 29: 377–87. An excellent review of the physiological processes assumed to be partially responsible for the health impact of social support. It examines evidence linking social support to changes in cardiovascular, neuroendocrine and immune function.

CHAPTER

8

The role of social psychology in health promotion

The epidemiological data presented in this book have identified health-impairing behaviour and psychosocial stress as important factors contributing to ill health. Social psychological knowledge can potentially be used to change health behaviour patterns and to reduce psychosocial stress, thus enabling social psychologists to make a major contribution to the public health effort. In this final chapter I would like to present my personal view on some of the more controversial aspects of the role of social psychology in health promotion.

Limits to persuasion

Despite substantial developments in our understanding of the principles that underlie the formation and change of attitudes, the impact of programmes of health education on health behaviour patterns has sometimes been disappointing. Attempts at persuading people to change their lifestyle have been hampered by three factors:

1 It is difficult to convince people that they are vulnerable to a health risk.
2 Even if we do convince them that they are vulnerable, this may not be sufficient to motivate them to change.
3 Even if individuals are persuaded to change health-impairing behaviours, they often find it difficult to act on these intentions.

As discussed in Chapter 3, there is a discrepancy between individual and population perspectives of health risk. While public health policies are guided by the population attributable risk, that is, the number of excess cases of disease in a population that can be attributed to a given risk factor, individual decision-making is determined by absolute and relative risk. The problem with many health-impairing behaviour patterns is that the relative risk, that is, the ratio of chance of the disease for individuals who engage in a risky behaviour vs. those who do not, is rather low. For example, even though drinking a bottle of wine every day or having a sedentary lifestyle increases the risk of morbidity and premature mortality, the relative risk is modest. And yet, because these habits are very common in western societies, the excess burden on the population attributable to these risk factors is quite high.

But even if the relative risk attributable to a given behaviour is high, as is the case with smoking, the absolute risk may still be low enough as to make it hardly seem worthwhile for the individual to change. For example, even though a smoker runs a much higher risk of developing lung cancer than does a non-smoker, the 10-year absolute risk of lung cancer for a 35-year-old man who is a heavy smoker is only about 0.3 per cent, and the risk of heart disease is only 0.9 per cent (Jeffery 1989). Nevertheless, these small numbers have a great significance from a population perspective. In a group of 1,000,000 male smokers aged 35, nearly 10,000 will die unnecessarily before the age of 45 due to their smoking habit. From the perspective of the individual, on the other hand, the odds are heavily in favour of individual survival, even in the absence of behaviour change.

Fortunately, from the perspective of public health policy and health promotion, individuals often seem to overestimate the risk attributable to the major behavioural risk factors. And even though they tend to estimate their own risk as considerably lower than that of their fellow citizens, these estimates still surpass by far their (likely) 'true risk'. Finally, there is suggestive evidence that relative risks may be more important than absolute risks in influencing health decisions. In other areas of judgement at least, people tend to under-use prior probabilities derived from base rates and the same may be true for health decisions.

What is difficult to accept for most public health professionals is that convincing people that they are at risk may not be sufficient to motivate them to abandon health-impairing in favour of health-enhancing habits. For example, the evidence on determinants of condom use among heterosexuals suggests that the perceived health threat of unsafe sex is not a good predictor of condom use. Although methodological factors may be contributing to this particular finding, it may also indicate that vulnerability to health threats has been overestimated as a target for health promotion. Since most people are aware of the risk they are taking when engaging in unprotected sex, those individuals who persist nevertheless often have other important reasons not to adopt safety measures. In the case of condom use, heterosexuals appear to be more concerned with sexual pleasure than with safety. Thus, as Becker (1976) so succinctly put it more than 30 years ago, good health and a long life may be important aims of most people, but they are not the only aim.

Even if health education is effective in motivating people to want to change, they often fail to act according to their intentions. Thus, the chances of smokers stopping smoking on their first attempt are very low. Most people relapse within the first few months and need repeated attempts before they succeed, if they succeed at all. This raises the question of why the coping skills people are taught during cognitive behaviour therapy (CBT) are of so limited use for resisting temptations in high risk situations. The application of methods and theories from social cognition research to health psychology has provided new answers to this old question. This research suggests that internal or environmental stimuli trigger automatic response tendencies or impulses (partially reflected by implicit attitudes), which often act outside people's awareness and/or control. According to the Reflective–Impulsive Model (RIM) (Strack and Deutsch 2004), self-regulation is a tug of war between impulses and reflective (i.e. deliberate) action, and impulses often win out, particularly when people's coping resources are depleted. Impulses are automatic responses to hedonic stimuli over which the individual has very little control. In contrast, reflective behaviour is controlled behaviour that can take account of long-term goals. Whereas the RIM assumes two different systems to explain the differences between impulses and reflective behaviour, our goal conflict model (e.g. Stroebe *et al.* 2008a) assumes that impulsive behaviour is the result of a goal conflict between the goal to enjoy the immediate pleasure of eating, drinking alcohol or smoking and the long-term advantages of losing weight, staying sober or staying healthy and enjoying a long life. People engage in impulsive behaviour when the enjoyment goal has become the overarching goal of controlling these urges.

Both theoretical approaches agree, however, that environmental stimuli can prime the automatic or impulsive response tendencies and that continuous priming is likely to result in a breakdown of reflective control. This is particularly likely when the individual's coping resources are depleted due to tiredness, alcohol consumption, distraction or depressed mood. Having identified automatic response tendencies triggered by internal or environmental stimuli as one of the reasons why people find it difficult to resist temptations in high risk situations, it also becomes apparent that cognitive skill training can only provide limited protection. Once people have been taught to recognize high risk situations, they can try to reduce their exposure to these situations. For example, people who intend to stop drinking alcohol or quit smoking can avoid joining their drinking friends in the neighbourhood bar. They can also stop stocking alcoholic beverages or cigarettes at home. But even though one can reduce exposure to risk situations, one can never fully avoid them. Furthermore, these impulses are not only triggered by external cues but also by internal urges and cravings.

Because automatic response tendencies or impulses are characterized by the lack of conscious control individuals can exert, it is important to develop techniques which operate at the same automatic level to inhibit these response tendencies. As we discussed in Chapter 3, such methods are being developed and some have already passed the first empirical test. In fact, there is already initial evidence that such methods can have long-term effects with a clinical population. However, more evidence is needed before these techniques can become a part of the clinical treatment of alcohol abusers, smokers or people with obesity.

Some side-effects of health education

There may also be unpleasant side-effects to health education which psychologists have been slow to recognize. By instilling in people the conviction that everybody is responsible for their own health, health education not only increases the motivation of people to improve their own behaviour, but may also motivate them to blame others who fail to live up to these new standards. This point became unpleasantly clear to me many years ago, when I had to undergo a coronary bypass operation. This is not a pleasant operation and I expected nothing but sympathy from my friends. I was more than a little surprised when I realized that many of them felt that I was myself largely to blame for my illness.

For a social psychologist, this should not have come as a surprise. This reaction could have been predicted from a number of social psychological theories. For example, attribution theory argues that perceptions of causality play an important role in determining affective reactions to an event as well as subsequent behaviour (Weiner *et al.* 1988). In the case of a serious physical illness, both the patient and the members of his or her social environment will search for reasons to account for onset of the illness. The outcome of this process of attribution will largely depend on the perceived controllability of the disease in question. If the disease is considered uncontrollable, the patient will be freed of any responsibility for falling ill, and everybody will be full of sympathy and pity. If, however, the disease is considered controllable, then the patient will be seen as responsible and blamed instead of pitied. Research on the perception of persons with AIDS has demonstrated that they are seen as responsible for their own illness and arouse anger rather than pity. These feelings can be changed by changing the attributions – for example, by telling people that the person in question contracted AIDS through a blood transfusion rather than sexual risk behaviour.

Although the contribution of behavioural causes is more substantial in the case of AIDS than it is for CHD, heart disease was rated in the middle range of controllability in a study conducted by Weiner *et al.* (1988). Furthermore, when participants were given the additional information that the person had been smoking and maintaining a poor diet, perceived controllability increased, and so did the level of blame for the patient.

There are a number of reasons why people may be particularly willing to blame patients for their illness. For example, the perception that a friend who is likely to be similar in many health-relevant characteristics has suddenly fallen ill with a serious illness is highly threatening. After all, if it happened to a friend it could also happen to me. People are therefore highly motivated to find reasons why it should happen to their friend and not to them. Attributing the disease to the friend's lifestyle would offer such a differentiating feature. Another reason why people may be highly motivated to blame others for their illness is that they themselves may have given up some pleasurable but health-impairing behaviour pattern, while the other person continued engaging in this behaviour. People who have stopped smoking may be particularly likely to blame others who continue and become sick. After all, by attributing the disease of smokers to their continued smoking, ex-smokers can justify the suffering they have undergone in abandoning the habit.

Unfortunately, this new puritanism may be the price we have to pay for emancipation. We cannot motivate people to change bad health habits and to adopt good ones without placing the responsibility for their health partly on to them. It is only human that, once they have accepted this responsibility, they will turn around and check whether others have also lived up to *their* responsibilities.

Beyond persuasion: changing the incentive structure

Many of the problems associated with health education can be avoided by changing the rewards and costs associated with a given behaviour. There is evidence that increases in the price of cigarettes or alcoholic beverages reduce the demand for these goods. Similarly, legal restrictions, like increasing the minimum age at which adolescents are allowed to purchase alcohol, or making seat belt use compulsory, also have a positive impact on behaviour. The advantage of legal and economic strategies is that they are useful for both influencing existing habits and preventing new health-impairing habits from developing.

However, there are also limits to the applicability of these strategies. Thus, economic incentives can only be employed in areas in which substances or goods have to be purchased in order to engage in certain health behaviours. And as the example of drug addiction demonstrates, high prices do not necessarily prevent people from abusive consumption. Similarly, legal sanctions can only be employed in areas where such sanctions are culturally acceptable and also enforceable. For example, a law prescribing that condoms must always be used in sexual intercourse would be neither socially acceptable nor enforceable.

The effectiveness of legal sanctions depends on the acceptance of the law and on individual perception that violation of the law is associated with a high risk of sanction. For example, it is quite likely that the introduction of a law making seat belt use compulsory would not have been as effective as it was if people had not accepted that such a law was in their own best interests. In fact, without the health education campaign that made it widely known that the wearing of seat belts substantially reduces the risk of injuries in traffic accidents, it is unlikely that such a law would have been passed by the UK Parliament. Similarly, the significant increases of state taxes for cigarettes in the USA were only possible after extensive health education campaigns changed the public climate regarding smoking. Thus, the war against smoking is an excellent example of the impact of a public health campaign that orchestrates persuasion with economic and legal means of changing health behaviour.

Freedom and constraint

The data presented in this book tend to support the argument developed by Gary Becker (1976) that most deaths are to some extent self-inflicted in the sense that they could have been postponed if people had engaged in a healthful lifestyle or abandoned health-impairing behaviour patterns. This has important implications for both individual decision-making and public health policy. At the individual level, the implication is that people are free to choose between lifestyles which differ in their impact on their health. For example, it is up to the individual to decide whether he or she wants to smoke and risk premature death or stop the habit and thereby substantially reduce the risk of morbidity and mortality from cancer and heart disease.

The important implication for public health policy is that it has to be ensured that the choices people make are well-informed ones. Individuals must be made to understand the health implications of their chosen lifestyle. But why should governments use legal measures and tax incentives to influence individual behaviour and thus infringe on the freedom of their citizens to live according to their chosen lifestyles? After all, the days when suicide was a criminal offence in many countries are over. Accordingly, one could argue that people should be free to choose slow methods of suicide such as chain-smoking cigarettes or drinking too much alcohol.

However, there are reasons for governments to impose some constraint on individual freedom. One reason is that governments tend to discourage individual behaviour which interferes with the health and well-being of others. For example, the laws which forbid people to drink and drive are usually justified with the argument that drunken drivers are a danger to their fellow citizens and actually kill many of them every year. Similarly, passive smoking has now been recognized as a health risk. It has been estimated, for example, that in Great Britain approximately 1000 people have died each year from passive smoking. According to one newspaper report, people who believe that their health was damaged in childhood by passive smoking have even taken legal advice about suing their parents (*Independent on Sunday*, 31 January 1993). This led to the restrictions that were imposed on smokers in aeroplanes, public buildings and offices, and finally to the introduction of laws that prohibit smoking in public places. Similar laws have been introduced in most European countries as well as the USA.

But is there any justification for constraining people's freedom to choose behaviour patterns that impair only their own health, such as imposing legal sanctions for failure to wear seat belts, or increasing taxes on cigarettes to reduce consumption? It has to be recognized that allowing individuals to impair their own health in this way also imposes a burden on their fellow citizens. Health, or more precisely the costs of illness, often constitute public goods. Public goods are goods for which it is not possible for those who supply or produce the good to exclude others who did not contribute from consumption. For example, clean air is a public good in the sense that people who incur costs or suffer discomfort to avoid contributing to pollution (e.g. by using public transport instead of their car) cannot prevent others, who do not incur such costs, from profiting from their actions (i.e. to free ride). Thus, there is a temptation to free ride. Similarly, health costs are a public good in countries in which there is full health insurance coverage, since contributions to insurance are usually independent of lifestyle factors. People who engage in health-impairing behaviour patterns and as a result incur higher health costs free ride to some extent on the healthful behaviour of others.

Summary and conclusions

In this book I have argued for integrated public health interventions that use both health education and fiscal and legal measures to influence a given behaviour. As the war against smoking has demonstrated, the two strategies should be seen as complementary. People are more willing to accept legal and fiscal measures if they know and accept the reasons which persuaded government agencies to introduce these measures. Wherever feasible, environmental changes should also be introduced to reduce or eliminate the need for behaviour change. For example, technical appliances should be constructed in ways that minimize the possibility of self-inflicted damage through careless operators.

Before 1950, most of the gains in life expectancy were due to the reduction in death rates at younger ages. In the second half of the twentieth century it was the improvements in survival after age 65 that increased life expectancy. And contrary to arguments that the rate at which the average life expectancy increased during the twentieth century declined sharply in the 1980s (Fries *et al.* 1989), there is now increasing evidence that the apparent levelling off is an 'artefact' (Oeppen and Vaupel 2002). As Oeppen and Vaupel demonstrate, best-performance life expectancy has steadily increased for 160 years and these authors see no evidence that it is approaching a ceiling. Furthermore, there is more to life than the absence of death. Healthy living may not only extend our lifespan, it is also likely to improve our quality of life and extend active life expectancy. The long-held conviction that disease and disability with advancing age results from inevitable, intrinsic ageing processes has been replaced by a view that lifestyle factors and the availability of a social support network can modify many of the usual ageing characteristics (Hansson and Carpenter 1994; Rowe and Kahn 1997). Thus, by adopting a healthy lifestyle when young, we can substantially increase our chances of successful ageing. Furthermore, by significantly reducing the average number of sick days, hospital days or illness symptoms, a healthy lifestyle will not only improve the quality of life for the individual, but it will also result in a significant reduction in population medical expenditure.

Glossary

Absolute risk: the probability that an event will occur, e.g. that an individual will become ill or die within a given period of time.

Acquired Immune Deficiency Syndrome (AIDS): an infectious disease caused by the human immunodeficiency virus (HIV) which attacks the human immune system.

Addiction: the condition of physical and psychological dependence on using a substance (e.g. alcohol, smoking).

Aerobic exercise: energetic and sustained physical exercise intended at increasing the body's capacity to use fuel oxygen; includes jogging, bicycling and swimming.

Affective priming technique: An implicit measure of attitudes. Individuals are presented with a 'prime' (i.e. name or picture of attitude object). Immediately afterwards they are presented with positive or negative adjectives (e.g. words such as useful, disgusting) and are asked to decide as fast as possible whether the adjective is positive or negative. The time it takes people to make this decision (response latency) constitutes the measure of attitude.

Alcohol abuse: a maladaptive pattern of alcohol use leading to clinically significant impairment or distress as manifested by one or more of a set of social or legal problems occurring within a 12-month period (e.g. repeated absence from work due to alcohol consumption, driving under the influence of alcohol, recurrent interpersonal problems due to alcohol).

Alcohol dependence: a more serious form of alcoholism than *alcohol abuse*. In addition to the symptoms of alcohol abuse, alcohol-dependent individuals show evidence of tolerance to the effects of alcohol and/or have experienced withdrawal symptoms.

Alcohol myopia: a narrowing of cognitive focus, as a result of a decrease in cognitive capacity due to alcohol consumption. Alcohol myopic individuals are unable to pay attention to any but the most salient features of a situation.

Angina pectoris: a chronic form of *coronary heart disease* marked by periodic attacks of chest pain. It is caused by brief and incomplete blockages of the blood supply to the heart due to *atherosclerosis*.

Antiretroviral drugs: see *highly active antiretroviral therapy*.

Atherosclerosis: a pathologic process affecting the large muscular and elastic arteries, in which the inner layer of the artery wall is thickened through the deposition of fatty and other materials (*plaque*). Atherosclerosis of the coronary arteries is the major cause of coronary heart disease.

Attitude: the tendency to evaluate a particular entity (e.g. person, group, object) with some degree of favour or disfavour.

Attribution: the process by which people interpret their own and other people's behaviour.

Attributional style: the tendency to make a particular kind of causal inference about behaviour across different situations and across time.

Automatic processes: processes that occur without intention, effort or awareness and do not interfere with other concurrent cognitive processes.

Aversion therapy: therapeutic technique which associates noxious stimuli (e.g. electric shock) with an unwanted behaviour (e.g. drinking alcohol) to arouse aversion to the unwanted behaviour.

Avoidant coping: dealing with a stressful encounter by avoiding confronting the problem or the emotions it arouses. This type of coping relies on strategies such as denial, distraction or wishful thinking.

Behaviour therapy: a set of therapeutic procedures, derived from basic research on human learning, that analyses and targets for modification the stimulus variables that cause and maintain maladaptive behaviour.

Behavioural intention: see *goal intention*.

Beliefs: the opinions, knowledge and thoughts someone has about some attitude object. Beliefs are perceived links between the attitude object and various attributes which are positively or negatively valued.

Binge eating: refers to consuming, in a discrete period of time, an amount of food which is definitely larger than most individuals would eat under similar circumstances.

Binge eating disorder: a newly described eating disorder characterized by frequent binge eating which is accompanied by emotional distress. These individuals do not engage in the compensatory behaviours (e.g. induced vomiting, use of laxatives) typical for *bulimia*.

Biomedical model: a scientific perspective which assumes that illness is solely the result of physical causes such as infection or injury. Psychological causes are not considered.

Biopsychosocial model: a scientific perspective which assumes that health and illness are the result of an interaction of social, psychological and biological factors.

BMI (body mass index): a height-specific standard for weight obtained by dividing weight in kilograms by height in metres squared [kg/m^2]. This index has a very high correlation with body fat.

Boundary model of eating: a cognitive theory of eating regulation developed to explain differences in the eating behaviour of normal and *restrained eaters*. The model assumes that biological pressures (hunger, satiation) keep food consumption within a certain range for all individuals. Due to their chronic dieting, this range is wider for restrained than unrestrained eaters. Restrained eaters regulate their eating in terms of a self-imposed diet boundary, a cognitive limit which marks their maximum desired consumption. Transgression of this diet boundary induces disinhibitory cognitions ('what the hell' cognitions) and subsequently leads to overeating.

Buffering hypothesis of social support: the hypothesis that social support protects the individual against the negative health impact of high levels of stress.

Cardiovascular reactivity: an exaggerated physiologic responsivity to behavioural challenges (e.g. stress experiences). Cardiovascular reactivity is measured by assessing the changes in heart rate, blood pressure or other cardiovascular variables in response to stress, as opposed to measuring only resting levels of these variables. It is suspected that this kind of reactivity is a factor contributing to the development of *coronary heart disease*.

Cardiovascular system: the system composed of the heart and the blood vessels.

Catecholamines: summary term which subsumes the *hormones epinephrine* and *norepinephrine* (also dopamine).

Cholesterol: a fat-like substance. Contained in most tissues, it is also the main component of deposits in the lining of arteries. It is carried in the blood mainly by two proteins, namely low-density and high-density *lipoproteins*. Cholesterol is also contained in food (e.g. egg yolk, milk, liver and kidneys).

Cirrhosis of the liver: a disorder of the liver in which healthy liver tissue has been damaged and replaced by fibrous scar tissue. The most common causes of cirrhosis are heavy drinking over years and malnutrition.

Classical conditioning: a kind of learning through which some neutral stimulus initially incapable of eliciting a particular response gradually acquires the ability to do so through repeated association with a stimulus that has already evoked that response.

Cognitive accessibility: refers to the ease and speed with which information stored in memory can be retrieved. The triggering stimuli that increase the accessibility of cognitive constructs are usually referred to as primes.

Cognitive appraisal: the evaluative process which determines why, and to what extent, a particular situation is perceived as stressful.

Cognitive–behavioural therapy (CBT): a hybrid form of psychological therapy which emphasizes the importance of cognitive processes and procedures in behaviour change. It places primary importance on cognitive processes and incorporates techniques to change aspects of cognitions as well as of behaviour.

Cognitive response model: the model assumes that attitude change is mediated by the thoughts, or 'cognitive responses', which recipients generate as they receive, and reflect upon, persuasive communications.

Cognitive restructuring: therapeutic technique which help patients to identify and correct self-defeating thought patterns which are frequently associated with emotional upset and *relapse* experiences.

Compatibility: measures of attitudes and behaviour are compatible to the extent that their target, action, context and time elements are assessed at identical levels of generality.

Confrontative coping: dealing with a stressful situation by trying to solve the problem and/or to confront the emotions it arouses.

Contingency contracting: a therapeutic technique where patients agree with some agency (usually the therapist) on a set of rewards/punishments that will be enacted contingent on their behaviour. For example, smokers who have stopped may forfeit a sum of money if they relapse.

Continuous abstinence: not smoking or drinking since the time of the stop attempt.

Coping: the cognitive and behavioural strategies which individuals use to manage both a stressful situation and the negative emotional reactions elicited by that event.

Coping resources: the extrapersonal (e.g. social support, financial resources) and intrapersonal resources (e.g. optimism, hardiness) available to the individual for *coping* with the demands of a stressful life event.

Coping strategy: the particular mode (or modes) of *coping* chosen by an individual to deal with a stressful situation.

Coping styles: preferred or habitual modes of *coping*.

Coronary angiography: cardiac catheterization to evaluate the extent of *atherosclerosis* or obstruction of the coronary arteries. Blood vessels are made visible to radiography by injecting into them a radio-opaque substance.

Coronary angioplasty: a method of treating blockage or narrowing of arteries in the heart by inserting (and then inflating) a balloon into the narrow passage to widen it. This is used as an alternative to *coronary bypass operations*.

Coronary heart disease (CHD): a disease of the arteries which feed the heart. It is almost always due to *atherosclerosis* causing inadequate blood supply to the heart muscles. There are two major forms of CHD, namely acute myocardial infarction and angina pectoris.

Correlation coefficient: a statistic that reflects the degree and direction of an association between two variables. Ranges from -1.00 (negative association) through 0.00 (no association) to $+1.00$ (positive association).

Cortisol: a *hormone* secreted by the adrenal cortex which promotes the synthesis and storage of glucose, suppresses inflammation and regulates the distribution of fat in the body.

Cross-sectional study: a research design by which variables are assessed in different groups at the same point in time. For example, the impact of a suspected risk factor on health is assessed by comparing the health of individuals exposed to the risk factor with that of individuals not exposed to the risk factor.

Daily hassles: minor stressors resulting from the irritations and frustrations of daily life.

Defence motivation: the desire to defend and maintain certain beliefs or attitudinal positions which are consistent with existing central attitudes and values.

Detoxification: the process of getting an addicted individual safely through withdrawal after stopping the use of the substance (e.g. drying out of alcoholics).

Disease concept of alcohol abuse: the view that alcoholism is a disease, caused by a psychological predisposition, an allergic reaction to alcohol or some nutritional deficits. Due to this disease, alcoholics suffer a loss of control when exposed to alcohol, which renders them unable to stop drinking. The only cure is total abstention.

Disulfiram: a drug which induces nausea and vomiting if one drinks alcohol in the days following ingestion of the drug. Administered to deter alcohol abusers from drinking alcohol.

Dual-process theories of persuasion: theories of persuasion (e.g. elaboration likelihood model, heuristic-systematic model) which postulate two modes of information processing that differ in the extent to which individuals engage in content-relevant thoughts. The mode of information processing used by an individual is assumed to depend on processing motivation and ability.

Emotion-focused coping: *coping* strategies which do not focus on the stressful event but on ameliorating the distressing emotional reactions to the event.

Endocrine system: the system of glands and other structures that produces and secretes *hormones* into the bloodstream.

Epidemiology: the study of the distribution and determinants of health-related states or events in specified populations.

Epinephrine: (US term for adrenaline) a *hormone* secreted by the adrenal medulla which stimulates the sympathetic nervous system. It stimulates the heart action and raises the blood pressure, releases glucose and increases its consumption, increases the circulation of the blood in the muscles, relaxes air passages and stimulates breathing. It prepares the body for physical action and at the same time inhibits digestion and excretion.

Expectancy–value models: models which assume that decisions between different courses of action are based on two types of cognitions, namely the subjective probability that a given action will lead to a set of expected outcomes and the valence of these outcomes. Individuals are assumed to choose the course of action which will be most likely to lead to positive consequences or avoid negative consequences.

Experiment: a controlled study where the experimenter deliberately introduces changes in the experimental condition but not the control condition to assess the effects of these changes on some variable of interest (i.e. the dependent variable). The control or comparison condition is comparable to the experimental condition in all respects, except that the changes have not been introduced. In true experiments respondents have to be randomly assigned to conditions.

Explicit measures of attitudes: are based on participants' self-reports of their attitudes.

Externality hypothesis: a cognitive theory of eating regulation which assumes differences in the cues that trigger the eating behaviour of obese and normal weight individuals. Whereas normal weight individuals respond mainly to internal, bodily cues in regulating their eating behaviour, the eating of overweight individuals is strongly influenced by external factors such as the sight and smell of food, social stimuli and habit.

Fear appeals: persuasive communications that attempt to motivate recipients to change behaviour deleterious to their health by inducing fear about the potential health hazards.

Foetal alcohol syndrome: distinct pattern of birth defects as a result of prenatal exposure to alcohol due to the mother's overconsumption of alcohol during pregnancy.

Functional measures of the immune system: measures of the performance of certain immune cells. The ability of lymphocytes to activate other cells to proliferate in the face of antigenic challenge, or to destroy invading cells, is essential to an adequate immune response. Lymphocytic proliferation is a test of cellular immunity that examines how effectively lymphocytes divide when stimulated through incubation with mitogens such as phytohemagglutinin (PHA) or concanavalin A (Con A). The ability of natural killer cells to destroy tumour cells is assessed by incubating natural killer cells with tumour cells.

Functional measures of social support: measures which assess the extent to which interpersonal relationships serve particular support functions (e.g. emotion, instrumental, information and appraisal support).

General adaptation syndrome (GAS): the stages of physiological reaction through which an organism moves when exposed to prolonged and intense stress. The stages consist of alarm, resistance and exhaustion.

Goals: cognitive representations of desired end-states.

Goal intentions: the intention to perform a specific behaviour. In contrast to *implementation intentions*, goal intentions leave time and situational context unspecified.

Habits: learned sequences of acts which have become automatic responses to specific cues and are functional in obtaining certain goals or end states.

Health: a state of physical, mental and social well-being which changes over time.

Health behaviour: defined either subjectively as behaviour undertaken by individuals to enhance or maintain their health or objectively as behaviours which have been shown to have beneficial health consequences.

Health belief model: the model assumes that people's health behaviour is determined by their perception of the threat of illness or injury and the advantages and disadvantages of taking action.

Health education: the provision of knowledge and/or training of skills which facilitate voluntary adoption of behaviour conducive to health.

Health promotion: any planned combination of educational, economic or environmental measures designed to reduce the vulnerability of individuals, groups or communities to disease in general, or to enhance their health.

Heuristic processing: mode of information processing which assesses the validity of a communication through reliance on heuristics (i.e. simple rules like 'doctors are always right') rather than a critical evaluation of the arguments.

Highly active antiretroviral therapy (HAART): effective therapy to control and HIV infection and to prevent the development of AIDS. Different antiretroviral drugs, which inhibit the retrovirus at different phases of its life-cycle, are taken in combination, because no single antiretroviral drug is likely to suppress the infection for long.

Hopelessness: a state characterized by negative expectations about the occurrence of highly valued outcomes (a negative outcome expectancy) and expectations of helplessness about changing the likelihood of occurrence of these outcomes (a helplessness expectancy).

Hormones: chemical substances which are released from an *endocrine* gland into the bloodstream and act on a distant target site.

Hostility: a personality trait that constitutes a risk factor for coronary heart disease. It reflects a negative attitude towards others involving cognitive (e.g. cynicism, mistrust), affective (e.g. anger) and behavioural components (e.g. aggression).

Human Immunodeficiency Virus (HIV): a virus which attacks and damages the immune system by infecting and killing *T-helper cells*.

Hypertension: high blood pressure.

Ileal bypass: a bypass of the end of the small intestines, used as surgical treatment in cases of extreme obesity.

Implementation intention: the intention to enact a specific behaviour in a specific situation at a specific time.

Implicit Association Test (IAT): a procedure developed to measure implicit attitudes using the strength of an association between two concepts with positive and negative evaluations. It uses response latencies to infer implicit evaluations.

Implicit attitude: automatic evaluative response to an attitude object.

Implicit measures of attitudes: unobtrusive and indirect measures that are not based on self-reports and mostly infer attitudes from response times.

Incidence: the number of new events (e.g. new cases of a disease in a defined population within a specified period of time).

Intention-to-treat analysis: a method to correct for the effects of drop-out in studies. With this analysis, results are based on all participants, even those who dropped out of the study. Estimates are used for the missing values of individuals who did not finish the study. One popular method is the 'last observation carried forward method', whereby the last known observation is used to fill in observations that are missing.

Learned helplessness: a condition of apathy and depression in reaction to repeated exposure to unavoidable stressors.

Lipoprotein: proteins that transport cholesterol in the blood. Classified into low-density and high-density lipoprotein. High levels of low-density lipoprotein contribute to plaque formation in atherosclerosis. High density lipoprotein may be involved in transporting surplus cholesterol back to the liver.

Longitudinal study: study in which a cohort of people is followed to allow repeated measurement of variables with the same individuals over time.

Mediating variable or process: a variable or process assumed to account for the cause–effect relationship between two other variables (e.g. differential knowledge about health risks is assumed to be one of the mediators of the relationship between social class and health). The mediating variable is assumed to be (at least partly) responsible for the effect of the cause (i.e. social class) on the outcome variable (i.e. health). To demonstrate that a variable is a mediator, one has to show that it covaries with both changes in the assumed cause and changes in the assumed outcome, and that statistically controlling for the mediator (e.g. through multiple regression) results in a substantial reduction, or even elimination, of the association between the assumed cause and the outcome.

Meta-analysis: a set of statistical techniques for integrating the results of independent studies of a given phenomenon in a common metric (effect size). Use of this common metric permits comparisons across studies and the examination of overall outcomes of findings of all studies combined.

Morbidity: any departure, subjective or objective, from a state of mental or physical well-being.

Mortality: death, usually calculated so that the number of deaths can be expressed as a ratio to number of persons at risk (i.e. still alive) in a specified population.

Myocardial infarction: an acute form of *coronary heart disease* which is commonly called a 'heart attack'. It reflects the death of a heart muscle (myocardium) due to severe and/or prolonged blockage of the blood supply to the tissue.

Negative affectivity: refers to a broad dimension of individual differences (reflected by measures of neuroticism) in the tendency to experience negative distressing emotions. Can affect responses to questionnaire items.

Negotiated safety: refers to agreements between partners to abstain from unprotected sex outside their relationship.

Nicotine regulation model: a theory of smoking which assumes that people smoke to regulate the level of nicotine in the internal milieu. Smoking is stimulated when the nicotine level falls below a certain set point.

Nicotine replacement therapy: nicotine replacement through nicotine chewing gum or nicotine patches helps people who have stopped smoking to overcome withdrawal symptoms.

Norepinephrine: (US term for noradrenaline) a hormone released by the adrenal medulla and by the synapses of sympathetic nerves. Whereas epinephrine prepares the body for physical action, norepinephrine deals with the routine jobs such as maintaining an even blood pressure.

Obesity: severe overweight due to excessive body fat. An individual is classified as obese with a body weight which is more than 20 per cent above the ideal weight or a BMI more than 30 kg/m².

Operant conditioning: modifies behaviour by manipulating the consequences of such behaviour.

Overweight: a body weight that is between the upper limit of normal and 20 per cent above that limit.

Passive smoking: breathing someone else's smoke in the environment.

Perceived social support: the perception that supportive others are available.

Perseverative cognition hypothesis: a hypothesis that assumes it is not stressful events themselves that are responsible for most of the stress-related physiological activity in daily life, but the thoughts and worries that these events stimulate.

Persuasion: the effects of exposure to relatively complex messages from other persons on the attitudes and beliefs of the recipients.

Placebo control groups: used to check whether the effect of a drug treatment is due to the active ingredient of the drug or some other effects of the treatment. Placebo control groups receive apparently the same drug treatment as the intervention group, except that the administered drug lacks the active ingredient.

Plaque: fatty material that may deposit in arteries. Responsible for narrowing of arteries.

Point prevalence abstinence: not smoking or not drinking around the time when the measurement is being taken.

Population attributable risk: refers to the number of excess cases of disease in a population that can be attributed to a given risk factor.

Prevalence: the number of events (e.g. instances of a given disease) in a given population at a given time.

Primary appraisal: evaluative process by which individuals categorize a given situation with respect to its significance for their well-being and decide whether the situation is irrelevant, positive or potentially harmful.

Primary prevention: actions undertaken to prevent health problems from occurring.

Priming: refers to the phenomenon that exposure to an object or a word in one context increases not only the accessibility of the mental representation of that object or concept in a person's mind but also the accessibility of related objects or concepts. As a result the activated concept exerts for some time an unintended influence of the individual's behaviour in subsequent unrelated contexts without the individual being aware of this influence.

Problem-focused coping: refers to instrumental behaviour aimed at reducing the risk of harmful consequences that might result from the stressful event.

Prospective study: longitudinal study where the risk factors or variables (e.g. stressful life events) which predict a certain future outcome (e.g. depression or heart disease) are measured first, and the outcome variables are then assessed at some future point in time.

Protection motivation theory: originally an attempt to specify the algebraic relationship between the components of the health belief model. In its most recent version the model assumes that the motivation to protect oneself from danger is a positive linear function of four beliefs: the threat is severe, one is personally vulnerable, one has the ability to perform the coping response, and the coping response is effective in reducing the threat. Two other beliefs have a negative effect on protection motivation: that engaging in the health impairing behaviour is rewarding; and that giving it up is costly.

Psychoneuroimmunology: studies the interaction between psychosocial processes and nervous, endocrine and immune system functioning.

Public health model: a term used here to refer to interventions aimed at changing health behaviour that rely on health promotion and are designed to change the behaviour of large groups.

Quantitative or enumerative tests of the immune system: involve counting the number or percentages of different types of immune cells such as helper T cells, suppressor/cytotoxic T cells, B cells and natural killer (NK) cells in the peripheral blood.

Rapid smoking: a clinical technique which creates aversion to smoking by instructing subjects to smoke continually, inhaling every six to eight seconds, until tolerance is reached.

Received social support: actual social support that has been received over a given period of time.

Relapse: reverting to the full-blown pattern of health-impairing or otherwise unwanted behaviour after beginning to change it.

Relative risk: the ratio of the risk of disease or death for individuals who engage in a risky behaviour and those who do not.

Restrained eaters: chronic dieters who try to restrict their food intake and suppress their weight.

Risk factor: any factor (e.g. aspect of personal behaviour, exposure) that increases the probability (determinant), or is associated with an increased probability of occurrence, of a disease (risk marker).

Rumination: an ineffective coping style associated with increased levels of depressive symptoms. Ruminators tend to focus passively on their symptoms of distress and the meaning and consequences of those symptoms.

Safe sex: sex which involves no risk of the partner being exposed to HIV. Sex is only safe if partners do not engage in any activities which result, or can result, in an exchange of blood, semen or vaginal secretions.

Safer sex: defined by activities (e.g. condom use) which substantially reduce the risk of infection.

Salient beliefs: a limited number of which are cognitively highly accessible in the situation, in which the individual responds to the attitude object.

Secondary appraisal: evaluation of the options available to meet the demands of the stressful situation and to avoid the threatened negative consequences.

Secondary prevention: actions undertaken to treat a disease in the early, non-symptomatic stages with the aim of arresting or reversing the condition.

Self-control dilemma: a decision between two alternatives, where one promises in immediate rewards, but endangers some long-term benefit (i.e. superordinate goal).

Self-efficacy: refers to beliefs in one's ability to carry out certain actions required to produce a given attainment. For example, the belief that one is capable of giving up smoking or going on a diet.

Self-management procedures: therapeutic procedures where clients are taught to analyse their own behaviour and to manage their own behaviour change.

Self-regulation: refers to the ability regulate behaviour, attention and emotion in the service of personal standards or goals. This involves overriding or changing one's inner responses, as well as interrupting undesired behavioural tendencies and refraining from acting on them.

Set point theory of weight regulation: proposes that each person has a physiologically based weight level (set point) which the body strives to maintain.

Skill training: therapeutic procedure based on the assumption that people engage in health-impairing behaviours because they lack certain skills, such as the skill to cope with stress or with negative emotional states.

Social support: reflects the information from others that one is loved and cared for, esteemed and valued, and part of a network of communication and mutual obligation. Such information can come from a spouse, a lover, children, friends or social and community contacts such as churches or social clubs.

Stage models of change: theories (e.g. transtheoretical model, precaution adoption process model) which assume that health behaviour change involves progression through a discernible number of stages from ignorance of a health threat to completed preventive action.

Stages of change: the stages through which individuals are assumed to move in their progression from ignorance of a health risk to taking protective action. The different stages are assumed to represent qualitatively different patterns of behaviour, beliefs and experience, and factors which produce transitions between stages vary depending on the specific stage transitions being considered.

Statins: a new generation of cholesterol-lowering drugs which block the endogenous synthesis of cholesterol in the liver.

Stress: the condition which arises when individuals perceive the demands of a situation as challenging or exceeding their resources and endangering their well-being.

Stressful life events: events which represent major changes in an individual's life that range from short-term to enduring and are potentially threatening.

Structural measures of social support: reflect the social integration or social embeddedness of individuals by assessing the existence or quantity of their social relationships.

Subjective norms: (normative) beliefs about how people who are important to us expect us to act weighted by our motivation to comply with their expectations.

Systematic processing: thorough, detailed processing of the information contained in a persuasive communication involving scrutinization of arguments and argument-relevant thinking.

Tailoring: a technique of personalizing persuasive communications on the basis of information about individuals gathered by questionnaire. This technique was originally developed to match persuasive communications to the *stages of change* of the individual, but it can be used to tailor the message to many more individual characteristics.

Tension reduction hypothesis: assumes that alcohol is consumed because it reduces tension. Increased tension constitutes a heightened drive state. By lowering tension and thus reducing this drive state, alcohol consumption has reinforcing properties.

T-helper cells: a class of lymphocytes which serves an important function in the regulation of the immune system by stimulating other cells to attack antigens.

Theory of planned behaviour: the extension of the theory of reasoned action. Besides attitudes and subjective norms, perceived behavioural control is incorporated as the third important predictor of behaviour.

Theory of reasoned action: a theory of the relationship between attitude and behaviour. Assumes that attitudes combine with subjective norms to influence behaviour.

Therapy model: a term used here to refer to interventions aimed at changing health behaviour that rely on methods of psychological therapy. This type of intervention typically involves a one-to-one relationship where 'patients' and therapists are in dyadic interaction, although group treatments and self-therapy programmes are also used.

Very low-calorie diets (VLCDs): supplemented fasts designed to spare the loss of lean body mass through the provision of 70 to 100g of protein a day in a total of 300 to 600 calories.

References

Aarts, H. and Dijksterhuis, A. (2000) Habits as knowledge structures: automaticity in goal-directed behavior. *Journal of Personality and Social Psychology*, 78: 53–63.

Aarts, H., Dijksterhuis, A. and Midden, K. (1998) To plan or not to plan? Goal achievement or interrupting the performance of mundane behaviors. *European Journal of Social Psychology*, 29: 971–9.

Abel, E.L. (1980) Fetal Alcohol Syndrome: behavioral teratology. *Psychological Bulletin*, 87: 29–50.

Abel, E.L. (1995) An update on incidence of FAS: FAS is not an equal opportunity birth defect. *Neurotoxicology and Teratology*, 17: 437–43.

Abraham, C., Sheeran, P., Spears, R. and Abrams, D. (1992) Health beliefs and the promotion of HIV-preventive intentions among teenagers: a Scottish perspective. *Health Psychology*, 11: 369–70.

Abramson, L., Seligman, M.E.P. and Teasdale, J.D. (1978) Learned helplessness in humans: critique and reformulation. *Journal of Abnormal Psychology*, 87: 49–74.

Abramson, L., Metalsky, G. and Alloy, L. (1989) Hopelessness depression: a theory-based subtype of depression. *Psychological Review*, 96: 358–72.

Adam, P.C.G., de Wit, J.B.F., Toskin, I. *et al.* (2009) Estimating levels of HIV testing, HIV prevention coverage, HIV knowledge, and condom use among men who have sex with men (MSM) in low-income and middle-income countries. *Journal of Acquired Immune Deficiency Syndrome*, 52: S143–51.

Adamson, S.J., Sellman, J.D. and Frampton, C.M.A. (2009) Patient predictors of alcohol treatment outcome: a systematic review. *Journal of Substance Abuse Treatment*, 36: 75–86.

Adler, M., Phillips, A. and Johnson, A. (1997) Communicable diseases: sexually transmitted disease, including AIDS, in J. Charlton and M. Murphy (eds) *The Health of Adult Britain 1941–1994*, 2: 21–9.

Adler, N.E., Boyce, T., Chesney, M.A. *et al.* (1994) Socioeconomic status and health: the challenge of the gradient. *American Psychologist*, 49: 15–24.

Adriaanse, M.A., De Ridder, D.T.D. and De Wit, J.B.F. (2009) Finding the critical cue: implementation intentions to change one's diet work best when tailored to personally relevant reasons for unhealthy eating. *Personality and Social Psychology Bulletin*, 35: 60–71.

Ajzen, I. (1988) *Attitudes, Personality and Behavior*. Chicago, IL: Dorsey.

Ajzen, I. (2005) *Attitudes, Personality and Behavior*, 2nd edn. Maidenhead: Open University Press.

Ajzen, I. and Fishbein, M. (1977) Attitude–behavior relations: a theoretical analysis and review of empirical research. *Psychological Bulletin*, 84: 888–918.

Ajzen, I. and Fishbein, M. (2000) Attitudes and the attitude–behavior relation: reasoned and automatic processes, in W. Stroebe and M. Hewstone (eds) *European Review of Social Psychology*, 11: 1–33.

Ajzen, I. and Madden, T.J. (1986) Prediction of goal-directed behavior: attitudes, intentions, and perceived behavioral control. *Journal of Experimental Social Psychology*, 22: 453–74.

Ajzen, I. and Timko, C. (1986) Correspondence between health attitudes and behavior. *Journal of Basic and Applied Psychology*, 42: 426–35.

Ajzen, I., Brown, T.C. and Carvajal, F. (2004) Explaining the discrepancy between intentions and actions: the case of hypothetical bias in contingent valuation. *Personality and Social Psychology Bulletin*, 30: 1108–21.

Ajzen, I., Czasch, C. and Flood, M. (2009) From intentions to behavior: implementation intention, commitment, and conscientiousness. *Journal of Applied Social Psychology*, 39, 1356–72.

Albarracin, D., Johnson, B.T., Fishbein, M. and Muellerleile, P.A. (2001) Theories of reasoned action and planned behavior as model of condom use: a meta-analysis. *Psychological Bulletin*, 127: 142–61.

Albarracin, D., Gillette, J.C., Earl, A.E. *et al.* (2006) A test of major assumptions about behavior change: a comprehensive look at the effects of passive and active HIV-prevention interventions since the beginning of the epidemic. *Psychological Bulletin*, 131: 856–97.

Albert, M.S., Savage, C.R., Jones, K. *et al.* (1995) Predictors of cognitive change in older persons: MacArthur studies of successful aging. *Psychology and Aging,* 10: 578–89.

Alcoholics Anonymous (1955) *The Story of How Many Thousands of Men and Women Have Recovered from Alcoholism.* New York: Alcoholics Anonymous Publishing.

Aldwin, C.M. and Revenson, T.A. (1987) Does coping help? A re-examination of the relation between coping and mental health. *Journal of Personality and Social Psychology,* 53: 337–48.

Allred, K.D. and Smith, T.W. (1989) The hardy personality: cognitive and physiological responses to evaluative threat. *Journal of Personality and Social Psychology,* 56: 257–66.

Alwin, D.F., Cohen, R.L. and Newcomb, T. (1991) *Political Attitudes Over a Life-span: The Bennington Women After Fifty Years.* Madison, WI: Madison University Press.

American Cancer Society (1986) *1986: Cancer, Fact and Figures.* New York: American Cancer Society.

Amirkhan, J.H. (1990) A factor analytically derived measure of coping: the coping strategy indicator. *Journal of Personality and Social Psychology,* 59: 1066–74.

Anderson, J.W., Konz, E.C., Frederich, R.C. and Wood, C.L. (2001) Long-term weight-loss maintenance: a meta-analysis of US studies. *American Journal of Clinical Nutrition,* 74: 579–84.

Anderson, R.N. and Smith, B.L. (2003) Deaths leading causes for 2001. National Vital Statistics reports: from the National Centers for Disease Control and Prevention, National Center for Health Statistics, *National Vital Statistics System,* 52: 1–85.

Antiretroviral Therapy Cohort Collaboration (2008) Life expectancy of individuals on combination antiretroviral therapy in high-income countries: a collaborative analysis of 14 cohort studies. *Lancet,* 327: 293–9.

Anton, R.F., O'Malley, S.S., Ciraulo, D. *et al.* (2006) Combined pharmacotherapies and behavioral interventions for alcohol dependence. The COMBINE Study: a randomized controlled trial. *Journal of the American Medical Association,* 295: 2003–17.

APA (American Psychiatric Association) (1994) *Diagnostic and Statistical Manual of Mental Disorders,* 4th edn. Washington, DC: American Psychiatric Association.

Archer, J. (1999) *The Nature of Grief: The Evolution and Psychology of Reactions to Loss.* London: Routledge.

Armitage, C.J. (2004) Evidence that implementation intention reduce dietary fat intake: a randomized trial. *Health Psychology,* 23: 319–23.

Armitage, C.J. (2005) Can the theory of planned behavior predict the maintenance of physical activity? *Health Psychology,* 24: 235–45.

Armitage, C.J. and Conner, M. (1999) The theory of planned behaviour: assessment of predictive validity and 'perceived control'. *British Journal of Social Psychology,* 38: 35–54.

Armitage, C.J. and Conner, M. (2001) Efficacy of the theory of planned behaviour. *British Journal of Social Psychology,* 40: 471–99.

Armstrong, G.L., Conn, L.A. and Pinner, R.W. (1999) Trends in infectious disease mortality in the United States during the 20th century. *Journal of the American Medical Association,* 281: 611–67.

Arrieta, A. and Russell, L.B. (2008) Effects of leisure and non-leisure physical activity on mortality in US adults over two decades. *Annals of Epidemiology,* 18: 889–95.

Ashley, M.J. and Rankin, J.G. (1988) A public health approach to the prevention of alcohol-related problems. *Annual Review of Public Health,* 9: 233–71.

Aspinwall, L.G. and Taylor, S.E. (1992) Modeling cognitive adaptation: a longitudinal investigation of the impact of individual differences and coping on college adjustment and performance. *Journal of Personality and Social Psychology,* 63: 989–1003.

Atkins, R (1999) *Dr. Atkins' New Diet Revolution.* South Dakota: Vermillion.

Attia, S., Eger, M., Müller, M., Zwahlen, M. and Low, N. (2009) Sexual transmission of HIV according to viral load and antiretroviral therapy: systematic review and meta-analysis. *AIDS,* 23: 1397–404.

Austenfel, J.L. and Stanton, A.L. (2004) Coping through emotional approach: a new look at emotional, coping, and health-related outcomes. *Journal of Personality,* 72: 1335–63.

Autorengruppe Nationales Forschungsprogramm (1984) *Wirksamkeit der Gemeindeorientierten Prävention Kardiovascularer Krankheiten (Effectiveness of Community-Oriented Prevention of Cardiovascular Diseases).* Bern: Hans Huber.

Avants, S.K., Warburton, L.A. and Margolin, A. (2001) How injection drug users coped with testing HIV-seropositive: implications for subsequent health-related behaviors. *AIDS Education and Prevention*, 13: 207–18.

Babor, T.F., Higgins-Biddle, J.C., Saunders, J.B. and Monteiro, M.G. (2001) *AUDIT: The Alcohol Use Disorders Identification Test*, 2nd edn. Geneva: WHO, http://whqlibdoc.who.int/hq/2001/who_msd_msb_01.6a.pdf (accessed August 2010).

Baer, J.S. and Lichtenstein, E. (1988) Classification and prediction of smoking relapse episodes: an exploration of individual differences. *Journal of Consulting and Clinical Psychology*, 56: 104–10.

Bahrke, M.S. and Morgan, W.P. (1978) Anxiety reduction following exercise and meditation. *Cognitive Therapy and Research*, 2: 323–33.

Bakker, A.B., Buunk, B.P. and Engles, R.C.M.E. (1994) Buitenechetlijke seks en AIDS-preventief gedrag: Een toets van het investeringsmodel, in P.A.M. van Lange, F.W. Siero, B. Verplanken and E.C.M. van Schie (eds) *Sociale psychologie en haar toepassingen*, pp. 40–53. Eburon: Delft.

Balldin, J., Berglund, M., Borg, S. *et al.* (2003) A 6-month controlled naltrexone study: combined effect with cognitive behavioural therapy in outpatient treatment of alcohol dependence. *Alcoholism: Clinical and Experimental Research*, 27: 1142–9.

Baltes, P.B. and Schaie, K.W. (1976) On the plasticity of intelligence in adulthood and old age: where Horn and Donaldson fail. *American Psychologist*, 31: 720–5.

Bandura, A. (1986) *Social Foundations of Thought and Action: A Cognitive Social Theory*. Englewood Cliffs, NJ: Prentice Hall.

Bandura, A. (1997) *Self-efficacy: The Exercise of Control*. New York, NY: Freeman.

Barefoot, J.C., Dodge, K.A., Peterson, B.L. *et al.* (1989) The Cook–Medley Hostility Scale: item content and ability to predict survival. *Psychosomatic Medicine*, 51: 46–57.

Barendregt, J.J., Bonneux, L. and van der Maas, P. (1997) The health costs of smoking. *New England Journal of Medicine*, 337: 1052–7.

Bargh, J.A. (2002) Losing consciousness: automatic influences on consumer judgment, behaviour and motivation. *Journal of Consumer Research*, 29: 280–5.

Bargh, J. and Chartrand, T.L. (1999) The unbearable automaticity of being. *American Psychologist*, 54: 462–79.

Bargh, J., Chen, M. and Burrows, L. (1996) The automaticity of social behavior: direct effects of trait construct and stereotype activation on action. *Journal of Personality and Social Psychology*, 71: 230–44.

Bargh, J.A.. Gollwitzer, P.M., Lee Chai, A. *et al.* (2001) The automated will: non-conscious activation and pursuit of behavioural goals. *Journal of Personality and Social Psychology*, 81: 1014–27.

Barrera Jr, M., Sandler, I.N. and Ramsey, T.B. (1981) Preliminary development of a scale of social support: studies on college students. *American Journal of Community Psychology*, 9: 435–47.

Baucom, D.H. and Aiken, P.A. (1981) Effect of depressed mood on eating among obese and nonobese dieting persons. *Journal of Personality and Social Psychology*, 41: 477–585.

Bauman, A.E., Bellew, B., Owen, N. and Vita, P. (2001) Impact of an Australian mass media campaign targetting physical activity in 1998. *American Journal of Preventive Medicine*, 21: 41–7.

Baumeister, R.F. (2002) Ego depletion and self-control failure: an energy model of the self's executive function. *Self and Identity*, 1: 129–36.

Baumeister, R.F., Bratslavsky, E., Muraven, M. and Tice, D.M. (1998) Ego depletion: is the active self a limited resource? *Journal of Personality and Social Psychology*, 74: 1252–65.

Barefoot, J.C., Dahlstrom, W.G. and Williams, R.B. (1987) Hostility, CHD incidence, and total mortality: a 25-year follow-up study of 255 physicians. *Psychosomatic Medicine*, 45: 59–63.

Barth, J., Schneider, S. and von Känel, R. (2010) Lack of social support in the etiology and the prognosis of coronary heart disease: a systematic review of meta-analysis. *Psychosomatic Medicine*, 72: 229–38.

Beck, A.T. (1976) *Cognitive Therapy and the Emotional Disorders*. New York: International Universities Press.

Becker, G.S. (1976) *The Economic Approach to Human Behavior*. Chicago: University of Chicago Press.

Becker, G.S., Grossman, M. and Murphy, K.M. (1994) An empirical analysis of cigarette addiction. *American Economic Review*, 84: 396–418.

Belloc, N.B. (1973) Relationship of health practices to mortality. *Preventive Medicine*, 2: 67–81.

Belloc, N.B. and Breslow, L. (1972) Relationship of physical health status and health practices. *Preventive Medicine*, 5: 409–21.

Bentler, P.M. and Speckart, G. (1979) Models of attitude–behavior relations. *Psychological Review*, 86: 452–64.

Bentler, P.M. and Speckart, G. (1981) Attitudes 'cause' behaviours: a structural equation analysis. *Journal of Personality and Social Psychology*, 40: 226–38.

Berg, D., LaBerg, J.C., Skutte, A. and Ohman, A. (1981) Instructed versus pharmacological effects of alcohol in alcoholics and social drinkers. *Behavioral Research and Therapy*, 19: 55–66.

Berg, F.M. (1999) Health risks associated with weight loss and obesity treatment programs. *Journal of Social Issues*, 55: 277–97.

Berkman, L.F. and Syme, S.L. (1979) Social networks, host resistance, and mortality: a nine-year follow-up of Alameda County residents. *American Journal of Epidemiology*, 109: 186–204.

Berkman, L.F., Glass, T., Brissette, I. and Seeman, T.E. (2000) From social integration to health: Durkheim in the new millennium. *Social Science & Medicine*, 51: 843–57.

Bernard, J. (1968) *The Sex Game*. Englewood Cliffs, NJ: Prentice Hall.

Bessenoff, G.R. and Sherman, J.W. (2000) Automatic and controlled components of prejudice toward fat people: evaluation versus stereotype activation. *Social Cognition*, 18: 329–53.

Best, J.A., Thompson, S.J., Santi, S.M. *et al.* (1988) Preventing cigarette-smoking among schoolchildren. *Annual Review of Public Health*, 9: 161–201.

Bewick, B.A., Trusler, K., Mulhern, B. *et al.* (2008) The feasibility and effectiveness of a web-based personalized feedback and social norms alcohol intervention in UK university students: a randomized control trial. *Addictive Behaviors*, 33: 1192–8.

Billman, G.E., Schwartz, P.J. and Stone, H.L. (1984) The effects of daily exercise on susceptibility to sudden cardiac death. *Circulation*, 69: 1182–9.

Bjartveit, K. and Tverdal, A. (2005) Health consequences of smoking 1–4 cigarettes per day. *Tobacco Control*, 14: 313–20.

Blackburn, G.L., Lynch, M.E. and Wong, S.L. (1986) The very-low-calorie diet: a weight-reduction technique, in K.D. Brownell and J.P. Foreyt (eds) *Handbook of Eating Disorders*, pp. 198–212. New York: Basic Books.

Blackburn, H. (1983) Diet and atherosclerosis: epidemiologic evidence and public health implications. *Preventive Medicine*, 12: 2–10.

Blair, S.N., Kohl, H.W., Paffenbarger Jr, R.S. *et al.* (1989) Physical fitness and all-cause mortality: a prospective study of healthy men and women. *Journal of the American Medical Association*, 3: 2395–401.

Blair, S.N., Kohl, H.W., Barlow, C.E. *et al.* (1995) Changes in physical fitness and all-cause mortality. *Journal of the American Medical Association*, 273: 1093–9.

Blalock, S., DeVellis, R.F., Giorgino, K.B. *et al.* (1996) Osteoporosis prevention in premenopausal women: using a stage model approach to examine the predictors of behaviour. *Health Psychology*, 15: 84–93.

Blascovich, J. and Katkin, E.S. (1995) *Cardiovascular Reactivity to Psychological Stress and Disease*. Washington, DC: American Psychological Association.

Blazer, D.G. (1982) Social support and mortality in an elderly community population. *American Journal of Epidemiology*, 115: 684–94.

Bliss, R.E., Garvey, A.J., Heinold, J.W. and Hitchcock, J.L. (1989) The influence of situation and coping on relapse crisis outcomes after smoking cessation. *Journal of Consulting and Clinical Psychology*, 57: 443–9.

Blissmer, B. and McAuley, E. (2002) Testing the requirements of stages of physical activity among adults: the comparative effectiveness of stage-matched, mismatched, standard care, and control interventions. *Annals of Behavioral Medicine*, 24: 181–9.

Bloss, G. (2006) Measuring the health consequences of alcohol consumption: current needs and methodological challenges. *Digestive Diseases*, 23: 162–9.

Blumenthal, J.A., Babyak, M.A., Doraiswamy, P. M. *et al.* (2007) Exercise and pharmacotherapy in the treatment of major depressive disorder. *Psychosomatic Medicine*, 69: 587–96.

Bohner, G. and Wänke, M. (2002) *Attitudes and Attitude Change*. Hove: Psychology Press.

Borgida, E. and Brekke, N. (1981) The base rate fallacy in attribution and prediction, in J.H. Harvey, W.J. Ickes and R.F. Kidd (eds) *New Directions in Attribution Research*, Vol. 3, pp. 63–95. Hillsdale, NJ: Lawrence Erlbaum.

Borland, R., Owen, N., Hill, D. and Schofield, P. (1991) Predicting attempts at sustained cessation of smoking after the introduction of workplace smoking bans. *Health Psychology*, 10: 336–42.

Botvin, G.J. *et al.* (1995) Long-term follow-up results of a randomized drug abuse prevention trial in a white middle-class population. *Journal of the American Medical Association*, 273: 1106–12.

Bouchard, C. (in press) BMI, fat mass, abdominal adiposity and visceral fat: where is the 'beef'? *International Journal of Obesity*, 31: 1552–3.

Brand, R.J., Paffenbarger, R.S., Sholtz, R.I. and Kampert, J.B. (1979) Work activity and fatal heart attack studied by multiple logistic risk analysis. *American Journal of Epidemiology*, 110: 52–62.

Braver, E.R., Shardell, M. and Teoh, E.R. (2010) How have changes in air bag designs affected frontal crash mortality? *Accident Analysis and Prevention*, 20: 499–510.

Breslow, L. (1990) The future of public health: prospects in the United States for the 1990s. *Annual Review of Public Health*, 11: 1–28.

Breslow, L. and Enstrom, J.E. (1980) Persistence of health habits and their relationship to mortality. *Preventive Medicine*, 9: 469–83.

Brewin, C.R. (1988) *Cognitive Foundations of Clinical Psychology*. London: Lawrence Erlbaum.

Brosschot, J.F., Gerin, W. and Thayer, J.F. (2006) The perseverative cognition hypothesis: a review of worry, prolonged stress-related physiological activation and health. *Journal of Psychosomatic Research*, 60: 113–24.

Brosschot, J.F., van Dijk, E. and Thayer, J.F. (2007) Daily worry is related to low heart rate variability during waking and subsequent nocturnal sleep period. *International Journal of Psychophysiology*, 63: 39–47.

Brown, G.W. and Harris, T. (1978) *Social Origins of Depression: A Study of Psychiatric Disorder in Women*. New York: Free Press.

Brown, G.W. and Harris, T.O. (eds) (1989) *Life Events and Illness*. New York: Guilford Press.

Brown, S.A., Goldman, M.S., Inn, A. and Anderson, L. (1980) Expectations of reinforcement from alcohol: their domain and relation to drinking patterns. *Journal of Consulting and Clinical Psychology*, 48: 419–26.

Brownell, K.D. (1995) Exercise in the treatment of obesity, in K.D. Brownell and C.G. Fairburn (eds) *Eating Disorders and Obesity*, pp. 473–8. New York: Guilford Press.

Brownell, K.D. and Rodin, J. (1994) The dieting maelstrom: is it possible and advisable to lose weight? *American Psychologist*, 49: 781–91.

Brownell, K.D., Stunkard, A.J. and Albaum, J.M. (1980) Evaluation and modification of exercise patterns in the natural environment. *American Journal of Psychiatry*, 137: 1540–5.

Brownell, K.D., Marlatt, G.A., Lichtenstein, E. and Wilson, G.T. (1986) Understanding and preventing relapse. *American Psychologist*, 41: 765–82.

Brownell, K.D., Puhl, R.M., Schwartz, M.B. and Rudd, L. (eds) (2005) *Weight Bias: Nature, Consequences and Remedies*. New York: Guilford.

Brownson, R.C., Eriksen, M.P., Davis, R.M. and Warner, K.E. (1997) Environmental tobacco smoke: health effects and policies to reduce exposure. *Annual Review of Public Health*, 18: 163–85.

Brownson, R.C., Hopkins, D.P. and Wakefield, M.A. (2002) Effects of smoking restriction in the workplace. *Annual Review of Public Health*, 23: 333–48.

Brownson, R.C., Haire-Joshu, D. and Luke, D.A. (2006) Shaping the context of health: a review of environmental and policy approaches in the prevention of chronic diseases. *Annual Review of Public Health*, 27: 341–70.

Bruch, H. (1961) The transformation of oral impulses in eating disorders: a conceptual approach. *Psychiatric Quarterly*, 35: 458–81.

Brunner, D., Manelis, G., Modan, M. and Levin, S. (1974) Physical activity at work and the incidence of myocardial infarction, angina pectoris and death due to ischemic heart disease. An epidemiological study in Israel collective settlements (kibbutzim). *Journal of Chronic Diseases*, 27: 217–33.

Brunstrom, J.M., Yates, H.M. and Witcomb, G.L. (2004) Dietary restrained and heightened reactivity to food, *Physiology and Behaviour*, 81: 85–90.

Bruun, K., Edwards, G., Lumio, M. *et al.* (1975) *Alcohol Control Policies and Public Health Perspective*, 25. Helsinki: Finnish Foundation for Alcohol Studies.

Buchhalter, A.R. *et al.* (2005) Tobacco abstinence symptom suppression: the role played by the smoking-related stimuli that are delivered by denicotinized cigarettes, *Addiction*, 100: 550–9.

Buchner, D.M., Beresford, S.A.A., Larson, E.B. *et al.* (1992) Effects of physical activity on health status in older adults II: intervention studies. *Annual Review of Public Health*, 13: 469–88.

Budd, R.J. and Rollnick, S. (1996) The structure of the readiness to change questionnaire: a test of Prochaska and DiClemente's transtheoretical model. *British Journal of Health Psychology*, 1: 365–76.

Butryn, M.L. and Wadden, T.A. (2005) Treatment of overweight in children an adolescents: does dieting increase the risk of eating disorders? *International Journal of Eating Disorders*, 37: 285–93.

Byers, T., Mullis, R., Anderson, J. *et al.* (1995) The cost and effects of a nutritional education program following work-site cholesterol screening. *American Journal of Public Health*, 85: 650–5.

Byrne, D. (1961) The repression–sensitization scale: rationale, reliability and validity. *Journal of Personality*, 29: 334–49.

Byrne, D.G., Whyte, H.M. and Butler, K.L. (1981) Illness behaviour and outcome following survived myocardial infarction: a prospective study. *Journal of Psychosomatic Research*, 25: 97–107.

Cambiano, V., Lampe, F.C., Rodger, A.J. *et al.* (2010) Long-term trends in adherence to antirretroviral therapy from start of HAART. *AIDS*, 24: 1153–62.

Canning, H. and Mayer, J. (1966) Obesity – its possible effect on college acceptance. *New England Journal of Medicine*, 275: 1172–4.

Cannon, W.B. (1929) *Bodily Changes in Pain, Hunger, Fear, and Rage*. Boston, MA: C.T. Branford.

Caplan, R.D. (1983) Person–environment fit: past, present and future, in C.L. Cooper (ed.) *Stress Research*, pp. 35–78. New York: Wiley.

Cappell, H. and Greeley, J. (1987) Alcohol and tension reduction: an update on research and theory, in H.T. Blane and K.E. Leonard (eds) *Psychological Theories of Drinking and Alcoholism*, pp. 15–54. New York: Guilford Press.

Carey, M.P., Kalra, D.L., Carey, K.B. *et al.* (1993) Stress and unaided smoking cessation: a prospective investigation. *Journal of Consulting and Clinical Psychology*, 61: 831–8.

Carleton, R.A., Lasater, T.M., Assaf, A.R. *et al.* (1995) The Pawtucket Heart Health Program: community changes in cardiovascular risk factors and projected disease risk. *American Journal of Public Health*, 85: 777–85.

Carver, C.S. and Scheier, M.F. (1990) Origins and functions of positive and negative affect: a control-process view. *Psychological Review*, 97: 19–35.

Carver, C.S., Pozo, C., Harris, S.D. *et al.* (1993) How coping mediates the effects of optimism on distress: a study of women with early stages breast cancer. *Journal of Personality and Social Psychology*, 65: 375–90.

Cataldo, M.F. and Coates, T.J. (eds) (1986) *Health and Industry: A Behavioral Medicine Perspective*. New York: Wiley.

Catley, D. and Grobe, J.E. (2008) Using basic laboratory research to understand scheduled smoking: a field investigation of the effects of manipulating controllability on subjective responses to smoking. *Health Psychology*, 27 (3 Suppl.): S189–96.

CDC AIDS Community Demonstration Projects Research Group (1999) Community-level HIV Intervention in 5 cities: final outcome data from the CDC AIDS community demonstration project. *American Journal of Public Health*, 89: 336–45.

CDC (Centers for Disease Control) (1994) Cigarette smoking among adults – United States, 1993. *Morbidity and Mortality Weekly Report*, 43: 925–30.

CDC (Centers for Disease Control) (2002) Cigarette smoking among adults – United States, 2000. *Morbidity and Mortality Weekly Report*, 51: 642–5.

CDC (Centers for Disease Control) (2008a) Cigarette smoking among adults – United States, 2007. *Morbidity and Mortality Weekly Report*, 57: 1221–6.

CDC (Centers for Disease Control) (2008b) Smoking-attributable mortality, years of potential life lost and productivity losses – United States, 2000–2004. *Morbidity and Mortality Weekly Report*, 57: 1226–8.

CDC (Centers for Disease Control) (2010) *National Vital Statistics Report*, 58: 19, http://www.cdc.gov/NCHS/data/nvsr/nvsr58/nvsr58_19.pdf.

Chaiken, S. (1980) Heuristic versus systematic information processing and the use of source versus message cues in persuasion. *Journal of Personality and Social Psychology*, 39: 725–66.

Chaiken, S. and Maheswaran, D. (1994) Heuristic processing can bias systematic processing: effects of source credibility, argument ambiguity, and task importance on attitude judgment. *Journal of Personality and Social Psychology*, 66: 460–73.

Chaiken, S., Giner-Sorolla, R. and Chen, S. (1996a) Beyond accuracy: defense and impression motives in heuristic and systematic information processing, in P.M. Gollwitzer and J.A. Bargh (eds) *The Psychology of Action: Linking Motivation and Cognition to Behavior*, pp. 553–78. New York: Guilford Press.

Chaiken, S., Wood, W. and Eagly, A. (1996b) Principles of persuasion, in E.T. Higgins and A.W. Kruglanski (eds) *Social Psychology: Handbook of Basic Principles*, pp. 702–44. New York: Guilford Press.

Chaney, E.F., O'Leary, M.R. and Marlatt, G.A. (1978) Skill training with alcoholics. *Journal of Consulting and Clinical Psychology*, 46: 1092–104.

Chang, E.C. (1998) Dispositional optimism and primary and secondary appraisal of a stressor: controlling for confounding influences and relations to coping and psychological adjustment. *Journal of Personality and Social Psychology*, 74: 1109–20.

Chapman, S. (2009) The inverse impact law of smoking cessation. *Lancet*, 373: 701–3.

Chassin, L., Presson, C.C., Sherman, S.J., Corty, E. and Olshavsky, R. (1984) Predicting the onset of cigarette smoking in adolescents: a longitudinal study. *Journal of Applied Social Psychology*, 14: 224–43.

Chassin, L., Presson, C.C., Sherman, S.J. and Edwards, D.A. (1990) The natural history of cigarette smoking: predicting young-adult smoking outcomes from adolescent smoking patterns. *Health Psychology*, 9: 701–16.

Chen, M. and Bargh, J.A. (1999) Consequences of automatic evaluation: immediate behavioural predisposition to approach or avoid the stimulus. *Personality and Social Psychology Bulletin*, 25: 215–24.

Chen, S. and Chaiken, S. (1999) The heuristic-systematic model in its broader context, in S. Chaiken and Y. Trope (eds) *Dual-process Theories in Social Psychology*, pp. 73–97. New York: Guilford.

Chesney, M. (2003). Adherence to HAART regimens. *AIDS Patient Care and STDs*, 17: 169–77.

Chida, Y. and Steptoe, A. (2009) The association of anger and hostility with future coronary heart disease: a meta-analytic review of prospective evidence. *Journal of the American College of Cardiology*, 53: 936–46.

Chiolero, A., Wietlisbach, V., Ruffieux, C. *et al.* (2006) Clustering of risk behavior with cigarette consumption: a population-based survey. *Preventive Medicine*, 42: 348–53.

Cholesterol Treatment Trialists' Collaborators (2005) Efficacy and safety of cholesterol-lowering treatment: prospective meta-analysis of data from 90,056 participants in 14 randomised trials of statins. *Lancet*, 366: 1267–78.

Christophersen, E.R. (1989) Injury control. *American Psychologist*, 44: 237–41.

Cinciripini, P.M., Lapitsky, L., Seay, S. *et al.* (1995) The effects of smoking schedules on cessation outcome: can we improve on common methods of gradual or abrupt nicotine withdrawal? *Journal of Consulting and Clinical Psychology*, 63: 388–99.

Clarkson, T.B., Manuck, S.B. and Kaplan, J.R. (1986) Potential role of cardiovascular reactivity in atherogenesis, in K.A. Matthews, S.M. Weiss, T. Detre *et al.* (eds) *Handbook of Stress, Reactivity and Cardiovascular Disease*, pp. 35–47. New York: Wiley.

Clarkson, T.B., Kaplan, J.R., Adams, M.R. and Manuck, S.B. (1987) Psychosocial influences on the pathogenesis of atherosclerosis among nonhuman primates. *Circulation*, 76 (Suppl. 1): 29–40.

Cloninger, C.R., Bohman, M. and Sigvardsson, S. (1981) Inheritance of alcohol abuse. *Archives of General Psychiatry*, 38: 861–8.

Coates, T., Stall, R., Catania, J., Dolcini, P. and Hoff, C. (1989) Prevention of HIV infection in high risk groups, in P. Volberding and M. Jacobson (eds) *1989 AIDS Clinical Review*. New York: Marcel Dekker.

Cobb, S. (1976) Social support as a moderator of life stress. *Psychosomatic Medicine*, 38: 300–14.

Cobb, S. and Lindemann, E. (1943) Neuropsychiatric observations after the Coconut Grove fire. *Annals of Surgery*, 117: 814–24.

Cohen, J. (1992) A power primer. *Psychological Bulletin*, 112: 155–9.

Cohen, S. (2004) Social relationships and health. *American Psychologist*, 59: 676–84.

Cohen, S. and Edwards, J.R. (1989) Personality characteristics as moderators of the relationship between stress and disorder, in R.W.J. Neufeld (ed.) *Advances in the Investigation of Psychological Stress*, pp. 235–83. New York: Wiley.

Cohen, S. and Herbert, T.B. (1996) Health psychology: psychological factors and physical disease from the perspective of human psychoneuroimmunology. *Annual Review of Psychology*, 47: 113–42.

Cohen, S. and McKay, G. (1984) Social support, stress, and the buffering hypothesis: a theoretical analysis, in A. Baum, J.E. Singer and S.E. Taylor (eds) *Handbook of Psychology and Health*, Vol. 4, pp. 253–67. Hillsdale, NJ: Lawrence Erlbaum.

Cohen, S. and Williamson, G.M. (1988) Perceived stress in a probability sample of the United States, in S. Spacapan and S. Oskamp (eds) *The Social Psychology of Health*, pp. 17–67. Newbury Park, CA: Sage.

Cohen, S. and Williamson, G.M. (1991) Stress and infectious disease in humans. *Psychological Bulletin*, 109: 5–24.

Cohen, S. and Wills, T.A. (1985) Stress, social support, and the buffering hypothesis. *Psychological Bulletin*, 98: 310–57.

Cohen, S., Mermelstein, R., Kamarck, T. and Hoberman, H.N. (1985) Measuring the functional components of social support, in I.G. Sarason and B.R. Sarason (eds) *Social Support: Theory, Research, and Applications*, pp. 73–94. Dordrecht: Martinus Nijhoff.

Cohen, S., Lichtenstein, E., Prochaska, J.O. *et al.* (1989) Debunking myths about self-quitting. *American Psychologist*, 44: 1355–65.

Cohen, S., Tyrell, D. and Smith, A. (1993) Negative life events, perceived stress, negative affect, and susceptibility to the common cold. *Journal of Personality and Social Psychology*, 64: 131–40.

Cohen, S., Frank, E., Doyle, W.J. *et al.* (1998) Types of stressors that increase susceptibility to the common cold in healthy adults. *Health Psychology*, 17: 214–23.

Cohen, S., Doyle, W.J., Turner, R. *et al.* (2003) Sociability and susceptibility to the common cold. *Psychological Science*, 14: 389–95.

Cole, P. and Rodu, B. (1996) Declining cancer mortality in the United States. *Cancer*, 78: 2045–8.

COMMIT Research Group (1995) Community intervention trial for smoking cessation (COMMIT): I. Cohort results from a four-year community intervention. *American Journal of Public Health*, 85: 183–92.

Committee on Diet and Health (1989) *Diet and Health*. Washington, DC: National Academy Press.

Committee on Trauma Research (1985) *Injury in America: A Continuing Public Health Problem*. Washington, DC: National Academy Press.

Condiotte, M.M. and Lichtenstein, E. (1981) Self-efficacy and relapse in smoking cessation programs. *Journal of Consulting and Clinical Psychology*, 49: 648–58.

Conner, M. and Sparks, P. (2005) Theory of planned behaviour and health behaviour, in M. Conner and P. Norman (eds) *Predicting Health Behavior*, pp. 170–222. Maidenhead: Open University Press.

Conner, M., Sandberg, T., McMillan, B. and Higgins, A. (2006) Role of anticipated regret, intention and intention stability in adolescent smoking initiation. *British Journal of Health Psychology*, 11: 85–101.

Cook, W. and Medley, D. (1954) Proposed hostility for Pharisaic-virtue-skills of the MMPI. *Journal of Applied Psychology*, 38: 414–18.

Cooney, N.L., Zweben, A. and Fleming, M.F. (1995) Screening for alcohol problems and at-risk drinking in health-care settings, in R.K. Hester and W.R. Miller (eds) *Handbook of Alcoholism Treatment Approaches*, 2nd edn, pp. 54–60. Boston, MA: Allyn & Bacon.

Cooper, M.L., Frone, M.R., Russell, M. and Mudar, P. (1995) Drinking regulates positive and negative emotions: a motivational model of alcohol use. *Journal of Personality and Social Psychology*, 69: 990–1005.

Corrao, G., Bgnardi, V., Zambon, A. and La Vecchia, C. (2004) A meta-analysis of alcohol consumption and the risk of 15 diseases. *Preventive Medicine*, 38: 613–19.

Craighead, L.W. (1984) Sequencing of behavior therapy and pharmacotherapy for obesity. *Journal of Consulting and Clinical Psychology*, 52: 190–9.

Craighead, L.W., Stunkard, A.J. and O'Brien, R. (1981) Behavior therapy and pharmacotherapy for obesity. *Archives of General Psychiatry*, 38: 763–8.

Crepaz, N., Hart, T.A. and Marks, G. (2004) Highly active antiretroviral therapy and sexual risk behavior: a meta-analytic review. *Journal of the American Medical Association*, 292: 224–36.

Cummings, K.M. and Hyland, A. (2005) Impact of nicotine replacement therapy on smoking behavior. *Annual Review of Public Health*, 26: 583–99.

Curran, J.W., Jaffe, H.W., Hardy, A.M. *et al.* (1988) Epidemiology of HIV infection and AIDS in the United States. *Science*, 239: 610–16.

Custers, R. and Aarts, R. (2005a) Positive affect as implicit motivator: on the nonconscious operation of behavioral goals. *Journal of Personality and Social Psychology*, 89: 129–42.

Custers, R. and Aarts, R. (2005b) Beyond priming effects: the role of positive affect and discrepancies in implicit processes of motivation and goal pursuit, in W. Stroebe and M. Hewstone (eds) *European Review of Social Psychology*, 16: 257–300.

Custers, R. and Aarts, H. (2007) In search of the nonconscious sources of goal pursuit: accessibility and positive affective valence of the goal state. *Journal of Experimental Social Psychology*, 43: 312–18.

Cutler, R.B. and Fishbain, D.A. (2005) Are alcoholism treatments effective? The Project MATCH data. *BMC Public Health*, 5: 75.

Dahlkoetter, J.A., Callahan, E.J. and Linton, J. (1979) Obesity and the unbalanced energy equation: exercise versus eating habit change. *Journal of Consulting and Clinical Psychology*, 47: 898–905.

Danner, U.H., Aarts, H. and deVries, N.K. (2008) Habit vs. intention in predicting future behaviour: the role of frequency, context stability and mental accessibility of past behaviour. *British Journal of Social Psychology*, 47: 245–65.

Dansinger, M.L. *et al.* (2005) Comparison of the Atkins, Ornish, Weight Watchers, and Zone diets for weight loss and heart disease risk reduction. *Journal of the American Medical Association*, 293: 43–53.

Das, E., DeWit, J. and Stroebe, W. (2003) Fear appeals motivate acceptance of action recommendations: evidence for a positive bias in the processing of persuasive messages. *Personality and Social Psychology Bulletin*, 29: 650–64.

Davis, R.M., Wakefield, M., Amos, A. and Gupta, P.C. (2007) The hitchhiker's guide to tobacco control: a global assessment of harms, remedies, and controversies. *Annual Review of Public Health*, 28: 171–94.

de Bruijn, G.-J. *et al.* (2007) Does habit strength moderate the intention-behaviour relationship in the Theory of Planned Behaviour? The case of fruit consumption. *Psychology and Health*, 22: 899–916.

de Hoog, N., Stroebe, W. and de Wit, J. (2005) The impact of fear appeals on processing and accepting action recommendations. *Personality and Social Psychology Bulletin*, 31, 24–33.

de Hoog, N., Stroebe, W. and de Wit, J. (2007) The impact of vulnerability to and severity of a health risk on processing and acceptance of fear-arousing communications: a meta-analysis. *Review of General Psychology*, 11: 258–85.

De Houwer, J., Teige-Mocigemba, S., Spruyt, A. and Moors, A. (2009) Implicit measures: a normative analysis and review. *Psychological Bulletin*, 135: 347–68.

DeJong, W. and Hingson, R. (1998) Strategies to reduce driving under the influence of alcohol. *Annual Review of Public Health*, 19: 359–78.

de Lint, J. (1976) Epidemiological aspects of alcoholism. *International Journal of Mental Health*, 5: 29–51.

DeLongis, A., Coyne, J.C., Dakof, G. *et al.* (1982) Relationship of daily hassles, uplifts, and major life events to health status. *Health Psychology*, 1: 119–36.

DeLongis, A., Folkman, S. and Lazarus, R.S. (1988) The impact of daily stress on health and mood: psychological and social resources as mediators. *Journal of Personality and Social Psychology*, 54: 486–95.

De Lorgeril, M., Salen, P., Martin, J-L., *et al.* (1999) Mediterranean diet, traditional risk factors, and the rate of cardiovascular complications after myocardial infarction: final report of the Lyon Diet Heart Study. *Circulation*, 99: 779–85.

Dépres, J.-P. and Krauss, R.M. (1988) Obesity and lipoprotein metabolism, in G.A. Bray, C. Bouchard and W.P.T. James (eds) *Handbook of Obesity*, pp. 651–76. New York: Dekker.

Detels, R., English, P., Visscher, B.R. *et al.* (1989) Seroconversion, sexual activity and condom use among 2915 HIV seronegative men followed for up to three years. *Journal of Acquired Immune Deficiency Syndromes*, 2: 77–83.

de Vet, E., de Nooijer, J., de Vries, N.K. and Brug, J. (2008) Testing the transtheoretical model for fruit intake: comparing web-based tailored stage-matched and stage mismatched feedback. *Health Education Research*, 23: 218–27.

De Vries, H., Backbier, E., Kok, G.J. and Dijkstra, A. (1995) The impact of social influences in the context of attitude, self-efficacy, intention and previous behavior as predictors of smoking onset. *Journal of Applied Social Psychology*, 25: 237–57.

de Vroome, E.M.M., Stroebe, W., Sandfort, T.G.M. *et al.* (2000) Safe sex in social context: individualistic and relational determinants of AIDS preventive behavior among gay men. *Journal of Applied Social Psychology*, 30: 2322–40.

de Wit, J.B.F., Kok, G.J., Timmermans, C.A.M. and Wijnsma, P. (1990) Determinanten van veilig vrijen en condoomgebruik bij jongeren. *Gedrag en Gezondheid*, 18: 121–33.

de Wit, J.B.F., de Vroome, E.M.M., Sandfort, T.G.M. *et al.* (1992) Safe sexual practices not reliably maintained by homosexual men. *American Journal of Public Health*, 82: 615–16.

de Wit, J.B.F., Sandfort, T.G.M., de Vroome, E., van Griensven, G.J.P. and Kok, G. (1993) The effectiveness of the use of condoms among homosexual men. *AIDS*, 7: 751–2.

de Wit, J., Stroebe, W., de Vroome, E.M.M. *et al.* (2000) Understanding AIDS preventive behavior in homosexual men: the theory of planned behavior and the information–motivation–skills model prospectively compared. *Psychology and Health*, 15: 325—340.

Dhabar, F.S. and McEwen, B.S. (1997) Acute stress enhances while chronic stress suppresses cell-mediated immunity in vivo: a potential role for lukocyte trafficking. *Brain, Behavior, and Immunity*, 11: 286–306.

Dickerson, S.S. and Kemeny, M.E. (2004) Acute stressors and cortisol response: a theoretical integration and synthesis of laboratory research. *Psychological Bulletin*, 130: 355–91.

Dijksterhuis, A. and van Knippenberg, A. (1998) The relation between perception and behavior, or how to win a game of Trivial Pursuit. *Journal of Personality and Social Psychology*, 74: 865–77.

Dijkstra, A., de Vries, H. and Parcel, G. (1992) The linkage approach applied to a school-based smoking prevention program in the Netherlands. *Journal of School Health*, 63: 339–42.

Dijkstra, A., de Vries, H., Roijackers, J. and van Breukelen (1996) Voorlichting op maat over stoppen met roken: een veldexperiment. *Gedrag and Gezondheid*, 24: 314–22.

Dijkstra, A., de Vries, H., Roijackers, J. and van Breukelen (1998) Tailored interventions to communicate stage-matched information to smokers in different motivational stages. *Journal of Consulting and Clinical Psychology*, 66: 549–57.

Dijkstra, A., Conijn, B. and de Vries, H. (2006) A match-mismatch test of a stage model of behaviour change in tobacco smoking. *Addiction*, 101: 1035–43.

Dilorio, C., McCarthy, F., DePadilla, L. *et al.* (2009) Adherence to antiretorviral medication regimens: a test of a psychosocial model. *AIDS Behavior*, 13: 10–22.

DiMatteo, M.R. (2004) Social support and patient adherence to medical treatment: a meta-analysis. *Health Psychology*, 23: 207–18.

Dimsdale, J.E. and Herd, A.J. (1982) Variability of plasma lipids in response to emotional arousal. *Psychosomatic Medicine*, 44: 413–30.

Dishman, R.K. (1982) Compliance/adherence in health-related exercise. *Health Psychology*, 1: 237–67.

Dishman, R.K. and Gettman, L.R. (1980) Psychobiologic influences on exercise adherence. *Journal of Sport Psychology*, 2: 295–310.

Djuric, Z. *et al.* (2002) Combining weight-loss counseling with the Weight Watchers plan for obese breast cancer survivors. *Obesity Research*, 10: 657–64.

Doherty, K., Militello, F.S., Kinnunen, T. and Garvey, A.J. (1996) Nicotine gum dose and weight gain after smoking cessation. *Journal of Consulting and Clinical Psychology*, 64: 799–807.

Dohrenwend, B.P. (1973) Social status and stressful life events. *Journal of Personality and Social Psychology*, 28: 225–35.

Dohrenwend, B.P. and Shrout, P.E. (1985) 'Hassles' in the conceptualization and measurement of life stress variables. *American Psychologist*, 40: 780–5.

Dohrenwend, B.S., Dohrenwend, B.P., Dodson, M. and Shrout, P.E. (1984) Symptoms, hassles, social supports, and life events: problem of confounded measures. *Journal of Abnormal Psychology*, 93: 222–30.

Donny, E.C., Houtsmuller, E. and Stitzer, M.L. (2006) Smoking in the absence of nicotine: behavioural, subjective and physiological effects over 11 days. *Addiction*, 102: 324–34.

Douglas, S. and Hariharan, G. (1993) The hazard of starting smoking: estimates from a split population duration model. *Journal of Health Economics*, 13: 213–30.

Dovidio, J.F. *et al.* (1997) The nature of prejudice: automatic and controlled processes. *Journal of Experimental Social Psychology*, 33: 510–40.

Dovidio, J.F., Kawakami, K. and Beach, K.R. (2001) Implicit and explicit attitudes: examination of the relationship, in R. Brown and S. Gaertner (eds) *Blackwell Handbook of Social Psychology*, pp. 175–97. Oxford: Blackwell.

Dunkel-Schetter, C. and Bennett, T.L. (1990) Differentiating the cognitive and behavioral aspects of social support, in B.R. Sarason, I.G. Sarason and G.R. Pierce (eds) *Social Support: An Interactional View*, pp. 267–96. New York: Wiley.

Dunn, A.L., Anderson, R.E. and Jakcic, J.M. (1998) Lifestyle physical activity interventions: history, short and long-term effects, and recommendations. *American Journal of Preventive Medicine*, 15: 398–412.

Dunn, A.L., Trivedi, M.H., Kampert, J.B. and Clark, C.G. (2005) Exercise treatment for depression: efficacy and dose response. *American Journal of Preventive Medicine*, 28: 1–8.

Eagly, A.H. and Chaiken, S. (1993) *The Psychology of Attitudes*. Fort Worth, TX: Harcourt Brace Jovanovich.

Eagly, A.H. and Chaiken, S. (2007) The advantage of an inclusive definition of attitude. *Social Cognition*, 25: 582–602.

Eaker, E.D., Pinsky, J. and Castelli, W.P. (1992) Myocardial infarction and coronary death among women: psychosocial predictors from a 20-year follow-up of women in the Framingham Study. *American Journal of Epidemiology*, 135: 854–64.

Earl, A. and Albarracin, D. (2007) Nature, decay, and spiraling of the effects of fear-inducing arguments and HIV counseling and testing: a meta-analysis of the short- and long-term outcomes of HIV-prevention interventions. *Health Psychology*, 26: 496–596.

Eckenrode, J. and Bolger, N. (1995) Daily and within-day event measurement, in S. Cohen, R.C. Kessler and L. Underwood Gordon (eds) *Measuring Stress*, pp. 80–101. New York: Oxford University Press.

Egger, G., Fitzgerald, W., Frape, G. *et al*. (1983) Result of large scale media antismoking campaign in Australia: North Coast 'Quit For Life' Programme. *British Medical Journal*, 286: 1125–8.

Elkins, R.L. (1980) Covert sensitization treatment for alcoholism: contributions of successful conditioning to subsequent abstinence maintenance. *Addictive Behaviors*, 5: 67–89.

Emrick, C.C., Tonigan, J.S. and Little, L. (1993) Alcoholics Anonymous: what is currently known? in B.S. McCready and W.R. Miller (eds) *Research in Alcoholics Anonymous*, pp. 41–76. Picataway, NJ: Rutgers Center for Alcohol Studies.

Endler, N.S. and Parker, J.D.A. (1990) Multidimensional assessment of coping: a critical evaluation. *Journal of Personality and Social Psychology*, 58: 844–54.

Engel, G.L. (1977) The need for a new medical model: a challenge for biomedicine. *Science*, 196: 129–36.

ENRICHD Investigators (2003) Effects of treating depression and low perceived social support on clinical events after myocardial infarction: the enhancing recovery in coronary heart disease patients (ENRICHD) randomized trial. *Journal of the American Medical Association*, 289: 3106–16.

Epping-Jordan, J.E., Compas, B.E. and Howell, D.C. (1994) Predictors of cancer progression in young adult men and women: avoidance, intrusive thoughts, and psychological symptoms. *Health Psychology*, 13: 539–47.

Epstein, L.H., Valoski, A., Wing, R.R. and McCurley, J. (1994) Ten-year outcomes of behavioral family-based treatment for childhood obesity. *Health Psychology*, 13: 373–83.

Epstein, S. (1979) The stability of behavior: on predicting most of the people much of the time. *Journal of Personality and Social Psychology*, 37: 1097–126.

Erber, M.W., Hodges, S.D. and Wilson, T.D. (1995) Attitude strength, attitude stability, and the effects of analyzing reasons, in R.E. Petty and J.A. Krosnick (eds) *Attitude Strength: Antecedents and Consequences*, pp. 433–54. Mawah, NJ: Erlbaum.

Estruch, R., Martinez-Gonzales, M.A., Corella, D. *et al*. (2006) Effects of a Mediterranean diet on cardiovascular risk factors: a randomized trial. *Annals of Internal Medicine*, 145: 1–11.

Evans, R.I., Rozelle, R.M., Mittelmark, M.D. *et al*. (1978) Deterring the onset of smoking in children: knowledge of immediate physiological effects and coping with peer pressure, media pressure, and parent modelling. *Journal of Applied Social Psychology*, 8: 126–35.

Ewing, J. (1984) Detecting alcoholism: the CAGE questionnaire. *Journal of the American Medical Association*, 252: 1905–7.

Fang, C.T., Chang, Y.Y., Hsu, H.M. *et al*. (2007) Life expectancy of patients with newly-diagnosed HIV infection in the era of highly active antiretroviral therapy. *QJM*, 100: 97–105.

Farber, P.D., Khavari, K.A. and Douglass, F.M. (1980) A factor analytic study of reasons for drinking: empirical validation of positive and negative reinforcement dimensions. *Journal of Consulting and Clinical Psychology*, 48: 780–1.

Farquhar, J.W., Maccoby, N., Wood, P.D. *et al*. (1977) Community education for cardiovascular health. *Lancet*, 4 June: 1192–5.

Farquhar, J.W., Fortman, S.P., Flora, J.A. *et al*. (1990) Effects of a communitywide education on cardiovascular disease risk factors: the Stanford Five-City project. *Journal of the American Medical Association*, 264: 359–65.

Farrell, P. and Fuchs, V. (1982) Schooling and health: the cigarette connection. *Journal of Health Economics*, 1: 217–30.

Fazio, R.H. (1990) Multiple processes by which attitudes guide behavior: the MODE model as an integrative framework, in M.P. Zanna (ed.) *Advances in Experimental Social Psychology*, Vol. 23, pp. 75–109. San Diego, CA: Academic Press.

Fazio, R.H. and Olson, M.A. (2003) Implicit measures in social cognition research: their meaning and use. *Annual Review of Psychology*, 54: 297–327.

Fazio, R.H. and Towles-Schwen, T. (1999) The MODE model of attitude behaviour processes, in S. Chaiken and Y. Trope (eds) *Dual-process Theories in Social Psychology*, pp. 97–115. New York: Guilford Press.

Fazio, R.H. and Williams, C.J. (1986) Attitude accessibility as moderator of the attitude-behavior relation: an investigation of the 1984 presidential election. *Journal of Personality and Social Psychology*, 51: 505–14.

Fazio, R.H., Sanbonmatsu, D.M., Powell, M.C. and Kardes, F.R. (1986) On the automatic activation of attitudes. *Journal of Personality and Social Psychology*, 50: 229–38.

Fazio, R.H., Jackson, J.R., Dunton, B.C. and Williams, C.J. (1995) Variability in automatic activation as an unobtrusive measure of racial attitudes: a bona fide pipeline? *Journal of Personality and Social Psychology*, 69: 1013–27.

Fedoroff, I.C., Polivy, J. and Herman, C.P. (1997) The effect of pre-exposure to food cues on the eating behavior of restrained and unrestrained eaters. *Appetite*, 28: 33–47.

Feng, J. *et al.* (2006) Cardiac sequelae in Brooklyn after the September 11 terrorist attacks. *Clinical Cardiology*, 29: 13–17.

Ferri, M., Amato, L. and Davoli, M. (2009) Alcoholics Anonymous and other 12-step programmes for alcohol dependence. *The Cochrane Library*, 3, http://onlinelibrary.wiley.com/o/cochrane/clsysrev/articles/CD005032/pdf_fs.html (accessed August 2010).

Festinger, L. (1954) A theory of social comparison processes. *Human Relations*, 7: 117–40.

Festinger, L. (1957) *A Theory of Cognitive Dissonance*. Palo Alto. CA: Stanford University Press.

Fhanér, G. and Hane, M. (1979) Seat belts: opinion effects of law-induced use. *Journal of Applied Psychology*, 64: 205–12.

Fidler, W. and Lambert, T. (2001) A prescription for health: a primary care based intervention to maintain the non-smoking status of young people. *Tobacco Control*, 10: 23–6.

Field, M., Kiernan, A., Eastwood, B. and Child, R. (2007) Rapid approach responses to alcohol cues in heavy drinkers. *Journal of Behavior Therapy and Experimental Psychiatry*, 39: 209–18.

Fielding, J.E. (1985) Smoking: health effects and control. *New England Journal of Medicine*, 313: 491–8.

Fielding, J.E. (1986) Evaluations, results and problems of worksite health promotion, in M.F. Cataldo and T.J. Coates (eds) *Health and Industry*, pp. 373–96. New York: Wiley.

Fielding, J.E. and Piserchia, P.V. (1989) Frequency of worksite health promotion activities. *American Journal of Public Health*, 78: 16–20.

Fikkan, J. and Rothblum, E. (2005) Weight bias in employment, in K.D. Brownell, R.M. Puhl, M.B. Schwartz and L. Rudd (eds) *Weight Bias: Nature, Consequences and Remedies*, pp. 15–28. New York: Guilford.

Fillmore, M.T. and Vogel-Sprott, M. (1995) Expectancies about alcohol-induced motor impairment predict individual differences in responses to alcohol and placebo. *Journal of Studies on Alcohol*, 56: 90–8.

Fillmore, M.T., Cascadden, J.L. and Vogel-Sprott, M. (1998) Alcohol, cognitive impairment and expectancies. *Journal of Studies on Alcohol*, 59: 174–9.

Fiore, M.C., Novotny, T.E., Pierce, J.P. *et al.* (1990) Methods used to quit smoking in the United States: do cessation programs work? *Journal of the American Medical Association*, 263: 2760–5.

Fishbach, A. and Shah, J.Y. (2006) Self-control in action: implicit dispositions towards goals and away from temptations. *Journal of Personality and Social Psychology*, 90: 820–32.

Fishbach, A., Friedman, R.S. and Kruglanski, A.W. (2003) Leading us not into temptation: momentary allurements elicit overriding goal activation. *Journal of Personality and Social Psychology*, 84: 296–309.

Fishbein, M. and Ajzen, I. (1975) *Belief, Attitude, Intention, and Behavior: An Introduction to Theory and Research*. Reading, MA: Addison-Wesley.

Fishbein, M., Middlestadt, S.E. and Hitchcock, P.J. (1994) Using information to change sexually transmitted disease-related behaviours: an analysis based on the theory of reasoned action, in R. DiClemente and J.L. Peterson (eds) *Preventing Aids: Theories and Methods of Behavioural Interventions*, pp. 61–78. New York: Plenum.

Fisher, J.D. and Fisher, W.A. (1992) Changing Aids-risk behavior. *Psychological Bulletin*, 111: 455–74.

Fisher, R.A. (1958) Cancer and smoking (letter). *Nature*, 182: 596.

Fisher, W.A., Fisher, J.D. and Rye, B.J. (1995) Understanding and promoting AIDS-preventive behavior: insights from the theory of reasoned action. *Health Psychology*, 14: 255–64.

Fitzgibbon, M.S., Stolley, M.R. and Kirschenbaum, D.S. (1994) Obese people who seek treatment have different characteristics than those who do not seek treatment. *Health Psychology*, 12: 342–5.

Flechtner-Mors, M. *et al.* (2000) Metabolic and weight loss effects of long-term dietary intervention in obese patients: four-year results. *Obesity Research*, 8: 399–402.

Fleischer, G.A. (1972) An experiment in the use of broadcast media in highway safety. Unpublished paper, University of Southern California, Department of Industrial Systems Engineering, Los Angeles (reported in Robertson 1987).

Floyd, D.L., Prentice-Dunn, S. and Rodgers, R.W. (2000) A meta-analysis of research on protection motivation theory. *Journal of Applied Social Psychology*, 30: 407–29.

Folkman, S. and Lazarus, R.S. (1980) An analysis of coping in a middle-aged community sample. *Journal of Health and Social Behavior*, 21: 219–39.

Folkman, S., Lazarus, R.S., Dunkel-Schetter, C. *et al.* (1986a) The dynamics of a stressful encounter. *Journal of Personality and Social Psychology*, 50: 992–1003.

Folkman, S., Lazarus, R.S., Gruen, R.J. and DeLongis, A. (1986b) Appraisal, coping, health status and psychological symptoms. *Journal of Personality and Social Psychology*, 50: 571–9.

Försterling, F. (1988) *Attribution Theory in Clinical Psychology*. Chichester: Wiley.

Foster, G.D., Wadden, T.A., Kendall, P.C. *et al.* (1996) Psychological effects of weight loss and regain: a prospective study. *Journal of Consulting and Clinical Psychology*, 64: 752–7.

Frattaroli, J. (2006) Experimental disclosure and its moderators: a meta-analysis. *Psychological Bulletin*, 132: 823–65.

Frederiksen, H. and Christensen, K. (2003) The influence of genetic factors on physical functioning and exercise in second half of life. *Scandinavian Journal of Medicine and Science in Sports*, 13: 9–18.

French, J.R.P. Jr. and Kahn, R.L. (1962) A problematic approach to studying the industrial environment and mental health. *Journal of Social Issues*, 18: 1–47.

French, S.A. and Jeffery, R.W. (1995) Weight concerns and smoking: a literature review. *Annals of Behavioral Medicine*, 17: 234–44.

French, S.A., Jeffery, R.W., Klesges, L.M. and Forster, J.L. (1995) Weight concerns and change in smoking behavior over two years in a working population. *American Journal of Public Health*, 85: 720–2.

French, S.A., Henrikus, D.J. and Jeffery, R.W. (1996) Smoking status, dietary intake, and physical activity in a sample of working adults. *Health Psychology*, 15: 448–54.

French, S.A. *et al.* (1997) A pricing strategy to promote low-fat snack choices through vending machines. *American Journal of Public Health*, 87: 849–51.

French, S.A., Story, M. and Jeffery, R.W. (2001) Environmental influences on eating and physical activity. *Annual Review of Public Health*, 22: 309–36.

Friedland, G.H. and Klein, R.S. (1987) Transmission of the HIV. *New England Journal of Medicine*, 317: 1125–35.

Friedman, M. and Rosenman, R.H. (1974) *Type A Behavior and Your Heart*. New York: Knopf.

Friedman, R.S., McCarthy, D.M., Förster, J. and Denzler, M. (2004) Automatic effects of alcohol cues on sexual atraction. *Addiction*, 100: 672–81.

Friedman, R.S., McCarthy, D.M., Förster, J. and Denzler, M. (2005) Automatic effects of alcohol cues on sexual attraction. *Addiction*, 100: 672–81.

Fries, J.F., Green, L.W. and Levine, S. (1989) Health promotion and the compression of morbidity. *Lancet*, I: 481–3.

Friese, M., Hofmann, W. and Schmitt, M. (2008a) When and why do implicit measures predict behaviour? Empirical evidence for the moderating role of opportunity, motivation, and process reliance. *European Review of Social Psychology*, 19: 285–338.

Friese, M., Hofmann, W. and Wänke, M. (2008b) When impulses take over: moderated predictive vadlidity of explicit and implicit attitude measures in predicting food choice and consumption behaviour. *British Journal of Social Psychology*, 47: 397–419.

Friese, M., Hofmann, W. and Wiers, R. (2010) On taming horses and strengthening the riders: recent developments in research on interventions to improve self-control in health behaviors, unpublished manuscript.

Frieze, I.H., Olson, J.E. and Good, D.C. (1990) Perceived and actual discrimination in the salaries of male and female managers. *Journal of Applied Social Psychology*, 20: 46–67.

Fuller, K. (1995) Antidipsotropic medication, in R.K. Hester and W.R. Miller (eds) *Handbook of Alcoholism Treatment Approaches*, 2nd edn, pp. 123–33. Boston, MA: Allyn & Bacon.

Funk, S.C. and Houston, B.K. (1987) A critical analysis of the hardiness scale's validity and utility. *Journal of Personality and Social Psychology*, 53: 572–8.

Furberg, C.D. (1994) Lipid-lowering trials: results and limitations. *American Heart Journal*, 128: 1304–8.

Furst, C.J. (1983) Estimating alcoholic prevalence, in M. Galanter (ed.) *Recent Developments in Alcoholism*, Vol. 1. New York, NY: Plenum.

Gallois, C. *et al.* (1994) Safe sexual intentions and behavior among heterosexual and homosexual men: testing the theory of reasoned action. *Psychology and Health*, 10: 1–16.

Ganellen, R.J. and Blaney, P.H. (1984) Hardiness and social support as moderators of the effects of life stress. *Journal of Personality and Social Psychology*, 47: 156–63.

Gardner, P., Rosenberg, H.M. and Wilson, R.W. (1996) *Leading Causes of Death by Age, Sex, Race, and Hispanic Origin: United States, 1992*. National Center for Health Statistics, *Vital and Health Statistics*, 20(29).

George, W.H. and Marlatt, G.A. (1983) Alcoholism: the evolution of a behavioral perspective, in M. Galanter (ed.) *Recent Developments in Alcoholism*, Vol. 1, pp. 105–38. New York: Plenum.

George, W.H., Frone, M.R., Cooper, M.L. *et al.* (1995) A revised alcohol expectancy questionnaire: factor structure confirmation and invariance in a general population. *Journal of Studies on Alcohol*, 56: 177–85.

Gerrard, M., Gibbons, F.X. and Bushman, B.J. (1996) Relation between perceived vulnerability to HIV and precautionary sexual behavior. *Psychological Bulletin*, 119: 390–409.

Glantz, S.A. and Mandel, L.L. (2005) Since school-based tobacco prevention programs do not work, what should we do? *Journal of Adolescent Health*, 36: 157–9.

Glaser, R. and Kiecolt-Glaser, J. (eds) (1994) *Handbook of Human Stress and Immunity*. San Diego, CA: Academic Press.

Glaser, R., Kiecolt-Glaser, J.K., Speicher, C.E. and Holliday, J.E. (1985) Stress, loneliness, and changes in herpes virus latency. *Journal of Behavioral Medicine*, 8: 249–60.

Glasgow, R.E., Terborg, J.R., Hollis, J.F. *et al.* (1995) Take Heart: results from the initial phase of a worksite wellness program. *American Journal of Public Health*, 85: 209–16.

Glasgow, R.E., Terborg, J.R., Strycker, L.A. *et al.* (1997) Take Heart II: replication of a worksite health promotion trial. *Journal of Behavioral Medicine*, 20: 143–61.

Godin, G. and Kok, G. (1996) The theory of planned behavior: a review of its applications to health-related behavior. *American Journal of Health Promotion*, 11: 87–97.

Godin, G., Sheeran, P., Conner, M. *et al.* (2010) Social structure, social cognition, and physical activity: a test of four models. *British Journal of Health Psychology*, 15: 79–95.

Goldberg, E.L. and Comstock, G.W. (1976) Life events and subsequent illness. *American Journal of Epidemiology*, 104: 146–58.

Goldman, L. and Cook, E.F. (1984) The decline in ischaemic heart disease mortality rates: an analysis of the comparative effects of medical interventions and changes in lifestyle. *Annals of Internal Medicine*, 101: 825–36.

Goldman, M.S., Brown, S.A. and Christiansen, B.A. (1987) Expectancy theory: thinking about drinking, in H.T. Blane and K.E. Leonard (eds) *Psychological Theories of Drinking and alcoholism*, pp. 181–226. New York: Guilford Press.

Goldman, R., Jaffa, M. and Schachter, S. (1968) Yom Kippur, Air France, dormitory food and the eating behavior of obese and normal persons. *Journal of Personality and Social Psychology*, 10: 117–23.

Gollwitzer, P.M. (1999) Implementation intentions: strong effects of simple plans. *American Psychologist*, 54: 493–503.

Gollwitzer, P.M. and Sheeran, P. (2006) Implementation intentions and goal achievement: a meta-analysis of effects and processes, in M.P. Zanna (ed.) *Advances in Experimental Social Psychology*, 38: 69–119. San Diego, CA: Elsevier.

Goodwin, D.W., Schulsinger, F., Hermansen, L. *et al.* (1973) Alcohol problems in adoptees raised apart from alcoholic biological parents. *Archives of General Psychiatry*, 28: 238–43.

Goodwin, D.W., Schulsinger, F., Moller, N. *et al.* (1974) Drinking problems in adopted and nonadopted sons of alcoholics. *Archives of General Psychiatry*, 31: 164–9.

Goodwin, P.J. *et al.* (2001) The effect of group psychosocial support on survival in metastatic breast cancer. *New England Journal of Medicine*, 345: 1719–26.

Gordon, T. and Kannel, W.B. (1973) The effects of overweight on cardiovascular disease. *Geriatrics*, 28: 80–8.

Gortmaker, S.L., Must, A., Perrin, J.M. *et al.* (1993) Social and economic consequences of overweight in adolescence and young adulthood. *New England Journal of Medicine*, 329: 1008–12.

Graham, J.D. (1993) Injuries from traffic crashes: meeting the challenge. *Annual Review of Public Health*, 14: 515–43.

Green, L.W. and Kreuter, M.W. (1991) *Health Promotion Planning: An Educational and Environmental Approach*. Mountain View, CA: Mayfield.

Greeno, C.G. and Wing, R.R. (1994) Stress-induced eating. *Psychological Bulletin*, 115: 444–64.

Greenwald, A.G. (1968) Cognitive learning, cognitive response to persuasion, and attitude change, in A.G. Greenwald, T.C. Brock and T.M. Ostrom (eds) *Psychological Foundations of Attitudes*, pp. 147–70. San Diego, CA: Academic Press.

Greenwald, A.G., McGhee, D.E. and Schwartz, J.L.K. (1998) Measuring individual differences in implicit cognition: the implicit association test. *Journal of Personality and Social Psychology*, 74: 1464–80.

Grilo, C.M. and Pogue-Geile, M.F. (1991) The nature of environmental influences on weight and obesity: a behavior genetic analysis. *Psychological Bulletin*, 110: 520–37.

Gu, M.O. and Conn, V. (2008) Meta-analysis of the effects of exercise interventions on functional status of older adults. *Research in Nursing and Health*, 31: 594–603.

Guo, B., Aveyard, P., Fielding, A. and Sutton, S. (2009) Do the transtheoretical models, processes of change, decisional balance and temptation predict stage movement? Evidence from smoking cessation in adolescents. *Addiction*, 104: 828–38.

Haberman, P.W. and Baden, M.M. (1978) *Alcohol, Other Drugs and Violent Death*. New York: Oxford University Press.

Haddon Jr, W. and Baker, S.P. (1981) Injury control, in D. Clark and B. MacMahon (eds) *Preventive and Community Medicine*, pp. 109–40. Boston, MA: Little, Brown.

Haddy, F.J. (1991) Roles of sodium, potassium, calcium, and natriuretic factors in hypertension. *Hypertension*, 18 (Suppl. III): 179–83.

Hagger, M.S., Chatzisarantis, N.L. and Biddle, S.H. (2002) Meta-analysis of the theories of reasoned action and planned behavior in physical activity: an examination of predictive validity and the contribution of additional variables. *Journal of Sport and Exercise Psychology*, 24: 3–32.

Hahn, M.E. (1966) *California Life Goals Evaluation Schedule*. Palo Alto, CA: Western Psychological Services.

Haines, A.P., Imeson, J.D. and Meade, T.W. (1987) Phobic anxiety and ischaemic heart disease. *British Medical Journal Clinical Research Ed.*, 295: 297–9.

Hajek, P. *et al.* (2009) Relapse prevention interventions for smoking cessation. The Cochrane Library, 1, http://onlinelibrary.wiley.com/o/cochrane/clsysrev/articles/CD003999/pdf_fs.html (accessed August 2010).

Hall, S.M., Tunstall, C.D., Vila, K.L. and Duffy, J. (1992) Weight gain and smoking cessation: cautionary findings. *American Journal of Public Health*, 82: 799–803.

Hammen, C. (2005) Stress and depression. *Annual Review of Clinical Psychology*, 1: 293–329.

Hansson, R.O. and Carpenter, B.N. (1994) *Relationships in Old Age: Coping with the Challenge of Transition*. New York: Guilford Press.

Harackiewicz, J.M. *et al.* (1987) Attributional processes in behavior change and maintenance: smoking cessation and continued abstinence. *Journal of Consulting and Clinical Psychology,* 55: 372–8.

Harrison, J.A., Mullen, P.D. and Green, L.W. (1992) A meta-analysis of studies of the health belief model with adults. *Health Education Research,* 7: 107–16.

Haskell, W.L. *et al.* (2007) Physical activity and public health: updated recommendations for adults from the American College of Sports Medicine and the American Heart Association. *Circulation,* 116: 1081–93.

Haugvedt, C.P. and Petty, R.E. (1992) Personality and persuasion: need for cognition moderates the persistence and resistance of attitude change. *Journal of Personality and Social Psychology,* 63: 308–19.

Hautzinger, M. *et al.* (2005) Rückfallverhinderung bei alkoholabhängigen Männern durch die Komibnation von SSRI und kognitiver. *Verhaltenstherapie Nervenartzt,* 76: 295–307.

He, J. *et al.* (1999) Passive smoking and the risks of coronary heart disease: a meta-analysis of epidemiologic studies. *New England Journal of Medicine,* 340: 920–6.

Heath, A.C. and Madden, P.A.F. (1994) Genetic influences on smoking behavior, in J.R. Turner, L.R. Cardon and J.K. Hewitt (eds) *Behavior Genetic Applications in Behavioral Medicine,* pp. 37–48. New York: Plenum.

Heath, A.C. and Martin, N.G. (1993) Genetic models for the natural history of smoking: evidence for a genetic influence on smoking persistence. *Addictive Behaviors,* 18: 19–34.

Heath, A.C. *et al.* (1997) Genetic and environmental contributions to alcohol dependence risk in a national twin sample: consistency of findings in women and men. *Psychological Medicine,* 27: 1381–96.

Heather, N. and Robertson, I. (1983) *Controlled Drinking.* London: Methuen.

Heather, N., Rollnick, S., Bell, A. and Richmond, R. (1996) Effects of brief counseling among male heavy drinkers identified on general hospital wards. *Drug Alcohol Review,* 15: 29–38.

Heatherton, T.F. and Baumeister, R.F. (1991) Binge eating as escape from self-awareness. *Psychological Bulletin,* 110: 86–108.

Heatherton, T.F. *et al.* (1988) The (mis)measurement of restraint: an analysis of conceptual and psychometric issues. *Journal of Abnormal Psychology,* 97: 19–28.

Heatherton, T.F., Herman, C.P. and Polivy, J. (1991) Effects of physical threat and ego threat on eating behavior. *Journal of Personality and Social Psychology,* 60: 138–43.

Hebel, M.R. and Mannix, L.M. (2003) The weight of obesity in evaluating others: a mere proximity effect. *Personality and Social Psychology Bulletin,* 29: 28–38.

Heckhausen, H. (1980) *Motivation und Handeln.* Heidelberg: Springer.

Heckman, B.D. *et al.* (2004) Coping and anxiety in women recalled for additional diagnostic procedures following an abnormal screening mammography. *Health Psychology,* 23: 42–8.

Heider, F. (1958) *The Psychology of Interpersonal Relations.* New York: Wiley.

Herd, A.J. (1978) Physiological correlates of coronary-prone behavior, in T.M. Dembrowski *et al.* (eds) *Coronary-prone Behavior.* New York: Springer.

Herman, C.P. and Mack, D. (1975) Restrained and unrestrained eating. *Journal of Personality,* 43: 647–60.

Herman, C.P. and Polivy, J. (1984) A boundary model for the regulation of eating, in A.J. Stunkard and E. Stellar (eds) *Eating and its Disorders,* pp. 141–56. New York: Raven Press.

Herttua, K., Mäkelä, P. and Martikainen, P. (2008) Changes in alcohol-related mortality and its socioeconomic differences after a large reduction in alcohol prices: a natural experiment based on register data. *American Journal of Epidemiology,* 168: 1110–18.

Herzog, T. *et al.* (1999) Do processes of change predict smoking stage movements? A prospective analysis of the transtheoretical model. *Health Psychology,* 18: 369–75.

Heshka, S. *et al.* (2003) Weight loss with self-help compared with a structured commercial program. *Journal of the American Medical Association,* 289: 1792–8.

Hester, R.K. and Miller, W.R. (eds) (2002) *Handbook of Alcoholism Treatment Approaches,* 2nd edn. Boston, MA: Allyn & Bacon.

Heymsfield, S.B. *et al.* (2003) Weight management using a meal replacement strategy: meta-analysis from six studies. *International Journal of Obeisity,* 27: 537–49.

Hibscher, J.A. and Herman, C.P. (1977) Obesity, dieting, and the expression of 'obese' characteristics. *Journal of Comparative and Physiological Psychology*, 91: 374–80.

Higuchi, S., Matsushita, S. and Kahsima, H. (2006) New findings on the genetic influences of alcohol abuse and dependence. *Current Opinion in Psychiatry*, 19: 253–65.

Hill, A. and Pozniak, A. (2010) A normal life expectancy, despite HIV infection? *AIDS*, 24: 1–2.

Hill, J.O., Wyatt, H., Phelan, S. and Wing, R.R. (2005) The National Weight Control Registry: is it useful in helping deal with our obesity epidemic? *Journal of Nutrition Education and Behavior*, 37: 206–10.

Hillsdon, M. *et al.* (2001) National level promotion of physical activity: research from England's ACTIVE for LIFE campaign. *Journal of Epidemiology and Community Health*, 55: 755–61.

Hiroto, D.S. (1974) Locus of control and learnt helplessness. *Journal of Experimental Psychology*, 102: 187–93.

Hiroto, D.S. and Seligman, M.E.P. (1975) Generality of learned helplessness in man. *Journal of Personality and Social Psychology*, 32: 311–27.

Hofmann, W. and Friese, M. (2008) Impulses go the better of me: alcohol moderates the influence of implicit attitudes towards food cues on eating behavior. *Journal of Abnormal Psychology*, 117: 420–7.

Hofmann, W., Friese, M. and Wiers, R. (2009) Impulsive versus reflective influences on health behavior: a theoretical framework and empirical review. *Health Psychology Review 2009*: 1–27.

Holland, R.W., Hendriks, M. and Aarts, H. (2005) Smells like clean spirit: non-conscious effects of scent on cognition and behavior. *Psychological Science*, 16: 689–93.

Hollis, J.F. *et al.* (2005) Teen reach: outcomes from a randomized controlled trial of tobacco reduction program for teens seen in primary medical care. *Pediatrics*, 115: 981–9.

Holmes, T.H. and Masuda, M. (1974) Life change and illness susceptibility, in W.S. Dohrenwend and B.P. Dohrenwend (eds) *Stress for Life Events*, pp. 45–72. New York: Wiley.

Holmes, T.H. and Rahe, R.H. (1967) The social readjustment rating-scale. *Journal of Psychosomatic Research*, 11: 213–18.

Hooper, L., Bartlett, C., Smith, G.D. and Ebrahim, S. (2002) Systematic review of long-term effects of advice to reduce dietary salt in adults. *British Medical Journal*, 325(7365): 628–32.

Houben, K. and Wiers, R.W. (2008) Implicitly positive about alcohol? Implicit positive associations predict drinking behavior. *Addictive Behavior*, 33: 979–86.

Houben, K., Havermans, R.C. and Wiers, R. (2010a) Learning to dislike alcohol: conditioning negative implicit attitudes towards alcohol and its effect on drinking behavior. *Psychopharmacology*, 211: 70–86.

Houben, K., Schoenmakers, T.M. and Wiers, R. (2010b) I didn't feel like drinking but I don't know why: the effects of evaluative conditioning on alcohol-related attitudes, craving and behavior. *Addictive Behaviors*, 35: 1161–3.

Houben, K., Nederkorn, C., Wiers, R.W. and Jansen, A. (2010c) Putting the brake on temptation: decreasing alcohol-related affect and drinking behavior by training response inhibition. Unpublished manuscript.

House, J.S. (1981) *Workstress and Social Support*. Reading, MA: Addison-Wesley.

House, J.S. and Kahn, R.L. (1985) Measures and concepts of social support, in S. Cohen and S.L. Syme (eds) *Social Support and Health*, pp. 83–108. Orlando, FL: Academic Press.

House, J.S., Robbins, C. and Metzner, H.L. (1982) The association of social relationships and activities with mortality: prospective evidence from the Tecumseh Community Health Study. *American Journal of Epidemiology*, 116: 123–40.

House, J.S., Landis, K.R. and Umberson, D. (1988) Social relationships and health. *Science*, 241: 540–5.

Houston, B.K. and Vavak, R.C. (1991) Hostility: developmental factors, psychosocial correlates, and health behaviors. *Health Psychology*, 10: 9–17.

Houston, D.J. and Richardson, L.E. (2005) Getting America to buckle up: the efficacy of state seat belt laws. *Accident Analysis and Prevention*, 37: 1114–20.

Houston, D.J. and Richardson, L.E. (2008) Motorcyclist fatality rates and mandatory helmet-use laws. *Accident Analysis and Prevention*, 40: 200–8.

Hovland, C.I., Janis, I.L. and Kelley, H.H. (1959) *Communication and Persuasion: Psychological Studies of Opinion Change.* New Haven, CT: Yale University Press.

Hughes, J.R., Keely, J. and Naud, S. (2004) Shape of the relapse curve and long-term abstinence among untreated smokers. *Addiction,* 99: 29–38.

Huhman, M.E. *et al.* (2007) Evaluation of a national physical activity intervention for children: VERB campaign, 2002–2004. *American Journal of Preventive Medicine,* 32: 38–43.

Huijding, J., De Jong, P.J., Wiers, R.W. and Verkooijen, K. (2005) Implicit and explicit attitudes toward smoking in a smoking and a nonsmoking setting. *Addictive Behaviors,* 30: 949–61.

Hull, J., van Teuren, R. and Virnelli, S. (1987) Hardiness and health: a critique and alternative approach. *Journal of Personality and Social Psychology,* 53: 518–30.

Hull, J.G. and Bond Jr, C.F. (1986) Social behavioral consequences of alcohol consumption and expectancy: a meta-analysis. *Psychological Bulletin,* 99: 347–60.

Hunninghake, D.B. *et al.* (1993) The efficacy of intensive dietary therapy alone or combined with lovastatin in outpatients with hypercholesterolemia. *New England Journal of Medicine,* 328: 1213–19.

Hurley, J. and Horowitz, J. (eds) (1990) *Alcohol and Health.* New York: Hemisphere.

Ikard, F.F. and Tomkins, S. (1973) The experience of affect as a determinant of smoking behavior: a series of validity studies. *Journal of Abnormal Psychology,* 81: 172–81.

Ikard, F.F., Green, D.E. and Horn, D.A. (1969) A scale to differentiate between types of smoking as related to management of affect. *International Journal of the Addictions,* 4: 649–59.

Imber, S. *et al.* (1976) The fate of the untreated alcoholic. *Journal of Nervous and Mental Disease,* 162: 238–47.

Injury Facts (2010) www.nsc.org/news_resources/injury_and_death_statistics/Documents/Summary_2010_Ed.pdf (accessed January 2011).

Irvin, J.E., Bowers, C., Dunn, M.E. and Wang, M.C. (1999) Efficacy of relapse prevention: a meta-analytic review. *Journal of Consulting and Clinical Psychology,* 67: 563–70.

Istvan, J. and Matarazzo, J.D. (1984) Tobacco, alcohol, and caffeine use: a review of their interrelationships. *Psychological Bulletin,* 95: 301–26.

Jacobs Jr, D.R. (1993) Why is low blood cholesterol associated with risk of non-atherosclerotic disease death? *Annual Review of Public Health,* 14: 95–114.

Jacobs, S. (1999) *Traumatic Grief: Diagnosis, Treatment, and Prevention.* Philadelphia, PA: Brunner/Mazel.

Janis, I.L. and Mann, L. (1977) *Decision Making: A Psychological Analysis of Conflict, Choice, and Commitment.* New York: Free Press.

Jansen, A. and Hout, van den H. (1991) On being led into temptation: 'counterregulation' of dieters after smelling a 'preload'. *Addictive Behaviors,* 16: 247–53.

Jansen, A. *et al.* (1988) Nonregulation of food intake in restrained emotional and external eaters. *Journal of Psychopathology and Behavioral Assessment,* 10: 345–53.

Janssen, M. *et al.* (1998a) Jonge homoseksuele mannen, voorlichtingsfolders en opvattingen over risico van HIV-infectie. Unpublished manuscript, University of Utrecht.

Janssen, M. *et al.* (1998b) Socioeconomic status and risk of HIV in young gay men. Unpublished manuscript, University of Utrecht.

Janz, N.K. and Becker, M.H. (1984) The health belief model: a decade later. *Health Education Quarterly,* 11: 1–47.

Jeffery, R.W. (1989) Risk behaviors and health: contrasting individual and population perspectives. *American Psychologist,* 44: 1194–202.

Jeffery, R.W. and Wing, R.R. (1995) Long-term treatment for weight loss. *Journal of Consulting and Clinical Psychology,* 63: 793–6.

Jeffery, R.W., Adlis, S.A. and Forster, J.L. (1991) Prevalence of dieting among working men and women: the healthy worker project. *Health Psychology,* 10: 274–81.

Jeffery, R.W. *et al.* (1993) Strengthening behavioral intentions for weight loss: a randomized trial of food provision and monetary incentives. *Journal of Consulting and Clinical Psychology,* 61: 1038–45.

Jeffery, R.W., Boles, S.M., Strycker, L.A. and Glasgow, R.E. (1997) Smoking specific weight gain concerns and smoking cessation in a working population. *Health Psychology*, 16: 487–9.

Jellinek, E.M. (1960) *The Disease Concept of Alcoholism*. Highland Park, NJ: Hillhouse.

Ji, M.F. and Wood, W. (2007) Purchase consumption habits: not necessarily what you intended. *Journal of Consumer Psychology*, 17: 261–76.

Jin, F. *et al.* (2009) Unprotected anal intercourse, risk reduction behaviours, and subsequent HIV infection in a cohort of homosexual men. *AIDS*, 23: 243–52.

Johnson, W.D. *et al.* (2008) Behavioral interventions to reduce risk for sexual transmission of HIV among men who have sex with men. *Cochrane Database of Systematic Reviews*, 3: CD001230.

Johnston, J.J., Hendricks, S.A. and Fike, J.M. (1994) The effectiveness of behavioural safety belt interventions. *Accident Analysis and Prevention*, 26: 315–23.

Jonas, K. (1995) Der Beitrag der Einstellungsforschung zur Vorhersage präventiven und riskanten gesundheitsbezogenen Verhaltens. Unveröggffentlichte Habilitation, Universität Tübingen.

Jones, B.T., Corbin, W. and Fromme K. (2001) A review of expectancy theory and alcohol consumption. *Addiction*, 96: 57–72.

Junger, M., Stroebe, W. and van der Laan, A. (1999) Delinquency, health behavior and health. Manuscript submitted for publication.

Kadden, R. *et al.* (eds) (2004) Cognitive-behavioral coping skills therapy manual. Project MATCH Monograph Series, Vol. 3, http://pubs.niaaa.nih.gov/publications/MATCHSeries3/Project%20MATCH%20Vol_3.pdf.

Kalichman, S.C. (1998) *Preventing AIDS: A Sourcebook for Behavioral Interventions*. Mahwah, NJ: Lawrence Erlbaum.

Kalichman, S.C. *et al.* (2007) Changes in HIV treatment beliefs and sexual risk behaviors among gay and bisexual men, 1997–2005. *Health Psychology*, 26.

Kaner, E.F.S. *et al.* (2007) Effectiveness of brief alcohol intervention in primary care populations. *Cochrane Review*, http://onlinelibrary.wiley.com/o/cochrane/clsysrev/articles/CD004148/pdf_fs.html (accessed August 2010).

Kanner, A.D., Coyne, J.C., Schaefer, C. and Lazarus, R.S. (1981) Comparison of two modes of stress measurement: daily hassles and uplifts versus major life events. *Journal of Behavioral Medicine*, 4: 1–39.

Kaplan, H.I. and Kaplan, H.S. (1957) The psychosomatic concept of obesity, *Journal of Nervous and Mental Disease*, 125: 181–201.

Kaplan, R.M. (1988) The value dimension in studies of health promotion, in S. Spacapan and S. Oskamp (eds) *The Social Psychology of Health*. Beverly Hills, CA: Sage.

Kaplan, R.M., Sallis, J.F. and Patterson, T.L. (1993) *Health and Human Behavior*. New York: McGraw-Hill.

Karnehed, N., Rasmussen, F., Hemingsson, T. and Tynelius, P. (2006) Obesity and attained education: cohort study of more than 700,000 Swedish men. *Obesity*, 14: 1421–8.

Karremans, J., Stroebe, W. and Claus, J. (2006) Beyond Vicary's fantasies: the impact of subliminal priming on brand choice, *Journal of Experimental Social Psychology*, 42: 792–8.

Kasl, S.V. and Cobb, S. (1970) Health behavior, illness behavior, and sick role behavior. *Archives of Environmental Health*, 12: 246–66.

Kawachi, I. *et al.* (1994a) Prospective study of phobic anxiety and risk of coronary heart disease in men. *Circulation*, 89: 1992–7.

Kawachi, I., Sparrow, D., Vokonas, P.S. and Weiss, S.T. (1994b) Symptoms of anxiety and risk of coronary heart disease: the Normative Aging Study. *Circulation*, 90: 2225–9.

Keesey, R.E. (1986) A set-point theory of obesity, in K.D. Brownell and J.P. Foreyt (eds) *The Physiology, Psychology, and Treatment of the Eating Disorders*, pp. 63–87. New York: Basic Books.

Kelley, G.A., Kelley, K.S., Hootman, J.M. and Jones, D.L. (2008) Exercise and health-related quality of life in older community-dwelling adults: a meta-analysis of randomized controlled trials. *Journal of Applied Gerontology*, 28: 369–94.

Kelly, J.A. and Kalichman, S.C. (1998) Reinforcement value of unsafe sex as a predictor of condom use and continued HIV/AIDS risk behavior among gay and bisexual men. *Health Psychology*, 17: 328–35.

Kemeny, M.E., Cohen, F., Zegans, L.A. and Conant, M.A. (1989) Psychological and immunological predictors of genital herpes recurrence. *Psychosomatic Medicine*, 51: 195–208.

Kendell, R.E. and Staton, M.C. (1966) The fate of untreated alcoholics. *Quarterly Journal of Studies in Alcohol*, 27: 30–41.

Kendler, K.S. *et al.* (1992) A population-based twin study of alcoholism in women. *Journal of the American Medical Association*, 268: 1877–82.

Kendler, K.S., Thornton, L.M. and Gardner, C.O. (2000) Stressful life events and previous episodes in the etiology of major depression in women: an evaluation of the 'kindling' hypothesis. *American Journal of Psychiatry*, 157: 1243–51.

Kenkel, D.S. (1991) Health behavior, health knowledge, and schooling. *Journal of Political Economy*, 99: 287–305.

Kenney, W.L. (1985) Parasympathetic control of resting heart rate: relationship to aerobic power. *Medicine and Science in Sports and Exercise*, 17: 451–55.

Kent, K.M., Smith, E.R., Redwood, D.R. and Epstein, S.E. (1973) Electrical stability of acutely ischemic myocardium: influences of heart rate and vagal stimulation. *Circulation*, 47: 291–8.

Kent, T.H. and Hart, M.N. (1987) *Introduction to Human Disease*, 2nd edn. East Norwalk, CT: Appleton-Century-Crofts.

Kessler, R.C. (1997) The effects of stressful life events on depression. *Annual Review of Psychology*, 48: 191–214.

Keys, A. (1980) *Seven Countries: A Multivariate Analysis of Death and Coronary Heart Disease.* Cambridge, MA: Harvard University Press.

Keys, A. *et al.* (1950) *The Biology of Human Starvation*, Vols. 1, 2. Minneapolis, MI: University of Minnesota Press.

Keys, A. *et al.* (1971) Mortality and coronary heart disease among men studied for 23 years. *Archives of Internal Medicine*, 128: 201–14.

Kiecolt-Glaser, J.K. and Glaser, R. (1991) Stress and immune function in humans, in R. Ader, D.L. Felten and N. Cohen (eds) *Psychoneuroimmunology*, 2nd edn, pp. 849–67. San Diego, CA: Academic Press/Harcourt Brace Jovanovich.

Kiecolt-Glaser, J.K. *et al.* (1987) Chronic stress and immunity in family caregivers of Alzheimers' disease victims. *Psychosomatic Medicine*, 49: 523–35.

Kiecolt-Glaser, J.K. *et al.* (1988) Marital discord and immunity in males. *Psychosomatic Medicine*, 50: 213–29.

Kiecolt-Glaser, J.K., McGuire, L., Robles, T.F. and Glaser, R. (2002) Emotions, morbidity, and mortality: new perspectives from psychneuroimmunology. *Annual Review of Psychology*, 53: 83–107.

Killen, J.D. *et al.* (1996) Weight concerns influence the development of eating disorders: a 4-year prospective study. *Journal of Consulting and Clinical Psychology*, 64: 936–40.

Killen, J.D. *et al.* (1997) Prospective study of risk factors for the initiation of cigarette smoking. *Journal of Consulting and Clinical Psychology*, 65: 1011–16.

Kim, D. and Kawachi, I. (2006) Food taxation and pricing strategies to 'thin out' the obesity epidemic. *American Journal of Preventive Medicine*, 30: 430–7.

Kippax, S. *et al.* (1997) Sexual negotiation in the AIDS era: negotiated safety revisited. *AIDS*, 11: 191–7.

Kirby, D. and DiClemente, R.J. (1994) School-based interventions to prevent unprotected sex and HIV among adolescents, in R.J. DiClemente and J.L.Peterson (eds) *Preventing AIDS: Theories and Methods of Behavioural Interventions*, pp. 117–39. New York: Plenum.

Kittel, F., Kornitzer, M., Dramaix, M. and Beriot, I. (1993) Health behavior in Belgian studies: who is doing best? Paper presented at the European Congress of Psychology, Tampere, Finland.

Klag, S. and Bradley, G. (2004) The role of hardiness in stress and illness: an exploration of the effect of negative affectivity and gender. *British Journal of Health Psychology*, 9: 137–61.

Klatsky, A.L. and Udaltsova, N. (2007) Alcohol drinking and total mortality risk. *Annals of Epidemiology*, 17, (5 Suppl.): S63–7.

Klem, M.L. *et al.* (1998) Psychological symptoms in individuals successful at long-term maintenance of weight loss. *Health Psychology*, 17: 336–45.

Klesges, R.C. *et al.* (1997) How much weight gain occurs following smoking cessation? A comparison of weight gain using both continuous and point prevalence abstinence. *Journal of Consulting and Clinical Psychology*, 65: 286–91.

Klesges, R.C. (1998) The relationship between smoking and body weight in a population of young military personnel. *Health Psychology*, 17: 454–8.

Kobasa, S.C. (1979) Stressful life events, personality, and health: an inquiry into hardiness. *Journal of Personality and Social Psychology*, 37: 1–11.

Kobasa, S.C., Maddi, S.R. and Courington, S. (1981) Personality and constitution as mediators in the stress–illness relationship. *Journal of Health and Social Behavior*, 22: 368–78.

Kobasa, S.C., Maddi, S.R. and Kahn, S. (1982) Hardiness and health: a prospective study. *Journal of Personality and Social Psychology*, 42: 168–77.

Koski, A., Sirén, R., Vuori, E. and Poikolainen, K. (2007) Alcohol tax cuts and increase in alcohol-positive sudden deaths – a time-series-intervention analysis. *Addiction*, 192: 362–8.

Kottke, T.E., Battista, R.N., DeFriese, G.H. and Brekke, M.L. (1988) Attributes of successful smoking cessation interventions in medical practice: a meta-analysis of 39 controlled trials. *Journal of the American Medical Association*, 259: 2883–9.

Kraft, P., Rise, J., Sutton, S. and Rosamb, E. (2005) Perceived difficulty in the theory of planned behaviour: perceived behavoural control or affective attitude? *British Journal of Social Psychology*, 44: 479–96.

Kramsch, D.M. *et al.* (1981) Reduction of coronary atherosclerosis by moderate conditioning exercise in monkeys on an atherogenic diet. *New England Journal of Medicine*, 303: 1483–9.

Kranzler, H.R. and Van Kirk, J. (2001) Efficacy of naltrexone and camprosate for alcoholism treatment: a meta-analysis. *Clinical and Experimental Research*, 25: 1335–41.

Kraus, S.J. (1995) Attitudes and the prediction of behavior: a meta-analysis of the empirical literature. *Personality and Social Psychology Bulletin*, 21: 58–75.

Krebs, P., Prochaska, J.O. and Rossi, J.S. (2010) A meta-analysis of computer-tailored interventions for health behavior change. *Preventive Medicine*, 51, 214–21.

Kruglanski, A.W. *et al.* (2002) A theory of goal systems. *Advances in Experimental Social Psychology*, 33: 331–78.

Kubzansky, L.D. *et al.* (1997) Is worrying bad for your heart? A prospective study of worry and coronary heart disease in the Normative Aging Study. *Circulation*, 95: 818–24.

Kung, H.C., Hoyert, D.L., Xu, J.Q. and Murphy, S.L. (2008) Deaths: final data for 2005. *National Vital Statistics Reports*, 56: 1–124.

Kyes, K.B. (1990) The effect of a 'safer sex' film as mediated by erotophobia and gender on attitudes towards condoms. *Journal of Sex Research*, 27: 297–303.

Lancaster, T. and Stead, L.F. (2002) Self-help intervention for smoking cessation. *Cochrane database of systematic reviews* (online), 3: CD001118.

Lapidus, L., Bengtsson, C. and Lissner, L. (1990) Distribution of adipose tissue in relation to cardiovascular and total mortality as observed during 20 years in a prospective population study of women in Gothenberg, Sweden. *Diabetes Research and Clinical Practice*, 10: S185–9.

LaPiére, R.T. (1934) Attitudes vs. Actions. *Social Forces*, 13: 230–7.

Larsson, B. *et al.* (1989) Obesity, adipose tissue distribution and health in men – the study of men born in 1913. *Appetite*, 13: 37–44.

Lazarus, R.S. and Folkman, S. (1984) *Stress, Appraisal, and Coping*. New York: Springer.

Lazarus, R.S., DeLongis, A., Folkman, S. and Gruen, R.J. (1985) Stress and adaptational outcomes: the problem of confounded measures. *American Psychologist*, 40: 770–9.

Ledermann, S. (1956) *Alcool, alcoolisme, alcoolisation: donées scientifiques de caractère physiologique, économique et social*. Institut National D'Études Démographiques. Travaux et Documents, Cahier No. 29. Paris: Presses Universitaires de France.

Ledermann, S. (1964) *Alcool, alcoolisme, alcoolisation. Mortalité, morbidité, accidents du travail.* Institut National D'Études Démographiques. Travaux et Documents, Cahier No. 41. Paris: Presses Universitaires de France.

Lee, I.M. and Skerrett, P.J. (2001). Physical activity and all-cause mortality: what is the dose-response relation? *Medicine & Science in Sports & Exercise*, 33(Suppl. 6): S459–71.

Leigh, B.C. (1989) In search of the seven dwarves: issues of measurement and meaning in alcohol expectancy research. *Psychological Bulletin,* 105: 361–73.

Leiker, M. and Hailey, B.J. (1988) A link between hostility and disease: poor health habits? *Behavioral Medicine*, 3: 129–33.

Leistikow, B.N. *et al.* (2000) Smoking as a risk factor for accident death: a meta-analysis of cohort studies. *Accident Analysis and Prevention*, 32: 397–405.

Lepper, M.R. and Greene, D. (1978) *The Hidden Cost of Reward*. New York: Wiley.

Leventhal, H. (1970) Findings and theory in the study of fear communication, in L. Berkowitz (ed.) *Advances in Experimental Social Psychology*, Vol. 5, pp. 119–86. New York: Academic Press.

Leventhal, H. and Avis, N. (1976) Pleasure, addiction, and habit: factors in verbal report or factors in smoking behavior? *Journal of Abnormal Psychology*, 85: 478–88.

Leventhal, H. and Cleary, P.D. (1980) The smoking problem: a review of the research and theory in behavioral risk modification. *Psychological Bulletin*, 88: 370–405.

Lichtenstein, E. (1982) The smoking problem: a behavioral perspective. *Journal of Consulting and Clinical Psychology*, 50: 804–19.

Lichtenstein, E. and Danaher, B.G. (1975) Modification of smoking behavior: a critical analysis of theory, research, and practice, in M. Hersen, R. Eisler and P. Miller (eds) *Progress in Behavior Modification*, Vol. 3, pp. 79–132. New York: Academic Press.

Locke, E.A. and Latham, G.P. (1990) *A Theory of Goal Setting and Task Performance*. Englewood Cliffs, NJ: Prentice Hall.

Lowe, M.R. (1993) The effects of dieting on eating behaviour: a three factor model. *Psychological Bulletin*, 114: 100–21.

Lowe, M.R., Miller-Kovach, K., Frye, N. and Phelan, S. (1999) An initial evaluation of a commercial weight loss program: short-term effects on weight, eating behavior, and mood. *Obesity Research*, 7: 51–9.

Luepker, R.V. *et al.* (1994) Community education for cardiovascular disease prevention: risk factor changes in the Minnesota Heart Health Program. *American Journal of Public Health*, 84: 1383–93.

Luft, F.C. (1997) Salt skirmishes. *Kidney-Blood-Pressure Research*, 20: 71–3.

Mann, T.A. *et al.* (2007) Medicare's search for effective obesity treatments: diets are not the answer. *American Psychologist*, 62: 220–33.

McCann, I.L. and Holmes, D.S. (1984) Influence of aerobics on depression. *Journal of Personality and Social Psychology*, 46: 1142–7.

McCarroll, J.R. and Haddon Jr, W. (1962) A controlled study of fatal motor vehicle crashes in New York City. *Journal of Chronic Diseases*, 15: 811–22.

McConnaughy, E., Prochaska, J.O. and Velicer, W.F. (1983) Stages of change in psychotherapy: measurement and sample profiles. *Psychotherapy*, 20: 368–75.

McConnaughy, E., DiClemente, C.C., Prochaska, J.O. and Velicer, W.F. (1989) Stages of change in psychotherapy: a follow-up report. *Psychotherapy*, 26: 494–503.

McCrady, S.B. and Delaney, S.I. (1995) Self-help groups, in R.K. Hester and W.R. Miller (eds) *Handbook of Alcoholism Treatment Approaches*, 2nd edn, pp. 160–75. Boston, MA: Allyn & Bacon.

McCrae, R.R. and Costa Jr, P.T. (1986) Personality, coping and coping effectiveness in an adult sample. *Journal of Personality*, 54: 385–405.

McDavid Harrison, K., Song, R. and Zhang, X. (2010). Life expectancy after HIV diagnosis based on national HIV surveillance data from 25 states, United States. *Journal of the Acquired Imune Deficiency Syndrome*, 53: 124–30.

McDonald, D.G. and Hodgdon, J.A. (1991) *Psychological Effects of Aerobic Fitness Training: Research and Theory*. New York: Springer.

MacDonald, T.K., Zanna, M.P. and Fong, G.T. (1995) Decision making in altered states: effects of alcohol on attitudes toward drinking and driving. *Journal of Personality and Social Psychology*, 68: 973–85.

MacDonald, T.K., MacDonald G., Zanna, M.P. and Fong, G.T. (2000) Alcohol, sexual arousal, and intentions to use condoms in young men: applying alcohol myopia theory to risky sexual behavior. *Health Psychology*, 19: 290–8.

McGee, D.L. (2005) Body mass index and mortality: a meta-analysis based on person-level data from twenty-six observational studies. *Annals of Epidemiology*, 15: 87–97.

McGinnis, J.M. and Foege, W.H. (1993) Actual causes of death in the United States. *Journal of the American Medical Association*, 270: 2207–12.

McGue, M. (1999) The behavioural genetics of alcoholism. *Current Direction in Psychological Science*, 8: 109–15.

McGuire, M.T., Wing, R.R. and Hill, J.O. (1999) The prevalence of weight loss maintenance among American adults. *International Journal of Obesity*, 23: 1314–19.

McGuire, R.J. and Vallance, M. (1964) Aversion therapy by electric shock: a simple technique. *British Medical Journal*, I: 151–3.

McGuire, W.J. (1985) Attitudes and attitude change, in G. Lindzey and E. Aronson (eds) *Handbook of Social Psychology*, 3rd edn, Vol. 2, pp. 233–346. New York: Random House.

MacKenzie, E.J. (2000). Epidemiology of injuries: current trends and future challenges. *Epidemiologic Review*, 22: 112–19.

McKeown, T. (1979) *The Role of Medicine*. Oxford: Blackwell.

McKinlay, J.B. and McKinlay, S.M. (1981) Medical measures and the decline of mortality, in P. Conrad and R. Kern (eds) *The Sociology of Health and Illness*, pp. 12–30. New York: St Martins.

McKinnon, W. *et al.* (1989) Chronic stress, leukocyte subpopulations, and humoral response to latent viruses. *Health Psychology*, 8: 389–402.

McKusick, L., Horstman, W. and Coates, T.J. (1985) AIDS and sexual behavior reported by gay men in San Francisco. *American Journal of Public Health*, 75 (15): 493–6.

McQueen, J., Howe, T.E., Allan, L. and Mains, D. (2009) Brief interventions for heavy alcohol uses admitted to general hospital wards. *Cochrance Library*, Issue 4, http://onlinelibrary.wiley.com/o/cochrane/clsysrev/articles/CD005191/pdf_fs.html.

Maddi, S.R., Kobasa, S.C. and Hoover, M. (1979) An alienation test. *Journal of Humanistic Psychology*, 19: 73–6.

Maddi, S.R., Bartone, P.T. and Puccetti, M.C. (1987) Stressful events are indeed a factor in physical illness: a reply to Schroeder and Costa (1984) *Journal of Personality and Social Psychology*, 52: 833–43.

Maddox, G.L., Back, K.W. and Liederman, V.R. (1968) Overweight and social deviance and disability. *Journal of Health and Social Behavior*, 9: 287–98.

Maes, S., Verhoeven, C., Kittel, F. and Scholten, H. (1998) Effects of a Dutch work-site wellness-health program: the Brabantia project. *American Journal of Public Health*, 88: 1037–41.

MAFF (Ministry of Agriculture, Fisheries and Food) (1995) *Manual of Nutrition*, 10th edn. London: The Stationery Office.

Magnus, K., Matross, A. and Stracker, J. (1979) Walking, cycling, or gardening with or without seasonal interruption, in relation to acute coronary events. *American Journal of Epidemiology*, 110: 724–33.

Mahoney, M.J. and Mahoney, K. (1976) *Permanent Weight Control: A Total Solution to a Dieter's Dilemma*. New York: W.W. Norton.

Maisto, S.A., Lauerman, R. and Adesso, V.J. (1977) A comparison of two experimental studies of the role of cognitive factors in alcoholics' drinking. *Journal of Studies on Alcohol*, 38: 145–9.

Mandler, G. (1975) *Mind and Emotion*. New York: Wiley.

Manini, T.M. *et al.* (2006) Daily activity energy expenditure and mortality among older adults. *Journal of the American Medical Association*, 296: 171–9.

Manning, W.G. *et al.* (1989) The taxes of sin: do smokers and drinkers pay their way? *Journal of the American Medical Association*, 261: 1604–9.

Manson, J.E. *et al.* (1995) Body weight and mortality among women. *New England Journal of Medicine*, 333: 677–85.

Manuck, S.B. and Krantz, D.S. (1986) Psychophysiological reactivity in coronary heart disease and essential hypertension, in K.A. Matthews *et al.* (eds) *Handbook of Stress, Reactivity and Cardiovascular Disease*, pp. 11–34. New York: Wiley.

Marks, G., Crepaz, N., Senterfitt, J.W. and Janssen, R.S. (2005) Meta-analysis of high-risk sexual behavior in persons aware and unaware they are infected with HIV in the United States. *Journal of Acquired Immune Deficiency Syndrome*, 39: 446–53.

Marlatt, G.A. (1985) Relapse prevention: theoretical rationale and overview of the model, in G.A. Marlatt and J.R. Gordon (eds) *Relapse Prevention*, pp. 3–70. New York: Guilford Press.

Marlatt, G.A. and Gordon, J.R. (1980) Determinants of relapse: implications for the maintenance of behavior change, in P.O. Davidson and S.M. Davidson (eds) *Behavioral Medicine*, pp. 410–52. New York: Brunner/Mazel.

Marlatt, G.A. and Rohsenow, D.J. (1980) Cognitive processes in alcohol use: expectancy and the balanced placebo design, in N.K. Mellow (ed.) *Advances in Substance Abuse*, Vol. 1, pp. 159–99. Greenwich, CT: JAI Press.

Marlatt, G.A., Demming, B. and Reid, J.B. (1973) Loss of control drinking in alcoholics: an experimental analogue. *Journal of Abnormal and Social Psychology*, 81: 233–41.

Martinsen, E.W. and Morgan, W.P. (1997) Antidepressant effects of physical activity, in W.P. Morgan (ed.) *Physical Activity and Mental Health*, pp. 93–106. Philadelphia, PA: Taylor & Francis.

Marwell, G., Aiken, M. and Demerath, N.J. (1987) The persistence of political attitudes among 1960s civil rights activists. *Public Opinion Quarterly*, 51: 359–75.

Mason, J.W. (1975) A historical view of the stress field (Parts I, II). *Journal of Human Stress*, 1: 6–12, 22–36.

Matarazzo, J.D. (1984) Behavioral health: a 1990 challenge for the health sciences professions, in J.D. Matarazzo *et al.* (eds) *Behavioral Health: A Handbook of Health Enhancement and Disease Prevention*, pp. 3–40. New York: Wiley.

Mattes, R.D. (1996) Dietary compensation by humans for supplemental energy provided as ethanol or carbohydrate in fluids. *Physiology and Behavior*, 59: 179–87.

Matthews, K.A., Glass, D.C., Rosenman, R.H. and Bortner, R.W. (1977) Competitive drive, pattern A, and coronary heart disease: a further analysis of some data from the Western Collaborative Group Study. *Journal of Chronic Disease*, 30: 489–98.

Mead, G.E. *et al.* (2009) Exercise for depression. *Cochrane Database of Systematic Reviews*, 3: CD004366.

Mechanic, D. (1978) *Medical Sociology*, 2nd edn. New York: Free Press.

Meichenbaum, P. (1977) *Cognitive Behavior Modification*. New York: Plenum.

Meisel, S.R. *et al.* (1991) Effect of Iraqi missile war on incidence of acute myocardial infarction and sudden death in Israeli civilians. *Lancet*, 338: 660–1.

Meyer, A.J. *et al.* (1980) Skills training in a cardiovascular health education campaign. *Journal of Consulting and Clinical Psychology*, 48: 129–42.

Meyers, A.W. *et al.* (1997) Are weight concerns predictive of smoking cessation? A prospective analysis. *Journal of Consulting and Clinical Psychology*, 65: 448–52.

Michie, S., Abraham, C., Wittington, C., McAteer, J. and Gupta, S. (2009) Effective techniques in healthy eating and physical activity interventions: a meta-regression. *Health Psychology*, 28: 690–701.

Miller, C.T. and Downey, K.T. (1999) A meta-analysis of heavyweight and self-esteem. *Personality and Social Psychology Review*, 3: 68–84.

Miller, G.E., Cohen, S. and Ritchey, A.K. (2002) Chronic psychological stress and the regulation of pro-inflammatory cytokines: a gulcocortoid-resistance model. *Health Pscyhology*, 21: 531–41.

Miller, G.E., Chen, E. and Zhou, E.S. (2007) If it goes up, it must come down? Chronic stress and the hypothalamic-pituitary-adrenocoritcal axis in humans. *Psychological Bulletin*, 133: 25–45.

Miller, S.M. (1980) Why having control reduces stress: if I can stop the roller coaster, I don't want to get off, in J. Garber and M.E.P. Selgiman (eds) *Human Helplessness: Theory and Applications*, pp. 71–95. New York: Academic Press.

Miller, T.Q. *et al.* (1996) A meta-analytic review of research on hostility and physical health. *Psychological Bulletin*, 119: 322–48.

Miller, W.R. (1995) Motivational enhancement therapy with drug abusers, www.motivationalinterview.org/clinical/METDrugAbuse.PDF (accessed July 2010).

Miller, W.R. and Hester, R.K. (1986) The effectiveness of alcoholism treatment: what research reveals, in W.R. Miller and N. Heather (eds) *Treating Addictive Behaviors: Processes of Change*, pp. 121–74. New York: Plenum.

Miller, W.R. and Munoz, R.F. (1976) *How to Control your Drinking?* Englewood Cliffs, NJ: Prentice Hall.

Milne, S., Sheeran, P. and Orbell, S. (2000) Prediction and intervention in health-related behavior: a meta-analytic review of protection motivation theory. *Journal of Applied Social Psychology*, 30: 106–43.

Mofenson, L.M. (2010) Prevention in neglected subpopulations: prevention of mother-to-child transmission of HIV infection. *Clinical Infection Diseases*, 50: S130–48.

Mokdad, A.H., Marks, J.S., Stroup, D.F. and Gerberding, J.L. (2004) Actual causes of death in the United States. *Journal of the American Medical Association*, 297: 1238–45.

Monroe, S.M. (1983) Major and minor life events as predictors of psychological distress: further issues and findings. *Journal of Behavioral Medicine*, 6: 189–205.

Monroe, S.M. and Harkness, K.L. (2005) Life stress, the 'kindling' hypothesis, and recurrence of depression: considerations from a life stress perspective. *Psychological Review*, 112: 417–45.

Mooney, A.J. (1982) Alcohol use, in R.B. Taylor (ed.) *Health Promotion: Principles and Clinical Applications*, pp. 233–58. New York: Appleton-Century-Crofts.

Mooney III, A.J. and Cross, G.M. (1988) Alcoholism and substance abuse, in L.B. Taylor (ed.) *Family Medicine*, 3rd edn, pp. 690–702. New York: Springer-Verlag.

Moore, M.H. and Gerstein, D.R. (eds) (1981) *Alcohol and Public Policy: Beyond the Shadow of Prohibition*. Washington, DC: National Academy Press.

Morgan, W.P. (ed.) (1997) *Physical Activity and Mental Health*. Philadelphia, PA: Taylor & Francis.

Morgenstern, J. and Longabaugh, R. (2000) Cognitive-behavioral treatment for alcohol dependence: a review of evidence for its hypothesized mechanisms of action. *Addiction*, 95: 1475–90.

Morris, J.N. *et al.* (1953) Coronary heart disease and physical activity of work. *Lancet*, 2: 1053–7, 1111–20.

Morris, J.N., Pollard, R., Everitt, M.G. and Chave, S.P.W. (1980) Vigorous exercise in leisure-time protection against coronary heart disease. *Lancet*, 2: 1207–10.

Morris, M.C., Ciesla, J.A. and Garber, J. (2010) A prospective study of stress autonomy versus stress sensitization in adolescents at varied risk for depression. *Journal of Abnormal Psychology*, 119: 341–54.

Mosing, M.A., *et al.* (2009) *Behavioral Genetics*, 39: 597–604.

Moskowitz, G.B. and Ignarri, C. (2009) Implicit volition and stereotype control, *European Review of Social Psychology*, 20: 97–145.

Müller-Rimenschneider, F. *et al.* (2008) Long-term effectiveness of behavioural interventions to prevent smoking among children and youth. *Tobacco Control*, 17: 301–12.

National Centers for Health Statistics (1989) *Health, United States 1988*. DHHS Publication No. (PHS) 89–1252. Washington, DC: US Government Printing Office.

National Heart, Lung, and Blood Institute (1998) Clinical guidelines on the identification, evaluation, and treatment of overweight and obesity in adults: the evidence report. *Obesity Research*, 6 (Suppl. 2): S51–210.

National Safety Council (1986) *Accident Facts – 1986*. Chicago, IL: National Safety Council.

National Task Force on the Prevention and Treatment of Obesity (2000) Dieting and the development of eating disorders in overweight and obese adults. *Archives of Internal Medicine*, 160: 2581–9.

Nausheen, B., Gidron, Y., Peveler, R. and Moss-Morris, R. (2009) Social support and cancer progression: a systematic review. *Journal of Psychosomatic Research*, 67: 403–15.

Neil, W.A. and Oxendine, J.M. (1979) Exercise can promote coronary collateral development without improving perfusion of ischemic myocardium. *Circulation*, 60: 1513–19.

Netz, Y., Wu, M.J., Becker, B.J. and Taenebaum, G. (2005) Physical actvity and psychological well-being in advanced age: a meta-analysis of intervention studies. *Psychology and Aging*, 20: 272–84.

Newcomb, M.D. (1990) What structural equation modelling can tell us about social support, in B.R. Sarason, I.G. Sarason and G.R. Pierce (eds) *Social Support: An Interactional View*, pp. 26–62. New York: Wiley.

NIAAA (2000) Alcohol Alert, 49, http:pubs.niaaa.nih.gov/publications/aa49.htm (accessed August 2010).

Nisbett, R.E. (1972) Hunger, obesity, and the ventromedial hypothalamus. *Psychological Review*, 79: 433–53.

Nisbett, R.E. and Wilson, T.D. (1977) Telling more than we can know: verbal reports on mental processes. *Psychological Review*, 84: 231–59.

Noar, S.M. (2008) Behavioral interventions to reduce HIV-related sexual risk behavior: a review and synthesis of meta-analytic evidence. *AIDS Behavior*, 12: 335–52.

Noar, S.M., Black, H.G. and Pierce, L.B. (2009) Efficacy of computer technology-based HIV prevention interventions: a meta-analysis, *AIDS*, 23: 107—115.

Nolen-Hoeksema, S. and Larson, J. (1999) *Coping with Loss*. Mahwah, NJ: Lawrence Erlbaum.

Nolen-Hoeksema, S., McBride, A. and Larson, J. (1997) Rumination and psychological distress among bereaved partners. *Journal of Personality and Social Psychology*, 72: 855–62.

Norman, P., Conner, M. and Bell, R. (1999) The theory of planned behavior and smoking cessation. *Health Psychology*, 18: 89–94.

Norman, P., Boer, H. and Seydel, E.R. (2005) Protection motivation theory, in M. Conner and P. Norman (eds) *Predicting Health Behaviour*, pp. 81–126. Maidenhead: Open University Press.

Novotny, T.E., Romano, R.A., Davis, R.M. and Mills, S.L. (1992) The public health practice of tobacco control: lessons learned and directions for the States in the 1990s. *Annual Review of Public Health*, 13: 287–318.

Nusselder, W.J. *et al.* (2000) Smoking and the compression of morbidity. *Journal of Epidemiology and Community Health*, 54: 566–74.

OECD Health Data (2005) How does Sweden compare? www.oecd.org/dataoecd/www.oecd.org/dataoecd/15/25/3497022.pdf.

OECD Health Data (2007) How does Germany compare? www.oecd.org/dataoecd/www.oecd.org/dataoecd/15-25-34970222.pdf.

OECD Health Data (2008a) How does Denmark compre? www.oecd.org/dataoecd/www.oecd.org/dataoecd/46/32/38979778.pdf.

OECD Health Data (2008b) How does the Netherlands compare? www.oecd.org/dataoecd/www.oecd.org/dataoecd/46/8/36980162.pdf.

Oeppen, J. and Vaupel, J.W. (2002) Broken limits to life expectancy. *Science*, 296: 1029–31.

Ogden, C.L. *et al.* (2006) Prevalence of overweight and obesity in the United States, 1999–2004. *Journal of the American Medical Association*, 295: 1549–55.

O'Leary, A.O. (1990) Stress, emotion, and human immune function. *Psychological Bulletin*, 108: 363–82.

Onyike, C.U. *et al.* (2003) Is obesity associated with major depression? Results from the third National Health and Nutrition Examination Survey, *American Journal of Epidemiology*, 158: 1139–47.

Ormel, J., Oldehinkel, A.J. and Brilman, E.I. (2001) The interplay and etiological continuity of neuroticism, difficulties, and life events in the etiology of major and subsyndromal, first and recurrent depressive episodes in later life. *American Journal of Psychiatry*, 158: 885–91.

Ostafin, B.D., Palfai, T.P. and Wechsler, C.E. (2003) The accessibility of motivational tendencies towards alcohol: approach, avoidance, and disinhibited drinking. *Experimental and Clinical Psychopharmacology*, 11: 294–301.

Ostafin, B.D., Marlatt, G.A. and Greenwald, A. (2008) Drinking without thinking: an implicit measure of alcohol motivation predicts failure to control alcohol use. *Behaviour Research and Therapy*, 46: 1210–19.

Ouimetter, P.C., Finney, J.W. and Moos, R.H. (1997) Twelve-step and cognitive-behavioral treatment for substance abuse: a comparison of treatment effectiveness. *Journal of Consulting and Clinical Psychology*, 65: 230–40.

Oulette, J. and Wood, E. (1998) Habit and intention in everyday life: the multiple processes by which past behavior predicts future behavior. *Psychological Bulletin*, 124: 54–74.

Paffenbarger Jr, R.S. and Hale, W.E. (1975) Work activity and coronary heart mortality. *New England Journal of Medicine*, 292: 545–50.

Paffenbarger Jr, R.S., Wing, A.L. and Hyde, R.T. (1978) Chronic disease in former college students, XVI: physical activity as an index of heart attack risk in college alumni. *American Journal of Epidemiology*, 108: 161–75.

Paffenbarger Jr, R.S., Hyde, R.T., Wing, A.L. and Hsieh, C. (1986) Cigarette smoking and cardiovascular disease, in D.G. Zaridze and R. Peto (eds) *A Major International Hazard* (IARC Scientific Publications No. 74). Lyon: International Agency for Research on Cancer.

Paffenbarger Jr, R.S., Lee, I.M. and Leung, R. (1994) Physical activitiy and personal characteristics associated with depression and suicide in American college men. *Acta Psychiatrica Scandinavia Supplementum*, 377: 16–22.

Palatini, P. and Julius, S. (1997) Heart rate and the cardiovascular risk. *Journal of Hypertension*, 15: 3–17.

Papies, E., Stroebe, W. and Aarts, H. (2007) Pleasure in the mind: restrained eating and spontaneous hedonic thoughts about food. *Journal of Experimental Social Psychology*, 43: 810–17.

Papies, E.K., Stroebe, W. and Aarts, H. (2008a) Understanding dieting: a social cognitive analysis of hedonic processes in self-regulation, in W. Stroebe and M. Hewstone (eds) *European Review of Social Psychology*, 19: 39–383.

Papies, E., Stroebe, W. and Aarts, H. (2008b) The allure of palatable food: biased selective attention among restrained eaters. *Journal of Experimental Social Psychology*, 44: 1283–92.

Papies, E.K., Stroebe, W. and Aarts, H. (2008c) Healthy cognition: processes of self-regulatory success in restrained eating. *Personality and Social Psychology Bulletin*, 34: 1290–300.

Parker, J.D.A. and Endler, N.S. (1992) Coping with coping assessment: a critical review. *European Journal of Personality*, 6: 321–44.

Parkes, C.M., Benjamin, B. and Fitzgerald, R.G. (1969) Broken heart: a statistical study of increased mortality among widowers. *British Medical Journal*, 1: 740–3.

Parrott, A.C. (1999) Does cigarette smoking cause stress? *American Psychologist*, 54: 817–20.

Parrott, A.C. (2005) Nicotine psychobiology: how chronic-dose prospectic studies can illuminate some of the theoretical issues from acute-dose research. *Psychopharmacology*, 184: 567–76.

Parrott, A.C. and Garnham, N.J. (1998) Comparative mood states and cognitive skills of cigarette smokers, deprived smokers and nonsmokers. *Human Psychopharmacology*, 13: 367–76.

Pasternak, R.C., Grundy, S.M., Levy, D. and Thompson, P.D. (1996) Task Force 3: spectrum of risk factors for coronary heart disease. *Journal of the American College of Cardiology*, 27: 978–90.

Payne, B.K., McClernon, F.J. and Dobbins, L.G. (2007) Automatic affective responses to smoking cues. *Experimental and Clinical Pharmacology*, 15: 400–9.

Pennebaker, J. (1989) Confession, inhibition, and disease, in L. Berkowitz (ed.) *Advances in Experimental Social Psychology*, Vol. 22, pp. 211–44. San Diego, CA: Academic Press.

Pennebaker, J. (1997) Writing about emotional experiences as a therapeutic process. *Psychological Sciences*, 8: 162–6.

Pennebaker, J.W., Kiecolt-Glaser, J.K. and Glaser, R. (1988) Disclosure of traumas and immune function: health implications for psychotherapy. *Journal of Consulting and Clinical Psychology*, 56: 239–45.

Pennebaker, J.W., Colder, M. and Sharp, L.K. (1990) Accelerating the coping process. *Journal of Personality and Social Psychology*, 58: 528–37.

Penwell, L.M. and Larkin, K.T. (2010) Social support and risk for cardiovascular disease and cancer: a qualitative review examining the role of inflammatory processes. *Health Psychology Review*, 4: 42–55.

Perkins, K.A. (1993) Weight gain following smoking cessation. *Journal of Consulting and Clinical Psychology*, 61: 768–77.

Perri, M.G. et al. (1997) Effects of group- versus home-based exercise in the treatment of obesity. *Journal of Consulting and Clinical Psychology*, 65: 278–85.

Perry, C.L. et al. (1996) Project Northland: outcomes of a community-wide alcohol use prevention program during early adolescence. *American Journal of Public Health*, 86: 956–65.

Peterson, C. and Seligman, M.E.P. (1987) Coarse explanations as a risk factor for depression: theory and evidence. *Psychological Review*, 91: 347–74.

Peterson, C., Seligman, M.E.P. and Vaillant, G.E. (1988) Pessimistic explanatory style is a risk factor for physical illness: a thirty-five-year longitudinal study. *Journal of Personality and Social Psychology*, 55: 23–7.

Peterson, C., Maier, S.F. and Seligman, M.E.P. (1993) *Learned Helplessness: A Theory for the Age of Personal Control*. New York: Oxford University Press.

Petty, R. and Cacioppo, J.T. (1986) *Communication and Persuasion: Central and Peripheral Routes to Attitude Change*. New York: Springer Verlag.

Petty, R. and Wegener, D.T. (1999) The elaboration likelihood model: current status and controversies, in S. Chaiken and Y. Trope (eds) *Dual-process Theories in Social Psychology*, pp. 37–72. New York: Guilford Press.

Petty, R., Wells, G.L. and Brock, T.C. (1976) Distraction can enhance or reduce yielding to propaganda: thought disruption versus effort justification. *Journal of Personality and Social Psychology*, 34: 874–84.

Petty, R., Cacioppo, J.T. and Goldman, R. (1981a) Personal involvement as a determinant of argument-based persuasion. *Journal of Personality and Social Psychology*, 41: 847–55.

Petty, R., Ostrom, T. and Brock, T.C. (1981b) Historical foundations of the cognitive response approach to attitudes and persuasion, in R.E. Petty, T.M. Ostrom and T.C. Brock (eds) *Cognitive Responses in Persuasion*, pp. 5–29. Hillsdale, NJ: Lawrence Erlbaum.

Petty, R., Wegener, D.T. and Fabrigar, L.R. (1997) Attitudes and attitude change. *Annual Review of Psychology*, 48: 609–47.

Pieper, S., Brosschot, J.F., van der Leeden, R. and Thayer, J. (2010) Prolonged cardiac effects of momentary assessed stressful events and worry episodes. *Psychosomatic Medicine*, 72: 570–7.

Pierie, P.L. et al. (1992) Smoking cessation in women concerned about weight. *American Journal of Public Health*, 82: 1238–43.

Pinkerton, S.D., Holtgrave, D.R. and Galletly, C.L. (2008) Infections prevented by increasing HIV serostatus awareness in the United States, 2001 to 2004. *Journal of Acquired Immune Deficiency Syndrome*, 47: 354–7.

Pinquart, M. and Duberstein, P.R. (2010) Association of social networks with cancer mortality: a meta-analysis. *Critical Reviews in Ocology/Hematology*, 75: 122–37.

Polich, J.M., Armor, D.J. and Braiker, H.B. (1981) *The Course of Alcoholism*. New York: Wiley.

Polivy, J. (1976) Perception of calories and regulation of intake in restrained and unrestrained subjects. *Addictive Behavior*, 1: 237–43.

Polivy, J. and Herman, C.P. (1976) Effects of alcohol on eating behavior: influence of mood and perceived intoxication. *Journal of Abnormal Psychology*, 85: 601–6.

Polivy, J. and Herman, C.P. (1987) Diagnosis and treatment of normal eating. *Journal of Consulting and Clinical Psychology*, 28: 341–3.

Pooling Project Research Group (1978) *Relationship of Blood Pressure, Serum Cholesterol, Smoking Habit, Relative Weight and ECG-abnormality to Incidence of Major Coronary Events: Final Report of the Pooling Project*. Dallas, TX: American Heart Association Monographs, No. 60.

Poortinga, W. (2007) The prevalence and clustering of four major lifestyle risk factors in an English adult population. *Preventive Medicine*, 44: 124–8.

Portnoy, D.B., Scott-Sheldon, L.A.J., Johnson, B.T. and Carey, M.P. (2008) Computer-delivered interventions for health promotional and behavioral risk reduction: a meta-analysis of 75 randomized controlled trials, 1988–2007. *Preventive Medicine*, 47: 3–16.

Powell, K.E., Thompson, P.D., Caspersen, C.J. and Kendrick, J.S. (1987) Physical activity and the incidence of coronary heart disease. *Annual Review of Public Health*, 8: 253–87.

Powers, M.B., Vedel, E. and Emmelkamp, P.M.G. (2008) Behavioral couples therapy (BCT) for alcohol and drug use disorders: a meta-analysis. *Clinical Psychology Reviewer*, 28: 952–62.

Prochaska, J.O. and DiClemente, C.C. (1983) Stages and processes of self-change of smoking: toward an integrative model of change. *Journal of Consulting and Clinical Psychology*, 51: 390–5.

Prochaska, J.O., DiClemente, C.C. and Norcross, J.C. (1992) In search of how people change: applications to addictive behaviour. *American Psychologist*, 47: 1102–14.

Prochaska, J.O. *et al.* (1994) Stages of change and decisional balance for 12 problem behaviors. *Health Psychology*, 13: 39–46.

Project MATCH Research Group (1998) Matching alcohol treatment to client heterogeneity: Project MATCH three-year drinking outcomes. *Alcoholism: Clinical and Experimental Research*, 22: 1300–11.

Puhl, R.M. and Latner, J.D. (2007) Stigma, obesity and the health of the nation's children. *Psychological Bulletin,* 133: 557–80.

Puska, P. *et al.* (1985) The community-based strategy to prevent coronary heart disease: conclusions from ten years of the North Karelia Project. *Annual Review of Public Health*, 6: 147–94.

Quinlan, K.B. and McCaul, K.D. (2000) Matched and mismatched interventions with young adult smokers: testing a stage theory. *Health Psychology*, 19: 165–71.

Rabkin, J.G. and Struening, E.L. (1976) Life events, stress, and illness. *Science*, 194: 1013–20.

Rahe, R.H. (1968) Life change measurement as a predictor of illness. *Proceedings of the Royal Society of Medicine*, 61: 124–6.

Rahe, R.H. and Lind, E. (1971) Psychosocial factors and sudden cardiac death: a pilot study. *Journal of Psychosomatic Research*, 15: 19–24.

Rahe, R.H. and Paasikivi, J. (1971) Psychosocial factors and myocardial infarction II: an outpatient study in Sweden. *Journal of Psychosomatic Research*, 15: 33–9.

Rahe, R.H., Romo, M., Bennett, L. and Siltanen, P. (1974) Subjects' recent life changes and myocardial infarction in Helsinki. *Archives of Internal Medicine*, 133: 222–8.

Ramstedt, M. (2001) Per capita alcohol consumption and liver cirrhosis mortality in 14 European countries. *Addiction*, 96 (1 Suppl.): S19–34.

Ramstedt, M. (2008) Alcohol and fatal accidents in the United States: a time series analysis for 1950–2002. *Accident Analysis and Prevention*, 40: 1273–81.

Randall, D.M. and Wolff, J.A. (1994) The time interval in the intention–behaviour relationship: meta-analysis. *British Journal of Social Psychology*, 33: 405–18.

Rankinen, T. and Bouchard, C. (2006) Genetics of food intake and eating behavior phenotypes in humans. *Annual Review of Nutrition,* 26: 413–34.

Ratneshwar, S. and Chaiken, S. (1991) Comprehension's role in persuasion: the case of its moderating effect on the persuasive impact of source cues. *Journal of Consumer Research*, 18: 52–62.

Ravussin, E., Burnand, B., Schutz, Y. and Jéquier, E. (1985) Energy expenditure before and during energy restriction in obese patients. *American Journal of Clinical Nutrition*, 41: 753–9.

Reblin, M. and Uchino, B.N. (2008) Social and emotional support and its implication for health. *Current Opinion in Psychiatry*, 21: 201–5.

Register, C.A. and Williams, D.R. (1990) Wage effects of obesity among young workers. *Social Science Quarterly*, 71: 131–41.

Rehm, J., Greenfield, T.K., and Rogers, J.D. (2001). Average volume of alcohol consumption, patterns of drinking, and all-cause mortality: results from the US national alcohol survey. *American Journal of Epidemiology*, 153: 64–71.

Remington, P.L. *et al.* (1985) Current smoking trends in the United States: the 1981–1983: behavioral risk factor surveys. *Journal of the American Medical Association*, 253: 2975–8.

Renehan, A.G. *et al.* (2008) Body-mass index and incidence of cancer: a systematic review and meta-analysis of prospective observational studies. *Lancet*, 371: 569–78.

Rennie, K.L. and Jebb, S.A. (2005) National prevalence of obesity: prevalence of obesity in Great Britain. *Obesity Reviews,* 6: 11–12.

Reynaud, M. *et al.* (2002) Alcohol is the main factor in excess traffic accident fatalities in France. *Alcoholism: Clinical and Experimental Research*, 26: 1833–9.

Rhodes, R.E., Plotnikoff, R.C. and Courneya, K.S. (2008) Predicting the physical activity intention–behavior profiles of adopters and maintainers using three social cognition models. *Annals of Behavioral Medicine*, 36: 244–52.

Rhodewalt, F. and Zone, J.B. (1989) Appraisal of life change, depression and illness in hardy and nonhardy women. *Journal of Personality and Social Psychology*, 56: 81–8.

Richard, R. and van der Pligt, J. (1991) Factors affecting condom use among adolescents. *Journal of Community and Applied Social Psychology*, 1: 105–16.

Riley, D.M. *et al.* (1987) Behavioral treatment of alcohol: a review and a comparison of behavioral and nonbehavioral studies, in M. Wilcox (ed.) *Treatment and Prevention of Alcohol Problems: A Resource Manual*, pp. 73–115. San Diego, CA: Academic Press.

Rippe, J.M. *et al.* (1998) Improved psychological well-being, quality of life, and health practice in moderately overweight women participating in a 12-week structured weight loss program. *Obesity*, 6: 208–18.

Rippetoe, P.A. and Rogers, R.W. (1987) Effects of components of protection motivation theory on adaptive and maladaptive coping with a health threat. *Journal of Personality and Social Psychology*, 52: 596–604.

Rise, J., Kovac, V., Kraft, P. and Moan, I.S. (2008) Predicting the intention to quit smoking and quitting behaviour: extending the theory of planned behaviour. *British Journal of Health Psychology*, 13: 291–310.

Roberts, R.E., Kaplan, G.E., Shema, S.J. and Strawbridge, W.J. (2002) Are the obese at greater risk for depression? *American Journal of Epidemiology*, 152: 163–70.

Robertson, K. *et al.* (1974) A controlled study of the effect of television messages on safety belt use. *American Journal of Public Health*, 64: 1071–80.

Robertson, L.S. (1984) Behavior and injury prevention: whose behavior? in J.D. Matarazzo *et al.* (eds) *Behavioral Health*, pp. 980–9. New York: Wiley.

Robertson, L.S. (1986) Behavioral and environmental interventions for reducing motor vehicle trauma, in L. Breslow, J.E. Fielding and L.B. Lave (eds) *Annual Review of Public Health*, pp. 13–34. Palo Alto, CA: Annual Reviews Inc.

Robertson, L.S. (1987) Injury prevention: limits to self-protective behavior, in N.D. Weinstein (ed.) *Taking Care*, pp. 280–97. New York: Cambridge University Press.

Rodgers, W.M., Conner, M. and Murray, T.C. (2008) Distinguishing among perceived control, perceived difficulty, and self-efficacy as determinants of intentions and behaviours. *British Journal of Social Psychology*, 47: 607–30.

Rodin, J. (1981) Current status of the internal–external hypothesis for obesity. *American Psychologist*, 36: 361–72.

Rodin, J., Slochower, J. and Fleming, B. (1977) The effects of degree of obesity, age of onset, and energy deficit on external responsiveness. *Journal of Comparative and Physiological Psychology*, 91: 586–97.

Rogers, P.J. and Blundell, J.E. (1980) Investigation of food selection and meal parameters during the development of dietary induced obesity (abstract). *Appetite*, 1: 85.

Rogers, R.W. (1983) Cognitive and physiological processes in fear appeals and attitude change: a revised theory of protection motivation, in J.T. Cacioppo and R.E. Petty (eds) *Social Psychophysiology: A Source Book*, pp. 153–76. New York: Guilford Press.

Rogers, R.W. and Mewborn, C.R. (1976) Fear appeals and attitude change: effects of anxiousness, probability of occurrence, and the efficacy of coping responses. *Journal of Personality and Social Psychology*, 34: 54–61.

Rooke, S. *et al.* (2010) Computer-delivered interventions for alcohol and tobacco use: a meta-analysis. *Addiction*, 105: 1381–90.

Rooney, B.L. and Murray, D.M. (1996) A meta-analysis of smoking prevention programs after adjustment for errors in the unit of analysis. *Health Education Quarterly*, 23: 48–64.

Rose, J.E. (2006) Nicotine and non-nicotine factors in cigarette addiction. *Psychopharmacology*, 184: 274–85.

Rose, J.S., Chassin, L., Presson, C.C. and Sherman, S.J. (1996) Prospective predictors of quit attempts and smoking cessation in young adults. *Health Psychology*, 15: 261–8.

Rosen, C.S. (2000) Is the sequencing of change processes by stages consistent across health problems? A meta-analysis. *Health Psychology*, 19: 593–604.

Rosenberg, H. (1993) Prediction of controlled drinking by alcoholics and problem drinkers. *Psychological Bulletin*, 113: 129–39.

Rosenberg, M.J. (1960) An analysis of affective–cognitive consistency, in C.I. Hovland and M.J. Rosenberg (eds) *Attitude Organization and Change*, pp. 15–64. New Haven, CT: Yale University Press.

Rosenberg, M.J. and Hovland, C.I. (1960) Cognitive, affective, and behavioral components of attitudes, in I. Hovland and M.J. Rosenberg (eds) *Attitude Organization and Change*, pp. 1–15. New Haven, CT: Yale University Press.

Rosenman, R.H. *et al.* (1975) Coronary heart disease in the Western Collaborative Group Study: final follow-up experience of 81–2 years. *Journal of the American Medical Association*, 223: 872–7.

Rosenstock, I. (1974) The health belief model and preventive health behavior. *Health Education Monographs*, 2: 354–86.

Ross, C.E. and Hayes, D. (1988) Exercise and psychological well-being in the community. *American Journal of Epidemiology*, 127: 762–71.

Ross, C.E. and Mirowsky, J. (1979) A comparison of life-event weighting schemes: change, undesirability, and effect-proportional indices. *Journal of Health and Social Behavior*, 20: 166–77.

Ross, S. and Peselow, E. (2009) Pharmacotherapy of addictive disorders, *Clinical Neuropharmacology*, 32: 277–89.

Roth, S. and Cohen, L.J. (1986). Approach, avoidance, and coping with stress. *American Psychologist*, 41: 813–19.

Rothacker, D.Q. (2000) Five-year self-management of weight using meal replacements: comparison with matched controls in rural Wisconsin. *Nutrition*, 16: 344–8.

Rothman, A.J. and Salovey, P. (2007) The reciprocal relation between principles and practice: social psychology and health behavior, in A.W. Kruglanski and E.T. Higgins (eds) *Social Psychology: Handbook of Basic Principles,* 2nd edn. pp. 826–49. New York: Guilford.

Rothman, A.J., Baldwin, A.S. and Hertel, A.W. (2004) Self-regulation and behavior change: distentangling behavioral initiation and behavioral maintenance, in R.F. Baumeister and K.D. Vohs (eds) *Handbook of Self-regulation*, pp. 130–48. New York: Guilford Press.

Rotter, J.B., Seeman, M. and Liverant, S. (1962) Internal vs. external locus of control of reinforcement: a major variable in behavior therapy, in N.F. Washburne (ed.) *Decisions, Values, and Groups*, pp. 473–516. London: Pergamon Press.

Rowe, J.W. and Kahn, R.L. (1987) Human aging: usual and successful. *Science*, 237: 143–9.

Rowe, J.W. and Kahn, R.L. (1997) Successful aging. *The Gerontologist*, 37: 433–40.

Ruberman, W., Weinblatt, E., Goldberg, J.D. and Chaudhary, B.S. (1984) Psychosocial influences on mortality after myocardial infarction. *New England Journal of Medicine*, 311: 552–9.

Rzewnicki, R. and Forgays, D. (1987) Recidivism and self-cure of smoking and obesity: an attempt to replicate. *American Psychologist*, 42: 97–100.

Saffer, H. (1991) Alcohol advertising bans and alcohol abuse: an international perspective. *Journal of Health Economics*, 10: 65–79.

Salina, D. *et al.* (1994) A follow-up of a media-based, worksite smoking cessation program. *American Journal of Community Psychology*, 22: 257–71.

Salonen, J.T., Puska, P. and Tuomilehto, J. (1982) Physical activity and risk of myocardial infarction, cerebral stroke and death: a longitudinal study in eastern Finland. *American Journal of Epidemiology*, 115: 526–37.

Saracco, A. *et al.* (1993) Man-to-woman sexual transmission of HIV: longitudinal study of 434 steady sexual partners of infected men. *Journal of Acquired Immune Deficiency Syndrome*, 6: 497–502.

Sarason, B.R., Shearin, E.N., Pierce, G.R. and Sarason, I.G. (1987) Interrelationships among social support measures: theoretical and practical implications. *Journal of Personality and Social Psychology*, 52: 813–32.

Sarason, B.R., Sarason, I.G. and Pierce, G.R. (1990) Traditional views of social support and their impact on assessment, in B.R. Sarason, I.G. Sarason and G.R. Pierce (eds) *Social Support: An Interactional View*, pp. 9–25. New York: Wiley.

Sarason, I.G., Levine, H.M., Basham, R.B. and Sarason, B.R. (1983) Assessing social support: the social support questionnaire. *Journal of Personality*, 44: 127–39.

Sax, P.E., Cohen, C.J. and Kuritzkas, D.R. (2010) *HIV Essentials*, 3rd edn. Sudbury, MA: Physician's Press.

Schaalma, H., Kok, G. and Peters, L. (1993) Determinants of consistent condom use by adolescents: the impact of experience of sexual intercourse. *Health Education Research*, 8: 255–69.

Schachter, S. (1959) *The Psychology of Affiliation*. Stanford, CA: Stanford University Press.

Schachter, S. (1971) *Emotion, Obesity, and Crime*. New York: Academic Press.

Schachter, S. (1977) Nicotine regulation in heavy and light smokers. *Journal of Experimental Psychology: General*, 106: 5–12.

Schachter, S. (1978) Pharmacological and psychological determinants of smoking. *Annals of Internal Medicine*, 88: 104–14.

Schachter, S. (1982) Recidivism and self-cure of smoking and obesity. *American Psychologist*, 37: 436–44.

Schachter, S. and Gross, R. (1968) Manipulated time and eating behavior. *Journal of Personality and Social Psychology*, 10: 98–106.

Schachter, S., Goldman, R. and Gordon, A. (1968) Effects of fear, food deprivation, and obesity on eating. *Journal of Personality and Social Psychology*, 10: 91–7.

Schachter, S., Kozlowski, L.T. and Silverstein, B. (1977a) Effects of urinary pH on secret smoking. *Journal of Experimental Psychology: General*, 106: 13–19.

Schachter, S., Silverstein, B. and Perlick, D. (1977b) Psychological and pharmacological explanations of smoking under stress. *Journal of Experimental Psychology: General*, 106: 31–40.

Scheier, M.F. and Carver, C.S. (1985) Optimism, coping, and health: assessment and implications of generalized outcome expectancies. *Health Psychology*, 4: 219–47.

Scheier, M.F. and Carver, C.S. (1987) Dispositional optimism and physical well-being: the influence of generalized outcome expectancies on health. *Journal of Personality*, 55: 169–210.

Scheier, M.F., Weintraub, J.K. and Carver, C.S. (1986) Coping with stress: divergent strategies of optimists and pessimists. *Journal of Personality and Social Psychology*, 51: 1257–64.

Scheier, M.F. et al. (1989) Dispositional optimism and recovery from coronary artery bypass surgery: the beneficial effects on physical and psychological well-being. *Journal of Personality and Social Psychology*, 57: 1024–40.

Scheier, M.F., Carver, C.S. and Bridges, M.W. (1994) Distinguishing optimism from neuroticism (and trait anxiety, self-mastery, and self-esteem): a reevaluation of the life orientation test. *Journal of Personality and Social Psychology*, 67: 1063–78.

Schifter, D.E. and Ajzen, I. (1985) Intention, perceived control, and weight loss: an application of the theory of planned behavior. *Journal of Personality and Social Psychology*, 49: 843–51.

Schmidt, W. and de Lint, J. (1970) Estimating the prevalence of alcoholism from alcohol consumption and mortality data. *Quarterly Journal of Studies on Alcohol*, 31: 957–64.

Schmied, L.A. and Lawler, K.A. (1986) Hardiness, Type A behavior, and the stress–illness relationship in working women. *Journal of Personality and Social Psychology*, 51: 1218–23.

Schmitz, K.H. and Jeffery, R.W. (2002) Prevention of obesity, in T.A. Wadden and A.J. Stunkard (eds) *Handbook of Obesity Treatment*, pp. 556–93). New York: Guilford.

Schneiderman, N., Ironson, G. and Siegel, S.D. (2005) Stress and health: psychological, behavioral, and biological determinants. *Annual Review of Clinical Psychology*, 1: 607–28.

Schoenbach, V.J., Kaplan, B.H., Fredman, L. and Kleinbaum, D.G. (1986) Social ties and mortality in Evans County, Georgia. *American Journal of Epidemiology*, 123: 577–91.

Schotte, D.E., Cools, J. and McNally, R.J. (1990) Induced anxiety triggering overeating in restrained eaters. *Journal of Abnormal Psychology*, 99: 317–20.

Schroeder, D.H. and Costa Jr, P.T. (1984) Influence of life events' stress on physical illness: substantive effects on methodological floors? *Journal of Personality and Social Psychology*, 46: 853–63.

Schuit, A.J., van Loonen, A.J.M., Tijhuis, M. and Ocké, M.C. (2002) Clustering of lifestyle risk factors in a general adult population. *Preventive Medicine*, 35: 219–24.

Schuler, G. *et al.* (1992) Regular physical exercise and low-fat diet: effects on progression of coronary artery disease. *Circulation*, 86: 1–11.

Schwartz, J.L. (1987) *Smoking Cessation Methods: The United States and Canada, 1978–1985.* Division of Cancer Prevention and Control, National Cancer Institute, US Department of Health and Human Services, Public Health Service (NIH Publication No. 87-2940). Washington, DC: US Government Printing Office.

Schwarz, N. (2007). Attitude construction: evaluation in context. *Social Cognition*, 25: 638–56.

Schwarz, N. and Bohner, G. (2001) The construction of attitudes, in A. Tesser and N. Schwarz (eds) *Blackwell Handbook of Social Psychology: Intraindividual Processes*, pp. 436–57. Oxford: Blackwell.

Schwarz, N. and Strack, F. (1991) Context effects in attitude surveys: applying cognitive theory to social research, in W. Stroebe and M. Hewstone (eds) *European Review of Social Psychology*, 2: 31–50.

Schwarzer, R. and Fuchs, R. (1996) Self-effiacy and health behaviours, in M. Conner and P. Norman, *Predicting Health Behaviour*, pp. 163–96. Buckingham: Open University Press.

Schwarzer, R. and Leppin, A. (1992) Social support and mental health: a conceptual and empirical overview, in L. Montada, S-H. Fillipp and M. Lerner (eds) *Life Crises and Experiences of Loss in Adult Life*, pp. 435–58. Hillsdale, NJ: Lawrence Erlbaum.

Segerstrom, S.C. and Miller, G.E. (2004) Psychological stress and the human immune system: a meta-analytic study of 30 years of inquiry. *Psychological Bulletin*, 130: 601–30.

Segerstrom, S.C., Taylor, S.E., Kemeny, M.E. and Fahey, J.L. (1998) Optimism is associated with mood, coping, and immune change in response to stress. *Journal of Personality and Social Psychology*, 74: 1646–55.

Seligman, M.E.P. (1975) *Helplessness.* San Francisco, CA: W.H. Freeman.

Selye, H. (1976) *The Stress of Life*, 2nd edn. New York: McGraw Hill.

Seydel, E., Taal, E. and Wiegman, O. (1990) Risk-appraisal, outcome and self-efficacy expectancies: cognitive factors in preventive behavior related to cancer. *Psychology and Health*, 4: 99–109.

Shah, J. (2003) The motivational looking glass: how significant others implicitly affect goal appraisal. *Journal of Personality and Social Psychology*, 85: 424–39.

Shaper, A.G., Wannamethee, G. and Walker, M. (1988) Alcohol and mortality in British men: explaining the U-shaped curve, *Lancet*, 3: 1267–73.

Sheeran, P. (2002) Intention-behavior relations: a conceptual and empirical review, in W. Stroebe and M. Hewstone (eds) *European Review of Social Psychology*, 12: 1–36.

Sheeran, P. and Abraham, C. (2005) The health belief model, in M. Conner and P. Norman, *Predicting Health Behaviour*, pp. 28–80. Maidenhead: Open University Press.

Sheeran, P. and Orbell, S. (1998) Do intentions predict condom use? Meta-analysis and examination of six moderator variables. *British Journal of Social Psychology*, 37: 231–50.

Sheeran, P. and Orbell, S. (2000) Using implementation intentions to increase attendance for cervical cancer screening. *Health Psychology*, 19: 283–9.

Sheeran, P., Abraham, C. and Orbell, S. (1999) Psychosocial correlates of heterosexual condom use: a meta-analysis. *Psychological Bulletin*, 125: 90–132.

Shekelle, R.B. *et al.* (1985) MRFIT Research Group: the MRFIT behavior pattern study, II. Type A behavior pattern and incidence of coronary heart disease. *American Journal of Epidemiology*, 122: 559–70.

Shen, B-J. *et al.* (2008) Anxiety characteristics independently and prospectively predict myocardial infarction in men. *Journal of the American College of Cardiology*, 51: 113–19.

Sherman, D.A., Nelson, L.D. and Steele, C.M. (2000) Do messages about health risk threaten the self? Increasing the acceptance of threatening health messages via self-affirmation, *Personality and Social Psychology Bulletin*, 26: 1046–58.

Shiffman, S. (1982) Relapse following smoking cessation: a situational analysis. *Journal of Consulting and Clinical Psychology*, 50: 71–86.

Shiffman, S. (1993) Assessing smoking patterns and motives. *Journal of Consulting and Clinical Psychology*, 61: 732–42.

Shiffman, S. *et al.* (1985) Preventing relapse in ex-smokers, in G.A. Marlatt and J. Gordon (eds) *Relapse Prevention: Maintenance Strategies in the Treatment of Addictive Behaviors*, pp. 472–520. New York: Guilford Press.

Sibai, A.M., Armenian, H.K. and Alam, S. (1989) Wartime determinants of arteriographically confirmed coronary artery disease in Beirut. *American Journal of Epidemiology*, 130: 623–31.

Siegel, J.M. and Kuykendall, D.H. (1990) Loss, widowhood, and psychological distress among the elderly. *Journal of Consulting and Clinical Psychology*, 58: 519–24.

Siegman, A.W. (1994) From Type A to hostility and anger: reflections on the history of coronary prone behavior, in A.W. Siegman and T.W. Smith (eds) *Anger, Hostility and the Heart*, pp. 1–22. Hillsdale, NJ: Lawrence Erlbaum.

Siegman, A.W. and Smith, T.W. (eds) (1994) *Anger, Hostility and the Heart*. Hillsdale, NJ: Lawrence Erlbaum.

Sigvardsson, S., Bohman, M. and Cloninger, R. (1996) Replication of the Stockholm adoption study of alcoholism. *Archives of General Psychiatry*, 53: 681–7.

Simoni, J.M., Frick, P.A. and Huang, B. (2006) A longitudinal evaluation of a social support model of medication adherence among HIV-positive men and women on antiretroviral therapy, *Health Psychology*, 25: 74–81.

Simopoulos, A.P. (1986) Obesity and body weight standards, in L. Breslow, J.E. Fielding and L.B. Lave (eds) *Annual Review of Public Health*, 7, pp. 475–92. Palo Alto, CA: Annual Reviews Inc.

Sims, E.A.H. and Horton, E.S. (1968) Endocrine and metabolic adaptation to obesity and starvation. *American Journal of Clinical Nutrition*, 21: 1455–70.

Singh, R.B. *et al.* (1992) Randomised controlled trial of cardioprotective diet in patients with recent acute myocardial infarction: results of one year follow up. *British Medical Journal*, 304: 1015–19.

Six, B. (1996) Attitude–behavior relations: a comprehensive meta-analysis of 887 studies published between 1927 and 1993. Paper presented at the XXVI International Congress of Psychology, Montreal, Canada.

Sleet, D.A., Ballesteros, M.F. and Borse, N.N. (2010) A review of unintentional injuries in adolescents. *Annual Review of Public Health*, 31: 195–212.

Smedslund, G., Fisher, K.J., Boles, S.M. and Lichtenstein, E. (2004) The effectiveness of workplace smoking cessation programmes: a meta-analysis of recent studies. *Tobacco Control*, 13: 197–204.

Smith, T.W. (1994) Concepts and methods in the study of anger, hostility, and health, in A.W. Siegman and T.W. Smith (eds) *Anger, Hostility and the Heart*, pp. 23–42. Hillsdale, NJ: Lawrence Erlbaum.

Smith, T.W. and MacKenzie, J. (2006) Personality and risk of physical illness. *Annual Review of Clinical Psychology*, 2: 435–67.

Smith, T.W., Pope, M.K., Rhodewalt, F. and Poulton, J.L. (1989) Optimism, neuroticism, coping, and symptom reports: an alternative interpretation of the Life Orientation Test. *Journal of Personality and Social Psychology*, 56: 640–8.

Society of Actuaries (1960) *Build and Blood Pressure Study, 1959*. Chicago: Society of Actuaries.

Society of Actuaries and Association of Life Insurance Medical Directors of America (1979) *Build Study*. Chicago: Society of Actuaries.

Sofi, F. *et al.* (2008) Adherence to Mediterranean diet and health status: meta-analysis. *British Medical Journal*, 337: 1344.

Sokol, R.J. *et al.* (1986) Significant determinants of susceptibility to alcohol teratogenicity. *Annals of the New York Academy of Sciences*, 477: 87–102.

Solberg Nes, L. and Segerstrom, S.C. (2006) Dispositional optimism and coping: a meta-analytic review. *Personality and Social Psychology Review*, 10: 235–51.

Solberg Nes, L., Evans, D.R. and Segerstrom, S.C. (2009) Optimism and college retention: mediation by motivation, performance, and adjsutment, *Journal of Applied Social Psychology*, 39: 1887–912.

Sonstroem, R.J. (1978) Physical estimation and attraction scales: rationale and research. *Medicine and Science in Sports*, 10: 97–102.

Sonstroem, R.J. (1988) Psychological models, in R.K. Dishman (ed.) *Exercise Adherence: Its Impact on Public Health*, pp. 125–53. Champaign, IL: Human Kinetics Books.

Sonstroem, R.J. and Kampper, K.P. (1980) Prediction of athletic participation in middle school males. *Research Quarterly for Exercise and Sport*, 51: 685–94.

Sorensen, G. *et al.* (1996) Work site-based cancer prevention: primary results from the Working Well Trial. *American Journal of Public Health*, 86: 939–47.

Sorensen, G., Emmons, K., Hunt, M.K. and Johnston, D. (1998) Implications of the results of community intervention trials. *Annual Review of Public Health*, 19: 379–416.

Spencer, J.A. and Fremouw, W.J. (1979) Binge eating as a function of restraint and weight classification. *Journal of Abnormal Psychology*, 88: 262–7.

Spielberger, C.D. (1986) Psychological determinants of smoking behavior, in L.D. Tollison (ed.) *Smoking and Society*, pp. 89–132. Lexington, MA: Heath.

Spittaels, H., De Bourdehuij, I., Brug, J. and Vandelanotte, C. (2007) Effectiveness of an online computer-tailored physical activity intervention in a real-life setting. *Health Education Research*, 22: 385–96.

Spring, B. *et al.* (2009) Behavioral intervention to promote smoking cessation and prevent weight gain: a systematic review and meta-analysis. *Addiction*, 104: 1472–86.

Stallones, R.A. (1983) Ischemic heart disease and lipids in blood and diet. *Annual Review of Nutrition*, 3: 155–85.

Stalonas, P.M., Johnson, W.G. and Christ, M. (1978) Behavior modification for obesity: the evaluation of exercise, contingency management and program adherence. *Journal of Consulting and Clinical Psychology*, 46: 463–9.

Stanton, A.L. and Snider, P.R. (1993) Coping with a breast cancer diagnosis: a prospective study. *Health Psychology*, 12: 16–23.

Stanton, A.L., Danoff-Burg, S., Cameron, C.L. and Ellis, A.P. (1994) Coping through emotional approach: problems of conceptualization and confounding. *Journal of Personality and Social Psychology*, 66: 350–62.

Stanton, A.L., Kirk, S.B., Cameron, C.L. and Danoff-Burg, S. (2000) Coping through emotional approach: scale construction and validation. *Journal of Personality and Social Psychology*, 78: 1150–69.

Stead, L.F., Bergson, G. and Lancaster, T. (2008) Physician advice for smoking cessation. *Cochrane Data Base of Systematic Reviews*, CD000165.

Steele, C.M. and Josephs, R.A. (1990) Alcohol myopia: its prized and dangerous effects. *American Psychologist*, 45: 921–33.

Stein, M., Keller, S.E. and Schleifer, S.J. (1985) Stress and immunomodulation: the role of depression and neuroendocrine function. *Journal of Immunology*, 135: 827s–33s.

Stephens, M.A.P., Druley, J.A. and Zautra, A.J. (2002) Older adults' recovery from surgery for osteoarthritis of the knee: psychosocial resources and constraints as predictors of outcomes. *Health Psychology*, 21: 377–83.

Sternberg, B. (1985) Relapse in weight control: definitions, processes, and prevention strategies, in G.A. Marlatt and J.R. Gordon (eds) *Relapse Prevention*, pp. 521–45. New York: Guilford Press.

Stice, E. (2002) Risk and maintenance factors for eating pathology: a meta-analytic review. *Psychological Bulletin*, 128: 825–48.

Stice, E. and Shaw, H. (2004) Eating disorder prevention programs: a meta-analytic review. *Psychological Bulletin*, 130: 206–27.

Stice, E., Presnell, K., Groesz, L. and Shaw, H. (2005) Effects of a weight maintenance diet on bulimic symptoms in adolescent girls: an experimental test of the dietary restraint theory. *Health Psychology*, 24: 402–12.

Stice, E., Shaw, H. and Marti, C.N. (2006) A meta-analytic review of obesity prevention programs for children and adolescents: the skinny on interventions that work. *Psychological Bulletin*, 132: 667–91.

Stokes, J.P. (1983) Predicting satisfaction with social support from social network structure. *American Journal of Community Psychology*, 11: 141–52.

Stolte, I.G. *et al.* (2004) Perceived load, but not actual HIV-1-R-RNA load, is associated with sexual risk behaviour. *AIDS*, 18: 1943–9.

Stone, A.A. *et al.* (1998) A comparison of coping assessed by ecological momentary assessment and retrospective recall. *Journal of Personality and Social Psychology*, 74: 1670–80.

Strack, F. and Deutsch, R. (2004) Reflective and impulsive determinants of social behavior. *Personality and Social Psychology Review*, 8: 220–47.

Strecher, V.J., Shiffman, S. and West, R. (2005) Randomized controlled trial of a web-based computer-tailored smoking cessation program as a supplement to nicotine patch therapy. *Addiction*, 100: 682–88.

Stroebe, M. (1992) Coping with bereavement: a review of the grief work hypothesis. *Omega*, 26: 19–42.

Stroebe, M. and Schut, H. (1999) The dual process model of coping with bereavement: rationale and description. *Death Studies*, 32: 197–224.

Stroebe, M. and Stroebe, W. (1993) Mortality of bereavement: a review, in M. Stroebe, W. Stroebe and R. Hansson (eds) *Handbook of Bereavement*, pp. 175–95. New York: Cambridge University Press.

Stroebe, M., Schut, H. and Stroebe, W. (2007) Health outcomes of bereavement. *Lancet*, 370: 1960–73.

Stroebe, W. (2000) *Social Psychology and Health*, 2nd edn. Buckingham: Open University Press.

Stroebe, W. (2002) Übergewicht als Schicksal: Die kognitive Steuerung des Eßverhaltens. *Psychologische Rundschau*, 53: 14–22.

Stroebe, W. (2008) *Dieting, Overweight And Obesity: Self-Regulation in a Food-Rich Environment*. Washington, D.C: American Psychological Association.

Stroebe, W. and Stroebe, M. (1987) *Bereavement and Health*. New York: Cambridge University Press.

Stroebe, W. and de Wit, J. (1996) Health-impairing behaviours, in G.R. Semin and K. Fiedler (eds) *Applied Social Psychology*, pp. 113–44. London: Sage.

Stroebe, W. and Schut, H. (2001) Risk factors in bereavement outcome: a methodological and empirical review, in M. Stroebe, R.O. Hansson, W. Stroebe and H. Schut (eds) *Handbook of Bereavement Research: Consequences, Coping and Care*, pp. 349–72. Washington, DC: American Psychological Association.

Stroebe, W. and Stroebe, M. (1987) *Bereavement and Health*. New York: Cambridge University Press.

Stroebe, W. and Stroebe, M. (1993) Determinants of adjustment to bereavement in younger widows and widowers, in M. Stroebe, W. Stroebe and R.O. Hansson (eds) *Handbook of Bereavement: Theory, Research, and Intervention*, pp. 208–26. New York: Cambridge University Press.

Stroebe, W. and Stroebe, M. (1996) The social psychology of social support, in E.T. Higgins and A.W. Kruglanski (eds) *Social Psychology: Handbook of Basic Principles*, pp. 597–621. New York: Guilford Press.

Stroebe, W., Stroebe, M. and Domittner, G. (1988) Individual and situational differences in recovery from bereavement: a risk group identified. *Journal of Social Issues*, 44: 143–58.

Stroebe, W. *et al.* (2008a) When dieters fail: a goal conflict model of eating. *Journal of Experimental Social Psychology,* 44: 26–36.

Stroebe, W. *et al.* (2008b) From homeostatic to hedonic theories of eating: self-regulatory failure in food-rich environments. *Applied Psychology: Health and Well-being*, 57: 172–93.

Stunkard, A.J. and Koch, C. (1964) The interpretation of gastric motility, I. Apparent bias in the reports of hunger by obese persons. *Archives of Genetic Psychiatry*, 11: 74–82.

Stunkard, A.J. and Sobal, J. (1995) Psychosocial consequences of obesity, in K.D. Kelley and C.G. Fairburn (eds) *Eating Disorders and Obesity*, pp. 417–21. New York: Guilford Press.

Suarez, E.C. (2003) Plasma interleukin-6 is associated with psychosocial risk factors of cardiovascular disease in apparently health adults. *Brain, Behavior, and Immunity*, 17: 296–303.

Suggs, L.S. and McIntyre, C. (2009) Are we there yet? An examination of online tailored health communication, *Health Education and Behavior*, 36: 278–88.

Sullivan, P.S., Salazar, L., Buchbinder, S. and Sanchez, T.H. (2009) Estimating the proportion of HIV transmissions from main sex partners among men who have sex with men in five US cities. *AIDS*, 23: 1153–62.

Suls, J. and Bunde, J. (2005) Anger, anxiety, and depression as risk factors for cardiovascular disease: the problems and implications of overlapping affective dispositions. *Psychological Bulletin*, 131: 260–300.

Sutton, S. (1982) Fear-arousing communications: a critical examination of theory and research, in J.R. Eiser (ed.) *Social Psychology and Behavioral Medicine*, pp. 303–37. Chichester: Wiley.

Sutton, S. (1987) Social-psychological approaches to understanding addictive behaviours: attitude–behaviour and decision-making models. *British Journal of Addiction*, 82: 355–70.

Sutton, S. (1989) Smoking attitudes and behavior: applications of Fishbein and Ajzen's theory of reasoned action to predicting and understanding smoking decisions, in T. Ney and A. Gale (eds) *Smoking and Human Behavior*, pp. 289–312. Chichester: Wiley.

Sutton, S. (1996) Can 'stages of change' provide guidance in the treatment of addiction? A critical examination of Prochaska and DiClemente's model, in G. Edwards and C. Dare (eds) *Psychotherapy, Psychological Treatment and the Addictions*, pp. 189–205. Cambridge: Cambridge University Press.

Sutton, S. (2005) Stage theories of health behaviour, in M. Conner and P. Norman (eds) *Predicting Health Behaviour*, 2nd edn, pp. 223–75. Maidenhead: Open University Press.

Sutton, S.R. and Hallett, R. (1989) Understanding the effect of fear-arousing communications: the role of cognitive factors and amount of fear aroused. *Journal of Behavioral Medicine*, 11: 353–60.

Sutton, S., McVey, D. and Glanz, A. (1999) A comparative test of the theory of reasoned action and the theory of planned behavior in the prediction of condom use intentions in a national sample of English young people. *Health Psychology*, 18: 72–81.

Svetkey, L.P. *et al.* (1999) Effects of dietary patterns on blood pressure: subgroup analysis of Dietary Approaches to Stop Hypertension (DASH) randomized clinical trial. *Archives of Internal Medicine*, 159: 285–93.

Swanson, N.A., Rudman, L.A. and Greenwald, A.G. (2001) Using the implicit association test to investigate attitude–behavior consistency for stigmatised behavior. *Cognition and Emotion*, 15: 207–30.

Sweeney, P., Anderson, K. and Bailey, S. (1986) Attributional style in depression: a meta-analytic review. *Journal of Personality and Social Psychology*, 50: 774–91.

Tajfel, H. (1978) Social categorization, social identity and social comparison, in H. Tajfel (ed.) *Differentiation Between Social Groups*. London: Academic Press.

Tang, J.L. *et al.* (1998) Systematic review of dietary intervention trials to lower blood total cholesterol in free-living subjects. *British Medical Journal*, 316: 1213–19.

Tanner, W.M. and Pollack, R.H. (1988) The effect of condom use and erotic instructions on attitudes towards condoms. *The Journal of Sex Research*, 25: 537–41.

Taubes, G. (1998) The (political) science of salt. *Science*, 281: 898–907.

Taylor, S.E. (2011) *Health Psychology*, 8th edn. New York: McGraw-Hill.

Terborg, J.R. (1988) The organisation as a context for health promotion, in S. Spacapan and S. Oskamp (eds) *The Social Psychology of Health*, pp. 129–74. Newbury Park, CA: Sage.

Terry, D.J. and Hynes, G.J. (1998) Adjustment to a low-control situation: re-examining the role of coping responses. *Journal of Personality and Social Psychology*, 74: 1078–92.

Terry, D.J. and O'Leary, J.E. (1995) The theory of planned behaviour: the effects of perceived behavioural control and self-efficacy. *British Journal of Social Psychology*, 34: 199–220.

Thayer, J. and Brosschot, J.F. (2010) Stress, health and illness: the effects of prolonged physiological activity and perseverative cognition, in D. French, A. Kaptein, K. Vedhara and J. Weinman (eds) *Health Psychology*, pp. 247–58. Oxford: Blackwell.

Theorell, T. and Rahe, R.H. (1971) Psychosocial factors and myocardial infarction, I. An inpatient study in Sweden. *Journal of Psychosomatic Research*, 15: 25–31.

Theorell, T., Lind, E. and Floderus, B. (1975) The relationship of disturbing life changes and emotions to the early development of myocardial infarction and other serious illnesses. *International Journal of Epidemiology*, 4: 281–93.

Thompson, E.L. (1978) Smoking education programs, 1960–1976. *American Journal of Public Health*, 68: 250–7.

Thompson, J.L., Manore, M.M. and Thomas, J.R. (1996) Effects of diet and diet-plus-exercise programs on resting metabolic rate: a meta-analysis. *International Journal of Sport Nutrition*, 6: 41–61.

Thompson, P.D. *et al.* (2003) Exercise and physical activity in the prevention and treatment of atherosclerotic cardiovascular disease. *Circulation*, 107: 3109–16.

Tiffany, S.T. (1990) A cognitive model of drug urges and drug-use behavior: role of automatic and nonautomatic processes. *Psychological Review*, 97: 147–68.

Troiano, R.P., Frongillo, E.A., Sobal, J. and Levitsky, D.A. (1996) The relationship between body weight and mortality: a quantitative analysis of combined information from existing studies. *International Journal of Obesity*, 20: 63–75.

Truby, H. *et al.* (2006) Randomised controlled trial of four commercial weight loss programmes in the UK: initial findings from the BBC 'diet trials'. *British Medical Journal*, 332: 1309–11.

Tsai, A.G. and Wadden, T.A. (2006) The evolution of very-low-calorie-diets: an update and meta-analysis. *Obesity*, 14: 1283–93.

Tsuji, H. *et al.* (1994) Reduced heart rate variability and mortality risk in an elderly cohort: the Framingham Study. *Circulation*, 90: 878–83.

Turner, J. and Wheaton, B. (1995) Checklist measurement of stressful life events, in S. Cohen, R.C. Kessler and L. Underwood Gordon (eds) *Measuring Stress*, pp. 29–58. New York: Oxford University Press.

Uchino, B.N. (2006) Social support and health: a review of physiological processes potentially underlying links to disease outcome. *Journal of Behavioral Medicine*, 29: 377–87.

Uchino, B.N. and Garvey, T.S. (1997) The availability of social support reduces cardiovascular reactivity to acute psychological stress. *Journal of Behavioral Medicine*, 20: 15–27.

Uchino, B.N., Cacioppo, J.T. and Kiecolt-Glaser, J.K. (1996) The relationship between social support and physiological processes: a review with emphasis on underlying mechanisms and implication for health. *Psychological Bulletin*, 119: 488–531.

Udry, J., Clark, L., Chase, C. and Levy, M. (1972) Can mass media advertising increase contraceptive use? *Family Planning Perspectives*, 4: 37–44.

UKATT Research Team (2007) UK alcohol treatment trial: client–treatment matching effects. *Addiction*, 103: 228–38.

Umberson, D., Wortman, C.B. and Kessler, R.C. (1992) Widowhood and depression: explaining long-term gender differences in vulnerability. *Journal of Health and Social Behavior*, 33: 10–24.

UNAIDS (2009) 09 Aids epidemics update, http://data.unaids.org/pub/Report/2009/JC1700_Epi_Update_2009_en.pdf (accessed June 2010).

USDHEW (US Department of Health, Education and Welfare) (1964) *Smoking and Health: A Report of the Surgeon General.* Washington, DC: US Government Printing Office.

USDHHS (US Department of Health and Human Services) (1984) *The Health Consequences of Smoking. Chronic Obstructive Lung Disease: A Report of the Surgeon General.* Washington, DC: US Government Printing Office.

USDHHS (US Department of Health and Human Services) (1985) *Fact Book, Fiscal Year 1985.* Bethesda, MD: National Heart, Lung, and Blood Institute.

USDHHS (US Department of Health and Human Services) (1986) *The Health Consequences of Involuntary Smoking: A Report of the Surgeon General.* Pub. No. (CDC) 87–8398. Washington, DC: US Government Printing Office.

USDHHS (US Department of Health and Human Services) (1990) *The Health Benefits of Smoking Cessation: A Report of the Surgeon General.* Rockville, MD: DHHS Publications.

USDHHS (US Department of Health and Human Services) (1996a) *Clinical Practice Guidelines: Smoking Cessation.* Pub. No. 96-0692. Rockville, MD: AHCPR.

USDHHS (US Department of Health and Human Services) (1996b) *Physical Activity and Health: A Report of the Surgeon General.* McLean, VA: International Medical Publishing.

USDHHS (US Department of Health and Human Services) (2000) *Treating Tobacco Use and Dependence: Clinical Practice Guidelines*, www.surgeongeneral.gov/tobacco/treating_tobacco_use.pdf (accessed Febuary 2009).

USDHHS (US Department of Health and Human Services) (2004) *The Health Consequences of Smoking: A Report of the Surgeon General*, www.cdc.gov/tobaco/data_statistics/sgr/sgr_2004/index. htm (accessed December 2006).

USDHHS (US Department of Health and Human Services) (2005) *Helping Patients Who Drink too Much: A Clinician's Guide*, http://pubs.niaaa.nih.gov/publications/practitioner/cliniciansguide2005/ clinicians_guide.htm (accessed August 2010).

USDHHS (US Department of Health and Human Services) (2006) *The Health Consequences of Involuntary Exposure to Tobacco Smoke: A Report of the Surgeon General*. Atlanta, GA: US Department of Health and Human Services, Centers for Disease Control and Prevention, Coordination Center for Health Promotion, National Center for Chronic Disease Prevention and Health Promotion, Office on Smoking and Health.

USDHHS (US Department of Health and Human Services) (2008) *Treating Tobacco Use and Dependence: 2008 Update*, www.surgeongeneral.gov/tobacco/treating_tobacco_use08.pdf (accessed February 2009).

Vaillant, G.E. (1983) *The Natural History of Alcoholism*. Cambridge, MA: Harvard University Press.

Van den Putte, B. (1991) 20 years of the theory of reasoned action of Fishbein and Ajzen: a meta-analysis, unpublished manuscript, University of Amsterdam.

van der Snoek, E.M., de Wit, J.B.F., Mulder, P.G.H. and van der Meijden, W.I. (2005) Incidence of sexually transmitted diseases and HIV infection related to perceived HIV/AIDS threat since highly active antiretroviral therapy availability in men who have sex with men. *Sexually Transmitted Diseases*, 32: 170–5.

van der Velde, F., van der Pligt, J. and Hooykaas, C. (1994) Perceiving AIDS-related risk: accuracy as a function of differences in actual risk. *Health Psychology*, 13: 25–33.

van Koningsbruggen, G., Stroebe, W., Aarts, H. and Papies, E. (in press) Thinking of dieting to resist temptations: behavioral control in food-rich environments. *European Journal of Social Psychology*.

van Koningsbruggen, G.M., Stroebe, W., Papies, E.K. and Aarts, H. (in press) Implementation intentions as goal primes: boosting self-control in tempting environments. Manuscript submitted for publication.

Van Wechem, S.N. *et al.* (1998) Fat watch: a nationwide campaign in the Netherlands to reduce fat intake – effect evaluation. *Nutrition and Health*, 12: 119–30.

Velicer, W., DiClemente, C.C., Prochaska, J.O. and Brandenburg, N. (1985) Decisional balance measure for assessing and predicting smoking status. *Journal of Personality and Social Psychology*, 48: 1279–89.

Veling, H. and Aarts, H. (2009) Putting behavior on hold decreases reward value of need-instrumental objects outside of awareness. *Journal of Experimental Psychology*, 45: 1020–3.

Vergidis, P.J. and Falagas, M.E. (2009) Meta-analyses of behavioural interventions to reduce the risk of transmission of HIV. *Infectious Disease Clinics of North America*, 23: 309–14.

Verplanken, B. and Aarts, H. (1999) Habit, attitude, planned behavior: is habit an empty construct or an interesting case of goal directed automaticity? in W. Stroebe and M. Hewstone (eds) *European Review of Social Psychology*, 10: 100–34.

Vickers Jr, R.R., Conway, T.L. and Hervig, L.K. (1990) Demonstrations of replicable dimensions of health behaviors. *Preventive Medicine*, 19: 377–401.

Viscusi, W.K. (1990) Do smokers underestimate risks? *Journal of Political Economy*, 98: 1253–69.

Vohs, K.D. and Heatherton, T.F. (2000) Self-regulatory failure: a resource-depletion approach. *Psychological Science*, 11: 249–54.

Wagenaar, A.C., Salois, M.J. and Komro, K.A. (2009) Effects of beverage alcohol prices and tax levels on drinking: a meta-analysis of 1003 estimates from 112 studies. *Addiction*, 104: 179–90.

Wagner, E.H., LaCroix, A.Z., Buchner, D.M. and Larson, E.B. (1992) Effects of physical activity on health status in older adults, I: observational studies. *Annual Review of Public Health*, 13: 451–68.

Waller, J.A. (1987) Injury: conceptual shifts and preventive implications. *Annual Review of Public Health*, 8: 21–49.

Walsh, D.C. and Gordon, N.P. (1986) Legal approaches to smoking deterrence, in L. Breslow, J.E. Fielding and L.B. Lave (eds) *Annual Review of Public Health*, Vol. 7: pp. 127–49. Palo Alto, CA: Annual Reviews Inc.

Walters, G.D. (2002) The heritability of alcohol abuse and dependence: a meta-analysis of behavior genetic research. *American Journal of Drug and Alcohol Abuse*, 28: 557–84.

Warner, K.E. (1981) Cigarette smoking in the 1970s: the impact of the antismoking campaigns on consumption. *Science*, 211: 729–31.

Warner, K.E. (1986) Smoking and health implications of a change in the Federal Cigarette Excise Tax. *Journal of the American Medical Association*, 255: 1028–32.

Warner, K.E. (2000) The economics of tobacco: myths and realities. *Tobacco Control*, 9: 78–89.

Waters, A.J. *et al.* (2007) Implicit attitudes to smoking are associated with craving and dependence. *Drug and Alcohol Dependence*, 91: 178–86.

Watson, D. and Pennebaker, J.W. (1989) Health complaints, stress, and distress: exploring the central role of negative effectivity. *Psychological Review*, 96: 234–54.

Watson, J.B. and Raynor, R. (1920) Conditioned emotional reactions. *Journal of Experimental Psychology*, 3: 1–14.

Weaver, K.E. *et al.* (2005) A stress and coping model of medication adherence and viral load in HIV-positive men and women on highly active antiretroviral therapy (HAART). *Health Psychology*, 24: 385–92.

Webb, T.L. and Sheeran, P. (2007) How do implementation intentions promote goal attainment? A test of component processes. *Journal of Experimental Social Psychology*, 43: 295–302.

Weekley, C.G., Klesges, R.C. and Relya, G. (1992) Smoking as a weight-control strategy and its relationship to smoking status. *Addictive Behaviours*, 17: 259–71.

Wegner, D.M. (1994) Ironic processes of mental control, *Psychological Review*, 101: 34–52.

Weinberger, M., Hiner, S.L. and Tierney, W.M. (1987) In support of hassles as measures of stress in predicting health outcomes. *Journal of Behavioral Medicine*, 10: 19–31.

Weiner, B., Perry, R.P. and Magnusson, J. (1988) An attributional analysis of reactions to stigma. *Journal of Personality and Social Psychology*, 55: 738–48.

Weinstein, N.D. (1987) Unrealistic optimism about susceptibility to health problems: conclusions from a community-wide sample. *Journal of Behavioral Medicine*, 10: 481–500.

Weinstein, N.D. (1988) The precaution adoption process. *Health Psychology*, 7: 355–86.

Weinstein, N.D. and Sandman, P.M. (1992) A model for the precaution adoption process: evidence from home radon testing. *Health Psychology*, 11: 170–80.

Weinstein, N.D., Rothman, A.J. and Sutton, S. (1998) Stage theories of health behavior: conceptual and methodological issues. *Health Psychology*, 17: 290–9.

Welin, L. *et al.* (1985) Prospective study of social influence on mortality. *Lancet*, 2: 915–18.

Wethington, E., Brown, G.W. and Kessler, R.C. (1995) Interview measures of stressful life events, in S. Cohen, R.C. Kessler and L. Underwood Gordon (eds) *Measuring Stress*, pp. 59–79. New York: Oxford University Press.

Weyerer, S. (1992) Physical inactivity and depression in the community. *International Journal of Sports Medicine*, 13: 492–6.

WHO (World Health Organization) (1948) *Constitution of the World Health Organization*. Geneva: WHO.

WHO (World Health Organization) (1982) *Prevention of Coronary Heart Disease: A Report of the WHO Expert Committee*. Geneva: WHO.

WHO (World Health Organization) (2000) *Obesity: Preventing and Managing the Global Epidemic*. Geneva: WHO

WHO (World Health Organization) (2008) *Violence, Injuries, and Disability: Biennial 2006–2007 Report*. Geneva: WHO.

Wicker, A.W. (1969) Attitudes versus actions: the relationship of verbal and overt behavioral responses to attitude objects. *Journal of Social Issues*, 25: 41–78.

Wiehe, S.E. *et al.* (2005) A systematic review of school-based smoking prevention trials with long-term follow up. *Journal of Adolecent Health*, 36: 162–9.

Wiers, R., van den Woerden, N., Smulders, F.T.Y. and de Jong, P. (2002) Implicit and explicit alcohol-related cognitions in heavy and light drinkers, *Journal of Abnormal Psychology*, 111: 648–58.

Wiers, R. *et al.* (2010a) Re-training automatic alcohol-approach tendencies in alcoholic patients increases abstinence. Unpublished manuscript.

Wiers, R. *et al.* (2010b) Retraining automatic action-tendencies to approach alcohol in hazardous drinkers. *Addiction*, 105: 279–87.

Willett, W.C. and Manson, J.E. (1996) Epidemiological studies of health risks due to excess weight, in K.D. Kelley and C.G. Fairburn (eds) *Eating Disorder and Obesity*, pp. 396–405. New York: Guilford Press.

Williams, D.M. *et al.* (2008) Comparing psychosocial predictors of physical activity adoption and maintenance. *Annals of Behavioral Medicine*, 36: 186–94.

Williams, D.R. and Collins, C. (1995) US socioeconomic and racial differences in health: patterns and explanations. *Annual Review of Sociology*, 21: 349–86.

Williams, G.D. and DeBakey, S.F. (1992) Changes in levels of alcohol consumption: United States, 1983–1988. *British Journal of Addiction*, 87: 643–8.

Williams Jr, R.B., Barefoot, J.C. and Shekelle, R.B. (1985) The health consequences of hostility, in M.A. Chesney and R.H. Rosenman (eds) *Anger and Hostility in Cardiovascular and Behavioral Disorders*, pp. 173–85. New York: McGraw Hill.

Williams Jr, R.B. *et al.* (1992) Prognostic importance of social and economic resources among medically treated patients with angiographically documented coronary artery disease. *Journal of the American Medical Association*, 267: 520–4.

Williamson, D.F. (1991) Epidemiological analysis of weight gain in U.S. adults. *Nutrition*, 7: 285–6.

Williamson, D.F. (1995) The association of weight loss with morbidity and mortality, in K.D. Brownell and C.G. Fairburn (eds) *Eating Disorders and Obesity*, pp. 411–16. New York: Guilford Press.

Williamson, D.F. *et al.* (1992) Weight loss attempts in adults: goals, duration, and rate of weight loss. *American Journal of Public Health*, 82: 1251–7.

Wilson, M. and Baker, S. (1987) Structural approach to injury control. *Journal of Social Issues*, 43: 73–86.

Wilson, T.D. and Kraft, D. (1993) Why do I love thee: effects of repeated introspections about a dating relationship on attitudes towards that relationship. *Personality and Social Psychology Bulletin*, 19: 409–18

Wilson, T.D., Kraft, D. and Dunn, D.S. (1989) The disruptive effects of explaining attitudes: the moderating effects of knowledge about the attitude object. *Journal of Experimental Social Psychology*, 25: 379–400.

Wilson, T.D., Lindzey, S. and Schooler, T.Y. (2000) A model for dual attitudes. *Psychological Review*, 107: 101–26.

Wing, R.R. (2004) Behavioral approaches to the treatment of obesity, in G.A. Bray and C. Bouchard (eds) *Handbook of Obesity: Clinical Applications*, 2nd edn, pp. 147–67. New York: Dekker.

Wing, R.R. and Hill, J.O. (2001) Successful weight loss maintenance. *Annual Review of Nutrition*, 21: 323–41.

Wing, R.R. and Phelan, S. (2005) Long-term weight loss maintenance. *American Journal of Clinical Nutrition*, 82: 222S–5S.

Wing, R.R., Jeffery, R.W., Hellerstedt, W.L. and Burton, L.R. (1996) Effects of frequent phone contact and optional food provision on maintenance of weight loss. *Annals of Behavioral Medicine*, 18: 172–6.

Winkelstein, W. *et al.* (1987) The San Francisco Men's Health Study, III. Reduction in HIV transmission among gay and bisexual men, 1982–86. *American Journal of Public Health*, 76: 685–9.

Winkleby, M.A., Taylor, B., Jatulis, D. and Fortmann, S.P. (1996) The long-term effects of a cardiovascular disease prevention trial: the Stanford Five City Project. *American Journal of Public Health*, 86: 1773–9.

Witkiewitz, K. and Marlatt, G.A. (2004) Relapse prevention for alcohol and drug problems. *American Psychologist*, 59: 224–35.

Witte, K. (1992) Putting the fear back into fear appeals: the extended parallel process model, *Communication Monograph*, 59: 329–49.

Witte, K. and Allen, M. (2000) A meta-analysis of fear appeals: implications for effective public health campaigns, *Health Education and Behavior*, 27: 591–616.

Wood, W. and Kallgren, C.A. (1988) Communicator attributes and persuasion: recipients' access to attitude-relevant information in memory. *Personality and Social Psychology Bulletin*, 14: 172–82.

Wood, W., Kallgren, C.A. and Preisler, R. (1985) Access to atttitude-relevant information in memory as a determinant of persuasion: the role of message attributes. *Journal of Experimental Social Psychology*, 21: 73–85.

Wood, W., Tam, L. and Guerrero Wit, M. (2005) Changing circumstances, disrupting habits. *Journal of Personality and Social Psychology*, 88: 918–33.

Wroe, A.L. and Thomas, M.G. (2003) Intentional and unintentional nonadherence in patients prescribed HAART treatment regimens. *Psychology, Health & Medicine*, 8: 453–63.

Wurtele, S.K. (1988) Increasing women's calcium intake: the role of health beliefs, intentions and health value. *Journal of Applied Social Psychology*, 18: 627–39.

Wurtele, S.K. and Maddux, J.E. (1987) Relative contributions of protection motivation theory components in predicting exercise intentions and behavior. *Health Psychology*, 6: 453–66.

Wurtele, S.K., Roberts, M.C. and Leeper, J.D. (1982) Health beliefs and intentions: predictors of return compliance in a tuberculosis detection drive. *Journal of Applied Social Psychology*, 12: 128–36.

Yeomans, M.R., Blundell, J.E. and Leshem, M. (2004) Palatability: response to nutritional need or need-free stimulation of appetite? *British Journal of Nutrition*, 92(Suppl. 1): S3–14.

Yu-Poth, S. *et al.* (1999) Effects of the national cholesterol education program's step I and step II dietary intervention programs on cardiovascular disease risk factors: a meta-analysis. *American Journal of Clinical Nutrition*, 69: 632–46.

Zanna, M.P. and Rempel, J.K. (1988) Attitudes: a new look at an old concept, in D. Bar-Tal and A.W. Kruglanski (eds) *The Social Psychology of Knowledge*, pp. 315–34. Cambridge: Cambridge University Press.

Zarski, J.J. (1984) Hassles and health: a replication. *Health Psychology*, 3: 243–51.

Author Index

Subject Index

EATING BEHAVIOUR

Terence M. Dovey

9780335235834 (Paperback)
2010

eBook also available

This text provides readers with a concise introduction to the psychology of eating focussing on the psychological and biological processes that underlie eating behaviour. While insights into eating behaviour that has gone wrong, such as anorexia nervosa and bulimia, are offered, the primary focus is on 'normal' eating behaviour.

Key features:

- Covers the subject of eating and food related behaviour from the five main areas of psychology, developmental, cognitive, social, biological, and psychopathological perspectives
- Written in a lively, accessible style
- Highlights the way that the brain and body control eating

www.openup.co.uk

 **OPEN UNIVERSITY PRESS**
McGraw - Hill Education

SOCIAL PSYCHOLOGY MATTERS

Wendy Hollway, Helen Lucey
and Ann Phoenix

9780335221035 (Paperback)
2006

eBook also available

Social Psychology Matters explores the significance of social
psychology in the twenty-first century and the important contribution it
can and does make to understanding ourselves and others in today's
world. This book is designed to help the reader navigate the complex
and ever-changing nature of the discipline and gain an overview of
the key concepts, methods and theories.

Key features:

- Provides an in-depth look at social psychological topics of
  significance
- Uses real-life experience to demonstrate why social psychology
  matters
- Explores four theoretical perspectives – cognitive social,
  discursive psychological, phenomenological and social
  psychoanalytic

www.openup.co.uk

OPEN UNIVERSITY PRESS
McGraw - Hill Education

ESSENTIAL READINGS IN HEALTH PSYCHOLOGY

Jane Ogden

9780335211388 (Paperback)
2007

eBook also available

Essential Readings in Health Psychology is a collection of key papers brought together for the first time in a single volume which complements Jane Ogden's bestselling textbook, Health Psychology. The reader focuses on the key areas highlighted by the British Psychological Society as central to health psychology, providing an ideal resource for any undergraduate or postgraduate course in health psychology as well as for students of medicine, nursing and allied health.

Key features:

- Employs different theories and methods which offer a different perspective
- Offers case examples of health psychology work that illustrate what health psychology research can (and cannot) achieve
- Framed by editorial discussions which will help students to understand the context, meaning and contribution of each paper to the discipline of Health Psychology as a whole

www.openup.co.uk

OPEN UNIVERSITY PRESS
McGraw - Hill Education

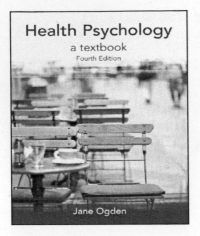

HEALTH PSYCHOLOGY
A Textbook
Fourth Edition

Jane Ogden

9780335222636 (Paperback)
2007

eBook also available

The market leading textbook in the field, *Health Psychology* by Jane Ogden is essential reading for all students and researchers of health psychology. It will also be invaluable to students of medicine, nursing and allied health. Retaining the breadth of coverage, clarity and relevance that has made it a favourite with students and lecturers, this fourth edition has been thoroughly revised and updated.

Key features:

- New chapter on women's health issues, exploring recent research into pregnancy, miscarriage, birth, menopause and related areas
- Updated "Focus on Research" examples to introduce contemporary topics and emerging areas for research in health psychology, including exercise, smoking and pain
- Includes new data, graphs and further reading plus suggestions about where to access the most recent publications and other data

www.openup.co.uk

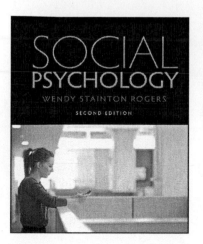

Social Psychology
Second Edition

Wendy Stainton-Rogers

9780335240999 (Paperback)
June 2011

eBook also available

Social Psychology is an introductory text, uniquely acknowledging that there are two different approaches to social psychology - experimental and critical. The new edition explores the increasing dominance of the critical approach, while still providing the reader with a holistic view and understanding of social psychology.

Key features:

- Introduces a new Online Learning Centre
- Provides up-to-date coverage of developments in the field
- Includes a new chapter exploring values, culture and 'otherness'

www.openup.co.uk

OPEN UNIVERSITY PRESS
McGraw - Hill Education

HEALTH PROMOTION
A Psychosocial Approach

Christine Stephens

9780335222087 (Paperback)
2008

eBook also available

Can the health of individuals be improved through community health programmes?

How can community health promotion programmes be more effective?

How is health awareness measured and evaluated?

In recent years, health promoters have focused their attention not just on individual lifestyle change, but on daily social and physical conditions that surround the individual. They are now looking towards lifestyle change based on community or socially-based interventions.

Key features:

- Argues for the importance of theoretical explanations that inform investigations of the social context of daily life
- Includes a practical grounding, using examples of community health promotion practice, such as community arts and local community models, based on material and research from Britain, New Zealand, Canada, the USA and South America
- Investigates the media's role in health promotion

www.openup.co.uk